MANNERS & CUSTOMS OF THE BIBLE

Oriental Street Scene.

MANNERS & CUSTOMS

OF THE

BIBLE

JAMES M. FREEMAN

Whitaker House

Unless otherwise indicated, all Scripture quotations are taken from the *King James Version* (KJV) of the Bible.

MANNERS AND CUSTOMS OF THE BIBLE

ISBN: 0-88368-290-7
Printed in the United States of America
Copyright © 1996 by Whitaker House

Whitaker House
30 Hunt Valley Circle
New Kensington, PA 15068

5 6 7 8 9 10 11 12 13 / 06 05 04 03 02 01 00

PREFACE.

THOUGH the Bible is adapted to all nations, it is in many respects an Oriental book.. It represents the modes of thought and the peculiar customs of a people who, in their habits, widely differ from us. One who lived among them for many years has graphically said: "Modes, customs, usages, all that you can set down to the score of the national, the social, or the conventional, are precisely as different from yours as the east is different from the west. They sit when you stand; they lie when you sit; they do to the head what you do to the feet; they use fire when you use water; you shave the beard, they shave the head; you move the hat, they touch the breast; you use the lips in salutation, they touch the forehead and the cheek; your house looks outwards, their house looks inwards; you go *out* to take a walk, they go *up* to enjoy the fresh air; you drain your land, they sigh for water; you bring your daughters out, they keep their wives and daughters in; your ladies go barefaced through the streets, their ladies are always covered." *

The Oriental customs of to-day are, mainly, the same as those of ancient times. It is said by a recent writer that "the Classical world has passed away. We must reproduce it if we wish to see it as it was." While this fact must be remembered in the interpretation of some New Testament passages, it is nevertheless true that many ancient customs still exist in their primitive integrity. If a knowledge of Oriental customs is essential to a right understanding of numerous Scripture passages, it is a cause of rejoicing that these customs are so stereotyped in their character that we have but to visit the Bible lands of the present day to see the modes of life of patriarchal times.

The design of this volume is to illustrate the Bible by an explanation of the Oriental customs to which it refers. The Bible becomes more than ever a *real* book when we can read it understandingly. While this is eminently true of its doctrines, it is also true of its facts. A distinguished author has

* THE JORDAN AND THE RHINE, by the Rev. W. Graham, p. 4.

aptly said: "In studying the Bible the Dictionary of Things is almost as important as the Dictionary of Words." It is a part of this "Dictionary of Things" that we propose to furnish in this book, though not in the form of a dictionary. The texts illustrated are arranged in the order in which they occur in the Bible, and are accompanied by explanations of the customs to which they allude. This method seems to be the most natural for Bible study, and is the plan followed by Burder, Rosenmüller, and Roberts.

The materials for a work of this character are more abundant now than ever. Supplementing the labors of those who in former days visited Egypt and Syria, travelers have, within a few years, entered new regions and brought to light facts hitherto unknown. The explorations of such men as Botta, Layard, Loftus, and Smith, and the labors of the Palestine Exploration Societies, both of England and America, have been productive of rich results, and, without doubt, results yet more valuable are to follow. The pick and the spade are to be the humble instruments of illustrating and authenticating the Word of God. Already, through their agency, important discoveries have been made. Ancient tablets covered with strange characters have been brought to light; by patient labor and wonderful ingenuity these characters have been deciphered, and made to tell the secrets which for ages they had kept concealed. The tombs of Egypt, the palaces of Assyria, and the royal records of Moab, have been compelled to speak, and now, in different languages, they bear testimony for God and his truth.

Of this varied and valuable material we have endeavored to make diligent use in the preparation of this volume. As it would encumber the work with multitudinous notes of reference to give, in every instance, the authority for the statements made, a list of the principal authors consulted is appended.

Should this volume aid the student in obtaining a better understanding of the Bible, the labor of the writer will not have been in vain.

LIST OF AUTHORITIES

CONSULTED IN THE PREPARATION OF THIS VOLUME.

———————•—◆—•———————

IN addition to those commentaries, books of travel, and other works which are specially mentioned where they are quoted, the materials for this volume have been obtained chiefly from the following authorities:

ALFORD, DR. HENRY—Greek Testament. Four volumes. London, 1872.

ANDERSON, REV. JOSEPH—Bible Light from Bible Lands. New York, 1856.

AYRE, REV. JOHN—The Treasury of Bible Knowledge. London, 1870.

BINGHAM, REV. JOSEPH—*Origines Ecclesiasticæ.* The Antiquities of the Christian Church. Two volumes. London, 1870.

BLOOMFIELD, DR. S. T.—Greek Testament. Two volumes. Ninth edition. London, 1855.

BONOMI, JOSEPH—Nineveh and its Palaces. London, 1865.

BROWN, DR. WILLIAM—Antiquities of the Jews. London, 1820.

BURDER, REV. SAMUEL—Oriental Customs. Two volumes. Sixth edition. London, 1822.

BURDER, REV. SAMUEL—Oriental Literature. Two volumes. London, 1822.

BUSH, REV. GEORGE—Illustrations of the Holy Scriptures. Philadelphia, 1848.

CALMET—Dictionary of the Holy Bible, (Ed., Taylor.) Five volumes. Fourth edition. London, 1823.

CHARDIN, JOHN—Travels into Persia and the East Indies. London, 1636.

FABER, DR. G. S.—The Origin of Pagan Idolatry, ascertained from Historical Testimony and Circumstantial Evidence. Three volumes. London, 1816.

FAIRBAIRN, DR. PATRICK—The Imperial Bible Dictionary. Two volumes. London, 1864, 1866.

FAIRBAIRN, DR. PATRICK—The Typology of Scripture. Two volumes. Third edition. Philadelphia, 1865.

FORBES. JAMES—Oriental Memoirs. Four volumes. London, 1813.

GALE, REV. THEOPHILUS—The Court of the Gentiles. Oxford, 1672.

GODWYN, DR. THOMAS—Moses and Aaron ; or, The Civil and Ecclesiastical Rites used by the Ancient Hebrews. London, 1678.

GRAHAM, REV. WILLIAM—The Jordan and the Rhine. London, 1854.

HACKETT, DR. H. B.—Illustrations of Scripture. Boston, 1855.

HARMER, REV. THOMAS—Observations on Various Passages of Scripture. (Ed., Dr. Clarke.) Four volumes. Fourth edition. London, 1808.

HENGSTENBERG, E. W.—Egypt and the Books of Moses. Translated by Prof. Robbins. Andover, 1843.

HERZOG, DR.—Real-Encyklopädie. (Twenty-two volumes.) Hamburg, Stuttgart, and Gotha, 1854–1868.

JAHN—Biblical Archæology. Translated by Prof. Upham. Fifth edition. New York, 1866.

JAMIESON, REV. ROBERT—Eastern Manners illustrative of Old Testament History. Two volumes. Edinburgh, 1836, 1838.

JENNINGS, DR. DAVID—Jewish Antiquities. Tenth edition. London, 1839.

JOWETT, REV. W.—Christian Researches in Syria and the Holy Land. Boston, 1826.

KEIL, DR. KARL FRIEDRICH—Handbuch der biblischen Archäologie. (Two volumes.) Frankfurt-am-Main and Erlangen, 1858, 1859.

KITTO, DR. JOHN—A Cyclopædia of Biblical Literature, (Ed., Dr. Alexander.) Three volumes. Third edition. Philadelphia. 1866.

KITTO, DR. JOHN—Daily Bible Illustrations. Eight volumes. New York, 1867.

KURTZ, DR. J. H.—Sacrificial Worship of the Old Testament. Translated by Martin. Edinburgh, 1873. (Clark's Foreign Theological Library.)

LANE, E. W.—An Account of the Manners and Customs of the Modern Egyptians. Two volumes. Third edition. London, 1842.

LAYARD, H. A.—Nineveh and its Remains. Two volumes. London, 1849.

LAYARD, H. A.—Monuments of Nineveh. London, 1849.

LAYARD, H. A.—Discoveries in the Ruins of Nineveh and Babylon. London, 1853.

LAYARD, H. A.—Monuments of Nineveh. Second series. London, 1853.

LIGHTFOOT, DR. JOHN—Works, (Ed., Pitman.) Twelve volumes. London, 1823.

LOFTUS, W. K.—Travels and Researches in Chaldæa and Susiana. New York, 1857.

MADDEN, F. W.—History of Jewish Coinage, and of Money in the Old and New Testament. London, 1864.

MAIMONIDES—The Reasons of the Laws of Moses. Translated by Dr. Townley. London, 1827.

MAUNDRELL, HENRY—A Journey from Aleppo to Jerusalem at Easter, A. D. 1697. London, 1810. (This edition contains PITTS' *Religion and Manners of the Mahometans*, to which we refer in several instances.)

M'CLINTOCK AND STRONG—Cyclopædia of Biblical, Theological, and Ecclesiastical Literature. Five volumes, [A to Mc.] New York, 1867–1873.
[Not yet completed.]

MEYER, JOHANN FRIEDRICH—Bibeldeutungen. Frankfurt-am-Main, 1812.

MICHÆLIS, J. D.—Commentaries on the Laws of Moses. Four volumes.
London, 1814.

MORIER, JAMES—Second Journey through Persia, Armenia, and Asia Minor.
London, 1818.

MORRISON, WALTER (Editor)—The Recovery of Jerusalem. (Palestine Exploration Fund.) New York, 1871.

NICHOLS, T. A.—Handy-Book of the British Museum. London, 1870.

PALMER, E. H.—The Desert of the Exodus. Two volumes. Cambridge,
(England,) 1871.

PORTER, REV. J. L.—The Giant Cities of Bashan and Syria's Holy Places.
New York, 1866.

RAWLINSON, G.—The History of Herodotus. Four volumes. London,
1858–1860.

RAWLINSON, G.—The Five Great Monarchies of the Ancient Eastern World.
Three volumes. Second edition. London, 1871.

ROBERTS, REV. J.—Oriental Illustrations of the Sacred Scriptures. London, 1844.

ROBINSON, DR. E.—Biblical Researches in Palestine and in the Adjacent
Regions. Three volumes. Second edition. Boston, 1856.

ROGERS, MISS MARY E.—Domestic Life in Palestine. Cincinnati, 1869.

ROSENMÜLLER, E. F. K.—Das alte und neue Morgenland. (Six volumes.)
Leipzig, 1818–1820.

SHARPE, SAMUEL—Texts from the Holy Bible explained by the Help of the
Ancient Monuments. Second edition. London, 1869.

SHAW, DR. THOMAS—Travels; or, Observations relating to Several Parts of
Barbary and the Levant. Second edition. London, 1757.

SMITH, DR. WILLIAM—A Dictionary of Greek and Roman Antiquities. Third
American edition. New York, 1855.

SMITH, DR. WILLIAM—A Dictionary of the Bible. Three volumes. Boston, 1863.

THOMSON, DR. W. M.—The Land and the Book. Two volumes. New York,
1860.

WILKINSON, J. G.—Manners and Customs of the Ancient Egyptians. Three
volumes. London, 1837.

WILKINSON, J. G.—A Second Series of the Manners and Customs of the
Ancient Egyptians. Three volumes. London, 1841.

WINER, DR. G. B.—Biblisches Realwœrterbuch. (Two volumes. Third
edition.) Leipzig, 1847, 1848.

LIST OF ENGRAVINGS.

HAND-BOOK

OF

BIBLE MANNERS AND CUSTOMS.

————◦•◦•◦————

GENESIS.

1.—USE OF THE TERM FATHER.

IV, 20, 21. Adah bare Jabal: he was the father of such as dwell in tents, and of such as have cattle. And his brother's name was Jubal: he was the father of all such as handle the harp and organ.

IN the East the originator of any custom is frequently spoken of as the "father" of that custom; so, also, a man is often described by representing him to be the "father" of some peculiarity which distinguishes him from others. A man of very long beard is called "the father of a beard." One of the Arabs who accompanied Palmer in his journey across the desert of the Exodus was called "the father of the top-knot," because the lock of hair on top of his head was of unusual size. A celebrated Arab chief was called "the father of the ostrich," because of the fleetness of the favorite horse which he rode. Dr. Thomson was once called by the mischievous young Arabs "the father of a saucepan," because they fancied that his black hat resembled that culinary utensil. When Loftus was in Chaldea his negro cook on one occasion killed two lion cubs. The Arabs, from that time forth, saluted him as "Abú Sebá'ín," that is, "the father of the two lions."

The name "father" is also applied to beasts or birds, and even to inanimate things. In Egypt the kite is sometimes called "the father of the air," because of its power of flight. An African city was called *Boo Hadgar*, "the father of stone"—that is, a stony city. There is a Turkish coin called "the father of a cannon," because of the representation of a cannon which is upon it.

In like manner Jabal was called "the father of such as dwell in tents," because he was probably the inventor of tents; and Jubal, "the father of all such as handle the harp and organ," because he invented those instruments.

This use of the term "father" is found, also, in other parts of the Bible.

In Isa. ix, 6, the Messiah is called "the everlasting Father," or "the Father of eternity;" that is, he is the giver of eternal life: in John viii, 44, the devil is called "the father of lies;" in Rom. iv, 12, Abraham is said to be "the father of circumcision;" in 2 Cor. i, 3, God is called "the father of mercies;" and in Eph. i, 17, "the father of glory." There is a corresponding use of the word *children.* See note on Matt. ix, 15.

2.—BABYLONIAN BRICKS—BITUMEN.

XI, 3. **They said one to another, Go to, let us make brick, and burn them thoroughly. And they had brick for stone, and slime had they for mortar.**

1. The soil of Babylonia is an alluvial deposit, rich and tenacious, and well adapted for brick-making. While many of the bricks of that country were

merely sun-dried, others were burned, as were those in the tower of Babel. Fire-burnt bricks were sometimes laid as an outer covering to walls of sun-dried brick. The finest quality of bricks was of a yellow color, resembling our fire-bricks; another very hard kind was of a dark blue; the commoner and coarser sorts were pink or red.

Amid the ruins of Babylonia ancient bricks have been discovered, in large quantities, stamped with inscriptions of

1.—Babylonian Brick.

great value to the archæologist. The ordinary size of these bricks is twelve to fourteen inches square, and three to four inches thick. At the corners of buildings half-bricks were used in the alternate rows.

2. The "slime" here spoken of is bitumen, which is still found bubbling from the ground in the neighborhood of ancient Babylon, where it is now used for mortar, as in former times. It is also found in some parts of Palestine. At Hasbeiya, near the source of the Jordan, there are wells or pits dug, in which bitumen collects, exuding from the crevices in the rocks. The "slime-pits" mentioned in Gen. xiv, 10, may have been similar to these. They were near the Dead Sea, where bitumen is still to be found.

Loftus (*Travels in Chaldea and Susiana,* p. 31) approves the suggestion of Captain Newbold, that the ancient Babylonians in some instances burned their bricks in the walls of their buildings, to render them more durable. The rude walls, erected with unburnt brick, cemented with hot bitumen, are supposed to have been exposed to the action of a furnace heat until they became a solid vitrified mass. This is indeed burning "thoroughly," and it may have been the method which the Babel-builders intended to pursue had they been permitted to finish their tower; as they said, according to the marginal reading, "Let us make brick, and burn them to a burning."

3.—PHARAOH.

XII, 15. The princes also of Pharaoh saw her.

Pharaoh is the common title of the native Egyptian kings mentioned in Scripture. The word itself does not mean king, as was formerly supposed; recent investigations have satisfied Egyptologists that it means the sun. This title was given to the king because he was considered the representative on earth of the God RA, or the sun. It is difficult to tell what particular Pharaoh or king is referred to here.

2.—PA-OURO.

4.—USE OF THE TERM BROTHER.

XIV, 16. And also brought again his brother Lot.

In chapter xi, 31 Lot is said to be the nephew, not the brother, of Abram. In like manner Jacob told Rachel (Gen. xxix, 12) that he was her father's brother; whereas, according to Gen. xxviii, 5, he was the son of her father's sister; that is, her father's nephew. This elastic use of the word brother is quite common in the East, however strange it may seem to us; yet we have a usage somewhat similar in the application of the term to persons not in any way related to us. We call fellow-countrymen, or fellow-craftsmen, or fellow churchmen, brothers. The Orientals apply the term to their kinsmen of whatever relation.

5.—UPLIFTED HAND.

XIV, 22. And Abram said to the king of Sodom, I have lift up mine hand unto the Lord, the most high God, the possessor of heaven and earth.

This was Abram's method of taking a solemn oath; a mode still practiced in the East, and to some extent in the West. It is said in Isa. lxii, 8, "The Lord hath sworn by his right hand." See also Dan. xii, 7; Rev. x, 5, 6; the note on Prov. xi, 21; and also on Ezek. xxi, 14.

6.—BURNING LAMP.

XV, 17. And it came to pass, that, when the sun went down, and it was dark, behold a smoking furnace, and a burning lamp that passed between those pieces.

The "burning lamp" is supposed to have been an emblem of the Divine presence, as fire is represented to be in other parts of the Scriptures. Roberts says that in India the burning lamp or fire is still used in confirmation of a covenant. If one's promise is doubted he will point to the flame of the lamp, saying, "That is the witness." The marriages of the East Indian gods and demi-gods are described as being performed in the presence of the God of fire; and it is to this day a general practice at the celebration of a marriage to have fire as a witness of the transaction. "Fire is the witness of their covenant, and, if they break it, fire will be their destruction." —*Orient. Illus.*, p. 21.

7.—RELIGION OF NAMES.

XVI, 13. And she called the name of the Lord that spake unto her, Thou God seest me.

One of the most prevalent superstitions in Egypt was connected with the religion of names. The Egyptians gave to each of their gods a name indicative of specific office and attributes. It was thus perfectly natural that Hagar, who was an Egyptian, should give a title of honor to Him who appeared to her in the wilderness. Some suppose that the Israelites were influenced by this superstition during their long bondage in Egypt, and that it is to this that Moses refers in Exod. iii, 13; and, further, that out of indulgence to this weakness God was pleased to give himself a name—one expressive of his eternal self-existence, Exod. iii, 14. This ancient Egyptian custom found its way to other nations. Zechariah, alluding to this, speaks of the time when "there shall be one Lord, and his name one." Zech. xiv, 9.

8.—TENT DOOR—TIME OF REST.

XVIII, 1. And he sat in the tent door in the heat of the day.

1. The "door of the tent" is a fold of the lower part, of the tent, which is fastened by a loop to the post near by. It may thus be opened or closed at pleasure. For the sake of light and air, it is generally thrown back during the day.

2. Noon is the hour of rest among the Orientals. When the sun is at its height the wind often becomes softer and the heat more oppressive. Then the dwellers in tents may be seen sitting "in the door," or reclining in the shade of the tent. It is also the hour for dinner. See Gen. xliii, 16, 25. Some travelers say that the Arabs eat by the door of the tent in order to notice the stranger passing by, and to invite him to eat with them. In the case mentioned in the text Abraham had probably dined, and was resting after dinner.

9.—BOWING—HOSPITALITY.

XVIII, 2, 3. And when he saw them, he ran to meet them from the tent door, and bowed himself toward the ground, and said, My Lord, if now I have found favor in thy sight, pass not away, I pray thee, from thy servant.

1. There are different modes of bowing in the East. In this case the word used (*shachah*) denotes complete prostration of the body. In this the person falls upon the knees, and then gradually inclines the body until the head touches the ground. See also Gen. xxiii, 7, 12; xlii, 6; xliii, 26.

2. There is in this text a beautiful illustration of Oriental hospitality. The company of the travelers is solicited as a personal favor to the host, and all the resources of the establishment are used for their entertainment. See Gen. xix, 2, 3; Judges vi, 18; xiii, 15; Job xxxi, 32. Modern travelers often refer to the earnestness with which this hospitality is urged upon them at the present day. It is not always, however, to be regarded as unselfish; in many instances a return being expected from the traveler who is thus entertained. A recent writer says, "Arabs are still as fond as ever of exercising the virtue of hospitality. As they practice it, it is a lucrative spec-

3.—ORIENTAL BOWING. (See p. 16.)

ulation. The Bedawî sheikh, knowing that he must not nowadays expect to entertain angels unawares, takes a special care to entertain only such as can pay a round sum for the accommodation, or give their host a good dinner in return. The casual and impecunious stranger may, it is true, claim the traditional three days' board and lodging; but he must be content with the scraps 'that fall from the rich man's table,' and prepare to hear very outspoken hints of the undesirability of his presence."—PALMER'S *Desert of the Exodus*, p. 486

10.—FEET-WASHING.

XVIII, 4. Let a little water, I pray you, be fetched, and wash your feet, and rest yourselves under the tree.

Where the soil is dry and dusty, and the feet shod with sandals, frequent washing of the feet becomes not only a luxury, but a necessity for comfort and health. It is as much a part of hospitality, under these circumstances, for a host to see that his guests' feet are washed, as it is to provide them with food, or to furnish them a place for repose. See Gen. xxiv, 32. The steward of Joseph gave to Joseph's brethren water for their feet. Gen. xliii, 24. Among the ancient Egyptians the basins kept in the houses of the rich for this purpose were sometimes of gold.

To this custom of feet-washing the Saviour refers when he mildly reproves Simon the Pharisee, at whose house he was a guest, for neglecting to give him water for this purpose. Luke vii, 44. Paul, when writing to Timothy concerning the qualifications necessary for the aged widows who are to be recipients of the charity of the Church, names this among others: "if she have washed the saints' feet." 1 Tim. v, 10. This work was the duty of a servant, (see 1 Sam. xxv, 41;) and it is this fact which gives force to the beautiful symbolic action of our Lord, as recorded in John xiii, 4–15. The Master of all became a servant to all.

Feet were washed on returning from a journey and on retiring to bed. See Gen. xix, 2; 2 Sam. xi, 8; Sol. Song v, 3.

11.—BREAD MAKING.

XVIII, 6. And Abraham hastened into the tent unto Sarah, and said, Make ready quickly three measures of fine meal, knead it, and make cakes upon the hearth.

1. Bread in the East is made from wheat or barley, rye being but little cultivated. The "fine meal" here spoken of is wheat flour finely sifted, and is considered very choice.

2. The "three measures" were equal to an ephah, which is supposed to have contained a little less than a bushel. It was an ordinary quantity for baking. See Judges vi, 19; 1 Sam. i, 24; Matt. xiii, 33. The *seah* or "measure" is also mentioned in 2 Kings vii, 1, 16.

3. From the haste with which this bread was prepared it was evidently unleavened. The flour and water were hastily mixed, and the thin dough was either laid on heated stones, where the cakes would soon bake, or the "hearth" in the text was a smooth spot of ground on which fire had been kindled and the embers brushed off, when the dough was placed on the ground and the embers raked over it. In either way the bread would soon be ready for the guests. See also 1 Kings xvii, 12, 13; xix, 6.

Palmer, while visiting the outlying districts of Sinai, found, upon the watershed of Wady el-Hebeibeh, the remains of a large and evidently ancient encampment. "The small stones which formerly served, as they do in the present day, for hearths, in many places still showed signs of the action of fire, and on digging beneath the surface we found pieces of charcoal in great abundance."—*Desert of the Exodus*, p. 258. What gives peculiar interest to this discovery is the fact that Mr. Palmer thinks that he here discovered the remains of the ancient Israelitish camp at Kibroth-Hattaavah. A detail of the reasoning by which he reaches this conclusion would be out of place here. The curious reader is referred to Palmer's interesting work, pp. 260, 312, 507, 508.

12.—HOSTS—FLESH FOOD.

XVIII, 7. Abraham ran unto the herd, and fetched a calf . . . and gave it unto a young man; and he hasted to dress it.

1. The primitive manner in which Abraham and Sarah personally attended to the wants of their guests, finds illustration in what Dr. Shaw says of the Arab chiéftains in Barbary. There the greatest prince is not ashamed to bring a lamb from the flock and kill it, while the princess, his wife, prepares the fire and cooks it.

2. This meat was cooked as soon as the animal was killed, in accordance with the oriental usage. A common method of preparing a hasty meal among the Arabs is to cut up the meat into small pieces, run them on small spits or skewers, and broil them over the fire.

13.—BUTTER—FEASTS.

XVIII, 8. And he took butter, and milk, and the calf which he had dressed, and set it before them; and he stood by them under the tree, and they did eat.

1. The word here rendered butter (*chemah*) is said usually to signify curdled milk. It is also supposed that it was this which Jael gave to Sisera "in a lordly dish." Judges v, 25. It is at this day frequently used in eastern countries under the name of *leben*.

2. A description of an Arab feast, as given by modern travelers, will illustrate the mode of preparing and eating food. The meat is boiled with camel's milk, and with wheat which has been previously boiled and then dried in the sun. It is served up in a large wooden dish, in the center of which the boiled wheat is placed, and the meat around the edge. A wooden bowl containing the melted fat of the animal is pressed down in the midst of the boiled wheat, and every morsel is dipped into this melted fat before being swallowed. A bowl of camel's milk is handed round after the meal. It is not certain that milk was formerly used in cooking meat, as is here seen to be the modern Bedawin custom.

3. It is common still in the East to see travelers and guests eating under the shade of trees.

14.—TENT PARTITION.

XVIII, 10. Sarah heard it in the tent-door . . . behind him.

This was not the tent door referred to in verse 1, but the partition separating the women's part of the tent from that belonging to the men. Such partitions are often seen in modern Bedawin tents. For description of these tents, see note on Solomon's Song i, 5.

15.—GATES.

XIX, 1. And Lot sat in the gate of Sodom.

The gateways of walled cities, as well as the open spaces near them, were popular places of resort, being vaulted and cool, and convenient for the meeting of friends, or for a view of strangers, since all who went in or out

4.—City Gate.

must pass that way. They often resembled large stone halls, and had sufficient area to accommodate large assemblages. There the people assembled at the close of the day to tell the news, and to discuss various topics of interest. Thus it was that Lot at evening happened to be in the city gate when the strangers came by. In this position he readily saw them as they entered. Allusion to this use of the gate may be found in numerous other passages See Gen. xxiii, 10; xxxiv, 20; 1 Sam. iv. 18; Job xxix, 7; Psa. lxix, 12; cxxvii, 5; Prov. i, 21. Other uses of the gate will be noticed further on.

16.—TOWN-QUARTERS.

XIX, 4. But before they lay down, the men of the city, even the men of Sodom, compassed the house round, both old and young, all the people from every quarter.

In Eastern cities there are different quarters where people live according to their nation, religion, or occupation. These quarters are named after the occupants: as "The Christian quarter," "The Jews' quarter," "The Franks' quarter," "The quarter of the water-carriers," and the like. This usage may have existed at a very early age, and if so, it probably is referred to in the text. The merchants and tradesmen of Sodom came from the different "quarters" where they lived and surrounded Lot's house. There may also be a reference to this custom in Isa. xlvii, 15; lvi, 11. In Jer. xxxvii, 21, "the bakers' street" is spoken of.

17.—LOOKING BEHIND.

XIX, 26. But his wife looked back from behind him, and she became a pillar of salt.

1. Roberts says, that the expression "from behind him," seems to imply that she was following her husband, which to this day is the custom in India.

2. He also states that when men or women leave the house they never look back, as "it would be very unfortunate." Should a man on going to

his work leave any thing which his wife knows he will require, she will not call after him lest he turn or look back, but will either take the article herself or send it by another. If a palankeen come up behind any persons who are walking in the road they will not look behind to see it, but carefully step a little on one side until it has passed, when they will gratify their curiosity.

18.—CAVE-DWELLINGS.

XIX, 30. He [Lot] dwelt in a cave, he and his two daughters.

The country of Judea being mountainous and rocky is full of caverns. Caves and clefts in the rock were probably among the earliest dwelling-places of man. The inhabitants of Mount Taurus, even to this day, live in caves, as do many of the wandering shepherds of Arabia Petrea. Thus Lot found a home for himself and his daughters. Some of these caves are of immense size, capable of holding hundreds, and even thousands, of people, and might easily be converted into strongholds for troops. It was in this way that the children of Israel sheltered themselves from the Midianites, (Judges vi, 2,) and from the Philistines, 1 Sam. xiii, 6. It was thus that David, with four hundred men, was concealed in the cave Adullam, (1 Sam. xxii, 1, 2,) and afterward with six hundred in Ziph, and in En-gedi, 1 Sam. xxiii, 13, 14, 29; xxiv, 3. Caves have been common places of resort for the persecuted people of God in all ages. See Heb. xi, 38.

19.—WEANING-FEAST.

XXI, 8. Abraham made a great feast the same day that Isaac was weaned.

It is still customary in the East to have a festive gathering at the time a child is weaned. Among the Hindoos, when the time for weaning has come, the event is accompanied with feasting and religious ceremonies during which rice is formally presented to the child.

20.—BURDEN ON SHOULDER.

XXI, 14. Putting it on her shoulder.

It was an ancient Egyptian custom for the women to carry burdens on the shoulder, and for the men to carry them on the head. The women in Palestine, to this day, carry the water skins and earthen jars upon the shoulder. It was thus that Rebecca carried her water pitcher. Gen. xxiv, 15. Sometimes they carry these jars on the head. It is said by some writers, that in India the women of high rank carry the water jars on the shoulder, and the common women carry them on the head.

21.—EARLY RISING—SADDLES.

XXII, 3. Abraham rose up early . . . and saddled his ass.

1. The habit of early rising is all but universal in Palestine. The climate makes this a necessity for the greater part of the year, the heat being so great that hard labor is oppressive a few hours after sunrise. At early dawn laborers go to their work and travelers start on their journeys. The Scripture references to this custom are numerous. See, for instance, Gen. xix, 2; xxi, 14; xxviii, 18; Exod. xxxiv, 4; Job i, 5; Psa. lxiii, 1.

2. We are not to imagine by the term "saddle" any thing similar to what we call by that name. The ancient saddle was merely a piece of cloth thrown over the back of the animal on which the rider sat. See Matt. xxi, 7. "No nation of antiquity knew the use of either saddles or stirrups." (GOGUET, *Origin of Laws.* Cited by BURDER.)

22.—GOING AND COMING.

XXII, 5. I and the lad will go . . . and come again.

Roberts says, that the people of the East never say, as we do when taking leave, "I will go," or, "I am going," but, "I go and return."

23.—CEREMONIAL MOURNING.

XXIII, 2. Abraham came to mourn for Sarah, and to weep for her.

We shall have occasion, in noticing other passages, to refer to the different modes of manifesting grief at times of bereavement; it is only necessary to say here, that there is in this text an evident allusion to a ceremonial mourning. The word "came" indicates this. The passage shows the antiquity of the custom of formal manifestation of sorrow in honor of the dead.

24.—MODE OF BARGAINING.

XXIII, 5, 6. The children of Heth answered Abraham, saying unto him, Hear us, my lord: thou art a mighty prince among us: in the choice of our sepulchers bury thy dead; none of us shall withhold from thee his sepulcher, but that thou mayest bury thy dead.

We have in the interesting narrative of this business transaction an exact representation of the Oriental mode of trafficking. Abraham, a great prince, but a stranger, wishes to buy a piece of land for a family burial place. He makes the proposition to those members of the tribe of Hittites in whose territory the land lies. They respond by offering him the use of any one of their own sepulchers which he may select. This generosity, however, is a mere ceremony preliminary to driving a bargain in which they mean to make as much as possible out of the rich stranger. So, also, when Ephron is approached in reference to selling the lot which Abraham desires, he says, (v, 11,) "Nay, my lord, hear me: the field *give* I thee, and the cave that is therein, I *give* it thee; in the presence of the sons of my people give I it thee: bury thy dead." This seems to be a wonderful liberality on the part of this Hittite, but he does not expect that his offer will be accepted; or, if actually accepted, he expects in return a present that shall be worth more than his gift.

25.—MIDDLEMEN.

XXIII, 8. Entreat for me to Ephron the son of Zohar.

Abraham does not go directly to Ephron, but he gets some of the Hittites to plead for him. No business of importance can to this day be transacted in the East without middlemen.

26.—HOW MONEY WAS USED.

XXIII, 16. Abraham hearkened unto Ephron; and Abraham weighed to Ephron the silver, which he had named in the audience of the sons of Heth, four hundred shekels of silver, current money with the merchant.

1. The Hebrews probably learned the use of metallic money from the Phenicians, among whom their ancestors dwelt, and who are said to have been the inventors of silver money. Other nations for a long time made oxen and sheep the standard of value. Silver was the metal at first generally used for currency, gold being kept for articles of jewelry. Gold money is first mentioned in 1 Chron. xxi, 25. though, of course, it may have been used before the time there referred to. Some suppose that in early times gold jewelry was made of specified weight, so that it might be used for money. See Gen. xxiv, 22.

5.—WEIGHING MONEY. (See page 24.)

2. Ancient money, being uncoined, was weighed instead of being counted. Even to this day Oriental merchants weigh the silver and gold which are the medium of traffic; not only the bullion, but the coined pieces also, lest some dishonest trader might pass upon them a coin of light weight. The ancient Egyptians, and some other nations, used rings of gold and of silver for the same purposes that coins are now used. These rings were weighed, the weights being in the form of oxen, lions, geese, sheep, and other animals. Some of these weights have been found; they are made of bronze, and with a ring projecting from the back for a handle.

6.—LION-WEIGHT. FROM KHORSABAD.

The weighing of money is also referred to in Jer. xxxii, 9, 10, and in Zech. xi, 12.

3. The word shekel (from *shakal*, to weigh) indicates the original mode of reckoning money by weight rather than by count; and when coined money was introduced it was natural that the name originally applied to what was weighed should be given to what was counted. Thus we find in the Bible a shekel of weight and a shekel of money. The exact weight of the shekel is not known. It is estimated to have been between nine and ten pennyweights, and is supposed to have been worth nearly sixty cents. This would make the value of the field Abraham bought of Ephron nearly two hundred and forty dollars.

4. The expression "current," seems to indicate some understood standard of value, either as to the purity of the silver or the weight, or both. "The Phenician merchants usually tried the silver themselves, and then, after dividing a bar into smaller pieces, put the mark upon them." (*Michælis.*) There may also have been a mark on the bar or on the ring money to indicate its weight.

27.—TRANSFER OF PROPERTY.

XXIII, 17, 18. **The field of Ephron, which was in Machpelah, which was before Mamre, the field, and the cave which was therein, and all the trees that were in the field, that were in all the borders round about, were made sure unto Abraham for a possession in the presence of the children of Heth, before all that went in at the gate of his city.**

1. All the details of the contract are here given as is still customary in an Oriental bargain. Every thing appertaining to the lot is here put down; field, cave, trees, every thing "in all the borders round about." Dr. Thom-

son says, "The contract must mention every thing that belongs to it, (the lot,) and certify that fountains or wells in it, trees upon it, etc., are sold with the field. If you rent a house, not only the building itself, but every room in it, above and below, down to the kitchen, pantry, stable, and hen-coop, must be specified."—*The Land and the Book*, vol. ii, p. 383.

2. There is no evidence here of any written contract, and probably there was none. The bargain was made "sure" by being consummated in the presence of the crowd assembled at the gate, as bargains often are now in the same country, the number of the witnesses precluding any withdrawing from the contract on either side.

3. We may now notice the steps by which the end of this bargain was gradually reached. How much time was consumed we are not told, but that there was a great deal of talking there can be no doubt. The whole scene vividly illustrates what many modern travelers describe from their own observation. 1. Abraham asks the Hittites the privilege of buying a place of burial, (verse 4.) 2. They offer him the free use of any one of their own sepulchers that he may choose, (verse 6.) 3. Abraham bows before them in acknowledgment of their courtesy, (verse 7.) 4. He asks them to use their influence with Ephron to effect a sale, (verse 8.) 5. Ephron offers to make him a present of the whole field and the cave, and calls on the people to be witnesses of his generosity and sincerity, (verse 11.) 6. Abraham bows again before them, (verse 12.) 7. He declines to take it as a gift, and offers to pay for it, (verse 13.) (See a parallel instance in 1 Chron. xxi, 22–25) 8. Ephron names his price, (three or four times what the land was worth, if the ancient usages were the same as the modern,) and intimates that such a price is a small matter for so great a prince as he is dealing with, (verse 15.) 9. Abraham, not being in a condition to insist on lower terms, accepts the offer. (verse 16.) 10. The money is weighed, and the land becomes the property of Abraham, (verse 16.)

28.—CAVE SEPULCHERS.

XXIII, 19. Abraham buried Sarah his wife in the cave of the field of Machpelah.

Sepulchral caves are still found in many parts of the East. Sometimes a natural cave is used, with such modifications as necessity may require. The place where Abraham buried Sarah was undoubtedly a natural cave. Tombs were frequently hewn out of the rock. See note on Isa. xxii, 16.

29.—CHIEF SERVANT—MODE OF SWEARING.

XXIV, 2, 8. Abraham said unto his eldest servant . . . Put, I pray thee, thy hand under my thigh, and . . . swear, etc.

1. The most intelligent and faithful servant in the household was appointed overseer of the others. The word "eldest" is not of necessity

expressive of age, but of authority. This was the head servant, chief of all the rest, though some of them may have been over others. In a similar way we use the word "elder" in an official sense, even when applied to young men. Such head-servants or stewards may still be seen portrayed on Egyptian tombs, with their secretaries, implements of writing, stewards' account books, and articles for domestic use. This was the position which Joseph filled. Gen. xxxix, 4.

2. The mode of swearing here spoken of seems to have been peculiar to the patriarcns. Jacob required Joseph thus to swear to him. Gen. xlvii, 29. Various conjectures have been made as to the precise position of the hand or hands in taking this oath, for which, as well as for the supposed significance of the oath, commentators may be consulted.

30.—BRIDE CHOSEN BY PARENTS.

XXIV, 4. Thou shalt go unto my country, and to my kindred, and take a wife unto my son Isaac.

The bridegroom does not make choice of his bride; the parents negotiate this important business between themselves, and the young people are expected to acquiesce in the arrangement. In this instance Abraham sends a trusty servant hundreds of miles away to select for his son a wife whom he never saw. Hagar chose a wife for Ishmael. Gen. xxi, 21. Isaac gave command to Jacob on this important subject. Gen. xxviii, 1. Judah selected a wife for Er. Gen. xxxviii, 6. Young men who chose wives for themselves without parental mediation usually afflicted their parents in so doing. Gen. xxvi, 35; xxvii, 46. The sons, however, had sometimes the privilege of suggesting their personal preferences to their parents. Thus Shechem did (Gen. xxxiv, 4;) and also Samson. Judges xiv, 2.

31.—WELLS.

XXIV, 11. He made his camels to kneel down without the city by a well of water at the time of the evening, even the time that women go out to draw water.

"A modern guide-book could hardly furnish a truer picture of what occurs at the close of every day in the vicinity of Eastern villages than this description, written so many thousand years ago."—HACKETT, *Illustrations of Scripture*, p. 89.

1. The position of a camel when at rest is kneeling. These animals are taught it when young.

2. Villages are built near wells or springs for convenience, but not near enough to be discommoded by the noise and dust and crowds which are sure to be drawn to such places.

3. The work of carrying water is done almost invariably by women,

7.—At the Well. (Gen. xxiv, 11.)

excepting in some large Oriental cities, where men as well as women become water carriers. See Gen. xxix, 10; Exod. ii, 16; 1 Sam. ix, 11.

4. Evening and early morning are the usual times for visiting the well for a supply of water.

32.—PITCHERS.

XXIV, 15. With her pitcher upon her shoulder.

The ancient pitchers were of earthenware. Lam. iv, 2. See also Judges vii, 20, where it is said that Gideon's men brake theirs. Such are used now for drawing water. Some have one handle, and others have two.

33.—HOW WELLS ARE USED.

XXIV, 16. She went down to the well, and filled her pitcher, and came up.

The wells are usually approached by flights of steps, so that the women may dip their pitchers directly into the water. In some cases the wells are dug deep, and require a rope, or some simple machinery, for raising the water. See note on John iv, 11.

34.—TROUGHS.

XXIV, 20. She hasted, and emptied her pitcher into the trough.

These troughs are placed near the wells for convenience in watering cattle. They are made of wood or stone. Sometimes a long stone block is hollowed out, from which a number of animals can drink at once; and sometimes the troughs are smaller, several of them lying about the same well, each so small as to accommodate only one animal at a time.

See also Gen. xxx, 38; Exod. ii, 16.

35.—NOSE–JEWELS—BRACELETS.

XXIV, 22. It came to pass, as the camels had done drinking, that the man took a golden ear-ring of half a shekel weight, and two bracelets for her hands of ten shekels weight of gold.

1. The "ear-ring" here spoken of (*nezem*) is more properly a nose-ring. The servant says, (verse 47,) "I put the ear-ring upon her face." The present of a single ear-ring would be strange; to put it on the *face* would be stranger still. Nose-jewels are referred to in Prov. xi, 22, Isa. iii, 21, and Ezek. xvi, 12, where for "forehead" in the text the margin has "nose."

8.—NOSE-RINGS OF MODERN EGYPT. (HALF SIZE.)

The nose-ring is made generally of silver or gold, but sometimes of coral, mother-of-pearl, or even of horn, according to the taste or means of the wearer.   This curious ornament varies considerably in size and thickness. The metal rings are usually from one inch to one inch and a half in diameter, and sometimes are as large as three inches.   Beads, coral, or jewels, are strung upon them.   They are usually hung from the right nostril, though sometimes from the left, and occasionally they are suspended from the middle filament of the nose.   In India, according to Roberts, the nose-jewels are of different shapes, resembling a swan, a serpent, or a flower. Anderson saw them in Egypt, made of brass, but worn only by women of the lower class.   Graham says that in Syria, as well as in Egypt, these ornaments are not worn among the respectable classes of society, but are found among the Africans and slaves; so that the fashion seems to have changed since Rebekah's day, and since the time when Isaiah wrote.

2. The weight of the nose-jewel given to Rebekah (a half shekel) was nearly a quarter of an ounce, troy.

3. Bracelets are almost universally worn by women in the East.   They are sometimes made of gold, sometimes of mother-of-pearl, but usually of silver.   The poorer women wear them made of plated steel, horn, brass, copper, and occasionally nothing but simple strings of beads.   The arms are

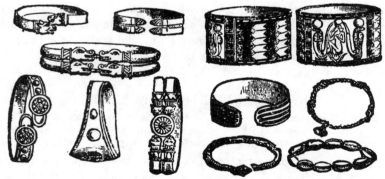

9.—ASSYRIAN BRACELETS.   EGYPTIAN BRACELETS.

sometimes crowded with them from wrist to elbow.   They are sometimes flat, but more frequently round or semicircular, and are often made hollow to give, by their bulk, the appearance of greater weight.   Bracelets (*tsemedim*) are also referred to in Num. xxxi, 50; Ezek. xvi, 11; xxiii, 42.   The other passages in which "bracelets" occur have different words in the original, which will be explained under the several texts where they are used.

4. The weight of the bracelets presented to Rebekah (ten shekels) was over four and a half ounces.   They are sometimes worn heavier than this, so as to seem more like manacles than bracelets.

36.—BRIDAL PRESENTS.

XXIV, 53. The servant brought forth jewels of silver, and jewels of gold, and raiment, and gave them to Rebekah.

1. Rich and splendid apparel, especially such as was adorned with gold, was very general among Eastern nations from earliest times, and is still quite common. Reference is made to this in Psa. xlv, 9, 13 : "Upon thy right hand did stand the queen in gold of Ophir."—"Her clothing is of wrought gold."

2. These beautiful and costly bridal-presents are given to the intended bride by the expectant bridegroom for the purpose of binding the contract. See note on Matt. i, 18.

37.—THE NURSE.

XXIV, 59. They sent away Rebekah their sister, and her nurse.

In an Eastern family the nurse is a very important personage. She is esteemed almost as a parent; and, accompanying the bride to her new home, there remains with her. She becomes the adviser, the assistant, and the friend of the bride. To the nurse, as to a mother, the bride will confide her greatest secrets. Thus Rebekah took with her on her long journey to her future home the nurse who had cared for her since childhood, so that, besides the female servants she took with her, (verse 61,) she might have one intimate familiar friend among strangers.

38.—UPLIFTED EYES — MARK OF RESPECT.

XXIV, 64. Rebekah lifted up her eyes, and when she saw Isaac, she lighted off the camel.

1. The expression "lifted up" is often met with in the Scriptures in connection with the eyes. It does not always mean to look upward, but sometimes to look directly and earnestly at an object. Roberts says, it is to this day a common form of speech in India. We have in this text an illustration. Isaac may have looked upward when "he lifted up his eyes" and saw the caravan coming, for he was walking in the field, engaged in meditation, (verse 63,) and very likely had his head inclined, and his eyes downward; but Rebekah, on the back of a camel, could hardly have looked upward when she saw Isaac. She simply looked directly and earnestly at him.

2. She quickly "lighted off" the camel when she discerned Isaac, thus giving him a customary mark of respect. In like manner Achsah alighted in the presence of Othniel and of Caleb, (Josh. xv, 18 ;) Abigail thus alighted in the presence of David, (1 Sam. xxv, 23;) and even the haughty Naaman was so happy over his wonderful cure that he alighted from his chariot in the presence of Elisha's servant, (2 Kings v, 21,) showing Gehazi the respect he would have shown to his master had he been present. Travelers tell us that this custom is still practiced.

39.—THE VAIL.

XXIV, 65. The servant had said, It is my master: therefore she took a vail and covered herself.

1. The custom of vailing the face of women, now so common in the East, was not general in the days of the patriarchs, nor for a long time after. The women usually appeared in public with faces exposed. Much of the modern Oriental scrupulousness on this subject is due to Mohammedan influence, the Koran forbidding women to appear unvailed except in the presence only of their nearest relatives. No representations of vails are found on either the Assyrian or the Egyptian monuments; yet the Egyptians, as well as the Hebrews, did use the vail on special occasions. Wilkinson says, that the ancient Egyptian vail was not so thick as the *boorko* of modern Egypt; but was thin enough to be seen through, like that of the Wahábees. The vailing of the bride before coming into the presence of the bridegroom is a very ancient custom, indicating modesty, and subjection to the husband.

It is claimed by some, however, that the *tsaiph*—both here and in Gen. xxxviii, 14, rendered " vail "—was not properly a vail, but rather a large wrapper which was worn out of doors; a light summer dress, of handsome appearance and of ample dimensions, so that it might be thrown over the head at pleasure. Thus, when she saw Isaac, Rebekah slipped the upper part of her loose flowing robe over her head, thereby concealing her face from her expectant lover.

40.—WOMAN'S TENT — MARRIAGE.

XXIV, 67. Isaac brought her into his mother Sarah's tent, and took Rebekah, and she became his wife.

1. The expression "Sarah's tent" may mean nothing more than her apartment in the principal tent of the encampment, (see Gen xviii, 9, 10; Judges iv, 18; and see note on Sol. Song i, 5;) though it is sometimes customary for the women to have separate tents of their own, as seems to have been the case with Leah and Rachel. Gen. xxxi, 33. This would doubtless be desirable where there were more wives than one.

2. There is no evidence of any special religious forms in these primitive marriages. The preliminaries referring to dowry and similar financial matters being satisfactorily arranged, the man took his wife as Isaac took Rebekah. The essence of the marriage ceremony consisted in the removal of the bride from her father's house to that of the bridegroom or of his father.

41.—BIRTHRIGHT.

XXV, 81, 83. Jacob said, Sell me this day thy birthright. . . . And he sold his birthright.

Great respect was paid by the household to the first-born son. He had headship over his brothers; he succeeded to the father's official authority;

he had a special claim to the father's benediction; in him was the progenitorship of the Messiah; the domestic priesthood belonged to him, according to some authorities, though this is denied by others.   Under the Mosaic law he received a double portion of the father's goods.   This birthright could be transferred to another for a consideration, or withheld by the father for cause.

42.—POTTAGE.

XXV, 34. Jacob gave Esau bread and pottage of lentiles; and he did eat and drink, and rose up, and went his way. Thus Esau despised his birthright.

Pottage was often made of lentiles, and is so made at this day.   Dr. Shaw says that they are cooked like beans, which they very much resemble, " dissolving easily into a mass, and making a pottage of a chocolate color."

In India this sort of food is considered so cheap and common that it represents, in proverbial speech, any thing that is worthless. "The fellow has sold his land for pottage; " that is, for an insignificant consideration. "The learned one has fallen into the pottage-pot; " that is, the wise man has done what was not expected of him—a mean thing. "He is trying to procure rubies by pottage; " that is, he wishes to get great things by small means. —*Roberts.*   These expressions illustrate the despicable conduct of Esau, who sold his priceless birthright for a mess of mean food, the emblem of worthlessness.

43.— CUSTOMS CONCERNING WELLS.

XXVI, 15. All the wells which his father's servants had digged in the days of Abraham his father, the Philistines had stopped them, and filled them with earth.

In the East, digging wells gives title to unoccupied lands.   Isaac therefore owned by inheritance the land in the vicinity of which these wells had been dug by his father's direction.   In a pastoral country it is a serious matter to choke up the wells which have been dug for the convenience of flocks and herds.   It is, in fact, a declaration of war, and has always been considered a hostile act.   Thus the Israelites did according to Divine command when they invaded Moab.. 2 Kings iii, 19, 25.   In some parts of Persia the people have a way of concealing their wells with boards covered with sand, so as to conceal them from the eye of an enemy.

44.—STRIFE AT WELLS.

XXVI, 20. The herdmen of Gerar did strive with Isaac's herdmen, saying, The water is ours.

These contests between rival herdmen for the possession of wells are still common in the land.   Water is so necessary, and yet sometimes so hard to get, that it is no wonder there are battles waged for it.   Some travelers state that the Bedâwin would give a stranger milk to drink rather than water, the latter being more valuable. A contest similar to the one noticed in the text took place between the servants of Abraham and those of Abimelech. Gen. xxi, 25.

45.—COVENANT FEASTS.

XXVI, 80, 81. He made them a feast, and they did eat and drink. And they rose up betimes . . . and sware one to another.

It was customary among the Hebrews, and also among the heathen nations, to eat together when entering into a covenant. When Jacob made his covenant with Laban he made a feast for his brethren. Gen. xxxi, 54. Many allusions to this custom are made by classical writers.

46.—SEASONED FOOD.

XXVII, 8, 4. Go out to the field, and take me some venison ; and make me savory meat, such as I love, and bring it to me, that I may eat.

This means a dish prepared in any appetizing way, but especially by means of condiments. The Orientals are fond of highly seasoned food. Salt, spices, onions, garlic, and various aromatic herbs, such as saffron and mint, are used as seasoning for their meats.

Some commentators suppose a connection between this feast and the former patriarchal blessing. They regard it as a solemn covenant ceremony—a sacrifice which ratifies the blessing. Such covenant solemnities were usually associated with a meal among the Orientals.

47.—TIME FOR MOURNING.

XXVII, 41. The days of mourning for my father are at hand.

This alludes to the formal ceremonious mourning for the dead, which usually lasted seven days, (Gen. l, 10; 1 Sam. xxxi, 13; Job ii, 13,) though it was sometimes continued for a longer period.

See note on John xi, 17.

48.—SLEEPING OUT OF DOORS.

XXVIII, 11. He lighted upon a certain place, and tarried there all night . . . and he took of the stones of that place, and put them for his pillows, and lay down in that place to sleep.

1. Sleeping out of doors all night could have been no hardship to a man inured to a shepherd's life, for this was a shepherd's custom.

2. It is not likely, as many seem to imagine, that his head rested on the naked stone. His outer mantle could easily have been drawn up over his head, and its folds would have made an excellent pillow on the stone headrest, the hardness of which could be further modified by the covering he usually wore on his head.

49.—MONUMENTAL STONES.

XXVIII, 18. Jacob rose up early in the morning, and took the stone that he had put for his pillows, and set it up for a pillar, and poured oil upon the top of it.

1. This stone was set up as a monument of God's wonderful revelation to him, and of his vow. Verse 20. Thirty years later he repeated this solemn act in the same place. Gen. xxxv, 14. Moses likewise built twelve pillars at Sinai as a sign of God's covenant. Exod. xxiv, 4. So Joshua set up a monument of stones in commemoration of the passage of the Jordan. Josh. iv, 3–9. At Shechem also he set up a stone under an oak as a memorial of the covenant between God and his people. Josh. xxiv, 26. In like manner Samuel erected a stone between Mizpeh and Shen to commemorate his victory over the Philistines. 1 Sam. vii, 12. As these stone pillars were all erected as testimonies of some great events, it has been suggested that Paul in 1 Tim. iii, 15 designs to represent the Church as a pillar of testimony for the truth, God having founded and reared the Church as a monument for that purpose.

There existed in heathen countries a practice similar to the one referred to in the text. Morier gives a good illustration of our text in a little incident he saw while traveling in Persia. He says: "I remarked that our old guide, every here and there, placed a stone on a conspicuous bit of rock, or two stones one upon the other, at the same time uttering some words, which I learned were a prayer for our safe return."—*Second Journey through Persia*, p. 85. He had frequently seen similar stones without knowing their design.

2. The anointing of the stone by Jacob was doubtless designed as a solemn act of consecration of this stone to its monumental purposes; just as subsequently Moses, by command of God, anointed the tabernacle and its furniture. Num. vii, 1. This act of the patriarch is not to be confounded with the idolatrous practice, common among heathens, of pouring oil upon stones and worshiping them. See note on Isa. lvii, 6.

50.—WELL-STONES.

XXIX, 2. Out of that well they watered the flocks: and a great stone was upon the well's mouth.

This was to protect the water from impurity, and from shifting sands, which without such protection would soon choke it. Modern travelers make frequent mention of the stone covers to wells and cisterns. Some of these stones are so large and heavy as to require the united strength of several men to remove them. May there not be reference to this custom in Job xxxviii, 30: "The waters are hid as with a stone, and the face of the deep is frozen?"

51.—WELLS OPENED.

XXIX, 8. Thither were all the flocks gathered: and they rolled the stone from the well's mouth, and watered the sheep, and put the stone again upon the well's mouth in his place.

This is not a part of the history; since all the flocks were not actually gathered and the stone removed until Rachel came. Verse 10. The verse is meant to describe the general custom of the country. It was usual to wait until all the flocks were gathered, and then the stone was taken off and the work of watering began. Verse 8. Harmer refers to the statement of Sir John Chardin, that he had known wells or cisterns locked up in the East, and accepts Chardin's explanation that this may have been the case in this instance, and that Rachel probably had the key, and that for that reason they were all obliged to wait until she came. But we see no reason for supposing any lock and key in the case; no mention is made of them in the narrative. The reason assigned in verse 8 for waiting for Rachel is, not that she had any special means for opening the well, but that it was customary for all the flocks to be gathered before the stone was rolled away.

52.—NAMES FROM ANIMALS.

XXIX, 6. Behold Rachel his daughter cometh with the sheep.

Burder calls attention to the fact that the name Rachel signifies, in Hebrew, a *sheep*, and says, " It was anciently the custom to give names even to families from cattle, both great and small."—*Oriental Customs*, No. 48. This ancient custom is no more singular than that which is common among us, of naming families after all sorts of beasts and birds, wild and tame; for example, Wolf, Fox, Lion, Bear, Bull, Nightingale, Jay, Hawk, Finch, etc.

53.—MEN KISSING.

XXIX, 13. And it came to pass, when Laban heard the tidings of Jacob his sister's son, that he ran to meet him, and embraced him, and kissed him.

This custom of embraces and kisses among men, though strange to us, is common enough in the East. Jacob kissed his father. Gen. xxvii, 27. Esau embraced and kissed Jacob. Gen. xxxiii, 4. Joseph kissed all his brethren. Gen. xlv, 15. Jacob kissed and embraced Joseph's sons. Gen. xlviii, 10. Aaron kissed Moses. Exod. iv, 27. Moses kissed Jethro. Exod. xviii, 7. David and Jonathan kissed each other. 1 Sam. xx, 41. The father of the prodigal is represented as kissing him when he returned home. Luke xv, 20. The elders at Miletus fell on Paul's neck and kissed him. Acts xx, 37. Modern travelers make frequent mention of this custom.

54.—WEAK EYES.

XXIX, 17. Leah was tender-eyed.

That is, she had weak or dull eyes, which, according to the Oriental standard of beauty, is a great blemish.

55.—RELATIVES PREFERRED.

XXIX, 19. It is better that I give her to thee, than that I should give her to another man.

It is still customary among many Eastern tribes to give the preference in marriage to a cousin. It is expected that a man will marry his cousin. He is not compelled to do it, but he has the right, and she is not allowed to marry any other without his consent.

56.—BRIDES BOUGHT.

XXIX, 20. Jacob served seven years for Rachel.

The dowry comes not *with* the bride, but *for* the bride. In Oriental marriages the bride is given only on receipt of a consideration. In many cases the transaction amounts to actual bargain and sale; this, however, is not necessarily the case. Custom regards the father of the bride as entitled to some compensation for the trouble had in her training, and for the loss of service experienced by her departure from home. If this compensation cannot be rendered in money, jewels, or cattle, it may be given in labor. It was in this way that Jacob became herdman to Laban. Moses probably served Jethro in a similar manner, for the sake of having Zipporah. Comp. Exod. ii, 21; iii, 1. Shechem offered to Jacob and his sons any amount of dowry he was pleased to ask for Dinah. Gen. xxxiv, 12.

57.—MARRIAGE FEAST.

XXIX, 22. Laban gathered together all the men of the place and made a feast.

The usual duration of a marriage feast was a week. Thus, "Fulfill her week," in verse 27, means, "Wait until the week's festivities are over." This was the duration of Samson's marriage feast. Judges xiv, 12.

58.—THE ELDER FIRST.

XXIX, 26. Laban said, It must not be so done in our country, to give the younger before the first-born.

This ancient custom still exists in India, and is sometimes observed in Egypt. It also prevailed in old imperial Germany. In India it is considered disgraceful in the extreme, and according to the Gentoo law a crime, for a father to permit a younger daughter to get married before the elder, or for a younger son to be married while his elder brother remains single. If the eldest daughter be deformed, or blind, or deaf, or dumb, then the

3

younger may be married first. If a father have an opportunity to marry one of his younger daughters advantageously, he will first do all he can to get the elder one married, and until this can be done the younger cannot be married.

59.—SIGNIFICANT NAMES.

XXIX, 32. She called his name Reuben; for she said, Surely the Lord hath looked upon my affliction.

Reuben, that is, *See! a son!* This was in joyful acknowledgment of this evidence of God's goodness. Many of the proper names in the Scriptures have a meaning in some way connected with the persons bearing them. Other people besides the Jews have had this custom: Africans, Arabs, East Indians, and the aborigines of our own land. Thus a certain Abyssinian was named *Omazena*, because of a wart on his hand; an Arab boy was called *Duman*, because he was born before the gate Bab-el-Duma at Damascus. Among the Hindoos we find *Ani Muttoo*, the precious pearl; *Pun Amma*, the golden lady; *Chinny Tamby*, the little friend. Among the North American Indians we have *Kosh-kin-ne-kait*, the cut-off arm; *Wah-ge-kaut*, crooked legs; *Wau-zhe-gaw-maish-kum*, he that walks along the shore.

60.—TERAPHIM.

XXXI, 19. Rachel had stolen the images that were her father's.

These "images" (*teraphim*) are supposed to have been rude representations of the human form; perhaps the statuettes of deceased ancestors. Nothing definite is known as to their size. They could not have been very large, or Rachel would not have been able to conceal them under the baggage;

nor could they have been very small, or they would not have served Michal's purpose of deception. See 1 Sam. xix, 13, 16. They may have been of different sizes. Their use is very ancient; the Israelites adopted them from the Arameans. They were household gods which were consulted as oracles. Micah the Ephraimite placed them in his "house of gods." Judg. xvii, 5; xviii, 14, 17, 18, 20.

Some Jewish writers believe that the teraphim were supposed, on consultation, to be able to give any information desired, and that Rachel stole them from her father for fear he should learn, by consulting them, what route Jacob and his family had taken. Whether or not the

10.—TERAPHIM.

teraphim were actually worshiped is a disputed question. The Hebrews certainly kept up the worship of Jehovah in connection with the use of the teraphim. It was not until the reign of Josiah that this singular custom was abolished. 2 Kings xxiii, 24. We even find traces of it afterward as late as the time of Hosea. Hosea iii, 4. The practice became deeply rooted, and extended over large regions of country. The Lares and Penates of the Romans are supposed to have been used for the same purposes as these teraphim. "The Penates were divinities or household gods, who were believed to be the creators or dispensers of all the well-being and gifts of fortune enjoyed by a family, as well as an entire community." "Every family worshiped one or more of these, whose images were kept in the inner part of the house." The Lares were "guardian spirits whose place was the chimney-piece, and whose altar was the domestic hearth." Lares and Penates were worshiped "in the form of little figures or images of wax, earthenware, or terra cotta, and of metal, more especially silver."—BARKER'S *Lares and Penates*, pp. 146, 147.

Faber supposes the teraphim to be identical with the cherubim. He thinks that those which belonged to Laban were images resembling the cherubim which were afterward put on the ark.—*Origin of Pagan Idolatry*, vol. iii, p. 621.

61.—TABRET AND HARP.

XXXI, 27. I might have sent thee away with mirth, and with songs, with tabret, and with harp.

1. The word *toph*, here and in other places rendered "tabret," and in a number of texts translated "timbrel," represents a very ancient musical instrument of percussion. There are three varieties depicted on the Egyptian monuments: one circular, another square or oblong, and a third consisting of two squares separated by a bar. Over these frames parchment was stretched, and in the rim were small bells or pieces of tinkling brass. The *toph* was used on occasions of joy, and was generally played by women, and often accompanied by dancing. It is reproduced in the "tambourine" which is occasionally seen in the streets of our large cities in the hands of itinerant musicians as an accompaniment to the barrel-organ.

2. The word *kinnor*, which frequently occurs in the Old Testament, and is translated "harp," has given rise to considerable discussion. It was undoubtedly the earliest musical instrument made, (Gen. iv, 21,) though some suppose that the text referred to is meant to show that Jubal was the inventor of stringed instruments generally, without referring to any particular kind. As to the shape of this ancient instrument there is no certainty. It has been variously represented by different writers as shaped like the lyre, the Greek letter Δ, the guitar, and the modern harp. There is

equal variety of opinion as to the number of strings. Seven, ten, twenty-four, and forty-seven have been named. It has also been asserted by some that it was played by means of a plectrum, while others assert that it was played by hand. These conflicting statements may all be harmonized by supposing that the shape varied at different times, or that the word *kinnor* was the generic term for all instruments of the lyre kind; that the number of strings varied at different periods, or with the size of the instrument; that the instruments were of different sizes; and that they were sometimes played with a plectrum and sometimes by hand. The *kinnor* was a very popular instrument with the Hebrews, and was used at jubilees and festivals. Its use was also practiced by other nations.

62.—CAMELS' FURNITURE.

XXXI, 34. Rachel had taken the images, and put them in the camel's furniture, and sat upon them.

It is not known whether this "furniture" was simply the cloth which covered the camel's back, or a couch which might be used at night for

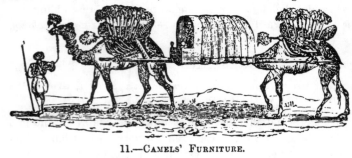

11.—CAMELS' FURNITURE.

a bed, or a fixture resembling the wicker-work chair or cage, covered with a canopy, which is used by the modern Arab ladies when they ride on camels. Whether Rachel made use of any such arrangement or not, the place where the teraphim were concealed was evidently in the article, whatever it was, which took the place of a saddle, and on which Rachel sat. It is at this day common for the Arabs to hide stolen property under the padding of their saddles.

63.—COVENANT STONES.

XXXI, 48. Laban said, This heap is a witness between me and thee this day.

The use of stones in making a covenant is referred to in the Bible on several occasions. Herodotus speaks of a similar custom among the ancient Arabians. He says: "When two men would swear a friendship, they stand on each side of a third. He, with a sharp stone, makes a cut on the inside of the hand of each, near the middle finger, and taking a piece from their dress dips it in the blood of each, and moistens therewith seven

stones lying in the midst, calling meanwhile on Bacchus and Urania."—
RAWLINSON's *Herodotus*, ii, p. 401.

Some think that Job refers to this custom when he speaks of "a days-
man." See Job ix, 33.

64.—PRESENTS.

**XXXIII, 10. Jacob said, Nay, I pray thee, if now I have found
grace in thy sight, then receive my present at my hand.**

The giving of presents is far more common in the East, and has more significance, than with us. Hardly any transaction of importance can take
place without a gift. The formal visits which friends make to each other
are preceded by presents of fowls, sheep, rice, coffee, and other provisions.
Sir John Chardin notices that in Persia every one gives what is most at
hand, and has a relation to his profession, and those who have no particular
profession give money. A refusal to receive a present is, throughout the
East, interpreted as an evidence of enmity. Hence Jacob's anxiety that
Esau should accept the gift he offered. See also Gen. xliii, 11; Judges
iii, 18; 1 Sam. ix, 7; x, 27; 2 Sam. xvii, 27–29; 1 Kings x, 2, 10; xiv, 3;
2 Kings v, 5, 15; viii, 9; 2 Chron. ix, 24; Psa. lxxii, 10; lxxvi, 11; Prov.
xviii, 16; Matt. ii, 11.

65.—KESITAH.

**XXXIII, 19. He bought a parcel of a field, where he had spread
his tent, at the hand of the children of Hamor, Shechem's
father, for a hundred pieces of money.**

Under the impression that the word *kesitah*, here rendered "pieces of
money," means a lamb, many of the ancient commentators supposed that
here was an evidence of early coinage; the "pieces of money" being coins
having on them the impress of a lamb. Stanley (*Hist. Jewish Church*,
Lect. III,) adopts this theory, and some other writers of our time agree with
him. Coins have indeed been found with the figure of a lamb upon them,
but they were not struck until later than B.C. 450, and, according to the
best numismatists, probably belonged to Cyprus. Madden affirms that the
earliest coined money was in the eighth century before Christ, and that
"the use of coined money in Palestine cannot have existed till after the
taking of Samaria by the Assyrians (in B.C. 721.)"—*Jewish Coinage*, p. 14.

Other interpreters have supposed the *kesitah* to be a *weight* made in the
form of a lamb, as ancient weights have been found in the shape of bulls,
lions, and other animals. See note on Gen. xxiii, 16.

Some of the recent philologists, however, deny that *kesitah* means a lamb.
They derive it from a root signifying *to weigh*, and suppose it to have been
a piece of silver of unknown weight or size.

The same word is used in Job xlii, 11.

66.—EAR-RINGS.

XXXV, 4. They gave unto Jacob all the strange gods which were in their hand, and all their ear-rings which were in their ears; and Jacob hid them under the oak which was by Shechem.

Ear-rings were of various sizes, shapes, and material. At the present day, among the Orientals, they are of gold, silver, brass, ivory, horn, and wood; they are sometimes plain, and sometimes adorned with precious stones·

12.—EGYPTIAN EAR-RING AMULETS.

Some are small, and fit closely to the ear, leaving no intermediate space; while others are large and heavy, and drop some distance below the ear. Some of these, by their weight, make a disagreeable-looking hole in the part of the ear whence they hang. MacGregor saw some men near Lake Huleh with ear-rings "not in the lobe of the ear, but in the projecting flesh."—*Rob Roy on the Jordan*, p. 150. It is supposed by some that the use of ear-rings among the Hebrews was confined to the women. If so there must have been exceptions. See Exod. xxxii, 2.

It is evident from this text that it was customary to connect the use of ear-rings with idolatry. This is further intimated in Hosea ii, 13, where the wearing of ear-rings is associated with burning incense to Baal. Isa. iii, 20 is also supposed to refer to idolatrous practices. Ear-rings were doubtless used as amulets. With strange figures and characters engraved upon them they were considered as charms warding off evil. They are still thus used in the East. Jacob, being commanded to go to Bethel to renew his covenant with God, desired to put away every vestige of idolatry from the people, and for this reason buried these ear-ring amulets with the teraphim under the oak.

67.—COAT OF PIECES.

XXXVII, 3. Israel loved Joseph: and he made him a coat of many colors.

Or, "a coat of pieces." The ordinary tunic was a garment worn next to the skin, reaching to the knees, and usually without sleeves. Joseph's coat is supposed to have had sleeves, and to have reached to the wrists and ankles; a luxurious robe, and a mark of distinction such as, in later times, Tamar and the other daughters of the king wore. 2 Sam. xiii, 18. The "pieces" may have been different pieces of cloth variously colored, and of which the garment was made; or they may have been various colored threads, stripes, or plaids. In India coats of different colored patchwork are made for favorite children, pieces of crimson, purple, and other colors being sewed together. Jackets are sometimes embroidered with gold and silk of various colors. It is believed that a child thus clad will be saved from evil spirits, since the attention of the spirits will be diverted from the child by the beauty of the garment. There is no evidence of any such superstition in the case of Jacob. It was merely an instance of parental favoritism.

68.—CISTERNS.

XXXVII, 24. They took him, and cast him into a pit: and the pit was empty, there was no water in it.

There are numerous pits or cisterns still to be found in Palestine. They are often hewn out of the solid rock, and, being narrower at the mouth than at the bottom, it is not an easy thing to get out unaided, if one should be so unfortunate as to get in. Dr. Thomson mentions the case of an acquaintance who fell into one of these pits, or empty cisterns, and, being unable to extricate himself, passed two dreadful days and nights before he was discovered and drawn out, more dead than alive.

These cisterns, when dry, were sometimes used as dungeons for prisoners, and thus Joseph's brethren put him into one. The prophet Jeremiah was also imprisoned in a cistern which had been dug in the court-yard of the prison. See Jer. xxxviii, 6, where the word *bor* is translated "dungeon." This is the same word that in the text is rendered "pit," and in some other places "cistern."

See also Jer. xiv, 3, Zech. ix, 11, and the note on Jer. ii, 13.

69.—CARAVANS.

XXXVII, 25. They sat down to eat bread: and they lifted up their eyes and looked, and, behold, a company of Ishmaelites came from Gilead, with their camels bearing spicery and balm and myrrh, going to carry it down to Egypt.

This was a caravan of Arabian merchants on their way to Egypt with such drugs as the Egyptians used for embalming and for medicinal purposes. The Egyptians depended on these itinerant Arab merchants for their supplies of this nature. See note on James iv, 13. The mode of traveling in a caravan is peculiar. Pitts describes it as he saw it in the great caravan which was journeying to Mecca on a religious pilgrimage. It was undoubtedly longer than this commercial caravan, yet this was probably arranged on a similar plan. "They travel four camels abreast, which are all tied one after the other, like as in teams. The whole body is called a caravan, which is divided into several *cottors*, or companies, each of which hath its name, and consists, it may be, of several thousand camels; and they move, one *cottor* after another, like distinct troops."—*Religion and Manners of the Mahometans*, p. 430. He also states that the camels have bells about their necks, which, with the singing of the camel drivers, who travel

13.—CARAVAN.

on foot, make pleasant music. Though there is great confusion at the setting out of a caravan, its different companies and divisions soon settle down into a condition of order.

The caravan is also referred to in Isa. xxi, 13, Luke ii, 44.

70.—MOURNING.

XXXVII, 34. Jacob rent his clothes, and put sackcloth upon his loins, and mourned for his son many days.

1. Rending the clothes as a token of grief is a very ancient custom, and is often referred to in the Bible. See Josh. vii, 6; 1 Sam. iv, 12; 2 Sam. i, 11; iii, 31; xiii, 31; 2 Kings ii, 12; xviii, 37; xix, 1; Ezra ix, 3; Job i, 20. A Jewish writer, quoted by Burder, says that this ceremony was performed in the following manner: "They take a knife, and holding the blade downward, do give the upper garment a cut on the right side, and then rend it a hand's breadth. This is done for the five following relations, brother, sister, son, daughter, or wife; but for father or mother the rent is on the left side, and in all the garments."—*Oriental Customs*, No. 65.

2. Sackcloth is also frequently mentioned. It was generally made of the hair of goats or of camels, and was coarse and black. It was used for straining liquids, for sacks, and for mourning garments. When used for

mourning it was sometimes worn next to the skin, which it must have chafed by its harshness, and at other times it was hung like a sack over the outer garments, or instead of them. A girdle of similar material confined its loose folds. Ahab, on one occasion, appears to have worn sackcloth next to his skin all night. See 1 Kings xxi, 27. In Rev. vi, 12, in the darkness accompanying an earthquake, the sun is said to have become "as black as sackcloth of hair."

71.—CAPTAIN OF THE GUARD.

XXXVII, 36. The Midianites sold him into Egypt unto Potiphar, an officer of Pharaoh's, and captain of the guard.

Literally, "captain of the executioners." He was responsible for the safe-keeping of state prisoners, and for the execution of sentence upon them. In cases of treason he sometimes executed the sentence himself. He was the official guardian of the person of the king—the chief of his body-guard.

The king of Babylon had a similar officer in his service. See 2 Kings xxv, 8; Jer. xxxix, 13; Dan. ii, 14. In the ruins of the hall of judgment of the palace at Khorsabad, Assyria, there is on the wall a representation of a naked man with limbs stretched out, and arms and ankles fastened to the floor or table, while a tall, bearded man is in the act of flaying him alive. This is supposed to be "the chief of the executioners" engaged at his horrid work; and some commentators interpret the expression "cut in pieces," in Dan. iii, 29, to refer to this act of flaying alive. See also Micah iii, 3.

72.—PRISONS.

XL, 3. He put them in ward in the house of the captain of the guard, into the prison, the place where Joseph was bound.

According to the Eastern custom, the state-prison formed a part of the dwelling-house of the chief of the executioners, or of some other prominent personage. See Jer. xxxvii, 15. Sometimes even the king's palace was so used. See Jer. xxxii, 2.

73.—USE OF WINE.

XL, 11. Pharaoh's cup was in my hand: and I took the grapes, and pressed them into Pharaoh's cup, and I gave the cup into Pharaoh's hand.

It has been supposed by some that the ancient Egyptians drank no wine, though they did not object to drinking the unfermented juice of the grape, and this text is referred to as an illustration. It was evidently a part of the duty of Pharaoh's butler to press the grapes into the cup that the king might drink; but it by no means follows that because of this no fermented wine was used. A passage in Herodotus is usually cited as an evidence that only fresh must was allowed. On the other hand, there is other ancient testimony that establishes the fact that the Egyptians used fermented wine. This testimony is corroborated by the old monuments, which have representations of different articles employed in making wine, wine-presses in operation, and drunken men and women.

74.—BURDENS ON THE HEAD.

XL, 16. I also was in my dream, and, behold, I had three white baskets on my head.

It is quite common in the East to carry burdens on the head. Thus the head and neck become so strong that it is not uncommon for a man to carry a weight which requires the united strength of three men to lift from the ground. Women and children, as well as men, carry loads in this way. In ancient Egypt only men carried burdens on the head. The women carried them on the shoulder. See note on Gen. xxi, 14.

75.—BIRTHDAY FEAST.

XL, 20. It came to pass the third day, which was Pharaoh's birthday, that he made a feast unto all his servants.

The Eastern kings celebrated their birthdays by holding feasts and granting pardon to offenders. On the occasion referred to in the text the king availed himself of this custom to pardon the chief butler; although, for some reason not stated, he refused to grant the same clemency to the chief baker. See also Matt. xiv, 6; Mark vi, 21.

76.—EGYPTIAN MAGICIANS.

XLI, 8. He sent and called for all the magicians of Egypt.

These magicians (*chartummim*) were an order of Egyptian priests who understood the sacred hieroglyphic writings. They cultivated a knowledge of art and science, interpreted dreams, practiced soothsaying and divination, and were supposed to possess secret arts. They were men of great influence in Egypt, much esteemed, and highly honored. They were applied to for direction and assistance on all subjects outside the ordinary range of knowledge. Hence Pharaoh sent for them when he desired an interpretation of his strange dreams. Moses in after years met this same class of men. Exod. vii, 11, 22. The same term is applied to the magicians in Babylon. Dan. i, 20; ii, 2.

77.—SHAVING AMONG THE EGYPTIANS.

XLI, 14. Pharaoh sent and called Joseph, and they brought him hastily out of the dungeon : and he shaved himself.

Contrary to the custom of the Hebrews and other Orientals, the Egyptians shaved closely, only allowing the beard to grow as a sign of mourning; thus reversing the custom of the Hebrews, who shaved as a token of mourning. See note on Isaiah xv, 2. Strange to say, the Egyptians, while so careful to shave the beard, sometimes fastened false beards to the chin. These were made of plaited hair, and were of different shapes and sizes, according to the rank of the wearer.

14.—EGYPTIAN BARBERS.

Joseph, while in prison, allowed his beard to grow; now that he is released he shaves, according to the Egyptian custom, as it would have been a disgrace for him to appear with a beard in the presence of the king.

78.—ELEVATION OF SLAVES.

XLI, 41. Pharaoh said unto Joseph, See, I have set thee over all the land of Egypt.

This elevation of a slave to a position of high office, though uncommon among Western nations, was not so rare in the East. There, change of fortune was so sudden that the beggar of to-day might be the noble of to-morrow. Many of the most prominent characters in Oriental history were once slaves. The history of Joseph has in this respect often been paralleled. A most curious illustration of this is given by Harmer in his account of Ali Bey, who was stolen from his native place in Lesser Asia, near the Black Sea, in 1741, when he was thirteen years old, and was carried into Egypt, where, after varied fortunes, he reached a position next in power to the Pasha.—*Observations*, vol. ii, p. 520.

79.—SIGNETS—ROBES—NECKLACES.

XLI, 42. Pharaoh took off his ring from his hand, and put it upon Joseph's hand, and arrayed him in vestures of fine linen, and put a gold chain about his neck.

1. Great importance was attached to the signet ring, which contained the owner's name, and the impression of which was of the same validity as a written signature is among us. Hence the gift of this royal signet ring was a transfer of royal authority to Joseph. Thus Ahasuerus gave his ring to Haman, and the document which Haman signed with it was considered as coming from the king. Esther iii, 10–12. The same ring was afterward

given to Mordecai, who used it in the same way. Esther viii, 2, 8, 10. The value and importance attached to the signet ring are referred to in Jeremiah

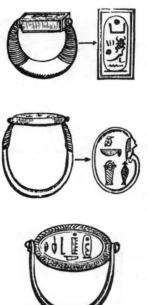

xxii, 24, and in Haggai ii, 23. Some valuable specimens of ancient signet rings have been found by antiquaries. One of the most remarkable of these is now in the Abbott Collection of Egyptian Antiquities, in the Museum of the New York Historical Society. It is in most excellent preservation and of very high antiquity, bearing the name of Shoofoo, the Suphis of the Greeks, who reigned before the time of Joseph. It was found in a tomb at Gizeh, and is of fine gold, weighing nearly three sovereigns.

For description of other kinds of seals see note on 1 Kings xxi, 8.

2. The fine (or, literally, *white*) linen robes were worn by the Egyptian priests, which fact has given some occasion to think that Joseph was received into the caste of priests, which was of the highest rank in Egypt, as it was the one to which the king himself belonged.

3. The gold chain was another mark of distinction, since none but persons of high rank

15.—Rings and Signets.   were permitted to wear such ornaments. There is in the Abbott Collection a gold necklace which has on it the name of Menes, the first Pharaoh of Egypt, and who reigned several hundred years before Shoofoo. The necklace has a pair of ear-rings to match. The signet and the necklace are no doubt similar in general appearance to those with which Joseph was invested. See also note on Sol. Song i, 10.

80.—SECOND CHARIOT—CALL FOR PROSTRATION.

XLI, 43. He made him to ride in the second chariot which he had; and they cried before him, Bow the knee.

1. The "second chariot" was either the one which followed immediately after the king's in state processions, or it was an extra chariot used by the king as a reserve in case of emergency. See 2 Chron. xxxv, 24.

2. The streets of modern Egyptian cities are so narrow that when an ordinary carriage passes through them it is customary to have an usher run before it to warn the people to get out of the way. In the case of Joseph, the command was to prostrate themselves, as they would do in the presence of royalty itself.

81.—GRANARIES.

XLI, 48. He gathered up all the food of the seven years, which were in the land of Egypt, and laid up the food in the cities.

Granaries were often very extensive in Egypt, and every facility was made for the housing and subsequent delivery of the grain. The monuments have many illustrations of the different styles of store-houses that were in use, by which we can obtain some idea of the manner in which the ancient Egyptians received and delivered their grain. Some of these store-houses

16.—EGYPTIAN GRANARY.

were evidently low flat-roofed buildings, divided into rooms or vaults, into which the grain was poured from bags. Similar structures were also used in Palestine, though we have no detailed account of the mode in which they were arranged. The Romans sometimes built store-houses for grain on stone pillars. The "barns" mentioned in Luke xii, 18, were evidently above ground, since they were to be pulled down. Subterranean store-houses were also common in the East. See note on Jer. xli, 8.

82.—SACKS, OF TWO KINDS.

XLII, 25. Joseph commanded to fill their sacks with corn, and to restore every man's money into his sack.

The sacks (*keleihem*) which were filled with corn, and the sack (*sak*) which had the money put into it, are supposed to have been of two different kinds. The latter is thought to have been a bag for holding the provender for the journey; while the former (more properly rendered *vessels* than *sacks*) were larger, and were filled with the grain that they were carrying to Canaan.

83.—EGYPTIAN DINNERS.

XLIII, 16. Bring these men home, and slay, and make ready; for these men shall dine with me at noon.

The ancient Egyptians had the beasts they desired for food slaughtered in the court-yard of the dwelling. While the monuments give representations of poulterers' shops, they do not show any shops for the sale of butchers' meat, but represent the slaying, in private houses, of quadrupeds intended for food. The cause of this is not positively known. As poultry, fish, and vegetables formed the principal food of the people, it may be that there was not sufficient demand for the flesh of beasts to warrant the establishing of butcher-shops, such flesh perhaps being reserved for great feasts. The slaughter of animals for the table is a common subject of representation on these monuments. The four legs of the animal were tied together, and it was then thrown to the ground. Here it was held by assistants while the butcher cut the throat from ear to ear. The blood was caught in vessels, and set aside for food. The animal was then flayed, and dressed, and cut into pieces, which were carried in trays to the kitchen, where the cook immediately began to get them ready for the table. In this text we find Joseph issuing his orders to "slay and make ready" for the noon-dinner; so that not much time elapsed between the slaughter of the victims and their appearance on the tables ready for eating. See also 1 Sam. xxviii, 24.

84.—FORM OF SALUTATION.

XLIII, 29. Is this your younger brother, of whom ye spake unto me? And he said, God be gracious unto thee, my son.

This is not a benediction, but one of the numerous forms of Oriental salutation used in meeting or in taking leave of an acquaintance.

85.—BREAD THE PRINCIPAL FOOD.

XLIII, 31. He washed his face, and went out, and refrained himself, and said, Set on bread.

Orientals in general are great eaters of bread. It has been computed that three persons in four live entirely upon it, or else upon such compositions as are made of barley or wheat flour. No doubt the term "bread" was often used to denote food in general; but this was because bread was more generally used than any other article of diet. When Joseph's brethren had cast him into the pit, "they sat down to eat bread." Gen. xxxvii, 25. When Moses was in Midian he was invited to "eat bread." Exod. ii, 20. The witch of En-dor "set a morsel of bread" before Saul and his servants. 1 Sam. xxviii, 22–25.

86.—EGYPTIAN MODE OF DINING.

XLIII, 32. They set on for him by himself, and for them by themselves, and for the Egyptians, which did eat with him, by themselves: because the Egyptians might not eat bread with the Hebrews; for that is an abomination unto the Egyptians.

1. The Egyptian tables were placed along the sides of the room, the guests having their faces toward the wall. In this case Joseph probably sat at one end of the hall and his brethren at the other end, (they " sat before him," verse 33,) while the Egyptians sat on either side. The ancient Egyptian table was a round tray fixed on a pillar or leg, which was often in the form of a man, usually a captive, who was represented as holding the burden of the table on his head and shoulders. The entire structure was of stone or of some hard wood. These tables were sometimes brought in and removed with the dishes upon them. One or two guests sat at each table.

17.—MODERN EGYPTIANS AT DINNER.

2. The Egyptians considered all foreigners unclean. No Egyptian would consent to kiss a Greek, nor to use any culinary utensil which belonged to one, nor to eat the flesh of any animal, even though a clean animal, which had been cut up with a Grecian knife. This was because foreigners ate animals which the Egyptians regarded either as unclean or as sacred. The Hebrews, for instance, slaughtered and ate the cow, which was sacred in the eyes of the Egyptians, and by them, on that account, exempt from slaughter. For this reason the representatives of the two nations could not eat together. Joseph ate by himself because he belonged to a higher caste than the Egyptians around him, and was above them all in social rank.

87.—POSITION OF GUESTS AT TABLE.

XLIII, 33. They sat before him, the first-born according to his birthright, and the youngest according to his youth.

1. The Egyptians sat at their meals; reclining was a Persian custom brought in at a later age. See note on Matt. xxvi, 7. They used chairs of various kinds, and stools, and sometimes sat on the floor with the left leg drawn under them and the right foot planted on the floor, thus elevating the right knee.

2. The guests were placed according to the rank they occupied. This does not imply the use of long tables, since even at the present day there are posts of honor at the round tables of the modern Egyptians.

88.—MODE OF DISTRIBUTING FOOD.

XLIII, 34. He took and sent messes unto them from before him: but Benjamin's mess was five times so much as any of theirs.

1. The ancient Egyptian mode of dining seems to have resembled the Persian rather than the Turkish. Different kinds of food were taken from the large dishes on which the cook had placed them, and were put on one smaller dish which was carried by a servant to the guest. In this instance Joseph saw that his brethren were well supplied from his own table.

2. Special respect was shown to guests of distinction by sending them some choice dainty, or a larger portion of food than was given to the others. Thus Joseph honored Benjamin with a five-fold portion, which must be considered the greater honor when we learn that a double portion was regarded sufficiently complimentary to a king. In Joseph's estimation his brother Benjamin was worth more than two kings.

89.—THE BOWL.

XLIV, 2. Put my cup, the silver cup, in the sack's mouth of the youngest.

The *gabia*, here rendered "cup," was more properly a bowl, and was distinguished from the *kosoth*, or smaller cups, into which the liquid was poured from the *gabia*. The distinction is made in Jer. xxxv, 5, where the two words are used.

90.—THE DIVINING CUP.

XLIV, 5. Is not this it in which my lord drinketh, and whereby indeed he divineth?

The question whether Joseph actually practiced divination, or only pretended to do so, or merely instructed his steward to ask an ironical question, or whether the original words may not have a different interpretation from that which the translators have put upon them, is one which concerns the commentator rather than the archæologist. It is an admitted fact that divining cups were used among the Egyptians and other nations. These cups bore certain magical inscriptions, and when used were filled with pure water. Authorities all agree as far as this, but they differ as to the use which was

18.—EGYPTIAN DIVINING CUP.

made of the cup after the water was poured into it. We give the statements of various writers, and it is quite' probable that they are all correct, different modes being used at different times.

1. The divination was performed by means of the figures which were reflected by the rays of light which were permitted to fall on the water. 2. Melted wax was poured into the water, and the will of the gods was interpreted by the variously shaped figures formed in this way. 3. The cup was shaken, and the position, size, or number of the bubbles which rose to the surface was considered. 4. There were thrown into the water plates of gold and of silver, and precious stones, with magical characters engraved on them. Words of incantation were muttered. Then some of the signs engraved on the stones were reflected in the water, or a voice was supposed to be heard, or the likeness of the deceased person concerning whom the inquiry was made was thought to appear in the water. 5. The

4

inquirer fixed his eye on some particular point in the cup until he was thrown into a dream-like or clairvoyant state, when he could see things strange and indescribable.

91.—LOUD WEEPING.

XLV, 2. He wept aloud: and the Egyptians and the house of Pharaoh heard.

In the East emotions of joy as well as of sorrow are expressed by loud cries. Sir John Chardin (cited by Harmer, *Observations*, vol. iii, p. 17) says, "Their sentiments of joy or of grief are properly transports; and their transports are ungoverned, excessive, and truly outrageous." He also states that when any one returns from a long journey his family burst into cries that may be heard twenty doors off. In like manner Joseph and his brethren, in their joy at meeting, indulged in excessive weeping.

92.—EGYPTIAN WAGONS.

XLV, 19. Take you wagons out of the land of Egypt for your little ones, and for your wives, and bring your father, and come.

Wilkinson supposes these wagons to have been similar to the war chariots, but with the sides closed. They had wheels with six spokes, and were drawn by oxen, which were harnessed the same as horses for the war chariots. In traveling the wagon was furnished with a sort of umbrella. It is evident from the narrative that wagons were at that time strange in Canaan. The sight of these Egyptian conveyances confirmed to the mind of Jacob the statement of his sons. See verse 27. Rosenmuller aptly suggests that Egypt was more likely than Canaan to develop the idea of a wagon, because it was a great plain.—*Morgenland*, vol. i, p. 212.

93.—GIFTS OF RAIMENT.

XLV, 22. To all of them he gave each man changes of raiment; but to Benjamin he gave three hundred pieces of silver, and five changes of raiment.

Presents of costly and beautiful garments are among the modes of complimenting in use by the Orientals. Since the fashions of dress do not change as with us, these gifts are valuable as long as they last. These "changes of raiment" were designed to be worn on special occasions. Other biblical references are made to this custom of presenting gifts of clothing. Samson offered raiment to any who should guess his riddle. Judges xiv, 12, 13, 19. When Naaman visited Elisha he took with him, among other gifts, "ten changes of raiment." 2 Kings v, 5. Even Solomon did not disdain to receive such presents. 2 Chron. ix, 24. Daniel was clothed with scarlet as a reward for interpreting the king's dream. Dan. v, 29. It is said of an illustrious Oriental poet of the ninth century, that he had so many presents made him during his life-time that at his death he had one hundred complete suits of clothes, two hundred shirts, and five hundred turbans. The Hindoos, at the close of a feast, commonly give to each guest a present of new garments. See also the notes on 1 Sam. xix, 24; Esther vi, 8; and Job xxvii, 16.

94.—EYES CLOSED.

XLVI, 4. **Joseph shall put his hand upon thine eyes.**

It was an ancient custom that the nearest of kin should close the eyes of a deceased person, and give a parting kiss to the corpse. It was a comforting assurance to Jacob that his beloved Joseph, whom he had for many years mourned as dead, should perform this filial office for him. At Jacob's death we are told that Joseph kissed him, (Gen. l, 1,) and it is to be presumed that he also closed the eyes of the patriarch, as God had promised.

95.—HATRED OF SHEPHERDS.

XLVI, 34. **Every shepherd is an abomination unto the Egyptians.**

Frequent illustrations of the contempt in which the Egyptians held shepherds are seen on the ancient monuments: the shepherds being invariably represented as lank, withered, distorted, emaciated specimens of humanity. Concerning the cause of this feeling there are different opinions. It is certain that cattle were not by any means considered unclean by the Egyptians: The cow was sacred to Isis, and oxen were used for food and for labor; it is not likely, therefore, that taking care of them could have been considered polluting. The objection was not to the tending of cattle—which in itself is as necessary as the cultivation of the soil—but rather to the vagrant mode of life to which the shepherds were addicted, and which was opposed to the designs and policy of the ruling caste. When the foundations of the state rested on agriculture the Egyptians associated rudeness and barbarism with the name of shepherd.

Besides this, Egypt had at one time been invaded by a horde of wandering shepherds, descended from Cush. They established themselves in the country and had a succession of kings. They fought the Egyptians, burned some of their principal cities, committed great cruelties, and were not driven out until they and their descendants had occupied the country for hundreds of years. Some suppose that their expulsion took place only a short time before Joseph's day.

Joseph skillfully availed himself of this well-known Egyptian hatred of shepherds for the purpose of having his brethren settled in a rich pastoral region, and isolated from the native Egyptians, thus keeping them a peculiar people

96.—TOKEN OF TRIUMPH.

XLIX, 8. Thy hand shall be in the neck of thine enemies.

This expression is intended to denote superiority and triumph. Job makes use of a similar figure where he represents God as taking him by the neck and shaking him to pieces. Job xvi, 12. David says, "Thou hast also given me the necks of mine enemies." 2 Sam. xxii, 41; Psalm xviii, 40. Jeremiah, lamenting the desolations of his people, says, "Our necks are under persecution." Lam. v, 5. The ancient Franks had a custom of putting the arm around the neck as a mark of superiority. An insolvent debtor gave himself up to his creditor as a slave, and as a token of submission he took the arm of his new master and put it around his neck.

Compare notes on Josh. x, 24, and 1 Cor. xv, 25.

97.—MILK HIGHLY ESTEEMED.

XLIX, 12. His teeth white with milk.

This is meant to represent the pastoral wealth of Judah. Milk is, in the East, a very important and highly valued article of diet. In India it is sometimes said of a rich man, "He has abundance of milk." A saying somewhat similar to this, but more closely resembling the text, is applied to one who has a plentiful supply of milk: "His mouth smells of milk."

98.—EMBALMING—MOURNING.

L, 2, 8. Joseph commanded his servants the physicians to embalm his father: and the physicians embalmed Israel. And forty days were fulfilled for him; for so are fulfilled the days of those which are embalmed: and the Egyptians mourned for him threescore and ten days.

1. Among the ancient Egyptians there were numerous classes of physicians, divided according to the various diseases which were their special subjects of study. They were not general practitioners, but specialists; hence their number was large. Joseph had them among his retainers. The *Taricheuta*, who superintended the process of embalming, were included among physicians as a special but subordinate class. They, in common with the higher class of physicians, belonged to the sacerdotal order.

2. There were different processes of embalming, varying according to the means at the disposal of the family of the deceased. The most expensive (and doubtless the mode by which Jacob and Joseph were embalmed) is estimated to have cost what would be equivalent to about twelve hundred and fifty dollars of our money. Preparatory to this process, the brain was removed by means of a crooked wire inserted through the nose. An incision was then made in the left side of the abdomen with a stone knife, the

use of metal not being permitted.*   Through this incision the viscera were drawn. with the exception of the heart and kidneys.   They were sometimes replaced after being prepared for preservation, and in other instances were put into vases.   Some authorities assert that they were thrown into the river Nile; but this is denied by others.

After the removal of the viscera the body was carefully washed externally with water, and internally with palm-wine, oil of cedar, and other antiseptic preparations.   The cavities of the head and abdomen were filled with myrrh, cassia, cinnamon, and other aromatic substances, and the incision in the abdomen was sewed up.   The body was then steeped in a strong infusion of niter.   The time occupied by this steeping process is variously stated at thirty, forty, and seventy days.   It may have varied at different periods of Egyptian history, or in different parts of the land at the same time.   Some have supposed that forty days were allowed for the embalming proper, and thirty for the steeping in niter.

When this process was completed the body and limbs were carefully wrapped in bandages of fine linen, plastered on the underside with gum. These bandages were seven or eight inches in width, and were sometimes six or seven hundred feet long.   At this stage of the process the body seems to have been in some way subjected to extreme heat, precisely how is not

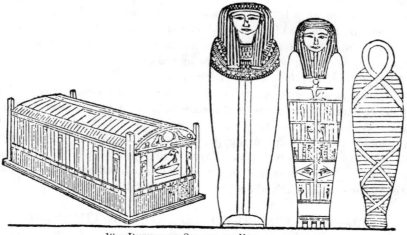

19.—DIFFERENT STAGES OF EMBALMING.

known.   Some have conjectured that it was soaked in pitch, boiling hot; others that it was put into a stove or oven.   That extreme heat was applied in some way is evident from the charred bandages and from the appearance of the bones.

* Three of these ancient stone knives are now in the Abbott collection, and also a saucer containing a gray embalming powder.

Layers of cloth, plastered with lime on the inside, were next placed on the body in a damped condition, fitting exactly to its shape, These layers were put on in sufficient numbers to make a thick case, which, when it was finished, was taken off until it became hardened, when it was replaced, and sewed up at the back. It was painted and ornamented with various figures, and in many instances was gilded. The part immediately over the face was made to resemble, as near as possible, the features of the deceased. The whole was then put into another case made of sycamore or cedar, and sometimes there was in addition an outside case made of the same material, or a sarcophagus of stone.

It is not positively known why the Egyptians embalmed the bodies of their dead. Some think that they believed the existence of the soul depended on that of the body, and hence desired to preserve the body as long as possible. Others suppose that they expected the soul at some distant future day to return to the body, and for that reason wished to preserve the body for its reception.

The oldest mummy known to the civilized world is now in the British Museum. "It is supposed to be that of Pharaoh Mycerinus, (Menkare,) of the fourth dynasty, the builder of the third great Pyramid at Gizeh, with whose coffin it was found by Colonel Vyse, in 1837. What is left of the coffin lies close by; it is unquestionably a very early piece of Egyptian work; wooden pegs instead of nails kept it together. Hieroglyphics are still seen on a portion of the lid and on the foot-piece; these, and especially the oval containing the name of Mycerinus, have been preserved with a freshness which is only to be accounted for by the extreme dryness of the climate of Egypt."—*Handy Book of the British Museum*, by T. Nichols, p. 145.

3. There is a special significance in the seventy days' mourning for Jacob if the custom at that time were the same as in the days of Diodorus Siculus, who was in Egypt about forty years before the time of Christ. He says that on the death of a king the Egyptians put on mourning apparel and closed all their temples for seventy-two days, during which time the embalming proceeded. It would seem, therefore, that Pharaoh ordered royal honors on the occasion of the death of his prime minister's father.

99.—WHY JOSEPH COULD NOT SEE THE KING.

L, 4. When the days of his mourning were past, Joseph spake unto the house of Pharaoh.

The reason why Joseph did not himself prefer his request to the king, but solicited the intervention of his friends, is to be found in the fact that, having allowed his hair and beard to grow during the seventy days of mourning, he was not in a condition to appear before Pharaoh in the manner required by the etiquette of the court. See note on Gen. xli, 14.

100.—LARGE FUNERALS.

L, 9. There went up with him . . . a very great company.

This not only shows the high esteem in which Joseph was held, but it also furnishes an illustration of the Egyptian fashion of large and stately

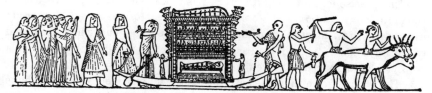

20.—Ancient Egyptian Funeral Procession.

funeral processions. The custom existed in every province in Egypt, and in every age of its history.

101.—THRESHING—FLOORS.

L, 10. They came to the threshing-floor of Atad, which is beyond Jordan.

The "threshing-floor" was not a shed, or a building, or any place covered with roof and surrounded by walls, but a circular piece of ground from fifty to a hundred feet in diameter. in the open air, on elevated ground, and made smooth, hardy, and clean. Here the grain was threshed and winnowed.

102.—EGYPTIAN COFFINS.

L, 26. So Joseph died, being a hundred and ten years old: and they embalmed him, and he was put in a coffin in Egypt.

Though so much care was taken in ancient Egypt to embalm the body, there were many who were buried without coffins. The mention of the fact here that "Joseph was put in a coffin," shows the high rank to which he had attained. His coffin was probably the outside receptacle or sarcophagus described in the note on Gen. l, 2, 3. Whether it was of wood or of stone we have no means of knowing; the latter material would more probably be used for so exalted a personage.

EXODUS.

103.—ARK—USE OF BITUMEN.

II, 8. She took for him an ark of bulrushes, and daubed it with slime and with pitch.

1. The precise form of this little "ark" is unknown. It may have been a basket, a boat, or a box. It was made of the leaf of the papyrus, a reedy plant which grew plentifully on the banks of the Nile, and which was used by the Egyptians for cordage, baskets, boats, sails, writing material, and a variety of other purposes; even sometimes for food.

2. The "slime" or bitumen is described in the note on Gen. xi, 3. We have here an illustration of the manner of its use. Though melting easily and running freely, when cold it is very brittle; but if mixed with tar it becomes tenacious when set, and makes a firm cement. In preparing the little vessel for the reception of the infant Moses, it is probable that the papyrus leaves were first plaited together, and then coated with a mixture of hot bitumen and tar, which when cold became firm and water-proof.

104.—BATHING IN THE NILE.

II, 5. The daughter of Pharaoh came down to wash herself at the river; and her maidens walked along by the river's side.

It would be quite inconsistent with modern Oriental ideas of propriety for women to bathe thus publicly; but among the ancient Egyptians it was admissible. Wilkinson (*Anc. Egypt*, vol. iii, p. 389) gives a picture from the monuments representing an Egyptian woman of rank bathing, attended by four female servants. The Nile was regarded as a sacred river, and divine honors were sometimes paid to it. Harmer (*Obs.*, vol. iii, p. 531) gives a quotation from Irwin's travels, in which the traveler tells of a company of dancing girls who went down to the Nile in the spring of the year to bathe in it, and to sing songs while marching along its banks, in honor of the fact that the waters of the river had begun their annual rise and overflow. It may have been some such sacred ceremony in which Pharaoh's daughter and her maidens were engaged at the time when Moses was found.

105.—AN EXCEPTIONAL MARRIAGE CUSTOM.

II, 21. He gave Moses Zipporah his daughter.

In general the proposal of marriage came from the family of the bridegroom; but occasionally this custom was reversed, as in the case referred to in the text. Caleb gave his daughter Achsah to Othniel. Josh. xv, 16, 17. Saul gave his daughter Michal to David. 1 Sam. xviii, 27.

106.—VARIED PASTURE GROUNDS.

III, 1. Moses kept the flock of Jethro his father-in-law, the priest of Midian: and he led the flock to the back side of the desert.

In Arabia shepherds do not limit the pasturage of their flocks to places near at home, but wander sometimes long distances, being gone from home for weeks and months in pursuit of new pasture grounds. The Midianites had the principal place of their residence somewhere on the eastern border of Edom, but they pastured their flocks as far as Gilead and Bashan on the north, and on the south they went along both shores of the Ælanitic Gulf.

107.—SHOES REMOVED.

III, 5. Put off thy shoes from off thy feet; for the place whereon thou standest is holy ground.

Orientals are as careful to remove their shoes or sandals before entering a house, or a place of worship, as we are to remove our hats. Piles of shoes, slippers, or sandals, may be seen at the doors of Mohammedan mosques and of Indian pagodas; it is a mark of respect due to those places. Moses was in this way directed to show his reverence for the Divine Presence. In like manner, when Joshua met "the captain of the Lord's host," near Jericho, he was required to re-

21.—Shoes Taken Off.

move his shoes. Josh. v, 15. It was so unusual a thing to wear shoes in the house that on one important occasion when it was to be done it was necessary especially to command it. See note on Exod. xii, 11.

108.—JEWELRY AT RELIGIOUS FEASTS.

III, 22. Every woman shall borrow of her neighbor, and of her that sojourneth in her house, jewels of silver, and jewels of gold, and raiment: and ye shall put them upon your sons, and upon your daughters; and ye shall spoil the Egyptians.

With the controversy that has arisen among commentators in reference to the meaning of the borrowing, the lending, and the spoiling, spoken of·in this text and in Exod. xi, 1–3; xii, 35, 36, we have nothing to do in this work.* We notice the text only as it has reference to Eastern customs. It must be remembered that the Israelites were about to go into the wilderness to sacrifice to Jehovah. Roberts says: "When the Orientals go to their sacred festivals they always put on their best jewels. Not to appear before the gods in such a way they consider would be disgraceful to themselves and displeasing to the deities. A person whose clothes or jewels are indifferent will *borrow* of his richer neighbors; and nothing is more common than to see poor people standing before the temples, or engaged in sacred ceremonies, well adorned with jewels."—*Oriental Illustrations*, p. 70.

If this custom obtained among the ancient Egyptians, the transaction recorded in the text would be perfectly natural.

109.—EGYPTIAN BRICKS.

V, 7. Ye shall no more give the people straw to make brick, as heretofore: let them go and gather straw for themselves.

The ancient Egyptian bricks were made of clay moistened with water and then put into molds. After they were sufficiently dry to be removed from the molds, they were laid in rows on a flat spot exposed to the sun, which gradually hardened them. Some were made with straw and some  without. Many had chopped barley and wheat straw; others bean haulm and stubble. The use of this crude brick was general in Egypt for dwellings, tombs, and ordinary buildings, walls of towers, fortresses, and sacred inclosures of temples. Even temples of a small size were sometimes built of unburnt brick, and several pyramids of this material are still to be seen in Egypt. The use of stone was confined mainly to temples, quays, and reservoirs.

22.—EGYPTIAN BRICK.   Egyptian bricks were frequently stamped with the

---

* Those who desire to see an exhaustive presentation of the various views of commentators on this subject may find it in KURTZ's *History of the Old Covenant*, (Clark's Foreign Theological Library,) vol. ii, pp. 319–334. KURTZ's conclusion is, "that the articles were not obtained by borrowing and purloining, but were spoils which came to the Israelites in the shape of presents, though they were forced from the Egyptians by moral constraint."

name of the king during whose reign they were made. They differ in size from the Babylonian bricks. They are from fourteen and a half to twenty inches long, from six and a half to eight and three quarter inches wide, and from four and a half to seven inches thick. Several bricks bearing the name of Thothmes III., and plainly showing the chopped straw used in their manufacture, are in the Abbott Collection, which also contains some of the ancient implements which were used in brick-making.

110.—HARD LABOR A PUNISHMENT.

V, 11. Go ye, get you straw where ye can find it: yet not aught of your work shall be diminished.

M. Chabas, a French Egyptologist, discovered some years since a papyrus the writing on which, when deciphered, proved to be the report of a scribe, to the effect that twelve workingmen who had been employed at brick-making had failed in their tasks, and had therefore been appointed to harder work as a punishment. There is no evidence that these workmen were Hebrews, but the fact shows that the cruelty inflicted on the Hebrews by their task-masters was in accordance with the customs of the country. See *Bibliotheca Sacra*, vol. xxii, p. 685.

111.—IRRIGATION.

VII, 19. ... upon the waters of Egypt, upon their streams, upon their rivers, and upon their ponds, and upon all their pools of water.

For purposes of irrigation canals were cut in various directions, and artificial pools were made to receive the waters of the Nile at its annual overflow. See notes on Deut. xi, 10, and Psa. i, 3.

112.—RECEPTACLES FOR NILE WATER.

VII, 19. That there may be blood throughout all the land of Egypt, both in vessels of wood and in vessels of stone.

These included all the vessels in which the Nile water was kept for daily use, among which were filtering pots of white earth. There were also stone reservoirs at the corners of the streets, and at other places, for the use of the poor.

113.—REVERENCE FOR RIVERS—ABHORRENCE OF BLOOD.

VII, 20. All the waters that were in the river were turned to blood.

1. Many ancient nations had great reverence for rivers. The Egyptians, sharing this feeling, regarded the Nile as a sacred stream, and worshiped it as a deity, calling it " the Father of life," and " the Father of the gods."

2. The Egyptians, especially the priests, were very particular in their external habits, and there was nothing which they held in greater abhorrence

than blood, seldom admitting any bloody sacrifices. Their horror must therefore have been extreme when they found the river, which they worshiped as a god, turned into blood, which they regarded with such utter disgust.

114.—NILE WATER.

VII, 21. The fish that was in the river died; and the river stank, and the Egyptians could not drink of the water of the river.

The extent of this calamity will be seen when it is remembered that the waters of the Nile were to the Egyptians then, as now, the great source of dependence for drinking and for culinary purposes. The spring water is hard and unwholesome, wells are seldom found, and rain water cannot be collected because it hardly ever rains. The inhabitants are therefore driven to the river, which all travelers agree in saying furnishes as sweet and wholesome water as can be found in the world. It is at first very thick and muddy, but can be readily filtered. The Egyptians say that "Nile-water is as sweet as honey and sugar." Great indeed must have been the misfortune when this universal supply of one of the greatest necessaries of life was cut off.

115.—ASHES USED IN CURSING.

IX, 8. Take to you handfuls of ashes of the furnace, and let Moses sprinkle it toward the heaven in the sight of Pharaoh.

"When the [East Indian] magicians pronounce an imprecation on an individual, a village, or a country, they take ashes of cow-dung, or those from a common fire, and throw them in the air, saying to the objects of their displeasure, 'Such a sickness or such a curse shall surely come upon you.'" —ROBERTS, *Oriental Illustrations*, p. 65.

116.—THE OUTSTRETCHED HAND.

X, 21. The Lord said unto Moses, Stretch out thine hand toward heaven.

This is the custom of the Indian magicians when they deliver their predictions. It is done to show that they have favor with their gods.

117.—SHOES WITHIN DOORS.

XII, 11. Thus shall ye eat it; with your loins girded, your shoes on your feet, and your staff in your hand; and ye shall eat it in haste.

1. While it would be quite superfluous to direct us to have shoes on while eating, the Israelites would not put them on without being ordered. This was in accordance with the custom referred to in the note on Exod. iii, 5, *q. v.* The reason for their violating their ordinary usage is here given: they were in haste.

2. Roberts mentions a sect in India called *Urechamanar*, who eat their food standing, having their sandals on their feet, and a staff or a bunch of peacock feathers in their hands.

118.—DOUGH—KNEADING-TROUGHS.

XII, 34. The people took their dough before it was leavened, their kneading-troughs being bound up in their clothes upon their shoulders.

1. The dough was made by mixing flour with water, or, perhaps, with milk. It was then kneaded with the hands; in Egypt the feet also were used. When the kneading was completed leaven was generally added. See note on Matt. xiii, 33.

2. The kneading-troughs were either small wooden bowls, such as the Arabs now use for kneading dough, and into which their bread is put after it is baked, or they may have been similar to the leather utensil described by Pococke, Niebuhr, and other travelers. It is a round piece of leather, having iron rings at certain distances around it, through which a chain is passed, so that it may, when not in use, be drawn together like a purse and hung up. The Arabs, when they travel, sometimes carry dough in it, and sometimes bread.

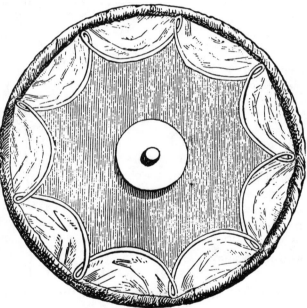

23.—KNEADING-TROUGH.

119.—EGYPTIAN CHARIOTS.

XIV, 6. He made ready his chariot.

The Egyptian chariot was a framework of wood, nearly semicircular in front, having straight sides and open behind. The front was of wood, and the sides were strengthened and ornamented with leather and metal bindings. The floor was of rope net-work, to give a springy footing. The fittings of the inside and the harness were of raw hide or tanned leather. On the sides quivers and bow-cases were fastened, crossing each other. The

24.—EGYPTIAN WAR-CHARIOT.

wheels were low, had six spokes, and were kept on the axle by a leather thong or linch-pin. There was no seat in the chariot. The number of horses to each chariot was two.

The chariot of the king did not differ materially from ordinary war-chariots. He, however, usually rode alone into battle, having the reins fastened around his waist, leaving both hands free to manage his weapons of war.

Jehu seems to have imitated the custom of Egyptian monarchs in driving his own chariot. See 2 Kings ix, 20.

120.—"THIRD MEN."

XIV, 7. He took six hundred chosen chariots, and all the chariots of Egypt, and captains over every one of them.

The word rendered captains is, literally, *third men*. Usually each war-chariot carried two men: the charioteer, who was an important character, and the warrior. Sometimes, however, there was a third man, who had direction of the two others. The strength of Pharaoh's chariot force is seen, then, in this, that he had, besides the usual pair of men to each chariot, a third man or "captain." Thus one might act as charioteer, one as warrior, and one as shield-bearer.

121.—NIGHT-WATCHES.

XIV, 24. It came to pass, that in the morning watch the Lord looked unto the host of the Egyptians.

Before the captivity, the Hebrews divided the night into three watches. The first was from sunset to ten o'clock; the second from ten o'clock to two; the third from two o'clock to sunrise. The first was called the "beginning of the watches." Lam. ii, 19. The second was called the "middle watch." Judges vii, 19. The third was called the "morning watch," as in the text, and also in 1 Sam. xi, 11.

This mode of dividing time is also referred to in Psa. lxiii, 6; cxix, 148. The Psalmist meditated on God and his word in the "night-watches."

For a later method of dividing the watches, see note on Mark xiii, 35.

122.—EGYPTIAN CAVALRY.

XV, 1. The horse and his rider hath he thrown into the sea.

Archæologists are not agreed as to the existence of cavalry among the ancient Egyptians. This passage and others similar seem to refer to cavalry, but it is said by some to have reference only to chariot warriors, in distinction from foot soldiers. All agree in admitting that there are no representations of cavalry on the monuments. Why they are not represented, if they were known, it is hard to say. Wilkinson insists, however, that there must have been Egyptian cavalry notwithstanding there are no monumental pictures of them. He refers to 2 Chron. xii, 3, where it is said that Shishak, king of Egypt, had twelve hundred chariots and sixty thousand horsemen. These horsemen are by far too numerous to be the occupants of the number of chariots given; so that, however it may have been in the time of the Exodus, there must have been Egyptian cavalry five hundred years later. He further says that the hieroglyphics notice the "command of the cavalry" as a very honorable position, generally held by the most distinguished of the king's sons, and he also refers to ancient profane authors who speak of Egyptian cavalry. See *Ancient Egyptians*, vol. i, pp. 288, 292.

123.—DANCING.

XV, 20. All the women went out after her with timbrels and with dances.

Dancing was performed at first on sacred occasions only. It was a part of the religious ceremonies of the Egyptians as well as of the Hebrews, and was engaged in by many idolatrous nations, and often accompanied with scenes of debauchery. Among the Hebrews it was joined with sacred song, and was usually participated in by the women only. When the men danced it was in companies separate from the women, promiscuous dancing not being practiced. If the ancient Hebrew dances were like those of the modern Arabs, we can understand how Miriam led in the dance. One leads off in the step, and the others follow in exact imitation of all the varied movements that she makes. These movements are entirely extemporaneous, governed by no fixed rule, but varied at the pleasure of the leader. Dancing was usually performed by the Hebrews in the day-time, and in the open air. It was an outward expression of tumultuous joy. When Jephthah returned from his conquest over the Ammonites "his daughter came out to meet him with timbrels and with dances." Judges xi, 34. When the men of Benjamin surprised the daughters of Shiloh the latter were dancing at "a feast of the Lord." Judges xxi, 19-21. When David returned after the slaughter of Goliath, the Israelitish women met him with singing and dancing. 1 Sam. xviii, 6. When the ark was brought home, David danced before it "with all his might." 2 Sam. vi, 14. Some suppose that the reason why Michal was offended at this was, not only because of his scanty costume, (as intimated in 2 Sam. vi, 20,) but also because he engaged in a service that usually pertained to women only, and hence was undignified and unbecoming in a king. On several occasions God's people are exhorted to praise the Lord in the dance. See Psa. cxlix, 3; cl, 4.

124.—FLESH-POTS—DIET.

XVI, 8. When we sat by the flesh-pots, and when we did eat bread to the full.

1. The flesh-pot was a three-legged vessel of bronze, which the Egyptians used for culinary purposes.

2. The ancient Egyptians were fond of animal food. They chiefly ate beef and goose, and also had an abundance of fish. The cow was sacred, and was not eaten. Some writers assert that sheep were not eaten; but the contrary is affirmed by others.

3. Bread here is a generic term denoting vegetable diet. This the Egyptians had in large variety. See Num. xi, 5.

125.—OMER—EPHAH.

XVI, 36. Now an omer is the tenth part of an ephah.

1. The omer or gomer was a dry measure supposed to contain two quarts, one pint, and one tenth, English corn measure.

2. The ephah is supposed to have contained three pecks, one quart, and a pint.

126.—CLEANLINESS IN WORSHIP.

XIX, 10. The Lord said unto Moses, Go unto the people, and sanctify them to-day and to-morrow, and let them wash their clothes.

This was considered a necessary preparation for meeting Jehovah. Pagans have similar ceremonies in connection with their worship. Roberts says: "No man can go to the temple wearing a dirty cloth: he must either put on a clean one, or go himself to a tank and wash it, if it be soiled; or he must put on one which is quite new. Near the temples men may be often seen washing their clothes, in order to prepare themselves for some religious ceremony."—*Oriental Illustrations.* Jacob commanded his household to be clean and change their garments when they went up to Bethel to build an altar to Jehovah. Gen. xxxv, 2.

127.—THORN-FIRES—GRAIN-HEAPS.

XXII, 6. If fire break out, and catch in thorns, so that the stacks of corn, or the standing corn, or the field, be consumed therewith, he that kindled the fire shall surely make restitution.

1. Thorns grow plentifully around the edges of the fields, and intermingle with the wheat. "By harvest-time they are not only dry themselves, but are choked up with tall grass dry as powder. Fire, therefore, catches in them easily, and spreads with great rapidity and uncontrollable fury; and as the grain is dead ripe, it is impossible to extinguish it."—THOMSON. *The Land and the Book*, i, 529. The farmers are exceedingly careful of fire at such times The Arabs in the valley of the Jordan, according to Burckhardt, invariably put to death any person who fires the grass, even though it be done innocently. After the harvest, and before the autumnal rains set in, it is quite common to set the dry thorns and weeds on fire in order to clear the land for plowing, and to furnish a fertilizer from the ashes.

2. The word "stacks" would be better rendered by *heaps*, since the grain was not put into stacks as with us; but being left uncut until fully ripe, it was, as soon as cut, gathered into heaps, ready for the threshing floor.

128.—BEASTS TO BE HELPED.

XXIII, 5. If thou see the ass of him that hateth thee lying under his burden, and wouldest forbear to help him, thou shalt surely help with him.

By reason of the roughness of the way, it was an easy matter for an ass, especially when overburdened, as was often the case, to fall to the ground, and it was also very difficult for the poor brute to extricate himself from the stones and hollows among which he fell. Hence this merciful law, requiring a man to help even his enemy when he finds him thus trying to aid an unfortunate brute. Wordsworth aptly suggests that this law sets the conduct of the priest and the Levite, in the parable of the Good Samaritan, in a most unenviable light, inasmuch as it shows them to have treated a fellow-being with less regard than their law required them to treat an enemy's ass. Luke x, 31, 32.

129.—PREPARATION FOR FESTIVALS.

XXIII, 14. Three times thou shalt keep a feast unto me in the year.

1. It is curious to notice how, at a time considerably later than the origin of these public festivals, the exact day of their occurrence was made known. In these days of almanacs and of exact astronomical calculations, we can hardly appreciate the difficulties they encountered in finding the right time. The

5

first appearance of the new moon was the starting-point. To ascertain this the Sanhedrin took the deposition of two impartial witnesses as to the time they had seen it. They next spread the intelligence through the country by means of beacons. A person with a bundle of brushwood or straw went to the top of Mount Olivet, where he kindled his torch and waved it back and forth till he was answered by fires of a similar nature from the surrounding hills. From these, in like manner, the intelligence was spread to others until the whole land was notified. After a time the Samaritans imitated the signs, thus making great confusion. This made it necessary to send messengers all over the country. These, however, did not go abroad at every new moon, but only seven times during the year. In this way the time for these three great feasts—Passover, Pentecost, and Tabernacles—as well as for other important occasions, was published to the people. See citation from Maimonides in BROWN'S *Antiquities of the Jews*, vol. i, p. 424.

2. These three festivals were preceded by a season of preparation, called *peres*, which lasted fifteen days. During this time each person was expected to meditate on the solemnity of the feast, and to undergo whatever legal purifications might be necessary. This is referred to in John xi, 55. Roads, bridges, streets, and public water-tanks were repaired for the convenience of travelers.

3. All the males of Israel were expected to attend, excepting the aged, the infirm, and infants who could not walk alone. They were commanded to bring offerings with them.

130.—THE PASSOVER.

XXIII, 15. Thou shalt keep the feast of unleavened bread.

This, the first of the three great feasts, is usually called the Passover, in commemoration of the passing over of the houses of the Israelites by the destroying angel, at the time when the first-born of the Egyptians were slain. The ancient Jewish canons distinguish between what they term "the Egyptian Passover" and "the Permanent Passover;" the former signifying the feast in its original form, and the latter representing it as modified in the subsequent years of the history of the people. The essential parts of the feast, were however, the same. It took place during the month Abib, or, as it was subsequently called, Nisan, corresponding very nearly with April of our calendar. See note on Deut. xvi, 1. While it lasted great care was taken to abstain from leaven. A he-lamb or kid of the first year was selected by the head of the family and was slain, its blood being sprinkled originally on the door-posts, and subsequently on the bottom of the altar. The animal was then roasted whole with fire, and eaten with unleavened bread and a salad of bitter herbs. It could not be boiled, nor must a bone of it be broken. When they first ate it in Egypt the Israelites had their loins girt and their shoes on, all ready for a journey, and they partook of it stand-ing, as if in haste to be away. In after years this position was changed to sitting or reclining. Not fewer than ten, nor more than twenty, persons were admitted to one of these feasts. Stanley (in his *History of the Jewish Church*, vol. i, p. 559, Am. ed.) gives a deeply interesting account, from his personal observation, of the modern observance of the Passover by the Samaritans. For the mode of observing the Passover in our Lord's time, see notes on Matt. xxvi, 19, 20.

It is supposed by some writers that, aside from the general design of the Passover, as already stated, there was in some of its ceremonies an inten-tional Divine rebuke of the idolatry of heathen nations, and especially of that of the Egyptians. One of their deities was represented by a human body with a ram's head. To have a lamb slain, and its blood sprinkled on the door-posts, was an act of contempt against this deity. Some heathen people ate raw flesh in connection with their festivities. The passover lamb was to be cooked. This cooking was by roasting, for the Egyptians and Syrians some-times boiled the flesh of their sacrificial victims in water, and sometimes in milk. It was to be roasted with fire, for the Egyptians, Chaldeans, and ancient Persians are said to have roasted their sacrifices in the sun. It was to be roasted whole, even to the intestines, for the heathen were in the habit of looking into these for omens, and sometimes even ate them raw.

131.—FEAST OF HARVEST—FEAST OF TABERNACLES.

XXIII. 16. The feast of harvest, the first-fruits of thy labors, which thou hast sown in the field: and the feast of ingather-ing, which is in the end of the year, when thou hast gathered in thy labors out of the field.

1. The Feast of Harvest is sometimes called the Feast of Weeks, because of the "seven weeks" by which its time was determined. Deut. xvi, 9, 10. It is also called the Day of First-fruits, (Num. xxvi i, 26,) because on that day the first loaves made from the wheat harvest were offered to the Lord. Its later name was Pentecost, because it occurred fifty days after Passover. These fifty days began with the offering of the first sheaf of the barley harvest during Passover week, (Lev. xxiii, 10,) and ended with the Feast of Harvest. This feast took place after the corn harvest, and before the vintage.

Its design was primarily to give an expression of gratitude to God for the harvest which had been gathered; but the Jews assert, that in addition to this, it was intended to celebrate the giving of the law on Siniai, which took place fifty days after the Passover. Maimonides says that the reason why the feast occupied but one day was because that was all the time occupied in giving the law.

On this day the people rested from all labor. Two loaves, made of the new wheat, were offered before the Lord. These were leavened, in distinction to the Passover bread, which was unleavened. Lev. xxiii, 17. The Jews say that this was because the Passover was a memorial of the haste in which they departed from Egypt, when they had not time to get their bread leavened; while the Feast of Harvest was a token of thankfulness to God for their ordinary food. In addition to this offering of the loaves, every person was required to bring in a basket a portion of the first-fruits of the earth, and offer it unto the Lord. Deut. xxvi, 1–10. At the same time there was a burnt offering of seven young lambs, one young bullock, and two rams. A kid was given as a sin-offering, and two young lambs for a peace-offering. Lev. xxiii, 18, 19.

2. The Feast of Ingathering, more generally known as the Feast of Tabernacles, (Lev. xxiii, 34,) was instituted to remind the people that their fathers dwelt in tents in the wilderness, (Lev. xxiii, 43;) and also to be an annual thanksgiving after all the products of the earth—corn, fruit, wine, and oil—were gathered for the year. Lev. xxiii, 39. It was held in the seventh month, Tizri, or Ethanim, corresponding to our October, and lasted for eight days; during which time the people dwelt in booths made of the branches of palm, willow, and other trees. Lev. xxiii, 39–43. On each day there were offered in sacrifice two rams, fourteen lambs, and a kid for a burnt-offering. During the continuance of the feast seventy bullocks were offered, thirteen on the first day, twelve on the second, eleven on the third, and so on, the number being diminished by one on each day until the seventh day, when only seven were offered. The eighth day was a day of peculiar solemnity, and had for its special offerings a bullock, a ram, and seven lambs for a burnt-offering, and a goat for a sin-offering. Num. xxix, 12–38. On the Sabbatical year, the Feast of Tabernacles was still further celebrated by a public reading of the law. Deut. xxxi, 10–13. Whether this was intended to include the whole law, or only certain portions, and if so, what portions, is matter of dispute.

Other ceremonies than these, originally instituted, were afterward added. See note on John vii, 37.

These festivals at the gathering of harvests were not peculiar to the Hebrews, but were in use among many Gentile nations. "The ancient sacrifices, assemblies, and conventions for sacrifices, were made at the gathering in of the fruits and productions of the earth, as the season of greatest leisure and rest." ARISTOTLE, cited by MAIMONIDES, *Reasons, etc.*, p. 257.

132.—ANNUAL PILGRIMAGES.

XXIII, 17. **Three times in the year all thy males shall appear before the Lord God.**

This great and sudden increase in the population of the sacred city—for it was to Jerusalem that the male inhabitants went, after they were settled in Canaan—could be accommodated much more easily than at first might be supposed. Three times a year these pilgrims were looked for, and every arrangement was doubtless made for their reception, while those who could not find room in the houses could pitch their tents in the streets or on the outskirts of the city. When the Mohammedans, in countless numbers, make their great pilgrimage to Mecca, they carry with them provisions enough to last during the journey both ways, and also during their stay in the city. They take from their homes butter, honey, oil, olives, rice, and bread, besides provender for camels and asses. They dwell in tents until their return.

133.—FORBIDDEN SEETHING.

XXIII, 19. Thou shalt not seethe a kid in his mother's milk.

As this injunction is put in connection with sacrifices and festivals, it seems to have referred to some idolatrous practices of the heathen. Cudworth says, on the authority of an ancient Karaite Comment on the Pentateuch, that it was an ancient heathen custom to boil a kid in the dam's milk, and then besprinkle with it all the trees, fields, gardens, and orchards. This was done at the close of their harvests for the purpose of making trees and fields more fruitful the following year. It will be noticed that the injunction of the text is given in connection with the feast of harvest.

Thomson says, that the Arabs "select a young kid, fat and tender, dress it carefully, and then stew it in milk, generally sour, mixed with onions and hot spices such as they relish. They call it Lebn immû—kid, 'in his mother's milk.' The Jews, however, will not eat it."—*The Land and the Book*, vol. i, 135.

134.—THE CUBIT.

XXV, 10. Two cubits and a half shall be the length thereof, and a cubit and a half the breadth thereof, and a cubit and a half the height thereof.

The word cubit is derived directly from the Latin *cubitus*, the lower arm. The Hebrew word is *ammah*, the *mother* of the arm, that is, the fore-arm. It is evidently a measure taken from the human body; as were other measures of length among the Hebrews and other nations. There seem to be two kinds of cubits, and some say three kinds, mentioned in Scripture. In Deut. iii, 11, we read of "the cubit of a man." In 2 Chron. iii, 3, "cubits after the first [or old] measure" are spoken of. In Ezek. xli, 8, we are told of "great cubits," each one of which, according to Ezek. xl, 5, measured a "cubit and a handbreadth." Some writers suppose these to represent three different measures of length; while others regard the first and second as identical, thus making but two kinds of cubits. Whether two or three cannot now be determined. It is no easier to decide as to the length of any one of the cubits named. Various estimates of the Mosaic cubit have been given, varying from twelve inches to twenty-two. The ancient Egyptian cubit was nearly twenty-one inches, which some of the best authorities now estimate as the length of the Mosaic. Other authorities, however, equally worthy of consideration, claim that the length of the Mosaic cubit, as applied to the Tabernacle and Temple, was eighteen inches; and that the Jews did not use the cubit of twenty-one inches—which was Babylonian as well as Egyptian—until after the captivity.

135.—BEATEN OIL.

XXVII, 20. Pure oil-olive beaten for the light.

This is supposed to have been oil which was obtained from olives not fully ripe, and pounded in a mortar instead of being put into a press. It was considered the best and purest, having a whiter color and better flavor, and yielding a clearer light than the ordinary oil from the press. Solomon made an annual present of this sort of oil to Hiram. 1 Kings v, 11. It is also mentioned in Exod. xxix, 40; Lev. xxiv, 2; Num. xxviii, 5. It may have been what is known as "cold drawn oil." See note on Psa. xcii, 10.

136.—THE SPAN.

XXVIII, 16. A span shall be the length thereof, and a span shall be the breadth thereof.

The span (zereth) is the distance between the extremities of the thumb and outside finger of the outstretched hand. It is half a cubit.

137.—METALLIC IDOLS.

XXXII, 4. He received them at their hand, and fashioned it with a graving tool, after he had made it a molten calf.

Most of the large idols worshiped by the ancients were first made of wood and then covered with plates of metal. We find illustrations of this in Isa. xxx, 22, and xl, 19. See also Nahum i, 14; Hab. ii, 18. A wooden image (or one of stone; see Hab. ii, 19) was first prepared, and the gold was then cast into a flat sheet which the goldsmith hammered and spread out into plating which was fastened on the wooden form. Thus the goldsmith first melted the gold, and then used "a graving tool" to fashion it to the shape of the image. Aaron's molten calf seems to have been made in this manner. "This is evident from the way in which it was destroyed: the image was first of all burnt, and then beaten or crushed to pieces, and pounded or ground to powder, (Deut. ix, 21;) that is, the wooden center was first burnt into charcoal, and then the golden covering beaten or rubbed to pieces; verse 20, compared with Deut. ix, 21."—KEIL.

See further note on Isa. xliv, 10.

138.—CALF WORSHIP.

XXXII, 6. They rose up early on the morrow, and offered burnt offerings; and brought peace offerings; and the people sat down to eat and to drink, and rose up to play.

"This expression [play—Heb. *tsachek,* to laugh; and so rendered in Gen. xxi, 6] often signifies dancing among the ancients. It probably refers here to some mystic dance which imitated the course of the stars. The sun-god was represented by the ancients by the image of a bull. Its worship was well known to the Israelites because the Egyptians paid honor to the bull Apis in Memphis; and earlier than this to the bull Mnevis in On, by which name the Greek Heliopolis (City of the Sun) was called. On was near the land of Goshen, which was given to the Israelites when they were

25.—CALF IDOL.

brought from Canaan to Egypt."— STOLLBERG'S *History of Religion,* vol. ii, p. 127; cit. by ROSENMÜLLER, *Morgenland,* vol. ii, p. 134.

The Egyptian idolaters worshiped deity under animal forms, thus differing from many other nations of antiquity whose deities were in human form. They kept live animals in some of their temples, and exhibited representations of them in others. The worship was accompanied with lascivious dances and other obscene practices. This is probably referred to in the twenty-fifth verse.

Reference is made to the Egyptian origin of this calf-worship in Ezek. xx, 6–8, and in Acts vii, 39, 40. Jeroboam, who afterward set up the two golden calves, (1 Kings xii, 28,) had lived in Egypt. 1 Kings xii, 2.

139.—MIRRORS.

XXXVIII. 8. He made the laver of brass, and the foot of it of brass, of the looking-glasses of the women assembling, which assembled at the door of the tabernacle of the congregation.

Ancient mirrors were metallic. The mirrors of the Egyptians were made of a mixed metal, chiefly copper, and were admirably polished. They were usually small, being in size and in general shape what would now be called hand-mirrors. They were wrought with great skill, and the handles, which were of wood, stone, or metal, were artistically shaped and highly ornamented. The Egyptian women were in the habit of carrying a mirror in one hand when they went to their temples to worship. It may be that the Hebrew women imitated this custom when they brought their mirrors to "the door of the tabernacle of the congregation."

Dr. Shaw (*Travels*, p. 24) says that the Moorish women he saw made their mirrors a part of the ornaments of their costume, hanging them on the breast, and wearing them with their other ornaments even when engaged in severest drudgery.

Allusion is made to metallic mirrors in Job xxxvii, 18; Isa. iii, 23; 2 Cor. iii, 18; James i, 23.

140.—TALENTS.

XXXVIII, 24. Twenty and nine talents.

The gold talent, which is here spoken of, is supposed to have weighed 1,320,000 grains, or very nearly 230 pounds troy. Its money value is reckoned at £5,475, or over $27,000. The silver talent, mentioned in verse 25, was half the weight, that is, 660,000 grains, or almost 115 pounds troy. Its value is estimated at £340, or $1,700. Of course there was no coin which represented this sum. The word was used to designate large amounts of money. See Matt. xxv, 15.

141.—THE JEWISH TABERNACLE.

XL, 2. On the first day of the first month shalt thou set up the tabernacle of the tent of the congregation.

This was thirty cubits long by ten wide, and was ten cubits in height. Exod. xxxvi, 20–30. It was made of boards of shittim or acacia wood, every board being ten cubits long, and one cubit and a half wide. Exod. xxxvi, 21. The thickness is not mentioned in the Bible, but Josephus says that each of these boards was four fingers thick, excepting the two corners of the west end, which were each a cubit in thickness.—*Ant. of the Jews*, Book III, chap. vi, § 3. Each board had two tenons at the base, (Exod. xxxvi, 22,) which fitted into silver mortises. Exod. xxxvi, 24. These mortises in turn were fastened to the ground by means of brass pins, (Exod. xxxviii, 20,) which, according to Josephus, were each a cubit in length. The boards were held together by means of wooden bars covered with gold. Exod. xxxvi, 31–34.

Several kinds of curtains and coverings were made for the Tabernacle. One was of fine linen, the threads being "blue, purple. and scarlet," and on the curtains were figures of cherubim, either woven or embroidered. Exod. xxxvi, 8–13. Another was of goats' hair, spun and woven into cloth. Exod. xxxv, 26; xxxvi, 14. Another was of "rams' skins dyed red," and a fourth was of the skins of the *tachash*, or "badger," (Exod. xxxvi, 19,) though precisely what animal is meant by that name is not known.

The design and arrangement of these different curtains and coverings are a subject of dispute among restorers of the Tabernacle. Some regard them as coverings thrown over the tabernacle, the figured-curtain being the first, and making a beautiful ceiling, the goats' hair next, the dyed rams' skins next, and over all the *tachash* skins.   Others think that the figured curtains not only made a ceiling, but also were suspended on the inside, either partially or entirely covering the gilded boards.

Connected with this question is that of the shape of the Tabernacle roof, whether flat, like Oriental houses, or peaked and slanting, like Oriental tents. Great names might be mentioned on both sides.   Fergusson, the celebrated English architect, presents a very strong plea in favor of the tent theory in Smith's *Dictionary of the Bible*, art. "Temple."   Some very strong arguments against his plan of restoration may be found in a recent work by a learned Scotch layman. *The Tabernacle and its Priests and Services*, etc., by William Brown, Edinburgh, 1871.   One of the most original treatises on the subject

26.—The Tabernacle, according to Paine.

is to be found in *Solomon's Temple*, etc., by the Rev. T. O. Paine, Boston, 1861.   Mr. Paine adopts the tent-theory, but, as we shall presently see, has a method of restoration entirely his own.

Fergusson supposes that the Tabernacle of gilded boards was entirely uncovered within and without, and that above this, and stretching beyond it on either side, so as completely to cover and protect it, were the curtains and coverings, in the form of a tent.   The beautiful figured curtain was first thrown over the ridge pole, and was thus visible from the inside of the Tabernacle. Over this was the cloth of goats' hair, and over this the "rams' skins dyed red." The *tachash* skins he places along the ridge pole as a protection to the joint of the ram-skin covering.

Mr. Paine supposes that the linen curtains were hung *in festoons* on the inside of the gilded boards, four cubits from the bottom, thus leaving six cubits of gilded boards uncovered. Stretched over the Tabernacle, in tent form, was a double covering, made of goats' hair, spun and woven into cloth of a dark brown color. This made the roof of the tent, and it came down close to the boarded sides of the Tabernacle. Fergusson's tent, it will be remembered, stretches some distance beyond. Next to the gilded planks, on the outside, Paine puts the *tachash* skins, and over these the skins of the rams, with the wool on and dyed red. Thus "the Tabernacle had red sides and end, and a brown roof and gable, nearly black."—*Solomon's Temple*, p. 16. He makes the front entirely open above the low entrance vail, and also has a small opening in the rear, or west end, between the top of the gable and the peak of the roof. See engraving on p. 77.

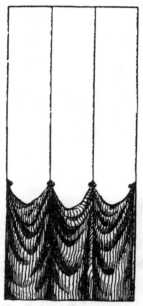

27.—TABERNACLE CURTAINS.

Nothing is said of the floor of the Tabernacle; whether of earth or boards is not known. In front were five pillars, over which was hung an embroidered curtain for a door. Exod. xxxvi, 37, 38. There was also a vail dividing the interior into two rooms. This vail was of embroidery and hung on four pillars. Exod. xxxvi, 35, 36. The precise length of each of these two rooms is not given, though, from the analogy between the Tabernacle and the Temple, two thirds of the space are supposed to have been given to the first room and the remaining third to the second. See 1 Kings vi, 17–20.

The first room, which was called the Holy Place, (Exod. xxviii, 29,) contained on one side the table of show-bread, on the other the golden candlestick, (Exod. xxvi, 35,) and, in front of the vail, the golden altar of incense. Exod. xxx, 6. Behind the vail was the second room, supposed to have been in the form of a perfect cube. It contained the ark, and was called the Most Holy Place. Exod. xxvi, 33, 34.

In this Tabernacle of the Israelites there was a general resemblance to the temples of other ancient nations. This resemblance is to be seen, among other things, in the secret place where no one was permitted to enter, the special shrine of the Deity.

The wandering tribes of Asia have tents for their temples. They are larger than their dwelling-tents, and of better material and workmanship.

142.—THE ARK OF THE COVENANT.

XL, 8. Thou shalt put therein the ark of the testimony, and cover the ark with the vail.

This is called elsewhere the "ark of the covenant," (Deut. xxxi, 26,) and "the ark of God." 1 Sam. iii, 3. It was made of acacia wood, overlaid with gold within and without. It was two cubits and a half long, one cubit and a half in width, and the same in height. An ornamental cornice, or "crown," of gold ran around the top. In each corner of the ark was a gold ring, and through the rings two gilded staves were kept for the purpose of carrying it when the Tabernacle was removed. Exod. xxv, 10–15.

In the work by Brown, referred to in the last note, the author expresses the opinion that the ark had feet, and that the rings were put into these feet in order, by means of the staves, to lift the ark on high when it was carried. He contends that *peamoth*, "corners," in Exod. xxv, 12, should be rendered "feet." Gesenius also gives this definition to the word.

The ark was put into the Most Holy Place. Exod. xxvi, 34. In it were placed the two tables of the law, for whose reception it was specially designed. Exod. xxv, 16. According to Heb. ix, 4, there were in addition to these a golden pot of manna and Aaron's rod which budded. Some think, however, that this is not in accordance with 1 Kings viii, 9, and that these two objects were laid up by the side of the ark. The passage referred to does not prove that the manna and the rod were never in the ark, but only that they were not there at the time the ark was put into Solomon's Temple; they may have been previously destroyed. It has also been supposed by some that a complete copy of the law was placed within the ark. See Deut. xxxi, 24–26. Others claim that "*in* the side" should be "*by* the side."

The cover was of solid gold, and was called "the mercy-seat." Exod. xxv, 17, 21. Springing from the ends of this cover were two golden cherubim with outstretched wings. Exod. xxv, 18–20. No particular description is given, here or elsewhere, of their size, shape, or general appearance. We do not know how to account for this failure to describe them, especially as all other articles connected with the Tabernacle are minutely described. Whether the form of the cherubim was so generally known as to make description unnecessary, or whether the description was purposely concealed, as among the secrets of Jehovah, cannot now be known. From the account given by Ezekiel in chapter i, 4–11, the cherubim seem to have been composite figures; but these could not have been in all respects like the cherubim over the ark, for Ezekiel represents them with four wings, each, two of which covered their bodies; while Moses speaks of the wings being stretched forth on high, "covering the mercy-seat," thus implying that they had but two wings each. More particular description is given of the colossal cherubim in the Temple of Solomon, which were probably patterned after those of the Tabernacle. These are distinctly stated to have had two wings each, and to have stood with their wings outstretched, and their faces turned inward. 2 Chron. iii, 10–13. However composite the form, it was doubtless more human than any thing else; in this respect differing from the winged figures of other nations. According to the Jewish tradition the cherubim over the mercy-seat had human faces.

Most of the nations of antiquity had arks, in which they preserved some secret things connected with their religion. These arks were likewise commonly surmounted with winged figures, but in spiritual meaning they are not worthy of comparison with the ark of the Hebrews. Clement of Alexandria, speaking of the Egyptians, says: "The innermost sanctuary of their temples is overhung with gilded tapestry; but let the priest remove the covering, and there appears a cat, or a crocodile, or a domesticated serpent wrapped in purple." How different this from the tables of the law, the Divine covenant!

143.—THE TABLE OF SHOW-BREAD—THE GOLDEN CANDLESTICK.

XL, 4. Thou shalt bring in the table, and set in order the things that are to be set in order upon it; and thou shalt bring in the candlestick, and light the lamps thereof.

1. The "table of show-bread" was on the north side of the Holy Place. Exod. xxvi, 35. It was made of acacia wood overlaid with gold, was two cubits long, one cubit wide, and a cubit and a half high. It had an ornamental cornice of gold around the top, and was furnished with rings of gold and gilded staves. Exod. xxv, 23–28. On it were placed twelve loaves of bread in two rows or piles, and on each row frankincense was put. The bread was changed every Sabbath. Lev. xxiv, 5–9. There were also golden vessels of various kinds, (Exod. xxv, 29,) probably for the bread, frankincense, and wine.

28.—TABLE OF SHOW-BREAD.

The shape of the table of show-bread in Herod's Temple is preserved to us in the celebrated triumphal arch erected in Rome to commemorate the destruction of Jerusalem by Titus. Among the spoils of war represented on it are those taken from the Temple. These articles probably bore some general resemblance to those in Solomon's Temple and in the Tabernacle.

29.—GOLDEN CANDLESTICK.

2. The "candlestick" consisted of a standard with three branches on each side, thus affording room for seven lamps, which were supplied with olive oil. The candlestick stood on the south side of the Holy Place, and with its snuffers and tongs was made of gold. Exod. xxv, 31–40. Nothing is known of its size, or of the formation of its base, or of the exact position of the six branches. Whether the tops of these branches were on a level, or in the form of an arch; and whether the branches extended in the same plane or in different planes is not known.

144.—THE GOLDEN ALTAR OF INCENSE.

XL, 5. Thou shalt set the altar of gold for the incense before the ark of the testimony.

This was made of acacia wood covered with gold. It was two cubits high, one cubit in length, and one in breadth. It had four "horns" or projections on the four corners at the top, and, like the ark and the table of show-bread, it had a cornice of gold, and rings and staves for transportation. The rings were of gold, and the staves of acacia wood covered with gold. Exod. xxxvii, 25–28. Its position was in the west end of the Holy Place, near the vail which concealed the Most Holy Place. Exod. xl, 26. It was thus immediately in front of the Ark of the Covenant, though separated from it by the vail.

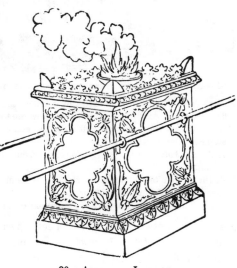

30.—ALTAR OF INCENSE.

145.—THE GREAT ALTAR OF BURNT-OFFERING.

XL, 6. Thou shalt set the altar of the burnt offering before the door of the tabernacle of the tent of the congregation.

This altar was placed in the court, not far from the entrance to the Tabernacle. Exod. xl, 6, 29. It was made of acacia wood, and covered with plates of brass. It was five cubits long, five cubits broad, and three cubits high, and had four horns at the four corners. It had brazen rings, and staves covered with brass were provided for moving it. It was hollow, and is supposed to have been filled with earth, thus complying with the command in Exod. xx, 24. See also Exod. xxxviii, 1–7.

Around the altar, midway from the bottom, was a projecting ledge on which the priest stood while offering sacrifice. This is represented in the word *karkob*, rendered "compass," in Exod. xxvii, 5, and xxxviii, 4; a word which Gesenius renders *margin* or *border*. It is supposed that an inclined plane of earth led to this on one side, probably the south. Thus we may see how Aaron could "come down" from the altar. Lev. ix, 22.

Various views have been entertained in reference to the grating or network spoken of in Exod. xxvii, 4, 5, and xxxviii, 4. Some place it at the top of the altar, supposing that the fire and the sacrifice were put upon it; but if the altar was filled with earth, as we have supposed, there would scarcely

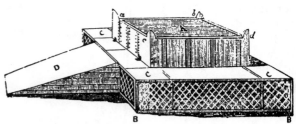

81.—ALTAR OF BURNT-OFFERING, ACCORDING TO MEYER.

have been any need of a grating for such a purpose. Others suppose the altar to have been only half-filled with earth, and that this grating was placed inside of the altar half way to the bottom, for the purpose of holding the earth. Both these theories assume that the grating occupied a horizontal position. Some archæologists, however, suppose this

A is the space between the boards, over which the utensils for fire and ashes were placed, while within were stones or earth.
B B is the network grating, with the projecting ledge, as described in Exod. xxvii, 4, 5.
C is the *karkob*, or ledge itself, projecting from the middle of the altar.
D is the incline toward it on one side, for the officiating priest to ascend by, formed of earth or stones.
a b c d are the horns or corner projections of the altar.

grating or network to have been perpendicular, and to have dropped from the edge of the *karkob*, or projecting ledge, to the ground. Thus in Exod. xxvii, 5, it is said, "And thou shalt put it [that is, the "grate of network of brass," verse 4] under the compass [*karkob*] of the altar beneath, that the net may be even to the midst of the altar."

Meyer is very decidedly in favor of this view; indeed we are not sure but he ought to be credited with having first suggested it. After speaking of the *karkob*, or ledge, he says: "Under the outer edge of this bench was the copper lattice work, which extended from it to the ground on all four sides, just as the body of the chest extended from the inner edge of the bench. It formed, with the bench or the *karkob* around, an expanding set-off, by reason of which the under half of the altar, on all sides, appeared wider than the upper. On the *karkob*, bench, or passage-way, the priest walked in order to attend to the sacrifice, to lay wood upon the altar, or to officiate in other ways. . . . The grating served to preserve the base of the altar from the sprinkled blood of the sacrifices, (see Exod. xxix, 12; Lev. iv, 7,) and to keep away from the sacred altar men and the beasts to be offered in sacrifice."—*Bibeldeutungen,* pp. 201–211.

146.—THE BRAZEN LAVER.

XL, 7. Thou shalt set the laver between the tent of the congregation and the altar, and shalt put water therein.

This was made out of the "brazen* mirrors" of the women, (Exod. xxxviii, 8,) and was used for the ablutions of the priests. Exod. xxx, 17–21. The better to accomplish this purpose it was placed between the brazen altar and the door of the Tabernacle. Exod. xl, 30–32. No description is given of its shape or size, but it is supposed to have been circular. In connection with the laver frequent mention is made of what is called its "foot." See Exod. xxx, 18, 28; xxxi, 9; xxxv, 16; xxxix, 39; xl, 11; Lev. viii, 11. This has led some commentators to believe that the "foot" was something more than a mere pedestal for the support of the laver, and they suppose that it may have been a lower basin to catch the water which flowed through taps or otherwise from the laver, thus making a convenient arrangement for washing the hands and feet of the priests.

147.—THE OUTER COURT.

XL, 8. Thou shalt set up the court round about, and hang up the hanging at the court gate.

This outer court which inclosed the Tabernacle was one hundred cubits long and fifty cubits wide. It was surrounded by a canvas wall five cubits high. The sides and ends, excepting the entrance, were made of fine linen curtains, which were hung on fillets, or, more properly, rods, made of silver. These silver rods were supported by pillars of brass, being connected to them by hooks of silver. There were twenty pillars on each side and ten on each end, all of them fitted into brazen sockets. At the east end of the court was the entrance. It occupied three panels, and was twenty cubits wide, thus taking up two fifths of the front. The curtains of the gate were made of the richest kind of needlework, and were wrought in colors. Exod. xxvii, 9–19. The frail walls of the Tabernacle were steadied by cords, which were fastened into the ground at suitable distances by means of tent-pins. See Exod. xxxv, 18.

* *Copper* is probably meant by the original word. See note on Dan. v, 4.

148.—PRIESTLY GARMENTS.

XL, 13. Thou shalt put upon Aaron the holy garments.

We shall first notice the garments which the high priest wore in common with the other priests:—

1. *Linen drawers,* reaching from the loins to the thighs. Exod. xxviii, 42 Maimonides (*Reasons,* etc., p. 267) says, that these were to be worn as an evidence that the divine worship sanctioned no such impurities as were associated with idolatrous worship, and that this is also the reason for the command in Exod. xx, 26.

2. *A tunic,* or *shirt,* of white linen. It was made of one piece, (see note on John xix, 23,) had sleeves, and is supposed to have reached to the ankles, and to have been of a checker pattern. Exod. xxviii, 39, 40; xxix, 5.

3. *A girdle.* This was wound around the tunic between the waist and the shoulders. Josephus says it was four fingers broad, and "so loosely woven that you would think it were the skin of a serpent."—*Ant.,* Book III, chap. 7, § 3. It was embroidered in colors. Exod. xxviii, 39.

4. *The miter,* or *turban,* made of linen, called a bonnet in Exod. xxxix, 28, and elsewhere.

We now notice the articles of dress which were peculiar to the high priest:—

1. *The robe.* This was woven of blue stuff, in one piece, with an opening by which it might be put on over the head. It was worn over the tunic, but whether it reached to the knees or to the ankles is uncertain. It was beautifully ornamented at the bottom with pomegranates in purple and scarlet. Little gold bells were hung between these, and made a tinkling sound whenever the wearer moved. Exod. xxxix, 22–26.

2. *The ephod.* The ordinary priest also wore an ephod, (see 1 Sam. xxii, 18,) but it was different in material and in style from that of the high priest. This was made of beautifully colored woven work, variegated with gold threads, the art of weaving which was known to the ancient Egyptians, from whom the Israelites may have learned it. These threads were made from thin plates of gold which were cut into wires. Exod. xxxix, 3. The ephod was in two pieces, one for the back and the other for the breast. The two pieces were joined by "shoulder pieces," which were a continuation of the front part of the ephod. Exod. xxviii, 6, 7; xxxix, 4. On the shoulder pieces were two precious stones, each having the names of six of the tribes of Israel. These stones were placed in gold settings, which some think made clasps for fastening the shoulder pieces together. Exod. xxviii, 9–12. The two parts of the ephod were fastened around the body by means of a girdle, which was really a portion of the front part of the ephod. Exod. xxviii, 8. The ephod had no sleeves.

3. *The breastplate.* This was made of the same material as the ephod It was half a cubit wide and a cubit in length, but being doubled, it became a half cubit square, and formed a pouch or pocket. On the front of this were four rows of precious stones, three in each row, and on them were engraved the names of the twelve tribes. These stones were set in gold. The breastplate was fastened to the ephod by golden chains. Exod. xxviii, 15–29. Connected with this breastplate were the Urim and Thummim —Lights and Perfections— but precisely what these were no man knows. They were used as a means of consulting Jehovah in cases of doubt. Numb. xxvii, 21; 1 Sam. xxviii, 6. How they were used cannot now be told. Some think that the twelve stones were the Urim and Thummim. the stones themselves being the Urim, or, Lights, and the names of the tribes engraven on them being the Thummim, or Perfections, because they represented the tribes in their tribal integrity.

32.—The High-Priest in his Robes.

From the fact that the Urim and Thummim are said to be *in* the breastplate, others again think that they were separate from the twelve stones and were put into the pocket behind them. Some suppose them to have been three precious stones which were placed in this pouch of the breastplate to be used for casting lots to decide questions of doubt; and that on one of the stones was engraven *Yes*, on another *No*, the third being without any inscription. The stone drawn out by the high priest would indicate the answer: affirmative, negative, or no answer to be given. This may have been so, but there is no proof of it. Trench, acting on the suggestion of Züllig, supposes the Urim and Thummim to have been a diamond, kept in the pouch of the breastplate, and having the ineffable

6

name of the Deity inscribed on it. He thinks this is the "white stone" referred to in Rev. ii, 17. See Trench on the *Epistles to the Seven Churches*, (American Edition,) p. 177.

4. *The diadem.* This was a plate of pure gold fastened around the miter by blue ribbons, and having engraved on it the words "HOLINESS TO THE LORD." (See page 84.)

LEVITICUS.

149.—FORBIDDEN OFFERINGS.

II, 11. Ye shall burn no leaven, nor any honey, in any offering of the Lord made by fire.

Maimonides assigns as a reason for this law that it was "the practice of the idolaters to offer only leavened bread, and to choose sweet things for their oblations, and to anoint or besmear them with honey."—*Reasons*, etc., p. 275.

150.—USE OF SALT.

II, 13. Every oblation of thy meat offering shalt thou season with salt; neither shalt thou suffer the salt of the covenant of thy God to be lacking from thy meat offering: with all thine offerings thou shalt offer salt.

The reason for this law, according to Maimonides, was found in the fact that the heathen never offered salt in sacrifices. If this were the case in the time of Moses, their custom must have changed subsequently, since there is abundant evidence of this use of salt among heathen of a later day. Some suppose that they imitated in this the Jewish sacrifices.

The partaking of salt by different persons together is regarded among the Arabs as a pledge of friendship. It is equivalent to a most solemn covenant. Numerous instances are recorded by travelers illustrative of this. So deeply rooted is this sentiment, that intended robbery has been abandoned when the robber has accidentally eaten salt while getting his plunder. Travelers have sometimes secured their safety in the midst of wild Bedawin by using stratagem in getting the Arabs to eat salt with them. Macgregor tells how he thus outwitted a sheikh who had made him a prisoner, and whose disposition seemed to be unfriendly. "We had now eaten salt together, and in his own tent, and so he was bound by the strongest tie, and he knew it."—*The Rob Roy on the Jordan*, p. 260.

By thus using salt in their sacrifices the people were bound to Jehovah in most solemn covenant. Hence we read of the "covenant of salt." Num. xviii, 19· 2 Chron. xiii, 5.

151.—THE BURNT–OFFERING.

VI, 9. This is the law of the burnt–offering: It is the burnt–offering, because of the burning upon the altar all night unto the morning, and the fire of the altar shall be burning in it.

The different victims for the burnt-offering were bullocks, sheep, goats, turtle doves, and young pigeons. The person making this voluntary offering, when he offered a bullock, put his hand on the victim's head, and then slew the animal. The priests took the blood and sprinkled it all around the great altar. In Solomon's Temple there was a red line half way up the sides of the great altar; some of the blood was sprinkled above and some below this line. See LIGHTFOOT, *Works*, (*Ed. Pitman,*) ix, 75. After the blood was sprinkled the person offering flayed the animal and cut him in pieces. In after times the priests and Levites sometimes did this. 2 Chron. xxix, 34. The entire offering was then burnt by the priests. If the offering consisted of a goat, a sheep, or fowls, the ceremony was slightly changed.

The burnt-offering was the only offering that was entirely burnt. Thus it is sometimes called the "whole" burnt-offering. Deut. xxxiii, 10; Psa. li, 19. The burning was to be so gradual that it should last from morning to evening, or from one daily sacrifice to the next. It was commanded that the fire on the altar should never go out.

The burnt-offering is described in detail in Lev. i, 1–17; vi, 8–13.

The design of the burnt-offering is not clearly stated in the Bible, and learned Jews differ in reference to it; some affirming that it was for evil thoughts, others that it was for a violation of affirmative precepts. Many Christian divines regard it as a symbol of entire and perpetual consecration to God; self-dedication, following upon and growing out of pardon and acceptance with God. See FAIRBAIRN'S *Typology*, vol. ii, p. 316.

152.—THE MEAT–OFFERING.

VI, 14. This is the law of the meat-offering.

The meat-offering was wholly vegetable in its nature, and was sometimes presented in a raw state and sometimes baked. Specific directions were given concerning the ceremonies to be observed in either case. A portion only was consumed in the fire, and the rest was given to the priest. Neither leaven nor honey was allowed to be mixed with it. It usually accompanied and was subsidiary to the sin and burnt offerings, and the quantity offered was graduated according to the victim presented as a burnt-offering. Num. xv, 4, 5, 6, 9.

It is supposed that oil was used to give the meat-offering a grateful relish; and frankincense to make a sweet odor in the court of the Tabernacle. Paul alludes to the fragrant meat-offering in Phil. iv, 18. The heathen used oil in their sacrifices, not mixed with flour, but poured over the burnt-offerings, to make the burning better. They likewise made free use of frankincense in their sacrifices. Full directions concerning the meat-offering are given in Lev. ii, 1–16; vi, 14–23.

153.—THE SIN-OFFERING.

VI, 25. This is the law of the sin-offering.

There were two kinds of sin-offering: one for the whole congregation and the other for individuals. For the first kind a young bullock was brought into the outer court of the Tabernacle, where the elders laid their hands upon his head and he was killed. The high priest then took the blood into the Holy Place and sprinkled it seven times before the vail, putting some on the horns of the golden altar of incense. The remainder of the blood was then poured out at the foot of the altar of burnt-offering. The fat of the animal was burnt upon the altar, and the rest of the body was taken without the camp and burnt. Lev. iv, 13–21.

Of the second kind of sin-offering there were three varieties. The first was for the high priest. The ceremonies only slightly varied from those just described. Lev. iv, 3–12. The second was for any of the rulers of the people. A kid was killed instead of a bullock. The priest did not enter the Holy Place, but merely put some of the blood on the horns of the altar of burnt-offering, and poured the rest out by the foot of the altar. The fat was burned upon the altar. Lev. iv, 22–26. The third was for any of the common people. A female kid or lamb was brought and treated as in the case just described. Lev. iv, 27–35. If poverty prevented the procuring of kid or lamb, two turtle doves or two young pigeons could be substituted; and for the very poorest a small offering of fine flour. Lev. v, 7–13.

What was left of the sin-offering for one of the rulers or for one of the common people was not burned without the camp, as in the two other instances, but was eaten by the priests and their sons. It was considered peculiarly holy, and special directions were given concerning the vessels in which it was cooked. Lev. vi, 24–30. The sin-offering was offered for sins of ignorance against negative precepts. Lev. iv, 2, 13, 22, 27.

154.—THE TRESPASS-OFFERING.

VII, 1. This is the law of the trespass-offering.

The trespass-offering was similar to the sin-offering; yet there were several important points of distinction. In the trespass-offering rams were offered, and the blood was sprinkled around the altar of burnt-offering. Lev. v, 18; vii, 2. The priest was required to make a special valuation of the ram offered. Lev. v, 15, 16.

The trespass-offering was offered in cases of trespass committed in holy things: dishonesty or falsehood in a trust; robbery joined with deceit; dishonesty and falsehood in reference to things found.   Lev. v, 15–vi, 7.

155.—OVEN—FRYING–PAN—PAN.

VII, 9.   All the meat-offering that is baken in the oven, and all that is dressed in the frying-pan, and in the pan, shall be the priest's that offereth it.

1. One form of oven common in the East consists of a hole dug in the ground four or five feet deep and three feet in diameter, and well plastered. When the oven is thoroughly heated the dough is rolled out no thicker than a finger, and is stuck against the sides of the oven, where it is instantly baked.   Another oven is made of a great stone pitcher, in the bottom of which a fire is made among small flints which retain the heat. On these the dough is placed and is soon baked.   Sometimes it is rolled out very thin, and is stuck on the outside of the heated pitcher, whence it instantly falls, baked through.   It

83.—ARAB OVEN.

is thought by some that reference is made to this pitcher-oven in Lev. ii, 4, and that the "unleavened cakes of fine flour mixed with oil" were to be baked inside the pitcher, and the "unleavened wafers anointed with oil" were to be baked on the outside; the "cakes" being mixed with oil, while the "wafers," rolled out thinner, were only smeared with it.

2. The "frying-pan" (*marchesheth*) was a deep vessel of iron used for boiling meat, and which could also be used for baking bread.

3. The "pan" was a thin flat plate of iron on which bread could be quickly baked as on our griddles.   This is the utensil referred to in Ezek. iv, 3.

156.—THE PEACE–OFFERING.

VII, 11.   This is the law of the sacrifice of peace-offerings.

Peace-offerings were of three kinds: 1. Thank-offerings; 2. Free-will offerings; 3. Offerings for vows. Lev. vii, 12, 16.   The peace-offering might be either of the herd or of the flock, and either male or female. Lev. iii, 1, 7, 12.   The offerings were accompanied by the imposition of hands, and by the sprinkling of blood around the great altar, on which the fat and the parts accompanying were burnt. Lev. iii, 1–5.   When offered for a thanksgiving a meat-offering was presented with it. Lev. vii, 12, 13.   A peculiarity of the peace-offering was, that the breast was waved and the shoulder heaved. Lev. vii, 34.   According to Jewish tradition this ceremony was performed by laying the parts on the hands of the offerer, the priest putting his hands again underneath, and then moving them in a horizontal direction for the waving, and in a vertical direction for the heaving. This is supposed to have been intended as a presentation of the parts to God as the supreme Ruler in heaven and on earth. The "wave-breast" and the "heave-shoulder" were the perquisites of the priests. Lev. vii, 31–34. The remainder of the victim, excepting what was burnt, was consumed by the offerer and his family, under certain restrictions. Lev. vii, 19–21. It has been suggested that this ceremony of eating the peace-offerings by the offerer and his family may have given rise to the custom among the heathen of eating flesh offered to idols in an idol temple. 1 Cor. viii, 10. See BROWN'S *Antiq. Jews*, i, 376.

157.—EARTHENWARE UNCLEAN.

XI, 33. Every earthen vessel, whereinto any of them [that is, the weasel, the mouse, etc., named in verses 29, 30,] falleth, whatsoever is in it shall be unclean ; and ye shall break it.

This is an illustration of the great attention paid by the Jews to ceremonial purity. Earthenware, being porous, was capable of absorbing any uncleanness, and hence mere washing or scouring was not sufficient to purify it: it must be destroyed. For a reason precisely opposite to this, earthen vessels used in connection with the sin-offering were destroyed, lest afterward any unclean thing should be put into them. See Lev. vi, 28.

158.—RANGES.

XI, 35. Whether it be oven, or ranges for pots, they shall be broken down.

Some think that instead of "ranges for pots," we should read "pots with lids." Others refer the words to some arrangement by which two or more cooking vessels could be used at once, thus economizing fuel. RAUWOLFF (cited by HARMER, *Obs.*, i, 465) describes an apparatus he saw among the Arabs which may have been similar to the "ranges" spoken of here. A hole was dug in the ground about a foot and a half deep, into which the earthen pipkins were put filled with meat and with covers on. Stones were piled around the pots on three sides of the little pit, and on the fourth side the Arabs threw the fuel. In a short time the heat was intense, and the meat cooked. The expression "broken down," in the text, may refer to the taking apart of the rude structure.

159.—MORTAR.

XIV, 42. He shall take other mortar, and shall plaster the house.

There were several kinds of mortar used by the Hebrews. Sometimes they used common mud and clay, mixed with straw chopped and beaten small. This may have been the kind especially referred to in the text. *Aphar*, "mortar," is frequently rendered "dust," and indeed is so translated in the verse preceding, where reference is made to the coating of old mortar which was scraped from the outside of the house. They also had several varieties of calcareous earth, any of which, mixed with ashes, made a good mortar. They likewise prepared an excellent cement of one part sand, two parts ashes, and three parts lime. These ingredients were well pounded, and were sometimes mixed with oil, while at other times the oil was put on as an outer coating.

Mortar was usually mixed by being trodden with the feet, but wheels were sometimes used.

160.—THE VICTIM'S HEAD.

XVI, 21. Both his hands upon the head of the live goat.

It was customary among the Egyptians for the person offering sacrifice to wish that all evil might be kept from him and fall on the head of his victim. For this reason the Egyptians would not eat the head of any animal, but sold it to the Greeks or else threw it into the river.

161.—THE GREAT DAY OF ATONEMENT.

XVI, 34. This shall be an everlasting statute unto you, to make an atonement for the children of Israel for all their sins once a year.

The Great Day of Atonement took place on the tenth day of the seventh month, Tisri, corresponding to our October. It was a day of great solemnity, especially designated and kept as a fast day, (see Lev. xxiii, 27; Num. xxix, 7; comp. Psa. xxxv, 13; Isa. lviii, 5,) and in later times was known by the name of The Fast. Acts xxvii, 9. On this day the high priest, clad in plain white linen garments, brought for himself a young bullock for a sin-offering and a ram for a burnt-offering; and for the people two young goats for a sin-offering, and a ram for a burnt-offering. The two goats were brought before the door of the Tabernacle, and by the casting of lots one was designated for sacrifice and the other for a scape-goat. The high priest then slaughtered the bullock and made a sin-offering for himself and family. He next entered the Most Holy Place for the first time, bearing a censer with burning coals, with which he filled the place with incense. Taking the blood of the slain bullock, he entered the Most Holy Place the second time, and there sprinkled the blood before the mercy-seat. He next killed the goat which was for the people's sin-offering, and, entering the Most Holy Place the third time, sprinkled its blood as he had sprinkled that of the bullock. Some of the blood of the two animals was then put on the horns of the altar of incense, and sprinkled on the altar itself. After this the high priest, putting his hands on the head of the scape-goat, confessed the sins of the people, and then sent him off into the wilderness. He then washed himself, and changed his garments, arraying himself in the beautiful robes of his high office, and offered the two rams as burnt-offerings for himself and for the people. Lev. xvi.

162.—GOAT-WORSHIP.

XVII, 7. They shall no more offer their sacrifices unto devils.

Seirim, here and in 2 Chron. **xi,** 15 rendered "devils," is derived from a word signifying *hairy, shaggy, rough,* from which it is used to designate he-goats. The Egyptians worshiped the goat under the name of *Mendes,* by which name a province in Egypt was called. The goat was worshiped as a personification of the fructifying power of nature, and was reckoned among the eight principal gods of Egypt. A splendid temple was dedicated to *Mendes,* and statues of the god were erected in many places. The Israelites doubtless learned the worship of the *Seirim* among the Egyptians. It was accompanied with the vilest acts of bestiality.

163.—MOLECH.

XVIII, 21. Thou shalt not let any of thy seed pass through the fire to Molech.

Molech (sometimes written Moloch) was an old Canaanitish idol, into whose worship the Israelites gradually became drawn. Similar rites were performed among other nations, probably varying at different times and in different places. The usual description given of this god is that of a hollow image made of brass, and having a human body with the head of an ox. The idol sat on a brazen throne with hands extended. In sacrificing to it the image was heated to redness by a fire built within. The parents then placed their children in the heated arms, while the noise of drums and cymbals drowned the cries of the little sufferers. It is also said that there were seven chapels connected with the idol, which were to be entered according to the relative value of the offering presented; only those who offered children being allowed to enter the seventh. Miniatures of these are supposed to be the "tabernacle" referred to in Amos v, 26; Acts vii, 43. Others think the "tabernacle" was a shrine or ark in which the god was carried in procession.

Some eminent writers deny that the description above given refers to the Molech of the Old Testament. The Bible itself gives no account of the idol save that children were made to "pass through the fire" to it. A diversity of opinion prevails as to the meaning of this expression. Most Jewish writers claim that it does not imply the actual sacrificing or burning of the children, but merely an idolatrous ceremonial purification; a fire baptism, which was accomplished by carrying the children between fires, or leaping over fires with them, or causing them to do the same. However this may have been in earlier times, it is certain that the service of Molech implied more than this at some periods of Jewish history. In the days of Ezekiel God's testimony was, "Thou hast slain my children, and delivered them to cause them to pass through the fire for them." Ezek. xvi, 21. Here passing through the fire is evidently synonymous with death. See also 2 Chron. xxviii, 3; Psa. cvi, 37, 38; Jer. vii, 31.

Frequent reference is made in the Scriptures to this heathen abomination. See 2 Kings xvi, 3; xvii, 17; xxi, 6; xxiii, 10; Jer. xxxii, 35; Ezek. xx, 31. The crime was threatened with the severest punishment. Lev. xx, 1–5.

Human sacrifices were anciently known to the Phenicians, Egyptians, Carthaginians, and other nations.

Some writers have sought to identify the worship of Molech with that of Baal. Others suppose that, according to the well-known astrological character of the Phenician and Syrian religions, Molech was the planet Saturn. Winer says: "The dearest ones might well be sacrificed to a star so dreaded as Saturn, in order to appease it, especially by nations who were by no means strangers to human sacrifices."—*Biblisch. Realw.*, s. v. Molech.

164.—FRUIT OF YOUNG TREES FORBIDDEN.

XIX, 23. Ye shall count the fruit thereof as uncircumcised : three years shall it be as uncircumcised unto you : it shall not be eaten of.

The fruit of young trees was not to be eaten until the fourth year after being planted, because of certain heathen superstitions. Maimonides says that the idolaters believed that unless the first-fruits of every tree were used in connection with certain idolatrous ceremonies the tree would suffer some great harm, and perhaps die. They further made use of magical rites for the purpose of hastening the bearing of fruit. The law in the text was aimed at this folly, for as no fruit could be touched until the fourth year, the Hebrews could not offer the first of the fruit as the idolaters did; nor would it be of any use to seek, by incantations and sprinklings, to hasten the coming of the fruit, since they could not eat it before the time designated, and long before that it would come naturally.

165.—IDOLATROUS USE OF HAIR.

XIX, 27. Ye shall not round the corners of your heads, neither shalt thou mar the corners of thy beard.

Among the ancients the hair was often used in divination. The worshipers of the stars and planets cut their hair evenly around, trimming the extremities. According to Herodotus the Arabs were accustomed to shave the hair around the head, and let a tuft stand up on the crown in honor of Bacchus. He says the same thing concerning the Macians, a people of

Northern Africa. This custom is at present common in India and China. The Chinese let the tuft grow until it is long enough to be plaited into a tail.

By the idolaters the beard was also carefully trimmed round and even. This was forbidden to the Jews. Dr. Robinson says, that to this day the Jews in the East are distinguished in this respect from the Mohammedans the latter trimming their beard, the former allowing the extremities to grow naturally.

It was also an ancient superstitious custom to cut off the hair at the death of friends and throw it into the sepulcher on the corpse. It was sometimes laid on the face and breast of the deceased as an offering to the infernal gods. From the verse following it would seem that this custom, as well as the other, may be referred to in the text.

The express on "utmost corners" in Jer. ix, 26; xxv, 23; xlix, 32 refers not to any dwelling-place, but to the custom forbidden in Leviticus; and accordingly the margin reads, "cut off into corners, or having the corners [of their hair] polled."

166.—MEMORIAL CUTTINGS—TATTOOING.

XIX, 28. Ye shall not make any cuttings in your flesh for the dead, nor print any marks upon you.

1. The custom of scratching the arms, hands, and face as tokens of mourning for the dead is said to have existed among the Babylonians, Armenians, Scythians, and Romans, and is practiced by the Arabs, Persians, and Abyssinians of the present day, and also by the New Zealanders. It was sometimes accompanied by shaving the hair from the forehead. See Lev. xxi, 5; Deut. xiv, 1; Jer. xvi, 6; xlviii, 37. Some suppose that reference is made in Zech. xiii, 6, to this custom of cutting the hands as a token of mourning.

2. The Orientals are very fond of tattooing. Figures of birds, trees, flowers, temples, and gods are carefully and painfully marked in their flesh with colors by the puncturing of sharp needles. This is still done in India for idolatrous purposes, and, in the time of Moses, probably had some connection with idolatry. Others do it for eccentric desire of adornment, as we sometimes find our own sailors printing their names and making representations of ships, anchors, and other objects on their arms by means of needles and india-ink, the latter mingling with the blood drawn by the needles, and leaving an indelible mark of a light blue. See note on Isa. xlix, 16, and also on Gal. vi, 17.

167.—THE HIN.

XIX, 36. A just hin.

The hin was a liquid measure containing about ten pints.

168.—FORBIDDEN FOOD.

XXII, 8. That which dieth of itself, or is torn with beasts, he shall not eat to defile himself therewith.

1. It might not be necessary among us to forbid the eating of animals which have died of disease, but in the East the lower classes will eat such food. Tavernier noticed that in Ispahan dead horses, camels, and mules were bought by people who made hashes of the meat, which they sold to the poor day-laborers.

2. The ancient Greeks prohibited the eating of the flesh of animals which had been torn by wild beasts. The Mohammedans have a similar rule. Some commentators suppose this prohibition to be grounded on the fact that the animals thus torn may have been killed by wolves, dogs, or foxes which were mad, and the flesh in this way rendered unwholesome.

The text is specially addressed to the priests; so also is Ezek. xliv, 31 A similar command, directed to the people at large, is found in Exod. xxii, 31, and Lev. xvii, 15.

169.—DRINK-OFFERINGS.

XXIII, 18. They shall be for a burnt-offering unto the Lord with their meat-offering, and their drink-offerings.

Accompanying other offerings was the drink-offering, which consisted of a certain quantity of wine, proportioned to the nature of the sacrifice. This was taken by the priest, and poured out like the blood at the foot of the altar of burnt-offering. For a bullock, half a hin (five pints) of wine was used; for a ram, a third of a hin; and for a lamb or kid, a fourth of a hin. See Num. xv, 4–12. In the temple service the pouring out of the wine of the drink-offering at the morning and evening sacrifice was the signal for the priests and Levites to begin their song of praise to God.

170.—THE FEAST OF TRUMPETS.

XXIII, 24. In the seventh month, in the first day of the month, shall ye have a sabbath, a memorial of blowing of trumpets, a holy convocation.

This festival, commonly called the " Feast of Trumpets," is universally regarded by the Jews as the Festival of the New Year, which began with the seventh month, Tisri. As it occurred at the new moon, and on the first day of the month in which the Great Day of Atonement and the Feast of Tabernacles took place, it was an occasion of great interest. It has ever been observed by the Jews as connected with the Day of Atonement, and the ten days between the two are considered days of preparation for the solemn day. The silver trumpets, which were ordered to be prepared for the purpose of calling the people together, (Num. x, 1–10,) were blown on this day more than at other times, because the new year and the new month began together.   Hence the name by which the feast is commonly called.

The day was kept as a Sabbath, no work being performed.   The usual daily morning sacrifice was offered, then the monthly sacrifice of the new moon, and then the sacrifice peculiar to the day, which consisted of a bullock, a ram, and seven lambs for a burnt-offering, and a kid for a sin-offering.   Num. xxix, 1–6.

171.—THE SABBATICAL YEAR.

XXV, 4. The seventh year shall be a sabbath of rest unto the land, a sabbath for the Lord: thou shalt neither sow thy field, nor prune thy vineyard.

Every seventh year was to be a time of recuperation to the soil.   The spontaneous produce of this Sabbatical Year was free to all comers, but especially to the poor.   Exod. xxiii, 11; Lev. xxv, 6.   It was also a time for the debtor to be released by his creditor.   Deut. xv, 1, 2.   During the Feast of Tabernacles of this year the law was publicly read to the people.   Deut. xxxi, 10–13.

172.—THE YEAR OF JUBILEE.

XXV, 10. Ye shall hallow the fiftieth year, and proclaim liberty throughout all the land unto all the inhabitants thereof: it shall be a jubilee unto you.

The Year of Jubilee was ushered in by the sound of trumpets through the land. every fiftieth year, on the Great Day of Atonement.   Like the Sabbatical Year, it was a year of rest to the soil.   Lev. xxv, 11.   Thus two idle years came together every fifty years, and God promised by special providence to give such a plentiful harvest during the sixth year that there should be enough until the harvest of the ninth year could be gathered.   Lev. xxv, 20–22.   See also 2 Kings xix, 29; Isa. xxxvii, 30.   A similar providence no doubt watched over the productions of the season before the Sabbatical Year, in addition to the spontaneous growth of that year.   All their transfers of real estate were made in reference to the Year of Jubilee, and the poor and unfortunate were specially favored.   Lev. xxv.

173.—STONE IDOLS.

XXVI, 1. Neither shall ye set up any image of stone in your land, to bow down unto it: for I am the Lord your God.´

Maskith, here rendered "image," is in Num. xxxiii, 52, (where the word is in the plural) translated "pictures."   Some writers suppose that *eben maskith*, "figure stone," is a stone formed into a figure; that is, an idol of stone in distinction to one made of iron or of wood.   See Keil, *Com. in loco.*

Others, however, regard it as referring to stones with figures or hieroglyphic inscriptions on them; "pictured" or "engraven stones," which in that age of idolatry were liable to be worshiped.

174.—HIGH PLACES—SUN-IMAGES.

XXVI, 30. **I will destroy your high places, and cut down your images.**

1. Frequent mention is made in the Scriptures of the "high places" of the heathen, where they were accustomed to worship their gods, supposing themselves there to be nearer to them, and more likely to be heard by them. This practice was imitated by the Hebrews, though denounced in their laws. They sometimes worshiped on their house-tops as a substitute for hills or mountains. See Jer. xix, 13; xxxii, 29; Zeph. i, 5.

2. The "images" (*chammanim*) here spoken of are called "sun images" in the margin, in several places where the word is used. They are supposed to have been identical with the sun-god Baal. From 2 Chron. xxxiv, 4, it would seem that they were sometimes placed on top of the altars of Baal, from which it is thought that they may have resembled rising flames. In some places where their destruction is spoken of they are represented as being "cut down," (Ezek. vi, 4,) and in other places they are said to be "broken." Ezek. vi, 6. Thus they may sometimes have been made of wood, and sometimes of stone. Perhaps they were made of stone when placed as a fixture on the altar, and of wood when put in other positions.

175.—SHEKEL—GERAH.

XXVII, 25. **All thy estimations shall be according to the shekel of the sanctuary: twenty gerahs shall be the shekel.**

1. What the "shekel of the sanctuary" was is not definitely stated. There are those who think it was worth double the value of the ordinary shekel. Others, again, suppose that "the shekel of the sanctuary" was the standard to which all shekels must conform if of full weight. See note on Gen. xxiii, 16.

2. The gerah was the smallest weight known to the Hebrews, and the smallest piece of money used by them. It weighed between eleven and twelve grains, and was in value about three cents.

176.—THE TITHING ROD.

XXVII, 32. **Whatsoever passeth under the rod.**

The reference here is to the Jewish mode of tithing sheep. As the sheep passed through a narrow gate, one by one, the person counting stood by, holding in his hand a rod colored with ochre. Every tenth one he touched with his rod, thus putting a mark upon it. Jeremiah alludes to this method of counting sheep in chap. xxxiii, 13. So also does Ezekiel, in chap. xx, 37.

NUMBERS.

177.—STANDARDS.

II, 2. Every man of the children of Israel shall pitch by his own standard, with the ensign of their father's house.

The. *degel*, "standard," was the large field sign which belonged to each division of three tribes, and was also the banner of the tribe at the head of that division. The *oth*, "ensign," was the small flag or banner which was carried

34.—EGYPTIAN STANDARDS.

at the head of each tribe and of each subdivision of a tribe. The Bible gives us no intimation of the form of these different signals. They probably bore some general resemblance to the Egyptian military signals, representations of which are to be found on the monuments. These were not at all like our modern flags or banners. They were made of wood or metal, and ornamented with various devices, and shaped in the form of some sacred emblem. Some illustration of the mode of using these signals may perhaps be obtained from the account which Pitts gives of the signals which are carried on the top of high poles in an Arabian caravan, not only by day, but also at night, at which time they are illuminated. "They are somewhat like iron stoves, into which they put short dry wood, which some of the camels are loaded with; it is carried in great sacks, which have a hole near the bottom, where the servants take it out as they see the fires need a recruit. Every *cottor* [i. e., company] hath one of these poles belonging to it, some of which have ten, some twelve, of these lights on their tops, more or less. They are likewise of different figures as well as numbers; one, perhaps, oval way, like a gate; another triangular, or like an N or an M, etc.; so that every one knows by them his respective *cottor*."
—*Religion and Manners of the Mahometans*, p. 43.

178.—THE LEVITES.

III, 6. Bring the tribe of Levi near, and present them before Aaron the priest, that they may minister unto him.

The family of Aaron were set apart especially to the duties of the priesthood. The rest of the tribe of Levi were consecrated to special services in connection with the worship of Jehovah. Each of the three families had its particular duties assigned. The Kohathites had charge of the sacred utensils of the Tabernacle. They saw that they were properly removed when on the march, and that they were put into their appropriate places when the encampment was again fixed. Num. iv, 4–15. The Gershonites took care of the hangings and curtains of the Tabernacle. Num. iv, 21–28. The Merarites were required to look after the boards, sockets, pillars, pins, and cords of the Tabernacle. Num. iv, 29–33. Moses also gave the Levites judicial authority, (Deut. xvii, 8–12,) and made them keepers of the book of the law. Deut. xxxi, 9, 25, 26. After the temple was built they acted as porters, musicians, and assistants to the priests.

The first Levites who were appointed began their service at thirty years of age, (Num. iv, 23, 30, 35;) but it was ordered that after that the age for commencing should be twenty-five years. Num. viii, 24. In David's time they began serving at twenty. 1 Chron. xxiii, 24–27. They were released from all obligation to serve when they became fifty years old. Num. viii, 25.

Forty-eight cities were set apart for their residence in the Land of Promise. Six of these were also cities of refuge, and thirteen of them they shared with the priests. Num. xxxv, 1–8; Josh. xxi, 13–19; 1 Chron. vi, 54–60.

179.—FULLNESS OF FOOD.

XI, 20. Until it come out at your nostrils.

Roberts says, that this figure of speech is used in India to convey the idea of being filled to satiety. A host says to his guests, "Now, friends, eat *mookamattam :* to the nose. That is, Eat until you are filled to the nose. Of a glutton it is said, "That fellow always fills up to the nose."

180.—THE STAFF OF INHERITANCE.

XVII, 2. Take of every one of them a rod, according to the house of their fathers.

In the pictures on the walls of the ancient Egyptian tombs the chief person is always represented with a long staff—the mark of his rank as a land owner, and as the head of his family. In the Abbott Collection there are fragments of two of these rods with hieroglyphic inscriptions.

In the engraving this staff is seen in the left hand. The stick in the right hand is supposed to be a scepter. Sharpe represents this man as "an Egyptian of the reign of Amunmai Thori II., who lived at least two centuries before the time of Moses."—*Bible Texts*, etc., p. 46.

85.—STAFF OF INHERITANCE.

181.—SACRIFICE OF THE RED HEIFER.

XIX, 2. Speak unto the children of Israel, that they bring thee a red heifer without spot, wherein is no blemish, and upon which never came yoke.

The sacrifice of the red heifer was a peculiar ceremony designed to purify from the ceremonial defilement resulting from contact with a corpse. Num. xix, 11–16. A heifer perfectly red, and which had never borne the yoke, was selected by the people, and brought to Eleazar the priest. She was then taken outside the camp and slaughtered. Eleazar sprinkled her blood seven times before the Tabernacle, after which the entire carcass was burnt, the priest throwing into the fire cedar, and hyssop, and scarlet. The ashes were then carefully collected and laid up in a suitable place for future use. Num. xix, 1–10. When purification from the defilement of a corpse became necessary, the ashes were made into a lye by means of running water, and the water was sprinkled from a bunch of hyssop on the person, the tent, the bed, or the utensils which had been defiled. Num. xix, 17–19

This sacrifice differed from all others in several important particulars. The victim was not slaughtered in the court, nor was it burnt on the altar; it was killed and burnt outside the camp. Neither the high priest nor any ordinary priest officiated, but the presumptive successor of the high priest. The animal chosen was not a bullock, as in other sacrifices, but a heifer, and the precise color was specified. The ashes were carefully preserved.

Much has been written on these subjects, and various attempts have been made to give full explanations of all the minutiæ of the ceremonies, but some things connected with them are not easily explained. The Jews are represented as saying, that Solomon himself, with all his wisdom, did not fully understand them.

The general design, doubtless, was to keep in remembrance the awful fact of sin, which brought death into the world, and the necessity of purification from its pollution. Paul makes reference to this in Heb. ix, 13, 14. As Kurtz remarks, " This idea of an antidote against the defilement of death was the regulating principle of the whole institution, determining not only the choice of the sacrificial animal, but what should be added to it, and all that should be done with it."—*Sacrificial Worship of the Old Testament*, p. 426.

182.—PROPHETS' MANTLES.

XX, 28. Moses stripped Aaron of his garments, and put them upon Eleazar his son.

This was the formal initiation of Eleazar into the sacred office. We find, also, that Elijah threw his mantle over Elisha, when, in obedience to divine command, he called him to the prophet's work. 1 Kings xix, 19. This mantle Elisha took up as soon as Elijah was translated. 2 Kings ii, 13, 14. In a similar way Eliakim was appointed the successor of Shebna. Isa. xxii, 15, 20, 21.

Among the Persians the prophet's mantle is a symbol of spiritual power, and is transferred from a prophet to his successor. Among the Hindoos when a Brahmin is inducted into the sacred office he is always covered with a yellow mantle.

183.—CHEMOSH.

XXI, 29. Woe to thee, Moab! thou art undone, O people of Chemosh.

Chemosh was the national god of the Moabites, and hence they are called in this text, and in Jer. xlviii, 46, "the people of Chemosh." He was also worshiped by the Ammonites. Judges xi, 24. Solomon built high places for Chemosh and Molech in the neighborhood of Jerusalem. 1 Kings xi, 7. Nothing definite is known concerning this god, or the mode of his worship. There is an old Jewish tradition that he was worshiped under the form of a black stone; and another that his worshipers went bare-headed, and refused to wear garments that were made by use of a needle. Chemosh is also mentioned in Jer. xlviii, 7, 13. His name is found on the celebrated Moabite Stone.

184.—BAAL.

XXII, 41. It came to pass on the morrow, that Balak took Balaam, and brought him up into the high places of Baal.

The word Baal signifies lord, not so much in the sense of ruler, as possessor, or owner. The name was given to the principal male deity of the Phenicians, corresponding to Bel or Belus of the Babylonians. See note on Isa. xlvi, 1. The name of the female deity associated with Baal was Astarte. The worship of Baal was of great antiquity, and was accompanied with splendid ceremonies. Priests and prophets were consecrated to his service. 2 Kings x, 19. Incense (Jer. vii, 9) and prayers (1 Kings xviii, 26) were offered. The worshipers prostrated themselves before the idol and kissed it, (1 Kings xix, 18,) perhaps at the same time kissing the hand toward the sun. See note on Deut. iv, 19. They danced with shouts, and cut themselves with knives. 1 Kings xviii, 26–28. The offerings were sometimes vegetable (Hosea ii, 8) and sometimes animal. 1 Kings xviii, 23. Human sacrifices were also offered. Jer. xix, 5.

Efforts have been made to identify Baal with one of the gods of classical mythology, but the results are by no means satisfactory. The Greek Zeus, the Roman Jupiter, Cronos or Saturn, Ares or Mars, and Hercules, have each been supposed by different writers to be the same as Baal. In reference to

7

the astrological nature of the worship, the most prevalent opinion is, that Baal represented the sun, while Astarte, his companion, represented the moon; but Gesenius and others assert that the two terms respectively stood for Jupiter and Venus. Baal and Gad are considered by some to be identical. See note on Isa. lxv, 11.

The ordinary symbol of Baal was a bull.

185.—BAAL–PEOR.

XXV, 8. Israel joined himself unto Baal-peor.

The worship of this special form of Baal is generally supposed to have been accompanied with obscene rites. This seems to be indicated in this chapter. Some consider Baal-peor to be the same as Chemosh.

DEUTERONOMY.

186.—CAMPING–GROUNDS.

II, 23. The Avim which dwelt in Hazerim.

Hazerim is not the name of a place, as it appears to be in the text. The same word occurs in Gen. xxv, 16, where it is translated "towns," and in Psa. x, 8, and Isa. xlii, 11, where it is translated "villages." In the text it is untranslated. The *hazerim* are supposed to have been the camping-grounds of wandering tribes, with a stone wall around them for protection. Mr. Palmer, in endeavoring to trace the route of the Israelites across the desert, found remains of some camping-grounds, evidently of ancient origin. The Maghrabim, or African Arabs, have their encampments on this principle at the present day. "When a camping-ground has been selected, cattle, as the most precious possession of the tribe, are collected together in one place, and the huts or tents are pitched in a circle round them; the whole is then fenced in with a low wall of stones, in which are inserted thick bundles of thorny acacia, the tangled branches and long needle-like spikes forming a perfectly impenetrable hedge around the encampment. These are called *Dowárs*, and there can be but little doubt that they are the same with the *Hazeroth*, or 'field inclosures,' used by the pastoral tribes mentioned in the Bible."—*Desert of the Exodus*, p. 321.

187.—STONE CITIES.

III, 5. All these cities were fenced with high walls, gates, and bars ; beside unwalled towns a great many.

These cities of Bashan, which are also referred to in 1 Kings iv, 13, seem to have astonished their conquerors. "Why were these cities, with their walls and gates, something so remarkable to the Israelites? Because they had come from the Red Sea through the wilderness, until near the Mandhur, [that is, the Hieromax,] almost exclusively through a limestone region, in which, until this day, the troglodyte-life predominates; the soft limestone being adapted to the excavation of artificial caverns. That, in a land of hard basalt, is not to be thought of. There, in order to obtain the security which the caverns afford, it is necessary to build cities, walled around and provided with strong gates. To the astonishment of European travelers, there remain to-day large numbers of the walled cities of Bashan, with their black basalt houses, gates, doors, and bolts."—RAUMER; *Palästina*, pp. 78, 79.

Recent travelers tell marvelous stories of these unoccupied stone cities, which are still in excellent preservation. Porter believes that some of them are the veritable cities taken by the Hebrews at the time referred to in the text. He says: "Time produces little effect on such buildings as these. The heavy stone slabs of the roofs resting on the massive walls make the structure as firm as if built of solid masonry; and the black basalt used is almost as hard as iron. There can scarcely be a doubt, therefore, that these are the very cities erected and inhabited by the Rephaim, the aboriginal occupants of Bashan."—*Giant Cities of Bashan*, p. 84.

Macgregor also speaks of the immense slabs of stone which were used in the construction of these black basalt houses. He saw double doors made of slabs seven feet high and six inches thick, and with pivots about four inches long and three in diameter, turning in stone sockets; and stone window shutters, in size four feet by three. The room in which he slept was fourteen feet long, nine wide, and eleven high. Stone rafters supported a stone roof. The walls were from four to six feet thick. Many of the houses were two stories high, and a few three stories. See *The Rob Roy on the Jordan*, pp. 175–179.

The high antiquity claimed for these houses has been disputed, though all agree that they are of great age; but, whether they are the same buildings which the Hebrew warriors saw, or are of more recent date, they are undoubtedly similar in construction and in general appearance to the dwellings which made up the cities spoken of in the text.

188.—BEDSTEADS.

III, 11. Behold, his bedstead was a bedstead of iron.

Bedsteads are less common in the East than with us, the bed being usually made on the divan, or platform around the room. Frames, however, are sometimes used. In Palestine, Syria, and Persia, these are made of boards. In Egypt they are made of palm-sticks, and probably were so made in Palestine in the time of King Og, when the palm was more plentiful than now.

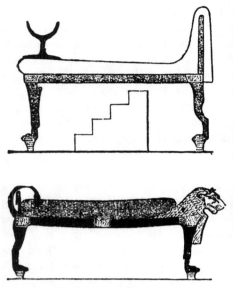

36.—Egyptian Bedsteads.

The palm-sticks, however, would make rather a rickety bedstead for a heavy man, and hence the giant-king needed something more substantial. Bedsteads of metal seem to have been in more common use in the East formerly than at present, though their use in ancient times appears to have been limited mainly to princes and persons of distinction. Bedsteads of gold, and also of silver, are spoken of by heathen writers. Some of these were used in temples, and some in palaces. Mention is likewise made of such in Esther i, 6, where see the note. Bedsteads of brass and of iron are also mentioned by ancient writers.

189.—ZABAISM.

IV, 19. Lest thou lift up thine eyes unto heaven, and when thou seest the sun, and the moon, and the stars, even all the host of heaven, shouldest be driven to worship them, and serve them.

The worship of the heavenly bodies is the most ancient and widely spread form of idolatry, and frequent allusions are made to it in the Scriptures. Its chief promoters were called Sabians. and sometimes Zabians; and the idolatry itself is known as Sabaism or Zabaism: probably from the Hebrew *tsaba*, a host. Thus in the name of the system the objects of worship are indicated: the "hosts of heaven."

It is supposed that many of the precepts in the Mosaic law were directed against Zabaism in its various corrupt forms. The text is an illustration. Besides the direct reference to this superstition in this and in other passages, occasional allusion to it may be found elsewhere. The many texts in which the expression "the Lord of hosts" occurs, seem to be directly leveled at Zabaism; teaching that there is a being superior to the hosts the Zabians worshiped, and to all hosts, whether of heaven or earth. Thus we read in Genesis ii, 1: "Thus the heavens and the earth were finished, and all the hosts of them;" and in Job ix, 7–9: "Which commandeth the sun, and it riseth not; and sealeth up the stars; which alone spreadeth out the heavens, and treadeth upon the waves of the sea; which maketh Arcturus, Orion, and Pleiades, and the chambers of the south." In these and similar passages God is declared to be the Creator of the heavenly bodies, and therefore far above them.   There is also an allusion to Zabaism in Job xxxi, 26–28: "If I beheld the sun when it shined, or the moon walking in brightness; and my heart hath been secretly enticed, or my mouth hath kissed my hand; this also were an iniquity to be punished by the judge: for I should have denied the God that is above."   Kissing the hand was a mark of respect to superiors, and was also an ancient idolatrous rite.   1 Kings xix, 18, may also refer to this custom, as well as to that of actually kissing the idol.   An old writer, speaking of these two texts, says: "These places refer to the Gentiles' mode of adoring the sun by lifting the right hand to their mouth; of which there is frequent mention among Pagan writers."—GALE'S *Court of the Gentiles*, vol. I, book ii, chap. 8.—Mollerus quaintly suggests that as "men could not attain to kiss the sun and moon with their mouth, they extended their hand to those celestial bodies, and thence moving it back to their mouth, they kissed it in token of homage and worship."

According to Maimonides the Zabians made images of the sun in gold and of the moon in silver.   They built chapels and placed these images in them, believing that the power of the stars flowed into them.   They offered to the sun at certain times "seven bats, seven mice, and seven reptiles, together with certain other matters."

Zabaism is likewise referred to in Deut. xvii, 3; 2 Kings xvii, 16; xxi, 3; xxiii, 5; Jer. viii, 2.

190.—PORTAL INSCRIPTIONS.

VI, 9.   Thou shalt write them upon the posts of thy house, and on thy gates.

It was a common custom among the ancient Egyptians to write inscriptions on the doors of their houses.   Besides the names of the dwellers, lucky sentences were written.   The Mohammedans write passages from the Koran on their doors.   "O God!" is written on some; "the Excellent Creator is the Everlasting," is also seen.   The modern Jews have in some places an arrangement equivalent to this.   The passages in Deut. vi, 4–9, and xi, 13–21, are written on one side of a piece of parchment which is prepared especially for the purpose, while on the other side is written שַׁדַּי, *the Almighty*.   The parchment is then rolled up, so that the sacred name shall be on the outside, and is put into a reed or metallic cylinder, which has in it a hole just large enough to show the שַׁדַּי upon the parchment.   This hole is covered by a piece of glass.   Such a cylinder, with its parchment roll, is known by the name of *Mezeuza*, and is fastened to the right-hand door-post of every door in the house, so that it is in full sight, and may be touched or kissed as the dwellers in the house go in and out.   The Jews from a very early period believed that the *Mezeuza* guarded the house against the entrance of diseases and evil spirits.

191.—WATERING WITH THE FOOT.

XI, 10. Not as the land of Egypt, from whence ye came out, where thou sowedst thy seed, and wateredst it with thy foot.

Two interpretations are given of this passage, either of which can find illustration in Oriental customs, and in the fact that from the absence of rain in Egypt, and the great breadth of plain country unbroken by hills, it has ever been necessary to water the land by artificial means. 1. One ancient mode of raising water from the Nile, or from the canals which were cut through Egypt, was by means of a wheel which was worked by the feet. Dr. Robinson saw in Palestine several of these wheels which were used to draw water from wells. In describing one he says: "On the platform was fixed a small reel for the rope, which a man, seated on a level with the axis, wound up, by pulling the upper part of the reel toward him with his hands, while he at the same time pushed the lower part from him with the feet."— *Bibl. Res. in Palestine*, vol. ii, p. 22. 2. For crops which required to be frequently watered the fields were divided into square beds, surrounded by raised borders of earth, to keep in the water, which was introduced by channels or poured in from buckets. The water could easily be turned from one square to another by making an opening in the border, the soft soil readily yielding to the pressure of the foot. This mode is also practiced in India.

Allusion to one or the other of these customs is made in 2 Kings xix, 24.

192.—IDOLATROUS USE OF BLOOD.

XII, 23, 24. Only be sure that thou eat not the blood: for the blood is the life; and thou mayest not eat the life with the flesh. Thou shalt not eat it; thou shalt pour it upon the earth as water. See also Gen. ix, 4; Lev. vii, 26, 27; xvii, 10-14.

The discussion which has risen on the various reasons for this prohibition of blood for food, so far as it concerns the physical consequences of such diet, or the typical character of sacrificial blood, or the relation of the blood to the life, can have no place here. There are, however, reasons for the law which may have been drawn from ancient idolatrous and cruel customs to which we may with propriety refer. R. Moses Bar Nachman, an old Jewish writer, says that the Zabians "gathered together blood for the devils, their idol gods, and then came themselves and ate of that blood with them as being the devil's guests, and invited to eat at the table of devils, and so were joined in federal society with them; and by this kind of communion with devils they were able to prophesy and foretell things to come."—TOWN-LEY'S *Maimonides*, p. 76.

The sacred books of the Hindoos exhibit traces of the same infernal mode of worship. They give directions concerning various oblations of blood, the different animals from which it may be drawn, and the different vessels in which it may be offered, positively forbidding, however, to pour it on the ground. If a similar prohibition existed among the Zabians, verse 24 may be a reference to it, commanding the Hebrews to do what the Zabians were forbidden. Hindoo devotees drink the reeking blood from newly killed buffaloes and fowls.

"Drink offerings of blood" are spoken of in Psa. xvi, 4; and in Zech. ix, 7, there is evident allusion to the idolatrous use of blood.

In addition to this, the old Jewish rabbins say that this prohibition against blood was made on account of an ancient custom of eating raw flesh, especially the flesh of living animals cut or torn from them, and devoured while reeking with the warm blood. Bruce tells of a similar custom among the modern Abyssinians, and his statement, though at first received with ridicule, has been confirmed by other travelers. The hungry Israelites, after defeating the Philistines between Michmash and Aijalon, seem from the narrative in 1 Sam. xiv, 32–34, to have indulged in a similar horrid practice.

193.—ABIB.

XVI, 1. The month of Abib.

Abib means *a green ear*. This denotes the condition of the barley in Palestine and Egypt during this month. It was the first month of the Jewish ecclesiastical year, and was in later times called Nisan. See Neh. ii, 1; Esther iii, 7. It corresponded.nearly to our month of April.

194.—IDOL GROVES.

XVI, 21. Thou shalt not plant thee a grove of any trees near unto the altar of the Lord thy God, which thou shalt make thee.

Idol temples and altars were surrounded by thick groves and trees, which became the resort of the abandoned of both sexes, and in which, under plea of idolatrous worship, excesses of the vilest kind were perpetrated. For this reason God forbade the planting of trees near his altars, lest his people should become, or seem to be, like the heathen. See also Isa. lvii, 5; lxv, 3; lxvi, 17; Jer. ii, 20; iii, 6; Ezek. vi, 13; xx, 28; Hos. iv, 13. Some suppose the word "grove" here to mean a high wooden pillar, planted in the ground. See note on Judges iii, 7.

195.—VARIOUS KINDS OF DIVINATION.

XVIII, 10, 11. . . . That useth divination, or an observer of times, or an enchanter, or a witch, or a charmer, or a consulter with familiar spirits, or a wizard, or a necromancer.

The word divination (*kosem kesamim*, "divining divinations") may here be taken as a generic term, of which the seven terms following represent the species. This might be more clearly shown by a slight change in the punctuation, and an omission of the word *or*, which was supplied by the translators; *e. g.*, "that useth divination: an observer of times, or an enchanter," etc.

By divination, as the term is used in the text, we understand an attempt to penetrate the mysteries of the future by using magical arts, or superstitious incantations, or by the arbitrary interpretation of natural signs. Its practice was very prevalent in the time of Moses among all idolatrous nations, as indeed it is to this day. We have occasional illustrations of it in Christian lands. It became necessary, therefore, to warn the Hebrews against the fascinating influence of this ungodly habit. God provided certain lawful means by which his will was revealed, such as by urim and thummim, by dreams, by prophecies, and by several other modes, so that there was no excuse for resorting to the practices of the heathen. These are spoken of under the following heads.

1. An observer of times, "*meonen:*" one that distinguishes lucky from unlucky days, recommending certain days for the commencement of enterprises, and forbidding other days; deciding also on the good or bad luck of certain months, and even of years. This sort of diviners often made their predictions by noticing the clouds. Some would refer this to divination by means of words, of which we have illustration in more modern times in bibliomancy, that is, opening a book at random and taking, for the will of God, the first words seen. Still others suppose that *meonen* has reference to fascination by means of "the evil eye."

2. An enchanter, "*menachesh.*" This may refer to divination by the cup, as already explained in the note on Gen. xliv, 5, in which passage the word *nachesh* is used. The Septuagint translators supposed it to mean divination by watching the flight of birds; while some later interpreters refer it to the divination by means of serpents, which were charmed by music.

3. A witch, "*mekashsheph.*" This word is used in the plural in Exod. vii, 11, to denote the "magicians" of Pharaoh, who were well versed in the arts of wonder-working. In Exod. xxii, 18 the word is used in the feminine, and is translated witch, as in the text. Maimonides informs us that the greater number of works of divination were practiced by women.

4. A charmer, "*chober:*" (from the root *chabar*, to bind.) This was one who used "a species of magic which was practiced by binding magic knots."— *Gesenius.* Some think it may have been one who practiced a kind of divination which drew or bound together noxious creatures for purposes of sorcery; others, that it was one who used a magic ring for divination.

5. A consulter with familar spirits, "*shoel ob.*" This may have reference to a species of divination in which ventriloquism was used. The primary meaning of the word *ob* is a leathern bottle, which has led some authorities to think that this divination was one which called up departed spirits, and

that the use of the word *ob* " probably arose from regarding the conjuroɪ, while possessed by the demon, as a *bottle*, that is, vessel, case, in which the demon was contained."—*Gesenius*.   Or, the word may have been used because these necromancers inflated themselves in the act of divination, like a skin bottle stretched to its utmost capacity, (see Job xxxii, 19 ;) as if they were filled with inspiration from supernatural powers.   See Wordsworth on Lev. xix, 31.   The woman of Endor who was consulted by Saul when the Philistines were about to attack him belonged to this class.   Saul asked her to divine to him by the *ob:* (" the familiar spirit.")   1 Sam. xxviii, 7, 8.

6. A wizard, "*yiddeoni:*" (the knowing one.)   This may have indicated any one who was unusually expert in the various magical tricks of divination.

7. A necromancer, "*doresh el hammethim:*" (one who seeks unto the dead.)   The necromancers had various modes of divination by the dead.   They sometimes made use of a bone or a vein of a dead body; and sometimes poured warm blood into a corpse, as if to renew life.   They pretended to raise ghosts by various incantations and other magical ceremonies.

196.—AXES.

XIX, 5.   His hand fetcheth a stroke with the axe to cut down the tree, and the head slippeth from the helve.

There were doubtless different forms of axe in use among the Hebrews, as different words are used to signify the instrument.   *Garzen*, the word used here and in Deut. xx, 19; 1 Kings vi, 7; and Isa. x, 15, was probably an axe which was used for felling trees and for hewing large timber.   Representations of ancient Assyrian and Egyptian axes have come down to us.   Some of these axes are fastened to the handle by means of thongs.   There is one kind, however, which is not so fastened, but which has an opening in it into which the helve is inserted, as with us.   It bears a close resemblance to a modern axe, and from the reference in the text to the head slipping off seems to have been the *garzen* here spoken of.   Egyptian axes were made of bronze, and perhaps of iron also.   That some, at

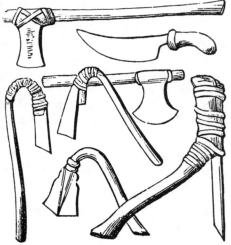

87.—Ancient Axes.

least, of the axes of the Hebrews were made of iron is evident from 2 Kings vi, 5, 6.

197.—LANDMARKS.

XIX, 14. **Thou shalt not remove thy neighbor's landmark, which they of old time have set in thine inheritance.**

In the East the fields of different owners are not marked by fences, as with us, but the boundaries are indicated by heaps of small stones, or by a ridge, or by posts, or by single stones set upright about a rod apart. It is easy for a dishonest man to remove these landmarks, little by little each year, and thus gradually encroach upon his neighbor. This practice is alluded to in Job xxiv, 2, and is forbidden in Prov. xxii, 28 and xxiii, 10, as in our text. A curse was pronounced upon those who removed landmarks. Deut. xxvii, 17. A figurative allusion is made to this crime in Hosea v, 10.

Not only the Jews, but other ancient nations, especially the Romans, had stringent laws against the removal of landmarks. In the British Museum are two or three very curious Babylonian monuments which are supposed to have been landmarks, and to be covered with curses on those who remove them. One of them is of marble, in shape of a massive fish. On the head is the figure of a serpent, and various other characters; and on the sides, in arrow-headed letters, are the curses.

198.—DEDICATION OF HOUSES.

XX, 5. **What man is there that hath built a new house and hath not dedicated it.**

We are not informed as to the ceremonies accompanying the dedication of a dwelling; they were probably a combination of social and devotional. The title of the thirtieth Psalm is, "A Psalm or Song at the Dedication of the House of David." The completion of the wall of Jerusalem in the time of Nehemiah was celebrated by a dedication, at which there was great rejoicing. Neh. xii, 27. The rabbins say that not only was a newly built house to be dedicated, but a house lately obtained, whether by inheritance, purchase, or gift. Houses that were not suitable for habitation, and that could not be made so, were not dedicated; but houses such as granaries and barns, that could in case of necessity be converted into dwellings, were dedicated.

The custom of dedicating dwelling-houses was common among the ancient Egyptians, and is practiced to this day among the Hindoos.

199.—THE GATE A PLACE OF JUSTICE.

XXI, 19. **Then shall his father and his mother lay hold on him, and bring him out unto the elders of his city, and unto the gate of his place.**

As the vicinity of the gate was a place of popular resort, (see note on Gen. xix, 1,) it became a convenient place for the administration of justice. Here courts were held, and disputes were settled. See Deut. xvi, 18;

xxv, 7; Josh. xx, 4; Ruth iv, 1; Job v, 4; xxxi, 21; Psa. cxxvii, 5; Prov. xxii, 22; xxxi, 23; Jer. xxxviii, 7; Lam. v, 14; Amos v, 12; Zech. viii, 16. From the fact that princes and judges thus sat at the gate in the discharge of their official duties, the word gate became a synonym for power or authority. This is illustrated in Matt. xvi, 18, where the expression "gates of hell" means *powers* of hell. We find it also in the title given to the government of the Turkish Empire, "the Ottoman Porte" or "the Sublime Porte;" (*porta*, a gate.) "The Gate of Judgment" is a term still common among the Arabians to express a court of justice, and was introduced into Spain by the Saracens.

Modern Oriental travelers speak of the existence at this day of the custom mentioned in the text.

200.—DISTINCTION IN DRESS.

XXII, 5. The woman shall not wear that which pertaineth unto a man, neither shall a man put on a woman's garment: for all that do so are abomination unto the Lord thy God.

The distinction between the dress of the sexes being less than with us, there was the greater need of this regulation. There is reason to believe that the law was made not merely to preserve decency, but because the heathen were in the habit of pursuing a different course as a part of their idolatrous worship. Maimonides says: "In the books of the idolaters it is commanded that when a man presents himself before the Star of Venus, he shall wear the colored dress of a woman; and when a woman adores the Star of Mars, she shall appear in armor." Pagan idols were frequently represented with the features of one sex and the dress of the other, and their worshipers endeavored to be like them. It is not at all unlikely that this custom was as old as the time of Moses, and was a partial reason for the enacting of this law.

201.—BATTLEMENTS.

XXII, 8. When thou buildest a new house, then thou shalt make a battlement for thy roof, that thou bring not blood upon thine house, if any man fall from thence.

The roofs of Eastern houses are flat, having a slight declivity from the center. As they are used for a variety of purposes by day, and often for sleeping at night, (1 Sam. ix, 26,) it becomes necessary to guard them by means of a wall. Almost every Eastern house has a parapet, the Moslems making theirs very high, to screen their women from observation.

The houses of Christians are sometimes built without parapets, and serious accidents occur. Dr. Shaw describes the battlements on the roofs of the houses in Barbary as very low on the side next the street, and also when they make partitions from the roofs of neighbors. He says of this outside wall that it is "frequently so low that one may easily climb over it."—*Travels*, p. 210. He also states that the inside parapet, next to the court of the house, is always breast high. There is sometimes here only a balustrade or lattice-work. In Syria, however, the higher battlement is next to the street, and the lower one next to the court.

202.—MINGLED SEED.

XXII, 9. Thou shalt not sow thy vineyard with divers seeds: lest the fruit of thy seed which thou hast sown, and the fruit of thy vineyard, be defiled.

The Zabians were accustomed to sow barley and dried grapes together, believing that without this union there would not be a good vintage; but that with it the gods would be propitious to them. Bishop Patrick observes, that if the Israelites had done this the fruits of the harvest would have been impure, because associated with idolatry. The first-fruits would not have been accepted by God, and hence the whole crop would have been useless.

203.—MIXED CLOTH.

XXII, 11. Thou shalt not wear a garment of divers sorts, as of woolen and linen together.

This was in opposition to the Zabian priests, who wore robes of woolen and linen, perhaps hoping thereby to have the benefit of some lucky conjunction of planets, which would bring a blessing on their sheep and their flax. It is said that the pious Jews would not sew a garment of woolen with a linen thread, and that if one saw an Israelite wearing a garment of mixed cloth it was lawful for him to fall upon him and tear the forbidden garment to pieces.

204.—DEBTORS PROTECTED.

XXIV, 10, 11. When thou dost lend thy brother any thing, thou shalt not go into his house to fetch his pledge. Thou shalt stand abroad, and the man to whom thou dost lend shall bring out the pledge abroad unto thee.

This was a humane law designed to protect the poor man from the intrusion of the money lender. "The strict laws regulating Oriental intercourse sufficiently guard the harems of all but the very poor. When the money lender goes to any respectable house he never rudely enters, but stands 'abroad' and calls, and the owner comes forth to meet him."—THOMSON, *The Land and the Book*, vol. i, p. 500. Another advantage of this law was, that it prevented the usurer from selecting his pledge, giving the choice to the poor debtor. He could "bring out" what he pleased, provided its value was sufficient to meet the claim of the creditor. The latter was compelled to accept it, whether pleased with it or not.

205.—THE OUTER GARMENT.

XXIV, 12, 18. If the man be poor, thou shalt not sleep with his pledge: in any case thou shalt deliver him the pledge again when the sun goeth down, that he may sleep in his own raiment.

From this it would seem that the most common article of pledge was a part of the clothing. The words *salmah* and *simlah*, (as it is in the parallel passage, Exod. xxii, 26,) were used to denote clothing in general, but especially the large outer garment, or wrapper, which was skillfully wound around the person, and was as useful at night for a bed covering as during the day for clothing. This is the "raiment" of the text. The Orientals do not change their clothes on retiring to rest, and hence this large outer garment becomes very serviceable. To keep such a garment from a poor man over night was indeed an act of inhumanity which is justly condemned by the law. The consequences of such cruelty are touchingly described by Job where he speaks of the works of wicked men: "They cause

38.—OUTER GARMENT.

the naked to lodge without clothing, that they have no covering in the cold. They are wet with the showers of the mountains, and embrace the rock for want of a shelter." Job xxiv, 7, 8.

The *abba* of the modern Bedawí is supposed to bear a close resemblance to the ancient garment spoken of. It is made of wool and hair, of various degrees of fineness; is sometimes entirely black, and sometimes entirely white; and is marked with two broad stripes. It is altogether shapeless, being like a square sack, with an opening in front, and with slits at the sides to let out the arms. Very similar to this is the *hyke*, which is worn by the Moors of Northern Africa, and used by them for a covering at night and for a cloak by day. Dr. Shaw speaks of several varieties of the *hyke*, both as to size and quality. It is a loose but troublesome garment, being frequently disconcerted and falling to the ground; so that the person who wears it is every moment obliged to tuck it up and fold it anew about his body."— *Travels*, p. 224. It is often used to wrap up burdens that are to be carried, and in this way the Israelites carried their kneading troughs wrapped up in the folds of their outer garments, and borne on their shoulders. Exod. xii, 34.

The outer garment is in the New Testament represented by the word ἱμάτιον, which in the Septuagint is the word used in this text and in Exod. xxii, 26. It is called a *cloak* in Matt. v, 40; *raiment* in Matt. xxvii, 31; *vesture* in Rev. xix, 13; *garment* in Matt. xiv, 36. In most of the passages in the New Testament where the word "garment" is used this is the article meant.

This outer garment was easily and frequently laid aside. See Matt. xxi, 7, 8; xxiv, 18; John xiii, 4, 12; Acts vii, 58; xxii, 20, 23.

206.—OLIVE GATHERING.

XXIV, 20. When thou beatest thine olive tree, thou shalt not go over the boughs again: it shall be for the stranger, for the fatherless, and for the widow.

This refers to one of the modes of gathering olives still practiced in the East, that is, by beating the branches with sticks. It was mercifully ordered that the Israelites should give the trees but one beating, leaving for the poor gleaners all the fruit that did not by this means drop off.

Olives are gathered also by shaking the trees. This is referred to in Isa. xvii, 6, and xxiv, 13. In these passages the mode of gleaning seems to be referred to.

207.—THRESHING BY OXEN.

XXV, 4. Thou shalt not muzzle the ox when he treadeth out the corn.

Threshing was sometimes done by instruments, (see note on Isa. xxviii, 27, 28,) and sometimes by having the grain trampled under foot

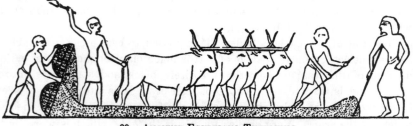

89.—ANCIENT EGYPTIANS THRESHING.

by horses or oxen. This is still a common mode in the East. The cattle are driven over the grain, treading heavily as they go, and in this rude, wasteful manner the threshing is accomplished. In general, the patient beasts are allowed to eat of the grain they tread out, though sometimes they are muzzled by parsimonious masters. See also Hosea x, 11. Paul from this law enforces the duty of ministerial support. 1 Cor. ix, 9.

208.—BAREFOOT.

XXV, 10. His name shall be called in Israel, The house of him that hath his shoe loosed.

To go barefoot was a sign of distress and humiliation. Thus David went up Mount Olivet when he left Jerusalem at the time of Absalom's rebellion. 2 Sam. xv, 30. The humiliation of the Egyptians was represented by the prediction of their walking barefoot. Isa. xx, 2-4. When Ezekiel was directed to cease his mourning he was told to put on his shoes. Ezek. xxiv, 17. Michælis says, "Barefooted was a term of reproach, and probably signified a man who had sold everything, a spendthrift and a bankrupt."—*Com. Laws Moses,* vol. i, p. 435. In this way the man who refused to marry his brother's childless widow was considered a worthless fellow.

209.—WEIGHTS.

XXV, 13. Thou shalt not have in thy bag divers weights, a great and a small.

1. The marginal reading for "divers weights" is "a stone and a stone," which is a literal rendering of the Hebrew. See also Prov. xi, 1; xvi, 11. Weights were no doubt originally made of different-sized stones, from which fact *eben,* a stone, was used to signify a weight, even after other materials were used for weights. We have the word "stone" in our own language to denote a weight of a certain size, and the Germans use the corresponding word *stein* for a similar purpose.

2. Oriental peddlers still have, as in ancient times, two sets of weights, one for buying and the other for selling. Allusion is made to this species of dishonesty in Prov. xx, 10, and in Micah vi, 11.

210.—FUNERAL FEASTS.

XXVI, 14. I have not eaten thereof in my mourning, neither have I taken away aught thereof for any unclean use, nor given aught thereof for the dead.

There is no evidence of any allusion here to idolatrous customs. The reference is probably to the feasts which were given on funeral occasions to the friends assembled. See Hosea ix, 4. The custom still exists in Palestine. The phrase "given aught thereof for the dead" may have reference to the practice of sending provisions into a house of mourning; to which custom allusion is supposed to be made in 2 Sam. iii, 35, where David, on occasion of Abner's death, refused to eat the food which was set before him. The expression "Eat not the bread of men," in Ezek. xxiv, 17, is thought to refer to the same custom. See also Jer. xvi, 7, 8. Dr. Thomson, however, furnishes a different explanation to this giving for the dead. He says: "On certain days after the funeral large quantities of corn and other food are cooked in a particular manner, and sent to all the friends, however numerous, *in the name of the dead.* I have had many such presents, but my dislike of the practice, or something else, renders these dishes peculiarly disgusting to me."—*The Land and the Book*, vol. i, p. 150.

211.—PLASTERED MONUMENTS.

XXVII, 2, 3. **Thou shalt set thee up great stones, and plaster them with plaster: and thou shalt write upon them all the words of this law.**

Michælis supposed that the letters were first cut in the stone and then covered entirely with plaster, so that in the coming ages, when the cement should crumble off, the law might be found in all its integrity. In this he has been followed by some commentators. The probability, however, is, that the lime was first spread over the stones, and the words of the law then cut into the plaster or painted on it. Such stones thus prepared, two thousand years ago or longer, are still in existence in Palestine. The Egyptians are said to have spread a kind of stucco over sandstone, and even over granite, before the paintings were made. Prokesch found in the tombs in the pyramids of Dashoor a stone on which red mortar had first been laid, and then the hieroglyphics and a figure of Apis impressed on the coating.

212.—IDOLATROUS SPOTS.

XXXII, 5. **They have corrupted themselves, their spot is not the spot of his children.**

The spot or blot here spoken of is said to be something that does not belong to the children of God. "Their spot is not of his children." Allusion is supposed to be made here to the marks which idolaters put upon their persons, particularly on their foreheads, in honor of their deities. It is a very ancient practice, and probably existed before Moses' time. Forbes, in his *Oriental Memoirs*, says that in India different idolatrous sects have different marks. These are specially common among the two principal sects, the worshipers of Siva and the worshipers of Vishnoo. The marks are horizontal and perpendicular lines; crescents or circles; or representations of leaves, eyes, and other objects. They are impressed on the forehead by the officiating Brahmin with a composition of sandal-wood dust and oil, or the ashes of cow-dung and turmeric. The colors are red, black, white, and yellow. In·many cases these marks are renewed daily.

Zophar may have referred to a similar custom when he spoke to Job about lifting up his face without spot. Job xi, 15. Eliphaz also spoke of lifting up the face to God. Job xxii, 26. Job himself subsequently denied that any blot was on his hands. Job xxxi, 7. In the Revelation of St. John there are several references to idolatrous marks on the forehead and hands. See Rev. xiii, 16; xiv, 9; xix, 20; xx, 4.

213.—TREADING OLIVES.

XXXIII, 24. Let him be acceptable to his brethren, and let him dip his foot in oil.

This refers to the primitive method of treading the olives in order to express the oil. It is not now practiced, and could only be done when the olives were very soft. There is a similar allusion in Micah vi, 15. See also the note on Job xxix, 6.

214.—THE EVERLASTING ARMS.

XXXIII, 27. The eternal God is thy refuge, and underneath are the everlasting arms.

By this bold image Moses represents the protecting power of God; thus reversing the idea of the Egyptians, who had pictures of the god Horus with inverted head and outstretched arms *over* the earth. This was one mode by which they represented the vault of heaven, as is shown in the engraving.

40.—EGYPTIAN GOD HORUS.

The beetle, or scarabæus, is the hieroglyphic for the name of Horus.

8

JOSHUA.

215.—ROOFS USED FOR STORAGE.

II, 6. She had brought them up to the roof of the house, and hid them with the stalks of flax, which she had laid in order upon the roof.

The flat roofs of Eastern houses, being exposed to sun and air, are well adapted for the reception of grain or fruit, which may be placed there to ripen or to be dried. The flax-stalks, piled upon the roof to dry in the sunshine, would afford a very good hiding-place for the spies.

216.—KNIVES.

V, 2. At that time the Lord said unto Joshua, Make thee sharp knives.

Knives were made of flint, bone, copper, iron, or steel. Specimens of ancient Egyptian and Assyrian knives are to be found in museums, and they probably have a general resemblance to those used by the Hebrews. They are of various shapes, according to the purpose for which they were made. Knives were not much used at meals. Even to this day the Orientals prefer dividing their meat with the fingers.

217.—STONE HEAPS.

VII, 26. And they raised over him a great heap of stones.

It was customary to heap up stones as rude monuments of important events. See Gen. xxxi, 46 ; Josh. iv, 3, 6. In the case of noted criminals this was done, not merely to mark the spot of their burial, but as a monument of the popular abhorrence of their crimes. This case of Achan is an illustration. Another instance may be found in the case of Absalom. 2 Sam. xviii, 17. When Joshua captured and hanged the king of Ai, he commanded a heap of stones to be raised over his grave. Travelers tell us that it is still customary in Palestine to cast stones upon the graves of criminals, the passers-by adding to the heap for a long time afterward. In the valley of Jehoshaphat is a monument popularly known by the name of "Absalom's Tomb," and supposed to mark the site of the "pillar" which Absalom set up for himself "in the king's dale." 2 Sam. xviii, 18. Mohammedans and Jews have for very many years been in the habit of casting stones at it as they pass, in token of their detestation of the crime of the rebellious son.

218.—RENT BOTTLES.

IX, 4. Wine bottles, old, and rent, and bound up.

Bottles made of skins when they get old are liable to be torn. The rents are repaired by sewing the broken edges together, by letting in a piece of leather, by putting in a round piece of wood, or by gathering up the rent place like a purse.

For a description of skin bottles, see note on Matt. ix, 17.

219.—DEGRADING SERVICE.

IX, 21. **Let them be hewers of wood and drawers of water.**

This was a degradation that must have been greatly felt by the Gibeonites, since it compelled them to relinquish the duties of soldiers, and take upon themselves menial services usually performed by women.

220.—ENEMIES TRODDEN ON.

X, 24. **Come near, put your feet upon the necks of these kings. And they came near, and put their feet upon the necks of them.**

This is an ancient Oriental mode of treating captured kings, not as an act of cruelty, but as a symbolical representation of complete subjugation. Compare notes on Gen. xlix, 8, and 1 Cor. xv, 25.

Roberts says of the East Indians: "When people are disputing, should one be a little pressed, and the other begins to triumph, the former will say, 'I will tread upon thy neck, and after that beat thee.' A low-caste man insulting one who is high, is sure to hear some one say to the offended individual, 'Put your feet on his neck.'"—*Oriental Illustrations,* p. 135.

41.—ASSYRIAN KING PLACING THE FOOT ON THE NECK OF AN ENEMY.

JUDGES.

221.—MUTILATION OF CAPTIVES.

I, 6. **They pursued after him, and caught him, and cut off his thumbs and his great toes.**

This was an ancient method of treating captured enemies. It rendered them permanently incapable of performing the duties of a soldier. According to his own confession, (verse 7,) Adoni-bezek had practiced the same cruelties on many of the royal captives whom he had taken in battle. The

Assyrian kings were addicted to similar cruelties. One of the ancient monuments bears an inscription which was put upon it by order of Asshur-izir-
pal, who began his reign B. C. 883. In this he says, speaking of a captured
city, "Their men, young and old, I took prisoners. Of some I cut off the
feet and hands; of others I cut off the noses, ears, and lips; of the young
men's ears I made a heap; of the old men's heads I built a minaret."—
RAWLINSON'S *Five Great Monarchies*, vol. ii, p. 85, *note.*

222.—BAALIM—ASHEROTH.

III, 7. **The children of Israel did evil in the sight of the Lord,
and forgat the Lord their God, and served Baalim and the
groves.**

1. Baalim is the plural of Baal. Gesenius defines it "images of Baal."
Against this, however, it has been said that the verbs which are associated
in the Bible with the word Baalim are not verbs which are used in connection with images, such as "set up," "cast down," "adorn," or "break
in pieces;" but rather verbs which are used in connection with heathen deities, *e. g.*, "to serve," "worship," "seek to," "go after," "put away." See
Fairbairn's Imp. Bib. Dict., vol. i, pp. 137, 167. Some of these latter terms,
however, can be used as properly in reference to images as to deities.

Some writers explain the word as indicating or including the various
modifications of Baal, such as Baal-Peor, Baal-Berith, Baal-Zebub. This
might find illustration in Hosea ii, 17 : "For I will take away the names
of Baalim out of her mouth, and they shall no more be remembered by their
name."

Others suppose Baalim to be what the old grammarians called the *pluralis
excellentiæ;* a form of speech designed to describe the god in the wide extent
of his influence and the various modes of his manifestation. The word is
of frequent occurrence in the Old Testament. See Judges ii, 11; viii, 33 ;
x, 10; 1 Sam. vii, 4; xii, 10; 2 Chron. xxiv, 7 ; Jer. ii, 23 ; ix, 14; etc.

2. The word *asheroth*, here rendered "groves," is often found either in
singular or plural form. In most places where it is used, the word "groves"
is evidently inappropriate, though in this our English translation is like the
Septuagint and the Vulgate. Selden, the eminent lawyer and antiquarian,
in his work *De Diis Syris Syntagmata Duo*, published in 1617, was the first
to suggest that the word must be understood to mean, at least in some
places, not groves, but images of Ashtoreth, the companion deity to Baal.
This is the view now entertained by some of the best critics. It is certainly more correct to speak of making *images* than to say that *groves*
were made. If the words "image of Ashtoreth" or "images of Ashtoreth" are substituted for the word "grove" or "groves" in the following
passages the sense will be much clearer: 1 Kings xvi, 33; 2 Kings

xvii, 16; xxi, 3; 2 Chron. xxxiii, 3. So in 2 Kings xvii, 10, and in 2 Chron. xxxiii, 19, it is said that *asheroth* were set up; that is, these wooden figures of Ashtoreth, in addition to the graven images also mentioned. In the days of Josiah there was an *asherah* in God's house. We are told in 2 Kings xxiii, 6, what the good king did with it; "And he brought out the grove from the house of the Lord, without Jerusalem, unto the brook Kidron, and burned it at the brook Kidron, and stamped it small to powder, and cast the powder thereof upon the graves of the children of the people." All this is much more appropriately said of an image than of a grove. This *asherah* likewise had over it a canopy or tent. woven by the women. 2 Kings xxiii, 7. It was doubtless the same image which Manasseh had put into the house of the Lord. 2 Kings xxi, 7. From Judges vi, 25–30, and from other passages which speak of the *asheroth* as cut or burnt, it appears that they were made of wood. Some suppose that the expression "stamped it small to powder," in the text above quoted, indicates that the *asherah* in that instance was made of metal, since otherwise there would have been no need of stamping it after burning; but the king may have pulverized the burnt wood in order more deeply to express his detestation of the idolatry which had occasioned its erection.

The *asherah* of the Phenicians is thought by some writers to be connected with the "sacred tree" of the Assyrians, an object which appears very frequently on the Assyrian monuments. If this conjecture be based on fact we may find in the representations of the sacred tree which have come down to us a picture of the *asherah* which the idolatrous Jews worshiped.

Another opinion, which has found favor in some quarters, is, that *Asherah* was the name of a goddess worshiped by the Canaanites, either Ashtoreth or some other. The word "served" in the text, and in 2 Chron. xxiv, 18, seems at first to sanction this view; but as the passages previously quoted evidently speak of wooden images, it is probable that in these two texts the symbol is put, by metonymy, for the divinity.

A learned English writer, some years ago, advanced a very singular idea in reference to the *asherah*. He suggested that it was "an armillary and

42.—SYMBOLIC TREE.

astronomical machine or instrument, erected long, very long ago—quite in the primitive ages;" that it was used for purposes of divination in connection with idolatrous worship; that it was probably about the height of a man, and had small balls branching off curvedly from the sustaining rod or axis; and that this axis was made of iron and brass, the bottom being set in a socket of stone, in which it turned as a pivot, requiring oil for lubrication. In proof of this last assertion he refers to the blessing which Moses pronounced on Asher. Deut. xxxiii, 24. 25. He assumes that the word Asher in that text has reference to the *asherah;* that the shoes of iron and brass refer to the axis of the armillary machine, the foot of which is dipped in oil, that it may revolve more easily! The reasoning of his lengthy dissertation is more curious than conclusive. See *Sabæan Researches,* by JOHN LANDSEER, Essay VIII.

223.—LOCKS.

III, 23. Then Ehud went forth through the porch, and shut the doors of the parlor upon him, and locked them.

The early Oriental lock consisted merely of a wooden slide drawn into its place by a string, and fastened there by teeth or catches. The lock commonly used in Egypt and Palestine is a long hollow piece of wood fixed in the door and sliding back and forth. A hole is made for it in the door post, and when it is pushed into this hole small bolts of iron wire fall into holes which are made for them in the top of the lock. The lock is placed on the inside of the door, and a hole is made in the door near the lock, through which the hand can be passed, and the key inserted. This will explain Solomon's Song v, 4, "My beloved put in his hand by the hole of the door." Some of these locks are very large and heavy.

224.—KEYS.

III, 25. Behold, he opened not the doors of the parlor: therefore they took a key and opened them.

The key was usually of wood, though some have been found in Egypt of

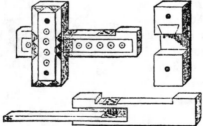

iron and bronze. The ordinary wooden key is from six inches to two feet in length, often having a handle of brass or silver, ornamented with filagree work. At the end there are wire pins, which are designed to loosen the fastenings of the lock. The key was anciently borne on the shoulder. See note on Isaiah xxii, 22.

43.—EGYPTIAN WOODEN LOCK AND KEY.

225.—OX-GOADS.

III, 31. Shamgar the son of Anath, which slew of the Philistines six hundred men with an ox-goad.

This must have been a formidable weapon if, as is doubtless the case, the goad of that day was similar to the one now used in Palestine. It is a strong pole about eight feet long and two inches in diameter. At one end is a sharp point for pricking the oxen when their movements become intolerably slow, and at the other end is a broad chisel-like blade, which is used to clear the plowshare of the roots and thorns which impede it or of the stiff clay which adheres to it. The pointed end of this instrument is alluded to in Acts ix, 5; xxvi, 14.

226.—WHITE ASSES.

V, 10. **Speak, ye that ride on white asses, ye that sit in judgment, and walk by the way.**

There is no reason to interpret, as some writers do, the expression "white asses," to mean asses covered with white caparisons. The intention is to indicate the wealth and luxury of the riders; and as asses wholly white, or even nearly so, are rare and costly, the men who own them must be classed among the rich and influential. Morier says that in Persia the Mollahs, or men of the law, consider it a dignity suited to their character to ride on white asses.

227.—AMBUSH NEAR WATER.

V, 11. **They that are delivered from the noise of archers in the places of drawing water, there shall they rehearse the righteous acts of the Lord.**

This refers to the practice of lying in ambush near wells and springs for the purpose of seizing flocks and herds when brought thither for water. Moses defended his future wife and her sisters against those who attacked them at the well. Exod. ii, 17. Dr. Shaw saw, near the coast of the western province of Algiers, a basin of Roman workmanship, which received the water of a beautiful rill, and which was called by the suggestive title of *Shrub we krub*, that is, *Drink and away*. The name was given on account of robbers, who lurked for booty near the drinkng-place.

228.—WINDOWS.

V, 28. **The mother of Sisera looked out at a window, and cried through the lattice.**

The walls of Oriental houses present but few windows to the street, and these are high up from the ground. They very seldom have glass in them, but are made of lattice-work, which is arranged for coolness, and also to give the inmates an opportunity of seeing without being seen. These windows are sometimes thrown out from the wall like our bay-windows, and thus afford a good opportunity of seeing what is going on in the street below. They are not hung like our ordinary sashes, but open and shut like doors. The window spoken of in the text was evidently on the street side of the house. So also was the window from which Michal saw David, (2 Sam.

vi, 16;) the window from which Joash shot the arrows, (2 Kings xiii, 17;) the window spoken of in Prov. vii, 6, and in Sol. Song ii, 9; and probably the windows which Daniel opened when he prayed. Dan. vi, 10. The window from which Jezebel was hurled may have opened into the street or into the court, (2 Kings ix, 30–33;) so may also the window from which Euty-chus fell. Acts xx, 9.

229.—EMBROIDERED GARMENTS.

V, 30. To Sisera a prey of divers colors, a prey of divers colors of needlework, of divers colors of needlework on both sides.

Rikmah, here rendered "needlework," means work made in different colors, whether by means of the needle or the loom. Precisely how this beautiful cloth was made is not now known. The Israelites were doubtless able to make figured cloth either with the needle or by weaving, since there is evidence from the Egyptian monuments that both methods were very ancient. The Israelites could therefore have learned the art in Egypt. Elegant and highly ornamented garments have ever been greatly prized by the Orientals. Babylon was anciently specially famous for their manufacture; whence the expression, "Babylonish garments." Josh. vii, 21. In the sacking of cities or camps all these variegated cloths were considered highly desirable booty. Thus Deborah, in this fine battle-poem, represents the ladies who attended on the mother of Sisera as suggesting to her that her son was detained because of the valuable spoil he had taken. Gold thread was sometimes used in the manufacture of beautiful garments. See Psa. xlv, 13, 14. The prophet Ezekiel refers to the fondness of the Assyrians for costly clothing. See Ezek. xxiii, 12, and the note on that passage.

230.—TORCHES.

VII, 16. He divided the three hundred men into three companies, and he put a trumpet in every man's hand, with empty pitchers, and lamps within the pitchers.

These "lamps" were probably torches, which could be quickly prepared for the use of the three hundred men. Lane says, that in the streets of Cairo the *Agha* of the police goes about at night accompanied by an executioner and a torch bearer, the latter of whom carries with him a torch which is called "shealeh." "This torch burns, soon after it is lighted, without a flame, excepting when it is waved through the air, when it suddenly blazes forth; it therefore answers the same purpose as our dark lantern. The burning end is sometimes concealed in a small pot or jar, or covered with something else when not required to give light."—*Manners and Customs of the Modern Egyptians,* vol. i, p. 178.

231.—ORNAMENTS.

VIII, 21. The ornaments that were on their camels' necks.

Saharonim, here translated ornaments, is in Isa. jii, 18, rendered "round tires like the moon." In Judges viii, 26, it is said that there were chains about the camels' necks. It thus appears that these camels had gold chains around their necks on which were the *saharonim*, or little moons, probably gold ornaments shaped like a moon either full or crescent. "Perhaps they were made in honor of the moon-faced Astarte, and intimated that they who bore them were placed under her protection. The taking

44.—CAMELS' ORNAMENTS.

away of these ornaments would thus be a removal of *idolatrous* objects."— *Wordsworth*. The Arabs of the present day are accustomed to hang ornaments around the necks of their camels. Some are shaped like crescents, and are made of cowrie shells sewed on a band of leather or cloth.

232.—BAAL-BERITH.

VIII, 33. The children of Israel ... made Baal-berith their god.

Baal-berith, or the covenant Baal, was one of the numerous Baalim that the Israelites worshiped at different times. We have no definite description of this god. A temple was built for him at Shechem, (Judges ix, 46,) but what were the special ceremonies we do not know. The worship is supposed to have been an imitation of the worship of Jehovah; an adulteration of that worship, in which Baal was put in the place of Jehovah.

233.—BETROTHAL AND MARRIAGE.

XIV, 7, 8. He went down, and talked with the woman; and she pleased Samson well. And after a time he returned to take her.

The former part of this passage has reference, doubtless, to the betrothal; the latter part, to the marriage. About a year usually elapsed between betrothal and marriage, though this was not always the case. The expression "after a time," literally, *after days*, is sometimes equivalent to a year.

See also note on Matt. i, 18.

234.—RIDDLES.

XIV, 12. Samson said unto them, I will now put forth a riddle unto you.

The Hebrews, in common with all Oriental people, were very fond of riddles, and amused themselves with them, especially at ordinary meals and feasts. Even princes sometimes competed in their solution. The queen of Sheba tested Solomon's wisdom with them. See 1 Kings x, 1, where the plural of the word which is here *rendered* riddle is translated "hard questions."

235.—GRINDING, A PUNISHMENT.

XVI, 21. The Philistines... bound him with fetters of brass; and he did grind in the prison house.

Grinding a hand mill was the lowest kind of slave labor. Among the Greeks and Romans slaves were sometimes compelled to do this as a punishment. It was doubtless considered equally degrading in the days of Samson, and for this reason the Philistines condemned him to it after they destroyed his sight. Some have endeavored to illustrate this scene by a pictorial representation of the Hebrew giant harnessed in leather bands to a huge wooden lever which is connected with a mill! Nothing of the sort is referred to in the text. The "ass's mill" was probably the invention of a later age, and even if it existed in Samson's day, how could he use it when he was "bound with fetters?" He was simply compelled to do the degrading work of a woman or a slave at the ordinary hand-mill, which is described in the note on Matt. xxiv, 41. Jeremiah laments the same fate which befell the young men of his people. Lam. v, 13.

236.—DAGON.

XVI, 23. The lords of the Philistines gathered them together for to offer a great sacrifice unto Dagon their god.

Dagon was the national god of the Philistines. The name is derived from *dag*, a fish. *Dagon* is the diminutive of *dag*, and signifies "little fish;" not

45.—DAGON.

so much, however, in reference to size, as to the affection entertained for it; so that some would render it, "dear little fish." From the description given in 1 Sam. v, 4, the idol is supposed to have been a combination of the human form with that of a fish. "And when they arose early on the morrow morning, behold, Dagon was fallen upon his face to the ground before the ark of the Lord; and the head of Dagon and both the palms of his hands were cut off upon the threshold; only the stump of Dagon was left to him." Omitting the words supplied by the translators ["the stump of"] and we find that the human part, consisting of the head and hands, was cut off, while *dagon*, or the fish part, remained. This description is corroborated by ancient traditions. The Babylonians believed that a being part man and part fish emerged from the Erythræan Sea, and appeared in Babylonia in the early days of its history, and taught the people various arts necessary for their well-being. Representations of this fish-god have been found among the sculptures of Nineveh. The Philistian Dagon was of a similar character. The deity is supposed to have been intended to represent the vivifying and productive powers of nature. The fish was an appropriate image to be used for this purpose, by reason of its rapid and enormous multiplication.

237.—SPORTS WITNESSED FROM THE ROOF.

XVI, 27. **Now the house was full of men and women; and all the lords of the Philistines were there; and there were upon the roof about three thousand men and women, that beheld while Samson made sport.**

This building must have been of great size to have gathered on its flat roof three thousand people. The blind Samson probably "made sport" on one side of the inclosed court-yard, where the spectators on the roof and the crowds within could see him at the same time. In Algiers, on occasions of public festivity, the courtyard of the palace is covered with sand for the accommodation of the wrestlers, who are brought there to amuse the crowd. Dr. Shaw says, "I have often seen numbers of people diverted in this manner upon the roof of the dey's palace at Algiers."—*Travels*, p. 217.

238.—THE MIDDLE PILLARS.

XVI, 29. **Samson took hold of the two middle pillars upon which the house stood, and on which it was borne up.**

The two "middle pillars" here spoken of constituted the key of the entire building : these falling, the house would be destroyed. Pliny mentions two large theaters built of wood, and planned with such ingenuity that each of them depended on *one hinge*. Dr. Thomson suggests, from his observations of the peculiar topography of Gaza, that the building was erected on a side-hill, having a steep declivity, and in such a position that the removal of the central columns would precipitate the whole edifice down the hill in ruinous confusion.—*The Land and the Book*, vol. ii, p. 342.

RUTH.

239.—GLEANING.

II, 3. **She went, and came, and gleaned in the field after the reapers.**

The Israelites were commanded by their law to be merciful to the poor. The corners of the fields were not to be reaped. Lev. xix, 9; xxiii, 22. If a sheaf should be accidentally left in the field it was to be allowed to remain there. Deut. xxiv, 19. This grain in the corners, and these odd sheaves in the field, were for the poor. The story of Ruth is a most beautiful illustration of this law. Reference is supposed to be made to this custom in Job xxiv, 10, " They take away the sheaf from the hungry."

240.—MUTUAL SALUTATIONS.

II, 4. Behold, Boaz came from Bethlehem, and said unto the reapers, The Lord be with you. And they answered him, The Lord bless thee.

These salutations are heard at this day in the East. The Psalmist prays that the haters of Zion may be like grass upon the house tops, and not like the grain which is reaped in the harvest field amid these mutual benedictions of employer and laborer. Psa. cxxix, 6–8.

241.—VINEGAR—PARCHED CORN.

II, 14. Boaz said unto her, At meal-time come thou hither, and eat of the bread, and dip thy morsel in the vinegar. And she sat beside the reapers: and he reached her parched corn, and she did eat, and was sufficed, and left.

1. *Chomets*—"vinegar "—was a beverage consisting generally of wine or strong drink turned sour. At present it is made in the East by pouring water on grape juice and leaving it to ferment. The Nazarites were forbidden to drink it. Num. vi, 3. It was doubtless excessively sour. Prov. x, 26. It was similar to the *posea* of the Romans, which was a thin sour wine, unintoxicating, and used only by the poor. This is what is referred to under the name of vinegar in the narrative of the crucifixion of our Lord. See Matt. xxvii, 34, 48; Luke xxiii, 36; John xix, 29, 30.

In Turkey grape juice is boiled from four to five hours, until it is reduced to one fourth the quantity put in. This is called *Nardenk*. It is of a dark color, has an agreeable sour-sweet taste, is turbid, and not intoxicating. It is sometimes used in the manner in which the *chomets* is said in the text to be used: the bread is dipped into it. It is thought by some to be the "vinegar" referred to in this passage.—See *Bibliotheca Sacra*, vol. v, p. 289.

2. The "parched corn " is prepared from grains of wheat not yet fully ripe. These are sometimes roasted in a pan or on an iron plate; sometimes the stalks are tied in small bundles, by which the ears are held in a blazing fire until roasted. Grain thus parched may be eaten with bread or without. In Lev. xxiii, 14, it is classed with bread and with green ears. Jesse sent an ephah of it and ten loaves of bread to his sons in the army, by the hand of David. 1 Sam. xvii, 17. Abigail took five measures of it as part of her present to David. 1 Sam. xxv, 18. David also received it with other provision from the hands of his friends when he was in want, after having

fled from his rebellious son Absalom. 2 Sam. xvii, 28. In Lev. ii, 14, it is called "green ears of corn dried by the fire." It is a common article of food in Palestine and in Egypt to this day.

242.—RUDE THRESHING.

II, 17. So she gleaned in the field until even, and beat out that she had gleaned.

This is still done by the gleaners at the close of their day's work, sticks or stones being used as convenient though rude instruments for threshing the grain they have gathered.

243.—THE TIME FOR WINNOWING.

III, 2. Behold, he winnoweth barley to-night in the threshing floor.

The evening was selected not only because it was cooler than the day, but because of the increase of wind which enabled the husbandmen to winnow more thoroughly. For the Oriental mode of winnowing see note on Amos ix, 9, and on Matt. iii, 12.

244.—WATCHING THE GRAIN.

III, 7. When Boaz had eaten and drunk, and his heart was merry, he went to lie down at the end of the heap of corn.

The threshing floor being uninclosed, (see note on Gen l, 10,) and exposed to robbers, it was necessary for the proprietor or some trusty servant to keep up a watch. We therefore find Boaz taking his supper and sleeping at the end of the heap of corn. This is still done by the proprietors of threshing floors in Palestine. The grain is carefully watched until it is all threshed, winnowed, and garnered.

245.—SIGN OF MARRIAGE—THE GOEL.

III, 9. Spread therefore thy skirt over thine handmaid; for thou art a near kinsman.

1. The expression "spread thy skirt" imports protection, and here signifies protection of a conjugal character. When marriages are solemnized among the Jews the man throws the skirt of his *talith* or robe over his wife and covers her head with it.

2. *Goel,* "kinsman," is, literally, "one who redeems." When a Hebrew was obliged to sell his inheritance on account of poverty, it was the duty of the nearest relative to redeem it for him. Lev. xxv, 25. Hence the word *goel* came to signify kinsman. The *goel* also became the recipient of property which had been unjustly kept from a deceased kinsman. Num. v, 6–8. It was likewise his duty to avenge the blood of his next of kin by seeking the life of the murderer. Gen. ix, 5, 6; Num. xxxv, 19; 2 Sam. xiv, 7.

Some have supposed from the association of the *goel* with marriage, as in this history of Ruth, that it was his duty to marry the widow of a deceased kinsman: but according to Deut. xxv, 5, this duty was only obligatory on a brother-in-law, which relation to Ruth was certainly not sustained by Boaz. Nor is there any evidence that it was sustained by the unnamed kinsman spoken of by Boaz in verse 12. Had this nearer *goel* been a brother-in-law Boaz would not have begun by asking him to redeem the property, (Ruth iv, 4,) but would instantly have demanded that he should marry the widow, on refusing to do which he was liable to judicial disgrace. Deut. xxv, 7–10. But in the case of the *goel* it was not until he redeemed the property of his relative, dying without a son, that he was under obligation to marry the widow. As Winer says, " The latter was to him the consequence of the former and not the reverse, as in the case of the *levir*, [brother-in-law.] Should he refuse to take possession of the property he was under no obligation to marry the widow. In so refusing he incurred no judicial disgrace, because he did not fail to discharge a duty, but only relinquished a right. The law had expressly imposed the duty of marriage on the *levir* only, and beyond him the obligation did not extend."—REALWÖRTERBUCH, *s. v. Ruth.*

Boaz had no right to redeem the property until the nearer kinsman refused, and neither he nor the other kinsman was under any obligation to do it; but having once assumed the redemption, the one thus exercising his right was by that act under obligation to marry the widow.

246.—THE VAIL.

46.—OUTER GARMENT OF WOMEN.

III, 15. Also he said, Bring the vail that thou hast upon thee, and hold it. And when she held it, he measured six measures of barley, and laid it on her.

Mitpachath, vail, is called mantle in Isaiah iii, 22, and some lexicographers assert that this is its meaning; that it does not signify what is commonly understood by a vail, but simply a large outer mantle or cloak, in one corner of which Ruth received the barley. Others, however, and among them Dr. Kitto, insist that a vail is meant; one made of strong cotton cloth and used for out-door wear.

The engraving represents a large vail, or mantle, which is worn by Egyptian women at the present day. It is called *milayeh.*

247.—THE SIGN OF THE SHOE.

IV, 7. Now this was the manner in former time in Israel concerning redeeming and concerning changing, for to confirm all things; a man plucked off his shoe, and gave it to his neighbor: and this was a testimony in Israel.

There was no divine law ordaining this; it was simply an ancient custom. It is not to be confounded with the law in reference to levirate marriages in Deut. xxv, 7-10. It probably originated from the fact that the right to tread the soil belonged only to the owner of it, and hence the transfer of a sandal was a very appropriate representation of the transfer of property. Allusion to this custom is doubtless intended in Psa. lx, 8, "Over Edom will I cast out my shoe;" that is, I will transfer it to myself. The custom was prevalent among the Indians and ancient Germans, and is said still to exist in the East.

I. SAMUEL.

248.—THE SEAT OF JUDGMENT.

I, 9. Now Eli the priest sat upon a seat by a post of the temple of the Lord.

In some parts of the East a seat is placed in the court-yard, where the master of the house may sit and give judgment on all domestic affairs. This seat is usually placed in some shady part of the court, against a wall or column. Thus in the text, Eli "sat upon a seat by a post." So David sat upon a seat by the wall. 1 Sam. xx, 25. These seats probably had no backs, and were therefore placed near the post or wall for support. Thus we are told that Eli fell backward from his seat at the gate and died. 1 Sam. iv, 18. The Assyrian monuments have many representations of such backless seats.

249.—THE HORN.

II, 1. Hannah prayed, and said, My heart rejoiceth in the Lord, mine horn is exalted in the Lord.

The horn is an emblem of power and of dignity; the exaltation of the horn therefore expresses elevation of privilege and honor, and its depression represents the opposite. See also 1 Sam. ii, 10; Job xvi, 15; Psa. lxxv, 4, 5; lxxxix, 17, 24; xcii, 10; cxii, 9. The Druse ladies on Mount Lebanon wear a horn as a part of their head-dress. These horns are made of various materials according to the wealth of the owner: dough, pasteboard, pottery, tin, silver, and gold. They vary in length from six inches to two feet and a half, and are three or four inches in diameter at the base, tapering almost to a point. The vail is thrown over the horn, and from it flows gracefully down. When once put on, the horn is never taken off; it remains on the wearer's head by day and at night, through sickness and health, even down to death.

It has been supposed by many writers that the passages above cited all refer to this article of costume, and it is frequently spoken of as an illustration of them. It should be borne in mind, however, that some of the most judicious critics deny all such reference, there being no evidence that the horn was ever used by the Hebrews. It appears rather to be a fashion of comparatively modern date. As good an interpretation of the above passages can be given by supposing the horn to refer to the natural weapon of beasts, and to be used in a figurative sense, as by imagining it to refer to an artificial ornament for human beings.

250.—TALISMANIC IMAGES.

VI, 5. **Wherefore ye shall make images of your emerods, and images of your mice that mar the land.**

These were doubtless talismanic figures made according to some occult laws of astrology. Such talismans are very ancient. They were supposed to cure diseases and to ward off evils. The learned Gregory thinks that they originated in false views entertained by the Gentiles concerning the brazen serpent. His theory is, that their astrologers, finding that among the Israelites the bite of serpents had been cured by the image of a serpent, concluded that all sorts of evils might be remedied, provided corresponding images were made under proper astrological conditions. Whether this theory be correct or not, there is abundant evidence of the ancient prevalence of this superstition. It still exists in India. Talismans, generally of silver, are carried to the heathen temples. These images represent as nearly as may be the diseases or the special troubles under which the offerers suffer. It is

47.—TALISMANIC IMAGES.

supposed that the gods will be propitious on seeing them, and give the sufferer the relief sought. Roberts (*Oriental Illustrations*, pp. 158, 159) has cuts of some of these little images which came into his possession by the gift of a friend. We here insert three of these, representing a deformed boy, an infant, and an old man. Images of eyes, ears, mouth, nose, and hands are also hung up in the temples.

Some commentators suppose that "the blind and the lame," mentioned in 2 Sam. v, 6–8, were talismanic images set up in the fort by the Jebusites for their protection.

251.—HELMETS—CUIRASSES.

XVII, 5. He had a helmet of brass upon his head, and he was armed with a coat of mail.

1. In the earliest times helmets were made of osier or rushes, and were in the form of bee-hives or skull-caps. The skins of the heads of animals were sometimes used. Various other materials were employed at different times. The ancient Egyptian helmet was usually made of linen cloth quilted. It was thick and well padded, sometimes coming down to the shoulder, and sometimes only a little below the ear. The cloth used was colored green, or red, or black. The helmet had no crest, but the summit was an obtuse point ornamented with two tassels. The Assyrian helmet was a cap of iron terminating above in a point, and sometimes furnished with flaps, covered with metal scales and protecting the neck. The Philistine helmet, as represented on ancient monuments, was of unique form. From the head-band there arose curved lines, by which the outline of the helmet was hollowed on the sides and rounded on top. Goliath's helmet was doubtless of this

48.—ANCIENT HELMETS.

shape, and, being made of brass, must have presented a beautiful appearance. The form of the Hebrew helmets is unknown; but they probably did not vary widely from the Egyptian. As is seen in verse 38 they were sometimes made of brass. The helmet is also mentioned in 2 Chron. xxvi, 14; Jer. xlvi, 4; Ezek. xxiii, 24; xxvii, 10; xxxviii, 5.

2. For the body, the skins of beasts were probably the earliest protection in battle. Felt or quilted linen was also used subsequently. The ancient Egyptians had horizontal rows of metal plates well secured by brass pins. The ancient Assyrians had scales of iron fastened on felt or linen. Iron rings

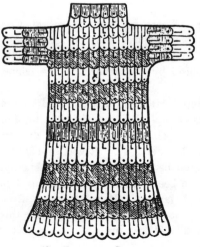

49.—EGYPTIAN CUIRASS.

9

closely locked together were likewise used by different nations. Scales made of small pieces of horn or hoof were also used. Sometimes a very serviceable armor was made of small plates of metal, each having a button and a slit, fitting into the corresponding slit and button of the plate next to it. It is supposed that Ahab had on armor of this sort when he was slain; the "joints of the harness" being the grooves or slits in the metallic plates, or the place between, where they did not overlap. 1 Kings xxii, 34; 2 Chron. xviii, 33. Goliath's "coat of mail" was scale armor, (*shiryon kaskassim:* "armor of scales.") This kind of armor consisted of metallic scales rounded at the bottom and squared at the top, and sewed on linen or felt. The Philistine corselet covered the chest only. On the bas-relief at Nineveh are seen warriors with coats of scale armor which descend to the knees or ankles. In one of the palaces Mr. Layard discovered a number of the scales used for this armor. Each scale was of iron two to three inches long, rounded at one end and squared at the other, with a raised or embossed line in the center, and some were inlaid with copper. At a later period the Assyrian armor was made of smaller scales, which were pointed and ornamented with raised figures, and the coat of mail reached no lower than the waist.

In several passages *shiryon* is rendered in our version "habergeon." See 2 Chron. xxvi, 14; Neh. iv, 16.

The *lorica* of the Romans and the *thorax* of the Greeks—rendered "breastplate" in Eph. vi, 14 and 1 Thess. v. 8—were scale armor covering breast and back.

252.—GREAVES—JAVELIN.

XVII, 6. **He had greaves of brass upon his legs, and a target of brass between his shoulders.**

1. Greaves were coverings for the legs. There are none represented on the Egyptian monuments, but they are seen on the Assyrian sculptures.

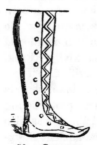

They were of leather, wood, or, as in the case of Goliath, of brass, and were bound by thongs around the calves and above the ankles.

2. *Kidon,* here rendered "target," is translated by the word "shield" in verse 45 of this chapter, and in Job xxxix, 23; "spear" in Josh. viii, 18, 26; Job xli, 29; Jer. vi, 23; and "lance" in Jer l, 42. It was probably a light javelin, which could be easily hurled at an enemy. Some suppose it to have been decorated with a flag, like the lances of the Polish lancers. It would seem from this verse that when not in actual use it was carried on the back; for this is the meaning of "between the shoulders." It was probably slung across the shoulders by means of a leathern strap.

50.—GREAVE.

253.—SPEAR—LARGE SHIELD.

XVII, 7. The staff of his spear was like a weaver's beam; and his spear's head weighed six hundred shekels of iron: and one bearing a shield went before him.

1. The *chanith*, "spear," was a heavier weapon than the *kidon*. See preceding note. The word is rendered both "spear," and "javelin." It was the *chanith* with which Saul endeavored to strike David, (1 Sam. xviii, 10, 11; xix, 9, 10,) and which at another time he aimed at Jonathan. 1 Sam. xx, 33. This heavy spear had at its lower extremity a point by which it could be stuck into the ground. It was in this way that the position of Saul was marked while he lay sleeping in the camp at Hachilah, his spear being his standard. 1 Sam. xxvi, 7. This lower point of the spear was almost as formidable as the head. The Arab riders of to-day sometimes use it to strike backward at pursuers, and it was with this "hinder end of the spear" that Abner killed Asahel. 2 Sam. ii, 23. The size of Goliath's *chanith* is expressed by the description of the staff and of the head; the latter being of iron, in contrast to the brass head of his *kidon*, and to his brazen helmet, cuirass, and greaves. See also note on Jer. xlvi, 4.

2. The *tsinnah*, "shield," was the largest kind of shield, and was designed to protect the whole body. This shield, as represented on the Egyptian monuments, was about five feet high, with a pointed arch above and square below. The great shield of the Assyrians, as is shown by their sculptures, was taller, and of an oblong shape, and sometimes had at the top an inward curve. The large shields were generally made of wicker work or of light wood covered with hides.

51.—EGYPTIAN LARGE SHIELD.

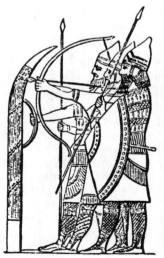

52.—ASSYRIAN LARGE SHIELD.

They were grasped by a handle of wood or of leather. Goliath had a man to bear his great shield before him. In the Assyrian sculptures there are representations of warriors fighting in this manner, with men before them holding the large shields, with the bottom resting on the ground, thus forming movable breastworks. The great shields of the Philistines seem to have been of circular shape.

The beauty of the figure used in Psa. v, 12 is heightened by the fact that the *tsinnah* is the shield there spoken of. The Lord uses the great buckler for the protection of his people.

254.—CHEESE—PLEDGE.

XVII, 18. Carry these ten cheeses unto the captain of their thousand, and look how thy brethren fare, and take their pledge.

1. The cheese used in the East is made up into small cakes, strongly salted, soft when new, but soon becoming dry and hard. It is greatly inferior to either English or Dutch cheese. Burckhardt speaks of a kind of cheese made of coagulated buttermilk, which is dried until it becomes quite hard, and is then ground. The Arabs eat it mixed with butter.

2. By the expression "take their pledge," is probably meant, Bring some token from them that they are yet alive and well. Roberts says that among the Hindoos a person in a distant country sends to those who are interested in his welfare a ring, a lock of hair, or a piece of his nail, as a "pledge" of his health and prosperity.

255.—THE SWORD.

XVII, 39. David girded his sword upon his armor, and he assayed to go.

The sword was one of the earliest weapons in use. The Egyptian sword

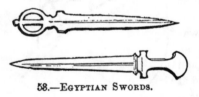

58.—EGYPTIAN SWORDS.

was short and straight, two and a half to three feet long, and double-edged. The handle was plain and hollowed in the center, the better to 'afford a firm grasp. The Hebrew sword probably resembled it.

256.—STAFF—SCRIP—SLING.

XVII, 40. He took his staff in his hand, and chose him five smooth stones out of the brook, and put them in a shepherd's bag which he had, even in a scrip; and his sling was in his hand.

1. The shepherd carries a staff which he holds in the center. It is used not only as a support in climbing hills, but for the purpose of beating bushes and low brushwood in which the flocks stray, and where snakes and other reptiles abound. It may also be used for correcting the shepherd-dogs, and keeping them in subjection. Thus Goliath says, " Am I a dog, that

thou comest to me with staves ? " verse 43. This useful accompaniment of shepherd-life is mentioned in Gen. xxxii, 10; Psa. xxiii, 4; Micah vii, 14, and in other passages.

2. The scrip was a bag of leather thrown over the shoulder, and used by shepherds and travelers to carry provision. It is still used by Eastern shepherds, and is made of the skin of a kid stripped off whole and tanned. This is the only passage in the Old Testament where it is mentioned, but reference is made to it in several places in the New Testament. Matt. x, 10; Mark vi, 8; Luke ix, 3; x, 4; xxii, 35, 36.

3. The sling was made of leather, or of plaited work of wool, rushes, hair, or sinews. The middle part, where the stone lay, was called the cup, (*caph*,) because of its cup-like depression. It was wider than the ends, but the sling gradually narrowed toward the extremities, so that it could be easily handled. In the Egyptian sling, which probably was the same as the Hebrew, there was a loop at one end which was placed over the thumb, in order to retain the weapon when the stone was hurled and the other end became free. The sling was used by shepherds to keep the beasts of prey from the flock, and also to keep the sheep from straying. Husbandmen likewise used it to drive away birds from the fields of corn. In war it was a formidable weapon in skillful hands. The Egyptian slinger carried a bag of

54.—EGYPTIAN SLINGER.

round stones depending from his shoulder, as David did. The Assyrians, however, according to their sculptures, had lying at their feet a heap of pebbles, which they picked up as they were needed. In using the sling, the stone was put into the broad hollowed part, the ends were grasped together in the hand, and after a few whirls around the head to give impetus, the stone was d scharged, frequently with force enough to penetrate helmet or shield.

A weapon so peculiar in its formation and so great in its power was appropriately referred to as an illustration of swift and certain destruction. Thus Abigail said to David, "The souls of thine enemies, them shall he sling out, as out of the middle of a sling." 1 Sam. xxv, 29. Thus the Lord said to Jeremiah, "I will sling out the inhabitants of the land at this once, and will distress them." Jer. x, 18. The figure in both these passages is drawn, not from the destructive power of the sling, but from the ease and rapidity with which, by a practiced hand, the stone was hurled from it.

The Benjamites were so skillful in the use of this weapon that some of them "could sling stones at a hair, and not miss." Judges xx, 16. The youthful David showed great skill, since he hurled the pebble with such aim and force that it smote the giant in the forehead and brought him to the ground. Verses 49, 50.

257.—PRINCELY ROBES.

XVIII, 4. Jonathan stripped himself of the robe that was up-on him, and gave it to David, and his garments, even to his sword, and to his bow, and to his girdle.

It is considered in the East a special mark of respect to be presented by a prince with some of the garments he has for his own wearing. The gift of a girdle is a token of the greatest confidence and affection, and is very highly prized. Joab expressed his intense desire for the death of Absalom by his willingness to give a girdle to the man who would murder him. 2 Sam. xviii, 11. Morier gives a curious instance of the estimation placed on the possession of garments which had once covered, and of weapons which had once adorned, the person of royalty. He says that when the treaty was made between Russia and Persia in 1814, the Persian plenipo-tentiary, who had been honored by various gifts of weapons and clothing from his sovereign, designated himself in the preamble of the treaty as "endowed with the special gifts of the Monarch, lord of the dagger set in jewels, of the sword adorned with gems, and of the shawl-coat already worn."—*Second Journey through Persia, etc.*, p. 299. It was in this way that the shepherd-warrior was honored by Jonathan. See also note on Esther vi, 8.

258.—JOY IN VICTORY—SHALISHIM.

XVIII, 6. It came to pass as they came, when David was returned from the slaughter of the Philistine, that the women came out of all cities of Israel, singing and dancing, to meet king Saul, with tabrets, with joy, and with instruments of music.

1. It was customary for the women to express their delight in victory by songs and music, and dancing in the presence of the conquerors. See Exod. xv, 20 ; Judges xi, 34.

2. Precisely what is meant by *shalishim*, which in our version is rendered "instruments of music," is not known. From the construction of the word there was evidently a triple arrangement of some sort in the formation of the *shalishim*. The margin of our English Bibles has "three-stringed instru-ments." They may have been harps of three strings, or of triangular shape ; but most authorities now agree in supposing them to have been triangles. These instruments of percussion are said to have originated in Syria, and if so may have been known to the ancient Hebrews. They were well adapted for the ringing music of a military triumph.

259.—RESPONSIVE SINGING.

XVIII, 7. **The women answered one another as they played, and said, Saul hath slain his thousands, and David his ten thousands.**

One part of the women probably sang, "Saul hath slain his thousands," and the others responded, "and David his ten thousands." This responsive chorus-singing is very ancient. Over four hundred years before this Miriam had led the women in the responsive chorus of victory on the occasion of the destruction of Pharaoh's army, the men and women alternating in their song. Exod. xv, 21. It is supposed to have been an Egyptian custom. See also Ezra iii, 11; Isa. vi, 3; Rev. iv, 8–11; v, 9–14.

260.—FLEEING FROM THE DART.

XIX, 10. **Saul sought to smite David even to the wall with the javelin; but he slipped away out of Saul's presence, and he smote the javelin into the wall: and David fled, and escaped that night.**

According to an ancient Asiatic custom, when a dart was thrown at a freedman, and he escaped from it by flight, he was thereby absolved from all allegiance to his master. Thus Saul by his murderous fury gave complete liberty to David, whose subsequent acts of war against the king could not be considered rebellion. From that hour he was no longer a subject of King Saul.—See KITTO's *Cyclopædia of Biblical Literature*, vol. i, p. 225.

261.—USE OF THE TERM NAKED.

XIX, 24. **He stripped off his clothes also, and prophesied before Samuel in like manner, and lay down naked all that day and all that night.**

This does not mean absolutely without any clothing. A person was called naked whose outer garments were thrown aside, leaving nothing but the tunic and girdle. See note on John xix, 23. Thus Isaiah was naked by simply removing his sackcloth mantle. Isa. xx, 2. This is also the meaning of "flee away naked" in Amos ii, 16. The young man who followed Jesus at the time of his arrest was probably "naked" in this sense. Mark xiv, 51, 52. Peter was also "naked" in the same way at the time he cast himself into the sea to meet the Lord. John xxi, 7. Compare 2 Sam. vi, 14, 20.

262.—RELATIVES CURSED.

XX, 30. **Saul's anger was kindled against Jonathan, and he said unto him, Thou son of the perverse rebellious woman.**

This is a favorite Oriental mode of abuse. It is supposed that an indignity offered to a man's mother will give him greater pain than one offered to himself. "Strike *me*," said the servant of Mungo Park, "but do not curse my mother." Sir W. Ouseley tells of a man who, seeking for wine, put to his lips a bottle of some nauseous medicine, and immediately cursed, not the man who made the disgusting draught, but all the female relatives in whose welfare he had the greatest interest; his wives, mother, daughters, and sisters.—BURDER, *Oriental Customs*, No. 312. Professor Hackett, having incautiously approached a large flock of sheep for the purpose of getting a better view, was assailed by the three women who were watching them, with "a volley of words almost terrific." They cursed his father, his mother, his grandfather, and all his ancestors.—*Illustrations of Scripture*, p. 106.

263.—VALUABLES WRAPPED IN CLOTHES.

XXI, 9. **The priest said, The sword of Goliath the Philistine, whom thou slewest in the valley of Elah, behold, it is here wrapped in a cloth behind the ephod.**

It is customary to wrap in cloths all articles which are esteemed specially valuable or sacred. Sacred books are inclosed in rich cases of brocade silk or costly velvet. Harmer suggests that the *simlah*, "cloth," in which the sword of Goliath was wrapped, may have been a part of some magnificent dress of David.—*Observations*, vol. ii, p. 517.

Money was sometimes put aside in a similar way. The unfaithful servant laid up his lord's money in a napkin, or handkerchief. See Luke xix, 20.

264.—THE SPEAKER MENTIONED FIRST.

XXIV, 12. **The Lord judge between me and thee, and the Lord avenge me of thee: but mine hand shall not be upon thee.**

With us it is a marked want of etiquette for the speaker to mention himself first, especially when speaking to or of those of superior rank or position. Chardin, however, says that among the Persians it is customary for the speaker to name himself first. From this text it seems to have been considered perfectly respectful in the days of David, and we have instances more ancient still. When Ephron the Hittite was bargaining with Abraham for the sale of the cave of Machpelah he said, "What is that betwixt me and thee?" Gen. xxiii, 15. So also Sarai said to her husband Abram, "The Lord judge between me and thee." Gen. xvi, 5. So Laban said to Jacob, "The Lord watch between me and thee." Gen. xxxi, 49.

265.—HOUSES OF THE DEAD.

XXV, 1. **Samuel died; and all the Israelites were gathered together, and lamented him, and buried him in his house at Ramah.**

Some commentators assert that Samuel was placed in a tomb erected in the house he occupied during his life, or in its court. Of this, however, there is no evidence.   Long before Samuel's time the grave was spoken of as "the house appointed for all living." See Job xxx, 23.   So afterward Joab "was buried in his own house in the wilderness." 1 Kings ii, 34.   It is much more probable that a tomb for the dead should be called a house than that a dwelling-place built for the living should be used as a tomb.   An American missionary in Syria says that at *Deir el Kamr*, on Mount Lebanon, he found a number of small solid stone buildings, having neither doors nor windows.   These were the "houses of the dead."   It was necessary to open the dead walls every time an interment took place.—JOWETT'S *Researches*, p. 207.

In India it is quite common to build a house in a retired place over the remains of the dead, where also the rest of the family, when they die, are interred.   In some of these houses the funeral car, or palanquin in which the body was borne to its burial, is suspended from the ceiling.   Great pains are taken to keep these houses of the dead in good repair, and some of them are built in a most magnificent manner.

266.—CHIEFTAIN'S SPEAR—CRUSE.

XXVI, 11. **Take thou now the spear that is at his bolster, and the cruse of water, and let us go.**

1. The spear here spoken of is the *chanith*, already described in the note on chap. xvii, 7.   In the Arab encampments of the present day the sheikh's tent is always recognized by a tall spear stuck in the ground in front of it; and the place where the sheikh reclines to rest when halting on a march is designated in like manner.

2. It is not known what was the precise shape of the cruse, (*tsappachath*,) or the material of which it consisted.   Some suppose it to have been made of iron plates shaped like a shallow cup or bowl.   The vessel at present used in the East for the purposes of a cruse or flask is globular in shape, and is made of blue porous clay.   It is nine inches in diameter, with a neck three inches long.   At the lower part is a small handle, and opposite is a straight spout having an orifice about the size of a straw, through which water is sucked.   The *tsappachath* is spoken of in the Bible as a receptacle for oil, (1 Kings xvii, 12,) and also for water.   See text and 1 Kings xix, 6.

The "cruse" mentioned in 1 Kings xiv, 3, and the one in 2 Kings ii, 20, are different vessels from the cruse of this text, and the words themselves are different in the original.   See notes on those passages.

II. SAMUEL.

267.—ARMLETS.

I, 10. I took . . . the bracelet that was on his arm.

Etsadah, "bracelet," is, according to Gesenius, more properly an anklet than a bracelet; yet as it is here spoken of in connection with the arm it doubt-

less means an armlet. The word occurs also in Num. xxxi, 50, where it is associated with *tsamid,* (bracelet,) and is rendered "chains." Saul's armlet is supposed to have been a part of the insignia of his royalty. Egyptian monarchs are often represented on the monuments wearing armlets and bracelets. The Persian kings often wore them, and they are still common among Oriental sovereigns, many of them being elaborately wrought and richly ornamented with jewels. From Sol. Song viii, 6, it appears that the signet was sometimes placed

55.—EGYPTIAN ARMLETS.

in the armlet: "As a seal upon thine arm."

268.—RECESS IN GATEWAY.

III, 27. Joab took him aside in the gate to speak with him quietly.

The expression "in the gate," is literally *in the midst of the gate,* and probably refers to some dark corner in the vaulted gateway where two persons might retire and converse unseen. To some such recess Joab invited Abner, avowedly for conversation, but really to kill him.

269.—BEDS FOR BIERS.

III, 31. Rend your clothes, and gird you with sackcloth, and mourn before Abner. And king David himself followed the bier.

Mittah, "bier," would be better rendered by *bed.* Persons of distinction were sometimes carried to the grave on their beds. Josephus describes minutely the preparations which were made by Archelaus for the funeral of his father Herod. The body was placed on a gilded bed, which was richly adorned with precious stones.—*Antiquities,* book xvii, chapter 8, § 3.

270.—PRISONERS FETTERED.

III, 34. Thy hands were not bound, nor thy feet put into fetters.

Strigelius supposes that David meant, by using this language, to distinguish Abner from those criminals who are carried to execution with their hands tied behind them; and from soldiers who are taken captive in war, and have their feet fastened by fetters to prevent their running away.

For a description of fetters see note on 2 Kings xxv, 7.

271.—STORING AND GRINDING GRAIN.

IV, 6. **They came thither into the midst of the house, as though they would have fetched wheat.**

Harmer (*Observations*, vol. i, p. 435) suggests that the pretense of these men that they went into the house for wheat, was rendered plausible by the fact that it was necessary to obtain the grain in the afternoon in order to have it ready for grinding early the next morning, according to daily custom. All suspicion of their murderous intention was thus avoided. Ishbosheth was taking his usual daily nap after the noon meal, (verse 5.) They went toward the place where the grain was stored, and thus gained access to the apartment of the sleeping king and murdered him.

272.—THE SISTRUM.

VI, 5. **David and all the house of Israel played before the Lord on all manner of instruments made of fir wood, even on . . . cornets.**

This is the only place where the word *menaanim* appears. The instrument it represents bore no resemblance to a cornet or to any other wind instrument. Gesenius describes it as "a musical instrument or rattle, which gave a tinkling sound on being *shaken*." He supposes it to have been the ancient sistrum. Other authorities agree with this interpretation, though some discard it. The sistrum was used in the worship of the ancient Egyptians. It was "generally from eight to sixteen or eighteen inches in length, and entirely of bronze or brass. It was sometimes inlaid with silvergilt, or otherwise ornamented, and, being held upright, was shaken, the rings moving to and fro upon the brass."—KITTO.

The other instruments named in this verse are described in other places. See Index.

56.—SISTRUM.

273.—THE BEARD CUT OFF.

X, 4. **Wherefore Hanun took David's servants, and shaved off the one half of their beards.**

According to Oriental sentiment a greater indignity could not have been put upon them. The beard is considered a symbol of manhood, and, in some places, of freedom—slaves being compelled to shave their beards in token of servitude. By shaving half their beard Hanun not only treated David's embassadors with contempt, but made them objects of ridicule. The beard is usually kept with care and neatness; and thus when David feigned madness in the presence of Achish, king of Gath, he " let his spittle fall down upon his beard," which convinced the beholders that he must be bereft of his senses. 1 Sam. xxi, 13. So disgraceful is it considered to have the beard cut off, that some of the Orientals would prefer death to such a punishment. Niebuhr, in his *Description of Arabia*, relates that in the year 1764, Kerim Kahn, one of the three rebels who at that time desired to obtain dominion over Persia, sent embassadors to Mir Mahenna, the prince of a little independent territory on the Persian Gulf, to demand a large tribute, and threatened to come to him with his army if he did not conduct himself as an obedient subject. Mahenna, however, treated the embassadors with great contempt, which was especially marked in cutting off their beards. Upon hearing of this, Kerim Kahn was so indignant that he sent a large army which subdued the territory.

274.—SPRING, THE SEASON FOR WAR.

XI, 1. It came to pass, after the year was expired, at the time when kings go forth.

" After the year was expired " is literally " at the return of the year," that is, in the spring. This was the time of the year for the commencement or renewal of military movements, the season for severe storms being over.

275.—PROMENADE ON THE ROOF.

XI, 2. It came to pass in an eveningtide, that David arose from off his bed, and walked upon the roof of the king's house : and from the roof he saw a woman washing herself.

1. After his customary afternoon rest had been taken, David walked on the flat roof of his palace. In the cool of the evening the roofs of the houses are occupied by family groups who go there for air and exercise. In Dan. iv, 29 we have an account of the walk of another king. Instead of walked *in* the palace, the marginal reading is, *upon* the palace. It was on the roof that Nebuchadnezzar walked, and from there he obtained that view of his great city which lifted his heart with pride and made him forget God.

2. The bath in which Bathsheba was washing was in the court-yard, secluded from all ordinary observation, but yet visible from the palace roof.

276.—ANIMALS PETTED.

XII, 3. It grew up together with him, and with his children ; it did eat of his own meat, and drank of his own cup, and lay in his bosom, and was unto him as a daughter.

There is a beautiful touch of nature about this; for though uttered in a parable the words are in truthful accordance with Eastern manners.

Bochart says that anciently not only lambs, but other animals, were by many persons allowed to eat with them at their tables, and to lie with them in their beds. The Arabs of to-day keep pet-lambs as we keep lap-dogs.

277.—FASTING FOR BEREAVEMENT.

XII, 21. **Then said his servants unto him, What thing is this that thou hast done? thou didst fast and weep for the child, while it was alive; but when the child was dead, thou didst rise and eat bread.**

What astonished the servants of David was, that their master should act so contrary to old-established customs of mourning in time of bereavement. Sir John Chardin says, "The practice of the East is to leave a relation of the deceased person to weep and mourn, till on the third or fourth day at furthest the relatives and friends go to see him, cause him to eat, lead him to a bath, and cause him to put on new vestments, he having before thrown himself on the ground."—HARMER, *Observations*, vol. iv, p. 424. David, on the contrary, changed his apparel and ate food as soon as he learned of the death of the boy.

278.—COVERING THE HEAD.

XV, 30. **David went up by the ascent of mount Olivet, and wept as he went up, and had his head covered, and he went up barefoot.**

Covering the head, as well as uncovering the feet, (see note on Deut. xxv, 10,) was a token of great distress. It was probably done by drawing a fold of the outer garment over the head. When Haman mourned over his great discomfiture his head was covered. Esther vi, 12. Jeremiah pathetically represents the plowmen as mourning in this way because of the severe drought. "Because the ground is chapped, for there was no rain in the earth, the plowmen were ashamed, they covered their heads." Jer. xiv, 4.

279.—EARTH ON THE HEAD.

XV, 32. **Hushai the Archite came to meet him with his coat rent, and earth upon his head.**

His rent coat signified mourning, (see note on Gen. xxxvii, 34,) as did also the earth on his head. In the British Museum is a tombstone from Abydos, on which is a representation of a funeral procession, the mourners in which show their grief by throwing dust on their heads. There was an ancient tradition among the Egyptians that, in the infancy of their history as a people, their god Noum had taught their fathers that they were but clay or dust. The practice of putting dust on their heads is supposed to have been originally designed to be symbolical of their origin from dust, and to convey the idea of their humility in view of that fact. We find frequent scriptural reference to the custom. When the Israelites were defeated at Ai, Joshua and the elders "put dust upon their heads." Josh. vii, 6. The Benjamite who brought to Eli the news of the death of his sons came to Shiloh "with earth upon his head." 1 Sam. iv, 12. The young Amalekite who brought to David the tidings of Saul's death had "earth upon his head." 2 Sam. i, 2. Tamar, dishonored, "put ashes on her head." 2 Sam. xiii, 19. In the great fast which was held in Nehemiah's time in Jerusalem, the children of Israel had "earth upon them." Neh. ix, 1. When Job's three friends mourned with him in his great troubles, they "sprinkled dust upon their heads toward heaven." Job ii, 12. This shows the great antiquity of the practice. Jeremiah, in lamenting over the desolations of Zion, says that the elders "have cast up dust upon their heads." Lam. ii, 10. Ezekiel, in predicting the destruction of Tyrian commerce, represents the sailors as casting up "dust upon their heads." Ezek. xxvii, 30. See also Rev. xviii, 19.

280.—DUST-THROWING.

XVI, 13. As David and his men went by the way, Shimei went along on the hill's side over against him, and cursed as he went, and threw stones at him, and cast dust.

Throwing dust at a person is an Oriental mode of expressing anger and contempt. In addition to the instance here given we find another in the history of Paul. The mob whom he addressed in Jerusalem became very much excited at his speech and sought to destroy him, declaring that he was not fit to live, and as evidence of their fury they "threw dust into the air." Acts xxii, 23. The precise meaning of this symbolic action we do not know. There may, however, be some connection between this custom and the practice of persons in trouble putting dust on their own heads in token of grief. See the preceding note. Throwing dust at others may be a symbolic mode of wishing them such trouble and grief that they may feel like covering themselves with dust, as an expression of their sorrow.

281.—CISTERN IN THE COURT-YARD:

XVII, 18, 19. But they went both of them away quickly, and came to a man's house in Bahurim, which had a well in his court; whither they went down. And the woman took and spread a covering over the well's mouth, and spread ground corn thereon; and the thing was not known.

The well (beer) here spoken of was not a living fountain, but simply a cistern or reservoir dug in the court-yard, as is often the case in the East at the present day. Such cisterns sometimes become dry, and then make excellent hiding-places for fugitives. The mouth being on a level with the ground, could be easily covered by a mat or some other article, and the corn being spread over this, suspicion would be disarmed. For description of the "court," see note on Esther i, 5.

282.—DOUBLE GATES.

XVIII, 24. David sat between the two gates: and the watchman went up to the roof over the gate.

At the gateways of walled cities special care was taken to increase the strength of the wall and the power of resistance, since the most formidable attacks of the enemy would probably be made there. The ordinary thickness of wall not being sufficient it was here widened, or, more properly, doubled. Considerable space was included between the outer and the inner wall, and to each of these walls there was a gate. It was in the room thus made that "David sat between the two gates."

283.—WATCHMAN—PORTER.

XVIII, 26. The watchman saw another man running: and the watchman called unto the porter.

1. Even strong walls and double gates would not of themselves secure a city from the enemy. Men were therefore employed to watch day and night on the top of the walls, and especially by the gates. It was thus that the messengers from the army were seen long before they reached the place where David anxiously sat. In like manner the watchman of Jezreel saw in the distance the company of Jehu driving furiously. 2 Kings ix, 17–20. So Isaiah in one of his sublime visions saw a watchman standing by his tower day and night. Isa. xxi, 5–12. A figurative use of the watchman and his work is beautifully made in Isa. lxii, 6; Ezek. xxxiii, 2, 6, 7; Hab. ii, 1.

2. It was the business of the porter to open and shut the gates at the proper time. In this case the porter, being in a convenient position below, could receive the intelligence from the watchman above and communicate the same to David. In 2 Kings vii, 10 this officer is called "the porter of the city." Porters are spoken of in connection with the rebuilding of the walls by Nehemiah. Neh. vii, 1. In Solomon's Temple there were four thousand of them, (1 Chron. xxiii, 5,) who were divided into courses, (2 Chron. viii, 14,) and had their posts assigned by lot. 1 Chron. xxvi, 13.

284.—THE CHAMBER OVER THE GATE.

XVIII, 33. The king was much moved, and went up to the chamber over the gate, and wept.

This chamber was a second story, which was built over the room referred to in the note on verse 24, and corresponded to it in size. It communicated with it by a stairway, and David retired there that he might have greater privacy in his grief. It was on the roof above this, which was a higher point of observation than the ordinary height of the wall, that the watchman stood when he saw the messengers coming. Verse 24.

285.—LAMENTATIONS OVER THE DEAD.

XIX, 4. The king covered his face, and the king cried with a loud voice, O my son Absalom! O Absalom, my son, my son!

Though concealed from sight in the upper chamber, the lamentations of the bereaved king could be easily heard by his followers, for he " cried with a loud voice." These loud exclamations are alluded to in several other places. At Jacob's funeral there was "a great and very sore lamentation." Gen. l, 10. When Jephthah, after his vow, saw his daughter coming, he cried, as if she were already dead, " Alas, my daughter!" Judges xi, 35. When the old prophet of Bethel buried in his own grave the disobedient prophet whom he had deceived to his death, he cried out, " Alas, my brother!" 1 Kings xiii, 30. It was among the curses heaped on Jehoiakim that he should have "the burial of an ass," and not be consigned to the grave with the usual lamentations. "Therefore thus saith the Lord concerning Jehoiakim the son of Josiah king of Judah; They shall not lament for him, saying, Ah my brother! or, Ah sister! they shall not lament for him, saying, Ah lord! or, Ah his glory!" Jer. xxii, 18. Somewhat similar to these are the cries of the Egyptian mourners at the present time. When the master of a house dies, the wives, children, and servants cry out, "O my master!" "O my camel!" "O my lion!" "O camel of the house!" "O my glory!" "O my resource!" "O my father!" "O my misfortune!" —LANE'S *Modern Egyptians*, vol. ii, p. 318.

Roberts, in his *Oriental Illustrations*, pp. 236–241, gives a number of striking specimens of Hindoo lamentations over the dead. Among them are the expressions of grief uttered by a husband on the loss of his wife: " What, the apple of my eye gone! my swan, my parrot, my deer, my Lechimy! Her color was like gold; her gait was like the stately swan; her waist was like lightning; her teeth were like pearls; her eyes like the kiyal-fish (oval); her eyebrows like the bow; and her countenance like the full-blown lotus. Yes, she has gone, the mother of my children! No more welcome, no more smiles in the evening when I return. All the world to me is now as the place of burning. Get ready the wood for *my* pile. O my wife, my wife! listen to the voice of your husband."

A father also says over the body of his son, " My son, my son! art thou gone? What! am I left in my old age? My lion, my arrow, my blood, my body, my soul, my third eye! Gone, gone, gone!"

286.—FERRY-BOATS.

XIX, 18. There went over a ferry-boat to carry over the king's household.

This is the only passage where a ferry-boat is named, and some critics think that a mere crossing of a ford is meant. The Hebrews could not have been ignorant of the use of boats, since they were employed by the Egyptians, as is evident from the monuments. The king's servants may have used rafts, or flat-bottomed boats, for conveying his household over the river. See, further, the note on Isaiah xviii, 2.

287.—CHERETHITES AND PELETHITES.

XX, 7. There went out after him Joab's men, and the Chere-thites, and the Pelethites, and all the mighty men.

Commentators and philologists are divided in the interpretation of these terms. Lakemacher was the first to advance the idea that the *Crethi* and the *Plethi* were Philistine soldiers whom David had enlisted in his army. This opinion was adopted by Ewald, and has since been agreed to by many eminent scholars and theologians, and is the view taken by Fuerst in his Hebrew Lexicon. On the other hand, others, equally eminent, contend that David would not have employed foreign soldiers as his body guard, as it is evident the *Crethi* and the *Plethi* were. Compare 2 Sam. xx, 23, with xxiii, 23. Some, however, attempt to meet this objection by supposing that they were Israelites who, from a lengthy residence in foreign parts, had attracted to themselves a foreign name. See FAIRBAIRN'S *Imp. Bib. Dict.*, s. v. *Cherethites.* Gesenius defines the *Crethi* to be executioners, and the *Plethi* runners or couriers; the duty of the former being to administer capital punishment, and of the latter to convey the king's orders wherever he chose to send them. Benaiah, who commanded them, (verse 23,) held an office similar to that of Potiphar under Pharaoh, (Gen. xxxvii, 36,) and Arioch under Nebuchadnezzar. Dan. ii, 14.

288.—TOUCHING THE BEARD.

XX, 9. Joab said to Amasa, Art thou in health, my brother? And Joab took Amasa by the beard with the right hand to kiss him.

To touch the beard of another was an insult, unless done as an act of friendship and a token of respect. Joab therefore showed the base treachery of his heart by coming to Amasa in the manner of a friend, thus entirely concealing his murderous intent. He inquired after his health, gently touched his beard as if to give a kiss, and then suddenly grasped it with his right hand and quickly stabbed the unsuspecting Amasa with the unnoticed sword which he held in his left.

289.—CIRCLING NETS.

XXII, 6. The sorrows of hell compassed me about; the snares of death prevented me.

The margin has "cords," instead of sorrows, which is a better rendering, because more consistent with the figure employed in the text. The allusion

10

is to an ancient mode of hunting, still in use. A certain tract of land, where wild beasts are known to be, is surrounded by a circle of nets, which is gradually contracted as the animals are driven in, until they are all brought to one common center, when escape is impossible. Similar reference is made in Psa. xviii, 5; cxvi, 3; Isa. li, 20. Representations of this mode of hunting are found on the Egyptian and Assyrian monuments.

I KINGS.

290.—THE PIPE.

I, 40. The people piped with pipes, and rejoiced with great joy.

The pipe was one of the most ancient, as it was one of the simplest, of instruments. It was originally merely a reed with holes perforated at certain distances, whence it derived its Hebrew name, *chalil: bored through*. As its use became more general it was made with greater care, and sometimes of other materials, such as brass, box-wood, horn, bone, or ivory. Sometimes a double pipe was used, one part being played with the right hand and the other with the left, and both uniting at the mouth-piece. The pipe was used for seasons of merriment or of joy. See 1 Sam. x, 5; Isa. v, 12; Luke vii, 32. It also served to enliven the journeys to the great feasts, (Isa. xxx, 29,) as music is now used in the East to entertain great companies of travelers. Sometimes, by reason of its soft wailing tones, it was used at funerals. Jer. xlviii, 36; Matt. ix, 23.

291.—THE ASYLUM.

I, 50. Adonijah feared because of Solomon, and arose, and went, and caught hold on the horns of the altar.

The right of asylum in sacred places was common to all nations, and though nowhere formally declared in the Mosaic law, it was clearly recognized, as is evident from Exod. xxi, 14, where it is directed to be refused under certain extreme circumstances. It would seem from the text, and also from chapter ii, 28, that if an accused person could take hold of the horns of the altar he was safe unless his crime were of a peculiarly glaring character. The "Cities of Refuge" were appointed for a similar purpose. See Numbers xxxv, 15–32.

292.—RARITY OF BURIAL IN CITIES.

II, 10. So David slept with his fathers, and was buried in the city of David.

This was a departure from the ordinary custom, as the dead were usually buried outside the cities. It was therefore a mark of high honor to the remains of the departed king that he was buried within the city; the strong-hold of Zion which was called after his name. Here, also, Solomon was afterward buried. 1 Kings xi, 43. Ahaz was likewise buried in the city, though not in the tomb of the kings. 2 Chron. xxviii, 27. Hezekiah, his son, was buried "in the chiefest of the sepulchers of the sons of David." 2 Chron. xxxii, 33. Manasseh, who succeeded him, and Amon, his son, were both buried in Jerusalem, in the garden of Uzza. 2 Kings xxi, 18, 26.

The sepulcher of David was known in apostolic times. Acts ii, 29. Its location is pointed out in the present day on the southern hill of Jerusalem, commonly called Mount Zion, under the Mosque of David. It is jealously guarded by Mohammedans from all intrusion. Dr. Barclay thinks that "the Tomb of David is several hundred yards east of the traditional locality." —*City of the Great King*, p. 215.

293.—FODDER.

IV, 28. **Barley also and straw for the horses and dromedaries.**

Barley was the usual fodder for cattle. They were also fed with a mixture of chopped straw, barley, beans, and pounded date kernels.

294.—RAFTS.

V, 9. **I will convey them by sea in floats unto the place that thou shalt appoint me.**

See also 2 Chron. ii, 16. These are what we call rafts, consisting of a number of planks fastened together and launched upon the water. The practice is an ancient one, and it is said that the earliest boats were nothing more than mere rafts made in this way, though there is another form of raft that is very ancient. See note on Isa. xviii, 2.

295.—SOLOMON'S TEMPLE.

VI, 2. **The house which king Solomon built for the Lord, the length thereof was threescore cubits, and the breadth thereof twenty cubits, and the height thereof thirty cubits.**

The idea of the temple did not originate with Solomon, but with David, who was not permitted to carry out his intention because he had been a man of war. 1 Chron. xxviii, 2, 3. God gave him a plan for the temple, as he had previously given Moses the plan for the tabernacle. This plan David communicated to Solomon, directing him to erect the building. 1 Chron. xxviii, 11–19.

It was built on Mount Moriah, on the site of the altar which David erected on the threshing floor of Araunah the Jebusite. 2 Sam. xxiv, 21–25; 2 Chron. iii, 1. It stood on the boundary line of Judah and Benjamin. According to Jewish authorities, the greater space of the courts was in Judah, but the temple and altar were in Benjamin. The hill being uneven, the top was leveled, and walls were built on the sloping sides up to a level with the summit, the intervening space being filled partly with vaults and partly with earth.

The temple had the same general arrangements as the tabernacle, being designed for the same purpose; the difference between the two structures being mainly such as would be suggested by the fact that the tabernacle was merely temporary and movable, while the temple was permanent and fixed. The dimensions of the temple were double those of the tabernacle. Like that, it faced the east, having the Most Holy Place in the west.

Its length (including the porch) was seventy cubits. Of this length the porch had ten cubits, the Holy Place forty, and the Most Holy Place twenty. 1 Kings vi, 3, 17, 20. The width of the building on the ground was twenty cubits, but to this there was added to the house proper a width of five cubits, for three stories of chambers which were built adjoining all the walls of the temple, excepting the porch. At the height of every five cubits the temple wall receded a cubit until half the height was reached; thus making each story of chambers a cubit wider than the one below it. 1 Kings vi, 5, 6, 10. The chambers on the west side must also have added five cubits to the length. The height of the building varied in different parts. The chambers were fifteen cubits high, the Most Holy Place twenty, the Holy Place thirty, and the porch one hundred and twenty. 1 Kings vi, 3, 20; 2 Chron. iii, 4. It is thought by some critics that this last measurement is an error in the copying of some ancient manuscript. Eighty has been suggested by some as the correct reading, and twenty by others.

In the porch were the two celebrated pillars called Jachin and Boaz. These were made of brass and highly ornamented. 1 Kings vii, 15–22. It is not definitely stated that they were placed in the porch as a support to that part of the building, but this would seem to be probable, though it is denied by some. Crossing the porch, which was ten cubits by twenty, we find folding doors of fir or cypress, having posts of olive wood. These doors were ornamented with carved cherubim, palm trees, and flowers, all of which were covered with gold. 1 Kings vi, 33–35. Within the doors was the Holy Place, forty cubits long, twenty wide, and thirty high. There were windows in this, probably of lattice work. 1 Kings vi, 4. These windows must have been in the upper part of the room, since the three stories of the chambers reached on the outside half way up the height. The stone walls were completely covered on the inside with wainscoting of cedar. The floor was made of cedar covered with cypress, which in turn was covered with gold. 1 Kings vi, 15, 30. The ceiling was cypress overlaid with gold. 2 Chron. iii, 5. The sides were elegantly carved with cherubim, palms, and flowers, covered over with gold. 1 Kings vi, 18; 2 Chron. iii, 7.

In the Holy Place there were ten golden candlesticks, five on each side, and ten tables of show-bread, arranged in a similar way. 2 Chron. iv, 7, 8. It is supposed by some that only one candlestick and one table were in use at a time. See 2 Chron. xiii, 11 ; xxix, 18 ; where the words are in the singular number. There we e snuffers, tongs, basins, and all other necessary articles, also of gold. 1 Kings vii, 50. The altar of incense, which was in this part of the temple, was made of cedar and covered with gold. 1 Kings vi, 20.

Between the Sanctuary, or Holy Place and the Oracle, or Most Holy Place, there was a partition, in which were double doors made of olive-wood carved and overlaid with gold. 1 Kings vi, 31, 32. There was also a rich vail of embroidery at this doorway. 2 Chron. iii, 14. The Oracle, like the Most Holy Place of the tabernacle, was a perfect cube. It was twenty cubits in length, breadth, and height. 1 Kings vi, 20. Floor, sides, and ceiling were of wood, with carved cherubim, palm-trees, and flowers, all overlaid with gold. 1 Kings vi, 29, 30. There were no windows here; Jehovah dwells in "thick darkness." 1 Kings viii, 12. Two gigantic cherubim, made of olive-wood and covered with gold, were in the Oracle. They were ten cubits high, and their outstretched wings, touching each other at the tips, reached entirely across the width of the room. 1 Kings vi, 23–28. They were in a standing position, and had their faces turned toward the vail. 2 Chron. iii, 10–13. The ark of the covenant, which had been in the tabernacle, was put into the Oracle under the wings of the cherubim after the temple was finished. 1 Kings viii, 6. No doubt the original cherubim and the mercy-seat accompanied it, though this is nowhere expressly stated. It may be inferred, however, from the fact that after the temple was built Jehovah is represented, as in the days of the tabernacle, "dwelling between the cherubim." Compare 1 Sam. iv, 4; 2 Sam. vi, 2; Psa. lxxx, 1; xcix, 1, with 2 Kings xix, 15 ; Isa. xxxvii, 16.

No definite account is given of the court or courts surrounding the temple. In 1 Kings vi, 36 the "inner court" is spoken of. This was doubtless the space immediately around the sacred edifice. Its dimensions are not given, nor is it certain what is meant by the text just referred to: "He built the inner court with three rows of hewed stone, and a row of cedar beams." Some commentators suppose this to mean that the inner court was surrounded by a wall consisting of three courses of stone capped with cedar beams. Others suppose that the inner court was a raised platform elevated to the height of three courses of stone with a coping of cedar, and they refer to Jer. xxxvi, 10, where this is called "the higher court."

This court, which was also called the "Court of the priests," (2 Chron. iv, 9,) contained the brazen altar of burnt offering, which was much larger than the one in the court of the tabernacle, being twenty cubits in length and in breadth, and ten in height. There was also here a circular "molten sea," ten cubits in diameter and five in height.   It stood on twelve brazen oxen, three facing each point of the compass.   On each side of the altar there were five brazen lavers. 2 Chron. iv, 1–6.

Around this court was another and a larger one, called the "Great Court," in 2 Chron. iv, 9; the "Outer Court," in Ezek. xlvi, 21; and the "Court of the Lord's House," in Jer. xix, 14; xxvi, 2.   This was the Court of the People, and was surrounded by strong walls, in which were gates of brass. 2 Chron. iv, 9.

The foregoing description of Solomon's temple coincides in the main with the accounts usually given by commentators.   It is proper, however, to notice the ingenious theory advanced by the Rev T. O. Paine, in his *Solomon's Temple*, already referred to in the note on Exod. xl, 2.   Mr. Paine has evidently studied the subject with much care, and has given the results of his investigations in an interesting monograph.   He assumes that the description given by Ezekiel in chapter xl, *et seq.*, is not the description of an ideal temple, but of Solomon's temple as it actually appeared before its destruction; and that it is designed to be a complement to the account given in the books of Kings and Chronicles, the one narrative detailing points omitted by the other.   He asserts that the building, contrary to the usual opinion, was wider at the top than at the bottom, and refers to Ezek. xli, 7 for proof; that the "chambers" mentioned as running around the building were galleries, and that these were supported by columns, the galleries increasing in distance from the temple-wall as they rose.   He contends that "all pictures of the temple which represent it as widest on the ground and narrower upward are bottom upward."—*Solomon's Temple*, p. 2.   (See the engravings on the opposite page.)

296.—THE MONTH ZIF.

VI, 37. In the fourth year was the foundation of the house of the Lord laid, in the month Zif.

This was the second month of the sacred year of the Hebrews, and corresponded nearly to our month of May.

297.—THE MONTH BUL.

˙VI, 38. In the eleventh year, in the month Bul, which is the eighth month, was the house finished.

This was the eighth month of the sacred year, and answered nearly to our November.

298.—SAWS.

VII, 9. All these were of costly stones, according to the measures of hewed stones, sawed with saws.

When the saw was invented is not known.   It is seen on the Egyptian monuments, and also on the Assyrian.   The saws referred to in the text

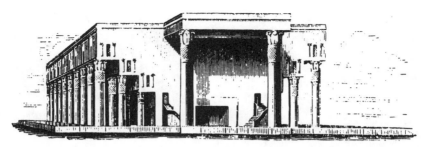

57.—FRONT VIEW.

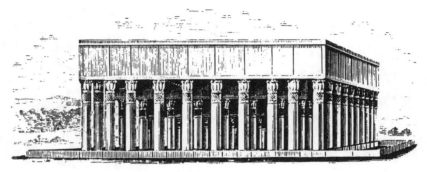

58.—WEST END.

59.—INTERIOR.

Solomon's Temple according to Paine.

were doubtless double-handed, since they were used for sawing stones. A striking peculiarity of the Oriental saw is that the teeth usually incline toward the handle instead of from it, as in the saws used among us.

299.—THE MONTH ETHANIM.

VIII, 2. **All the men of Israel assembled themselves unto king Solomon at the feast in the month Ethanim, which is the seventh month.**

Ethanim was the seventh month of the sacred year, and the first of the civil year, and corresponded nearly with our month of October. The great day of atonement and the feast of tabernacles took place during this month. It is to this feast that reference is made in the text.

300.—UPLIFTED HANDS IN PRAYER.

VIII, 22. **Solomon stood before the altar of the Lord in the presence of all the congregation of Israel, and spread forth his hands toward heaven.**

This was an ancient custom in prayer, not only among the Hebrews, but among the heathen. At the present day a favorite praying posture with Mohammedans is standing with hands uplifted. The allusions to it in classic writers are frequent, and so also are the references in Scripture. See Exod. ix, 29, 33 ; 2 Chron. vi, 12 ; Ezra ix, 5 ; Job xi, 13 ; Psa. xxviii, 2 ; xliv, 20 ; lxviii, 31 ; lxxxviii, 9 ; cxxxiv, 2 ; cxli, 2 ; cxliii, 6 ; Isa. i, 15.

301.—LARGE GOLDEN SHIELDS.

X, 16. **King Solomon made two hundred targets of beaten gold : six hundred shekels of gold went to one target.**

The "target" here is different from the one spoken of in 1 Sam. xvii, 6, where see the note. There it is *kidon*, a javelin ; here it is *tsinnah*, a large shield, for the description of which see note on 1 Sam. xvii, 7. These great golden shields of Solomon were probably made of wood, and covered with plates of gold instead of leather. See also 2 Chron. ix, 15.

302.—SMALL GOLDEN SHIELDS.

X, 17. **He made three hundred shields of beaten gold : three pounds of gold went to one shield.**

These shields were of a smaller size than those referred to in the sixteenth verse. The Hebrew *magen* is in some places rendered "buckler," (2 Sam. xxii, 31 ; 2 Chron. xxiii, 9,) and, on the other hand, buckler is sometimes the rendering of *tsinnah*. See note on 1 Sam. xvii, 7. While, however, the two words are thus interchanged by the translators, there was an essential difference in the size and weight of the two objects represented by them. The *tsinnah*, in verse 16, was for heavy troops, and was large enough to protect the entire person; while the *magen*, in this verse, was a shield which only protected a part of the person, could be carried on the arm, and was used by light troops. See also 2 Chron. ix, 16.

303.—SOLOMON'S THRONE.

X, 18. Moreover, the king made a great throne of ivory, and overlaid it with the best gold.

The body of the throne was probably of wood, entirely covered with ivory and gold, both being visible and relieving each other. Judging from the description given of this throne it must have been one of extraordinary magnificence. It had, by the two arms, lions such as are represented on the monumental pictures of ancient Egyptian and Assyrian thrones. Six steps reached to the platform on which it was placed, and on either side of each step was an image of a standing lion. Thus the upward passage to the throne was guarded by twelve lions, six on either side. Oriental monarchs have always been noted for the splendor of their thrones. Gold and precious stones of every kind, and wrought by the most elaborate workmanship into forms of rarest beauty, are described by travelers as dazzling the eye by the brilliancy of their appearance. We are told of thrones that are covered with diamonds, rubies, emeralds, and pearls, of almost fabulous size, and fashioned in the semblance of birds, beasts, trees, and vines with leaves and fruit. See also 2 Chron. ix, 17.

304.—ASHTORETH—MILCOM.

XI, 5. For Solomon went after Ashtoreth the goddess of the Zidonians, and after Milcom the abomination of the Ammonites.

1. Ashtoreth was the companion deity to Baal. See note on Num. xxii, 41. This text, verse 33 of this chapter, and 2 Kings xxiii, 13, are the only places where the word is used in the singular. In all other passages it is Ashtaroth, which is a term probably corresponding to Baalim, the plural of Baal. See note on Judges iii, 7. The two words are in several places coupled together. See Judges x, 6; 1 Sam. vii, 4; xii, 10. Ashtoreth, or Astarte, was a goddess of the Sidonians, and also of the Philistines. 1 Sam. xxxi, 10. Under different names she was worshiped in all the countries and colonies of the Syro-Arabian nations. As Baal is supposed to have represented the sun, so Astarte is thought to have represented the moon; though some take the two to stand for Jupiter and Venus. The worship of Astarte is very ancient, and was undoubtedly connected with impure rites. But little is known of the form of the goddess or of the mode of worship. She is sometimes seen represented with the head and horns of a cow, and sometimes with a woman's head having horns. We read in Gen. xiv, 5, of the city of Ashteroth Karnaim, that is, the horned Ashtaroth. As the city was

doubtless named because of the worship of Astarte, the word *Karnaim* (horns) is thought to have reference to the horns of the goddess, either lunar or bovine, or both. If "the queen of heaven" spoken of by Jeremiah was meant for Astarte, as many suppose, we have a little light thrown on the mode of her worship. "Seest thou not what they do in the cities of Judah and in the streets of Jerusalem? The children gather wood, and the fathers kindle the fire, and the women knead their dough, to make cakes to the queen of heaven, and to pour out drink-offerings unto other gods, that they may provoke me to anger." Jer. vii, 17, 18. See also Jer. xliv, 17–19. Here a whole family is represented as engaging in the worship of the goddess. They present to her meat-offerings and drink-offerings, and burn incense. The worship of Astarte is also referred to in Judges ii, 13; 1 Sam. vii, 3; xii, 10. . See likewise note on Isa. lxv, 11.

2. Milcom, also called Malcham, (Zeph. i, 5,) is another name for Molech. See note on Lev. xviii, 21.

305.—CRACKNELS.

XIV, 3. Take with thee ten loaves, and cracknels, and a cruse of honey, and go to him.

Cracknels (*nikkuddim*) were some sort of thin hard biscuit carried by the common people on their journeys. Their name (from *nakad*, to mark with points) may indicate thin punctured biscuits, or those which will easily crumble.

306.—A MONSTROUS IDOL.

XV, 13. Also Maachah his mother, even her he removed from being queen, because she had made an idol in a grove; and Asa destroyed her idol, and burnt it by the brook Kidron.

Miphletseth, here, and in the parallel passage in 2 Chron. xv, 16, rendered "idol," is defined by Fuerst, "horror, terror, monstrosity." From the mode of its destruction here noticed this image was evidently of wood. It is supposed to have been an obscene figure, the worship of which shows the demoralizing influence of idolatry. Such figures were often worshiped among the ancient idolaters, and are still worshiped in India.

307.—STICKS FOR FUEL.

XVII, 10. When he came to the gate of the city, behold, the widow woman was there gathering of sticks.

There seems to have been a scarcity of fuel in Palestine then as now. Twigs, branches, sticks of all kinds, and even thorns, (Psa. lviii, 9,) are carefully gathered for making fires, and the greatest economy is practiced in their use.

See note on Psa. lviii, 9, and also on Matt. vi, 30.

308.—THE MEAL JAR.

XVII, 12. She said, As the Lord thy God liveth, I have not a cake, but a handful of meal in a barrel.

The *kad* was not what we understand by a barrel, a wooden vessel with staves and hoops, but a vessel made of clay. The same word is translated "pitcher" in several other places. It is still common in the East to keep grain in earthen jars. The same sort of vessel which was used for meal by this widow was afterward used for water on the occasion of Elijah's sacrifice. 1 Kings xviii, 33.

309.—THE HABITS OF A HEATHEN GOD.

XVIII, 27. It came to pass at noon, that Elijah mocked them, and said, Cry aloud: for he is a god; either he is talking, or he is pursuing, or he is in a journey, or peradventure he sleepeth, and must be awaked.

Faber maintains the identity of Baal with the Hindoo deity Jagan Nath, the "lord of the universe," who is represented by his followers as sometimes wrapped in profound meditation, sometimes sleeping, and sometimes taking long journeys. He says, "Elijah is not simply ridiculing the worship of the idolatrous priests; he is not taunting them, as it were, at random; but he is ridiculing their senseless adoration, *upon their own acknowledged principles*."— *Origin of Pagan Idolatry*, vol. ii, p. 503.

310.—LACERATIONS IN IDOL–WORSHIP.

XVIII, 28. They cried aloud, and cut themselves after their manner with knives and lancets, till the blood gushed out upon them.

It was customary among the heathen to make lacerations in their flesh, not only as a mark of mourning for the dead, as shown in the note on Lev. xix, 28, but also as an act of idolatrous worship. This custom was not, however, of Egyptian origin, as were many of the customs practiced in Canaan. Wilkinson says that the Egyptians beat themselves at the close of their sacrifices, as is shown by paintings in the tombs. He also says that the custom of cutting was from Syria. The same practice is followed at the present day among idolaters of different nations. They cut their flesh in various ways until they are streaming with blood. They consider that this voluntary blood-shedding is meritorious, and will help to wash away their sins.

311.—HOUR OF EVENING SACRIFICE.

XVIII, 36. It came to pass at the time of the offering of the evening sacrifice that Elijah the prophet came near.

The precise time at which that sacrifice was offered is a matter of dispute. In Exod. xxix, 39, it is directed to be offered "at even;" literally, *between the two evenings.* On the meaning of this expression the controversy turns. Some suppose the first evening to have been at sunset, and the second at the time when the stars became visible. The two evenings must have been earlier than this in Elijah's time, since the events which took place after his sacrifice on this occasion required a longer period of daylight than can be found so late in the day. See 1 Kings xviii, 40–46. The tradition among the Jews is that the first evening was at the time the sun began to decline toward the west; that is, shortly after noon. The second evening was the time the sun set. The time of the evening sacrifice would thus be midway between noon and sunset, or from half past two to half past three o'clock. This was about the time of its offering in the days of Christ.

312.—THE SOUND OF RAIN.

XVIII, 41. Elijah said unto Ahab, Get thee up, eat and drink; for there is a sound of abundance of rain.

In India, according to Roberts, it is as common to say, *sound* of rain, as with us to say, appearance of rain. This expression sometimes refers to the thunder which precedes rain, and sometimes to a blowing noise in the clouds which shows the approach of rain.

313.—THE FACE BETWEEN THE KNEES.

XVIII, 42. He cast himself down upon the earth, and put his face between his knees.

This is not, as some commentators have thought, a posture obtained by kneeling on the ground and then bending the face over to the earth. It refers to a common Oriental position for meditation and devotion. The person sits with the feet drawn close to the body, thus bringing the knees nearly on a level with the chin. In Egypt there are many statues of men in this position. Specimens of these can be seen in museums of Egyptian antiquities; there are several such in the Abbott Collection in New York, and a number in the British Museum, one of which is made of black basalt. This was undoubtedly the posture of Elijah, who, in addition to sitting in this peculiar manner, inclined his head forward until his face was literally "between his knees." Dr. Shaw found this to be an occasional posture of the Turks and Moors in Barbary while engaged in their devotions. Rosenmüller tells of a Persian poet who was so lost in religious contemplation, with his head upon his knees, that he failed to hear the voice of a friend who accosted him.—*Morgenland,* vol. iii, p. 194. In India this posture is likewise common for those who are engaged in deep meditation or who are in great sorrow. Roberts gives several illustrations of it: "This morning, as I passed the garden of Chinnan, I saw him on the ground with his face between his knees. I wonder what plans he was forming! It must have been something very important to cause him thus to meditate." "Kandan is sick or in trouble, for he has got his face between his knees."—*Oriental Illustrations*, p. 205.

314.—GIRDLE—RUNNING FOOTMEN.

XVIII, 46. **He girded up his loins, and ran before Ahab to the entrance of Jezreel.**

1. The girdle is one of the most useful articles of Eastern costume, and frequently the most ornamental of them all. With the long loose dress of the Orientals it becomes a necessity, since it would be difficult to walk or run unless the dress were tightened. Hence Elijah "girded up his loins" as a preparation for running. See also 2 Kings iv, 29; ix, 1. Thus the Israelites prepared for their exodus. Exod. xii, 11. It is also thought to give strength to the body while engaged in severe bodily labor or exercise, and hence the word is sometimes used figuratively to denote strength. See Job xl, 7; Psa. lxv, 6; xciii, 1.

Girdles are of various sizes, and are made of different materials, from calico to cashmere. The rich use silk or linen, and sometimes decorate their girdles with gold, silver, and precious stones. The poor have them of coarser materials, leather being very commonly used. Elijah's girdle was of leather, (2 Kings i, 8;) so also was that of John the Baptist. Matt. iii, 4.

60.—RUNNING FOOTMEN. (See next page.)

Graham thus describes the mode of putting on the girdle. "The girdle is put on thus: your slave having folded it the right breadth, holds it at one end, while you take the other and lay it upon your side, and roll yourself round and round, as tight as possible, till you·arrive at the slave, who remains immovable.   If you have no slaves, a hook or the branch of a tree will answer the same purpose."—*The Jordan and the Rhine*, p. 163.   When running, the ends of the outer garment are tucked into the girdle.

2. It is still customary to do honor to a king by running before his chariot; and the same honor is conferred upon persons of less distinction. When Mohammed Ali came to Jaffa, some years ago, with a large army, to quell the rebellion in Palestine, he had his quarters inside the city, while the camp was on the sand-hills to the south.   The officers in their passage from camp to headquarters " were preceded by runners, who always kept just ahead of the horses, no matter how furiously they were ridden ; and in order to run with the greater ease, they not only girded their loins very tightly, but also tucked up their loose garments under the girdle, lest they should be incommoded by them."—THOMSON, *The Land and the Book*, vol. ii, p. 227.

Allusion is also made to this custom in 1 Sam. viii, 11; 2 Sam. xv, 1; 1 Kings i, 5.   (See the engraving on the opposite page.)

315.—DAY'S JOURNEY.

XIX, 4. But he himself went a day's journey into the wilderness.

This is a very ancient mode of estimating distances, and is still in use.   A " day's journey " varies, according to circumstances, from eighteen miles to thirty.   The ordinary day's journey of Scripture is probably not far from twenty miles.   See also Gen. xxx, 36; xxxi, 23; Exod. v, 3; viii, 27; Num. xi, 31; Deut. i, 2; 2 Kings iii, 9; Luke ii, 44.

The "Sabbath day's journey" was a less distance.   See note on Acts i, 12.

316.—COVERING THE FACE.

XIX, 13. It was so, when Elijah heard it, that he wrapped his face in his mantle, and went out, and stood in the entering in of the cave.

Covering the face was a sign of reverence in the presence of God.   Thus Moses, when the Lord appeared to him in the burning bush, "hid his face, for he was afraid to look upon God."   Exod. iii, 6.   So the seraphim seen by Isaiah in his temple-vision covered their faces with two of their wings. Isa. vi, 2.

317.—PLOWING.

XIX 19. So he departed thence, and found Elisha the son of Shaphat, who was plowing with twelve yoke of oxen before him, and he with the twelfth.

The Eastern plow is a rude affair, far inferior to the one in use in our country.   It does not enter deep into the soil, and is of very light and simple construction, sometimes being made merely of the trunk of a young tree having two branches running in opposite directions. There are many plows, however, not quite so primitive in structure as this. See note on Isa. ii, 4. Some of them have one handle and some have two handles, and they are usually drawn by two oxen. The plowmen often plow in company. Dr. Thomson says he has seen more than a dozen plows at work in the same field, each having its plowman and yoke of oxen, and all moving along in single file. Anderson makes a similar statement. We can thus see how Elijah "was plowing with twelve yoke of oxen before him." He had not, as some have imagined, twenty-four oxen yoked to a single plow, but there were twelve plows in a file, each having its own oxen and plowman, and he was "with the twelfth;" that is, he had charge of the last plow in the file.

318.—MILITARY GIRDLES.

XX, 11. Let not him that girdeth on his harness boast himself as he that putteth it off.

The girdle is used as a convenient place for carrying different weapons. The sword, the dagger, and in modern times the pistol, are placed there.

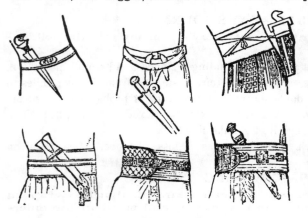

It was thus that Ehud carried his dagger. Judges iii, 16. We are told in 1 Sam. xxv, 13, that David and his men girded on their swords. Similar allusions to this use of the girdle are made in Deut. i, 41; Psa. xlv, 3; Sol. Song iii, 8; Isa. viii, 9.

The military girdle was not, however, a mere sword-sash, but

61.—ANCIENT MILITARY GIRDLES.

a strong belt, designed to sustain the body, and at the same time to cover such portion of the abdomen as might be unprotected by the cuirass. Some girdles, indeed, seem to have been a constituent part of the cuirass, intended to fasten it more firmly. The importance of the girdle as a piece of armor is seen in the fact that thorough preparation for the fight is called "girding on." Paul says: "Stand therefore, having your loins girt about with truth." Eph. vi, 14.

Military girdles were made of stronger materials than those designed for common purposes. Leather, iron, and bronze were used in their construction, and, where rich ornament was required, silver and gold.

319.—PAVILIONS.

XX, 16. But Ben-hadad was drinking himself drunk in the pavilions, he and the kings, the thirty and two kings that helped him.

It is not necessary to associate any idea of splendor with these "pavilions." They were merely booths, (*succoth,*) as the word is rendered in Gen. xxxiii, 17; Job xxvii, 18; Jonah iv, 5. In Isaiah i, 8, the same word is translated "lodge;" in Amos ix, 11 it is "tabernacle." Such "pavilions" were nothing but temporary structures of boughs erected to keep off the heat, and even kings were not ashamed to make use of them. It is said that such are still erected for Turkish pashas while on warlike expeditions.

320.—GODS FOR HILLS AND VALLEYS.

XX, 28. The Syrians have said, The Lord is God of the hills, but he is not God of the valleys.

There seems to be an allusion here to the opinion, prevalent among all heathen nations, that the different parts of the earth had different divinities. They had gods for the woods, for the mountains, for the seas, for the heavens, and for the lower regions. The Syrians seem to have received the impression that Jehovah was specially the God of the mountains; but he manifested to them that he ruled every-where.

321.—TOKEN OF ABASEMENT.

XX, 32. So they girded sackcloth on their loins, and put ropes on their heads, and came to the king of Israel.

This was a sign of deep abasement and submission. It was a Persian custom for persons desiring clemency from the sovereign to approach him with a sword suspended from the neck. The same practice has also been noticed in Egypt. Harmer suggests that these servants of Ben-hadad appear before Ahab with ropes around their necks from which their swords hung. Others suppose that these ropes were halters.

322.—SALE OF PATRIMONY.

XXI, 3. Naboth said to Ahab, The Lord forbid it me, that I should give the inheritance of my fathers unto thee.

The law of Moses would not permit the sale of one's patrimony, except in cases of extreme destitution. See Lev. xxv, 23, 25; Num. xxxvi, 7. Roberts gives an interesting description of an Eastern garden, and speaks of the high value placed on it by its owner, who has inherited it from his ancestors, and whose dearest associations in life are connected with it. "To part with such a place is, to the people of the East, like parting with life itself."— *Oriental Illustrations*, p. 208.

323.—SEALS.

XXI, 8. So she wrote letters in Ahab's name, and sealed them with his seal.

The seal is, in the East, of more importance than the signature, and indeed is often used in place of a signature. No document is of any validity without it. The ordinary mode of using it is to cover it with ink, and press it on the paper. The seal is often connected with a ring, and worn on the finger. See note on Gen. xli, 42.

Ancient seals have been found of various shapes—cylindrical. square, pyramidal, oval, and round. A very common style of seal among the ancient Egyptians was one made of stone, rounded on one side and flat on

62.—EGYPTIAN SIGNET RINGS.

the other. The inscription for the seal was on the flat surface, and the convex surface was skillfully wrought into the form of a scarabæus or beetle.

Since the beetle was worshiped by the Egyptians, whose example was followed by the Phenicians, after whose deities Ahab had gone, some have thought that Ahab's seal was of this description.

Seals that were not set in rings were perforated with a hole through which a string passed, by means of which the seal was suspended from the neck. It is supposed that Judah's was worn in this way. Gen. xxxviii, 18. Many ancient seals were in shape of a cylinder, and some of these were set in a frame which enabled the seal to revolve as the impression was made. Some beautiful specimens of this kind of seal have been found among the ruins in Chaldea and Assyria.

The figures engraved on seals were various. Modern Oriental seals have usually the name of the owner on them, and often a sentence from the Koran. The ancient seals had devices of symbolical meaning, and letters either hieroglyphic or cuneiform.

63.—SEAL, WITH FRAME.

Seals are made of brass, silver, gold, pottery, and stone, either precious or common, set in metal. The art of engraving stones is very ancient. See Exod. xxviii, 11, 36; xxxix, 6.

See also note on Neh. vi, 5, and on Job xxxviii, 14.

II KINGS.

324.—THE FLY-GOD.

I, 2. He sent messengers, and said unto them, Go, inquire of Baal-zebub the god of Ekron whether I shall recover of this disease.

Baal-zebub is, literally, "the fly-god;" but whether this name was given in honor or in contempt is not known. It may have been at first a name of contempt, which afterward, by general use, lost its original significance. Some suppose this god to have been one of the medical idols of the Philistines, receiving its title from its imaginary influence over pestiferous insects which are said to infest Philistia. In Taylor's Calmet there is a curious picture of an antique paste representing a head of Jupiter, and having the appearance of a huge fly.

Gale says: "The Phenicians styled their principal god Baal Samen, 'the lord of heaven,' (in the Phenician language.) The Jews called him Baal-zebub, 'lord of a fly.' Scaliger supposes that the original name was Baal-zebahim, 'lord of sacrifices,' contracted, by way of contempt, to Baal-zebub, 'lord of flies;' *i. e.*, he could not keep flies away from his sacrifices." — *Court of the Gentiles,* book ii, c. vii, p. 80.

64.—THE FLY-GOD.

It is thought that Beelzebul is a contemptuous designation of this Philistine Baal, he by it being called *dung-god.* See Matt. x, 25; xii, 24; Mark iii, 22; Luke xi, 15, 18, 19, where, according to the best authorities, Beelzebub should read Beelzebul. The Jews, being fond of playing upon words, may have intentionally altered the name of this god. Some, however, define Beelzebul to mean "the lord of the dwelling," and deny any connection between Beelzebul of the New Testament and Baalzebub of the Old.

325.—THE DIVAN.

I, 4. Thou shalt not come down from that bed on which thou art gone up, but shalt surely die.

The royal bed was probably made, as beds are now in the houses of wealthy Orientals, on the *divan*, which is a platform about three to four feet in width, extending sometimes across one end of the room and sometimes around three sides. It is used as a sofa by day, and as a sleeping-place at

65.—MODERN SYRIAN HOUSE—INTERIOR, SHOWING THE DIVAN.

night. It is usually elevated from six inches to a foot from the floor, though Professor Hackett found one instance at least in which the height of the *divan* was such that it was necessary to mount to it by two or three steps. In the palace of a king it would probably be higher than in ordinary dwellings, and thus Ahaziah literally went "up" to his bed. In like manner David speaks of going "up" into his bed. Psa. cxxxii, 3.

326.—SCHOOLS OF THE PROPHETS.

II, 3. And the sons of the prophets that were at Bethel came forth to Elisha.

The disciples of the prophets were called sons, as teachers are sometimes called fathers. 2 Kings ii, 12; vi, 21. These "sons of the prophets" formed a peculiar order, whose mission seems to have been to assist the prophets in their duties, and in time to succeed them. They were not a monastic order, as some suppose, nor were they merely theological students, though they probably studied the law and the history of God's people, together with sacred poetry and music.

The "schools of the prophets" in which these "sons" were trained are supposed to have been founded by the prophet Samuel, though their origin and history are involved in obscurity. They were located not only in Bethel, as appears from the text, but also in Rama, (1 Sam. xix, 19, 20,) in Jericho, (2 Kings ii, 5,) in Gilgal, (2 Kings iv, 38,) and probably in other places. See 1 Sam. x, 5, 10, and 2 Kings vi, 1. Their members were numerous; a hundred are spoken of in Gilgal, (2 Kings iv, 43,) and at least fifty in Jericho. 2 Kings ii, 7.

Some of "the sons of the prophets" were married, and probably lived in houses of their own. 2 Kings iv, 1, 2. Others were unmarried and occupied a building in common, (2 Kings vi, 1, 2,) and ate at a common table. 2 Kings iv, 38.

How long the "schools of the prophets" lasted is not definitely known. They seem to have flourished most in the time of Samuel, Elijah, and Elisha. Fifty years after Elisha's death Amos prophesied; and, according to his statement, he had no training in a prophetic school, though it does not follow that none existed in his day. See Amos vii, 14.

An extended account of these schools may be found in *Keil's Commentary* on 1 Sam. xix, 18–24.

327.—THE CRUSE.

II, 20. He said, Bring me a new cruse, and put salt therein. And they brought it to him.

Tselochith, here translated "cruse," is rendered "dish" in 2 Kings xxi, 13; "pan," in 2 Chron. xxxv, 13; and "bosom," in Prov. xix, 24; xxvi, 15. It is supposed to have been a flat metal dish.

328.—BALDNESS.

II, 23. There came forth little children out of the city, and mocked him, and said unto him, Go up, thou bald head; go up, thou bald head.

In India the expression "bald-head" has no special reference to a lack of hair, but is often applied to men who have an abundance. It is rather a term of contempt, intended to signify a mean and worthless fellow.

The Hebrews valued a good head of hair, and greatly deprecated baldness. See Isa. xv, 2, and note.

399.—WASHING HANDS.

III, 11. Here is Elisha the son of Shaphat, which poured water on the hands of Elijah.

As no knives or forks are used in the East, it is absolutely necessary to have a plentiful supply of water for the hands at the close of every meal.

For this a pitcher and basin are provided. The hands are held over the basin while a servant pours water from the pitcher. The basin has a

double bottom, the upper part of which is full of holes, through which the water as soon as used passes out of sight into the lower part. From the center of the bottom there rises a small projection which is used as a receptacle for the soap. The expression in the text, "poured water on the hands," is intended to show that Elisha performed the work

66.—MODE OF WASHING HANDS.

·of a servant for Elijah. He was Elijah's assistant as well as his disciple.

330.—HUMAN SACRIFICES.

III, 27. Then he took his eldest son, that should have reigned in his stead, and offered him for a burnt offering upon the wall.

The offering of human sacrifices is a very ancient custom, and was practiced at different times among many nations. Burder, in an elaborate note, (*Oriental Literature*, No. 570,) gives a long list of nations who offered human sacrifices. Among these are the Ethiopians, the Phenicians, the Scythians, the Egyptians, the Chinese, the Persians, the Indians, the Gauls, the Goths, the Carthaginians, the Britons, the Arabians, and the Romans. These sacrifices were offered in various ways. Some were slaughtered by the knife; some were drowned; some were burned; some were buried alive. In some instances, as in the case recorded in the text, parents sacrificed their own offspring. The idolatrous Israelites followed the example of their Phenician neighbors in this respect. See Jer. xix, 5. Allusion is made to this custom in Micah vi, 7.

A few years since an inscription was discovered in Behistun, which, according to the rendering of Professor Grotefend of Hanover, contained an offer of Nebuchadnezzar to let his son be burned to death in order to ward off the affliction of Babylon.—SAVILE'S *Truth of the Bible*, p. 281.

331.—RIGHTS OF CREDITORS.

IV, 1. The creditor is come to take unto him my two sons to be bondmen.

The Mosaic law gave the creditor the right to claim the person and children of the debtor who could not pay that they, might serve him until the year of Jubilee, when they again became free. See Lev. xxv, 39-41. Reference is made to this custom in Neh. v, 5, 8; Job xxiv, 9; Isa. l, 1.

There was a similar, though severer, law among other nations, who are supposed to have derived the idea from the Hebrews. See Matt. xviii, 25.

332.—VESSEL FOR OIL.

IV, 2. She said, Thine handmaid hath not any thing in the house, save a pot of oil.

Asuk, pot, is supposed to have been an earthen jar, deep and narrow, with a pointed bottom which was inserted into a stand of wood or stone, or stuck into the ground like the Roman and Egyptian *amphora*. Phillott (SMITH'S *Dictionary of the Bible*, s. v. POT) thinks that the *asuk* had no handles, while the *amphora* had a handle on each side. *Amphoræ* were used for containing or carrying oil, wine, or water. Though usually of earthenware, they were sometimes made of metal. The "pitcher" referred to in Mark xiv, 13, and in Luke xxii, 10, is supposed to have been an *amphora*.

67.—AMPHORÆ.

333.—ALIYAH—STOOL.

IV, 10. Let us make a little chamber, I pray thee, on the wall; and let us set for him there a bed, and a table, and a stool, and a candlestick.

1. The *aliyah*. "chamber," is an upper room of an Eastern house, being sometimes built on the roof, and sometimes making a second story to the porch, to which it has access by stairs. It is hence called in 2 Sam. xviii, 33, "the chamber over the gate." See note on that text. In the text it is called a chamber "in the wall," probably because its window, opening to the street, made a break in the dead wall, and was thus about the only evidence to an outside spectator of the existence of rooms in the house. It is usually well furnished, and kept as a room for the entertainment of honored guests. Thus the Shunammite entertained Elisha, as related in the text. It was in such a room that Elijah dwelt in Zarephath at the house of the widow. 1 Kings xvii, 19, 23. In the first of these two verses we have the word "loft" as a translation of the word *aliyah*, thus conveying to

many minds the idea of a bare, desolate garret, which is very far from the fact. Further than this, Dr. Thomson states that the poorer kind of houses have no *aliyah*, which leads him to the conclusion "that this widow woman was not originally among the very poorest classes, but that her extreme destitution was owing to the dreadful famine which then prevailed."—*The Land and the Book*, vol. i, p. 285.

Such a room makes a desirable place of retirement for the master of the house. Ahaziah was in an *aliyah*, in his palace of Samaria, when he fell through the lattice-work of the window and injured himself. 2 Kings i, 2. Eglon, King of Moab, was in a room of this description when he was assassinated by Ehud. Judges iii, 20. *Aliyah* is in this text rendered "summer parlor;" the marginal reading is "a parlor of cooling." Doubtless the latticed windows were so arranged as to keep the room as cool and comfortable as possible.

It was on the roof of an *aliyah* in the palace of Ahaz that the kings of Judah had erected altars for idolatrous worship. 2 Kings xxiii, 12. It was in an *aliyah* where, in the midst of idolaters, Daniel prayed three times daily to the one true God. Dan. vi, 10. *Aliyoth* are also referred to in Jer. xxii, 13, 14, and in Psa. civ, 3, 13, where the word is most beautifully used in a figurative sense.

In the New Testament the *aliyah* is referred to under the name of "upper room," (ὑπερῷον, which is the Septuagint rendering of *aliyah*.) It was in such a place that the disciples gathered immediately after the ascension of the Saviour. Acts i, 13. In a room of this kind the corpse of Tabitha or Dorcas was placed   Here the widows whom she had helped wept over her, and here Peter restored her to life. Acts ix, 37, 39. In a similar place, in the city of Troas, Paul once preached until midnight. Acts xx, 7, 8.

It is also supposed by some commentators that the "upper room" where Jesus ate the passover with his disciples was a room of this description. Mark xiv, 15; Luke xxii, 12. Others, however, deny this, since ὑπερῷον is not the word used to denote the room. See note on Mark xiv, 15.

2. "Stool." here, like "loft" in 1 Kings xvii, 19, seems to indicate something very rude; but in reality the original word (*kisse*) is the very word that is used in some other passages to designate a throne. The seat for the prophet was probably the very best that could be procured.

334.—LADIES RIDING.

IV, 22. **She called unto her husband, and said, Send me, I pray thee, one of the young men, and one of the asses, that I may run to the man of God, and come again.**

Ladies of the higher class in the East seldom walk, but almost always ride on asses, which are there more frequently used for riding than with us. The rider is attended by a servant who runs behind, and, with a whip or stick, drives or goads the animal forward at whatever pace may be desired. Solomon is thought to refer to this custom in Eccles. x, 5–7.

335.—TIMES OF PUBLIC INSTRUCTION.

IV, 23. **He said, Wherefore wilt thou go to him to day? it is neither new moon, nor sabbath.**

The prophets were probably accustomed at the new moon and on the Sabbath-day to assemble the people for instruction and edification. The question of the husband of the Shunammite woman appears, therefore, to express his astonishment that she should go to the prophet at a time which was neither new moon nor Sabbath. The prophet Amos represents the greedy, sordid men of his day as saying, "When will the new moon be gone, that we may sell corn? and the Sabbath, that we may set forth wheat?" Amos viii, 5. They preferred their worldly business to the keeping of sacred days, or listening to the instructions of the men of God.

336.—FORMAL SALUTATION.

IV, 26. **Run now, I pray thee, to meet her, and say unto her, Is it well with thee? Is it well with thy husband? Is it well with the child? And she answered, It is well.**

These are merely the customary formal salutations which are so profusely used by Orientals. Dr. Thomson says, "If you ask after a person whom you know to be sick, the reply at first will invariably be *well, thank God*, even when the next sentence is to inform you that he is dying."—*The Land and the Book*, vol. ii, p. 177. The expression is also used without any reference to the state of one's health; as in verse 23, when the husband expressed his surprise at his wife's going to see the prophet at that time, her only answer was, "Well." The salutation is the same in form as that of "Peace," so often spoken of in the Bible. See note on John xx, 19.

337.—RIMMON—ETIQUETTE.

V, 18. **When my master goeth into the house of Rimmon to worship there, and he leaneth on my hand.**

1. Rimmon is supposed to have been a prominent deity of the Syrians. Traces of the name are found in Tabrimon, the father of Benhadad, king of Syria, (1 Kings xv, 18,) and perhaps in Hadadrimmon. Zech. xii, 11. Nothing definite is known of this deity or of the nature of his worship, and the derivation of the word is uncertain. Some suppose it to be the application to a deity of the word *rimmon*, a pomegranate. Stollberg in his *History of Religion*, (cited by Rosenmüller, *Morgenland*, vol. iii, p. 231,) says that the Orientals consider apples as symbols of the sun, and on this account certain

court servants of the king of Persia carried a staff with a golden apple on the point. Others derive the word from *ramam*, to be high, or lifted up. This again would point to the sun; and it is highly probable that the worship of Rimmon had some connection with that adoration of the sun so common among the heathen nations of the East.

2. It was probably a part of the court etiquette that the king should lean on the arm of one of his chief officers. The king of Israel had this custom as well as the king of Syria. 2 Kings vii, 2, 17. The Jews have a tradition that two young women waited on Esther when she was queen of Persia, one to hold up her train, and the other for her to lean upon.

338.—THE CAB.

VI, 25. The fourth part of a cab of dove's dung for five pieces of silver.

The cab was a dry measure holding nearly two quarts.

339.—MARKET AT THE GATE.

VII, 1. To-morrow about this time shall a measure of fine flour be sold for a shekel, and two measures of barley for a shekel, in the gate of Samaria.

The vicinity of the gate was a convenient place for the sale of produce, since what was for sale would be exposed to the view of all passing in or out. Reference is made to this in Neh. xiii, 20, 21. Layard, speaking of the vaulted recesses in the gateways of Assyrian cities, says, " Frequently in the gates of cities, as at Mosul, these recesses are used as shops for the sale of wheat and barley, bread and grocery."—*Nineveh and Babylon*, p. 57, (note.)

340.—OSTENTATION IN MAKING PRESENTS.

VIII, 9. So Hazael went to meet him, and took a present with him, even of every good thing of Damascus, forty camels' burden, and came and stood before him.

There is no reason to suppose, as some commentators have done, that these camels were loaded with all that they could carry " of every good thing of Damascus." It was merely the Oriental desire for display which sent the forty camels. No doubt the royal present was really valuable, but the different articles of which it was composed were probably so distributed that each camel had but a small portion, and thus a caravan was brought into use. Maillet (cited by Harmer, vol. ii, p. 313) says, speaking of bridal presents, "Through ostentation, they never fail to load upon four or five horses what might easily be carried by one; in like manner, as to the jewels, trinkets, and other things of value, they place in fifteen dishes what a single plate would very well hold."

Probably the present which the children of Israel sent to Eglon, king of Moab, was accompanied with a similar parade. It is said of Ehud that " when he had made an end to offer the present, he sent away the people that bare the present." Judges iii, 18. This indicates that a number of persons were called into requisition to convey the gift. It is said to be a custom in Persia, when a present is brought to the king, not to permit any person to carry more than one article, no matter how small it may be.

341.—OIL VESSEL.

IX, 1. **Gird up thy loins, and take this box of oil in thine hand, and go to Ramoth-gilead.**

We have no account of the material or shape of the *pak*, which is here called " box," and in 1 Sam. x, 1, " vial." Gesenius derives it from *pakah*, " to drop." This would seem to indicate a flask with a narrow mouth, from which oil or perfumery might be dropped. Such flasks have been found among Egyptian and Assyrian remains.

342.—EYE PAINTING.

IX, 80. **When Jehu was come to Jezreel, Jezebel heard of it; and she painted her face, and tired her head, and looked out at a window.**

This is literally, " put her eyes in paint," and alludes to the very ancient custom, still observed in the East, of coloring the eyes with a black powder called *kohl*. Graham says: " It is probable that stibium or antimony was formerly used for this purpose, and in some places it may be so used still, especially for painting the edges of the eyelids. Kohl, the substance now in general use for blackening the eyes and the eyebrows, is produced by burning *liban*, a kind of frankincense, and by burning the shells of almonds This kind is merely ornamental; but the kohl, formed from the powder of the ore of lead, is used as much for its supposed medicinal as its beautifying properties. The arch of the eyebrow is much darkened and elongated, and the edges of the eyelids, both above and below, tinged with the dark hues of the kohl, which is supposed to add to the natural beauty of the counte-nance by the effects of contrast."—*The Jordan and the Rhine*, p. 190.

In Jer. iv, 30 reference is made to this practice: "Though thou rentest thy face with painting." The marginal reading is *eyes*, instead of "face," and the allusion is to the effect of the powder on the eye. Being astringent, it contracts the eyelids, and by con-trast of color makes the white of the eye look larger, thus "rending" or widening the eye. Prov. vi, 25, is also supposed to allude to this custom; and there is a reference to it in Ezek. xxiii, 40. Some think the

68.—Two Styles of Eye Painting.

practice was common as far back as the days of Job, from the fact that one of his daughters was called Keren-happuch, that is, *paint-horn.* Job xlii, 14.

The powder is kept in glass vessels, and was anciently kept in boxes of wood, stone, or pottery of various shapes; some of them highly ornamented, and having from two to five different compartments. Several of these curious boxes, brought from Egypt, and very ancient, are now in the Abbott Collection, New York.

The kohl is applied to the eyelids by a small piece of wood, ivory, or silver, made for the purpose, and in shape not unlike a bodkin. This is

69.—KOHL BOXES AND IMPLEMENTS.

moistened in rose-water and dipped into the black powder and then drawn under the eyelids.

343.—ENEMIES BEHEADED.

X, 8. There came a messenger, and told him, saying, They have brought the heads of the king's sons. And he said, Lay ye them in two heaps at the entering in of the gate until the morning.

Beheading enemies is a very ancient custom. Thus David cut off the head of Goliath and carried it to Saul. 1 Sam. xvii, 51, 57. So also the Philistines cut off the head of Saul. 1 Sam. xxxi, 9. Layard found at Nineveh representations of scenes which well illustrate the text. Heads of slain enemies are collected and brought to the king, or to the officer appointed to take account of their number. Morier, in his narrative of his second journey through Persia, states that prisoners have been known to be put to death in cold blood in order to increase the number of heads of the slain which are deposited in heaps at the palace gate. Many such heaps of heads are piled up in Persia. Sir William Ousely, who was in Persia in the early part of this century, saw the remains of some of these heaps on which the skulls seemed to be stuck together in a mass of clay or mortar. Similar accounts are given by later travelers.

344.—PRIESTLY ROBES.

X, 22. He said unto him that was over the vestry, Bring forth vestments for all the worshipers of Baal. And he brought them forth vestments.

Like the priests of almost all nations, the priests of Baal had their particular sacred robes which they used only while officiating. They were made probably of white byssus, and were kept in a particular wardrobe of the temple under the care of some person appointed for the purpose.

345.—STORAGE FOR BEDS.

XI, 2. **They hid him, even him and his nurse, in the bed-chamber.**

Literally, *in the chamber of beds*, which was a room, not for sleeping, but for storing beds, whence they could be brought out when needed for use. Their place of concealment was thus less likely to be discovered than if they had been hidden in a mere sleeping-room. See also 2 Chron. xxii, 11.

346.—CORONATION CEREMONIES.

XI, 12. **He brought forth the king's son, and put the crown upon him, and gave him the testimony; and they made him king, and anointed him; and they clapped their hands, and said, God save the king.**

We have here noted the most important ceremonies connected with the coronation of a Hebrew king. See also 2 Chron. xxiii, 11.

1. The crown was put upon him. We have no definite knowledge of the shape of the crowns which were worn by the Hebrew kings. The original word used here is the same that is used to denote the diadem of the high priest, which was a plate of gold tied around the head with a ribbon. Exod. xxxix, 30, 31. Doubtless there were other forms of crowns, as other words are used in various passages.

2. They gave him the "testimony." That is, they made to him a formal presentation of a manuscript roll of the Divine law, as an indication that this was to be his guide in administering the government.

3. They anointed him. This was not done in every case of coronation, and from the expression "they made him king," which precedes the statement of his anointing, it has been inferred that the essential parts of the coronation ceremony were those connected with the crown and the "testimony;" the anointing of the founder of a dynasty being considered all that was necessary so long as the succession was unbroken in his family. Saul was thus anointed, (1 Sam. x, 1,) and so also was David. 2 Sam. ii, 4. Solomon was likewise anointed, (1 Kings i, 39,) because there was a probability that his right to the throne would be disputed; and Joash, in the text, was anointed for the same reason. Anointing was a ceremony connected with coronation before the Jews ever had a king, as is evident from Judges ix, 8, 15. It was by Divine command that the people of God adopted it. See 1 Sam. ix, 16; x, 1; 1 Kings i, 34, 39. From this circumstance the king was called "the Lord's anointed." See 1 Sam. xii, 3, 5; 2 Sam. i, 14, 16; Psa. ii, 2; Hab. iii, 13, etc.

4. The people then clapped their hands and shouted, "Live the king." This was their part of the ceremony, and denoted their approbation of the newly crowned sovereign. Mr. Harmer (*Observations*, vol. ii, p. 433) calls attention to the fact that the Hebrew text in this place, and in Psa. xlvii, 1, and Isa. lv, 12, has *hand* instead of *hands*, as our translators have it. He suggests that a different sort of clapping may have been meant by this than what is ordinarily understood by clapping hands, where one hand is forcibly struck upon another, though that is practiced in the East. He refers to an Oriental custom of striking the fingers of one hand gently and rapidly upon the lips as a token of joy, and supposes that the expression clap the *hand*, in distinction from clap the *hands*, refers to some similar custom observed by the Hebrews.

347.---THE KING'S PLACE.

XI, 14. The king stood by a pillar as the manner was.

This "pillar" was some prominent place which the king was in the habit of occupying in the temple. It is also referred to in 2 Kings xxiii, 3. It is said in 2 Chron. xxxiv, 31, that king Josiah "stood in his *place*." The same word is there used that is here rendered "pillar." It is supposed to have been an elevated stand or platform, and some commentators think it identical with the brazen scaffold which Solomon built in the center of the temple court. See 2 Chron. vi, 13; xxiii, 13.

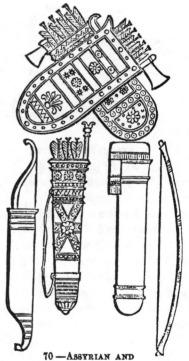

70—ASSYRIAN AND EGYPTIAN QUIVERS AND BOWS.

348.—BOW AND ARROWS.

XIII, 15. Elisha said unto him, Take bow and arrows. And he took unto him bow and arrows.

1. The bow is a very ancient weapon, and early mention is made of it in the Bible. Ishmael became an archer. Gen. xxi, 20. Isaac sent Esau to get venison by means of the bow. Gen. xxvii, 3. It also came into early use as a weapon of war. Gen. xlviii, 22. Bows were made of various materials: wood, horn, and even ivory, were used. Sometimes the wood and horn were united in the bow, the wood being backed with horn. Metallic bows were

also used. See Job xx, 24 ; Psa. xviii, 34. Bows were of various shapes. The Egyptian bow—a round piece of wood from five feet to five and a half long—was either nearly straight, with a slight curve at each end, or else showed a deep curve in the center when unstrung.

Assyrian bows were sometimes curved and sometimes angular. They were shorter than the Egyptian bows. The strings of ancient bows were of leather thongs, horse hair, hide, or catgut. Various modes were adopted for bending the bow, the hand, the knee, or the foot being used. It was probably most usually bent by the aid of the foot, since *darak*, the word commonly used in speaking of bending the bow, literally means to "tread."

2. The arrows were made of reed or wood and tipped with metal or horn. They were sometimes feathered, though not always. From Psa. xxxviii, 2, we infer that they sometimes had barbed points.

349.—MODE OF DECLARING WAR.

XIII, 17. He said, Open the window eastward. And he opened it. Then Elisha said, Shoot. And he shot.

This was an ancient method of declaring war, and is often referred to in ancient and classical writings. A herald came to the confines of the enemy's territory, and, after observing certain solemnities, cried with a loud voice, "I wage war against you," at the same time assigning the reasons for the war. He then shot an arrow or threw a spear into the country to be invaded, which was considered sufficient warning of warlike intentions. Thirty days were allowed for peaceable settlement; if no such settlement was reached during that time, hostilities began at the expiration of it.

350.—HEBREW MODE OF BURIAL.

XIII, 21. It came to pass, as they were burying a man, that, behold, they spied a band of men ; and they cast the man into the sepulcher of Elisha : and when the man was let down, and touched the bones of Elisha, he revived, and stood up on his feet.

To understand this text fully, it is necessary to remember that among the Israelites the dead were not buried in coffins as with us. The Egyptians sometimes used coffins, (see note on Gen. l, 26 ;) but the Israelites, who brought many Egyptian customs with them into Palestine, did not adopt this custom. They wrapped their dead in linen cloths and laid them in the tomb. See note on John xix, 40. Thus the man mentioned in the text was about to be buried when his friends saw the Moabites. Seeing that they could not reach the grave prepared for him without being perceived by the enemy, they quickly rolled away the stone from Elisha's sepulcher, near which they were, and put the corpse there. As there was no coffin for either body, the body of the newly dead could easily touch the bones of the buried prophet.

351.—SUCCOTH-BENOTH—HEATHEN GODS.

XVII, 30, 31. The men of Babylon made Succoth-benoth, and the men of Cuth made Nergal, and the men of Hamath made Ashima. And the Avites made Nibhaz and Tartak, and the Sepharvites burnt their children in fire to Adrammelech and Anammelech, the gods of Sepharvaim.

1. The precise meaning of *Succoth-benoth* is not known. Its literal signification is, "booths of the daughters;" and it is supposed to be, not the name of a god, but of places where women abandoned themselves to impure rites connected with the worship of Babylonian deities. Sir H. Rawlinson believes that the word represents the Chaldee goddess Zir-banit, worshiped at Babylon and called queen of the place. Gesenius suggests that "perhaps it should read *Succoth-bamoth, the booths in high places,* consecrated to idols."

2. *Nergal* was a well-known Assyrian deity. The word signifies "great man" or "hero." He is called by various names on the monuments: "the great brother;" "the storm ruler;" "the god of battles;" "the god of the chase." The last is his principal title, and he seems to have been the chief patron of hunting, which fact has led some to believe that he represented the deified hero Nimrod. The name of Nergal often appears on Assyrian seals and cylinders, and his symbol was a man-lion, or human-headed lion with eagle's wings. Astronomically, Nergal corresponds to Mars.

3. *Ashima* was a god of the people of Hamath. The majority of Jewish writers assert that this deity was worshiped under the form of a goat without wool; others say under the form of a lamb. The goat is found among sacred animals on Babylonian monuments. This would make Ashima correspond to the Egyptian Mendes and the Greek Pan. It is also supposed by some writers that Ashima was the same as the Phenician god Esmun, the Phenician Esculapius, to whom were also attributed the characteristics of Pan.

4. *Nibhaz* was a god of the Avites, but nothing is known with certainty of the peculiarities of the deity or the shape of the idol. The Hebrew interpreters say that the idol was in the form of a man with the head of a dog. The Egyptians worshiped the dog, and, according to some writers, their god Anubis was represented by a man with a dog's head, though Wilkinson asserts that the head is that of a jackal. The family relation of the two animals is, however, sufficiently near for the purposes of idolatry.

5. *Tartak* was another Avite deity. Some Jewish writers suppose the idol to have been in the form of an ass; but others assert that this is mere conjecture, and that the name, which they render *hero of darkness*, has, reference to some planet of supposed malign influence, such as Mars or Saturn.

6. *Adrammelech* was a god of the Sepharvites, and is supposed to be iden-

tical with Molech, for a description of which deity see note on Lev. xviii, 21. Rawlinson identifies Adrammelech with the Chaldean god San or Sansi.

7. *Anammelech* was also a god of the Sepharvites. No satisfactory etymology of the name has been found. Some suppose this deity to be represented by the Arabian constellation Cepheus, containing the shepherd and the sheep. Some authorities give the idol the figure of a horse, others that of a pheasant or a quail. Human sacrifices were offered to this god as well as to Adrammelech.

352.—DEPORTATION.

XVIII, 11. **The king of Assyria did carry away Israel unto Assyria, and put them in Halah and in Habor by the river of Gozan, and in the cities of the Medes.**

The practice of carrying into captivity all the inhabitants of a city or of a section of country was in use by the Assyrians from a very early period of their history, and is frequently referred to and illustrated on their monuments. "In the most flourishing period of their dominion—the reigns of Sargon, Sennacherib, and Esar-haddon—it prevailed most widely, and was carried to the greatest extent. Chaldeans were transported into Armenia; Jews and Israelites into Assyria and Media; Arabians, Babylonians, Lusianians, and Persians into Palestine—the most distant portions of the empire changed inhabitants, and no sooner did a people become troublesome from its patriotism and love of independence than it was weakened by dispersion, and its spirit subdued by a severance of all its social associations."—RAWLINSON, *Five Great Monarchies*, vol. ii, p. 238.

Tiglath Pileser carried a large number of captives to Assyria twenty years before the captivity referred to in the text. See 2 Kings xv, 29. Eight years after this Sennacherib took "the fenced cities of Judah." 2 Kings xviii, 13. An account of this event is given on one of the Assyrian monuments. The king claims to have carried away over two hundred thousand of the inhabitants. More than a hundred years after this Nebuchadnezzar, king of Babylon, invaded Judea, and by several distinct deportations carried the people into captivity. See 2 Kings xxiv, 14; xxv, 11; 2 Chron. xxxvi, 20; Jer. lii, 28—30.

353.—VARIOUS USES OF THE GRAPE.

XVIII, 32. **A land of corn and wine, a land of bread and vineyards, a land of oil olive and of honey.**

An American missionary in Turkey states that in some districts grapes are so plentiful that, with oil and bread, they form the chief nourishment of the people. Thus it was, according to the text, in Palestine and in Assyria in the days of Hezekiah. Each was "a land of bread and vineyards."

The same writer, in speaking of the various uses of the grape as a staple food of the people, enumerates fifteen different articles made from that fruit.

Among them are preserves, jellies, and confectionery, made of the fresh juice; pickles, molasses, and sugar; besides wine and brandy, and other more familiar preparations. See *Bibliotheca Sacra*, vol. v, pp. 283, 287.

354.—CAPTIVE GODS.

XVIII, 34. **Where are the gods of Hamath, and of Arpad? where are the gods of Sepharvaim, Hena, and Ivah?**

The Assyrian monuments give evidence of a custom which illustrates the haughty language of this text. It was the practice of Assyrian conquerors to take the idols which they found in the temples of the people whom they subdued and convey them to Assyria, where they were assigned a place in Assyrian temples as captive gods. Hence Sennacherib spoke to the Jews by his embassador informing them that the Assyrian deity was so powerful that none other could cope with him. The gods of all other people against whom the Assyrians had fought had been captured, and it was in vain for the Jews to expect their god to save them.

355.—NISROCH.

XIX, 87. **As he was worshiping in the house of Nisroch his god.**

Nisroch was an idol of Nineveh, concerning which there have been various conjectures. The rabbins affirmed that it was made out of one of the planks of Noah's ark. Others supposed it to be an image of the dove which Noah sent out from the ark. Some have thought the planet Saturn to be represented by it, and some the constellation of the eagle. Others have supposed Nisroch to be a representation of Asshur, the deified patriarch and head of the Assyrian pantheon.

These various opinions are sufficient to show the obscurity connected with the subject. The etymology of the word, which occurs only here and in Isa. xxxvii, 38, is uncertain. Some philologists think that Nisroch is not a correct reading, while others suppose the word to mean the *great eagle*. This bird was held in great veneration by the ancient Persians, and was also worshiped by the Arabians before the time of Mohammed. From the frequent appearance on the Assyrian sculptures of a human figure with the head of an eagle or a hawk, Layard conjectured that this was the representation of Nisroch, and this has so often been asserted that many imagine that whenever they see a picture of one of these hawk-headed figures they see a picture of Nisroch. Rawlinson, however, asserts the contrary, and says that the hawk-headed figure is more like a subordinate character, an attendant genius, than a god. No name of any god has yet been discovered on the monuments which bears any resemblance to Nisroch.

356.—SUN-DIALS.

XX, 11. Isaiah the prophet cried unto the Lord: and he brought the shadow ten degrees backward, by which it had gone down in the dial of Ahaz.

Maăloth, "dial," is the same word that is rendered "degrees" in this verse, and "stairs" in 2 Kings ix, 13. This and the parallel passage in Isa. xxxviii, 8, are the only places where the word "dial" occurs. Our translators probably judged correctly in supposing from the context that by *maaloth* in this place some instrument for measuring time is meant; but what was its peculiar shape is left to conjecture. The Babylonians were doubtless the originators of the sun-dial. Herodotus states that the Greeks derived it from them, (*Euterpé,* chap. cix;) and it is highly probable that king Ahaz, after whom this dial in the palace court was named, obtained the idea from Babylon.

Some think this dial was a hemispherical cavity in a horizontal square stone, with the gnomon in the middle, the shadow of which, falling on different lines cut in the hollow surface, marked the hours of the day. Others imagine a vertical index surrounded by twelve concentric lines. It may have been, as some suppose, a pillar set up in an open elevated place, with encircling steps on which the shadows fell; or stairs so constructed that the shadow of an obelisk or of a gnomon on the top platform might indicate the hours.

The "degrees," however, must have marked shorter periods than hours, since ten forward and ten backward are spoken of as only a part of the whole number of degrees. See KEIL, *Commentary, in loco.*

It has been suggested that the "stairs" from which Jehu was proclaimed king, as recorded in 2 Kings ix, 13, were the same as the "dial" of Ahaz. As already noted, the same word, *maaloth,* represents both. The idea is that Jehu was taken up the different steps of the dial until he reached the top platform, where he was placed by the side of the gnomon, when the trumpets were blown and the formal announcement was made, "Jehu is king." See CLARKE, *Commentary* on 2 Kings ix, 13.

357.—ROYAL TREASURES.

XX, 13. Hezekiah hearkened unto them, and showed them all the house of his precious things, the silver, and the gold, and the spices, and the precious ointment, and all the house of his armor, and all that was found in his treasures.

It has long been the custom for Eastern princes to amass great quantities of treasure merely for ostentation. The kings of Judah may have had a similar custom. Burder (*Oriental Customs,* No. 433) tells of the treasure of an Eastern monarch which was so immense that two unusually large cellars or warehouses were not sufficient to hold it. It consisted of precious stones,

12

plates of gold, and gold coin enough to load a hundred mules. It had been collected by twelve of his predecessors, and it was said that he had in his treasury a coffer three spans long and two broad full of precious stones of incalculable value.

358.—HORSES USED FOR IDOLATROUS PURPOSES.

XXIII, 11. He took away the horses that the kings of Judah had given to the sun.

Allusion is here made to a peculiar form of sun-worship. Among the Persians horses were considered sacred to the sun. The king of Persia when he sacrificed offered a white horse to that luminary. The people, when they wished to sacrifice to the sun, mounted their horses in the early morning and rode toward the rising orb as if to salute it, and then offered the noble victims to it in sacrifice. See GALE'S *Court of the Gentiles*, book ii, chap. viii, p. 115.

The kings of Judah had evidently heard of this custom, and imitated it; though some commentators doubt that they actually slew the animals, supposing that they simply went in state in the early morning to see the sun rise and to adore it. Some have even imagined that these horses were not real, but merely statues, made of wood, stone, or metal, which stood at the entrance of the temple. The mention made of the " chariots of the sun " in the latter part of the verse seems, however, to indicate that living animals were intended, and that they were harnessed to these chariots. Whether they were really sacrificed or not, they were kept and used for idolatrous purposes, and therefore became proper subjects of confiscation.

359.—GRAVE-STONES.

XXIII, 17. He said, What title is that that I see ? And the men of the city told him, It is the sepulcher of the man of God.

This refers to the custom of marking the graves of the dead by some distinguishing sign. The word here rendered "title" is the same that in Ezek. xxxix, 15, is rendered "sign." It means a pillar set up to designate a grave, and served the twofold purpose of a tablet for an epitaph, and also as a sign to warn all passers-by lest they should become ceremonially unclean by touching the grave. The absence of any such sign is what is referred to in Luke xi, 44: "Woe unto you, scribes and Pharisees, hypocrites! for ye are as graves which appear not, and the men that walk over them are not aware of them."

Dr. Shaw says of the cemeteries in Barbary: "The graves are all distinct and separate; each of them having a stone, placed upright, both at the head and feet, inscribed with the name of the deceased.—*Travels*, p. 219.

360.—PRISONERS BLINDED—FETTERS.

XXV, 7. They slew the sons of Zedekiah before his eyes, and put out the eyes of Zedekiah, and bound him with fetters of brass, and carried him to Babylon. See also Jer. xxxix, 7; lii, 11.

1. Blinding has long been a common Oriental punishment. See Judg. xvi, 21; 1 Sam. xi, 2. In Persia, during the time of the younger Cyrus, men deprived of their sight for crimes were a common spectacle along the highway. This penalty is still inflicted by the Persians on princes who are declared to have forfeited their right to the throne. Chardin states that one mode of blinding was by passing a red-hot copper plate before the eyes. This did not always produce total blindness, and sometimes the point of a dagger or of a spear was thrust into the eye. The Babylonians and the Assyrians, as well as the Persians, made use

71.—BLINDING A PRISONER.

of the same cruel punishment. Frequent representations of it are found on the ancient sculptures. The engraving represents part of a scene from a marble slab discovered at Khorsabad. The Assyrian king has several prisoners brought before him to be blinded. In his left hand he holds the cords at the end of which are hooks inserted in the prisoner's lips. See note on Isa. xxxvii, 29. In his right hand is a spear, which he thrusts into the eyes

2. Fetters were of various shapes and materials. Those which were put on Zedekiah were made of brass or copper; so also were those with which Samson was fastened. Judges xvi, 21. There is in the British Museum a pair of bronze fetters, brought from Nineveh, wh ch weigh eight pounds eleven

72.—BRONZE FETTERS FROM NINEVEH.

ounces, and measure sixteen and a half inches in length. These probably resemble the fetters put on Zedekiah. "The rings which inclose the ankles are thinner than the other part, so that they could be hammered smaller after the feet had been passed through them. One of these rings has been broken, and when whole the fetters may have weighed about nine pounds."—SHARPE'S *Bible Texts Illustrated.*

I. CHRONICLES.

361.—MARRIAGE OF SLAVE TO MASTER'S DAUGHTER.

II, 34, 35. Now Sheshan had no sons, but daughters. And Sheshan had a servant, an Egyptian, whose name was Jarha. And Sheshan gave his daughter to Jarha his servant to wife.

According to the Mosaic law, daughters were not to be married out of the tribe to which they belonged. This was commanded in order to keep the inheritance of each tribe to itself. See Numbers, chapter xxxvi. In the text, Sheshan, who had no sons, is represented as marrying his daughter to an Egyptian, and that Egyptian a servant. Harmer states that though this may have been contrary to the law of Moses, it was in accordance with a custom frequently practiced in the East. He quotes from one of Maillet's letters, in which an account is given of one Hassan, who had been a slave to Kamel, the "Kiaia of the Asaphs of Cairo, that is, colonel of four or five thousand men who go under that name." "Kamel," says Maillet, "according to the custom of the country, gave him one of his daughters in marriage, and left him at his death one part of the great riches he had amassed together in the course of a long and prosperous life." He also succeeded his master in his office.—*Observations*, vol. iv, p. 298.

362.—TIDINGS CARRIED TO IDOLS.

X, 9. They took his head, and his armor, and sent into the land of the Philistines round about to carry tidings unto their idols.

The Hindoos have a custom corresponding to this. When they gain a victory over their enemies they carry the tidings to their idols with great pomp and ceremony. In the common affairs of life the same practice is resorted to. A man delivered from prison, or from the wicked scheme of his enemies, always goes to his gods to carry the news. Roberts gives the following as a specimen of the formal speech used on such occasions: "Ah! Swamy, you know Muttoo wanted to ruin me; he therefore forged a deed in my name, and tried to get my estates. But I resisted him, and it has just been decided before the court that he is guilty. I am therefore come to praise you, O Swamy!"—*Oriental Illustrations*, p. 229.

363.—STONE-BOWS.

XII, 2. They were armed with bows, and could use both the right hand and the left in hurling stones and shooting arrows out of a bow.

It will be noticed that the words *hurling* and *shooting* have been supplied by the translators. Without them the reading would be, "could use both the right hand and the left in stones and arrows out of a bow." This has led some to think that there was in use among the Hebrews a kind of bow for shooting stones as well as arrows; an instrument corresponding to the stone-bow in use in the Middle Ages. These stone-bows of David's men may have suggested the invention, two hundred and fifty years' later, of the heavier instruments of a similar character to be used in sieges. See note on 2 Chron. xxvi, 15.

364.—AMEN.

XVI, 36. All the people said, Amen, and praised the Lord.

Amen literally means firm, from *aman*, to prop, to support. Its figurative meaning is *faithful*. Its use is designed as a confirmatory response, and the custom is very ancient. See Num. v, 22 ; Deut. xxvii, 15–26.

"The Jewish doctors give three rules for pronouncing the word: 1. That it be not pronounced too hastily and swiftly, but with a grave and distinct voice. 2. That it be not louder than the tone of him that blessed. 3. It was to be expressed in faith, with a certain persuasion that God would bless them and hear their prayer."—BURDER, *Oriental Customs*, No. 438.

It is also customary for the Mohammedans, at the close of every public prayer, to say, Amen.

365.—THE HORN.

XXV, 5. All these were the sons of Heman the king's seer in the words of God, to lift up the horn.

Some of the earliest wind instruments were no doubt made of the horns of animals, and when afterward metals were used in their manufacture they retained more or less of the original shape, and continued to be called by the original name. The difference between the *keren*, "horn," and the *shophar*, "trumpet," "cornet," is supposed to have been principally in the shape, the latter having less of a curved shape than the former. See note on Psa. xcviii, 6. The *keren* is mentioned as a musical instrument in Josh. vi, 5, and in Dan. iii, 5, 7, 10, 15. In the passage in Daniel it is translated "cornet."

II. CHRONICLES.

366.—FORTIFIED CITIES.

VIII, 5. Also he built Beth-horon the upper, and Beth-horon the nether, fenced cities, with walls, gates, and bars.

1. Fortifications are as ancient as cities ; indeed, some writers assert that the difference, anciently, between cities and villages was simply the differ-

ence between walled and unwalled towns. The Egyptian and Assyrian sculptures contain representations of "fenced cities" with walls of squared

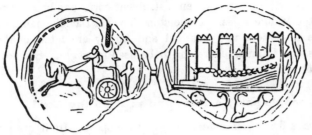

stone or squared timber on the summit of scarped rocks. Some of the fenced cities of Scripture are thought to have been protected by stockades of wood. Sometimes there was more than one

78.—WALLS AND TOWERS; FROM BABYLONIAN COINS.

wall to a fortified city. It was thus with Jerusalem. See 2 Kings xxv, 4; 2 Chron. xxxii, 5. Sometimes there was a ditch outside the wall, and a low wall or rampart protecting that. At regular distances on the wall there were towers for the purposes of watching and defense. See 2 Kings ix, 17; 2 Chron. xxvi, 15. The gates were strongly protected with bolts or bars of brass or iron. Sometimes there was built at some central point within the city a citadel or stronghold which might resist attack even after the walls were destroyed.

2. To "build" a city often meant not to give a new town a location, and to erect the houses, but to build walls around a town already inhabited. It was thus that Solomon built the two Beth-horons mentioned in the text. Thus Rehoboam "built" the cities named in 2 Chron. xi, 5–10. So Jeroboam "built" Shechem and Penuel, (1 Kings xii, 25,) and Hiel "built" Jericho, (1 Kings xvi, 34,) a city which had been inhabited long before. Judges i, 16; iii, 13.

367.—CREMATION.

XVI, 14. Laid him in the bed which was filled with sweet odors and divers kinds of spices prepared by the apothecaries' art: and they made a very great burning for him.

There is a division of opinion among commentators concerning the meaning of the last clause in this verse. Some of the best authorities believe that the "very great burning" was the burning of the odoriferous substances which were brought together. They understand that a large quantity of these substances was collected and placed in the sepulcher of Asa, and that after these were burned the body of the dead king was laid upon the perfumed ashes, as on a bed. This is also referred to in the promise which was made to Zedekiah concerning his burial. Jer. xxxiv, 5. It is likewise thought to have been this which was denied to Jehoram, on the occasion of his death, because of his wickedness. 2 Chron. xxi, 19.

On the other hand, it is asserted that burning spices and perfumes in this way for the dead does not find a parallel in the customs of any nation ancient or modern; and that these various passages refer to the burning of the body together with the spices on a funeral pile. Jahn says, "The *ancient* Hebrews considered burning the body a matter of very great reproach, and rarely did it except when they wished, together with the greatest punishment, to inflict the greatest ignominy." Gen. xxxviii, 24. He considers the burning of Saul and of his sons (1 Sam. xxxi, 12) an exceptional instance, designed by their friends to prevent any further indignities from the Philistines. The sentiment in reference to the burning of bodies afterward underwent a change. A hundred and forty years after Saul's death the body of Asa was burnt, and the event is spoken of by the historian not as a new thing, but as a custom already established. Over a century later we find the same custom referred to. See Amos vi, 10. In time the revolution of sentiment became so complete that while burning was considered the most distinguished honor, *not* to be burned was regarded the most signal disgrace, as in the case of Jehoram already mentioned. Another change of sentiment eventually took place. After the captivity the Jews conceived a great hatred to this rite, and the Talmudists endeavored to explain the passages respecting it as referring to the burning of the aromatic substances alone. See Jahn's *Archæology*, § 210.

Roberts takes substantially the same view, and gives a detailed account of the Hindoo method of cremation. The Hindoos burn the bodies of nearly all their illustrious dead, and it is considered disgraceful not to have the ceremony performed. They first wash the corpse with water mingled with fragrant oils and scented waters. The body is then placed on a bed, or on a chariot covered with crimson cloth, and is carried on men's shoulders to the place of burning. The funeral pile is seldom more than five feet high, and when prepared for a great man is made of sandal and other aromatic woods, to which are added sweet odors and spices. The body is then placed on the pile, and the son or nearest relative has his head shaved. Then the son takes a torch and, turning his head away from the pile, sets fire to it, and returns home. Those who remain to see the corpse consumed throw clarified butter and oils on the fire to hasten the combustion. See Roberts' *Oriental Illustrations*, p. 234.

368.—DEATH BY BEING THROWN FROM A ROCK.

XXV, 12. Brought them unto the top of the rock, and cast them down from the top of the rock, that they all were broken in pieces.

This was a very ancient punishment, practiced among different nations. In Greece, according to the Delphian law, those who were guilty of sacrilege were punished in this manner. The Romans also inflicted the same punishment for various offenses. Among the Turks and the Persians a similar

mode of capital punishment was adopted.   Selden has suggested that the
mode of Jezebel's death is an illustration of this custom.   2 Kings ix, 33.

369.—TOWERS.

XXVI, 10. He built towers in the desert.

The duties of shepherds often led them into wild districts where their
lives were in danger from wandering brigands.   Hence it became necessary

to erect towers into
which they might re-
tire for safety from the
attacks of large forces,
and from which they
could drive off the
marauders.   The rea-
son assigned for build-
ing the towers by Uz-
ziah is the same as
that given for digging
the wells: "for he had
much cattle." See also
2 Chron. xxvii, 4.
A beautiful figurative
use is made of this
custom in Psa. lxi, 3,
and in Prov. xviii, 10.
Towers were also built
in vineyards. See note
on Matt. xxi, 33.

74.—Towers in the Desert.

370.—ENGINES OF WAR.

**XXVI, 15. He made in Jerusalem engines, invented by cunning
men, to be on the towers and upon the bulwarks, to shoot
arrows and great stones withal.**

The invention of these engines of war marks an era in warfare, since by
their use the power of an army was greatly increased whether for attack or
defense.   They were simply machine bows and slings, which, by the application of mechanical principles, were made to throw heavier projectiles than
the smaller weapons which were held in the hand.   We have here doubtless
the origin of the *balistæ* and *catapultæ* which afterward became so famous in
Roman warfare.   The *balista* was used to shoot stones; the *catapulta* projected darts.   Historians mention three sizes of *balistæ*, which were graded

according to the weight of the stones they threw, namely: a half hundred weight, a whole hundred weight, and three hundred weight. Occasionally there were some used which threw stones as light as two pounds. Several balls of limestone, which were found in the excavations in Jerusalem in 1869, are thought to have been used as missiles and hurled from a *balista*. *Catapultæ* were denominated according to the length of the darts thrown from them. No exact idea can now be had of the forms of these engines. The Romans classified them under the generic title of *tormentum*, because of the twisting of the hairs, thongs, and vegetable fibers from which the elastic string was made which gave impetus to the projectile. See SMITH's *Dict. Class. Antiq.*, s. v. *Tormentum.* These engines were often used from the top of a "mount" or inclined plane. See note on Ezek. iv, 2.

371.—CHANGE OF NAME.

XXXVI, 4. **The king of Egypt made Eliakim his brother king over Judah and Jerusalem, and turned his name to Jehoiakim.**

It has long been a custom among Eastern people to change their names on the occurrence of some great event in life. It was in accordance with the divine command at the time of the renewal of the covenant that the name of Abram was changed to Abraham, (Gen. xvii, 5; Neh. ix, 7,) and that of Sarai to Sarah. Gen. xvii, 15. Jacob's name was changed to Israel, in commemoration of his prevailing prayer. Gen. xxxii, 28; xxxv, 10. The king of Egypt changed the name of Joseph to Zaphnath-paaneah, because of his ability to reveal secrets. Gen. xli, 45. Another king of Egypt subsequently changed the name of Eliakim the son of Josiah to Jehoiakim, when he made him king of Judah, as narrated in the text, and also in 2 Kings xxiii, 34. So when the king of Babylon made Mattaniah king he changed his name to Zedekiah. 2 Kings xxiv, 17. In like manner the name of Hadassah was changed to Esther. Esth. ii, 7. So, also, when Nebuchadnezzar wished to have a few of the young Jewish prisoners taught in the Chaldean language and customs, he changed their names from Daniel, Hananiah, Mishael, and Azariah, to Belteshazzar, Shadrach, Meshach, and Abed-nego. Dan. i 6, 7.

The custom is further illustrated by Sir John Chardin in his *Travels in Persia.* He states that King Sefi, the first years of whose reign were unhappy on account of wars and famine in many of the Persian provinces, was persuaded by his counselors to change his name as a means of changing the tide of fortune, since there must be about the name of Sefi some hidden fatal power of evil. He was, therefore, crowned anew in the year 1666 under the name of Solyman III. All seals, coins, and other public symbols that had on them the name of Sefi, were broken, the same as if the king had been dead, and his successor had taken his place upon the throne.

EZRA.

372.—NETHINIM.

II, 43. The Nethinim.

These were men who assisted the Levites in performing the meanest offices connected with the temple service. Part of them lived in Jerusalem, and part were distributed among the Levitical cities. They are supposed to have been Canaanites reduced to servitude, (Josh. ix, 21–27,) and captives taken in war, who were set apart to this service, and therefore called *nethinim: the given, the devoted.* They were held in low esteem by the Jews, occupying a social position even lower than the *mamzer,* or illegitimate offspring.

373.—THE PERSIAN DARIC.

II, 69. Threescore and one thousand drams of gold.

The coin referred to here and in chapter viii, 27, and also in Neh. vii, 71, 72, is the Persian daric. It was a thick piece of gold having on

75.—PERSIAN DARIC.

one side the figure of a king with bow and javelin, or bow and dagger, and on the other an irregular oblong depression. The weight of the daric was from 124 to 129 grains troy. Its value has been variously estimated; it was probably not far from six dollars, gold.

374.—MONEY TABLETS.

III, 7. They gave money also unto the masons, and to the carpenters.

The particular kind of money which was given to these workmen is not here mentioned. It may have been gold and silver; perhaps it was clay; for it is a fact worth mentioning that in Babylonia and in Persia at that very time there were in use certain clay tablets which are supposed by some writers to have been used for the same purpose that we now use bank-notes! Among other curious things which Loftus unearthed at Warka were about forty "small tablets of unbaked clay, covered on both sides with minute characters." They were in length from two inches to four and a half, and in breadth from one inch to three. They had on them the names of various kings, and dates ranging from 626 to 525 B. C. Among these was the name of Cyrus, the king who directed the work for which the money was given according to the text. Sir Henry Rawlinson, who examined the inscriptions, says that the tablets "seemed to be notes issued by the government for the convenience of circulation, representing a certain value, which was always expressed in measures of weight, of gold or silver, and redeemable on presentation at the royal treasury." Loftus adds, "These tablets were, in point of fact, the equivalents of our own bank-notes, and prove that a system of artificial currency prevailed in Babylonia, and also in Persia, at an unprecedented early age—centuries before the introduction of paper or printing."—*Travels in Chaldea and Susiana*, p. 222.

375.—THE TEMPLE OF ZERUBBABEL.

VI, 3, 4. Let the house be builded, the place where they of-fered sacrifices, and let the foundations thereof be strongly laid; the height thereof threescore cubits, and the breadth thereof threescore cubits; with three rows of great stones, and a row of new timber.

This temple, sometimes called the second temple, and sometimes the temple of Zerubbabel, was built on the site of the first, or Solomon's temple. We have not so definite a description given of this as we have of Solomon's temple. The second temple was larger than the first. The "rows" of stones are supposed to refer to three stories of chambers, such as were attached to Solomon's temple, and on these was placed an additional story of wood. The temple of Zerubbabel, though of greater size than that of Solomon, was inferior to it in magnificence. According to Jewish author-ities its altar of burnt-offering was of stone instead of brass, and it had but one table of show-bread and but one candlestick. It is also said that the sanctuary was entirely empty, excepting that in place of the ark of the cov-enant a stone was set three fingers high, on which the high priest placed the censer and sprinkled the blood of atonement. Some suppose, however, that a new ark was made and set in the sanctuary. The rabbins reckon five different important features of the first temple which were wanting in the second: 1. The Ark of the Covenant. 2. The Sacred Fire. 3. The She-kinah. 4. The Holy Spirit. 5. The answer by Urim and Thummim. Some of these distinctions are, however, thought by more sober writers to be a little fanciful.

376.—ADAR.

VI, 15. This house was finished on the third day of the month Adar.

This was the closing month of the year, and corresponded very nearly to our month of March.

NEHEMIAH.

377.—CHISLEU.

I, 1. **It came to pass in the month Chisleu.**

This corresponded very nearly to our month of December.

378.—THE ROYAL BUTLER.

I, 11. **For I was the king's cup-bearer.**

The office of royal cup-bearer or butler is of high antiquity, and was a place of great honor in the Persian court. The cup-bearer, being in the daily

presence of the king, and seeing him at his seasons of relaxation from care, had many opportunities of ingratiating himself into the good-will of the monarch, and thus doubtless obtained many favors which were denied others. Cup-bearers were generally eunuchs, and are often found represented on Assyrian monuments. In these representations they hold the cup in the left hand, and in the right hand a fly-flap made of the split leaves of the palm. A long napkin, richly embroidered and fringed, is thrown over the left shoulder for the king to wipe his lips with. Among the Medes and Persians the cup-bearer, before serving the king, took the wine into the cup from the vessels, and then poured a little into the palm of his left hand and drank it; so that if the wine were poisoned the king might ascertain it without running any personal risk.

76.—The Royal Cup-bearer.

Pharaoh had cup-bearers to attend him. Gen. xl, 2. Solomon also had them. 1 Kings x, 5; 2 Chron. ix, 4.

379.—SAFE–CONDUCT.

II, 7. **Moreover I said unto the king, If it please the king, let letters be given me to the governors beyond the river, that they may convey me over till I come into Judah.**

It is still customary in many parts of the East to obtain letters of recommendation, or orders for safe conduct, when the traveler desires to visit different districts under one central authority. Without these he could not travel in comfort or safety; but having them, those to whom he presents them are bound to protect him. Thus Nehemiah was able to travel safely throughout the Persian empire.

380.—SHAKING THE LAP.

V, 13. Also I shook my lap, and said, So God shake out every man from his house, and from his labor, that performeth not this promise, even thus be he shaken out, and emptied.

The "lap" was a fold made in the outer garment, near the breast, for the reception of various articles. See note on Luke vi, 38. To shake this was equivalent to a curse, and to empty it was a significant suggestion of utter extermination. Roberts says that the natives of India always carry in their lap a pouch made of the leaf of cocoa or of some other tree, and that they are careful never to have the pouch entirely empty. They have in it money, areca nut, betel leaf, and tobacco. Even when they wish to find any article they never empty the pouch, but rather fumble about for a long time until they get hold of the object sought. They say if the pouch should become empty it might remain so for a long time. They also shake the lap of the robe when they curse each other.

When the Roman embassadors proposed the choice of peace or war to the Carthaginians they made use of a similar ceremony. "When the Roman embassadors entered the senate of Carthage they had their toga gathered up in their bosom. They said, 'We carry here peace and war; you may have which you will.' The senate answered, 'You may give which you please.' They then shook their toga, and said, 'We bring you war.' To which all the senate answered, 'We cheerfully accept it.'"—BURDER, *Oriental Illustrations*, No. 645.

It was in a similar way that Nehemiah significantly suggested to the usurers of his time their utter extermination if they failed to keep the covenant of restitution which they had made. See also Acts xviii, 6.

381.—LETTERS.

VI, 5. Then sent Sanballat his servant unto me in like manner the fifth time with an open letter in his hand.

1. The first mention that is made in Scripture of a letter is of that which David sent to Joab. 2 Sam. xi, 14. We also read of the letters which Jezebel wrote in the name of Ahab. 1 Kings xxi, 8. The king of Syria wrote a letter to the king of Israel. 2 Kings v, 5–7. Jehu also wrote letters. 2 Kings x, 1. Later on in the history more frequent mention is made of them.

On what substance these ancient letters were written it is now impossible to say. They may have been written on skins dressed for the purpose, on palm-leaves, or on papyrus, the use of which is now known to have been very ancient with the Egyptians, and from them neighboring nations may have learned it.

2. In Persia, as well as in some other Oriental lands, letters, when sent to persons of distinction, are generally, after being rolled up in a scroll, inclosed in a bag or purse, which is sometimes made of very elegant and costly material. The end of this purse is tied, closed over with clay or wax, and then sealed. See Isa. viii, 16; xxix, 11; Dan. xii, 4, 9; Rev. v, 4, 9; x, 4; xxii, 10. For the mode of sealing, see note on 1 Kings xxi, 8. This is considered a mark of respect, and a recognition of the rank or position of the person to whom it is sent. When sent to inferiors, or to persons whom the writer wishes to treat with contempt, the letters are uninclosed. This custom probably existed among the Persians in the time of Nehemiah, since special emphasis is in the text laid upon the fact that the letter was an *open* letter; that is, as we understand it, that it was not inclosed in a bag, and therefore indicated the contempt which Sanballat had for Nehemiah. He treated him as a person of inferior position.

382.—ELUL.

VI, 15. The twenty and fifth day of the month Elul.

This month corresponded very nearly with September of our calendar.

383.—TIRSHATHA.

VII, 65. And the Tirshatha said unto them.

This was the title of the Persian governor of Judea. Gesenius derives the word from the Persian *torsh :* "severe," "austere," which would make the meaning equivalent to *your Severity.* He compares it with the German *gestrenger Herr,* (that is, your "Worship;" but, literally, *Severe Master,*) a title which was formerly given to the magistrates of the free and imperial German cities. The English have a corresponding expression: "most *dread* Sovereign"

See also Ezra ii, 63; Neh. vii, 70; viii, 9; x, 1.

384.—SENDING PORTIONS.

VIII, 10. Go your way, eat the fat, and drink the sweet, and send portions unto them for whom nothing is prepared.

This has generally been interpreted to mean that the wants of the poor were to be supplied; but Harmer (*Observations,* vol. ii, p. 107) prefers to refer it to the custom of sending a portion of a feast to those who car not well come to it, especially to the relatives of those who give the feast, and to those in a state of mourning, who in their grief would make no preparation. In Esther ix, 19 it is said that among the ceremonies of the feast of Purim there was to be "sending portions one to another." In the twenty-second verse of the same chapter the order of Mordecai is given for keeping the feast, and it is directed "that they should make them days of feasting and joy, and of sending portions one to another, and gifts to the poor." From this verse it is evident that sending "gifts to the poor" is not the same thing as "sending portions one to another." This latter custom, however, may, in turn, be different from the one referred to in Nehemiah, and may mean that these pious Jews expressed their joy by a mutual exchange of the good things provided for the feast. This custom is alluded to in Rev. xi, 10, where the enemies of the "two witnesses" are represented as rejoicing over their death: "And they that dwell upon the earth shall rejoice over them, and make merry, and send gifts one to another; because these two prophets tormented them that dwelt on the earth."

385.—WOOD FOR THE SACRIFICES.

X, 34. We cast the lots among the priests, the Levites, and the people, for the wood offering, to bring it into the house of our God, after the houses of our fathers, at times appointed year by year, to burn upon the altar of the Lord our God, as it is written in the law.

The work of supplying the wood necessary for the altar fires was a part of the task assigned to the Nethinim. See note on Ezra ii, 43. On the occasion of the captivity these became scattered, and their organization was broken up, and though some Nethinim returned to Jerusalem, they were probably not so numerous as before. It became necessary, therefore, for all classes of the people to attend to this work, and the time of their doing it was regulated by lot. This work is what is called the "wood offering" in the text and in chapter xiii, 31. We have no further mention of it in the Scriptures, but the Jewish writers give additional accounts of the manner in which the work was done. Different families had different times of the year assigned them for their share in the work. This was the origin of a great festival which was known by the name of the feast of wood-carrying, and was celebrated annually on a certain day in Ab, (August.) This was the last day of the year on which wood could be cut for this purpose, and all the people without distinction of tribe or grade brought wood to the temple on that day. The festival was universally and joyously kept; no fasting or mourning was permitted.

386.—PLUCKING THE HAIR.

XIII, 25. I contended with them, and cursed them, and smote certain of them, and plucked off their hair.

This is equivalent to what we term "tearing the hair out by the roots." It was sometimes a self-inflicted suffering as a token of mourning, (see Ezra ix, 3,) sometimes an act of wanton persecution, (see Isa. l, 6,) and sometimes punishment, as represented in the text. It is said that the ancient Athenians punished adulterers by tearing the hair from the scalp and then covering the head with hot ashes.

———◆———

ESTHER.

387.—THE COURT OF THE HOUSE.

I, 5. In the court of the garden of the king's palace.

The "court" of an Oriental house is the open space around which the house is built. The outside of the building shows to the observer hardly

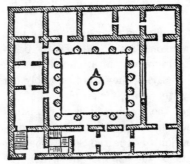

77.—GROUND-PLAN OF HOUSE.

anything but blank walls, the privacy of the people being such that the interior of their dwellings is completely hidden from public gaze. The ordinary houses have but one court, but houses of a better class have two or three, and some of the best houses in Damascus have seven courts. The palaces of kings had a number of courts.

The courts are sometimes laid out in beautiful gardens containing various fruits and flowers; and trees are often planted there: the palm, the cypress, the olive, the pomegranate. To this the Psalmist alludes when he says. "I am like a green olive-tree in the house of God." Psa. lii, 8. Again, "The righteous shall flourish like the palm-tree: he shall grow like a cedar in Lebanon. Those that be planted in the house of the Lord shall flourish in the courts of our God." Psa. xcii, 12, 13. Sometimes the court is handsomely paved with marble, (see verse 6,) and has a fountain in the center. Cisterns are also built here. See note on 2 Sam. xvii, 18, 19.

The court usually has a covered walk nine or ten feet wide projecting from the house. This walk is generally on the four sides of the court, though sometimes only on one side. If the house is over one story high, the roof of this covered walk forms a gallery, and is protected by a balustrade. This gallery is supported by pillars. Solomon is supposed to refer to this in Prov. ix, 1: "Wisdom hath builded her house, she hath hewn out her seven

78.—COURT OF A HOUSE IN DAMASCUS.

pillars." See also Job ix, 6; xxvi, 11; Psa. lxxv, 3; Gal. ii, 9; 1 Tim. iii, 15; but on this last text see note on Gen. xxviii, 18. On occasions of feasting, the guests are often assembled in the court, as is related in the text.

The rooms of the house open into the court. In some houses this opening is by means of doors; but in others the rooms are divided from the court by a low partition only. Where the house is more than one story in height the stairs to the upper apartments are usually, though not always, in one corner of the court.

The diagram on page 198 represents the ground-plan of an Oriental house. In the left-hand corner, at the bottom, is the door, which opens directly into the porch or entrance-hall. To enter the court it is necessary to cross this hall and go through an adjacent room. It can thus be seen how one might enter the porch and yet have no view of the interior arrangements of the house. In the center of the court, at the place marked A in the diagram, is the fountain or cistern. The small circles around the court mark the positions of the pillars which support the gallery above, and the square and oblong spaces represent various apartments. The engraving on page 199 gives a representation of the court of a house with tesselated marble pavement, garden, and fountain.

Reference is made to the court in 1 Kings vii, 8, 9, 12; Neh. viii, 16; Esth. vi, 4, 5, etc.

388.—CURTAINS—COUCHES.

I, 6. **Where were white, green, and blue hangings, fastened with cords of fine linen and purple to silver rings and pillars of marble : the beds were of gold and silver, upon a pavement of red, and blue, and white, and black marble.**

1. In the heat of summer an awning is sometimes stretched across the court from one gallery to another. Reference is thought to be made to this in Psa. civ, 2, and Isa. xlv, 12; and many writers think that the text speaks of an awning of variegated colors thrown over the court-yard of the palace. In the ruins of the palace at Khorsabad a small bronze lion was found of beautiful workmanship and fixed in a flagstone in the pavement of the court. At intervals there were similar flagstones in the pavement, where it is evident that other lions had been placed. From the fact that this lion had a ring rising from his back, resembling the rings in the animal-shaped weights which have been found, (see note on Gen. xxiii, 16,) it is supposed that these bronze images were used in the pavement to fasten the cords of the awning which was spread over the court.

Some authorities, however, suppose that the variegated hangings, instead of making an awning, were magnificent curtains suspended between the marble pillars of the court. This is the opinion of Professor Rawlinson, and also of Loftus. The latter excavated among the ruins of the great palace at

13

Susa, which he believes to have been the very palace referred to in the book of Esther. His investigations satisfied him that "the Great Hall at Susa consisted of several magnificent groups of columns, together having a frontage of three hundred and forty-three feet nine inches, and a depth of two hundred and forty-four feet. These groups were arranged into a central phalanx of thirty-six columns, (six rows of six each,) flanked on the west, north, and east by an equal number, disposed of in double rows of six each and distant from them sixty-four feet two inches."—*Travels in Chaldea and Susiana*, p. 367. He thinks that the colored curtains were hung around the central group of marble columns.

2. It is customary to spread mats and carpets on the court pavement for the accommodation of guests; Ahasuerus with kingly magnificence placed costly couches. These couches of "gold and silver," on which the guests reclined in the palace court while they feasted, (see note on Matt. xxvi, 7,) may have been covered with cloth in which these materials were interwoven, (see note on Prov. vii, 16,) or they may have been put on frames which were ornamented with the precious metals. Layard says that "chairs and couches adorned with feet of silver and other metals were looked upon as a great object of luxury in Persia."—*Nineveh and its Remains*, vol. ii, p. 300. According to Herodotus, the tables, thrones, and couches in the temple of Belus at Babylonia were of solid gold.

389.—DRINKING CUSTOMS.

I, 8. The drinking was according to the law ; none did compel: for so the king had appointed to all the officers of his house, that they should do according to every man's pleasure.

Revelers of all nations seem to have had their peculiar drinking customs which were as binding as laws. Among the Egyptians, wine was offered before dinner commenced, and the guests also drank during the repast. Among the Greeks, each guest was obliged to keep the round or leave the company. "Drink, or be gone," was the proverb. At the Roman feasts, a master of the feast was chosen by throwing dice. He prescribed rules to the company which all were obliged to observe. See note on John ii, 8.

Bishop Patrick, in his note on this place, suggests that the text means that though it was the custom to compel men to drink whether they would or not, yet the king on this occasion directed that each guest be left to his own discretion, and that none were obliged to drink according to this custom. Leaving out the word *was*, which the translators supplied; rendering the Hebrew word *dath*, "custom," instead of "law," as in our version; and slightly changing the punctuation, the Bishop translates: "The drinking according to custom, none did compel." Thus no one would incur displeasure who violated the ordinary rule of conviviality.

390.—FEASTS FOR THE WOMEN.

I, 9. Also Vashti the queen made a feast for the women in the royal house which belonged to king Ahasuerus.

The women in the East do not have their feasts in the same room with the men. This separation of the sexes is an ancient custom which was observed at this time at the court of Persia, though Jahn, speaking of the custom, says that "Babylon and Persia must, however, be looked upon as exceptions, where the ladies were not excluded from the festivals of the men, (Dan. v, 2;) and if we may believe the testimony of ancient authors, at Babylon they were not remarkable for their modesty on such occasions." *Archæology*, § 146.

As far as Babylon is concerned the remark is correct, and it serves to illustrate the relaxation of manners which showed itself among the dissolute Babylonians. It is not true, however, in reference to Persia, as is plainly seen by the indignation of Vashti when her drunken husband sent for her to come and display her beauty before the revelers. Her womanly spirit was aroused and she refused. See verse 12. This error as to the Persian custom probably rests on an oft-quoted story told by Herodotus, who says that seven Persian embassadors, being sent to Amyntas, a Grecian prince, were entertained by him at a feast, and told him when they began to drink that it was customary among their countrymen to introduce their concubines and young wives at their entertainments. Dr. Pusey says of this statement, "If historical, it was a shameless lie, to attain their end."—*Lectures on Daniel*, p. 461, note. Rawlinson represents the Oriental seclusion of women as carried to an excess among the ancient Persians. See *Five Ancient Monarchies*, vol. iii, p. 222.

391.—CHAMBERLAINS.

I, 10. The seven chamberlains that served in the presence of Ahasuerus the king.

Sarisim is variously rendered "chamberlains," "officers," and "eunuchs." They were emasculated persons who had charge of the harems of Oriental monarchs, and who were also employed by them in various offices about the court. They often became the confidential advisers of the monarch, and were frequently men of great influence, and sometimes had high military office. See Jer. xxxix, 3. This was especially the case in Persia, where they acquired great political power, and filled positions of great prominence, and sometimes engaged in conspiracy against the life of the king, an illustration of which may be found in chapter ii, verse 21.

The Hebrew monarchs had them in their courts. See 1 Sam. viii, 15;

1 Kings xxii, 9; 2 Kings viii, 6; ix, 32; xxiii, 11; xxv, 19; 1 Chron. xxviii, 1; Jer. xxix, 2; xxxiv, 19; xxxviii, 7; lii, 25.

Though it was the barbarous custom of Eastern sovereigns to mutilate many of their young prisoners in the manner here indicated, there is no evidence that the Hebrew kings ever did this. The eunuchs employed by them are supposed to have been imported. It is thought that Daniel and his companions were thus maltreated by the king of Babylon in fulfillment of the prediction contained in 2 Kings xx, 17, 18; Isa. xxxix, 7.

392.—THE ROYAL HAREM.

II, 18. **Out of the house of the women unto the king's house.**

The place appointed as a residence for the wives and concubines of the king was separated from the rest of the palace by a court. There were in it three sets of apartments: one set for the virgins who had not yet been sent for by the king, one for the concubines, and one for the queen and the other wives. The first is referred to in verse 8; it was under the charge of a special chamberlain. The second is mentioned in verse 14, and is spoken of as under the charge of another chamberlain. The third is mentioned in chapter i, 9, and was under the charge of the queen herself: she was not watched over by a chamberlain, but had one subject to her orders. See Esther iv, 5.

393.—TEBETH.

II, 16. **The tenth month, which is the month Tebeth.**

This corresponded very nearly to our month of January.

394.—THE PERSIAN QUEEN.

II, 17. **The king loved Esther above all the women, and she obtained grace and favor in his sight more than all the virgins; so that he set the royal crown upon her head, and made her queen instead of Vashti.**

There was one of the wives of the Persian monarchs who occupied a higher position than any of the others, and to her alone the title of "queen" belonged. "The chief wife or queen-consort was privileged to wear on her head a royal tiara or crown. She was the acknowledged head of the female apartments or Gynæceum, and the concubines recognized her dignity by actual prostration. On great occasions, when the king entertained the male part of the court, she feasted all the females in her own part of the palace. She had a large revenue of her own, assigned her, not so much by the will of her husband, as by an established law or custom. Her dress was splendid, and she was able to indulge freely that love of ornament of which few Oriental women are devoid."—RAWLINSON, *Five Ancient Monarchies*, vol. iii, p. 218.

This was the elevated position filled by Vashti, and afterward by Esther.

395.—ETIQUETTE OF THE PERSIAN COURT.

IV, 11. Whosoever, whether man or woman, shall come unto the king into the inner court, who is not called, there is one law of his to put him to death, except such to whom the king shall hold out the golden scepter, that he may live.

The etiquette of the Persian court was very strict. Except the " Seven Princes," no one could approach the king unless introduced by a court usher. To come into the king's presence without being summoned was a capital crime; and the severity of the Persian punishments may be seen in the fact that an act like this was followed by the same punishment as murder or rebellion. The intruder was instantly put to death by the attendants unless the king, by extending his golden scepter, showed his approval of the act. It was well understood, therefore, that whoever thus appeared before the king deliberately risked life; and it is an evidence of the influence which Esther had gained over Ahasuerus that, when she appeared, the scepter was extended. See chapter v, 2, and viii, 4.

396.—FEASTING WITH THE KING.

V, 12. To-morrow am I invited unto her also with the king.

It was a rare privilege for a subject, however high his station, to be permitted to banquet with the king. Occasionally, however, this was allowed, and Haman had reason to feel highly honored at the invitation he received from the queen by permission of the king. It must be understood, however, that when subjects were thus admitted to feast with royalty they were reminded of their inferior position. " The monarch reclined on a couch with golden feet, and sipped the rich wine of Helbon; the guests drank an inferior beverage, seated upon the floor."—*Five Monarchies*, vol. iii, p. 214. On some very special occasions the rigidity of this rule was relaxed. The king presided openly at a banquet where large numbers of dignitaries were assembled, and royal couches and royal wine were provided for them all. Such a feast is referred to in chapter i, 3.

397.—ROYAL HONORS GIVEN TO A SUBJECT.

VI, 8. Let the royal apparel be brought which the king useth to wear, and the horse which the king rideth upon, and the crown royal which is set upon his head.

1. Chardin says that when the grandees visited Solyman III., to congratulate him on his coronation, the king made every one of them a present of a *Calate*, or royal vest. " It is an infallible mark of the particular esteem which the sovereign has for the person to whom he sends it, and that he has

free liberty to approach his person."—*Travels in Persia*, p. 71.   See also note on 1 Sam. xviii, 4.

2. Herodotus states that the kings of Persia had horses of remarkable beauty and of a peculiar breed which were brought from Armenia.   To ride upon the king's horse was almost as great an honor as to sit upon his throne.

3. Some commentators think that by "the crown royal" is meant merely an ornament which was a part of the head-trappings of the horse; though why the horse's head-dress should deserve such special mention here it is not easy to tell.   It is more likely that the crown of the king is meant, and if so, it is probable, as some authorities suppose, that the crown was put, not on the head of Mordecai, but on the head of the horse.   It is said to have been a custom among the Persians, as well as some other nations, that the crown of the king was sometimes put on some favorite royal steed when the animal was led in state.

398.—SIGN OF ROYAL DISPLEASURE.

VII, 7. The king arising from the banquet of wine in his wrath went into the palace garden: and Haman stood up to make request for his life to Esther the queen; for he saw that there was evil determined against him by the king.

The rising of the king in this way was an evidence to Haman of his condemnation to death; it was the royal method of expressing displeasure and vengeance.   An instance is cited by Rosenmüller, from Olearius, which illustrates this Persian custom.   Schah Sefi once considered himself insulted by an unseemly jest which one of his favorites had permitted himself to relate in his presence.   The king suddenly arose and left the place, and the favorite saw that his fate was sealed.   He went home in dismay, and in a few hours the king sent for his head.—*Morgenland*, vol. iii, p. 314.

399.—THE FACE COVERED.

VII, 8. As the word went out of the king's mouth, they covered Haman's face.

The precise design of thus covering the face of a condemned criminal is not known, though it has been conjectured that it was intended to signify that the person condemned was not worthy again to look on the face of the king.   The custom was observed in other nations as well as among the Persians.

400.—SIVAN.

VIII, 9. In the third month, that is, the month Sivan.

Sivan corresponded nearly to our month of June.

401.—THE FEAST OF PURIM.

IX, 26. **Wherefore they called these days Purim after the name of Pur.**

Pur is a Persian word signifying a part, and thence denoting a lot. With the Hebrew plural termination it becomes *purim*, "lots." This is the name by which the feast is known which is kept to commemorate the deliverance of the Jews from the plot of Haman. It is called the Feast of Lots because Haman in his superstition resorted to divination for the purpose of ascertaining when he could most effectually destroy the Jews. See Esther iii, 7. Some think that the name was given in irony, as denoting the contempt in which the Jews held Haman and his divination.

There is a tradition that the introduction of this feast among the Jews met with some opposition, though it afterward became generally observed. The day before the feast is kept as a solemn fast. On the day of the feast the people assemble in the synagogue, where the book of Esther is read amid clapping of hands and stamping of feet, as demonstrations of contempt for Haman and of joy for the deliverance of the Jews. After leaving the synagogue there are great feasts at home, which have been sometimes carried to such excess that some writers have called the Feast of Purim the Bacchanalia of the Jews.

JOB.

402.—PASTORAL WEALTH.

I, 3. **His substance also was seven thousand sheep, and three thousand camels, and five hundred yoke of oxen, and five hundred she-asses.**

Among people of pastoral and nomadic habits it is natural to estimate wealth, not by houses and lands, but by the number of animals owned. Abram was very rich in cattle. Gen. xiii, 2. Lot had flocks and herds. Gen. xiii, 5 See also Gen. xxiv, 35. Job's wealth, on the return of his prosperity, was estimated in like manner. See Job xlii, 12. Special mention is made of she-asses because they were more highly valued than the males on account of their milk, a nourishing drink. To this day the riches of the Bedawîn are reckoned by the number and quality of their cattle.

403.—THE VALUE OF LIFE.

II, 4. **Skin for skin, yea, all that a man hath will he give for his life.**

Many interpretations have been given of this passage, which was evidently a familiar proverb in the early times when Job lived. It probably refers to some ancient custom of bartering by means of skins of animals slain in the chase. The hungry hunter trades with the grain grower, parting, for a supply of food, with the skins of the beasts he has slain, and if necessary he will exchange all he has in order to obtain bread. As Kitto says of this text. "It will then express the necessity of submitting to one great evil to avoid incurring a greater, answering to the Turkish proverb, ' We must give our beards to save our heads.' "—*Daily Bible Illustrations*, vol. v, p. 83.

404.—GRAIN AND THORNS.

V, 5. Whose harvest the hungry eateth up, and taketh it even out of the thorns, and the robber swalloweth up their substance.

This may refer either to the thief who takes all the grain, even that which is mixed with thorns, or to a custom which Dr. Thomson mentions as illustrating this text. He says, "The farmers, after they have threshed out the grain, frequently lay it aside in the chaff in some private place near the floor, and cover it up with thorn-bushes to keep it from being carried away or eaten by animals. Robbers who found and seized this would literally take it from among the thorns."—*The Land and the Book*, vol. i, p. 537.

405.—POISONED ARROWS.

VI, 4. For the arrows of the Almighty are within me, the poison whereof drinketh up my spirit.

An allusion is doubtless made here to the practice, common among barbarous nations of all times, of dipping the points of arrows into some poisonous substance for the purpose of insuring the death of the persons who might be struck with them.

406.—SHADOWS.

VII, 2. As a servant earnestly desireth the shadow, and as a hireling looketh for the reward of his work.

The lengthening shadow indicates the close of day and the termination of toil, and is therefore desired by the weary laborer. In India time is measured by the length of one's shadow. If a man is asked for the time of day, he stands erect in the sunshine, observes where his shadow terminates, and then paces the distance, and is able to tell the time with considerable accuracy. A person wishing to leave his work often exclaims, "How long my shadow is in coming!"—ROBERTS, *Oriental Customs*, p. 261.

407.—PRIMITIVE MAIL-CARRIERS.

IX, 25. My days are swifter than a post: they flee away, they see no good.

Swift runners were often employed in ancient times to convey important messages. Kings kept a number of such in their service as a part of the royal household. When Hezekiah sent invitations to the solemn passover which he designed holding at Jerusalem, it is said that "the posts went with the letters from the king and his princes throughout all Israel and Judah." 2 Chron. xxx, 6. In the time of Jeremiah there seems to have been a regular postal service established, for he says, in prophesying the destruction of Babylon: "One post shall run to meet another, and one messenger to meet another, to show the king of Babylon that his city is taken at one end." Jer. li, 31. The Persians also made use of swift messengers. The order commanding the murder of all the Jews in the empire was sent by this means. See Esth. iii, 13, 15. The order which neutralized the effect of this proclamation was sent by "posts that rode upon mules and camels." Esth. viii, 14.

While there may have been no systematic communication of this sort in the time of Job, yet it is evident from the text that men fleet of foot were employed when occasion required. The patriarch compares the rapid flight of his days to a post; literally, a runner, a man hastening with news. This was the swiftest mode of communication with which he was familiar, and his days went swifter still.

See further the note on Matt. v, 41.

408.—SUPPOSED VIRTUES OF SNOW WATER.

IX, 30. **If I wash myself with snow water, and make my hands never so clean.**

Snow water was anciently supposed to possess peculiar virtues for cleansing the skin. It was thought that the skin was whitened by it, and that it contracted the fibers and prevented perspiration. "In the fable of Lockman, No. 13, the black man rubs his body with snow in order to make it white. Therefore Mohammed prays, 'Lord, wash me from my sins white with water, snow, and ice.'"—UMBREIT, *Version of the Book of Job.*

409.—ROBBERS.

XII, 6. **The tabernacles of robbers prosper, and they that provoke God are secure.**

Robbery has from a very early period of history been a common occupation of lawless men, and has also often proved a profitable employment, as intimated by the text. Whole tribes, and in some instances entire nations, adopted it as a means of livelihood. The Sabeans stole Job's oxen and asses, and "the Chaldeans made out three bands and fell upon the camels." Job i, 15, 17. The Shechemites "set liers in wait" for Abimelech "in the top of the mountains, and they robbed all that came along that way by them." Judges ix, 25. The robbery mentioned in the parable of the Good Samaritan (Luke x, 30) frequently found its counterpart in facts, and at the present day travelers are sometimes robbed by predatory bands.

410.—BOSSES.

XV, 26. He runneth upon him, even on his neck, upon the thick bosses of his bucklers.

The boss was the external convex part of the round shield, its thickest and strongest portion. There were some shields whose shape was wholly convex, the center being an elevated point, as may be seen in the engraving, which represents an Assyrian convex shield.

There were also convex ornaments which were placed on the outside of shields, adding strength as well as beauty. Layard found at Nimroud circular bronze shields, each having an iron handle fastened by six nails. The heads of these nails formed bosses on the outside of the shield.

In the text Eliphaz expresses the uselessness of the attack which the wicked man makes on God, by representing him as running upon the most impenetrable part of the shield.

79.—CONVEX SHIELD.

411.—FRAIL HOUSES.

XV, 28. He dwelleth in desolate cities, and in houses which no man inhabiteth, which are ready to become heaps.

Many of the rude huts in the East are made of small stones or built of mud. The roof is made by covering the beams with brushwood, and this in turn with earth. The rain soaks into the earth, and the weight settling on brush and beams gradually breaks them down unless there is an industrious occupant (see Eccl. x, 18) to keep the roof in proper condition. When the roof is broken down the walls easily fall, and the whole house soon becomes a heap of ruins. But this is true not merely of such rude mud huts, but of large edifices, temples and palaces, built of sun-dried brick, as the ruins of Babylon and Nineveh amply testify.

412.—LIGHT AND DARKNESS AS EMBLEMS.

XVIII, 5, 6. Yea, the light of the wicked shall be put out, and the spark of his fire shall not shine. The light shall be dark in his tabernacle, and his candle shall be put out with him.

To the susceptible mind of the Oriental, light is an object of desire, and darkness something to be greatly dreaded. The lamp is usually kept burning in the house all night; and its light is used as an emblem of prosperity, and the extinguishment of it as an emblem of a great calamity. Thus Job speaks of the days of his prosperity when the candle of the Lord shone upon his head. Job xxix, 3. David says, "Thou wilt light my candle; the Lord my God will enlighten my darkness." Psa. xviii, 28. On the other hand, we find Job saying, as expressive of great affliction: "How oft is the candle of the wicked put out." Job xxi, 17. Solomon says, "Whoso curseth his father or his mother, his lamp shall be put out in obscure darkness." Prov. xx, 20. "The candle of the wicked shall be put out." Prov. xxiv, 20 The Saviour on two occasions refers to this Oriental dread of darkness where he represents the punishment of the wicked under the figure of "outer darkness." See Matt. viii, 12; xxii, 13. Both ideas are blended in Prov. xiii, 9: "The light of the righteous rejoiceth: but the lamp of the wicked shall be put out."

See also Jer. xxv, 10.

413.—THE NET IN COMBAT.

XIX, 6. Know now that God hath overthrown me, and hath compassed me with his net.

Some commentators find here an illustration of an ancient mode of com bat practiced among the Persians, Goths, and Romans. Among the Romans one of the combatants had a sword and shield, while the other had a trident and net. The latter endeavored to throw his net over the head of his adversary. If he succeeded in this, he immediately drew the net around his neck with a noose which was attached to it, pulled him to the ground and dispatched him with the trident. If he failed to throw the net over the head, he in turn ran the risk of being destroyed by his adversary while seeking his net for another throw. If Job knew of this custom in his day, he represents himself in this text as having engaged in a contest with God, and, being defeated, he now lies entangled in the net and completely at the mercy of his conqueror.

414.—BOOKS—TABLETS—MONUMENTS.

XIX, 23, 24. O that my words were now written! O that they were printed in a book! that they were graven with an iron pen and lead in the rock forever! See also Jer. xvii, 1.

Three different substances for the preservation of records are usually supposed to be referred to here:

1. *Books.* These were anciently made of linen or cotton cloth, skins, or the leaves of the papyrus. From the last word comes our English word, paper. The inner bark of trees was also sometimes used. The Latin word for bark being *liber*, this word at length came to signify a book; it is still found in the English word library. When made of cloth or skins the book was made up in the form of a roll. See note on Isa. xxxiv, 4.

2. *Leaden tablets.* These are of high antiquity. In 1699 Montfaucon bought at Rome a very old book entirely made of lead. It was about four inches long and three wide, and had a cover and six leaves or sheets. The hinges and nails were also made of lead. The volume contained Egyptian gnostic figures and inscriptions in Greek and Etruscan characters.

In a temple in the Carian city of Cnidus, erected in honor of Hades and Persephone, about the fourth century before Christ, the women were in the habit of depositing thin sheets of lead on which were written the names of persons they hated, together with their misdeeds. They also inscribed on the lead tablets imprecations against those who had thus injured them. Many of these tablets were discovered in 1858 when excavations were made in the ruins of the temple. They are now in the British Museum.

It is not, however, certain that Job in the text refers to leaden tablets or leaves on which inscriptions were made. He may have alluded to the custom of first cutting letters in stone and then filling them up with molten lead. There are indications that some of the incised letters in Assyrian monuments were filled with metal. M. Botta states that the letters on the pavement slabs of Khorsabad give evidence of having been filled with copper. See LAYARD'S *Nineveh and its Remains,* vol. ii, p. 188.

3. *Stone monuments.* The law was originally written on tables of stone "with the finger of God." Exod. xxxi, 18. The second set of tables were written by Moses by Divine command. Exod. xxxiv, 4, 28. Joshua copied the law on the stone altar at Mount Ebal. Josh. viii, 32. This mode of recording important truths or events was very common in ancient times. Job desires that his sentiments should be thus engraved, that generations to come might read the record.

The stone records of ancient Oriental nations, which modern discoveries have brought to light, are all illustrations of the custom which Job evidently had in mind. Many of these bear on Scripture facts and history, confirming and supplementing the sacred record. The most remarkable, in some respects, of any of these ancient monuments is the famous Moabite stone, the discovery of which in the year 1868 created such intense excitement among biblical scholars and antiquarians. This is the very oldest Semitic inscription of importance as yet discovered, and is the only one thus far found which reaches back to the age of the Jewish monarchy. It gives the Moabitish account of the conflict described in the third chapter of the Second Book of Kings.

415.—HOUSES OF CLAY.

XXIV, 16. **In the dark they dig through houses, which they had marked for themselves in the daytime.**

This refers to houses that are built of clay. Of these there are several varieties. Some have a framework of wicker hurdles thickly daubed with mud. In others the walls are made of layers of mud placed one over the other, each drying before the next is put on. Others still are made of sun-dried bricks. This style of building is very ancient, and is still common in many parts of the East. A thief might easily break through a wall of this kind, and modern thieves are as ready to do it as were the burglars who lived in the days of Job.

Houses like these are referred to by Eliphaz in Job iv, 19, where he speaks of "houses of clay, whose foundation is in the dust, which are crushed before the moth;" and also in Ezek. xii, 5, where the prophet is commanded, in a figurative way, to dig "through the wall." The Saviour also refers to them when he speaks of thieves breaking through to steal, (Matt. vi, 19,) and of the house which was broken up by the thief. Matt. xxiv, 43. The frailty of the walls of such houses is also probably referred to in Psa. lxii, 3, and Isa. xxx, 13.

416.—WORMS FEEDING ON THE BODY.

XXIV, 20. The worm shall feed sweetly on him; he shall be no more remembered.

It is an Oriental opinion that worms exist in the skin and in all parts of the body, and that they are among the principal causes of its destruction. Roberts (*Oriental Illustrations*, p. 271) quotes from an ancient Indian medical work in which eighteen kinds of worms are enumerated by the author in as many different parts of the body. In Job xix, 26, the translators have supplied the word *worms:* "Though after my skin worms destroy this body." Though the word is not in the original, yet the sentiment is in accordance with the text we are now illustrating and with several other passages. See Job vii, 5; xvii, 14; xxi, 26; Isa. xiv, 11. In India it is common for a sick man to say, "Ah, my body is but a nest for worms; they have paths in all parts of my frame!" "Ah, these worms are continually eating my flesh!"

417.—RAIMENT AS WEALTH.

XXVII, 16. Though he heap up silver as the dust, and prepare raiment as the clay.

The Eastern people have always reckoned collections of raiment among their choice treasures, and estimate them in the accounts of their wealth along with gold and silver. This is seen in the text, and is also to be found in the injunction of the Saviour in Matt. vi, 19, where, in speaking of the uncertain character of worldly wealth, he refers to the ravages of the moth upon the treasures of raiment. So Paul in his address at Miletus to the elders of Ephesus, says, "I have coveted no man's silver, or gold, or apparel." Acts xx, 33. He also refers to the value of garments in 1 Tim. ii, 9, where he speaks of "costly array." James likewise says in his epistle, chapter v, 2, "Your riches are corrupted and your garments are moth-eaten."

See also the note on Gen. xlv, 22.

418.—STONE OIL-PRESSES.

XXIX, 6. The rock poured me out rivers of oil.

Some think the reference here is to the fact that the olive-tree sometimes grows in very rocky soil; but allusion is more probably made to stone oil-

80.—ANCIENT OIL-PRESSES.

presses, from which the oil flowed like a river. See also Ezek. xxxii, 14. Moses speaks of oil being sucked " out of the flinty rock." Deut. xxxii, 13.

419.—EATING ALONE.

XXXI, 17. Or have eaten my morsel myself alone, and the fatherless hath not eaten thereof.

It is a part of Oriental etiquette to invite others to partake of food. See note on Gen. xviii, 2, 3. Dr. Shaw says, referring to his travels in Arabia: " No sooner was our food prepared, whether it was potted flesh boiled with rice, a lentil soup, or unleavened cakes served up with oil or honey, than one of the Arabs, (*not to eat his morsel alone,*) after having placed himself on the highest spot of ground in the neighborhood, calls out thrice, with a loud voice, to all his brethren, *The sons of the faithful,* to come and partake of it; though none of them were in view, or perhaps within a hundred miles of us. This custom, however, they maintain to be a token at least of their great benevolence, as indeed it would have been of their hospitality, provided they could have had an opportunity to show it."—*Travels,* Preface, p. xii.

420.—IMPRESSIONS OF SEALS.

XXXVIII, 14. It is turned as clay to the seal.

The bricks of Egypt, Babylonia, and Assyria bear marks which have evidently been made with a seal. Egyptian wine jars and mummy pits were sometimes sealed with clay. There have been found in Assyria public documents made of clay, and having the letters stamped in them, and the marks of official sealing. In the East, doors of granaries or of treasure rooms are to this day sometimes sealed with clay, so that it is impossible to enter without first breaking the seal. The sepulcher of Christ was probably sealed in this way. See note on Matt. xxvii, 66. Clay is used in preference to wax because the former hardens with the heat, while the latter melts. The engraving represents a lump of clay from Assyria, having several impressions of seals upon it.

For description of seals, see note on 1 Kings xxi, 8.

81.—IMPRESSIONS OF SEALS.

421.—CORDS AND RINGS.

XLI, 2. Canst thou put a hook into his nose? or bore his jaw through with a thorn?

1. *Agmon*, "hook," is more correctly a rush-cord or rope made of reeds, (Gesenius;) and the question of the text suggests the wonderful strength of the leviathan by the impossibility of putting a rope around his nose, thus binding his jaws.

2. *Choach*, "thorn," is really a ring; and the text probably refers to a custom, very ancient and still practiced, of inserting a strong iron ring into the jaw of a fish as soon as caught. A cord is fastened to the ring and the fish is let down into the water, where it remains until the fisherman has an opportunity of selling it.

422.—FISH-SPEARS.

XLI, 7. Canst thou fill his skin with barbed irons? or his head with fish-spears?

There is an allusion here to an instrument resembling the bident or two-tongued fish-spear in use by the Egyptians, and frequently depicted on the monuments. This spear was a slender rod some ten or twelve feet long, doubly feathered at the end, like a modern arrow. It had two sharp points about two feet in length, and on these the fish were impaled. The fisherman pushed along the Nile in a flat-bottomed boat among the papyrus reeds and lotus plants, and on seeing his finny prey drove the weapon with his right hand, steadying it through a curve in his left.

423.—ADVERSITY A PRISON

XLII, 10. The Lord turned the captivity of Job, when he prayed for his friends: also the Lord gave Job twice as much as he had before.

This, in the figurative language of the East, means that the Lord restored Job to his former prosperity. Roberts says, "A man formerly in great prosperity speaks of his present state as if he were in prison. 'I am now a captive. Yes, I am a slave.' If he be again providentially elevated, it is observed, 'His captivity is changed.'"—*Oriental Illustrations,* p. 302. David says, "Bring my soul out of prison, that I may praise thy name." Psa. cxlii, 7.

424.—PRESENTS TO THE AFFLICTED.

XLII, 11. Then came there unto him all his brethren, and all his sisters, and all they that had been of his acquaintance before, and did eat bread with him in his house. . . . Every man also gave him a piece of money, and every one an earring of gold.

1. It is said to be still a custom in some parts of the East for friends and relatives to visit, at some previously appointed time, a man in trouble, bringing with them presents to supply his wants, and to make up for whatever losses he may have sustained by his calamity. After partaking of a feast, prepared by the host, the guests leave their gifts, and express their desire for his future prosperity.

2. On the meaning of "a piece of money," (*kesitah,*) see note on Gen. xxxiii, 19.

425.—POETIC NAMES.

XLII, 14. He called the name of the first, Jemima; and the name of the second, Kezia; and the name of the third, Keren-happuch.

Rosenmüller has the following note on this verse: "A Jewish writer, Solomon Jarchi, correctly remarks that the names of the daughters of Job indicate their beauty, as it is said in the fifteenth verse: 'And in all the land were no women found so fair as the daughters of Job.' The first name, *Jemima,* means *resembling a clear day,* (with the brilliancy of its beauty)—fair as the day. So, according to *Hesychius, Hämera,* that is, day, was a surname of Diana. The second name, *Kezia,* means Cassia, one of the most valuable spices of antiquity. The third name, *Keren-happuch,* means *Horn of the Eye-paint,* that is, a vessel made of horn, wherein the Oriental women kept the paint which they used for their eyes. Thomas Roe, in his *Travels,* remarks that the Persians are accustomed to give their women names which mean spices, fragrant ointments, pearls or precious stones, or something otherwise beautiful and delightful."—*Morgenland,* vol. iii, p. 375.

It is proper to say, however, that the etymology above given is disputed by some authorities. Gesenius derives Jemima from an Arabic word signifying *dove.* Dr. Alexander, editor of *Kitto's Cyclopedia,* defines Keren-happuch, *Horn of adornment,* or *Horn of beauty.* These interpretations, as much as the others given, represent the names as names of beauty.

PSALMS.

426.—IRRIGATION OF GARDENS.

1, 8. **He shall be like a tree planted by the rivers of water, that bringeth forth his fruit in his season.**

Several commentators call attention to the fact that *palge-mayim*, here rendered "rivers of water," literally means *divisions of waters;* and reference is supposed to be made to a very favorite mode of irrigation in some Eastern countries. Canals are dug in every direction, and through these the

82.—A WATERED GARDEN.

water is carried, to the great improvement of vegetation. Egypt was once covered with these canals, and in this way the waters of the Nile were carried to every part of the valley through which the river ran. Some Eastern gardens are so arranged that water is conveyed around every plot, and even to every tree. Allusion is probably made to this custom in Ezek. xxxi, 3, 4, where "the Assyrian" is spoken of as "a cedar." "The waters made him great, the deep set him up on high with her rivers running around about his plants, and sent out her little rivers unto all the trees of the field." We do not know that this ancient custom existed so early as

14

the time of Job, but chapter xxxviii, 25, of the Book of Job seems to indicate it: "Who hath divided a watercourse for the overflowing of waters,"
etc. Solomon says, "The king's heart is in the hand of the Lord, as the
rivers of water: he turneth it whithersoever he will." Prov. xxi, 1. In
enumerating the many works of his reign the same king says, "I made me
gardens and orchards, and I planted trees in them of all kind of fruits. I
made me pools of water, to water therewith the wood that bringeth forth
trees." Eccles. ii, 5, 6.

See note on Deut. xi, 10. See also Isa. i, 30; lviii, 11; Jer. xvii, 8;
xxxi, 12.

Several methods are adopted for conveying the water from a river to the
canals which run through the gardens. Sometimes large wheels are so set
that while the bottom enters the water, the top is a little above the level
of the bank. The circumference of every wheel has earthen jugs fastened
to it. The turning of the wheel, either by the current or by oxen, plunges
the jugs under the water and fills them; when the jugs rise to the top of
the bank they empty themselves into a channel prepared for the purpose, and the water is thus conveyed to the garden. Sometimes the water
is raised from the river to the canal on the bank by means of a *shadoof,* or
well-sweep, very similar to the old-fashioned machine for drawing water
from wells in our own country—a horizontal pole, hung on a perpendicular
one, having a bucket at one end and a balance of stones at the other.

427.—KISSING AN ACT OF HOMAGE.

II, 12. **Kiss the Son, lest he be angry and ye perish from the
way; when his wrath is kindled but a little.**

When Samuel anointed Saul he kissed the newly make king. This act of
homage was a recognition of his royalty. 1 Sam. x, 1. It is a custom still
observed in India and Arabia. In this way the Psalmist desires all men to
recognize the royalty of the Son. Kissing was an act of worship among
idolaters. See 1 Kings xix, 18; Job xxxi, 27: Hosea xiii, 2. Instead of
worshiping idols, God would have us worship his son Jesus Christ.

An interesting incident is given in Irby and Mangle's Travels showing
how kissing was used as a token of reconciliation. The circumstance
recorded occurred near Petra.

"While we were deliberating on this subject, we saw a great cavalcade
entering our camp from the southward. There were many mounted Arabs
with lances, and we observed that there were some amongst the horsemen
who wore richer turbans, and of more gaudy colors, than is usual amongst
Bedouins or peasants. As the procession advanced, several of Abou
Raschid's Arabs went out and led the horses of the chiefs by the bridles
into the camp. The whole procession alighted at the tent of our chief, and

kissed his turban; this was the signal of pacification. Peace was immediately proclaimed throughout the camp, and notice was given that men bearing arms, who had come from a distance, many of whom had joined us that very morning, were to return to their respective homes."—*Travels in Egypt*, etc., p. 122.

428.—WAITING FOR BOOTY.

X, 8. He sitteth in the lurking places of the villages: in the secret places doth he murder the innocent.

This is an accurate description of the habit of the Bedawín of the present day. They watch for booty in villages, or "in the wilderness," (see Jer. iii, 2,) anywhere where they can be hidden from view and where they may hope to find an unwary passer-by. They do not hesitate to add murder to robbery if, in their opinion, necessity demands it.

See also Psa. lvi, 6; Prov. i, 11; Jer. v, 26.

429.—ANOINTING GUESTS.

XXIII, 5. Thou anointest my head with oil; my cup runneth over.

Anointing was an ancient custom practiced by the Egyptians, and afterward by the Greeks and Romans and other nations. Olive oil was used, (see note on Psa. xcii, 10,) either pure or mixed with fragrant and costly spices, often brought from a long distance. See note on Matt. xxvi, 7. The practice was in use, not only as a part of the ceremony in connection with the coronation of kings, (see note on 2 Kings xi, 12,) and at the installation of the High Priest, (Psa. cxxxiii, 2,) but as an act of courtesy and hospitality toward a guest. Thus, the Lord accuses Simon of a want of hospitality in neglecting to anoint the head of him whom he had invited to eat with him.

Luke vii, 46. There are pictures on the Egyptian monuments representing guests having their heads anointed. Oil was used for other parts of the body as well as for the head, and at home as well as when visiting. The biblical references to the custom are numerous. See Deut. xxviii, 40; Ruth iii, 3; Psa. xcii, 10; civ, 15; Eccl. ix, 8; Micah vi, 15; Matt. vi, 17. The neglect of anointing was considered a sign of mourning. See 2 Sam. xiv, 2; Dan. x, 3. An anointed face, on the other

83.—ANOINTING A GUEST.

hand, was a sign of joy; hence we read of being anointed with the "oil of gladness." Psa. xlv, 7; Heb. i, 9.

Tavernier states that he found the Arabs always ready to accept a present of olive oil.   As soon as one received it he lifted his turban and anointed his head, his face, and his beard, at the same time lifting his eyes to heaven and saying, "God be thanked!"

Captain Wilson, an Oriental traveler, speaking of the custom alluded to in this.passage, says: "I once had this ceremony performed on myself in the house of a great and rich Indian, in the presence of a large company.   The gentleman of the house poured upon my hands and arms a delightful odor-iferous perfume, put a golden cup into my hands, and poured wine into it until it ran over; assuring me, at the same time, that it was a great pleasure to him to receive me, and that I should find a rich supply in his house." —BURDER, *Oriental Customs*, No. 539.

The Psalmist in the text represents himself as an honored guest of Jehovah, who prepares a table for him, hospitably anoints him, and puts into his hands a full cup.

430.—CATARACTA.

XXIV, 7.   Lift up your heads, O ye gates ; and be ye lifted up, ye everlasting doors.

Allusion is thought to be made here to the custom of hanging gates so that, instead of opening in the ordinary way, they rise and fall as they open and shut.   A gate of this description was called *cataracta*, because of the force and noise with which it fell.   It was used in the fortification of towns, and corresponded to the portcullis of modern times; and is supposed to have been known in the time of David.   See SMITH'S *Dictionary of Greek and Roman Antiquities*, S. V. *Cataracta*.

431.—SYMBOLICAL HAND-WASHING.

XXVI, 6.   I will wash mine hands in innocency: so will I compass thine altar, O Lord.

There were several occasions on which the Jews were accustomed to wash their hands in connection with religious rites.   The Psalmist may have had one or all of these in mind when he uttered the text.   See also Psa. lxxiii, 13.

1. There was the washing required of the priests in the service of the tabernacle and temple.   The brazen laver was made for this purpose.   See Exod. xl, 30–32.   It is said to have been customary for the priests, when they had bound the sacrifice to the horns of the altar to march around it, after they had washed their hands.   Thus David says, "So will I compass thine altar, O Lord."

2. The Jews were also accustomed to wash their hands before engaging in prayer.   Paul is thought to refer to this in the expression "holy hands" in 1 Tim. ii, 8.

3. There were certain ceremonies directed to be observed in cases of murder where the murderer was unknown. The elders of the city nearest to which the body of the murdered man was found were directed to strike off a heifer's head, and then it is commanded that they "shall wash their hands over the heifer that is beheaded in the valley: and they shall answer and say, Our hands have not shed this blood, neither have our eyes seen it." Deut. xxi, 6, 7. This was considered a most solemn asseveration on their part of their innocence in the matter. Pilate, though a Gentile, had probably lived long enough among the Jews to understand this custom, and is, therefore, supposed to refer to it when, on the demand of the people that Barabbas be freed and Jesus crucified, "he took water, and washed his hands before the multitude, saying, I am innocent of the blood of this just person: see ye to it." Matt. xxvii, 24. The custom is said to have been Gentile as well as Jewish; but this is denied. See BLOOMFIELD, *Greek Testament; Note on Matt.* xxvii, 24.

Since David desires in this text to symbolize inward purity by outward washing, any one of these customs may serve for illustration.

432.—THE PSALTERY.

XXXIII, 2. Sing unto him with the psaltery, and an instrument of ten strings.

These two instruments, the "psaltery" and "the instrument of ten strings," (see also Psa. xcii, 3; cxliv, 9,) are supposed to have been the same, the one term being used to explain the other. The shape of the *nebel*, or psaltery, is unknown. Some suppose it to have been like an inverted Delta, ▽. Others, from the name, imagine that it was shaped like a leathern bottle, the word *nebel* having that signification. A skin bottle inverted and an inverted Delta would in general shape be similar, so that both ideas may be correct. Others think that it was shaped somewhat like a guitar, and that it resembled that instrument in its general style.

84.—ASSYRIAN TRIANGULAR LYRE. (KOYUNJIK.)

Josephus says. "The psaltery had twelve musical notes, and was played upon by the fingers."—*Antiquities*, Book vii, chapter 12, § 3. These twelve "notes" are supposed to have been represented by twelve strings, whereas the texts above cited speak of but ten. It may be that the number differed in different varieties of the instrument. If we suppose these varieties to have been designated by the number of their strings, we may find the reason for the explanatory clause of the Psalmist, the kind of psaltery to which he specially refers being the one known as " the ten-stringed." The strings, whatever their number, were stretched over a wooden frame. 2 Sam. vi, 5 ; 1 Kings x, 12.

85.—ASSYRIAN LYRE WITH TEN STRINGS.
(KHORSABAD.)

When the *nebel* was invented and when it came into use among the Hebrews is unknown. It is first mentioned in connection with the inauguration of King Saul. When the company of young prophets met him, shortly after Samuel had anointed him, one of the instruments on which they played was the *nebel.* 1 Sam. x, 5. It was used in Divine worship. See 2 Sam. vi, 5 ; 1 Chron. xiii, 8 ; xv, 16 ; xvi, 5 ; xxv, 1 ; Amos v, 23. It was also used on festive occasions. See Isa. v, 12 ; xiv, 11 ; Amos vi, 5. (In these last passages and in Amos v, 23, *nebel* is rendered *viol* in our English version.) From 1 Chron. xiii, 8 ; xv, 16, and Amos v, 23, it appears that the *nebel* was used to accompany the voice.

433.—POSTURE OF THE FACE IN PRAYER.

XXXV, 18. I humbled my soul with fasting, and my prayer returned into mine own bosom.

Reference is thought to be made here to the custom among Orientals of praying with the head inclined forward until the face is almost hidden in the bosom of the garment.

434.—THE SERVANT'S EARS.

XL, 6. Mine ears hast thou opened.

The Psalmist uses this expression to denote the fact that he is a servant of God, ready to do his will, as he further declares in the eighth verse. He seems to have in his mind the ceremony by which a Hebrew servant, if unwilling to leave his master, might be bound to him for life. "Then his master shall bring him unto the judges ; he shall also bring him to the door, or unto the door post ; and his master shall bore his ear through with an awl ; and he shall serve him for ever." Exod. xxi, 6. See also Deut. xv, 16, 17. This custom was observed, not only by the Jews, but also by many other ancient nations.

435.—ABUSE OF HOSPITALITY.

XLI, 9. Yea, mine own familiar friend, in whom I trusted, which did eat of my bread, hath lifted up his heel against me.

It is considered an act of great baseness among Eastern nations for any one to do an evil deed against those who have shared his hospitality. This feeling is very ancient, and is often alluded to by ancient authors. The Saviour refers to it when he mentions the baseness of Judas, and cites this very passage from the Psalmist. John xiii, 18. See also Obadiah 7. Similar to this notion of the sacredness of hospitality, though more binding in its nature, was "the covenant of salt." See note on Lev. ii, 13.

436.—PERFUMED GARMENTS.

XLV, 8. All thy garments smell of myrrh, and aloes, and cassia.

In many parts of the East the people are excessively fond of perfuming their garments, sometimes making the fragrance so strong that Europeans can scarcely endure it. They sprinkle their clothing with sweet scented oils extracted from spices or sandal wood, and with a great variety of strongly perfumed waters. They fumigate them with powerful incense or by burning scented woods. They make use of camphor, civet wood, sandal wood, aloes, and even sometimes sew chips of perfumed wood into the garments. Reference is made to this custom in Sol. Song iv, 11: "The smell of thy garments is like the smell of Lebanon;" and possibly in Hosea xiv, 6. Most commentators suppose an allusion to this custom to be made also in Gen. xxvii, 27, where Isaac kissed Jacob, and it is said, "he smelled the smell of his raiment, and blessed him and said, See, the smell of my son is as the smell of a field which the Lord hath blessed." This, however, is disputed by some. Kurtz refers to Tuch's view of the passage, and agrees with his interpretation. "We must, therefore, agree with Tuch, that an aromatic smell of the herbs, flowers, and other produce of the field, must have been felt off the garments of Esau, who was 'a man of the field;' a supposition this which involves no difficulty, considering that the country was so rich in aromatic and smelling herbs."—*History of the Old Covenant*, vol. i, p. 298.

437.—USE OF HYSSOP.

LI, 7. Purge me with hyssop and I shall be clean.

Hyssop was appointed to be used in ceremonial purification. It was used in connection with the passover, (Exod. xii, 22,) the cleansing of lepers, (Lev. xiv, 4, 6, 49, 51, 52,) and the sacrifice of the red heifer. Num. xix,

6, 18. See also Heb. ix, 19. Hyssop was anciently considered a means of actual bodily purification, and was even taken internally for that purpose.

438.—BOTTLED TEARS.

LVI, 8. Thou tellest my wanderings: put thou my tears into thy bottle: are they not in thy book?

Reference is usually thought to be made here to the lachrymatories or tear-bottles which have been found in ancient tombs, and which are supposed to have been used for the purpose of receiving the tears of mourning relatives and friends at the time of burial. These tear-bottles are made of various materials, such as glass and earthenware, and are of different shapes. The most of them are broad at the bottom, with long slender necks and funnel-shaped mouths. Morier says that in Persia, "in some of their mournful assemblies, it is the custom for a priest to go about to each person, at the height of his grief, with a piece of cotton in his hand, with which he carefully collects the falling tears, and which he then squeezes into a bottle, preserving them with the greatest caution." "Some Persians believe that, in the agony of death, when all medicines have failed, a drop of tears so collected put into the mouth of a dying man has been known to revive him; and it is for such use that they are collected."—*Second Journey through Persia*, p. 179.

Some commentators, however, deny that there is any reference in this text to the ancient lachrymatories, or that there is any evidence of their use among the Hebrews. Such affirm that the allusion here is to the custom of putting into bags, or small leathern bottles, articles of value for safe keeping. See note on Luke xii, 33. The idea would then be, "Treasure up these tears as something of great value."

439.—SERPENT CHARMING.

LVIII, 4, 5. They are like the deaf adder that stoppeth her ear; which will not hearken to the voice of charmers, charming never so wisely.

Serpent charming has from remote times been practiced among Oriental nations. While there is doubtless imposture often associated with the exhibitions of serpent charmers, yet there are many carefully observing travelers who give it as their opinion, from their own observation, that there are men who, in some way, can detect the presence of serpents in houses and old walls, and can draw them out and keep them from doing mischief by the power of shrill musical notes. Since none of the serpent tribe have any external ear, and consequently can only hear very sharp sounds, it is hardly necessary to explain the deafness of the adder as willful, occasioned, as some old travelers have gravely asserted, by putting one ear to the dust and stopping the other with its tail.

Some travelers give it as their opinion that all the serpents exhibited by the charmers have previously had their fangs extracted, while others assert that some of the serpents thus sported with have afterward given unmistakable evidence of still possessing the death-dealing power. Forbes gives a curious illustration of this. He once painted the picture of a *cobra de capello*, which a Hindoo snake charmer kept dancing on the table for a whole hour, while the artist was at his work. During this time he " frequently handled

86.—INDIAN SERPENT CHARMERS.

it to observe the beauty of the spots, and especially the spectacles on the hood, not doubting but that its venomous fangs had been previously extracted." The next morning his servant informed him, very much to his astonishment, that "while purchasing some fruit in the bazar he had observed the man who had been with me on the preceding evening entertaining the country people with his dancing snakes. They, according to their usual custom, sat on the ground around him, when, either from the music stopping too suddenly, or from some other cause irritating the vicious reptile which I had so often handled, it darted at the throat of a young woman, and inflicted a wound of which she died in about half an hour."—*Oriental Memoirs*, vol. i, p. 44.

Besides the text, reference is made to serpent charming in several other passages. Solomon refers to it in Eccl. x, 11: "Surely the serpent will bite without enchantment; and a babbler is no better." In the prophecy of Jeremiah, there is allusion made to the same custom: "For, behold, I will send serpents, cockatrices, among you, which will not be charmed, and they shall bite you, saith the Lord." Jer. viii, 17.

440.—BROKEN TEETH.

LVIII, 6. Break their teeth, O God, in their mouth : break out
the great teeth of the young lions, O Lord.

This is thought by some to be a continuation of the figure in the preceding verse, and to allude to the custom of snake charmers, who, it is said,
often break out the teeth of the serpents they wish to tame, and remove the
poisonous gland; though this is not always done, as the preceding note
shows.

This interpretation, however, supposes a "mixed figure" in the text: a
sudden transition from the serpent's teeth to the teeth of young lions.
Other interpreters therefore suppose that the reference to serpent charming closes with the fifth verse, and that in the sixth verse an allusion is made
to an ancient custom of heathen kings, who were in the habit of knocking
out the teeth of their prisoners, or of those who had offended them.

441.—THORNS FOR FUEL.

LVIII, 9. Before your pots can feel the thorns, he shall take
them away as with a whirlwind.

There is a great variety of thorny shrubs and plants abounding in Palestine. These the people gladly gather and use for fuel. They make a quick,
hot fire, which kindles easily and soon expires. The idea conveyed in the
text is that of swift destruction. The wicked are to be destroyed quicker
than the heat from a fire of thorns could reach the cooking vessels.

A similar figure is used in the prophecy of Isaiah: "And the people shall
be as the burnings of lime: as thorns cut up shall they be burned in the
fire." Isa. xxxiii, 12. It has been supposed from this text that thorns may
have been used in lime-kilns.

Allusion to the use of thorns for fuel is also made in 2 Sam. xxiii, 6, 7;
Psa. cxviii, 12; Eccl. vii, 6; Isa. ix, 18; x, 17; Nahum i, 10.

See note on 1 Kings xvii, 10, and also on Matt. vi, 30.

442.—LEATHER TABLES.

LXIX, 22. Let their table become a snare before them: and
that which should have been for their welfare, let it become a
trap.

The table of the modern Arabs is usually nothing but a piece of skin or
leather, a mat, or a linen cloth spread upon the ground. The ancient Hebrews are supposed to have used a table of this sort, and this is thought to
be referred to in the text. A table thus spread on the ground might easily
become a trap by which the feet of the unwary would be entangled so that
they should fall. For a description of the "snare" and "trap" referred to
here, see note on Psa. xci, 3.

443.—UNBURIED BODIES.

LXXIX, 2. The dead bodies of thy servants have they given to be meat unto the fowls of the heaven, the flesh of thy saints unto the beasts of the earth.

1. To be deprived of burial was considered by the Jews one of the greatest dishonors that could be inflicted on a human being. In this' they but shared the common feeling of civilized man. We find a number of scriptural references to this sentiment. The Psalmist, lamenting the desolations he beheld, says, "Our bones are scattered at the grave's mouth, as when one cutteth and cleaveth wood upon the earth." Psa. cxli, 7. Solomon speaks of it as a great disgrace that a man "have no burial." Eccl. vi, 3. The Lord said of Jehoiakim, "his dead body shall be cast out in the day to the heat, and in the night to the frost." Jer. xxxvi, 30. In the text the bodies are represented not only as unburied, but as further dishonored by being devoured by birds and beasts. This was one of the curses pronounced by Moses for disobedience to the Divine law. Deut. xxviii, 26. It was a threat mutually exchanged between David and Goliath. 1 Sam. xvii, 44–46. The prophet Jeremiah has several references to this dishonorable treatment of the bodies of the dead. See Jer. vii, 33; xvi, 4; xix, 7; xxxiv, 20.

2. In connection with this subject it may not be amiss to state that, on the other hand, the ancient Magi exposed the bodies of their dead, to be eaten by birds, as a matter of religious principle; their theory being that any other mode of disposing of a corpse would pollute at least one of the four so-called elements: earth, air, fire, and water. If living beings should devour the dead, this pollution would be prevented. At the present day the Guebres, or Fire-worshipers, the descendants of the ancient Persians, follow the same practice, and even have apparatus prepared for the purpose. "Round towers of considerable height, without either door or window, are constructed by the Guebres, having at the top a number of iron bars, which slope inwards. The towers are mounted by means of ladders, and the bodies are placed crossways upon the bars. The vultures and crows which hover about the towers soon strip the flesh from the bones, and these latter then fall through to the bottom. The Zendavesta contains particular directions for the construction of such towers, which are called *dakhmas*, or 'towers of silence.'"—RAWLINSON, *Five Great Monarchies*, vol. ii, p. 350, note 2.

444.—THE "PIT."

LXXXVIII, 4. I am counted with them that go down into the pit.

There are several Hebrew words which are rendered in our version by the word "pit." The ordinary method of burial being in a grave dug in the earth, or hewn out of the rock, the phrase "go down into the pit" became synonymous with death and the grave. Solomon represents those who are trying to entice the innocent youth into ways of wickedness as saying, "Let us swallow them up alive as the grave; and whole, as those that go down into the pit." Prov. i, 12. Hezekiah, in his song of thanksgiving for the recovery of his health, says, "For the grave cannot praise thee, death cannot celebrate thee; they that go down into the pit cannot hope for thy truth." Isa. xxxviii, 18. In these two passages the parallel members of the sentence explain each other. The phrase referred to is of frequent occurrence in Scripture. See, for example, Job xvii, 16; xxxiii, 24; Psa. xxviii, 1; xxx, 3; cxliii, 7; Ezek. xxvi, 20; xxviii, 8; xxxi, 14; xxxii, 18.

445.—BIRD-SNARES.

XCI, 8. **Surely he shall deliver thee from the snare of the fowler.**

Several different words are used in the Hebrew to denote various snares which were employed in fowling. The word *pach*, which is used in the text, denoted a spring, or trap-net, "in two parts, which, when set, were spread out upon the ground, and slightly fastened with a stick, (trap-stick;) so that as soon as a bird or beast touched the stick, the parts flew up and inclosed the bird in the net, or caught the foot of the animal. Job xviii, 9."—ROBINSON'S *Gesenius*. The word *mokesh* is also used to denote a snare of the same sort;

87.—ANCIENT EGYPTIAN SNARES.

though it is also sometimes used to signify a circle of nets for capturing beasts. See note on 2 Sam. xxii, 6.

Snares which were spread on the ground and caught the bird by the feet, or, loosing a spring, encircled it with a net, are often referred to by biblical writers as illustrative of the dangers which beset men. See Job xviii, 8–10, where several varieties seem to be named. The same is true of Psa. cxl, 5. See also Psa. cxxiv, 7; cxli, 9; cxlii, 3; Prov. vii, 23; xxii, 5; Hosea ix, 8; Amos iii, 5.

For another mode of catching birds, see note on Hosea vii, 12.

446.—GREEN OIL.

XCII, 10. I shall be anointed with fresh oil.

Literally, *green oil.* Some interpret this to mean oil newly made; others an oil made from green or unripe olives, like the beaten oil of the sanctuary. See note on Exod. xxvii, 20. Roberts suggests that it means "cold drawn oil," or that which is pressed from the nut without the process of boiling. He says: "The Orientals prefer this kind to all others for anointing themselves; it is considered the most precious, the most pure and efficacious. Nearly all their medicinal oils are thus extracted, and because they cannot gain so much by this method as by the boiling process oils so drawn are very dear. Hence their name for the article thus prepared is also *patche*, that is, 'green oil.'"—*Oriental Illustrations*, p. 339.

447.—TRUMPETS.

XCVIII, 6. With trumpets and sound of cornet make a joyful noise before the Lord, the King.

1. *Chatsotserah*, "trumpet," was a long, straight, and slender wind instrument, such as Moses was commanded to furnish for the service of the Israelites. Num. x, 2. Josephus gives this description of it: "In length it was little less than a cubit. It was composed of a narrow tube, somewhat thicker than a flute, but with so much breadth as was sufficient for admission of the breath of a man's mouth; it ended in the form of a bell, like common trumpets."—*Antiquities*, book iii, chap. 12, § 6.

The *chatsotserah* was used for notifying the people of the different feasts, for signaling the change of camp, and for sounding alarms in time of war. See Num. x, 1–10; Hosea v, 8. It was at first used in sacrificial rites only on special occasions, but in the time of David and Solomon its use for such purposes was very much extended.

2. It is impossible to give an accurate description of the *shophar*, here and in other passages rendered "cornet," but often translated "trumpet." Our translators render it "trumpet," except when, as in the text, they are compelled to make a distinction between it and *chatsotserah*, which they invariably render "trumpet." See 1 Chron. xv, 28; 2 Chron. xv, 14; Hosea v, 8. It is translated "trumpet" in Exod. xix, 16; Lev. xxv, 9; Job xxxix, 25; Joel ii, 1; Amos ii, 2.

Authorities differ as to its shape, some supposing it to have been straight, while others contend that it was more or less bent like a horn. The latter opinion would seem the more probable from the fact that the "horn," (*keren,*) in Josh. vi, 5, is elsewhere throughout that chapter spoken of as a *shophar*, or "trumpet." From its name, which means "bright," or "clear," the *shophar* is thought to have had a clear, shrill sound. It was used for announcing the beginning of the year of jubilee, and for other ceremonial purposes; for calling the attention of the people to important proclamations; for declaration of war; and for demonstrations of joy. See Lev. xxv, 9; Judges iii, 27; 1 Sam. xiii, 3; 2 Chron. xv, 24; Isa. xviii, 3.

448.—CALF-WORSHIP.

CVI, 19, 20. They made a calf in Horeb, and worshiped the molten image. Thus they changed their glory into the similitude of an ox that eateth grass.

There is thought to be an allusion here to a custom which was practiced in Egypt in connection with the worship of the sacred calf, Apis. Godwyn says: "The party that repaired unto him tendered a bottle of hay or grass; which, if he received, then it betokened a good and happy event; if, otherwise, he refused it, then it did portend some evil to come."—*Moses and Aaron*, book iv, chapter 5.

449.—OFFERINGS FOR THE DEAD.

CVI, 28. They joined themselves also unto Baal-peor, and ate the sacrifices of the dead.

Allusion is supposed to be made here to those sacrifices which were anciently offered by various nations to, or in honor of, the dead. Egyptian funeral tablets have representations of some of these feasts. The friends met together to eat the sacrifice or peace-offering, which consist-ed of various articles—meat, bread, vegetables, and liquids. What was left by the mourn-ers was eaten by the wild ani-mals; hence, in the hieroglyph-ical inscriptions the jackal is styled "the devourer of what is set out for the dead." The ancient Greeks had a similar custom. They met, after the funeral, at the house of the bereaved, and partook of an entertainment composed of a variety of animal and vegeta-

88.—Egyptian Offerings for the Dead.

ble substances. The broken morsels which fell from the table were looked on as sacred to the departed souls, and could not be lawfully eaten. "These fragments were carried to the tomb, and there left for the ghost to feast upon; whence, to denote extreme poverty, it was usual to say that a person *stole his meat from the graves*."—POTTER'S *Antiquities of Greece*, vol. ii, p. 230.

450.—SHRIVELED BOTTLES.

CXIX, 83. I am become like a bottle in the smoke.

Bottles made of skin (see note on Matt. ix, 17) are often hung up in Oriental tents. Here the smoke from the tent fire can freely act upon them, since there is no chimney to carry it away. Skins of wine were sometimes hung in the smoke to give the wine a peculiar flavor. When skin bottles are long exposed to smoke, they become hard, shriveled, and unsightly. This is the foundation of the striking figure of the text.

451.—WATCHFUL SERVANTS.

CXXIII, 2. Behold, as the eyes of servants look unto the hand of their masters, and as the eyes of a maiden unto the hand of her mistress, so our eyes wait upon the Lord our God, until that he have mercy upon us.

Servants in the East are not always spoken to when orders are given by the master or mistress. The wishes of the latter are made known by signs; hence it becomes necessary for the servants to watch the hand of the master to ascertain when they are wanted and what is required of them. The clapping of the hands may bring them when in an adjacent room, and a silent motion of the hand may express the master's wish. Servants are trained to watch for these signs and to obey them. This custom is doubtless the one alluded to in the text; and yet there is force in the suggestion of Harmer, that, in its special application here, the latter part of the verse must not be forgotten. He paraphrases the passage thus: "As a slave, ordered by a master or mistress to be chastised for a fault, turns his or her imploring eyes to that superior, till that motion of the hand appears which puts an end to the bitterness that is felt, so our eyes are put up to thee, our God, till thy hand shall give the signal for putting an end to our sorrows."—*Observations*, vol. ii, p. 430.

452.—GRASS ON HOUSETOPS.

CXXIX, 6. Let them be as the grass upon the housetops, which withereth afore it groweth up.

From the peculiar structure of the roofs of Eastern houses it can easily be seen how grass might there spring up and yet not have a flourishing growth. Dr. Robinson, speaking of the houses near Lebanon, says: "The flat roofs of the houses in this region are constructed by laying, first, large beams at intervals of several feet; then, rude joists; on which, again, are arranged small poles close together, or brush-wood; and upon this is spread earth or gravel rolled hard. This rolling is often repeated, especially after rain, for these roofs are apt to leak. For this purpose a roller of stone is kept ready for use on the roof of every house. Grass is often seen growing on these roofs." —*Biblical Researches*, vol. iii, p. 39.

The earth on the roof affords a starting place for the grass, but the frequent use of the roller and the trampling of feet give it but a poor chance for life. "It withereth afore it groweth up." The same figure is also used in 2 Kings xix, 26, and in Isa. xxxvii, 27.

Travelers who have visited Persia tell us of houses the roofs of which are covered with green sod, from which the grass grows luxuriantly. Hay is said to be gathered from these roofs, and lambs are turned out on them to pasture. The same is reported of northern Gothic countries. The psalmist however, could not, as some think, have had such roofs in mind, even admitting that he ever saw them, since the application of the illustration pre-supposes grass, not of luxuriant growth, but short-lived.

453.—OIL USED MEDICINALLY.

CXLI, 5. Let the righteous smite me; it shall be a kindness: and let him reprove me; it shall be an excellent oil, which shall not break my head.

Oil is used in the East not only for anointing, but also for medicinal purposes. There are some complaints in the head which are supposed to be specially relieved by the use of certain oils. Other kinds of oil, however, are said to produce delirium. The "excellent oil" in the text was the kind that cured. Roberts adds to this statement of the medicinal use of oils on the head the fact that in Judea "the crown of the head is the place selected for chastisement. Thus, owners of slaves, or husbands, or schoolmasters, beat the heads of the offenders with their knuckles." The Hindus have figurative forms of speech very similar to the text: "Let a holy man smite my head! and what of that? it is an excellent oil." "My master has been beating my head, but it has been good oil for me."

454.—CARYATIDES.

CXLIV, 12. That our daughters may be as corner-stones, polished after the similitude of a palace.

It is thought by some that reference is made here to the *Caryatides* or columns representing female figures. These were common in Egyptian architecture, and their appearance was doubtless familar to the Hebrews. The psalmist wishes the fair daughters of the land to be like "corner columns finely sculptured," thus combining strength with beauty. He desires that they may be noted, not merely for loveliness, but for usefulness, holding up the social fabric, as pillars sustain a temple.

455.—ORGANS.

CL, 4. Praise him with the timbrel and dance; praise him with stringed instruments and organs.

The *ugab* was one of the most ancient instruments, its invention being ascribed to Jubal. Gen. iv, 21. From Job xxi, 12, and xxx, 31, it appears to have been used on festive occasions. In the text it is spoken of as appropriate for use in the worship of God.

Various opinions have been expressed in reference to the character of this instrument. Winer, (*Bib. Realw.*,) and Leyrer, (in Herzog's *Real-Encyklopädie*,) following some very old authorities, suppose the *ugab* to have resembled the bagpipe. They represent it as consisting of two pipes fastened in a leather bag, one above and the other below. Through the upper pipe, which had a mouth-piece, the bag was filled with air, while the lower pipe had holes which were played on with the fingers like a flute, the bag meanwhile rising and falling like a bellows, by means of pressure.

Most authorities, however, identify the *ugab* with the syrinx or " Pandean pipes," which is undoubtedly a very ancient instrument, and is generally conceded to be the germ of the modern organ. Kitto says that the syrinx was the instrument which was meant by our translators when they used the word " organ; " thus relieving them from the charge of obscurity, that word having changed its meaning since their day.

The syrinx was used by the Arcadian and other Grecian shepherds, and was supposed by them to have been invented by Pan, their tutelary god, who was sometimes heard playing on it, as they imagined, on Mount Mænalus. It was made of cane, reed, or hemlock. " In general, seven hollow stems of these plants were fitted together by means of wax, having been previously cut to the proper length, and adjusted so as to form an octave; but sometimes nine were admitted, giving an equal number of notes. Another refinement in the construction of this instrument, which, however, was rarely practiced, was to arrange the pipes in a curve so as to fit the form of the lip, instead of arranging them in a plane."—SMITH, *Dict. Greek and Roman Ant.*

This instrument is still used in some parts of the East. The reeds are of unequal length, but of equal thickness, and vary in number from five to twenty-three. Specimens may be occasionally seen in European and American cities in the possession of itinerant street musicians.

456.—CYMBALS.

CL, 5. Praise him upon the loud cymbals; praise him upon the high-sounding cymbals.

The ancient cymbals resembled those in use in our day, consisting of two circular concave plates of brass, or other metal, and producing a clanging sound by being struck against each other.

15

Two kinds are supposed to be mentioned in the text. The "loud cymbals" are thought to have corresponded to the castanets which are used

by the Moors and Spaniards as an accompaniment to guitars and dances. Two of these small cymbals were held in each hand. The "high-sounding cymbals" are thought to have been the larger kind that we are accustomed to see in military bands. They were thus used in ancient times, and were also employed by the Hebrews in Divine worship as an accompaniment to the chorus of singers. 1 Chron. xv, 16; xxv, 6; 2 Chron. v, 13. Paul refers to this instrument in 1 Cor. xiii, 1: "Though I speak with the tongues of men and angels, and have not charity, I am become as sounding brass, or a tinkling cymbal."

89.—Eunuch Playing on the Cymbals, (Koyunjik.)

THE PROVERBS.

457.—EXTERNAL APPLICATIONS.

III, 8. It shall be health to thy navel, and marrow to thy bones.

Sir John Chardin supposes that allusion is here made to the custom, so prevalent in the East, of making external applications of oils, ointments, plasters, and frictions, especially on the stomach and abdomen. In addition to this the passage may obtain further illustration from a fact mentioned by Roberts. He says that in India "the navel is often spoken of as a criterion of prosperity;" and he gives several proverbial expressions which are frequently used to denote good fortune, in which a figure is brought out similar to that in the text.

458.—TALKING BY SIGNS.

VI, 13. He speaketh with his feet, he teacheth with his fingers.

Feet and fingers are frequently used in the East as a means of communicating ideas, especially when in the presence of those from whom it is intended to conceal the information imparted, and who might hear if words were uttered. Certain movements of hands and feet are understood to have a definite meaning, so that merchants have been known to bargain in the presence of others by sitting on the ground with a piece of cloth thrown over the lap, under which they arrange their terms by the movements of their fingers. In a similar way the Brahmins convey religious mysteries to their disciples, their hands·being concealed in the folds of their robes. Thus they teach "with their fingers." See also John xiii, 24.

Debauchees and dancing girls are in the habit of making gestures and movements with their feet. Some suppose Solomon to refer to these when he speaks of the "naughty person" as he does in the text. The practice was known among the ancient Romans and is described by classic authors.

459.—COVERINGS OF TAPESTRY.

VII, 16. I have decked my bed with coverings of tapestry, with carved works, with fine linen of Egypt.

Eres, "bed," is supposed by some writers to signify bedstead, and they think the text refers to a custom of hanging over the bedstead a canopy of richly woven stuff covering a frame. Others suppose the text to refer to the rich bed clothing which is found in the houses of wealthy Orientals. We are told by travelers of coverlets of green and crimson satin ornamented with gold embroidery, and presenting an appearance of great splendor; in fact, being more ornamental than useful, especially when it is considered that the large cushions which are used as pillows sometimes have embroidery upon them so thick as seriously to interfere with comfort when the head rests on it. "Coverings of tapestry" are also mentioned in Prov. xxxi, 22.

460.—MIXED WINE.

IX, 2. She hath killed her beasts, she hath mingled her wine, she hath also furnished her table.

Harmer supposes that by "mixed wine" is meant old wine that is drawn from jars where it becomes turbid and strong by being mingled with the lees. "Mixed wine" would then mean old or strong wine, and the announcement in the text that Wisdom "hath mingled her wine," means that she has opened the wine for use, the feast being ready. Bishop Lowth also supposes mixed wine to be strong wine, but made so, not in the way suggested by Harmer, but by the admixture of foreign substances; affirming that, "whereas the Greeks and Latins by *mixed wine* always understood wine diluted and lowered with water, the Hebrews, on the contrary, generally mean by it wine made stronger and more inebriating by the addition of higher and more powerful ingredients, such as honey, spices, defrutum, (or wine inspissated by boiling it down to two thirds or one half of the quantity,) myrrh, mandragora, opiates, and other strong drugs."—*Commentary on Isaiah* i, 22.

Kitto, on the other hand, gives it as his opinion that in most, if not all, cases where mixed wine is spoken of, wine mingled with water is meant; and he quotes Isaiah i, 22, as an illustration: "Thy silver is become dross, thy wine mixed with water." But he forgets that the prophet is there speaking, not of wine as ordinarily drank at feasts, but of wine that is deteriorated in quality. Gesenius expresses it, "adulterated, spoiled by mixing water with it." God's people had become debased, they were like wine mixed with water. The other passages which speak of mixed wine most certainly seem to refer to a liquor that is strengthened, rather than weakened, by that with which it is mixed. See Psa. lxxv, 8; Prov. xxiii, 30; Sol. Song viii, 2; Isa. v, 22.

461.—STRIKING HANDS.

XI, 21. **Though hand join in hand, the wicked shall not be unpunished.**

Literally, "hand to hand." Striking hands, or touching hands, is an Orien tal mode of sealing a bargain, and is sometimes practiced even in this country. "Give us your hand on that" is a colloquial expression occasionally heard among an inferior class of traders. In the East the parties making a contract touch each other's right hands, and then each raises his hand to his lips or forehead. Sometimes the hands are simply joined. The text, then, is expressive of a covenant. See also Ezra x, 19; Ezek. xvii, 18. A more solemn form of expressing faithfulness, amounting, indeed, to an oath, is seen in the uplifted hand. See note on Gen. xiv, 22, and also on Ezek. xxi, 14.

Joining hands was frequently practiced as a mode of pledging security, and is thus referred to in Job xvii, 3; Prov. vi, 1; xvii, 18; xxii, 26.

For remarks on "giving the hand" as a pledge of submission, see note on Jer. l, 15.

462.—LOW DOORWAYS.

XVII, 19. **He that exalteth his gate seeketh destruction.**

In the open country where the houses are exposed to the depredations of wandering Arabs the gates are made very low, so as to prevent the marauders from riding through the porch into the court. A high gate would be an invitation to enter. Even in cities the gates of houses are often made low and unattractive in appearance, affording no indication of the wealth which may be within, lest the cupidity of wicked rulers should be attracted. Travelers speak of house-gates as low as three feet from the ground. In Persia a lofty gate is one of the signs of royalty, which some of the subjects, in their vanity, imitate as far as they dare.

Anderson says: "The house in which I dwelt in Jerusalem had an arch, or gate-way, a few yards from the door, which was so low that a person on horseback could not pass under it. It was evidently built for the sake of security."—*Bible Light from Bible Lands*, p. 329.

The meaning of the text undoubtedly is, He who has a high gate to his house invites the robber by a show of prosperity and by affording facility of entrance. He thus "seeketh destruction."

463.—THE LOT.

XVIII, 18. **The lot causeth contentions to cease, and parteth between the mighty.** See also chap. xvi, 33.

The use of the lot, as a mode of settling disputed questions, is very ancient, and was practiced by most ancient nations. It was resorted to in reference to almost all the varied affairs of life. Magistrates and priests were appointed by it, and the land of conquered enemies was distributed by its means.

Among the Hebrews we find its use sanctioned by Divine authority. Thus the scape goat was selected by lot. Lev. xvi, 8. The inheritances of the tribes in the Land of Promise were determined in the same way. Num. xxxiv, 13; Josh. xiv, 2. The lot was used on various occasions subsequently. We cite a few instances. The men who attacked Gibeah were selected by lot. Judges xx, 9. In this. manner Jonathan was detected as the violator of Saul's command concerning fasting, in his fight with the Philistines. 1 Sam. xiv, 41, 42. In this way the positions of the porters in the temple were decided. 1 Chron. xxvi, 13. When the storm arose on board the ship where Jonah was. the heathen sailors cast lots to determine who had brought them into trouble. Jonah i, 7.

In the New Testament we have allusions to the same practice. The Roman soldiers divided the garments of the Saviour by lot. Matt. xxvii, 35; Mark xv, 24. In this manner Matthias was chosen to fill the place of Judas. Acts i, 26.

We have no information given in Scripture concerning the mode by which lots were cast. Among the Latins, especially where several parties were concerned, "little counters of wood, or of some other light material, were put into a jar (called *sitella*) with so narrow a neck that only one could come out at a time. After the jar had been filled with water and the contents shaken, the lots were determined by the order in which the bits of wood, representing the several parties, came out with the water. In other cases they were put into a wide, open jar and the counters were drawn out by the hand. Sometimes, again, they were cast in the manner of dice."—FAIRBAIRN, *Imperial Bible Dictionary, s. v.,* Lot.

Roberts describes the mode by which property is divided by lot in India, as follows: "They draw on the ground tne cardinal points, thus: They then

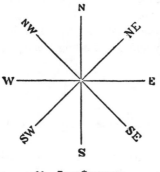

90.—Lot-Compass.

write the names of the parties on separate leaves and mix them all together. A little child is then called, and told to take one leaf and place it on any point of the compass he pleases; this being done, the leaf is opened, and to the person whose name is found therein will be given the field or garden which is in that direction."—*Oriental Illustrations*, p. 231.

He further states that the Hindus settle every disputed question by lot. They decide what physician they shall have, and what remedies, and even leave the selection of a wife to the same blind chance.

464.—DWELLING ON THE HOUSE-TOP.

XXI, 9. It is better to dwell in a corner of the house-top than with a brawling woman in a wide house. See also chap. xxv, 24.

It is customary to build on the flat roofs of Eastern houses arbors, or booths, (called "tabernacles" in Matt. xvii, 4,) for the purpose of resting from the heat of the day during the summer. They are also occupied as sleeping-chambers at night. Some suppose that Saul slept in a place of this sort, though he may have slept on the open roof. See 1 Sam. ix, 25, 26. These temporary structures serve an excellent purpose at the season of the year for which they are specially designed, but as a place in which to "dwell" permanently they are, of course, very undesirable. The rain and cold would soon drive the inhabitants from them. Yet in the estimation of the wise man, a cheerless spot like this is preferable as a place of residence to a large house with plenty of room and all conveniences, provided "a brawling woman" is in it!

465.—BEAUTIFUL WORK IN METAL.

XXV, 11. A word fitly spoken is like apples of gold in pictures of silver.

Maskiyoth, "pictures," is supposed by some to convey the idea of carved work, rather than that of painted work, and hence they would refer it in this place to something that is made by the skill of the carver or the engraver, such as a salver of silver with chased work upon it, and having fruit of gold. Others think that silver baskets of filigree work are meant, the fruit contained in them being real and of a golden color, or else artificial, and made of gold. Either of these interpretations would be consistent with Eastern customs. Roberts suggests that, inasmuch as in verses 6 and 7 mention is made of the manner in which one should approach a king, Solomon in this verse had before his mind the presents which are sometimes made to Oriental monarchs—golden ornaments in the shape of fruit, placed on highly polished silver salvers.

466.—SNOW USED IN SUMMER.

XXV, 13. As the cold of snow in the time of harvest, so is a faithful messenger to them that send him: for he refresheth the soul of his masters.

It is evident that this cannot refer to the coming of winter weather in summer, since the application of the figure supposes something desirable, which certainly could not be said of a fall of snow in harvest time. The custom, so common in the East to-day, of cooling wines with snow or ice, was doubtless practiced in the time of Solomon. Mount Lebanon supplies a large country in its neighborhood from the inexhaustible stores of snow upon its top. The snow is mixed with the wine, thus making the latter more palatable; so a faithful messenger is a source of refreshment to "the soul of his masters."

467.—HINGES.

XXVI, 14. As the door turneth upon his hinges, so doth the slothful upon his bed.

The hinges of Eastern houses are not like ours, but consist of pivots inserted into sockets both above and below. In the Hauran there are still standing stone houses with stone slabs for doors, having pivots cut out of the same and turning in sockets prepared for them in the wall of the house.

468.—THE NUMBER SEVEN.

XXVI, 25. When he speaketh fair, believe him not: for there are seven abominations in his heart.

The number *seven* is used frequently in Scripture, and expresses the idea of completeness or fullness. Thus the text represents the hypocrite as having a heart filled with abominations. This figurative use of the number *seven* obtains in some parts of the East at the present day. It is frequently employed to signify an indefinite number, but always a large number, and hence conveys the idea of sufficiency. The Scripture passages where the word "seven" is used are too numerous to be quoted here. They are scattered all through the Bible, especially in the prophetical books; the book of Revelation making most frequent symbolical use of the word.

The interesting question, Why the number seven should be regarded a perfect number? is one the discussion of which does not fall within the scope assigned to this work. Those who desire information on this subject, and also on the general question of the sacred numbers used in the Bible, may consult, in addition to the various Bible Dictionaries and Encyclopedias, *Stuart on the Apocalypse*, in his Introduction, § 7, "Numerosity of the Apocalypse," vol. i, p. 130; and in Excursus II, "On the Symbolical Use of Numbers in the Apocalypse," vol. ii, p. 409. Dr. Whedon also has a very valuable and characteristic note on the same subject in his *Commentary on the Gospels*, vol. ii, p. 77.

469.—LEAKY ROOFS.

XXVII, 15. A continual dropping in a very rainy day and a contentious woman are alike. See also chap. xix, 13.

Reference is undoubtedly made here to the frequent leaks to which the flat roofs of Eastern houses are subject. Having merely a covering of earth, rolled smooth and hard, (see note on Psa. cxxix, 6,) a heavy rain will soon succeed in finding its way through, when the drops will fall into the room below, thus making it uncomfortable, if not actually uninhabitable. Travelers are frequently disturbed in this manner during violent storms, sometimes being obliged to change their quarters in the middle of the night.

470.—MORTARS.

XXVII, 22. Though thou shouldest bray a fool in a mortar among wheat with a pestle, yet will not his foolishness depart from him.

91.—Egyptian Mortar.

Mortars, for cracking grain by pounding with a pestle, are often used in the East. They are made of metal, earthenware, wood, or stone, the last being the most common material. The pestle is usually about five feet long. Sometimes two pestles are used at the same time for one mortar, the two persons holding them striking alternate blows, like blacksmiths at an anvil. The ancient Israelites used the mortar for beating their manna. Num. xi, 8.

There is no evidence that the Hebrews ever administered punishment literally in the way indicated in the text, but it has been done among other nations. Beating to death in a mortar is a State punishment which is sometimes inflicted in Turkey and in India.

471.—BUTTER-MAKING.

XXX, 33. Surely the churning of milk bringeth forth butter, and the wringing of the nose bringeth forth blood: so the forcing of wrath bringeth forth strife.

There is but little in the Eastern mode of preparing butter that is similar to our churning. The milk is put into a bag or bottle, made of the skin of a goat or of a buffalo, and is agitated in various ways until the butter, such as it is, comes. See note on Gen. xviii, 8. Sometimes the skin containing the milk is shaken to and fro, or beaten with sticks. Sometimes it is placed on the ground and trodden upon. Thus Job says, " I washed my steps with butter." Job xxix, 6. Again, it is pressed or squeezed with the hands, so that the contents become agitated and gradually coagulate. This last method is probably referred to in the text. There is a beauty in the original which does not appear in our English version. The word *mits* is thrice repeated, but is translated by three different terms: "churning," "wringing," "forcing." It literally means "pressing" or "squeezing," just as the skin bag is pressed or squeezed for the production of butter. The nose treated in a similar manner will bleed, and wrath which is thus "pressed" will result in strife.

ECCLESIASTES.

472.—WHITE GARMENTS.

IX, 8. Let thy garments be always white.

In the warm countries of the East white clothing is more frequently and generally worn than with us. This allusion to white garments is a beautiful figurative exhortation to perpetual purity of character, and one that would be readily appreciated by the Oriental mind. " May God blacken his face " is a common imprecation in the East. Mohammed is often called " He of the white face." In the Bible there are a number of references to white garments as typical of purity. In Dan. vii, 9, the Deity is represented as clad in a "garment white as snow." When Jesus was transfigured "his raiment was white as the light." Matt. xvii, 2. The angels appeared in white robes when the disciples visited the tomb of their risen Lord, (Matt. xxviii, 3; Mark xvi, 5; Luke xxiv, 4; John xx, 12,) and also when he ascended into heaven. Acts i, 10. The redeemed are to be clothed in white. Rev. vii, 13; xix, 14.

473.—BREAD ON THE WATERS.

XI, 1. Cast thy bread upon the waters: for thou shalt find it after many days.

Many interpreters are of the opinion that there is here an allusion to the manner of sowing rice in Egypt, that is, by scattering it broadcast in the mud, or upon the overflowing waters of the Nile. Others, however, dispute this, claiming that there is no evidence of the cultivation of rice having been introduced into Egypt as early as the days of Solomon. These commentators consider the expression merely figurative without being based on any actual custom.

———◆———

THE SONG OF SOLOMON.

474.—TENTS.

I, 5. I am black, but comely, O ye daughters of Jerusalem, as the tents of Kedar, as the curtains of Solomon.

Tents were among the early habitations of man, though not the earliest, since they were not introduced until the time of Jabal, who was in the seventh generation from Adam. See Gen. iv, 20. The first tents were doubtless made of skins, though afterward when the process of weaving became known they were made, as they are at this day, of cloth of camels' hair, or of goats' hair, spun by the women. The latter is the material most commonly used by the Arabs, and since the goats are usually black, or a very dark brown, the tents exhibit the same appearance. It was thus in the days of Solomon with the tents made by the descendants of the Ishmaelitish Kedar. These tents individually are not very beautiful objects, but when arranged in the form of a circular encampment, with the cattle inclosed by the circle of tents, and the sheikh's tent in the center, they present a picturesque appearance. Balaam was impressed with the beauty of such a scene when he beheld the vast encampment of the Israelites, and exclaimed, "How goodly are thy tents, O Jacob, and thy tabernacles, O Israel!" Num. xxiv, 5.

The Arab tents are of various sizes, according to the number of the family or the wealth of the proprietor. The number of poles to a tent varies from one to nine. Some tents are circular in shape, some square, and others oblong. The covering is spread over the poles, which are fastened in the ground. The edges of the cover have leather loops, to which are attached the cords of the tent, which are sometimes stretched out tight and fastened

92.—TENTS.

to the ground by means of iron or wooden pins, or else are fastened to upright posts, on which a curtain is hung around the tent, forming the walls, which can be removed at pleasure without disturbing the rest of the tent. Other cords reach from the top of the tent to the ground, where they are fastened with pins, thus steadying the whole structure. It was one of these pins which Jael drove into the head of Sisera. Judges iv, 21.

The tent erected, and its cords stretched out, are often figuratively alluded to in the Bible. Thus Isaiah represents God as the one "that stretcheth out the heavens as a curtain, and spreadeth them out as a tent to dwell in." Isa. xl, 22. He also says, in speaking of the glorious prosperity of the Church and the need of enlargement, "Enlarge the place of thy tent, and let them stretch forth the curtains of thine habitations: spare not, lengthen thy cords, and strengthen thy stakes." Isa. liv, 2. See also Isa. xxxiii, 20.

It is a work of some effort to pitch a tent properly, especially a large one, requiring the united efforts of willing hands. Hence the pathetic language of Jeremiah in mourning over the desolations of God's people: "My tabernacle is spoiled, and all my cords are broken: my children are gone forth of me, and they are not: there is none to stretch forth my tent any more, and to set up my curtains." Jer. x, 20.

The large tents have nine poles, placed in three rows, covering sometimes a space twenty to twenty-five feet long, ten feet wide, and eight to ten-feet high in the middle, with the sides sloping. Such tents often have a curtain hung on the middle row of poles, dividing the tent into two parts, one for the men, and the other for the women. See notes on Gen. xviii, 10; xxiv, 67. The poles which thus uphold the tent and divide it into sections are further made useful by having hooks driven into them from which are suspended clothes, baskets, saddles, weapons, and various other articles of daily use.

These tents are rapidly struck and removed from place to place, so that the eye which to-day rests on a large encampment active with life may to-morrow behold nothing but a wilderness. Thus Isaiah says, "Mine age is departed, and is removed from me as a shepherd's tent." Isa. xxxviii, 12. The facility with which tents are taken down, and the frailty of their material, are beautifully alluded to by Paul in 2 Cor. v, 1. See also 2 Peter i, 13, 14.

Tents of cotton, linen, or silk are used for traveling or for holiday purposes, are of all colors, and are sometimes very magnificent. Stories which would be incredible if not from good authorities, are told of the splendor of state tents which have been reared by Oriental monarchs. Silver, gold, precious stones, silk, velvet, camels' hair cloth, and brocades, have combined to make these structures at once costly and splendid. The state tents of Támerlane are said to have had poles of silver inlaid with gold, curtains of velvet, and ropes of silk. Nadir Shah had a state tent the outside of which was of fine scarlet broadcloth, and the lining of violet-colored satin. On this lining were embroideries in pearls, diamonds, rubies, emeralds, amethysts, and other precious stones, representing birds, beasts, trees, and flowers.

No description is given us of Solomon's state tents; indeed, some suppose that the "curtains" mentioned in the text refer to some of the splendid hangings of his palace. The unity of the passage, however, suggests the idea of tents, and it is not at all improbable that Solomon, the luxurious monarch who spared no expense to gratify his taste, had tents of magnificence commensurate with his royal grandeur. The King of Babylon had a royal pavilion though no description is given of it. Jer. xliii, 10.

475.—SHEPHERDS' NOONING.

I, 7. Tell me, O thou whom my soul loveth, where thou feedest, where thou makest thy flock to rest at noon.

During the heat of the day the shepherds are in the habit of leading their flocks to some cool and shady spot, where they recline and rest until the shadows lengthen. The sheep sleep, or chew the cud, while the shepherds pass the time in some light employment, such as plaiting mats, or in musing or story telling.

476.—JEWELS—NECKLACES.

I, 10. Thy cheeks are comely with rows of jewels, thy neck with chains of gold.

1. Eastern women sometimes have a cord of gold around their head at the forehead, on which are strung precious stones of various sorts, which hang down over the cheeks of the fair wearers. Thus their "cheeks are comely with rows of jewels."

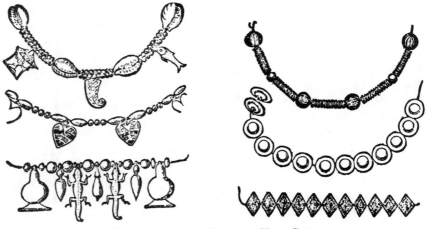

98.—ASSYRIAN AND EGYPTIAN NECK CHAINS.

2. Neck chains were made of gold or other metal, or else consisted of strings of pearls, corals, and precious stones. They were sometimes made of gold-pieces shaped like a half-moon. Such are referred to in Isa. iii, 18: "round tires like the moon." See also note on Judges viii, 21. These necklaces hung low down upon the breast, and were worn both by men and women. See Prov. i, 9; iii, 3. This was the custom among the Egyptians as well as the Hebrews; Joseph had a gold chain put around his neck by Pharaoh. Gen. xli, 42. The Medes, Persians, Babylonians, and other ancient nations, followed the same custom. See Dan. v, 7, 16, 29. Neck chains are also referred to in Sol. Song iv, 9; Ezek. xvi, 11.

477.—USE OF RAISINS.

II, 5. Stay me with flagons, comfort me with apples.

Ashishoth, "flagons," is conceded by the best authorities to mean, not drinking vessels, but cakes of pressed raisins, such as are often used in the East, by travelers, for refreshment. The word also occurs in 2 Sam. vi, 19; 1 Chron. xvi, 3; and Hosea iii, 1. In the last passage *anabim*, which is rendered " wine," should be translated " grapes," as it is in the margin. Instead of "flagons of wine," we should then read "cakes of grapes." Some think there is a reference in that passage to the custom of offering such cakes in sacrifice to heathen deities.

478.—THE ROYAL LITTER.

III, 9, 10. King Solomon made himself a chariot of the wood of Lebanon. He made the pillars thereof of silver, the bottom thereof of gold, the covering of it of purple.

Appiryon, "chariot," is a litter, or palanquin, a vehicle of very ancient use, and still common in the East. The same conveyance is referred to in the word *tsab* in Num. vii, 3, and Isa. lxvi, 20. In the former passage it is translated "wagon," in the latter "litter." The palanquin is made of a light framework of wood, and is covered with cloth, having a lattice door or window at each side. Two strong poles are fastened to it, which in India are borne on the

94.—Ancient Egyptian Litter or Palanquin.

shoulders of men, but in Western Asia are harnessed to mules, horses, or camels, one of the animals being at each end. Occasionally four beasts are employed, two at each end, and sometimes a litter is so contrived as to be fastened to the back of a single camel. Engraving number 11, p. 40, has a representation of a camel litter.

Litters are often of great magnificence, especially if they belong to royalty. The woodwork is richly carved, and ornamented with gold, and silver, and precious stones. The canopy is of silk, satin, or brocade, and ornamented with jewels. These conveyances are ordinarily shaped like a couch, and are so made that the traveler can lie down at full length if desired.

479.—CITY WATCHMEN.

V, 7. The watchmen that went about the city found me, they smote me, they wounded me ; the keepers of the walls took away my vail from me.

There were not only watchmen stationed on the walls to guard against the approach of enemies, (see note on 2 Sam. xviii, 26,) but there were others whose duty it was to patrol the streets of the city and preserve order. See Psa. cxxvii, 1; Sol. Song iii, 3. There are such in Oriental cities to-day, and they challenge all persons found abroad after certain hours of the night, arresting those that are not able to give a good account of themselves, and sometimes subjecting them to rough treatment.

ISAIAH.

480.—TREATMENT OF WOUNDS.

I, 6. They have not been closed, neither bound up, neither mollified with ointment.

The Hebrews had but little knowledge of surgery, less than the Egyptians. They seldom used inward remedies, but trusted mainly to outward applications. See note on Prov. iii, 8. The text illustrates the treatment of wounds; they were "closed," that is, the lips of the wound were pressed together and bound, that cohesion of the parts might be effected. "There was, and is, no sewing up of wounds in the East; and hence the edges, healing without being perfectly united, make the scar of a wound more conspicuous and disfiguring than with us. The only attempt to produce cohesion is by 'binding up' the wound, after the edges have been as far as possible 'closed' by simple pressure."—KITTO, *Daily Bible Illus.*, vol. vi, p: 25.

481.—LODGE IN A GARDEN.

I, 8. **The daughter of Zion is left as a cottage in a vineyard, as a lodge in a garden of cucumbers.**

As the fields were not always provided with fences it became necessary to have persons to watch them, especially while the fruit was ripening, in order to keep off all depredators, whether man, beast, or bird. These "keepers of a field" are referred to in Jer. iv, 17, and they are still to be seen in the East. During the ripening season they watch day and night and through all sorts of weather, and hence need some protection from excessive heat, dew, or storm. This protection is found in temporary huts, which are made of closely twined branches and leaves, or of pieces of matting thrown over a rude framework of poles. There is an allusion to such a frail structure in Job xxvii, 18, and also in Isa. xxiv, 20. When the crop is gathered and the field forsaken the deserted lodge soon leans and falls, and the whole scene is one of utter loneliness. It was such a picture of desolation to which the prophet compares "the daughter of Zion."

482.—PLOWSHARES.

II, 4. **They shall beat their swords into plowshares.** See also Joel iii, 10, and Micah iv, 3.

In the passage in Joel the expression is reversed: "Beat your plowshares into swords." Commentators are divided as to the meaning of *ittim*, variously rendering it "plowshares," "spades," "hoes," "mattocks." The word refers to instruments for stirring up the soil in some way, and, so far as concerns capability of conversion to swords, these may as well have been plowshares as any thing else. The plowshare was a small piece of iron, which somewhat resembled a short sword, and might easily have been beaten into one, and with equal facility a sword could have been changed into a plowshare.

483.—DANCING—GIRLS—ANKLETS.

III, 16. **Because the daughters of Zion are haughty, and walk with stretched-forth necks and wanton eyes, walking and mincing as they go, and making a tinkling with their feet.**

1. Roberts finds in this and in the following verses an accurate description of the Hindoo dancing-girls who are trained for service in idolatrous temples. "When these females dance they stretch forth their necks, and hold them awry, as if their heads were about to fall off their shoulders." "As the votaries glide along they roll their eyes, (which are painted,) and cast wanton glances on those around."—*Oriental Illustrations*, p. 386.

2. Some suppose the "mincing" refers to a tripping step in the dance; others think that the reference is to slender golden chains reaching from one ankle to another, and compelling them to take short and rapid steps. See note on verse 20.

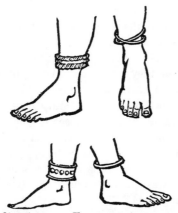

3. The "tinkling with their feet" may have been made simply by the striking of anklets one upon another, or by bells or other small ornaments attached to the anklets. These anklets were of gold, silver, or iron, according to the taste or means of the wearer, and are still worn by Oriental women. They are sometimes quite heavy, and special pains are taken to strike them together, in order to make a jingle. When they are hollow, as is often the case, the sharp sound is increased. In Egypt and in India some of the anklets have small round bells attached to them, and these bells sometimes have little pebbles in them, which

95.—Ancient Egyptian Anklets.

strike like tiny clappers. Leyrer (in Herzog's *Real. Ency.*, vol. vii, p. 731) suggests that it may have been in some such way that the wife of Jeroboam announced her presence, "when Abijah heard the sound of her feet, as she came in at the door." 1 Kings xiv, 6.

484.—CAULS—TIRES.

III, 18. Their cauls and their round tires like the moon.

1. What is meant by *shebisim*, "cauls," is not certain. The marginal reading is "net-works," and many writers suppose that nets for the hair are meant. These were anciently worn, as is evident from the Egyptian and Assyrian monuments, and from specimens which have found their way to museums. Others think that reference is made here to the mode of dressing

96.—Assyrian Nets for the Hair.

the hair, arranging it into tresses, and attaching to it golden ornaments and small coins, or so braiding it as to resemble checker-work. A German author (Schroeder) conjectures that *shebisim* were small metallic ornaments resembling the sun, and he would associate them with the moon-ornaments mentioned in the same verse. This interpretation is accepted by Fuerst and others, but rejected by authorities equally good.

2. *Saharonim*, "round tires like the moon," were metallic moon-shaped ornaments hung around the neck. Similar ornaments were sometimes hung about the necks of camels. See note on Judges viii, 21.

485.—JEWELRY AND VAILS.

III, 19. The chains and the bracelets and the mufflers.

1. *Netiphoth*, "chains," were properly pendents, or ear-drops. See note on Gen. xxxv, 4.

2. *Sheroth*, "bracelets," were probably bracelets made of gold wire, and wreathed or woven.

3. *Realoth*, "mufflers," were thin vails. The Hebrew name was given to them because of their tremulous or fluttering motion.

486.—SUNDRY ARTICLES, USEFUL AND ORNAMENTAL.

III, 20. The bonnets, and the ornaments of the legs, and the headbands, and the tablets, and the ear-rings.

1. The "bonnets" of the Oriental women, it is hardly necessary to say, bear no resemblance to the articles known by that name among us. They resemble the turbaned head-dresses of the men, but are less bulky and of finer materials. A cap is put on the head around which are wound rich handkerchiefs or shawls, folded high and flat. Gold and silver ornaments and jewels are added according to the taste of the wearer. The original word *peer* conveys the idea of ornament, and is rendered "beauty" in Isa. lxi, 3; "ornaments" in Isa. lxi, 10; and "tire" in Ezek. xxiv, 17, 23. Saalschütz supposes the *peer* to have been a metallic crown of filigree work, fastened around the cap.

2. "The ornaments of the legs" (*tseadoth*) were probably step-chains, that is, "short chains which Oriental females wore attached to the ankle-band of each foot, so as to compel them to take short and mincing steps, to walk mincingly."—GESENIUS.

3. *Kishshurim*, "headband," are supposed by some critics to denote fillets for the hair. Others, however, interpret them to mean girdles. The same word is rendered "attire" in Jer. ii, 32.

4. *Battey-hannephesh*, "tablets," is literally "houses of breath." The margin has, "houses of the soul." There is thought by some to be a reference here to boxes or bottles which were filled with perfume, and fastened to the necklace or the girdle. Chardin mentions having seen the women in Persia with small golden boxes of filigree work, which were filled with a black mixture of musk and amber.

Roberts, however, disputes this interpretation, and thinks these "houses of the soul" find their counterpart in certain ornaments which are worn by

16

Hindu women, and made of silver or gold, and richly adorned with precious stones. He says: "The dancing-girls, the wives of the pandārams, and

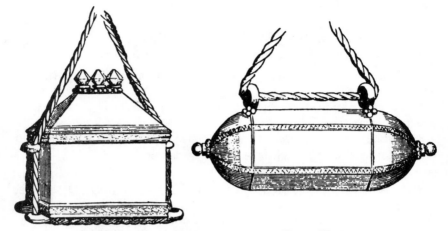

97.—HOUSES OF THE SOUL. WORN BY HINDU WOMEN.

many other women, wear an ornament resembling a house, and sometimes a temple, which contains an image corresponding with the Φαλλος of the Greeks and the Priapus of the Romans."—*Oriental Illustrations*, p. 388.

5. *Lechashim*, "ear-rings," are thought to have been charms or amulets made of gold, silver, or precious stones, perhaps in the shape of serpents, or with serpents engraven on them. They may have been used as ear-rings also. See note on Gen. xxxv, 4.

487.—APPAREL.

III, 22. The changeable suits of apparel, and the mantles, and the wimples, and the crisping pins.

1. *Machelatsoth*, "changeable suits of apparel," were costly garments of any kind which were used only on festival occasions, and put off when at home. The same word is rendered "change of raiment" in Zech. iii, 4.

2. *Maataphoth*, "mantles," are supposed by some to have been cloaks or mantles of ample folds, which were worn outside of the other garments; while others think that they were a fashionable sort of upper tunic.

3. *Mitpachoth*, "wimples," were wide upper garments, the distinction between which and *maataphoth* is not clear, unless the latter explanation above given is correct. The word is rendered "vail" in Ruth iii, 15, where see the note.

4. *Charitim*, "crisping-pins," are now thought by the best authorities to have had nothing to do with the hair, as our translators supposed, but to

have been richly ornamented purses of gold or embroidered work, long and round in form, perhaps like an inverted cone, and suspended from the girdle. We have the idea more correctly expressed in 2 Kings v, 23, where the same word is translated "bags."

488.—VARIOUS ARTICLES OF ATTIRE.

III, 23. The glasses, and the fine linen, and the hoods, and the vails.

1. *Gilyonim*, "glasses," are probably the small metallic mirrors wherewith Oriental women adorn their persons. See note on Exod. xxxviii, 8. The Septuagint, however, and a number of eminent commentators, understand the word to mean "transparent garments," referring to the garments of thin gauze or other material so delicately made as to reveal the form of the wearer. Such were the celebrated Coan garments of classic writers, and dresses of this sort are still used in the East, often richly ornamented with gold spangles.

2. *Sedinim*, "fine linen," is mentioned in Judges xiv, 12, 13, as a part of the gift which Samson offered to any who would guess his riddle. In our version the word is there rendered "sheets." It also occurs in Prov. xxxi, 24, in Solomon's description of "a virtuous woman." The *sedinim* were inner garments or tunics.

3. *Tseniphoth*, "hoods," were coverings for the head, the difference between which and the *peerim*, or "bonnets," of verse 20 it is not easy now to determine. The etymology of the two words would suggest that the *tseniphoth* were simply the turbaned wrappers which were wound around the heads, while the *peerim* were the same, with rich ornaments attached. Some writers, however, suppose the *tseniphoth* to have been merely ribbons for binding the hair or fastening the tiara. The word in the singular is rendered "diadem" in Job xxix, 14, and Isa. lxii, 3.

4. *Redidim*, "vails," differed somewhat from the *realoth*, "mufflers," of verse 19. Kitto supposes the "*radid* to have been a kind of head vail which ladies wear at home, and which, not being intended for concealment of the features, rests upon the head and falls down over the back. It is of very light texture, being usually a long strip of muslin embroidered with threads of colored silk and gold, forming altogether one of the most

98.—HEAD-DRESS.

graceful articles in the female attire of the East."—*Daily Bible Illustrations*, vol. vi, p. 53.

489.—HAIR-DRESSING—GIRDLE.

III, 24. Instead of well-set hair, baldness, and instead of a stomacher, a girding of sackcloth.

1. The women of the East have always paid special attention to dressing the hair. Folds, braids, and tresses in every variety are a source of pride. See note on 1 Peter iii, 3. On the other hand, baldness is considered a great calamity and is made an occasion for contempt. See note on 2 Kings ii, 23. Thus the change from " well-set hair " to " baldness " would be regarded as a serious misfortune.

2. *Pethigil,* " stomacher," is supposed by some to have been a girdle, made of beautiful and costly materials and richly embroidered. Others, from the etymology of the word, and from the contrast between the " stomacher " and the " girding of sackcloth," suppose it to have been a wide loose flowing mantle characteristic of luxury and wantonness.

99.—ANCIENT EGYPTIAN MODE OF WEARING THE HAIR.

490.—SITTING ON THE GROUND.

III, 26. Her gates shall lament and mourn; and she being desolate shall sit upon the ground.

Sitting on the ground was a posture which denoted deep distress. When Job's friends came to sympathize with him, "they sat down with him upon the ground seven days and seven nights, and none spake a word unto him: for they saw that his grief was very great." Job ii, 13. When the Jews were in captivity, it is said, "By the rivers of Babylon, there we sat down, yea, we wept, when we remembered Zion." Psa. cxxxvii, 1. Jeremiah also alludes to the same custom in Lam. ii, 10; iii, 28. The same idea is represented in a more intensified form in the expressions, "wallow thyself in ashes," Jer. vi, 26, and " roll thyself in the dust." Micah i, 10.

Most of the Roman coins which were struck in commemoration of the capture of Jerusalem have on one side the figure of a woman sitting on the ground, usually, though not in every instance, under the shade of a palm tree. The figure is generally represented with one hand to the head, which rests upon it inclining forward, and the other hanging over the knee, thus presenting a picture of great grief. In one instance, however, the hands are t'ed behind the back. These coins were issued during the reigns of Vespasian, Titus, and Domitian, some of them being struck in Judea, and some in Rome. They are of gold, silver, and brass, and give an apt illustration of the custom referred to in the text. Representations and descriptions of all these coins may be found in MADDEN's *History of Jewish Coinage*, etc., chap. viii.

491.—ATTENTION CALLED.

V, 26. He will lift up an ensign to the nations from far, and will hiss unto them from the end of the earth: and, behold, they shall come with speed swiftly.

Some commentators have supposed an allusion here, and in chap. vii, 18, to the custom of calling bees from their hives to the fields and back again by means of a hiss or whistle. Others, however, deny that any such custom existed, and claim that the allusion is to another custom prevalent in the East: that of calling the attention of any one in the street by a significant hiss. In the prophecy of Zechariah, the Lord says concerning the children of Ephraim, "I will hiss for them, and gather them." Zech. x, 8. Here there is doubtless a reference to the same custom of calling attention by a hiss.

492.—BUTTER AND HONEY.

VII, 15. Butter and honey shall he eat; that he may know to refuse the evil, and to choose the good.

See also verse 22. Honey is frequently mixed with various forms of milk-preparations and used upon bread. The Arabs in traveling often take leathern bottles full of honey for this purpose. It is considered very palatable, especially by the children. The context shows that the reference in the text is made particularly to the days of childhood. The fourteenth verse refers to the birth of a son, and the sixteenth to his early infancy. It is of this child that it is said, "Butter and honey shall he eat."

There may be in the mixture of these two substances a propriety founded on physiological facts. Wood, in speaking of the Musquaw, or American Black Bear, after giving an account of its method of obtaining the wild honey which is found in hollow trees, adds: "The hunters, who are equally fond of honey, find that if it is eaten in too great plenty it produces very unpleasant symptoms, which may be counteracted by mixing it with the oil which they extract from the fat of the bear."—*Illustrated Natural History*, vol. i, p. 397. We find in Prov. xxv, 16, 27, allusion to the disagreeable consequences of eating too much honey, and it is possible that experience had proved the oily nature of the butter a corrective of the honey.

Butter is mentioned in connection with honey in 2 Sam. xvii, 29; Job xx, 17; Sol. Song iv, 11. Honey and oil are named together in Deut. xxxii, 13.

493.—THE MATTOCK.

VII, 25. On all hills that shall be digged with the mattock.

This instrument was probably similar to our grub-ax, and was made of either wood or iron. It was used in mountainous places, where a plow could not be easily handled, for turning up the soil. This fact is referred to in the text.

494.—BALDNESS A SIGN OF MOURNING.

XV, 2. On all their heads shall be baldness, and every beard cut off.

To make the head bald, or to shave or pluck the beard, was a sign of mourning among the Hebrews and many other nations. See also Ezra ix, 3; Job i, 20; Isa. xxii, 12; Jer. vii, 29; xvi, 6; xli, 5; xlvii, 5; xlviii, 37; Micah i, 16.

495.—SINGING AT WORK.

XVI, 10. Gladness is taken away, and joy out of the plentiful field; and in the vineyards there shall be no singing, neither shall there be shouting; the treaders shall tread out no wine in their presses; I have made their vintage shouting to cease.

It was a common custom among the Egyptians to sing at their work. The Hebrews did the same, and were especially jubilant at the time of grape gathering. They plucked off the grapes with acclamations of joy, and carried them to the wine-press. There they alleviated the labor of treading the grapes by singing, accompanied with musical instruments and joyous shouts. Some authorities interpret *hedad*, "shouting," as an exclamation used by the grape treaders as they jumped up and down. Allusions are made to the joyful character of the work of vintage in Judges ix, 27; Jer. xxv, 30; xlviii, 33.

496.—PAPYRUS-BOATS.

XVIII, 2. That sendeth embassadors by the sea, even in vessels of bulrushes upon the waters.

The papyrus was used on the Nile for making boats. Sometimes bundles of the plant were rudely bound together in the form of a raft or boat; at other times the leaves were plaited, basket-fashion, and coated with bitumen and tar. See note on Exod. ii, 3. Similar boats are used on the Euphrates and Tigris. They are circular in shape, and are sometimes covered with leather instead of bitumen.

Another style of vessel is also used on the Nile. The leaves of the papyrus or the palm are placed as a floor upon rafts made of earthen jars which are tied together by the handles. These jars are made in Upper Egypt, and are thus floated down stream by the potters, who sell their ware and walk back to their homes.

On the Euphrates and Tigris the floats are made of inflated skins covered with a flooring of leaves and branches made into wicker work, and having a

100.—ASSYRIAN SKIN-BOAT.

raised bulwark of the same. These singular vessels are called *kelleks*, and are of various sizes, from the little family boat resting on three or four skins, to the great raft, forty feet or more in length, and of proportionate width. The latter sort float on several hundred skins, and bear an assorted cargo of merchandise besides passengers. When the cargo has reached its destination the woodwork is sold for fuel, and the skins are taken back by land to be re-formed into another vessel. Boats of this description have been used from early historic times, and are referred to by Herodotus and other ancient authors.

497.—EGYPTIAN FISHING.

XIX, 8. **The fishers also shall mourn, and all they that cast angle into the brooks shall lament, and they that spread nets upon the waters shall languish.**

Reference is made in this "burden of Egypt" (see verse 1) to the Egyptian fisheries. The Egyptians consumed enormous quantities of fish, which they obtained from the teeming waters of the Nile, and of the canals which irrigated the land. So important was the traffic in fish that at one time the royal profits from Lake Mœris alone amounted to a talent of silver a day, or about $350,000 a year. Large quantities of fish were salted; and sometimes the fish were simply dried in the sun. Two methods of Egyptian fishing are mentioned in the text.

1. *Chakkah*, "angle," is rendered "hook" in Job xli, 1. Angling was a favorite pastime with all ranks of the Egyptians. Their hooks were of

bronze, and were baited with ground bait. Sometimes a short pole was used, and sometimes the fisherman held the line in his hand.

2. *Mikmoreth,* "nets," was a drag-net, and is so rendered in Hab. i, 15, 16. It was of a lengthened form, having floats along one edge and weights along the other, with a rope at each end. It corresponded to our seine, and was sometimes cast by hand, the men wading out with it and dragging it back to the shore, bringing the fish with it. At other times a boat was used, the net being cast overboard as the boat was rowed along. The monuments give a number of illustrations of fishing by nets, as well as with the hook, though it is said that net-fishing is now unknown in Egypt.

498.—SHIELDS OILED.

XXI, 5. **Prepare the table, watch in the watch-tower, eat, drink: arise, ye princes, and anoint the shield.**

Shields were made of bull-hide, of two or more thicknesses, stretched over a frame of wood, and sometimes strengthened with metallic rims, and ornamented in various places by pieces of metal. An occasional rubbing with oil was necessary to prevent the leather from becoming dry and cracked, and to keep the metallic portions from rust. This was especially necessary on getting ready for battle, and hence to " anoint the shield " was equivalent to a preparation for war.

499.—ON THE ROOFS.

XXII, 1. **What aileth thee now, that thou art wholly gone up to the house-tops?**

This, as Alexander observes, (*com. in loco,*) is "a lively description of an Oriental city in commotion." The flat roofs were used not only for promenading, (see note on 2 Sam. xi, 2,) but also as places of general gathering in times of excitement, just as we gather in the streets. From the roofs the inhabitants were accustomed to look down into the streets or afar off on the roads. This they could not do from the windows, as these seldom opened on the street. The prophet represents the entire people assembled on the tops of their houses. The precise object of their gathering he does not state, nor is it here necessary to discuss. Whether for mere curiosity, or to assail the invaders, or to indulge in idolatrous worship, these gatherings on the housetops give a striking illustration of Oriental customs.

500.—QUIVERS—SHIELD-CASES.

XXII, 6. **Elam bare the quiver with chariots of men and horsemen, and Kir uncovered the shield.**

1. The quivers were commonly carried by the archers on their backs, the top being near the right shoulder, so that the arrows could be conveniently drawn. The quiver usually had two rings, one near the top and the other

101.—CORINTHIAN TOMB AT PETRA.

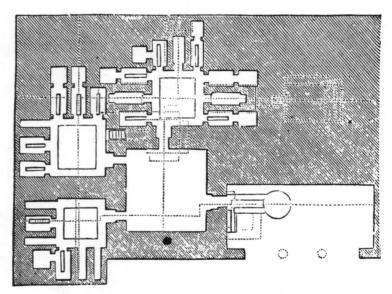

102.—PLAN OF THE TOMBS OF THE KINGS, AT JERUSALEM.

near the bottom, to which **was** fastened a strap which the archer slipped over his left arm and his head. Occasionally the quiver was thrust through one of the cross belts or attached to the body by a girdle-strap. In chariots the quivers were attached to the sides of the vehicle. Quivers were probably made of wood or of leather, and were often very highly ornamented. Representations of quivers may be found in cut No. 70, p. 178.

2. Shields, when not in use, were kept in cases, or covers, probably made of leather, to preserve them from dust. To "uncover the shield" would be equivalent to a preparation for battle, and is an expression having the same meaning as "anoint the shield" in chapter xxi, 5.

See also note on Hab. iii, 9.

501.—ROCK–SEPULCHERS.

XXII, 16. **What hast thou here, and whom hast thou here, that thou hast hewed thee out a sepulcher here, as he that heweth him out a sepulcher on high, and that graveth a habitation for himself in a rock.**

Sepulchers in the East were often hewn out of the solid rock, sometimes below the level of the ground, and frequently above ground and on the sides of mountains. Chambers were excavated in the rock, and on either side of these chambers were narrow cells in which the bodies of the dead were placed, each in its own receptacle. Sometimes the long side of the cell was cut at a right angle to the passage, so that the body of the dead was inserted lengthwise; at other times it was cut parallel to the passage, so that the body was inserted sidewise. In this latter mode our Lord seems to have been buried, since when Mary looked into the sepulcher she saw "two angels in white, sitting the one at the head, and the other at the feet, where the body of Jesus had lain." John xx, 12. Sometimes these rooms were without cells, and then the bodies rested on the floor. In the larger sepulchers were passage-ways leading to other chambers.

Many of these ancient sepulchers are still to be seen. The rock-tombs of Petra are among the most celebrated. A picture of the famous "Corinthian Tomb" is appended. Such sepulchers are also to be found in different parts of Palestine, but especially in the neighborhood of Jerusalem. The rocks south of the valley of Hinnom are full of them, and the valley of the Kidron contains a large number. The most celebrated of these sepulchers are those known by the names of "the Tombs of the Judges," at the head of the Valley of Jehoshaphat, containing sixty niches for bodies; "the Tombs of the Prophets, or Apostles," on the western declivity of the Mount of Olives, in which thirty cells have been discovered, though doubtless more are concealed by rubbish; and "the Tombs of the Kings," a half-mile north of the Damascus gate. There is no evidence that these tombs are rightly named, but they have all been at some time burial-places of great importance.

The last-named is especially rich in the ornamentation of its entrance, which is adorned with sculptures of fruit and flowers; and as an account of its internal arrangements will convey some idea of the plan of the best style of these rock-tombs, we give an abstract of Dr. Barclay's description of the so-called "Tombs of the Kings." They are situated " on the west side of a sunken court, about ninety feet square and upward of twenty feet deep. These finely-constructed catacombs are entered through a splendid, but now much decayed and defaced, portico, or portal and hall, on its western side, thirteen and a half feet high and twenty-eight and a half wide. Near its south-western corner is a door beneath the level of the floor, two and a half feet broad and less than three feet high, opening into an anteroom about nineteen feet square. In the western side of this room is a door leading into another room, thirteen and a half feet square, having in it about a dozen receptacles for the dead, and a passage leading by a stairway into a room ten feet by twelve, situated a story lower. There are two rooms entered from the south side of the anteroom or hall, each having half a dozen loculi; and from the north side of the westernmost one is a flight of steps conducting to another room in the lower story, ten feet square."—*City of the Great King*, p. 191.

When Maundrell visited these tombs in 1697 he found that "in every one of these rooms, except the first, were coffins of stone placed in niches in the sides of the chambers. They had been at first covered with handsome lids, and carved with garlands; but now most of them were broke to pieces by sacrilegious hands."—*Journey from Aleppo to Jerusalem*, under date of March 28. None of these sarcophagi are now remaining, though there are still richly carved fragments strewn about the rooms and the court. Fragments of elegantly paneled stone doors also lie scattered around. One of these was still hanging in its place at the time of Maundrell's visit. It was a slab of stone six inches in thickness, and in length and breadth about the size of an ordinary door. It turned on two hinges or pivots of stone, which were let into sockets cut out of the rock. These doors were for the interior rooms. The outer door-way was closed by a circular stone, for account of which see note on Matt. xxvii, 60.

502.—KEYS, HOW CARRIED.

XXII, 22. The key of the house of David will I lay upon his shoulder; so he shall open, and none shall shut; and he shall shut, and none shall open.

Oriental keys being usually large, (see note on Judges iii, 25,) it is often a matter of convenience to carry them on the shoulder. As the possession of a key may be taken as evidence of property or of trust, the key became an emblem of wealth or authority. Eastern merchants are often seen carrying keys on the shoulder. In the text, Shebna, the treasurer of Hezekiah, is warned that Eliakim shall carry " the keys of the house of David; " that is, that he should become treasurer in Shebna's place. This is a figurative way of expressing what is said in the twenty-first verse : " I will commit thy government into his hand," which expression is itself partly figurative, the hand being the emblem of power. The idea contained in both these passages is expressed in Isa. ix, 6, where it is said of the Messiah, " the government shall be upon his shoulder." The word keys is used figuratively to denote authority in Matt. xvi, 19, where Christ says to Peter: " I will give unto thee the keys of the kingdom of heaven: and whatsoever thou shalt bind on earth shall be bound in heaven; and whatsoever thou shalt loose on earth shall be loosed in heaven."

See also Rev. i, 18; iii, 7; ix, 1; xx, 1.

103—Keys Carried on the Shoulder.

503.—WOODEN PEGS.

XXII, 23. I will fasten him as a nail in a sure place, and he shall be for a glorious throne to his father's house.

The reference here is not to the tent-pins which are driven into the ground for the purpose of fastening the tent-cords, but to wooden pins or pegs which are put into the wall for the purpose of holding clothing and various household utensils. This is evident from the two following verses. When these pins are driven into the plastering of a house they are very insecure, and in a majority of instances fall out. To fasten them " in a sure place " they must be built into the wall as the house is built. They are then firm, and, being large, help to strengthen the walls and at the same time afford a useful support for the articles named. A beautiful reference to these house-pegs is made in Ezra ix, 8, where Ezra speaks of God's grace which had given the people " a nail in his holy place."

504.—GRAPE–GLEANING.

XXIV, 13. As the gleaning grapes when the vintage is done.

The Hebrews were directed not to pick their grapes closely, but to leave a few for the poor. See Lev. xix, 10; Deut. xxiv, 21. This merciful provision is referred to by Gideon when he represents " the gleaning of the grapes of Ephraim " as " better than the vintage of Abi-ezer." Judg. viii, 2.

505.—RESERVED FOR TRIUMPH.

XXIV, 22. They shall be gathered together, as prisoners are gathered in the pit, and shall be shut up in the prison, and after many days shall they be visited.

Lowth (W.) suggests that there is a reference here "to the custom of kings, who used to confine the chief commanders of their enemies whom they take prisoners and reserve them for some extraordinary day of triumph, and then bring them out to public punishment."—*Commentary in loco.*

506.—FILTERED WINE.

XXV, 6. A feast of wines on the lees, of fat things full of marrow, of wines on the lees well refined.

This refers to wines that are kept long with the dregs mixed with them, and therefore old and strong. They are refined or filtered by being strained through a cloth sieve, thus separating the liquor from the lees. The wine in the East is said to be usually turbid, and requires straining before it is fit for use.

507.—FUEL GATHERED BY WOMEN.

XXVII, 11. When the boughs thereof are withered, they shall be broken off: the women come, and set them on fire.

In the East it is the business of women and children to gather fuel. This is the reason the statement is so explicitly made here that "the women" shall come and set them on fire. It has an odd sound to us, for the question naturally arises why women rather than men are mentioned; but to the people of Isaiah's time the expression was perfectly natural, as it is to the people of the East to-day.

508.—THRESHING.

XXVIII, 27, 28. The fitches are not threshed with a threshing instrument, neither is a cart wheel turned about upon the cummin; but the fitches are beaten out with a staff, and the cummin with a rod. Bread corn is bruised; because he will not ever be threshing it, nor break it with the wheel of his cart, nor bruise it with his horsemen.

Four different modes of threshing are here referred to:

1. With a rod or flail. This was for the small delicate seeds, such as fitches and cummin. It was also used for grain when only a small quantity was to be threshed, or when it was necessary to conceal the operation from an enemy. It was doubtless in this manner that Ruth, when she was in the field of Boaz, "beat out" at evening what she had gleaned during the day.

See Ruth ii, 17. It was probably in the same way that Gideon " threshed wheat by the wine-press to hide it from the Midianites." Judges vi, 11. With a stick he could beat out a little at a time, and conceal it in the tub of the wine-press from the hostile Midianites.

2. With the *charuts*, " threshing instrument." This was a machine in some respects resembling the ordinary stone-sledge of American farmers. Professor Hackett describes one he saw at Beirut: " The frame was composed of thick pieces of plank, turned up in front like our stone-sledge, and perforated with holes underneath for holding the teeth. The teeth consisted of pieces of sharp basaltic rock about three inches long, and hardly less firm than iron itself. This machine is drawn over the grain by horses or oxen, and serves, together with the trampling of the feet of the animals, to beat out the kernels and cut up the straw preparatory to winnowing."—*Illustrations of Scripture*, p 161. The teeth were sometimes of iron. See Amos i, 3. The *tribulum* of the Romans resembled this instrument.

3. *Agalah*, " cart-wheel," is supposed to have been the same as the *morag*, " threshing instrument," mentioned in 2 Sam. xxiv, 22 ; 1 Chron. xxi, 23 ; and Isa. xli, 15, though some make the *morag* and the *charuts* the same.

This instrument is still known in Egypt by the name of *mow-rej*. It consists of three or four heavy rollers of wood, iron, or stone, roughly made and joined together in a square frame, which is in the form of a sledge or

104.—MODERN MODE OF THRESHING IN EGYPT WITH THE MOWREJ.

drag. The rollers are said to be like the barrels of an organ with their projections. The cylinders are parallel to each other, and are stuck full of spikes having sharp square points. It is used in the same way as the *charuts*. The driver sits on the machine, and with his weight helps to keep it down. This instrument is probably referred to in Prov. xx, 26, where it is said, " A wise king scattereth the wicked and bringeth the wheel over them."

(It is proper to say that authorities are not agreed as to the difference between the *charuts*, the *agalah*, and the *morag*. In the above account we have endeavored, as far as possible, to harmonize the conflicting opinions of various expositors.)

4. The last mode of threshing referred to in the text is that of treading out the grain, for an explanation of which see note on Deut. xxv, 4.

509.—SPIRIT-VOICES.

XXIX, 4. Thy voice shall be, as of one that hath a familiar spirit, out of the ground, and thy speech shall whisper out of the dust.

This is probably an allusion to the notion which was common to the ancient heathen, as well as to the Hebrews, that the souls of the dead had a weak, stridulous sound, entirely different from the voices of living men. The necromancers, who were chiefly women, spoke in a shrill, feigned voice, and may have practiced ventriloquism; in which case the voice would seem to come from the ground, where it was popularly supposed the disembodied spirits were. See also Isa. viii, 19.

510.—SOWING.

XXXII, 20. Blessed are ye that sow beside all waters, that send forth thither the feet of the ox and the ass.

There are two different opinions in reference to what customs are alluded to in this verse. Some think reference is made to the fields which are irrigated by artificial means, (see note on Psa. i, 3,) and to the practice of covering the seeds by plowing instead of by harrowing. The seed is sown in the irrigated fields, and the ox and the ass are used to draw the plow through the soil. Though oxen and asses were used for plowing, (see Isa. xxx, 20,) it was forbidden to plow with them together. See Deut. xxii, 10.

Others suppose reference to be made to the method of planting rice. Chardin says: "They sow it upon the water; and before sowing it, and while the earth is covered with water, they cause the ground to be trodden by oxen, horses, and asses, who go mid-leg deep, and this is the way of preparing the ground for sowing."—HARMER'S *Observations*, vol. i, p. 477.

511.—PARCHMENT ROLLS.

XXXIV, 4. All the host of heaven shall be dissolved, and the heavens shall be rolled together as a scroll.

Parchment books were rolled around a stick or cylinder, and, if very long, around two cylinders, from the two extremities. There is in the public library at Cambridge, England, an ancient manuscript roll of the Pentateuch. It is made of goats' skins dyed red, and measures forty-eight feet in length by about twenty-two inches in breadth. As the book of Leviticus and a part of Deuteronomy are wanting, it is calculated that the original length could not have been far from ninety feet. It consists of thirty-seven different skins, and contains one hundred and seventeen different columns of writing. These columns correspond to the pages of our books, are each about four inches wide, and contain from forty to fifty lines apiece. This manuscript is undoubtedly very ancient, though its date cannot now be ascertained. It was obtained by the Rev. Dr. Buchanan from the black Jews in Malabar.

The celebrated Samaritan Pentateuch is the oldest manuscript of which we have any knowledge. It consists of twenty-one skins of unequal size, most of which contain six, but some only five, columns. The columns are thirteen inches deep and seven and a half wide. Each contains from seventy to seventy-two lines, and the entire roll has one hundred and ten columns.

Ancient rolls were sometimes encased in a cover, which was more or less ornamented, and on which the title was sometimes written. This case corresponded to the envelopes in which their letters were put. See note on

105.—Parchment Scroll.

Neh. vi, 5. Some commentators think that this outside cover, with its title, is what is referred to in Psa. xl, 7: "In the volume of the book it is written of me." Others suppose that reference is made in that text to a small strip of parchment which was attached to each roll, and contained the title, so that the nature of the contents could be ascertained without the trouble of unrolling.

When the manuscript was used the reader unrolled it until he found the place, and when he had finished reading he rolled it up again. This is what is meant by opening and closing the book in Luke iv, 17, 20.

This style of book is often referred to in the Bible. See Ezra vi, 1, 2; Jer. xxxvi, 2, 23, 29; Ezek. ii, 9; iii, 1, 2; Zech. v, 1, 2; 2 Tim. iv, 13, and probably Rev. v, 1, etc., though some commentators think that a book of leaves is there meant.

512.—PRISONERS BRIDLED.

XXXVII, 29. Because thy rage against me, and thy tumult, is come up into mine ears, therefore will I put my hook in thy nose, and my bridle in thy lips.

Allusion is here made to the custom of inserting a ring in the nose of a refractory animal for the purpose of subduing and leading him. The metaphor is a favorite one with the Arabian poets. The language used here, however, is not altogether metaphorical in its reference to human beings. In the sculptures taken from Khorsabad there are representations of prisoners brought before the king, each prisoner having an iron ring thrust through his lower lip. To these rings cords are attached, which the king holds in his left hand, while in his right he holds a spear, which he thrusts into the

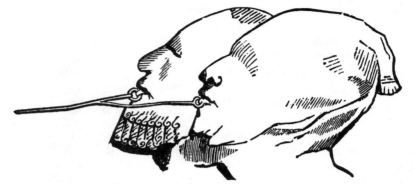

106.—MEN BRIDLED.

eyes of the poor prisoners. See note on 2 Kings xxv, 7. See also 2 Kings xix, 28; Ezek. xxix, 4; xxxviii, 4.

513.—PREPARING THE WAY OF THE KING.

XL, 8, 4. **The voice of him that crieth in the wilderness, Prepare ye the way of the Lord, make straight in the desert a highway for our God. Every valley shall be exalted, and every mountain and hill shall be made low: and the crooked shall be made straight, and the rough places plain.**

Roads of some kind must have existed in former times in Palestine, though nothing worthy of the name is to be found there to-day. The use of chariots, and the opening and preservation of the way to the Cities of Refuge, and such expressions as are found in this text, seem to imply a knowledge and a use of artificial roads.

It has been the custom from ancient times for Oriental monarchs, when wishing to travel through their dominions, to send men before them to prepare their way, by removing stones, (see Isa. lxii, 10,) leveling rough places, filling up hollows, and making the road pleasant and easy for the distinguished travelers. Semiramis, on one of her journeys, coming to a rough, mountainous region, ordered the hills leveled and the hollows filled, which was done at an enormous cost. Her object was not only to shorten the way, but to leave to posterity a lasting monument of herself. There have been modern instances of a similar character, though not involving so much labor and expense.

In Matt. iii, 3, Mark i, 3, Luke iii, 4, John i, 23, this passage is applied to John the Baptist, who, as a herald, (see note on 1 Cor. ix, 27,) preceded the Messiah to announce his coming and to have the way prepared.

514.—LAMP–WICKS.

XLII, 8. A bruised reed shall he not break, and the smoking flax shall he not quench.

Lamp-wicks were made of linen, and the allusion is to a wick that is burning with feeble flame from absence of oil, and just ready to expire. The readiness with which the light of such a wick can be put out is referred to in Isa. xliii, 17, "They are quenched as tow;" where *pishtah,* "tow," is the same word that is rendered "flax" in the text.

515.—A BATH BY POURING.

XLIV, 3. I will pour water upon him that is thirsty, and floods upon the dry ground.

Roberts thinks there is an allusion here to one mode of bathing practiced by Orientals, which is to have water poured on the body by an attendant. The Egyptian monuments give evidence that this mode was practiced in Egypt.

516.—HOW IDOLS WERE MADE.

XLIV, 10. Who hath formed a god, or molten a graven image that is profitable for nothing?

1. The term "molten" does not necessarily mean that the image was cast of solid metal. Such may sometimes have been made, especially of small size; but the metallic part of idols was usually a thin plating of metal on a wooden image. See note on Exod. xxxii, 4. Thus the carpenter and the goldsmith worked together. See Isa. xl, 19, 20; xli, 7; Jer. x, 3, 4.

2. The work of the carpenter was to take the rude log and fashion it into an image ready to receive the metallic plates. This is aptly described in the thirteenth verse of this chapter: "The carpenter stretcheth out his rule; he marketh it out with a line; he fitteth it with planes, and he marketh it out with the compass, and maketh it after the figure of a man, according to the beauty of a man; that it may remain in the house." The figure was first marked on the log with a chalk line, and then cut and carved with the proper tools until it assumed the shape and size required. Denon, in his *Travels in Egypt,* (cited by BURDER, *Oriental Customs,* No. 720,) speaks of an idol which he found "on one of the columns of the portico of Tentyra; it was covered with stucco and painted. The stucco being partly scaled off, gave me the opportunity of discovering *lines traced* as if with *red chalk.* Curiosity prompted me to take away the whole of the stucco, and I found the form of the figure sketched, with corrections of the outline; a division into twenty-two parts: the separation of the thighs being in the middle of the whole height of the figure, and the head comprising rather less than a seventh part."

It was after some such plan, probably, that idols were made in the time of Isaiah. The wooden image, once made, could be worshiped as it was, or it could be covered with plaster or with metal. On the other hand, the metallic outside might not always have had an interior of wood, but may sometimes have been filled with clay, as idols in India are at this day.

517.—EYES SEALED.

XLIV, 18. He hath shut their eyes that they cannot see, and their hearts that they cannot understand.

The margin has "daubed" instead of shut, and thus comes nearer to the original, *tach*, from *tuach*, which Gesenius defines "to spread over, to daub, to besmear, to plaster." The words convey the idea of something smeared over the eyes to close them. Harmer suggests, as an explanation of the expression, a reference to a custom followed in the East Indies. The Great Mogul once sealed up his son's eyes for three years as a punishment, and at the expiration of that time removed the seal. This is given on the authority of Sir Thomas Roe's chaplain, who does not tell us, however, what was put upon the eyes to produce this result. Dr. Russell tells of a Jewish wedding in Aleppo, where the eyelids of the bride were fastened together with gum, and only the bridegroom was to open them. It is possible that in Isaiah's day there was some mode of causing temporary blindness by smearing the eyes, and that this is referred to in the text.

518.—NEBO.

XLVI, 1. Bel boweth down, Nebo stoopeth.

Nebo was the last in order of the planetary gods of the Chaldeans, and was also worshiped by the Babylonians and the Assyrians, and by the Sabians in Arabia. He is supposed to have been of Babylonian origin. He corresponds to the Latin Mercury, the Greek Hermes, and the Egyptian Thoth. The name is supposed to be derived from *nabah*, to prophesy, and the office of this deity was that of interpreter for the gods. His symbol was a simple wedge or arrow-head. The same word (*Tir*) among the ancient Persians signified both "arrow-head" and the name of the planet nearest the sun, Mercury. The popularity of this god is seen in the combination of his name with the names of ancient kings: for example, *Nebu*chadnezzar, *Nebu*zaradan, *Nebu*hashban, *Nabo*nedus, *Nabo*nassar, *Nabu*rianus, *Nabo*nabus, *Nabo*polassar.

In the British Museum are statues of Nebo which were taken from Nimrud. They are partially covered with cuneiform inscriptions. There is also in the same Museum a block of black basalt, which was found at Hillah in 1862. It has on it an inscription of six hundred and twenty lines, divided into ten columns. In this inscription reference is made by Nebuchadnezzar, its author, to the god Nebo, in which, among other things, he says: "Nebo, the guardian of the hosts of heaven and earth, has committed to me the scepter of justice to govern men."

The expressions, "boweth down" and "stoopeth," evidently refer to the downfall of these idols, and of the system of idolatry of which they were the symbols. According to the prophecy this was to be accomplished by the Persian power. It is, therefore, proper to remark here, that though the Persians worshiped the sun, the moon, the earth, etc., images of gods were entirely unknown among them. Herodotus says of them, "They have no images of the gods, no temples nor altars, and consider the use of them a sign of folly."—Book i, chap. 131. Thus it was in perfect accordance with their own customs that the Persians should destroy the graven images of other nations. To Cyrus the Persian monarch, is assigned, in chapter xlv, 1, this work of destruction. So utterly helpless are Nebo and Bel, that they cannot deliver themselves from captivity, and so worthless that they are counted only as "a burden to the weary beast."

107.—NEBO. FROM STATUE IN BRITISH MUSEUM.

An account of Bel is given in the note on Jer. l, 2.

519.—MODE OF CARRYING IDOLS.

XLVI, 7. **They bear him upon the shoulder, they carry him, and set him in his place, and he standeth.**

It is precisely in this way that the Hindoos of the present day, according to Ward, carry their idols in procession and set them in the temples. There is an Assyrian marble which has on it, in bas-relief, a representation of a procession, in which four idols are carried on the shoulders of men.

520.—ASTROLOGERS.

XLVII, 18. **Let now the astrologers, the star-gazers, the monthly prognosticators, stand up, and save thee from these things that shall come upon thee.**

Efforts to foretell future events by watching the motions of the heavenly bodies are very ancient. The ancient Babylonians and Chaldeans were especially celebrated for their attempts in this direction. See Dan. ii, 2. In Chaldea the astrologers formed a particular caste, in which the knowledge acquired was transmitted from father to son. They taught that the universe was eternal, that a divine providence ruled over it, and that the movements of the heavenly bodies were directed according to the council of the gods. Their long observation had made them more competent than other men to calculate the movements and influence of the stars. From the rising and setting of the planets, their orbits and color, they predicted storms, heat, rain, comets, eclipses, and earthquakes; and from the varied appearances of the heavens they foretold events that not only affected lands and nations, but also brought happiness or unhappiness to kings and common people.

To assist them in making calculations from the stars the astrologers divided the heavens, visible and invisible, into twelve equal parts, six above the horizon and six below. These they called "houses," and the various subjects which affect the happiness of mankind, such as fortune, marriage, life, death, religion, etc., were distributed among them. From the position of the stars in these "houses" the calculations were made. The two words rendered "astrologers" in the text literally signify "dividers of the heavens."

521.—PICTURES ON THE HANDS.

XLIX, 16. Behold, I have graven thee upon the palms of my hands; thy walls are continually before me.

This is a figurative way of expressing that Jehovah will never forget Zion. The city is represented as graven on his hands, so that its walls are perpetually in his sight, and thus the people of God, who are figured by the city, are kept in everlasting remembrance. Roberts says that a similar form of speech is frequently used in India to express one's destiny. It is common to say, in reference to men or things, "They are written on the palms of his hands." Remembrance of an absent one is expressed by a figure similar to the one used in the latter part of the text:• "Ah, my friend, you have long since forgotten me !" *"Forgotten you! Never !* for your walls are ever before me."

Many writers, however, suppose that there is in the text something more than an allusion to a mere figure of speech; that an actual custom is referred to. It is thought that the Jews of that day were in the habit of tattooing on their hands or arms representations of the city or temple in order to keep before them something to remind them of the sacred places. This is Bishop Lowth's view, and it is accepted by many commentators. We have an illustration of it in modern times. Maundrell tells us that it was customary in his day for pilgrims to Jerusalem to have figures of various kinds marked on their arms as memorials of their visit. These representations were called "ensigns of Jerusalem." He describes the process as follows: "The artists who undertake the operation do it in this manner: they have stamps in wood of any figure that you desire, which they first print off upon your arm with powder and charcoal; then taking two very fine needles tied close together, and dipping them often, like a pen, in certain ink, compounded, as I was informed, of gunpowder and ox-gall, they make with them small punctures all along the lines of the figure they have printed; and then, washing the part in wine, conclude the work. These punctures they make with great quickness and dexterity, and with scarce any smart, seldom piercing so deep as to draw blood."—*Journey from Aleppo to Jerusalem,* under date of *March* 27.

See also notes on Lev. xix, 28, and Gal. vi, 17.

522.—MODES OF CARRYING CHILDREN.

XLIX, 22. They shall bring thy sons in their arms, and thy daughters shall be carried upon their shoulders.

Two modes of carrying children are here alluded to, though there is no reason to suppose that either was exclusively for one sex. In Deut. xxxiii, 12, Benjamin is represented as occupying the position here assigned to the daughters.

1. "In their arms" may also be rendered in their *bosom,* as it is in the margin. The large lap or pocket made by the folds of the outer garment (see note on Luke vi, 38) was a convenient and comfortable place for carrying a child. In Num. xi, 12, it is intimated that it was customary for fathers to carry their infants in this manner when going on a journey.

2. Another Oriental mode of carrying children is on the shoulders. This is sometimes done by placing them astride the neck. Thus, it is said of Benjamin, "he shall dwell between his shoulders." Deut. xxxiii, 12. At other times the child is placed astride one shoulder, usually the left, with one leg hanging down on the back and the other on the breast. In either case the child steadies itself by putting its arms around the parent's head, and by clinging with its feet. In Egypt women are often seen

108.—CARRYING CHILDREN.

carrying a child on one shoulder and a jar of water on the other.

For still another mode of carrying children see note on Isa. lx, 4.

523.—DUST SHAKEN OFF.

LII, 2. Shake thyself from the dust; arise, and sit down, O Jerusalem.

Jowett, in his *Christian Researches,* refers to the custom of Orientals sitting on the ground with their feet drawn under them, gradually gathering dust on their garments, and rising occasionally to shake it off, and then resuming their seats. This, however, is only a partial explanation of the allusions of the text. The "dust" referred to may be either that in which Jerusalem had been sitting, or that which she had put upon her head. In either case the idea of mourning would be represented. The mourner is exhorted to arise from the dust and take a higher position; not to sit down again in the dust. The language seems to embrace the idea of a throne, a high seat. Alexander agrees with some of the best expositors who adopt the interpretation of the Targum, *Sit upon thy throne.* From this Jerusalem is supposed to have been previously cast down. The ground was to be left, the dust shaken off, and the throne occupied. The mourning was to be changed for rejoicing.

524.—PREPARING FOR WAR.

LII, 10. The Lord hath made bare his holy arm in the eyes of all the nations.

To "make bare the arm" is a metaphorical expression denoting preparation

109.—THE ARM MADE BARE.

for active work, especially for war. The beauty of the figure is seen, not only in the fact that the arm is an appropriate emblem of power, but also in the additional fact that the Oriental costume permits the arm to be bared in an instant. Jowett says: "The loose sleeve of the Arab shirt, as well as of the outer garment, leaves the arm so completely free, that in an instant the left hand, passing up the right arm, makes it bare; and this is done when a person, a soldier, for example, about to strike with his sword, intends to give the arm full play."— *Christian Researches*, etc., p. 208.

Reference is also made to this baring of the arm in Isa. liii, 1, and also in Ezek. iv, 7. Classic writers likewise make frequent allusion to it.

525.—SPRINKLING.

LII, 15. So shall he sprinkle many nations.

Most commentators suppose the figure of sprinkling to be taken from the ceremonial sprinklings of the Mosaic law. It was customary to sprinkle blood in connection with different sacrifices. See notes on Exod. xxiii, 15; Lev. vi, 9; vi, 25; vii, 1; vii, 11; xvi, 34. In allusion to this custom the prophet, in the text, represents the Messiah as making atonement for the nations.

110.—PERFUME
SPRINKLER.

Some writers think there is an allusion to the custom of sprinkling guests at feasts with perfumed waters from a silver vessel of vase-like shape and with a perforated top, through which the fluid is thrown on the faces of the guests. This sprinkling is sometimes so copious as to cause embarrassment. Bruce, after describing an interview he once had with a certain dignitary, says: "Our coffee being done, I rose to take my leave, and was presently wet to the skin by deluges of orange-flower water." Niebuhr relates a similar instance: "The first time we were received with all the Eastern ceremonies, (it was at Rosetto, at a Greek merchant's house,) there was one of our company who was excessively surprised when a domestic placed himself before him and threw water over him, as well on his face as over his clothes." See TAYLOR'S *Calmet; Fragments.* No. XIV.

The engraving represents a perfume-sprinkler of beautiful form, such as is used in some parts of India.

526.—INVITATION TO BUY.

LV, 1. Ho, every one that thirsteth, come ye to the waters, and he that hath no money; come ye, buy, and eat; yea, come, buy wine and milk without money and without price.

A beautiful illustration of the customary mode of addressing purchasers in the East is given by Miss Rogers, who thus describes her walk through one of the streets of Jerusalem: "The shopkeepers were crying to the passers-by, 'Ho, every one that hath money, let him come and buy! Ho, such a one, come and buy!' But some of them seemed to be more disinterested, and one of the fruiterers, offering me preserves and fruit, said; 'O lady, take of our fruit without money and without price; it is yours, take all that you will,' and he would gladly have laden our *kawas* with the good things of his store and then have claimed double their value."—*Domestic Life in Palestine,* p. 49. There is more sincerity in the Gospel invitations than in those of the traders

527.—STONE-WORSHIP.

LVII, 6. Among the smooth stones of the stream is thy portion; they, they are thy lot: even to them hast thou poured a drink-offering, thou hast offered a meat-offering.

The worship of stone pillars is a practice of very great antiquity, and one to which many nations were formerly devoted. Some have strangely confounded the anointing of the stone at Bethel by Jacob with this superstitious practice; but we think the patriarch can be freed from the charge of idolatry on that occasion. See note on Gen. xxviii, 18. The worship of stones is referred to in Deut. vii, 5; xii, 3, and in many passages where the word "images" is used. It is very probable also that the allusion to the "rock" of the heathen in Deut. xxxii, 31, 37, is a reference to the same species of idolatry. "The image which fell down from Jupiter," and which was worshiped by the Ephesians, may furnish another illustration. See note on Acts xix, 35.

The old custom was to anoint the stones which were worshiped, and to present offerings to them. Clemens Alexandrinus speaks of a superstitious man as "a worshiper of every shining stone." Arnobius, who lived in the fifth century, said, after his conversion to Christianity, that when he was a heathen he never saw an oiled stone without addressing it and praying to it.

There are many monuments of this ancient idolatry still in existence; they are especially abundant on the western extremity of Europe, in Cornwall, and in the islands and promontories from the Land's End to Caithness and the Orkneys. In fact, evidences of this worship have come down to such recent times that it may well be doubted whether this species of idolatry has even yet ceased to exist in Europe. In the latter part of the seventeenth century it was practiced in Lapland, one of the deities of Scandinavian mythology being represented by a stone. In the early part of the following century there were pillar-stones held in great veneration among the inhabitants of the Western Islands of Scotland. One of these stones was swathed in flannel. Another, about eight feet high and two broad, was called "the bowing stone," because the people bowed before it in reverence and said the Lord's prayer. Within twenty years of the present time the same superstition has been known to exist in Ireland, and very probably is to be found there still. The Earl of Roden, in his *Progress of the Reformation in Ireland*, states that in the Island of Inniskea, off the coast of Mayo, the people worship a stone which is wrapped in flannel. Its power is believed to be immense. The people pray to it in time of sickness, and invoke it to raise a storm and send some hapless vessel a wreck on their barren coast that they may profit by the disaster! See an article in *Notes and Queries* for February 7, 1852, from the pen of Sir J. Emerson Tennent.

528.—THE ARM AN EMBLEM OF POWER.

LIX, 1. Behold, the Lord's hand is not shortened, that it cannot save.

As the arm is an emblem of power, so shortness of arm signifies diminished power, and length of arm an increase. Thus it is said that Artaxerxes Longimanus, that is, the Long-handed, was so called, not because of any peculiarity of body, but because of the vast extent of his power. There is an ancient Egyptian sculpture in which the same bold figure is employed as the one used by the prophet in the text. It represents Thannyras, the son of Inarus, whom Artaxerxes had made Satrap of Egypt, worshiping the sun as his god. In this he disregarded the religion of his own people, and adopted that of their conquerors. The sun is represented as sending his rays down on the earth, and at the end of every ray is a hand.

See also Num. xi, 23, and Isa. 1, 2.

111.—Egyptian Satrap Worshiping the Sun.

529.—MODE OF CARRYING CHILDREN.

LX, 4. Thy sons shall come from far, and thy daughters shall be nursed at thy side.

In the East, children are not only carried on the bosom and on the shoulders, (see note on Isa. xlix, 22,) but also on the hip, and reference is thought to be made to this custom in this text and in Isa. lxvi, 12. Chardin saw the mothers carrying their nursing children astride upon the hip with the arm around the body. Other travelers have noticed the same custom.

530.—PIGEON HOUSES.

LX, 8. Who are these that fly as a cloud, and as the doves to their windows.

Doves have always been favorite birds in the East. In Egypt, Syria, and Persia there are cotes built for their special accommodation. In the text the prophet represents the success of Christianity by the countless Gentiles who will seek admission into the Church. So numerous will these Gentiles be that they will appear like a cloud, just as the doves appear when they fly to the entrances to their habitations. The figure is very animated and beautiful.

Some of the dove houses are quite peculiar in their construction. Shaw represents them as a prominent feature in Egyptian villages. They are round, tall, and narrow, six or eight being grouped together. See *Travels*, plate facing p. 291.

Morier gives an interesting account of the pigeon houses of Persia, which are erected at intervals in the open country for the purpose of collecting the dung for manure. "They are large round towers, rather broader at the bottom than the top, and crowned by conical spiracles through which

the pigeons descend. Their interior resembles a honeycomb pierced with a thousand holes, each of which forms a snug retreat for a nest. More care appears to have been bestowed upon the outside than upon that of the generality of the dwelling-houses, for they are painted and ornamented. The extraordinary flights of pigeons

112.—PIGEON TOWERS IN PERSIA.

which I have seen alight upon one of these buildings afford perhaps a good illustration for the passage in Isa. lx, 8. . . . Their great numbers and the compactness of their mass literally look like a cloud at a distance, and obscure the sun in their passage."—*Second Journey*, etc., p. 140.

531.—THE OPEN GATES.

LX, 11. **Therefore thy gates shall be open continually; they shall not be shut day nor night.**

The gates of walled towns are shut at sundown, or shortly after. Travelers often hasten in their journey when they see the sun declining and the shadows lengthen, lest the day expire before they reach the city gates. It not uncommonly happens that, with all their exertions, they are too late; they are then compelled to spend the night outside, exposed to storms and robbers. The prophet represents the Church of Christ with her gates "open continually," in marked contrast to the custom with which Oriental people are familiar. A similar illustration is given by John in his beautiful description of the New Jerusalem: "And the gates of it shall not be shut at all by day: for there shall be no night there." Rev. xxi, 25.

532.—A DIADEM FOR ASHES.

LXI, 3. **To appoint unto them that mourn in Zion, to give unto them beauty for ashes, the oil of joy for mourning, the garment of praise for the spirit of heaviness.**

Peer, "beauty," is the same word that is rendered "bonnet" in Isa. iii, 20, where see the note. The prophet wishes to show the contrast between the time of mourning and that of rejoicing. The mourner sits with ashes on the head. See note on 2 Sam. xv, 32. When the mourning ceases and the joy comes the ashes are taken from the head, and, in the true spirit of rejoicing, a beautiful diadem is placed thereon instead.

533.—WEDDING JEWELRY.

LXI, 10. **As a bridegroom decketh himself with ornaments, and as a bride adorneth herself with her jewels.**

At Oriental weddings both bride and bridegroom are adorned with a profusion of jewelry of every kind. If too poor to purchase they borrow from neighbors and friends, that a splendid show may be made. See also Rev. xxi, 2.

534.—REPETITION.

LXII, 10. **Go through, go through the gates; prepare ye the way of the people; cast up, cast up the highway.**

We have here an illustration of the Oriental style of repetition in language, of which there are several other instances in this book.' Thus, in chapter xxiv, 19, 20, we read in our version, "The earth is utterly broken down, the earth is clean dissolved, the earth is moved exceedingly. The earth shall reel to and fro like a drunkard." This is more literally rendered by Alexander, "Broken, broken is the earth; shattered, shattered is the earth; shaken, shaken is the earth. The earth reels, reels like a drunken man." So also in chapter xxvi, 3, we have, "Thou wilt keep him in perfect peace." The margin gives the literal translation, "Peace, peace." See also Jer. xxii, 29; Ezek. xxi, 27.

This is not exclusively a Hebrew idiom. Chardin quotes from a Persian letter the words, "To whom I wish that all the world may pay homage," and says that the language is literally, "that all souls may serve his name, his name."

535.—IDOLATROUS FEASTS.

LXV, 11. **But ye are they that forsake the Lord, that forget my holy mountain, that prepare a table for that troop, and that furnish the drink-offering unto that number.**

For "troop" and "that number" the margin substitutes the original words *gad* and *meni.* The precise meaning of these two terms is a matter of diversified opinion. Gesenius defines *gad* to be the god Fortune, the same as Baal or Bel, that is, the planet Jupiter, which was regarded throughout the East as the giver of good fortune. There was a city called Baal-Gad in the valley of Lebanon under Mount Hermon. Gesenius gives to *meni* the definition of *fate, fortune, destiny,* and thinks the planet Venus was intended. Venus was identical with Astarte, and was regarded by the ancient Semitic nations as the source of good fortune, and as such was coupled with the planet Jupiter; Jupiter being the "Greater Good Fortune," and Venus the "Lesser Good Fortune." Fuerst is undecided whether *gad* refers to Jupiter or Venus; he supposes *meni* to refer to the moon, and that both were deities who were supposed to control fate.

Many interpreters have refused to render the two words as names of idols, and have "referred the whole clause either to convivial assemblies, perhaps connected with idolatrous worship, or to the troop of planets and the multitude of stars, as objects of such worship."—ALEXANDER, *Commentary in loco.*

All, however, are agreed on one point, that the whole passage has reference to idolatrous worship of some sort; the "table" and the "drink-offering" give evidence of that. The kind of offering referred to is supposed to be identical with the *lectisternia* of the Romans. These were feasts spread for the consumption of the gods on occasions of extraordinary solemnities. Images of the gods reclined on couches, while before them were placed tables filled with viands, as if the gods were really partaking of the things offered in sacrifice. The custom is thought to have been of Egyptian origin, and from the Egyptians the Hebrews probably learned it. Jerome states that in every city in Egypt, and especially in Alexandria, they were in the habit, on the last day of each year, of covering a table with dishes of various kinds, and with a cup filled with a liquor made of water, wine, and honey, either in acknowledgement of the fertility of the past year, or to implore fruitfulness for the year to come.

See also notes on Num. xxii, 41, and 1 Kings xi, 5.

———◆———

JEREMIAH.

536.—CISTERNS.

II, 18. They have forsaken me the fountain of living waters, and hewed them out cisterns, broken cisterns, that can hold no water.

The dryness of the summer months in Palestine, and the absence of large rivers, together with the scarcity of springs in many places, make it necessary to collect into cisterns the rains which fall, and the waters which fill the small streams in the rainy season. This has been the custom in that land from very early times. These cisterns are either dug in the earth or cut out of the soft limestone rock, and are of several kinds. Sometimes a shaft is sunk like a well, and the bottom widened into the shape of a jug. Excavations of this sort combine the characters of cisterns and wells, since they not only receive the rain which is conducted into them, but the water which percolates through the limestone. Another kind consists of chambers excavated out of the rock, with a hole in the roof. Again, an excavation is made perpendicularly, and the roof arched with masonry. Some are lined with wood or cement, while others are left in their natural state.

They are sometimes entirely open at the top, and are then entered by steps, or, in the case of large ones, (and some are very large,) by flights of stairs. Where they are roofed, a circular opening with a curb is at the top, and a wheel, with a rope and bucket, is provided. This is referred to in Eccl. xii, 6, "The wheel broken at the cistern." Jerusalem is abundantly supplied with water by means of cisterns, and during all its long and terrible sieges has never suffered for want of a supply.

It is to these different kinds of receptacles for water that the prophet refers in the text. Though with proper care the water may be kept sweet for a time, it is often in a filthy condition, not to be compared to the pure water from living fountains, and at any time the cisterns are liable to become "broken," and to leak. See also 2 Kings xviii, 31; Isa. xxxvi, 16.

537.—HANDS ON THE HEAD.

II, 37. Thou shalt go forth from him, and thine hands upon thine head.

This is an Oriental mode of expressing great grief, and is thought by some to signify that the heavy hand of God's affliction is resting on the mourner. This was one of the tokens of mourning adopted by Tamar after the cruel maltreatment she received from Amnon. See 2 Sam. xiii, 19. There is in the British Museum a sculptured slab representing Egyptian mourners at a funeral, with their hands on their heads. According to Roberts, this is a common mode of expressing grief in India. "When people are in great distress they put their hands on their head, the fingers being clasped on the top of the

118.—HANDS ON THE HEAD.

crown. Should a man who is plunged into wretchedness meet a friend, he immediately puts his hands on his head to illustrate his circumstances. When a person hears of the death of a relation or friend he forthwith clasps his hands and places them on his head. When boys have been punished at school, they run home with their hands on the same place."— *Oriental Illustrations*, p. 461.

See also note on 2 Sam. xv, 32.

538.—BELLOWS.

VI, 29. The bellows are burned, the lead is consumed of the fire.

The use of the bellows in the East is confined now, as it was in ancient

times, to the workers in metals, ordinary fires being regulated by fans. The ancient bellows consisted of a leathern bag in a wooden frame, with a long mouthpiece of reed tipped with metal to preserve it from the action of the fire. The operator stood with a bellows under each foot. In each hand, attached to the instrument under foot, was a string, by which he lifted the bag of skin when it became exhausted of air by the pressure of the foot.

114.—EGYPTIAN BELLOWS.

539.—MIRTH AT MARRIAGES.

VII, 34. Then will I cause to cease from the cities of Judah, and from the streets of Jerusalem, the voice of mirth, and the voice of gladness, the voice of the bridegroom, and the voice of the bride.

Marriages in the East are celebrated by processions of friends, who throng the streets and give noisy demonstrations of their joy. Singers and musicians accompany them, and the shouts and music are heard afar off. Miss Rogers gives a lively account of a wedding party she once met not far from Mount Carmel. "Pleasant sounds of voices, songs, bells, and laughter reached us, and we saw an animated little party approaching, mounted on camels, whose nodding heads and necks were decorated with beads, shells, crimson tassels, and strings of little tinkling bells."—*Domestic Life in Palestine*, p. 94.

Among the Mohammedans no marriages are allowed during the month of Ramadan, which is their solemn annual fast. The troubles to come upon Judah are represented in the text by the prediction of utter silence in the streets. See also Jer. xvi, 9; xxv, 10; xxxiii, 11; Rev. xviii, 23.

540.—LODGINGS.

IX, 2. **O that I had in the wilderness a lodging-place of way-faring men; that I might leave my people, and go from them!**

The prophet probably refers to those temporary lodging-places for travelers in the open country which private charity or municipal law sometimes provides in the East; or he may refer to the temporary hospitality which is considered in the East as a religious duty to be extended toward strangers. See note on Job xxxi, 17, and see Jer. xiv, 8. His idea is that the wilderness is better than the place where his people live, and the hospitality of strangers preferable to the society of his wicked friends. Roberts thinks there may here be reference to a custom he has noticed in India. When a man becomes angry with his family it is not uncommon for him to threaten to leave them and dwell in the wilderness. This threat is not always empty sound; for there are many in every town and village who thus leave their families and are absent for months or years, and some never return. The wilderness has many ascetics, who, from this and other causes, live retired from the haunts of men.

541.—MOURNING WOMEN.

IX, 17, 18. **Thus saith the Lord of hosts, Consider ye, and call for the mourning women, that they may come: and send for cunning women, that they may come; and let them make haste, and take up a wailing for us, that our eyes may run down with tears, and our eyelids gush out with waters.**

Not only are great lamentations made by the bereaved for their loved ones, but professed mourners, usually women, are hired for the purpose. They assemble in greater or less number, according to the ability which those who hire them have to pay for their services. Their hair is disheveled, their clothes torn, and their countenances daubed with paint and dirt. They sing in a sort of chorus, mingled with shrill screams and loud wailing, distorting their limbs frightfully, swaying their bodies to and fro, and moving in a kind of melancholy dance to the thrumming music of tambourines. They recount the virtues of the deceased, calling him by names of tenderest endearment, and plaintively inquiring of him why he left his family and friends! With wonderful ingenuity these hired mourners seek to make a genuine lamentation among the visitors who have come to the funeral, by alluding to any among them who have suffered bereavement, dwelling on its character and circumstances, and thus eliciting from the sorrowing ones cries of real grief.

Miss Rogers gives a thrilling account of a formal mourning which lasted for a week, and at which she was present for several hours. Three rows of women on the one side of the room faced three rows on the other side. They clapped their hands and struck their breasts in time to the monotonous melody they murmured. One side, led by a celebrated professional mourner, sang the praises of the dead man, while the other responded in chorus. After the singing they shrieked and made a rattling noise in their throats, while the widow kneeled, swayed her body backward and forward, and feebly joined in the wild cry.

"A minstrel woman began slowly beating a tambourine, and all the company clapped their hands in measure with it, singing, 'Alas for him! Alas for him! He was brave, he was good; alas for him!' Then three women rose, with naked swords in their hands, and stood at two or three yards distance from each other. They began dancing with slow and graceful movements, with their swords at first held low and their heads drooping. Each dancer kept within a circle of about a yard in diameter. By degrees the tambourine and the clapping of the hands and the songs grew louder, the steps of the dancers were quickened. They threw back their heads and gazed upward passionately, as if they would look into the very heavens. They flourished their uplifted swords, and as their movements became more wild and excited, the bright steel flashed, and bright eyes seemed to grow brighter. As one by one the dancers sank, overcome with fatigue, others rose to replace them. Thus passed seven days and nights. Professional mourners were in constant attendance to keep up the excitement, and dances and dirges succeeded each other, with intervals of wild and hysterical weeping and shrieking."—*Domestic Life in Palestine*, pp. 181, 182.

Shaw says that the hired mourners at Moorish funerals cry out in a deep and hollow voice, several times together, *Loo! loo! loo!* ending each period with "some ventriloquous sighs." See *Travels*, etc., p. 242.

To this singular custom of hiring mourners the prophet refers in the text, and also in the twentieth verse. These hired mourners were present at the burial of the good king Josiah. 2 Chron. xxxv, 25. Solomon refers to them in Eccl. xii, 5: "The mourners go about the streets." Amos speaks of "such as are skillful of lamentation." Amos v, 16. Hired mourners were present with their instruments of funeral music at the house of Jairus after the death of his daughter. See Matt. ix, 23; Mark v, 38.

See also note on 2 Sam. xix, 4.

542.—ADZE.

X, 3. For one cutteth a tree out of the forest, the work of the hands of the workman, with the axe.

Maätsad, "ax," is thought to have been a light kind of hewing instrument, similar to an adze, used for fashioning or carving wood into shape. It is rendered "tongs" in Isa. xliv, 12.

543.—WRITING ON THE GROUND.

XVII, 13. All that forsake thee shall be ashamed, and they that depart from me shall be written in the earth.

Some commentators suppose a reference is here made to names written on earth in opposition to names written in heaven; others think the reference is to words written in the dust in contrast to words engraven in the rock. As the former are easily obliterated and forgotten, so will be the fate of those who depart from the Lord.

We have no direct evidence that writing in the dust was actually practiced in the days of Jeremiah. The figure used in the text might readily suggest itself aside from any custom. It may not be inappropriate, however, to observe that this mode of writing has been practiced in some schools in the East. Harmer says that Peter della Vallé noticed a simple way of " writing short-lived memorandums in India, where he beheld children writing their lessons with their fingers on the ground, the pavement being for that purpose strewed all over with very fine sand. When the pavement was full they put the writings out; and, if need were, strewed new sand from a little heap they had before them wherewith to write farther."—*Observations,* vol. iii, p. 128, note.

The text brings to mind what is said of Jesus when the adulterous woman was brought into his presence in the temple. He "stooped down, and with his finger wrote on the ground." John viii, 6, 8.

544.—THE POTTER.

XVIII, 3. Then I went down to the potter's house, and, behold, he wrought a work on the wheels.

The potter's art has been practiced from very ancient times. The Egyptian monuments give evidence that it was known in Egypt before the entrance of the Hebrews into that country. Some expositors have inferred from Psa. lxxxi, 6, that the Israelites, when in bondage, were employed in pottery as well as in brickmaking: "I removed his shoulder from the burden; his hands were delivered from the pots." Others, however, give to the word *dud* the meaning of " basket," and make it refer to the baskets which were used by the brickmakers for carrying clay.

115.—Egyptian Potters.

The clay was first trodden with the feet by the potter, (Isa. xli, 25,) and when it became of the proper consistency it was put on the "wheels." These were originally of stone, and two in number, one above the other, like a pair of millstones; the lower one immovable, and the upper revolving on an axis and turned by the potter by means of a treadle, and sometimes by the hands of an attendant. In after times the wheels were made of wood. The softened clay was put upon the upper wheel, and fashioned by the potter's hand to any shape desired.

545.—EARTHEN BOTTLES.

XIX, 1. Thus saith the Lord, Go and get a potter's earthen bottle.

It is evident from this and other passages that it is a mistake to suppose that all Eastern bottles were made of skin. Ancient bottles of earthenware of various shapes are to be found in the museums, and are often depicted on the monuments. In 1 Kings xiv, 3, *bakbuk*, here rendered bottle, is spoken of as a "cruse" in which honey was kept.

546.—BOTTLES BROKEN.

XIX, 10. Then shalt thou break the bottle in the sight of the men that go with thee.

This action, so symbolical of utter destruction, is still used in the East to denote the same thing. Dr. Thomson says, "The people of this country have the same custom of breaking a jar when they wish to express their utmost detestation of any one. They come behind or near him and smash the jar to atoms, thus imprecating upon him and his a like hopeless ruin."— *The Land and the Book*, vol. ii, p. 497.

547.—TIDINGS OF A NEW-BORN SON.

XX, 15. Cursed be the man who brought tidings to my father, saying, A man-child is born unto thee; making him very glad.

The birth of a son is, in the East, considered a cause of special congratulation to the father. Its announcement makes him "very glad." In Persia it is associated with particular ceremonies. Morier says, "Some confidential servant about the harem is usually the first to get the information, when he runs in great haste to his master, and says, ' *Mujdeh*,' or ' Good news,' by which he secures to himself a gift, which generally follows the Mujdeh. Among the common people, the man who brings the Mujdeh frequently seizes on the cap or shawl, or any such article belonging to the father, as a security for the present, to which he holds himself entitled."—*Second Journey*, etc., p. 103.

548.—CEILINGS.

XXII, 14. That saith, I will build me a wide house and large chambers, and cutteth him out windows; and it is ceiled with cedar, and painted with vermilion.

The interiors of Oriental houses of the better class are often of a splendid character. The ceilings, panels, and doors are richly painted and gilded. Special pains are taken to ornament the ceilings. Tasteful interlaced patterns are used, often painted in brilliant colors: red, blue, gold, and green, being the favorites.

The prophet represents here the general luxuriance of the people, and the dishonesty which sometimes accompanied it. See verse 13. In another prophecy we read: "Is it time for you, O ye, to dwell in your ceiled houses, and this house lie waste?" Haggai i, 4.

116.—CEILING OF PALACE AT KONIEH.

549.—SMITING THE THIGH.

XXXI, 19. Surely after that I was turned, I repented; and after that I was instructed, I smote upon my thigh.

This was one method by which the Jews expressed deep sorrow in time of mourning. Ezekiel was commanded to act in a similar manner as a significant mode of expressing the sorrow that was to come on rebellious Israel. See Ezek. xxi, 12. The Greeks and Persians had a similar custom, and it is practiced in some parts of the East at the present day.

550.—EVIDENCES OF PURCHASE.

XXXII, 14. Take these evidences, this evidence of the purchase, both which is sealed, and this evidence which is open; and put them in an earthen vessel, that they may continue many days.

It is supposed that one of these documents was a duplicate of the other; and it may have been customary to carefully seal one copy and deposit it in a safe place, perhaps to bury it on a part of the land described in it, while the other was left unsealed in some public place designated for the purpose, where all persons interested might have access to it whenever they desired. Inasmuch, however, as the city was to be destroyed, the prophet was directed to have both copies put into an earthen vessel for preservation.

In Taylor's Calmet it is suggested that the earthen vessel containing these documents was to be buried in one corner of the land purchased, as a sort of hidden landmark of the property; and as a possible illustration the following passage is cited from the Gentoo laws of boundaries and limits: "Dust, or bonds, or *seboos*, (bran,) or cinders, or scraps of earthenware, or the hairs of a cow's tail, or the seed of the cotton-plant: all these things above-mentioned, being put into an earthen jar filled to the brim, a man must privately bury upon the confines of his own boundary; and there preserve stones also, or bricks, or sea-sand: either of these three things may be buried by way of Landmark of the limits; for all these things, upon remaining a long time in the ground, are not liable to rot, or to become putrid; any other thing, also, which will remain a long time in the ground without becoming rotten or putrid, may be buried for the same purpose. Those persons who, by any of these methods, can show the line of their boundaries, shall acquaint their sons with the respective Landmarks of those boundaries; and, in the same manner, those sons shall explain the signs of the limits to their children."—*Fragments*, No. LXXX. Taylor's *Calmet*, vol. iii, p. 138.

551.—CUTTING THE COVENANT.

XXXIV, 18. When they cut the calf in twain, and passed between the parts thereof.

This was a very ancient method of making a covenant. The two contracting parties slaughtered a victim, cut the body in two, and passed between the severed parts. Some writers hold that the design was to express a wish that, if the covenant should be broken, the same fate might befall the party violating it which had befallen the slain beast. Others think that it was intended to represent, that as the two divided parts belonged to one animal, so the two parties making the covenant were of one mind so far as the subject of the covenant was concerned. It is thought probable that the latter was the original design of the custom, and that the former notion was added to the meaning subsequently, or substituted for it when the original intention was forgotten. This old custom is referred to in the very expression which was used by the Hebrews to represent the making of a covenant. The phrase "make a covenant," which is so often used in the Old Testament, is literally, "to *cut* a covenant," (*karath berith*.)

This ceremony was used when Jehovah made a covenant with Abram. See Gen. xv, 10, 17. "Ephraem Syrus observes, that God condescended to

follow the custom of the Chaldeans, that he might in the most solemn manner confirm his oath to Abram the Chaldean."—KEIL and DELITZSCH, *Commentary in loco.* The custom was widespread among ancient nations, and is
often referred to by classical writers. There are traces of it even in modern
times. Pitts, after narrating some of the superstitious customs of the
Algerine pirates when a storm overtakes them at sea, continues: "If they
find no succor from their before-mentioned rites and superstitions, but that
the danger rather increases, then they go to sacrificing of a sheep, (or two
or three upon occasion, as they think needful,) which is done after this manner: having cut off the head with a knife, they immediately take out the
entrails, and throw them and the head overboard; and then with all the
speed they can (without skinning) they cut the body into two parts by the
middle, and throw one part over the right side of the ship and the other
over the left, into the sea, as a kind of propitiation."—*Religion and Manners
of the Mahometans,* chap. ii.

552.—INK.

XXXVI, 18. **He pronounced all these words unto me with his
mouth, and I wrote them with ink in the book.**

1. The ink of the ancients was usually composed of lampblack, soot, or
pulverized charcoal, prepared with gum and water. It was sold in small particles or grains. When needed for use some of the grains were put into the
inkhorn, (see note on Ezek. ix, 2,) and mixed with water until the mixture
became of the consistence of our modern printer's ink. It was of an intense
glossy black, retaining its color for ages, yet easily obliterated with sponge
and water. This is thought to be referred to in Num. v, 23, and Col. ii, 14.
The ink still used in the East is mostly of this character.

Ink is also mentioned in 2 Cor. iii, 3; 2 John 12, and 3 John 13.

2. For a description of books. see note on Job xix, 23, 24.

553.—THE HEARTH.

XXXVI, 22. **The king sat in the winter house in the ninth
month, and there was a fire on the hearth burning before
him.**

Ach, "hearth," is a portable furnace or stove. The rooms of Oriental
houses are sometimes warmed at the present day by means of such pots or
furnaces. "They have the form of a large pitcher, and are placed in a
cavity sunk in the middle of the apartment. When the fire has burnt down,
a frame like a table is placed over the pot, and the whole is then covered
with a carpet; and those who wish to warm themselves sit upon the floor
and thrust their feet and legs, and even the lower part of their bodies, under
the carpet."—ROBINSON'S *Gesenius.*

554.—BURIED TREASURES.

XLI, 8. We have treasures in the field, of wheat, and of barley, and of oil, and of honey.

1. It is a very ancient custom in many parts of the East to store grain in large pits or cisterns, dug in the ground for the purpose. In Syria these cisterns are sealed at the top with plaster, and covered with a deep bed of earth to keep out vermin. They are cool and dry and tight. Among the Moors the custom is to have a thick layer of straw on the bottom and a lining of straw on the sides. They cover the mouth with a stone, and sometimes build over it a small pyramid of earth to shed the rain. Very often, however, after closing the mouth, they cover the place with sod so skillfully that none but the initiated can tell where the pit is. Shaw says that in Barbary there are sometimes two or three hundred of these grain-pits together, the smallest of them holding four hundred bushels.

Burder (*Oriental Literature,* No. 621) gives a quotation from Chenier, a French traveler, who says that among the Moors the fathers of wealthy families fill a granary of this kind at the birth of every child, and empty it when the child becomes an adult and is married. He knew of corn which had been kept in such pits for twenty-five years and was still fit for use, though it had lost its whiteness.

These are doubtless he kind of places referred to in the text, where the treasures of wheat were kept. David also had "storehouses in the field." 1 Chron. xxvii, 25. Besides these subterranean granaries there were also barns. See note on Gen. xli, 48.

2. In like manner oil is sometimes kept in jars buried in the ground; and jars of honey might easily be kept in a similar manner. The ten men referred to in the text who sought to purchase their lives of Ishmael, had concealed their treasures in the field so that no one should rob them.

Some suppose that the "cellars of oil" belonging to David were merely places where oil jars were buried. See 1 Chron. xxvii, 28.

Other treasures besides those mentioned in the text are frequently buried in the East. See note on Matt. xiii, 44.

555.—SPEARS—SCALE ARMOR.

XLVI, 4. Furbish the spears and put on the brigandines.

1. *Romach* is rendered "spear" in Judges v, 8, and in several other texts; "javelin," in Num. xxv, 7; "buckler," in 1 Chron. xii, 8; (in the plural) "lancets," in 1 Kings xviii, 28. It is thought to have been a spear used by heavy-armed troops. Colonel Smith, in *Kitto's Cyclopædia,* (*s. v.* " Arms,") says, "Probably the shepherd Hebrews, like nations similarly situated in

northern Africa, anciently made use of the horn of an oryx, or a leucoryx, above three feet long, straightened in water, and sheathed upon a thorn-wood staff. When sharpened, this instrument would penetrate the hide of a bull, and, according to Strabo, even of an elephant; it was light, very difficult to break, resisted the blow of a battle-ax, and the animals which furnished it were abundant in Arabia and in the desert east of Palestine. At a later period the head was of brass, and afterward of iron." These horn spears were probably the original type from which the various kinds of spears were subsequently produced. Precisely how the *romach* differed from the other heavy spear, the *chanith*, (see note on 1 Sam. xvii, 7,) we cannot say.

2. *Siryon* ("brigandine" in the text, and in Jer. li, 3) was a coat of scale armor; the same as *shiryon*, which is rendered "coat of mail" in 1 Sam. xvii, 5, where see the note.

556.—HEAVY AXES.

XLVI, 22. **They shall march with an army and come against her with axes as hewers of wood.**

Kardom was a name given to an axe which seems to have been used especially for cutting down trees, and is thought to have had a heavier head than other axes. It is mentioned in Judges ix, 48; 1 Sam. xiii, 20, and Psa. lxxiv, 5.

557.—THE GOD AMMON.

XLVI, 25. **Behold, I will punish the multitude of No, and Pharaoh, and Egypt, with their gods, and their kings.**

The most of commentators now agree that *amon*, here rendered "multitude," should be taken as a proper name, and left untranslated. The original is *amon minno*, "Amon of No." By No is undoubtedly meant the celebrated Egyptian city of Thebes, which was situated on both sides of the Nile, and was noted for its hundred gates of brass, its numerous and splendid temples, obelisks, and statues. Amon was the name of an Egyptian deity, and probably of a Libyan and Ethiopian god, whose worship had its seat in Thebes, where was an oracle of the deity; for which reason the name of the city was joined to that of the god. This is to be noticed not only in this text, but also in Nahum iii, 8, where for the "populous No" of our version the original has *No Amon.* The Greeks likened this god to Zeus, and the Romans called him Jupiter Ammon or Hammon. He appears to have been a personification of the sun, and is thought to have corresponded to Baal of the Phenicians. The ancient Egyptian name is said to have been *Amen.* On the monuments it is written *Amn* or *Amn-Re*, Amon the Sun.

It was formerly supposed, and is still commonly asserted, that this god was represented under the figure of a human form with a ram's head. This, however, has of late been denied. Fairbairn says: "It was the god *Neph*,

sometimes written *Kneph*, and by the Greeks *Chnoubis*, who was so represented, and the proper seat of whose worship was not Thebes, but Meroë, and who also had a famous oracle in the Lybian desert. The Amon of Thebes, 'king of gods' as he was called, always had the form simply of a man assigned him, and in one of the characters under which he was worshiped appears to have been virtually identified with the sun, and in another with the Egyptian Pan."—*Imperial Bible Dictionary*.

Wilkinson says, "The figure of Amun was that of a man, with a head-dress surmounted by two long feathers; the color of his body was light blue, like the Indian Vishnoo, as if to indicate his peculiarly

117.—AMON.

exalted and heavenly nature; but he was not figured with the head or under the form of a ram, as the Greeks and Romans supposed."—*Manners and Customs of the Ancient Egyptians*, vol. iv, p. 246.

558.—POURING WINE.

XLVIII, 11. Moab hath been at ease from his youth, and he hath settled on his lees, and hath not been emptied from vessel to vessel, neither hath he gone into captivity: therefore his taste remaineth in him, and his scent is not changed.

It is customary to pour wine from one vessel to another to improve its quality. Chardin says: "They frequently pour wine from vessel to vessel in the East; for when they begin one, they are obliged immediately to empty it into smaller vessels, or into bottles, or it would grow sour."—HARMER'S *Observations*, vol. ii, p. 155. Dr. Clarke, in a note on the same page, adds: "From the *jars* (says Dr. Russell, MS. note) in which the wine ferments it is drawn off into *demyans*, which contain perhaps twenty quart bottles, and from those into bottles for use; but as these bottles are generally not well washed, the wine is often sour. The more careful use pint bottles, or half-pint bottles, and cover the surface with a little sweet oil."

A similar allusion to the pouring of wine from the lees is made in Isa. xxv, 6, where see the note. See also Zeph. i, 12, where, as in this text, being "on the lees" is figuratively used to express a sinful rest. Jeremiah carries the figure of the text into the following verse, where, instead of

" wanderers," many commentators render *tsaim* by the word " tilters." " I will send unto him *tilters*, who shall *tilt him up*." The act of pouring the wine off the lees from one vessel to another is thus represented.

559.—BEL.

L, 2. Babylon is taken, Bel is confounded, Merodach is broken in pieces; her idols are confounded, her images are broken in pieces.

1. Bel was the principal god of the Babylonians, and the third in rank among the Assyrians. The name is generally supposed to be the Chaldaic form of Baal, though this is disputed by some. For an account of Baal-worship see note on Num. xxii, 41. In addition to what is there stated, we may remark that the sacrifices offered to Bel consisted of adult cattle and their sucklings, together with incense. The horned cap, so frequently observed in Assyrian monuments, is supposed to have been the symbol of this god. Bel is also mentioned in Isa. xlvi, 1, and Jer. li, 44.

2. The origin and meaning of the name Merodach are doubtful. Instead of being a separate deity from Bel, he is supposed to be identical; the name being originally a descriptive epithet of Bel, which gradually became recognized as one of the names of that deity. On the monuments he is known as Bel Merodach. " Nebuchadnezzar calls him 'the king of the heavens and the earth,' 'the great lord,' 'the senior of the gods,' 'the most ancient,' 'the supporter of sovereignty,' 'the layer up of treasures,' etc., and ascribes to him all his glory and successes."—RAWLINSON'S *Five Great Monarchies*, vol. i, p. 135.

560.—SIGN OF SUBMISSION.

L, 15. She hath given her hand, her foundations are fallen, her walls are thrown down.

This is a beautiful Orientalism denoting submission, and probably has some relation to the custom of giving the hand in pledge of a covenant. See note on Prov. xi, 21. There are several texts where the expression is used: " We have given the hand to the Egyptians, and to the Assyrians to be satisfied with bread." Lam. v, 6. When Hezekiah sent throughout all Israel and Judah his proclamation for a passover, he said to the people, among other things, "yield yourselves to the Lord." 2 Chron. xxx, 8. This is literally, "give the hand to Jehovah." At the beginning of Solomon's reign it is said: " And all the princes, and the mighty men, and all the sons likewise of king David, submitted themselves unto Solomon the king." 1 Chron. xxix, 24. This is literally, "gave the hand under Solomon."

This identical form is said by Roberts to be used in India at the present time. When two have quarreled, and one makes acknowledgment, he is said to "put his hand under." The same is said when a rebellious son submits to his father. The expression is not altogether figurative. When

118.—SUBMISSION.

one submits to a superior he stoops, and moves his hands to the ground, saying, "I submit, my lord." Hence the appropriateness of the language used.

561.—BATTLE-AXES.

LI, 20. Thou art my battle-ax and weapons of war: for with thee will I break in pieces the nations, and with thee will I destroy kingdoms.

Mappets, "battle-ax," is defined by Gesenius to be "a mallet, a maul, a war-club;" and he makes it identical with *mephits*, which in Prov. xxv, 18,

319.—EGYPTIAN BATTLE-AXES.

is rendered "maul." Others, however, think that a heavy bladed instrument is meant. The Egyptian battle-ax was from two to two and a half feet in length, with a single blade, which was secured to the handle by bronze pins, while the handle in that part was bound with thongs to keep the wood from splitting. The soldier on a march either held it in his hand, or hung it on his back with the blade downward. The shape of the blade was the segment of a circle, divided at the back into two smaller segments whose points were fastened by the pins already named. The blade was made either of bronze or of steel. Another kind of battle-ax was about three feet in length, and had a large metal ball at the end, to which the blade was fixed. Either of these weapons was terrible, from the combination of weight with sharpness.

While the Persians often used the battle-ax it was rarely used by the Assyrians, though it is sometimes represented on the monuments. These weapons seem to have had short handles and large heads, and to have been wielded with one hand. Some of them had two heads, like the *bipennis* of the Romans and the *labra* of the Lydians and Carians. The Chaldeans and Babylonians also made use of battle-axes. One belonging to the former is represented on an ancient clay tablet as having the blade of the ax balanced by three heavy spikes on the opposite side of the handle.

LAMENTATIONS.

562.—HANGING BY THE HAND.

V, 12. Princes are hanged up by their hand.

By whose hand the princes were hung up has been a matter of discussion among commentators. Some suppose that the text means they hung themselves; others that they were hung by the hand of their enemies; others still that they were suspended by the hand, and in this helpless condition left to perish. In support of this last interpretation we give a statement by Roberts: "No punishment is more common than this in the East, especially for slaves and refractory children. Has a master an obstinate slave? has he committed some great offense with his hands? several men are called, who tie the offender's hands and hoist him to the roof, till he beg for forgiveness. School-boys who are in the habit of playing truant are also thus punished. To tell a man that you will hang him by the hands is extremely provoking."—*Oriental Customs*, p. 142.

If this custom was practiced in the time of Jeremiah we can see how great an indignity was put upon the princes when they were punished after the manner of slaves.

EZEKIEL.

563.—WRITING ON BOTH SIDES.

II, 10. He spread it before me; and it was written within and without: and there was written therein lamentations, and mourning, and woe.

The manuscript rolls were usually written only on one side, though sometimes both sides were used. This was the case with the roll which Ezekiel saw. So numerous were the troubles which were to come upon the children of Israel that the roll which contained an account of them was completely filled, it being necessary to write on both sides. Something like this is thought to be meant in Rev. v, 1. See note on Isa. xxxiv, 4.

564.—RECORDS ON POTTERY.

IV, 1. **Thou also, son of man, take thee a tile, and lay it before thee, and portray upon it the city, even Jerusalem.**

Assyrian and Babylonian records were kept, not only on sculptured slabs of stone, but also on pottery. There were "cylinders," as they are called, some barrel-shaped, and some hexagonal or octagonal. These were made of very fine, thin, and strong terra-cotta, and were hollow. They were from a foot and a half to three feet in height, and were closely covered with cuneiform writing, which was often in such small characters as to require the aid of a magnifying glass to decipher it. These cylinders were placed at the corners of the temples, where many of them have been discovered. They were written in columns, and contain histories of the monarchs who reigned when the temples were built.

120.—ASSYRIAN CLAY TABLETS.

In addition to these, clay tablets of various sizes were used, from nine inches by six and a half to one inch by one and a half. These were sometimes entirely covered with writing and pictorial representations. It was on such a tile that Ezekiel was directed to make a representation of Jerusalem.

When the clay was in a soft, moist state, in its mold or frame the characters were put upon it, perhaps in some instances by a stamp, but usually by means of a sharp edged bronze style about a foot long, by means of which each character was traced separately by hand, just as we use a pen. After the completion of the writing or pictures the clay was baked, and such was the perfection of the manufacture that many of these articles have been preserved from decay for three thousand years.

They vary in color, owing, as some suppose, to the varying length of time they were in the kiln, while others think that some coloring matter must have been mixed with the clay. They are bright brown, pale yellow, pink, red, and a very dark tint nearly black. Usually the cylinders found are of a pale yellow, and the tablets a light red or pink. Some of them are unglazed, and others are coated with a hard white enamel.

565.—MOUNTS—FORTS—RAMS.

IV, 2. And lay siege against it, and build a fort against it, and cast a mound against it; set the camp also against it, and set battering-rams against it round about.

Several important operations in ancient sieges are here noticed:

1. The "mount" was an inclined plane which the besiegers of a castle or a walled town built up to the walls so that they could bring their engines of war closer, and work them to greater advantage. The mount was made of all sorts of materials, earth, timber, boughs, and stones, the sides being walled up with brick or stone, and the inclined top made of layers of brick or stone, forming a paved road up which the war engines might be drawn. Some of these engines are described in the note on 2 Chronicles xxvi, 15; another is mentioned below. Mounts were used by the Assyrians, Babylonians, Egyptians, Jews, and Greeks, and are often referred to in the Old Testament under the name of "banks"

121.—Assault on a City—Artificial Mount.

or "bulwarks," as well as "mounts." See, among other passages, Deut. xx, 20; 2 Sam. xx, 15; 2 Kings xix, 32; Isa. xxxvii, 33; Jer. vi, 6; xxxiii, 4; Ezek. xvii, 17.

2. *Dayek*, "fort," was a watch-tower. Numbers of these towers were set up before a besieged city, for the purpose of watching and harassing the inhabitants. See also 2 Kings xxv, 1; Jer. lii, 4; Ezek. xvii, 17; xxi, 22; xxvi, 8.

3. The battering-ram is supposed to have been first used by the Phenicians. It consisted of a heavy beam of wood strengthened with iron plates, and terminating in an iron head made like that of a ram. Suspended from a wooden frame-work by ropes or chains, the beam was swung to and fro by the attacking party, and was struck against the wall with repeated blows until a breach was effected. The Assyrian armies were abundantly supplied with similar engines of war, though they were made after different patterns. It is to these that Ezekiel refers in the text. "Some had a head shaped like

122.—BATTERING-RAMS.

the point of a spear; others, one more resembling the end of a blunderbuss. All of them were covered with a frame-work, which was of ozier, wood, felt, or skins, for the better protection of those who worked the implement; but some appear to have been stationary, having their frame resting on the ground itself; while others were movable, being provided with wheels."— RAWLINSON, *Five Great Monarchies*, vol. i, p. 470.

To oppose the ram various inflammable substances, such as tow, were thrown upon the light frame-work, setting it on fire. To extinguish this, those who worked the ram carried a supply of water. Again, a chain was let down by the besieged, and the end of the ram was caught in it, and the force of the blow neutralized by drawing the ram upward. To counteract this some of the besieging party were stationed below the ram, and provided with strong hooks which they caught in the descending chains, hanging on them with all their weight.

Battering-rams were frequently used against walls from the ground, at the foot, but sometimes were drawn to the top of mounds such as have been just described. They are referred to, in addition to the text, in Ezek. xxi, 22, and probably in Ezek. xxvi, 9, under the name "engines of war." There may also be a reference to them in 2 Sam. xx, 15.

566.—CHAMBERS OF IMAGERY.

VIII, 10. So I went in and saw; and behold every form of creeping things, and abominable beasts, and all the idols of the house of Israel, portrayed upon the wall round about.

The vivid description of what the prophet saw in his vision, as recorded in this remarkable chapter, is doubtless an ideal representation. The imagery employed, however, is taken from scenes in actual life, and could find its realization in the temples of ancient Egypt, where the Israelites learned many of their idolatrous practices. The tombs of Egypt, which are now exposed to the view of the traveler, have painted on them, in colors that are still bright, representations of various animals, and also of the gods. Whether or not these tombs were ever used as places of worship is a disputed point. Their painted walls, however, cannot but suggest the "chambers of imagery" mentioned by the prophet. See verse 12. The walls of their temples were in a similar way adorned with pictorial representations of the animals and gods which they worshiped.

In like manner were the temples of other ancient nations ornamented. In the temple of Belus were sculptured representations of men with two wings, and others with four; some having two faces, others the legs and horns of goats, or the hoofs of horses. There were bulls also with the heads of men, and horses with the heads of dogs. It was doubtless similar monstrosities, and other figures too revolting for description, which Ezekiel saw.

567.—TAMMUZ.

VIII, 14. He brought me to the door of the gate of the Lord's house which was toward the north; and, behold, there sat women weeping for Tammuz.

Notwithstanding the numerous and ingenious conjectures of various critics, nothing is positively known concerning the origin and meaning of this word. The opinion commonly received by commentators is that Tammuz was the Syrian name of Adonis, under which title the Phenicians worshiped the sun. Adonis is the Phenician, or old Hebrew, for "Lord," or "my Lord," and is the same in meaning as Baal. The worship of Adonis, which spread through many lands, was Phenician in origin, and was celebrated chiefly in Byblus, and in the temples of Aphrodite. According to the legend, Adonis was killed by a boar and afterward rose from the dead. This is supposed to represent the sun's decline in winter and his returning strength in summer.

The ceremonies consisted in mourning over his death and searching for the idol which represented his body, after which there were festivities accompanied with gross debauchery.

Others, however, recognizing the article in the original, making it *the* Tammuz, have supposed the word to designate an idol set up for worship. An old Rabbinical commentator says that the image was made of metal, and was hollow. In the eye socket there was lead, which, on a fire being kindled within the hollow image, melted and ran down like tears. Another represents the Tammuz as a hollow image with holes through which water flowed. Those who adopt the idea that the image wept, whether from fire or water, render the text, "there sat women causing Tammuz to weep."

Another ancient tradition makes Tammuz the name of an old idolatrous prophet, who was put to death by a king whom he endeavored to persuade to worship the stars. On the night of his death all the images gathered from the ends of the earth to the temple of Babel, where was the golden image of the sun. This image, suspended between heaven and earth, fell down in the midst of the temple, and all the other images fell around it, and wept all night because of the death of the prophet. After this there was an annual mourning on account of his death.

Whether Tammuz was a myth, an idol, or a man, the women spoken of in the text were undoubtedly engaged in some acts of idolatrous worship which are called "abominations."

568.—POSTURE IN WORSHIP.

VIII, 16. **Five and twenty men, with their backs toward the temple of the Lord, and their faces toward the east; and they worshiped the sun toward the east.**

This shows their connection with the fire-worshipers. All nations who worshiped the sun prayed with their faces turned to the East. The oldest temples of the fire-worshipers were built in such a manner that the entrance was on the west side, so that the worshipers faced the East on entering. The temple of Jehovah was built with the entrance in the East and the Oracle in the West, so that the worshipers turned their backs on the place of the rising sun. The perverted priests mentioned in the text disrespectfully turned their backs on the Oracle, and faced the East like the fire-worshipers.

569. — TWIGS USED IN HEATHEN WORSHIP.

VIII, 17. **They put the branch to their nose,**

According to Strabo and others, when the fire-worshipers prayed before the sacred fire, they held in the left hand a little bunch of twigs called *barsom*, and applied it to their mouth when uttering prayer. Hengstenberg says: "The nose is derisively mentioned in place of the mouth, according to the leaning to irony and sarcasm, which appears so often in the prophets when they oppose and chastise superstitious folly."—*Commentary on Ezekiel.*

Some think the reference here is to the custom of divining by rods. See note on Hosea iv, 12.

570.—THE INKHORN.

IX, 2. One man among them was clothed with linen, with a writer's inkhorn by his side.

It is still customary in the East to put into the girdle the case containing writing implements. It consists of two parts, a receptacle for the pens,

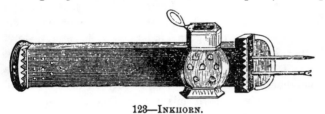

123—INKHORN.

and a box for the ink. It is sometimes made of ebony or some other hard wood, but generally of metal — brass, copper, or silver—often highly polished and of exquisite workmanship. It is about nine or ten inches long, one and a half or two inches wide, and half an inch deep. The hollow shaft contains pens of reed and a penknife, and has a lid. To the upper end of this case the inkstand is soldered if of metal. This is a small box, square, round, or polygonal; has a lid which moves on hinges, and fastens with a clasp. It is usually twice as heavy as the shaft. The projection of the inkstand is seen outside the girdle, while the shaft is concealed by its folds.

571.—MARKS OF CONSECRATION.

IX, 4. Set a mark upon the foreheads of the men that sigh and that cry for all the abominations that be done in the midst thereof.

This mark was to be put on these faithful ones for their protection when the faithless were to be destroyed. It showed that they belonged to God. The allusion is to a very ancient custom. In Egypt a runaway slave was freed from his master if he went to the temple and gave himself up to the god, receiving certain marks upon his person to denote his consecration to the deity there worshiped. Cain had a mark put on him for his protection, as an evidence of God's promise to spare his life notwithstanding his wickedness. Gen. iv, 15. To this day all Hindoos have some sort of mark upon their forehead signifying their consecration to their gods. Several passages in the book of Revelation represent the saints as having a mark on their

19

foreheads. See Rev. vii, 3; ix, 4. xiv, 1; xxii, 4. The followers of the "beast" are also said to be marked in the forehead or in the hands. See Rev. xiii, 16, 17; xiv, 9; xx, 4. The Romans marked their soldiers in the hand and their slaves in the forehead. The woman in scarlet, whom John saw, had a name written on her forehead. Rev. xvii, 5.

See also note on Gal. vi, 17.

572.—UNSTABLE WALLS.

XIII, 10. One built up a wall, and, lo, others daubed it with untempered mortar. See also Ezek. xxii, 28.

Kitto is of the opinion that reference is here made to "cob-walls;" that is, walls which are made of beaten earth rammed into molds or boxes, to give shape and consistence, and then emptied from the molds, layer by layer, on the wall, where it dries as the work goes on. Such walls cannot stand the effects of the weather, and houses built on this principle soon crumble and decay. See note on Job xv, 28. To protect them from the weather a very fine mortar is sometimes made, which is laid thickly on the outside of the walls. When this mortar is properly mixed with lime it answers the purpose designed; but where the lime is left out, as is often the case, the "untempered mortar" is no protection. For mode of making mortar, see note on Lev. xiv, 42.

Some commentators, however, translate *taphel*, which in our version is rendered "untempered mortar," by the word "whitewash." They represent the idea of the text to be the figure of a wall of unendurable material, and coated, not with cement which might protect it, but with a mere thin covering of lime, which gives the wall a finished durable appearance, which its real character does not warrant. Thus Paul calls the high priest, "thou whited wall." Acts xxiii, 3. See note on "whited sepulchers," under Matt. xxiii, 27.

573.—PILLOWS—KERCHIEFS.

XIII, 18. Woe to the women that sew pillows to all armholes, and make kerchiefs upon the head of every stature to hunt souls.

It is not by any means certain that the customs alluded to in this text can, at this late day, be explained.

1. The pillows sewed to the armholes, or to the "elbows," as the margin has it, are usually supposed to mean the soft cushions which are placed on Oriental divans. Among the poorer classes the skins of sheep or of goats were formerly used for pillows, being stuffed with chaff or wool for this purpose. The pillows of the wealthy were, of course, more luxurious in style and in finish. They were stuffed with some soft substance, and covered with

rich and costly materials.   These, placed on the bed on the divan, (see notes on 2 Kings i, 4, and on Amos iii, 12,) made a luxurious resting-place for the arms.

Other interpretations, however, have been given of the passage.   Instead of "armholes" or "elbows" some authorities have, as a more literal interpreta tion," joints of the hands."   See GESENIUS, *Lexicon*, and FAIRBAIRN, *Commentary*.   Others render *atstsile yadai*, "joints of *my* hands."   See Hengstenberg and Wordsworth, and the authorities cited by the latter.   These commentators suppose the meaning to be that, when God stretched forth his hands to punish sin, the false prophets covered them by their heterodox teaching, so that his hands would not seem to be able to grasp the rebellious offenders.

It has also been suggested by an old writer that the false prophetesses referred to in the text practiced divination, and that the pillows were amulets, which were fitted to their sleeves to aid them in their work.   We have not been able, however, to find any evidence of the existence of such a custom.   Verse 20 of this chapter seems to intimate that the pillows were not merely made *for* the arms, but fastened *to* the arms: "I will tear them from your arms."   We have no evidence, however, that it refers to divination.

2. *Mispachoth*, "kerchiefs," has been variously rendered "cushions," "quilts," "coverings for the head," and "long, flowing robes or mantles."

The word is generally thought to signify large and costly coverings for the head.   Some suppose these to have been designed to add to the luxury and attractiveness of the wicked prophetesses who wore them.   Kitto connects the practice with the worship of Astarte, in whose figures there is always something remarkable about the head-dress.   Others, however, who suppose the pillows to have been cushions covering the hand of Jehovah, as already noted, place these head-dresses on the heads of the ungodly people who merit Divine retribution, and regard the figure as further carrying out the idea that the wicked prophetesses endeavored to neutralize the blow of Jehovah's judgment, not only by covering his hands, but also by covering the heads of the guilty.

Another interpretation, however, makes these *mispachoth* similar to the *mitpachoth* of Isa. iii, 22, "wimples" in our version.   See the note on that text.   Dr. Alexander, editor of *Kitto's Cyclopedia*, calls attention to the affinity between the two words, and also notices the fact that, in verse 21, the *mispachoth* are shown to be articles that can be torn.   He therefore adopts the opinion of Kimchi, who says that the *mispachoth* were long loose robes such as the goddesses are represented as wearing, and in which the women referred to in the text wrapped themselves from head to foot.   For "kerchiefs upon the head of every stature," Dr. Alexander would read, "robes of every length on the head;" that is, these luxurious women made use of elegant and well-fitting robes.

574.—BABES SALTED.

XVI, 4. Thou wast not salted at all.

In ancient times new-born babes were rubbed with salt in order to harden their skin, as this operation was supposed to make it dry, tight, and firm. Galen mentions the practice, and it is also referred to by Jerome in his commentary on this passage. The salt may also have been applied as an emblem of purity and incorruption.

575.—PITFALLS.

XIX, 4. The nations also heard of him, he was taken in their pit.

There is thought to be an allusion here to the custom of assembling for the capture of a lion or other wild beast when the news of its depredations goes forth. All who hear of it are expected to aid in the capture.

The special mode of capture referred to in this text is by means of the pitfall. A hole is dug in the ground, and covered over with the branches of trees and with sod. The animal treading on this slight covering is precipitated into the pit, where it is either taken out alive or killed by the hunters on their arrival.

Figurative allusion is made to the pitfall in Psa. vii, 15; ix, 15; xxxv, 7; xciv, 13; Prov. xxvi, 27; Isa. xxxviii, 17.

576.—SCEPTERS.

XIX, 11. She had strong rods for the scepters of them that bare rule.

Scepters were originally nothing but simple rods cut from the branches of trees, and more or less ornamented. They were in later times more elaborately made, and sometimes, instead of wood, the material was gold. Esther v, 2. The opinion that the scepter originated with the shepherd's staff, because the first kings were mostly nomad princes, though entertained by some eminent authorities, is rejected by others equally eminent. The scepter of the ancient Egyptian kings is said, by Diodorus Siculus, to have resembled, not a shepherd's crook, but a plow. The scepter may have been originally used by kings and leaders simply because it was the most natural support and weapon; while subsequent circumstances changed its form and significance.

577.—SMITING THE HANDS.

XXI, 14. Thou, therefore, son of man, prophesy, and smite thine hands together.

Several different emotions seem to have been represented at different times by the action of smiting the hands, all of which we group in one note.

1. It was sometimes a sign of *contempt*. Of the wicked rich man Job says, "Men shall clap their hands at him, and shall hiss him out of his place." Job xxvii, 23. Jeremiah represents Jerusalem as so desolate that all the passers-by clap their hands at her. See Lam. ii, 15.

2. It was sometimes a sign of *anger*. When Balaam blessed Israel, instead of cursing them, "Balak's anger was kindled against Balaam, and he smote his hands together." Num. xxiv, 10. So when the Lord beheld the wickedness of the house of Israel, the representation of his kindled wrath is expressed in these words: "Behold, therefore I have smitten mine hand at thy dishonest gain which thou hast made, and at thy blood which hath been in the midst of thee." Ezek. xxii, 13.

3. It was sometimes a sign of *sorrow*. In sorrow, for the idolatry of Israel, the Lord commanded Ezekiel to smite with his hand. See Ezek. vi, 11.

4. It was sometimes a sign of *triumph*. In this manner the Ammonites rejoiced over fallen Israel. God says, "Thou hast clapped thine hands, and stamped with the feet, and rejoiced in heart with all thy despite against the land of Israel." Ezek. xxv, 6. It is to be noticed that in this text, and in the one last quoted, clapping the hand is connected with stamping the foot.

5. It was sometimes the sign of a *pledge* or an *oath*. The hand was used for this purpose by uplifting. See note on Gen. xiv, 22. A similar purpose was accomplished by two persons striking hands. See note on Prov. xi, 21. In addition to this, the striking of one hand upon another belonging to the same man was also considered as a pledge of earnestness and of truth. Thus Ezekiel is told in the text to smite his hands together, and in verse 17 the Lord promises to smite his hands together. In both instances there is a pledge to the performance of what is stated.

Smiting the hands together has the signification of an oath in some parts of the East to this day.

578.—THREE MODES OF DIVINATION.

XXI, 21. **For the king of Babylon stood at the parting of the way, at the head of the two ways, to use divination: he made his arrows bright, he consulted with images, he looked in the liver.**

Three modes of divination are here mentioned as having been practiced by the king of Babylon when he came to the junction of two ways and was unable to decide which to take.

1. *Belomancy*, or divination by arrows. *Kilkal bachitsim*, "he made his arrows bright," is literally, "he *shook* the arrows," alluding to the mode of using the arrows for the purpose of divination. According to Jerome, in the

case referred to in the text, each arrow to be used had on it the name of some town to be attacked. The arrows so marked were put into a quiver and shaken together, after which they were drawn one by one. The cities were to be attacked in the order in which the arrows were drawn. As " Jerusalem " was on the arrow first drawn, thither the king proceeded. Another old writer says that the arrows were thrown up to see which way they would fall, and in this manner the course to be taken was indicated.

Some of the sculptured slabs at Nimroud are supposed to represent divination of this sort, the king being seen with arrows in his hand.

This superstition was much practiced by the Arabs, notwithstanding it is prohibited in the Koran: " It is likewise unlawful for you to make division by casting lots with arrows. This is an impiety."—*Koran*, chap. v, (Sale's translation. See also Mr. SALE's *Preliminary Discourse*, § 5.)

The Arabs were in the habit of consulting their arrows before any thing of importance was undertaken. These arrows were parti-colored, were without heads or feathers, and were kept in some sacred place. Seven of them were kept in the temple at Mecca. In divination the Arabs generally used but three, though sometimes they used four. On one of the arrows was written, in Arabic, " My Lord hath bidden me ; " on the second, " My Lord hath forbidden me ; " the third was blank. If the first was drawn, the proposed enterprise was carried out ; if the second was drawn, the project was abandoned ; if the third was brought out, the arrows had to be again mixed and drawn until a decided answer was obtained.

2. Consultation of the *teraphim*. " He consulted with images." The Hebrew word is *teraphim*. Fairbairn says : " This is the only place where the use of teraphim is expressly ascribed to a heathen, though in 1 Sam. **xv**, 23, it is stigmatized as of an essentially heathen and, consequently, obnoxious character : ' Stubbornness is as iniquity and teraphim.' "— *Commentary in loco*. The Hebrews were very much addicted to this form of divination. See note on Gen. xxxi, 19.

3. *Hepatoscopy*, or inspection of the liver. This is a branch of *splanchnomancy*, or divination by inspection of the viscera, and is often referred to by classic writers. It is said that among the Lusitani the livers were obtained, not only from animals offered in sacrifice, but also *from prisoners taken in war !*

The Orientals considered the liver to be the most valuable of the viscera because they thought it most concerned in the formation of the blood, and they believed that in the blood is the life. The ancient Jews, Greeks, and Romans, and some other nations, supposed the liver to be the seat of the passions. In like manner the Arabs of the present day regard the liver as the seat of courage ; and among the Malay peoples the liver is considered the seat of all moral impressions and feelings. One names another caressingly,

" My liver ! " " My liver is sick " is, in other words, " I am angry." " My
liver is anxious," " my liver wishes," is absolutely equivalent, in other
words, to " my heart," " my soul." — See DELITZSCH'S *System of Biblical
Psychology*, p. 316.

This widely-diffused idea of antiquity, traces of which are still to be found,
may account for the fact that the liver was considered the most important
of the viscera for divining purposes. The lower part of the liver was the
portion which was used in divination, and there were certain signs which
were considered to be of good or bad omen. If the liver was of good size,
sound, and without spot or blemish, prosperity and success were expected.
If it was too dry, and had blisters, pustules, or any corrupt humors ; if it was
parched, thin, hard, or of an ugly black color, disappointment and adverse
fate were looked for.

This revolting mode of divination was practiced not only by the Babylonians, as indicated in the text, but by the Greeks and Romans also. There
is no evidence, however, of its existence among the Jews.

579.—ASSYRIAN GARMENTS.

**XXIII, 12. She doted upon the Assyrians her neighbors, cap-
tains and rulers clothed most gorgeously, horsemen riding
upon horses, all of them desirable young men.**

The Assyrians were famous for their rich and costly apparel. The expression " Assyrian garments " be-
came synonymous with elegant and
expensive clothing. Bonomi says:
" The robes of the Assyrians were
generally ample and flowing, but
differed in form from those of the
Egyptians and the Persians. They
consisted of tunics or robes varying
in length, in mantles of diverse
shapes, of long-fringed scarfs, and
of embroidered girdles. Ornaments
were scattered with profusion over
these dresses, some of which appear
to have been emblematic of certain dignities or employments."—
Nineveh and its Palaces, p. 431.

The figures sculptured on the
Assyrian marbles attest to the truth-
fulness of the description given in
the text. Bonomi gives an interesting extract from Mr. Smirk's re-

124.—ASSYRIAN FRINGED DRESS.

view of the Assyrian sculptures, which may serve to illustrate the subject: "The apparel of the Assyrians appears by these sculptures to have been almost always richly fringed, with wide borders ornamented with figures of men, animals, and foliage. The caparison of their horses is most gorgeous; every strap of their head and body-housings is enriched; to the chariot horses is usually seen attached, apparently either to the extremity of the pole or to the trappings of the neck, and to the front of the chariot itself, a long fish-shaped piece of drapery fringed and embroidered. Layard is at a loss to designate this object. Perhaps ' the precious clothes for chariots,' alluded to by Ezekiel (see Ezek. xxvii, 20) as being obtained by the people of Tyre from Dedan, may have reference to this singular piece of horse-furniture."—*Nineveh and its Palaces*, p. 437.

580.—MURAL SCULPTURES.

XXIII, 14. **She saw men portrayed upon the wall, the images of the Chaldeans portrayed with vermilion.**

Here is a manifest reference to those wonderful mural sculptures which, after being buried for centuries amid the ruins of the palaces and temples whose walls they once adorned, have been brought to light by the perseverance and skill of modern explorers. It is not at all improbable that Ezekiel himself once saw the very marbles that the eyes of this generation are permitted to behold.

The Assyrian and Chaldean sculptures were colored. Traces of red, blue, and black still remain on the beard and hair, and on some of the head-coverings. The Assyrian red was more brilliant than the Egyptian. It is almost vermilion in the sculptures of Khorsabad, and a brilliant crimson or lake-tint in those of Nimroud. Bonomi and some others suppose that there were originally other colors used on the sculptures, but that, being more destructible than those which remain, they have disappeared in the lapse of time. There is no positive evidence of this, though it is highly probable.

581.—MUTILATIONS.

XXIII, 25. **I will set my jealousy against thee, and they shall deal furiously with thee : they shall take away thy nose and thine ears.**

These mutilations were common among the Chaldeans and Persians. Among the former adulterers were punished in this manner, which fact is doubtless the basis of the reference in the text.

582.—WEAPONS BURIED.

XXXII, 27. **Which are gone down to hell with their weapons of war : and they have laid their swords under their heads.**

This is an allusion to an ancient custom of burying the weapons of war with the warrior. Chardin says that " in Mingrelia they all sleep with their swords under their heads and their other arms by their sides; and they bury them in the same manner, their arms being placed in the same position."—HARMER's *Observations*, vol. iii, p. 55.

583.—WRITING ON RODS.

XXXVII, 20. **The sticks whereon thou writest shall be in thine hand before their eyes.**

We find the practice of writing on rods alluded to as early as the time of Moses. See Num. xvii, 2. A similar practice was known among the Greeks. The laws of Solon, which were preserved at Athens, were written on billets of wood called *axones*. These were of a square or pyramidal form, and made to turn on an axis. The northern nations and the ancient Britons also wrote on sticks. Some of these were square and some three sided, and each side contained one line. These sticks were sometimes set in a framework which was called *Peithynen*, or the *Elucidator*. At one end of each stick was a knob projecting beyond the frame. By means of these knobs the sticks could be turned and the successive lines read. "Stick almanacs" were used in England almost to the fourteenth century. Some were large, and hung up on one side of the mantel-piece; while others were small enough to be carried in the pocket.

584.—THE BATH.

XLV, 10. **Ye shall have just balances, and a just ephah, and a just bath.**

The bath was a measure of liquids, such as wine and oil, and was of the same capacity as the ephah in dry measure. See note on Exod. xvi, 36. It is supposed to have contained nearly nine gallons. It is referred to also in Isa. v, 10. The "measures" mentioned in Luke xvi, 6, are baths.

See also note on John ii, 6.

585.—THE MANEH.

XLV, 12. **Twenty shekels, five-and-twenty shekels, fifteen shekels, shall be your maneh.**

Maneh is supposed by some to be the origin of the Latin *moneta* and the English *money;* though others give to the word a different etymology. It was the standard pound among Hebrew weights, and the word is rendered "pound" in several passages. See 1 Kings x, 17; Ezra ii, 69; Neh. vii, 71, 72. In this text it is untranslated. The word often occurs on the Assyrian inscriptions also.

The ordinary maneh in use among the Hebrews is supposed to have weighed a hundred shekels, or about one pound fourteen ounces avoirdupois.

In this text, however, another maneh seems to be mentioned. The passage is confessedly obscure, and various interpretations have been given of it.

Some think that three distinct manehs are referred to: one of twenty, one of twenty-five, and one of fifteen shekels. Hengstenberg suggests that the maneh was of foreign origin, and that the three different values here attached are the estimates put upon it in the different countries where it was used.

Others suppose that the text refers to but a single maneh of sixty shekels divided into three parts, 20+25+15. Chardin found this a customary mode of reckoning in the East; and though it seems strange to us, yet if the custom was practiced in Ezekiel's time, it was but natural that the maneh should be described in this way.

586.—THE COR.

XLV, 14. The Cor, which is a homer of ten baths.

The cor, or homer, was used for either dry or liquid measure. The liquid cor is supposed to have contained seventy-five gallons. The dry cor is supposed to have contained eight bushels and a pint. It is mentioned in 1 Kings iv, 22, and Luke xvi, 7, in both of which places it is rendered "measures."

DANIEL.

587.—TEMPLE TREASURES.

I, 2. He brought the vessels into the treasure-house of his God.

It is customary in every heathen temple to have a particular place for storing the sacred jewels and other valuables which are supposed to be the special property of the idol there worshiped. Nebuchadnezzar having brought from Jerusalem, as trophies of war, the sacred vessels of the temple, placed them in the temple of Belus at Babylon side by side with the costly ornaments and utensils which were appropriated to idolatrous worship.

There were also in the temple at Jerusalem rooms specially set apart for the reception of tithes, and for the storing of valuable articles belonging to the sacred edifice. See 1 Chron. ix, 26; 2 Chron. xxxi, 11; Neh. x, 38.

588.—BABYLONIAN MODE OF LIVING.

I, 5. The king appointed them a daily provision of the king's meat, and of the wine which he drank.

This would have been a very luxurious mode of living for these Hebrew lads, quite in contrast to what they had been accustomed to, and to the extremely plain diet which Daniel requested for himself and his companions. The Babylonian kings and nobles were noted for their high living. Their tables were loaded with wheaten bread, meats in great variety, luscious fruits, fish, and game. The usual beverage was wine of the best varieties, and they were fond of drinking to excess. The ancient Persian kings followed the custom of the Babylonian monarch, and fed their attendants from their own tables.

589.—PUNISHMENT OF CRIMINALS.

II, 5. **Ye shall be cut in pieces, and your houses shall be made a dunghill.** See also chap. iii, 29.

1. Cutting into pieces was a punishment common to many ancient nations. It was known to the Hebrews, and was inflicted by Samuel upon Agag. See 1 Sam. xv, 33. Some think that dichotomy, or sawing asunder, is the punishment here referred to. See note on Heb. xi, 37.

2. According to Babylonian customs the house in which the criminal lived was sometimes destroyed, and the very land on which his dwelling stood considered cursed forever. The custom was also known among the Persians. See the decree of Darius in Ezra vi, 11. It was likewise practiced at Athens. There were many spots in the midst of that populous city which were kept perpetually vacant by reason of a decree similar to that referred to in the text.

590.—MUSICAL INSTRUMENTS.

III, 5. **The sound of the cornet, flute, harp, sackbut, psaltery, dulcimer.** See verses 7, 10, and 15.

1. *Keren*, "cornet," is described in the note on 1 Chron. xxv, 5.

2. *Mashrokitha*, "flute," was an instrument supposed by some to have been like the *chalil*, "pipe." See note on 1 Kings i, 40. Others think it consisted of a number of pipes similar to the *ugab*, "organ." See note on Psa. cl, 4.

3. *Kathros*, "harp," is thought by Rawlinson to represent the Babylonian harp, which, he says, "would seem to have resembled the later harp of the Assyrians, but it had fewer strings, if we may judge from a representation upon a cylinder. Like the Assyrian, it was carried under one arm and was played by both hands, one on either side of the strings."—*Five Ancient Monarchies*, vol. iii, p. 20. It is thought by some to have less resembled the harp than the cithern or cittern, which was an instrument of Greek origin, and in use among the Chaldeans. It was of the guitar species, and is still used in many eastern countries. It has strings varying in number from three to twenty-four.

125.—BABYLONIAN HARP.

4. *Sabbeca*, "sackbut," is thought to have resembled the *sambuca* of the Romans. Rawlinson supposes it to have been a large harp, resting on the ground like the harps of the Egyptians. Wright (in SMITH'S *Dictionary of the Bible*) states that the *sambuca* was triangular in shape, having four or more strings; it was played by the fingers, and gave forth a shrill sound.

5. *Pesanterin*, "psaltery," was a species of harp, thought to be the same as the *nebel*. See note on Psa. xxxiii, 2. Rawlinson suggests that it may have resembled the modern *santour*, and if so, he supposes that he has found

126.—MUSICIAN PLAYING THE DULCIMER.

a representation of it on an Assyrian monument. It was a sort of dulcimer, which was suspended from the neck of the musician, and projected horizontally from his waist. "It consisted (apparently) of a number of strings, containing not fewer than ten, stretched over a hollow case or sounding-board. The musician seems to have struck the strings with a small bar or hammer held in his right hand, while, at the same time, he made some use of his left hand in pressing them so as to produce the right note."—*Five Ancient Monarchies*, vol. i, pp. 537, 538.

6. *Sumpongah*, "dulcimer," is variously thought to have been a lute, a crooked trumpet, a long drum, an organ, and a bagpipe. Gesenius, and others with him, suppose the last-named instrument to be meant. The bagpipe is, at the present day, called in Italy *sampogna*, and in Asia Minor *sambony*.

It may be noted, as a curious illustration of the wide difference of opinion in respect to many of the ancient musical instruments, that some authorities consider the bagpipe to be intended by the word *ugab*. See note on Psa. cl, 4.

The monuments amply testify to the fondness of the Babylonians for music. They had numerous instruments, and organized large bands. Annarus, a Babylonian noble, entertained his guests at a banquet with music, vocal and instrumental, performed by a band of one hundred and fifty women.

591.—HOUR—BURNING ALIVE.

III, 6. And whoso falleth not down and worshipeth shall the same hour be cast into the midst of a burning fiery furnace.

1. This is the first indication we have in sacred history of so short a division of time as an hour. *Shaah*, "hour," is supposed to be a vague expression for a short time, whose duration is not distinctly defined, rather than for the definite time which we understand by the word hour. Indeed, we ourselves use the word occasionally in an indefinite sense. The word is, however, worthy of notice here, because it is claimed that the Babylonians were the first to make a regular division of the day into hours. The Greeks learned it from them, (see *Herodotus*, ii, 109;) and probably the Jews did the same, since there is no allusion to hours among them before the time of the captivity, while afterward the use of this division of time is frequently noticed. See further note on John xi, 9.

2. Burning alive was a very ancient punishment among the Babylonians, and possibly among other nations. Jeremiah mentions two false prophets who were to be put to death in this manner. See Jer. xxix, 22. The custom has come down to modern times in Persia. Chardin says that, in 1668, he saw ovens in Ispahan heated by royal command to terrify certain bakers who were disposed to put a heavy charge on their bread in time of scarcity. He speaks of the punishment of burning as recognized at that time, refractory cooks being spitted and roasted, and bakers thrown into an oven. It is supposed by some that there is a reference to burning as a capital punishment in Psa. xxi, 9: "Thou shalt make them as a fiery oven in the time of thine anger: the Lord shall swallow them up in his wrath, and the fire shall devour them."

592.—"MIGHTY MEN."

III, 20. He commanded the most mighty men that were in his army to bind Shadrach, Meshach, and Abed-nego, and to cast them into the burning fiery furnace.

On the monuments discovered at Khorsabad there are representations of gigantic and muscular men, like the "mighty men" of the text, who seem to have been always in attendance on the king, waiting to execute his orders. Such men were selected from the army on account of their size and strength, just as it is customary in the present day in Europe, as well as in the East, to select men of unusual stature as porters or guards in the palaces of kings. The monuments represent these men as clad in a peculiar costume, beautiful in style, and rich in ornament. It was probably men of this description who, at the king's command, took the unfortunate captives and tossed them into the fiery furnace.

593.—VARIOUS GARMENTS.

III, 21. Then these men were bound in their coats, their
hosen, and their hats, and their other garments.

It is not easy to tell the precise articles of costume intended by the original
words which our translators have rendered as above, though the improved
sources of exposition in our day add to the knowledge which they possessed.
Bevan, in SMITH's *Dictionary of the Bible*, vol. i, p. 457, renders as follows:

1. *Sarbalin*, "coats," (*marg.*, "mantles,") were drawers, which made the
distinctive feature in the Persian as compared with the Hebrew dress.

2. *Patish*, "hosen," was an inner tunic.

3. *Carbala*, "hat," (*marg.*, "turban,") was an upper tunic.

4. *Lebush*, "garments," was a cloak which was worn over all.

594.—THE USE OF METAL.

V, 4. The gods of gold, and of silver, of brass, of iron.

The working of metal into various articles of ornament or of use is an art
as old as the days of Tubal-Cain. See Gen iv, 22. The different metals referred to in this text are frequently spoken of in the Bible. There is no
question as to their identity, except in the case of *nechash*, which is the
Chaldee form of *nechosheth*, and in the text is rendered "brass." The facti-
tious metal known by this name, and which is compounded of copper and
zinc, is said to be of a later date than the early historic times of the Bible.
It certainly cannot be intended by the word *nechosheth* in such passages as
Deut. viii, 9, and Job xxviii, 2. *Copper* is probably the metal there referred
to as being dug out of the earth. The same word is rendered "steel" in
2 Sam. xxii, 35; Job xx, 24; Psa. xviii, 34, and Jer. xv, 12. Inasmuch as
copper is better worked when alloyed, and as tin was known at a very early
day, (see Num. xxxi, 22,) it is supposed that a combination of these two
metals—that is, bronze—was used in the manufacture of different articles.
Tools, utensils, and ornaments of bronze are found among the Egyptian and
Assyrian remains. The vessels of the Tabernacle, which are represented in
our version as made of "brass," (*nechosheth*,) were probably either copper or
bronze. See Exod. xxxviii, 2–6, 8.

595.—PRAYER.

VI, 10. His windows being open in his chamber toward Jerusalem, he kneeled upon his knees three times a day, and
prayed, and gave thanks before his God, as he did aforetime.

1. For the position of this chamber, see note on 2 Kings iv, 10.

2. He did not look toward the sun, as the fire-worshipers did, (see note

on Ezek. viii, 16,) but toward Jerusalem, where the temple of Jehovah stood, and where the sacred Presence was in the Oracle. This seems to have been a custom among the Jews when they were away from the Holy City. See 1 Kings viii, 44, 48; 2 Chron. vi, 34; Psa. v, 7; xxviii, 2; cxxxviii, 2; Jonah ii, 4. See also note on Matt. iv, 23.

3. There was no legal prescription in the Jewish ritual of any hours for seasons of prayer. The hours of morning and evening sacrifice would naturally be suggested to the mind of a pious Jew as suitable times for prayer. To this might easily be added a time midway. This appears to have been the case with David, who says: " Evening, and morning, and at noon, will I pray, and cry aloud: and he shall hear my voice." Psa. lv, 17. The order in which these three seasons of prayer are named by the psalmist seems to indicate the origin of the custom as just suggested. In the text Daniel is said to have prayed " three times a day." From Dan. ix, 21, it appears that one of these seasons of prayer was at the time of evening sacrifice; the two others were probably the same as those mentioned by David. In later times the precise hour is more clearly indicated. Compare Acts ii, 15; x, 9; iii, 1.

596.—COURT ETIQUETTE—IRREVERSIBLE EDICTS.

VI, 15. **Know, O king, that the law of the Medes and Persians is, That no decree nor statute which the king establisheth may be changed. See also verses 8 and 12.**

1. Lowth (W.) calls attention to an illustration of court etiquette contained in this text as compared with Esther i, 19. Here the expression " Medes and Persians " is used, the Medes being named first because Darius was a Mede. In the other instance, in the book of Esther, the expression is "Persians and Medes," Persians being named first out of compliment to Ahasuerus, who was a Persian.

2. The strict etiquette of the Persian court obliged the king never to revoke an order once given, however much he might regret it, because in so doing he would contradict himself, and, according to Persian notions, the law could not contradict itself. A curious instance of the unchangeable character of the Medo-Persian law is here seen in the fact that, after Ahasuerus had issued the order directing the cruel slaughter of the Jews, (Esther iii, 13,) he would not reverse it, even at the urgent request of his queen, (Esther viii, 5;) but he issued another edict in which he granted the Jews permission "to gather themselves together, and to stand for their life." Esther viii, 11. Thus the first irreversible edict was completely neutralized by another just as irreversible as itself; and the king continued to act his part as a character but little short of divinity: infallible, immutable, and wholly free from the weakness of repentance!

HOSEA.

597.—DIVINATION BY RODS.

IV, 12. My people ask counsel at their stocks, and their staff declareth unto them.

Some commentators suppose that two distinct classes of divination are here referred to, represented by the words "stocks" and "staff." If this be so, the former would probably allude to the consultation of teraphim. See note on Gen. xxxi, 19. If but one mode of divination be intended, it is more definitely indicated by the latter word "staff," and doubtless refers to rhabdomancy, or divination by rods. According to Cyril of Alexandria, this custom had its origin among the Chaldeans. It was also practiced by the Scythians, Persians, Assyrians, and Arabians. In more recent times it has been found among the Chinese, the Africans, and the New Zealanders. Henderson, in his *Commentary on Hosea*, suggests that the Runic wands of the Scandinavian nations, on which were inscribed mysterious characters, and which were used for magical purposes, originated in this custom. Traces of it may also be found in England and in America in the occasional use of willow rods for discovering hidden treasure, or for finding mines of gold or silver, or wells of petroleum.

There were various methods of using the rods in divination, the mode differing in different countries. Herodotus states that, among the Scythians, the soothsayer brought a large bundle of rods and laid it on the ground. Then, while muttering over his prophecy, he untied the bundle and placed each wand in a position by itself, after which he gathered the rods together and tied them up again into a bundle. A divine power was supposed to rest in the rods, and to communicate wisdom to the magician. The Scythians used willow sticks, the Persian Magi used tamarisk, and carried the magical bundle with them on all occasions of ceremony. The rods were of different length, and varied in number, three, five, seven, or nine, an odd number in every instance.

Another mode of using the rods was for the magician to hold one of them in his hand while asking his questions, and then to stoop toward the ground as if to get an answer from some invisible source. This answer was always inaudible, and was supposed to be made known to the magician in spirit. Sometimes he leaned on the staff while making his consultations.

At other times the person consulting measured the rod by spans, or by the length of his finger, saying as he measured, "I will go," or "I will not go;" or else, "I will do," or "I will not do;" varying the phrase to suit the circumstances. In the way that the last span indicated, so he decided.

Some used this method of divination by taking a rod which was peeled on one side and throwing it at a distance. As the one or the other side fell uppermost, so the decision was made. In the Abbott Collection of Egyptian Antiquities are seven pieces of wood, which were found in a tomb at Sakkarah. Each stick is peeled in the manner above stated. Mr. Abbott supposed them to have been used by children in some ancient game, similar to one now played by the young Egyptians. The sticks are tossed in the air, and according to the way in which they fall the game is won or lost. These ancient sticks may, however, have been used for divination, and the modern game may thus have had its origin. Lane describes a game very common among the lower classes of Egyptians in which sticks are thrown, one side white and the other black. The game is called "táb."—See *Modern Egyptians*, vol. ii, pp. 59, 63.

598.—SNARES FOR BIRDS.

VII, 12. **When they shall go, I will spread my net upon them; I will bring them down as the fowls of the heaven.**

Resheth, "net," in this passage refers evidently to a net which was used to catch birds in the air. How it differed from other nets we are unable to say, and in what manner it was employed we can only surmise. From the way in which the word is used in Ezek. xii, 13; xvii, 20; xix, 8; xxxii, 3, the *resheth* is supposed to have been used to throw over animals walking on the earth, as well as to catch the inhabitants of the air. Jennings (in KITTO'S *Cyclopedia*, article "Fowling") intimates that the only use of this net was that represented in the texts quoted; but from other passages it is clear that the *resheth* was used also as a snare for the feet. See Job xviii, 8; Psa. ix, 15; xxxi, 4; lvii, 6; cxl, 5.

For other modes of snaring birds, see note on Psa. xci, 3.

599.—THE YOKE.

XI, 4. **I drew them with cords of a man, with bands of love: and I was to them as they that take off the yoke on their jaws, and I laid meat unto them.**

This is an agricultural simile, and refers to the custom of raising the yoke from the neck and cheeks of the oxen so that they can more readily eat their food. Henderson says: "The *ol*, yoke, not only included the piece of wood on the neck by which the animal was fastened to the pole, but also the whole of the harness about the head which was connected with it. The yokes used in the East are very heavy, and press so much upon the animals that they are unable to bend their necks."—*Commentary in loco.*

Compare this statement with what Jesus says about *his* yoke in Matthew xi, 2?–30.

20

600.—THE CHIMNEY.

XIII, 3. As the smoke out of the chimney.

This rendering conveys a wrong impression, since chimneys are comparatively a modern invention, and were entirely unknown to the Hebrews. In an Oriental dwelling the openings which let in the light are the same that let out the smoke; though it is said that in some houses there are, in addition to the lattice windows, holes near the ceiling specially designed for the escape of smoke. The fire being made on the "hearth" in the middle of the floor, (see the note on Jer. xxxvi, 22,) the smoke makes its way upward through the room and gets out through such apertures as it can find, usually the windows. *Arubbah*, here rendered "chimney," is in other places translated "window." It would be much more correct to read this text, "as the smoke out of the window," remembering meanwhile that the window is different from the kind we are accustomed to see. See note on Judges v, 28.

———◆———

AMOS.

601.—WORTHLESSNESS.

II, 6. They sold the righteous for silver, and the poor for a pair of shoes. See also chap. viii, 6.

Naal may be rendered either "shoe" or "sandal." From the form of expression here used the meanest, cheapest kind of sandal is evidently meant · the poor debtor was sold into slavery because he could not pay for so small a matter as a pair of sandals. A similar mode of speech is noticed in India at the present day. "When a person wishes to insult another in reference to the price of any article he says, 'I will give you my sandals for it.' 'That fellow is not worth the value of my sandals.'"—ROBERTS, *Oriental Illustrations*, p. 504.

See further note on Matt. iii, 11; and for a description of sandals, see note on Acts xii, 8.

602.—IDOLATROUS CUSTOMS.

II, 8. They lay themselves down upon clothes laid to pledge by every altar, and they drink the wine of the condemned in the house of their god.

Henderson's translation gives the sense of the passage more clearly than the authorized version. He renders it: "They stretch themselves upon pledged garments close to every altar, and drink the wine of the amerced in the house of their gods." The text refers to the unjust habits and to the idolatrous practices of the backslidden Israelites, especially of those in authority. They took money which they had exacted by the imposition of fines, which were in all probability fixed at an amount higher than justice demanded, and with it purchased wine, which is therefore called "the wine of the amerced." This wine they drank in heathen temples. In addition to this they took from the poor as a pledge for debts their outer garments, which were their covering through the night as well as during the day. Instead of returning these at sun-down, as the law required, (Deut. xxiv, 12; see also the note on that text,) they kept them all night, and stretched themselves upon them in the heathen temples. This stretching may refer either to the reclining at the idolatrous feasts, or to the custom, sometimes practiced among the heathen, of sleeping near the altars of their gods, that they might obtain communications in dreams.

Keil translates the verse: " And they stretch themselves upon pawned clothes by every altar, and they drink the wine of the punished in the house of their God." He does not believe that the prophet refers to feasts in idolatrous temples, but in drinking carousals which were held in the house of God. He says that "Amos had in his mind the sacred places in Bethel and Dan, in which the Israelites worshiped Jehovah as their God under the symbol of an ox, (*calf.*")—*Commentary in loco.*

603.—DAMASK COVERING.

III, 12. So shall the children of Israel be taken out that dwell in Samaria in the corner of a bed, and in Damascus in a couch.

Instead of "Damascus," some commentators read "damask," making the word refer to the rich silk-woven stuff with raised figures of flowers and other patterns, and not to the place where it was made, and whence it derived its name. Thus the text would read, "a damask couch," or "a couch of damask." The allusion here is to the luxurious couches which are on the divan in Eastern houses, for a description of which see note on 2 Kings i, 4. The corner of the divan is the most convenient place for repose, and is considered the place of honor. Hackett says: "A divan, which I saw in the palace of the late Mohammed Ali at Alexandria, furnishes an apt commentary on this verse. It was arranged, after the Oriental fashion, along the entire side of the room. It was capable of seating a great number of persons. A covering of the richest damask silk was spread over it, and hung in folds over the outward edge; while the magnificent cushions, adorned with threads of gold at the corners, distinguished those places above the others as the seats of special honor."—*Scripture Illustrations*, p. 61.

604.—PALACES.

III, 15. And I will smite the winter-house with the summer-house ; and the houses of ivory shall perish.

1. The expressions "winter-house" and "summer-house" do not of necessity imply two separate houses, but may mean separate suites of apartments in the same house. Thomson says: "Such language is easily understood by an Oriental. In common parlance, the lower apartments are simply *el beit*—the house; the upper is the *'alliyeh*, which is the summer-house. Every respectable dwelling has both, and they are familiarly called beît *shetawy* and beît *seîfy*—winter and summer house. If these are on the same story, then the external and airy apartment is the summer-*house*, and that for winter is the interior and more sheltered room. It is rare to meet a family that has an entirely separate dwelling for summer."—*The Land and the Book*, vol. i, p. 478. It may have been in the interior apartment that Jehoiakim sat when Jehudi read the roll in his presence. See Jer. xxxvi, 22.

2. By "houses of ivory" we are not to understand houses built of that material, but houses richly ornamented with it. The ancients decorated the ceilings, doors, and panels of their rooms with ivory. It was in this way that Ahab is said to have built an "ivory house." 1 Kings xxii, 39. Such houses are the "ivory palaces" mentioned in Psa. xlv, 8.

605.—CHIUN.

V, 26. Ye have borne the tabernacle of your Moloch and Chiun your images, the star of your god, which ye made to yourselves.

1. For a description of Moloch, see note on Lev. xviii, 21.

2. The majority of those interpreters who suppose Chiun to be a proper name take it to mean the planet Saturn. The Septuagint has 'Ραιφάν, which afterward became corrupted to 'Ρεμφάν, and is so used by Stephen in Acts vii, 43. Some have assumed that 'Ραιφάν was an Egyptian name of the planet Saturn, but others have denied this. Some commentators suppose that the word is not a proper name, but merely signifies a statue, an idol, or a pedestal on which an idol might be placed.

606.—BEDS OF IVORY.

VI, 4. That lie upon beds of ivory, and stretch themselves upon their couches.

The divan on which the beds were spread, or the frames on which they rested, were inlaid and ornamented with ivory. Compare the note on "houses of ivory," Amos iii, 15.

607.—HORSES, UNSHOD.

VI, 12. Shall horses run upon the rock?

This question has no pertinence in our times, since, by reason of being shod with iron, our horses do not injure their hoofs by running upon the rock. Horse-shoeing was, however, unknown to the Hebrews, and is of comparatively modern introduction. Bishop Lowth states that the shoes of leather and of iron mentioned by Greek and Roman writers, as well as the silver and the gold shoes with which Nero and Poppea shod their mules, inclosed the whole hoof as in a case, or as a shoe does a man's foot, and were bound or tied on, and even these were exceptional cases. In ordinary instances no shoes of any kind were used. We can thus see how, with hoofs unprotected, the horses could not be expected to run upon a rock. No doubt Amos had this in mind. Isaiah also, in describing the character of the army that should come with destructive judgments upon Judah, says that "their horses' hoofs shall be counted like flint." Isa. v, 28. A hard hoof must have been a very desirable quality in a horse, when the art of protecting the foot with iron shoes was unknown.

608.—CULTIVATION OF FIGS.

VII, 14. A gatherer of sycamore fruit.

This shows his humble position, since none but the poorest cultivate or use this fruit. Henderson, speaking of the word *boles*, "gatherer," says: "The particular mode in which the ancients cultivated fig-trees the LXX appear to have had in their eye when they rendered it by κνίζων, a *nipper or scratcher;* for we are informed by Theophrastus that iron nails or prongs were employed to make incisions or scratches in the tree, that, by letting out some of the sap, the fruit might be ripened."—*Commentary in loco.* Gesenius sustains this rendering of the Septuagint, but Keil dissents. He says that nipping cannot be shown to be implied by the word *boles*, and further declares that the eating, and not the cultivation, of the fruit is what is meant.

609.—THE SIEVE.

IX, 9. I will sift the house of Israel among all nations, like as corn is sifted in a sieve.

A part of the process of winnowing grain consisted in the use of a sieve, by which means the particles of earth, and other impurities which clung to the corn during the process of threshing, were separated from the grain. In addition to this text, reference is figuratively made to the sieve in Isa. xxx, 28, and Luke xxii, 31. See also note on Ruth iii, 2, and on Matt. iii, 12.

JONAH.

610.—CALLING ON THE GODS.

I, 5. Then the mariners were afraid, and cried every man unto his god.

As these sailors were probably Phenicians from different places, they worshiped different gods. Every man may have had his own special deity to whom he prayed when in trouble. Roberts found illustrations of this text on more than one occasion when in a storm at sea in a vessel with a heathen crew: "No sooner does danger appear than one begins to beat his head and cry aloud, 'Siva, Siva!' another beats his breast and piteously shrieks forth, ' Vishnoo!' and a third strikes his thigh and shouts out with all his might, 'Varuna!' "—*Oriental Illustrations*, p. 513.

611.—SAILORS' SUPERSTITIONS.

I, 7. Come, and let us cast lots, that we may know for whose cause this evil is upon us.

1. On the subject of lots, see note on Prov. xviii, 18.

2. It was a common opinion among sailors that the misconduct of one person might bring disaster on the whole company. This notion still prevails, not only among heathen mariners, but to some extent among sailors belonging to Christian nations, many of whom have strangely superstitious ideas. Rosenmüller says, in illustration of this ancient opinion: " Thus, (according to Cicero, *On the Nature of the Gods*, iii, 37,) the sailors considered Diagoras of Melos the cause of the storm which overtook them because he was an atheist, and had betrayed the Eleusinian mysteries."—*Morgenland*, vol. iv, p. 39°.

———◆———

MICAH.

612.—THE COVERED LIP.

III, 7. Then shall the seers be ashamed, and the diviners confounded: yea, they shall all cover their lips; for there is no answer of God.

The margin has "upper lip," that is, the lip-beard or mustache, as the word *sapham* is rendered by Gesenius and others. The Hebrews held the beard in high estimation as a mark of manliness. To cover the lip, and thus conceal the beard growing there, was a sign of sorrow or of mourning.

Thus, in the text, Micah represents the prophets as mourning because God refuses to reveal himself to them: " they shall all cover their lips." Thus also the leper was required to cover his upper lip. Lev. xiii, 45. An allusion to this custom is likewise made in Ezek. xxiv, 17, 22.

613.--SITTING IN THE SHADE.

IV, 4. **They shall sit every man under his vine, and under his fig-tree; and none shall make them afraid.**

This is a figurative expression used to denote a state of national peace and domestic happiness. See also 1 Kings iv, 25, and Zech. iii, 10. It is based on the custom of seeking a pleasant shade under fig-trees and vines. In the East the grape-vine is more extensively used for ornament and shade than the woodbine or ivy in our own country. The branches are frequently trained to run over a trellis in the court-yard of the house. The fig-tree, by its thick branches and broad leaf, makes a very agreeable natural shade. Nathanael was under a fig-tree enjoying its shade, and engaged probably in pious meditation, when Philip found him and brought him to Jesus. John i, 48.

NAHUM.

614.—NINEVITE CONVIVIALITY.

I, 10. **While they are drunken as drunkards.**

Henderson's translation is more graphic: "thoroughly soaked with their wine." The prophet here has reference to the drinking habits of the Nine-

127.—ASSYRIAN DRINKING-SCENE.

vites, of which the monuments give abundant illustration. Rawlinson says: "In the banquet-scenes of the sculptures it is drinking, and not eating, that is represented. Attendants dip the wine-cups into a huge bowl or vase, which stands on the ground and reaches as high as a man's chest, and carry them full of liquor to the guests, who straightway fall to a carouse. ... Every guest holds in his right hand a wine-cup of a most elegant shape, the lower part modeled into the form of a lion's head, from which the cup itself rises in a graceful curve. They all raise their cups to a level with their heads, and look as if they were either pledging each other or else one and all drinking the same toast."—*Five Great Monarchies*, vol. i, pp. 579, 580.

615.—ASSYRIAN WARRIORS.

II, 8. The shield of his mighty men is made red, the valiant men are in scarlet: the chariots shall be with flaming torches in the day of his preparation, and the fir-trees shall be terribly shaken.

This is a vivid description of ancient Assyrian warriors and their equipments.

1. The shields may have been reddened with paint, or with the copper with which they were overlaid.

2. The fighting costume of ancient warriors was of a blood-red color. It

128.—ASSYRIAN WAR-CHARIOT OF THE EARLY PERIOD. (NIMRUD.)

is said that one object of this was to conceal from the enemy the blood of their wounds, the sight of which might inspire them with new courage and hope.

3. By the "flaming torches" of the chariots, Michaelis, Ewald, Gesenius, and others, suppose to be meant the *falces* or scythes which were fastened

to the axle, and turned repeatedly with every revolution of the wheel. Henderson accordingly renders *esh-peladoth*, "fiery scythes." The fire of these scythes would be coruscations produced by their excessive brightness and the rapidity of their motion. Keil, however, (in his *Commentary*,) objects to this interpretation on the ground that "scythe-chariots were first introduced by Cyrus, and were unknown before his time to the Medes, the Assyrians, the Arabians, and also to the ancient Egyptians." He supposes *peladoth* to refer to the steel coverings of the Assyrian war-chariots, and appends the following interesting note from Strauss: "The chariots of the Assyrians, as we see them on the monuments, glare with shining things made either of iron or steel, battle-axes, bows, arrows, and shields, and all kinds of weapons; the horses are also ornamented with crowns and red fringes, and even the poles of the carriages are made resplendent with shining suns and moons; add to these the soldiers in armor riding in their chariots, and it could not but be the case that, when illumined by the rays of the sun above them, they would have all the appearance of flames as they flew hither and thither with great celerity." (See verse 4, *l. c.*)

4. By the "fir-trees," which were to be "terribly shaken," are probably meant the spears, darts, and lances, which had handles made of the wood of the cypress.

616.—TEMPERING CLAY.

III, 14. Go into clay, and tread the mortar.

This is an allusion to the ancient method of tempering the clay for making bricks. It was done by the feet of the laborer, and was very severe and fatiguing labor. *Tit*, "clay," may also be rendered "mire;" and *chomer*, "mortar," is not to be understood here in the sense of a cement for bricks, but rather of clay. Henderson accordingly translates the passage, "Enter the mire, and tread the clay." Keil has, "Tread in the mire, and stamp the clay." Potter's clay was tempered in a similar way. "He shall come upon princes as upon mortar, and as the potter treadeth clay." Isa. xli, 25.

HABAKKUK.

617.—WORSHIP OF WEAPONS.

I, 16. They sacrifice unto their net, and burn incense unto their drag.

These fishing implements are used figuratively to represent the weapons of war by means of which the Chaldeans designed to take the Jews. It was customary among some ancient nations to offer sacrifices to their weapons. The Scythians offered sacrifices to a sword which was set up as a symbol of Mars. Herodotus says: "Yearly sacrifices of cattle and of horses are made to it, and more victims are offered thus than to all the rest of their gods."—Book iv, chap. lxii. Grote, in speaking of the same people, says: "The Sword, in the literal sense of the word, was their chief god—an iron scimitar solemnly elevated upon a wide and lofty platform, which was supported on masses of faggots piled underneath—to whom sheep, horses, and a portion of their prisoners taken in war, were offered up in sacrifice." —*History of Greece*, part ii, chap. xvii. The Hindus, to this day, make offerings to their fishing tackle, to their weapons, and to their tools of various kinds.

618.—THE USE OF WOOD IN WALLS.

II, 11. **For the stone shall cry out of the wall, and the beam out of the timber shall answer it.**

Kaphis, "beam," is supposed by some to be a cross-beam for binding together the walls of a building. Jerome says it is "the beam which is placed in the middle of any building to hold the walls together, and is generally called ἱμάντωσις by the Greeks." Henderson, however, objects to this rendering. He says: "That it was not the wood itself is evident from the following: *from*, or *out of the wood*." He prefers the interpretation given by the Mishna, and followed by some Jewish writers. According to these *kaphis* signifies a half brick. Rashi, the celebrated commentator and Talmudist, explains it to be "half a brick, which is usually laid between two layers of wood."

There are numerous evidences to show that ancient architects used wood to unite and bind walls, and it may have been some such custom to which the prophet refers in the text.

619.—SILENCE.

II, 20. **But the Lord is in his holy temple: let all the earth keep silence before him.**

There may be a reference here to the profound and impressive silence which prevails in Oriental courts among the guards and officers who attend upon royal personages.

620.—THE NAKED BOW.

III, 9. **Thy bow was made quite naked.**

The bow was often kept in a case made of leather or of cloth. To make it "naked" meant to take it out of its case in order to use it. The expression signifies a preparation for war, and is of the same meaning as "uncovering the shield." See note on Isa. xxii, 6.

ZEPHANIAH.

621.—THE CHEMARIM.

I, 4. I will cut off the remnant of Baal from this place, and the name of the Chemarim with the priests.

The word *chemarim*, here untranslated, occurs also in 2 Kings xxiii, 5, where it is rendered "idolatrous priests;" and in Hosea x, 5, where it is rendered "priests." It signifies the priests of idolatrous worship. Keil does not include in the term the priests of Baal, but limits its application to "the priests appointed by the Kings of Judah for the worship of the high places and the idolatrous worship of Jehovah"—*Commentary in loco*. Gesenius thinks it is derived from *kamar*, to be burned, to be sad, and that it refers to the black garments worn by priests. Some, however, think this idea too modern for adoption. Keil says that this derivation "is decidedly opposed by the fact, that neither the priests of the idols nor of the high places were ascetics or monks, and in ancient times the priests from India to Gaul wore robes of a white, and if possible of a brilliant white, color. Compare BAHR'S *Symbol.*, ii, p. 87, f, and the works there quoted."—*Commentary on 2 Kings* xxiii, 5.

ZECHARIAH.

622.—THE MONTH SEBAT.

I, 7. The eleventh month, which is the month Sebat.

Sebat corresponds very nearly to our month of February.

623.—HEAVY STONES.

XII, 8. And in that day will I make Jerusalem a burdensome stone for all people: all that burden themselves with it shall be cut in pieces.

Jerome supposes an allusion here to a custom common in Judea in his day, and which he thinks was known in the time of Zechariah. The young men were in the habit of lifting heavy stones for exercise, and for a display of strength. They lifted them to various heights, according to the weight of the stones and their own strength: to the knees, the breast, the top of the head, and even above the head, at arms' length. Jerusalem is declared by the prophets to be such a "burdensome stone" that whosoever should undertake to lift it would be destroyed by its weight.

Most commentators have followed Jerome's interpretation, though some prefer to think that the reference is made merely to a heavy stone used in building.

624.—SEPARATION OF THE SEXES.

XII, 12. And the land shall mourn, every family apart; the family of the house of David apart, and their wives apart.

According to the Jewish custom, not only did the men and women dwell in separate apartments, but they also worshiped separately. In this text, the trouble that is to come upon the land is so great that every family shall be in mourning, the men mourning by themselves, and the women in like manner lamenting together.

625.—BELLS FOR HORSES.

XIV, 20. In that day shall there be upon the bells of the horses, Holiness unto the Lord.

It was quite common among ancient nations to have bells hung around the necks of horses, both by way of ornament and to accustom the war-horses to noise. At the present time bells are used in caravans for horses and

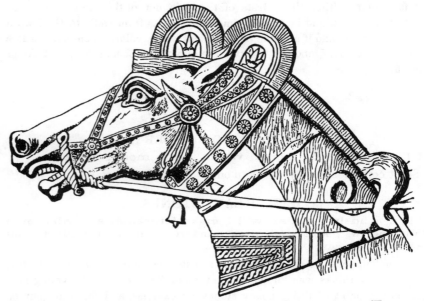

129.—HEAD OF A CHARIOT-HORSE, SHOWING COLLAR WITH BELLS ATTACHED. (KOYUNJIK.)

camels; sometimes being strung around the legs, as well as suspended from the neck. They are designed, not only for ornament, but also to encourage the animals by their sound, to frighten beasts of prey, and to keep the caravan together.

Some suppose that *metsilloth*, "bells," were small pieces of metal resembling cymbals, which made a tinkling noise by collision as the horses moved.

MALACHI.

626.—FULLING.

III, 2. He is like a refiner's fire, and like fullers' soap.

The precise character of all the articles used by the ancient fullers is unknown. They had mineral alkali in niter, to which reference is made in Prov. xxv, 20, and Jer. ii, 22. They obtained vegetable alkali, as the Arabs do at the present time, from the ashes of some plants and from the juices of others.

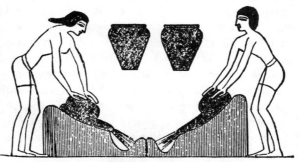

180.—Ancient Egyptian Fullers at Work.

They likewise used, for cleansing their cloth, urine and chalk, and bean-meal mixed with water.

The cloths are thought to have been first trodden by the feet. They were also rubbed with the knuckles. A subsequent operation probably consisted in rubbing the cloth on an inclined plane, after the manner still followed in the East, and one which was common among the ancient Egyptians.

627.—THE BOOK OF REMEMBRANCE.

III, 16. A book of remembrance was written before him for them that feared the Lord, and that thought upon his name.

The metaphor is supposed to be taken from the ancient Persian custom cf keeping a record of the names and deeds of any who had rendered special service to the king. It was in this way that the faithfulness of Mordecai in revealing to Ahasuerus the plot against his life was recorded and filed among the records of the court. See Esther vi, 1, 2.

628.—TREATMENT OF ENEMIES.

IV, 3. And ye shall tread down the wicked; for they shall be ashes under the soles of your feet.

Chardin supposes that allusion is here made to the mode of making mortar in the East. One kind is made of a mixture of sand, ashes, and lime, which ingredients are mixed by being trodden. See note on Lev. xiv, 42, and also on Nahum iii, 14. There is also reference to the custom of putting the feet on conquered enemies, for an account of which see note on 1 Cor. xv, 25.

MATTHEW.

629.—ESPOUSALS.

I, 18. Mary was espoused to Joseph.

Espousal among the Hebrews was something more than what a mere marriage engagement is with us. It was considered the beginning of marriage, was as legally binding as marriage itself, and could not be broken off save by a bill of divorce. Hence we find that Joseph is called the "husband" of Mary, (verse 19.) The betrothal was usually determined by the parents or brothers of the parties, and the engagement was made between a friend or legal representative of the bridegroom and the father of the bride. The espousals were made very early in life, though marriage did not take place before the bride was twelve years old. Even when the age was suitable, the marriage was not consummated for some time after the betrothal. See Judges xiv, 8. At least a year, or sometimes more, elapsed between the betrothal and the marriage of a maiden, to give time for preparing her outfit. In case of a widow marriage might take place thirty days after espousal. The betrothal was usually accompanied by a feast in the house of the bride.

The engagement, to be binding, must be either by written contract, or by the reception of presents by the bride from the bridegroom. When Abraham's servant received the consent of Rebekah's father and brother to make her the wife of his master's son, he presented to the maiden valuable gifts. See Gen. xxiv, 53. The reception of these made the contract binding. The bride remained at her father's house until the time of marriage, when the bridegroom came after her. This custom is referred to in Deut xx, 7. Meanwhile communication between her and the bridegroom was kept up by means of the "friend of the bridegroom." See note on John iii, 29.

630.—THE MAGI.

II, 1. Now when Jesus was born in Bethlehem of Judea in the days of Herod the king, behold, there came wise men from the East to Jerusalem.

These "wise men," or, more properly, *magi*, (*μάγοι*,) belonged to a numerous and influential order of men. The origin of Magism is involved in obscurity. It is thought to have had its beginning among either the Chaldeans or the Assyrians; more probably among the former. Starting in Chaldea, it would naturally make its way to Assyria, Media, and the adjoining countries. From Media it was brought into Persia, where it exerted a powerful influence in modifying the ancient religious faith of the people. Some profess to trace the Magian doctrines to Abraham, who, it is said, if he did not originate them, at least purified them from the errors of Zabaism. See note on Deut. iv, 19. After Abraham's time they became corrupted, and were again purified by Zoroaster, who is supposed to have been a descendant of the prophet Daniel.

We find in the Old Testament several references to the Magi. In Jer. xxxix, 3, 13, Nergal-sharezer is said to have been the *Rab-mag*, that is, the chief of the Magi. His name is supposed to be recorded in the Babylonian inscriptions, where mention is made of *Nergal-shar-uzur*, who is styled *Rabu-emga* or *Rab mag*. The *chakamim*, or "wise men," referred to in Jer. l, 35, were probably Magi.

In Daniel's time the Magi were very prominent in Babylon. In Dan. ii, 2, "magicians," "astrologers," "sorcerers," and "Chaldeans" are mentioned; while in the twenty-seventh verse of the same chapter "soothsayers" are named. These are represented by five different words in the original, and some writers think that five distinct classes of Magi are here referred to.

131.—CHALDEAN DIVINER.

It is difficult, however, at this late day to specify the difference between them, though the attempt has sometimes been made.

It has been supposed from Dan. v, 11, compared with ii, 48, and iv, 9, that Daniel himself was made a member of the Magian order, and its chief; but the expressions there used may only mean that the king regarded him as superior to all the magicians in his dominion, and as having authority over them. In any case, we cannot believe that Daniel embraced any theological notions of the Magi which were in opposition to Hebrew orthodoxy.

An account of the worship practiced by the Magi of Media will give us some idea of the peculiarities of the order. Rawlinson says: "Magism was essentially the worship of the elements, the recognition of fire, air, earth, and water as the only proper objects of human reverence. The Magi held no personal gods, and, therefore, naturally rejected temples, shrines, and images, as tending to encourage the notion that gods existed of a like nature with man; that is, possessing personality—living and intelligent beings. Theirs was a nature worship, but a nature worship of a very peculiar kind. They did not place gods over the different parts of nature, like the Greeks; they did not even personify the powers of nature, like the Hindoos; they paid their devotion to the actual material things themselves. Fire, as the most subtle and ethereal principle, and again as the most powerful agent, attracted their highest regards; and on their fire-altars the sacred flame, generally said to have been kindled from heaven, was kept burning uninterrupted from year to year and from age to age by bands of priests, whose special duty it was to see that the sacred spark was never extinguished." —*Five Ancient Monarchies*, vol. ii, p. 346.

The Magians were a priestly caste, and the office is supposed to have been hereditary. They uttered prophec.es, explained omens, interpreted dreams, and practiced rhabdomancy or divination by rods. See note on Hosea iv, 12. Their notion of the peculiar sanctity of the so-called elements led to a singular mode of disposing of the bodies of the dead. See note on Psa. lxxix, 2.

In Persia they became a powerful body under the guide of Zoroaster, and were divided into three classes: *Herbeds*, or disciples; *Mobeds*, or masters; and *Destur-mobeds*, or perfect masters. After a time the term Magi became more extended in its meaning. As the Magi were men of learning, devoting special attention to astronomy and the natural sciences, it happened that, after the lapse of years, men who became celebrated for learning were called Magi, whether belonging to the priestly order or not. So, as the Magi joined to the pursuits of science the arts of the soothsayer, in process of time mere conjurors who had no scientific knowledge were called Magi. Simon Magus (Acts viii, 9) and Bar-Jesus or Elymas (Acts xiii, 6, 8) were men of this sort.

The Magi who came to visit the infant Saviour were no doubt of the better class. The idea, however, that they were kings and three in number is mere imagination, and unsusceptible of proof. They were evidently skilled in astronomical knowledge, and were earnest seekers after the new-born king. Where they came from is a disputed question. Various writers have suggested that they were Babylonians, Arabians, Persians, Bactrians, Parthians, or even Brahmins from India. Matthew says they were from "the East," which was a geographical term of very elastic meaning.

One of the best dissertations on this subject is a monograph by Dr. Upham,* who claims a Persian nationality for these Magi. His opinion is indorsed by some of the best recent biblical critics.

631.—THE STAR OF THE KING.

II, 2. **Where is he that is born King of the Jews? for we have seen his star in the east, and are come to worship him.**

When the preparations were making for the coronation of Solyman III. as king of Persia in 1666, the astrologers had very important duties assigned them, according to the custom of their country. Sir John Chardin, who was

* The Wise Men: Who they Were; and How they Came to Jerusalem. By Francis W. Upham, LL.D. New York, 1873.

present, says that these astrologers were appointed "to observe the lucky hour, according to the position of the stars, for the performance of this weighty ceremony."—*Coronation of Solyman III.,* p. 36.

The wise men mentioned in the text may have supposed, from what they had seen of the star, that it was a favorable time for the coronation of the new-born King, and hence they came to worship him.

632.—ROUGH GARMENTS—LOCUST FOOD.

III, 4. The same John had his raiment of camel's hair, and a leathern girdle about his loins; and his meat was locusts and wild honey. See also Mark i, 6.

1. The "raiment of camel's hair" was a coarse, rough outer garment, such as is still worn by the Arabs. It is made of the thin coarse hair of the camel. Some think, because Elijah is called "a hairy man" in 2 Kings i, 8, that he wore a garment of this sort. A rough garment seems to have been characteristic of a prophet. See Zech. xiii, 4.

2. For a description of the girdle, see note on 1 Kings xviii, 46.

3. With many of the Bedawin on the frontiers locusts are still an article of food, though none but the poorest eat them. They are considered a very inferior sort of food. They are salted and dried, and eaten with butter or with wild honey. The fact that John ate this kind of food illustrates the extreme poverty of the forerunner of Christ, and shows the destitution he suffered by living in the wilderness far away from the haunts of men.

633.—CARRYING SANDALS.

III, 11. He that cometh after me is mightier than I, whose shoes I am not worthy to bear.

To carry the master's sandals was considered the most menial duty that could be performed. On entering a house the sandals are taken off by a servant, who takes care of them, and brings them again when needed. In India it is customary for a servant to accompany his master when he walks out. If the master desires to walk barefoot on the soft grass or the smooth ground the servant removes the sandals and carries them in his hand. John felt himself unworthy to do for Christ even the meanest work of a servant.

See also note on John i, 27.

634.—WINNOWING GRAIN.

III, 12. Whose fan is in his hand, and he will thoroughly purge his floor, and gather his wheat into the garner; but he will burn up the chaff with unquenchable fire. See also Luke iii, 17.

The grain in the East is threshed in the open air, (see note on Gen. l, 10.) by being trampled under the feet of oxen or horses, (see note on Deut.

xxv, 4,) or by means of instruments, as described in the note on Isa. xxviii, 27, 28. By these processes the straw becomes very much broken; and, to separate the grain from the hulls and straw the mingled mass is thrown against the wind by means of a wooden shovel, or else a wooden fork, having sometimes two prongs and sometimes three, and a handle three or four feet long. This is the "fan" alluded to in a number of Scripture passages. It is usually employed in the evening. See note on Ruth iii, 2. The wind carries the chaff away, while the grain falls to the ground. The grain is sometimes sifted after the winnowing. See note on Amos ix, 9. The chaff is burned and the grain is stored, either in subterranean granaries (see note on Jer. xli, 8) or in barns. See note on Gen. xli, 48.

The fan is referred to in Isa. xxx, 24, where it is mentioned in connection with the "shovel." The precise difference between the two instruments there indicated is not now known. See also Jer. iv, 11; xv, 7; li, 2. The scattering of the chaff by the wind after fanning is frequently alluded to figuratively. See Job xxi, 18; Psa. i, 4; Isa. xxix, 5; xli, 16; Dan. ii, 35; Hos. xiii, 3.

635.—THE PINNACLE OF THE TEMPLE.

IV, 5. Then the devil taketh him up into the holy city, and setteth him on a pinnacle of the temple. See also Luke iv, 9.

This is commonly supposed to have been the summit of the royal gallery built by Herod within the area of the temple buildings on the edge of the Kedron valley. Josephus says of it: "This cloister deserves to be mentioned better than any other under the sun; for, while the valley was very deep, and its bottom could not be seen if you looked from above into the depth, this farther vastly high elevation of the cloister stood upon that height, insomuch that if any one looked down from the top of the battlements, or down both those altitudes, he would be giddy, while his sight could not reach to such an immense depth."—*Antiquities*, Book XV, chap. xi, § 5. The extreme distance from the top of the battlement to the bottom of the valley is supposed to have been about seven hundred feet. See also note on Matt. xxiv, 1.

636.—THE SYNAGOGUE.

IV, 23. Teaching in their synagogues, and preaching the gospel of the kingdom. See also Mark i, 39; Luke iv, 44.

Jewish writers claim for the synagogue a very remote antiquity, but its origin probably dates during the captivity. There were no fixed proportions in the building, as there were in the tabernacle and in the temple. When a synagogue was to be built the highest ground that could be found in the vicinity was selected for the site, and, if possible, the top was erected above the roofs of surrounding buildings. Where this could not be done a tall pole was placed on the summit in order to make the building conspicuous. Synagogues were often built without roofs. They were also so constructed that the worshipers, as they entered and prayed, faced Jerusalem. See note on Dan. vi, 10. At the Jerusalem end was the chest or ark which contained the book of the law. Toward the middle of the building was a raised platform, and in the center of the platform was a pulpit. A low partition five or six feet high divided the men from the women.

The leading object of the synagogue was not worship, but instruction The *temple* was "the house of prayer." Matt. xxi, 13. The synagogue was never called by that name. Reading and expounding the law was the great business of the synagogue: and, though a liturgical service was connected with these, it was subordinate to them.

The priests had no official standing or privileges in the synagogue, though they were always honored when present. They were the hereditary officials of the temple, but the officers of the synagogue were elected either by the congregation or by the council.

The leader of the congregation might ask any suitable person to address the assembly. Persons who were known as learned men, or as the expounders of religious faith, were allowed to speak. Hence in the text and in the parallel passages we find Christ publicly speaking in the synagogue. See also Matt. xiii, 54; Mark vi, 2; Luke iv, 15; iv, 16–22; John xviii, 20. So also the apostles on their missionary journey addressed the people in these places of public gathering. See Acts xiii, 5, 15; xiv, 1; xvii, 10, 11; xvii, 17; xviii, 19.

637.—SAVORLESS SALT.

V. 13. If the salt have lost his savor, wherewith shall it be salted? it is thenceforth good for nothing, but to be cast out, and to be trodden under foot of men. See also Luke xiv, 34, 35.

Salt produced by the evaporation of sea-water in hot countries is said sometimes to lose its saline properties. The same result is also sometimes seen in impure rock-salt that has long been exposed to the air. When such is the case there can nothing be done with it but to throw it out into the highway, where men and beasts trample it down. Dr. Thomson tells of some salt which was brought from the marshes of Cyprus by a merchant of Sidon, and stored in small houses with earthen floors. "The salt next the ground in a few years entirely spoiled. I saw large quantities of it literally thrown into the street. to be trodden under foot of men and beasts. It was good for nothing."—*The Land and the Book*, vol. ii, p. 43.

Schöttgen supposes reference is here made to the bituminous salt from the Dead Sea, which, he says, was strewn over the sacrifices in the temple to neutralize the smell of the burning flesh, and when it became spoiled by exposure it was cast out upon the walks to prevent slipping in wet weather, and was thus literally "trodden under foot of men."

638.—LAMP—BUSHEL—LAMP-STAND.

V, 15. Neither do men light a candle, and put it under a bushel, but on a candlestick. See also Mark iv, 21; Luke viii, 16; xi, 33.

1. " Lamp " would be a better word here than " candle," since oil is what was used for illuminating purposes in Palestine. Though frequent reference is made in Scripture to the lamp, no description of it is given. Many ancient lamps of various shapes and material have been preserved to the present time, and doubtless give some idea of the sort of lamp used in our Saviour's time. The Egyptian monuments have also representations of still earlier lamps, such as were probably used by the Hebrews.

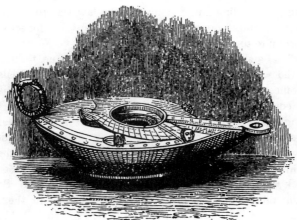

132.—ANCIENT LAMP.

The common lamps among the Greeks and Romans were made of clay, the more costly ones of bronze, and even sometimes of gold. Some of these were very beautiful. Most of the lamps were oval in shape and flat on top, on which there were often figures in relief. A wick floated in the oil or passed through holes in the lamp. The lamps received different names according to the number of holes which they had for the wicks.

See Job xviii, 6; Prov. xxxi, 18; Jer. xxv, 10; Zeph. i, 12; Luke xv, 8. See further note on Matt. xxv, 3.

2. Μόδιος, "bushel," represents the chief Roman dry-measure, the *modius*. Its capacity is reckoned at nearly one peck, English measure.

3. The candlestick or lamp-stand was as varied in shape and quality as the lamp. The rudest sort was to be found sometimes in houses with mud walls, where, in building up the wall, a portion of the clay was suffered to bulge out into the

133.—ANCIENT LAMP-STAND.

room at a suitable height. It was then hollowed; and, when the house was finished, the hollow was filled with oil, and a wick was made to float in it. This contrivance combined lamp and lamp-stand in one utensil. The ordinary lamp-stands were made of wood; the better kinds, of bronze. They were of various heights, and some of them of very beautiful form and workmanship. The lamp-stand is also referred to in Rev. ii. 5.

639.—JOT AND TITTLE.

V, 18. One jot or one tittle shall in no wise pass from the law, till all be fulfilled. See also Luke xvi, 17.

There may be allusion here to the great care taken by the copyists of the law to secure accuracy even to the smallest letters, or curves or points of letters. 'Ιῶτα, "jot," refers to the *yodh*, י, the smallest letter in the Hebrew alphabet; κεραία, "tittle," is an *apex* or *little horn*, and refers to the horn-like points which are seen on Hebrew letters, for example, ב, ד, ה, ח, ר. It is worthy of remark that the *yodh* has one of these points, and the meaning of the text may be, "Not even a *yodh*, nor the point of a *yodh*." The text under consideration is sometimes cited to prove that, in the time of Christ, copies of the law were written in the "square character."

Sometimes curved extensions resembling horns are attached to the letters by the copyists for ornamentation. Prof. Hackett found in one of the synagogues at Safet a scribe engaged in making a copy of the law. He says: "A more elegant Hebrew manuscript, a more perfect specimen of the calligraphic art, I never saw than that executed by this Jewish amanuensis. No printed page could surpass it in the beauty, symmetry, and distinctness with which the characters were drawn. One peculiarity that struck me at once, as I cast my eye over the parchment, was the horn-like appearance attached to some of the letters. I had seen the same mark before this in Hebrew manuscripts, but never where it was so prominent as here. The sign in question, as connected with the Hebrew letter Lamedh [ל] in particular, had almost the appearance of an intentional imitation of a ram's head."—*Illustrations of Scripture*, p. 225.

Dr. Ginsburg, in Kitto's *Cyclopedia*, (s. v., JOT AND TITTLE,) expresses the opinion that the "tittle" refers to certain small ornaments which the Talmudists were accustomed to place upon the tops of letters. They attached great importance to these ornaments, though they formed no special part of the letters.

640.—AGREEING WITH AN ADVERSARY.

V, 25. Agree with thine adversary quickly, while thou art in the way with him; lest at any time the adversary deliver thee to the judge. See also Luke xii, 58.

According to the Roman law, if a person had a quarrel which he could not settle privately he had the right to order his adversary to accompany him to

the prætor. If he refused, the prosecutor took some one present to witness by saying, "May I take you to witness?" If the person consented
he offered the tip of his ear, which the prosecutor touched; a form which
was observed toward witnesses in some other legal ceremonies among the
Romans. Then the plaintiff might drag the defendant to court by force in
any way, even by the neck, (see Matt. xviii, 28;) but worthless persons, such
as thieves and robbers, might be dragged before a judge without the formal-
ity of calling a witness. If on the way to the judge the difficulty was settled, no further legal steps were taken. See ADAM'S *Roman Antiquities*,
12th Ed., p. 98.

To this custom our Saviour refers in the text. When the accused is thus
legally seized by the accuser, he is urged to make up his quarrel while on
the way to the judge, so that no further legal process be had.

641.—PROFANITY.

V, 34. I say unto you, Swear not at all.

The Pharisees taught that there were two kinds of oaths—the violation of
one being perjury, and that of the other an innocent matter, or at most
but a slight offense. If the name of God was in the oath it was binding;
this the Saviour refers to in verse 33. If the name of God was not in the oath
it need not be kept. Jesus, on the other hand, objects to this distinction; and
further teaches that it is wrong to indulge in profanity. The Orientals
were very profuse in their swearing; and examples are found in classic
writers of the different sorts of oaths referred to in verses 34–36. The
habit has continued to the present day, as various travelers have testified.
Among others, Dr. Thomson says: "This people are fearfully profane.
Every body curses and swears when in a passion. No people that I have ever
known can compare with these Orientals for profaneness in the use of the
names and attributes of God. The evil habit seems inveterate and universal.
. . . The people now use the same sorts of oaths that are mentioned and
condemned by our Lord. They swear by the head, by their life, by heaven,
and by the temple, or, what is in its place, the Church. The forms of cursing and swearing, however, are almost infinite, and fall on the pained ear
all day long."—*The Land and the Book*, vol. i, p. 284.

642.—COMPULSORY HELP.

V, 41. Whosoever shall compel thee to go a mile, go with him
twain.

There is reference here to an ancient Persian custom, which was adopted by
the Persian government. The Persians introduced the use of regular couriers
to carry letters or news. See note on Job ix, 25. The king's courier had
absolute command of all help that was necessary in the performance of his

task. He could press horses into his service, and compel the owners to accompany him if he desired. To refuse compliance with his demands was an unpardonable offense against the king.

643.—ALMS-GIVING.

VI, 2. **When thou doest thine alms, do not sound a trumpet before thee, as the hypocrites do in the synagogues and in the streets, that they may have glory of men.**

1. Some have thought from these words that it was customary, literally, to sound a trumpet before an alms-giver. However this might have been in the streets, it certainly could not be permitted "in the synagogues," as it would disturb the services there. There is no evidence whatever that any such custom was ever practiced by alms-givers. The words are therefore to be understood in a figurative sense, which is based on the custom of heralds making public announcements; or there may be an allusion to the trumpet which was sounded before actors and gladiators when they were brought into the theater; or to the trumpet which was sounded six times from the roof of the synagogue to usher in the Sabbath. We have corresponding phrases in modern languages. "In German, *ausposaunen* and *an die grosse Glocke schlagen*; in English, 'to sound one's own trumpet,' 'to trumpet forth,' 'every man his own trumpet;' in French, *faire quelque chose tambour battant, trompetter*; in Italian, *trompetar, bucinar.*"—THOLUCK, *Sermon on the Mount,* p. 298. The idea of the text is simply that alms-giving should be unaccompanied by ostentation.

2. It was customary among the Jews to give alms to the poor who were assembled before the entrance to the temple or synagogue. This is referred to in Acts iii, 3, where the lame man asked alms of Peter and John as they were going into the temple. Chrysostom makes reference to the custom as afterward practiced in front of the early Christian churches. See BINGHAM, *Antiquities of the Christian Church,* Book XIII., chap. viii, § 14. It may be that in the text the word "streets" refers to the space in front of the synagogue.

In the synagogues there was a regular form of giving alms, the offerings being deposited in the alms-boxes before the prayers began. Thus the Saviour speaks first of alms-giving, and next of prayer. Sometimes, on special occasions, the congregation handed their alms to the proper officer.

644.—THE TWO HANDS.

VI, 3. **When thou doest alms, let not thy left hand know what thy right hand doeth.**

This is a proverbial expression, found also in classic and Rabbinical authors. We know of no custom alluded to in this proverb save the general habit of giving with the right hand, as it is more conveniently used than the other; but Mr. Jowett speaks of a custom he noticed in Palestine, which, if it existed in our Lord's time, might have suggested the saying of the text. In giving an account of his visit to Nablous, Mr. Jowett says: "The manner in which the Samaritan priest desired me, on parting, to express our mutual good-will, was by an action, than which there is not one more common in all the Levant. He put the forefinger of his right hand parallel to that of his left, and then rapidly rubbed them together, while I was expected to do the same, repeating the words, 'right, right;' or, in common acceptation, 'together, together.' It is in this manner that persons express their consent on all occasions: on concluding a bargain, on engaging to bear one another company, and on every kind of friendly agreement or good understanding." —*Christian Researches*, etc., p. 209.

The idea of the text may be, that alms-giving is not to be a matter where the hands are put together in token of an understanding with some one else, but it is to be done privately.

645.—REPETITIONS IN PRAYER.

VI, 7. When ye pray, use not vain repetitions, as the heathen do: for they think that they shall be heard for their much speaking.

Some of the rabbis in our Lord's time had taught that oft-repeated prayers were of certain efficacy, thus falling into an imitation of the heathen, who have ever been noted for unmeaning repetitions. When Elijah challenged the worshipers of Baal, they called on their god "from morning even unto noon, saying, O Baal, hear us." 1 Kings xviii, 26. When Paul excited the rage of Demetrius, who in turn aroused the mob at Ephesus, the angry crowd "all with one voice about the space of two hours cried out, Great is Diana of the Ephesians." Acts xix, 34. It would seem as if the further men become removed from true spiritual worship the greater estimate they put on oft-repeated forms. The Mohammedans equal the heathen in this respect. After the storming of Seringapatam, the body of Tippoo Sahib was found among the slain, and in his pocket was a book of devotion with various forms of prayer, and among them the following: "O God, O God, O God, O God! O Lord, O Lord, O Lord, O Lord! O Living, O Immortal! O Living, O Immortal! O Living, O Immortal! O Living, O Immortal! O Creator of the heavens and the earth! O thou who art endowed with majesty and authority! O wonderful," etc.—BURDER, *Oriental Customs*, No. 931.

The Hindus consider the repetition of the name of a god an act of worship. They say the name of God is like fire, through which all sins are consumed; hence the repetition of the names of their deities is a common practice. According to Ward, they even have rosaries, the beads of which

they count off in order to facilitate these repetitions. They imagine that by this easy process they can obtain any thing they desire.

646.—GRASS FOR FUEL.

VI, 30. **The grass of the field, which to-day is, and to-morrow is cast into the oven.** See also Luke xii, 28.

So great is the scarcity of fuel that even dried grass and withered flowers are used for making a fire. They are carefully gathered and carried in bundles, sometimes in the arms, and sometimes loaded on donkeys.

See also note on 1 Kings xvii, 10; and on Psa. lviii, 9.

647.—BREAD RESEMBLING STONES.

VII, 9. **What man is there of you, whom, if his son ask bread, will he give him a stone?** See also Luke xi, 11.

The point of this question will be more apparent when it is remembered that the loaves of bread bore some resemblance in general appearance to round, flat stones. A similar allusion may be noticed in the narrative of our Lord's temptation, where the devil suggests that Jesus change the stones into bread. See Matt. iv, 4; Luke iv, 4.

Some of the bread used in the East at the present time resembles stones in other respects than in mere appearance. Palmer represents the bread, which is daily doled out to the Arabs by the monks of St. Catharine's on Mount Sinai, as of decidedly stony character. He playfully says: "One of these loaves I brought back with me; an eminent geologist, to whom I submitted it, pronounced it 'a piece of metamorphic rock, containing fragments of quartz embedded in an amorphous paste.' No decently brought-up ostrich could swallow one without endangering his digestion for the term of his natural life."—*The Desert of the Exodus*, p. 61.

648.—THE SCRIBES.

VII, 29. **He taught them as one having authority, and not as the scribes.** See also Mark i, 22.

Anciently the scribes were merely officers whose duties included writing of various kinds; but, on the return of the Jews from the Babylonish captivity, the *sopherim*, as the scribes were called, were organized by Ezra into a distinct body, and they became interpreters of God's law as well as copyists. Among other duties, they copied the Pentateuch, the Phylacteries, (see note on Matt. xxiii, 5,) and the Mezuzoth. See note on Deut. vi, 9. So great was their care in copying that they counted and compared all the letters, to be sure that none were left out that belonged to the text, or none admitted improperly. On stated occasions they read the law in the synagogues. They also lectured to their disciples, and commented on the law.

The lawyers (see Matt. xxii, 35; Luke vii, 30; xi, 45; xiv, 3) and the doctors of the law (see Luke ii, 46; v, 17; Acts v, 34) were substantially the same as the scribes. Efforts have been made to show that different classes of duties were assigned to lawyers, doctors, and scribes, but without any very definite results. It may be, as some suppose, that the doctors were a higher grade than the ordinary scribes. The scribes were all carefully educated for their work from early life, and at an appropriate time— some say at the age of thirty—they were admitted to office with special forms of solemnity.

The scribes were not only copyists of the law, but they were also the keepers of the oral traditionary comments and additions to the law. Gradually accumulating with the progress of time these were numerous, and were regarded by many as of equal value with the law itself. To this Jesus alludes in Mark vii, 5–13. Paul represents himself as having been, before his conversion, "exceedingly zealous of the traditions" of his fathers. Gal. i, 14. The scribes also adopted forced interpretations of the law, endeavoring to find a special meaning in every word, syllable, and letter. Thus the Saviour charges them: "Woe unto you, lawyers! for ye have taken away the key of knowledge: ye entered not in yourselves, and them that were entering in ye hindered." Luke xi, 52.

At the time of Christ the people were increasingly dependent on the scribes for a knowledge of their Scriptures. The language of the Jews was passing into the Aramaic dialect, and the mass of the people, being unable to understand their own sacred books, were obliged to accept the interpretation which the scribes put upon them. Hence their astonishment, as indicated in the text, at the peculiar style of teaching adopted by Jesus, and especially illustrated in his Sermon on the Mount. The scribes repeated traditions; Jesus spake with authority: "I say unto you." They had but little sympathy with the masses; he went about mingling with the people, and explaining to them in a simple practical way the duties of religion.

649.—THE BED.

IX, 6. Arise, take up thy bed, and go unto thine house. See also Mark ii, 9–12.

The "bed" was simply a mat or blanket which could be carried in the hands. The poor sometimes had no other bed than the outer garment. See note on Deut. xxiv, 12, 13. The wealthier people in the East have quilts or mattresses filled with cotton, which are spread on the floor or on the divan. See note on 2 Kings i, 4. In the text the paralytic, being healed, was told to take up his bed and go home. All he had to do was to roll up his blanket

134—ROLLING UP A BED.

and depart. A similar incident took place at the pool of Bethesda. See John v, 8, 9, 11, 12. On such simple "beds" the sick were easily carried. This is referred to in Matt. ix, 2; Mark ii, 3, 4; Luke v, 18; Acts v, 15.

650.—USE OF THE TERM CHILDREN.

IX, 15. **Jesus said unto them, Can the children of the bride-chamber mourn, as long as the bridegroom is with them?** See also Mark ii, 19; Luke v, 84.

The "children of the bride-chamber" were the friends and acquaintances who participated in the marriage festivities. The expression "child" or "children," like that of "father," (see note on Gen. iv, 20, 21,) is an Oriental form of speech, and is designed to show some relation between the person to whom it is applied and certain qualities existing in that person, or certain circumstances connected with him; these qualities or circumstances being the result of that relation. Thus people who are brought together on occasion of a marriage-feast are called the "children of the bride-chamber." So when any passion or influence, good or bad, gets control of men, they are said to be the children of that passion or influence. Thus we have "children of wickedness," 2 Sam. vii, 10; "children of pride," Job xli, 34; "children of the kingdom," and "children of the wicked one," Matt. xiii, 38; "children of this world," and "children of light," Luke xvi, 8; "children of disobedience," Eph. ii, 2; Col. iii, 6; "children of wrath," Eph. ii, 3.

We find a similar idiom in the use of the word "son" and "daughter." We have "sons of Belial" in Judges xix, 22, and in several other passages; "sons of the mighty," Psa. lxxxix, 6; "sons of thunder," Mark iii, 17; "son of consolation," Acts iv, 36; "son of perdition," 2 Thess. ii, 3. We have also "daughter of Belial," 1 Sam. i, 16; "daughters of music," Eccl. xii, 4; "daughter of troops," Micah v, 1.

651.—SKIN-BOTTLES.

IX, 17. Neither do men put new wine into old bottles: else the bottles break, and the wine runneth out, and the bottles perish: but they put new wine into new bottles, and both are preserved. See also Mark ii, 22; Luke v, 37.

The use of bottles made from the skins of animals is very ancient, and is still practiced in the East. The skins of goats and kids are commonly taken for this purpose, and are usually so fashioned as to retain the figure of the animal. In preparing the bottle, the head and feet are cut off, and the skin

185.—ANCIENT SKIN-BOTTLES.

stripped whole from the body. The neck of the animal sometimes makes the neck of the bottle; in other cases one of the fore-legs is used as an aperture through which the liquid may be poured out. The thighs serve as handles; by attaching straps to them the bottle can be fastened to the saddle, or slung over the shoulder of the traveler. The Arabs tan the skins with Acacia bark and leave the hairy side out. For a large party, and for long journeys across the desert, the skins of camels or of oxen are used. Two of these, when filled with water, make a good load for a camel. They are smeared with grease to prevent leakage and evaporation. These water-skins, large and small, are much better than earthen jars or bottles for the rough experiences of Oriental traveling. Earthen bottles are, however, sometimes employed in domestic use. See note on Jer. xix, 1.

The "bottle" which Hagar carried into the wilderness, and from which she gave Ishmael drink, was probably a kid-skin. See Gen. xxi, 14. A similar scene is represented in the engraving,

136.—WOMAN GIVING DRINK TO A CHILD FROM A SKIN-BOTTLE.

from an ancient Assyrian sculpture. Skin-bottles were also used for milk (Judges iv, 19) and for wine (1 Sam. xvi, 20.) In the text and its parallels allusion is made to this use of skins. When the skin is green, it stretches by fermentation of the liquor and retains its integrity; but when it becomes old and dry, the fermentation of the new wine soon causes it to burst.

For the mode of repairing skin-bottles when broken, see note on Josh. ix, 4.

652.—FRINGES.

IX, 20. Came behind him, and touched the hem of his garment. See also Luke viii, 44.

According to the Mosaic law every Jew was obliged to wear a fringe or tassel at each of the four corners of the outer garment, one thread of each tassel to be deep blue. These tassels were to be to them a perpetual reminder of the law of God, and of their duty to keep it. See Num. xv, 38, 39; Deut. xxii, 12. This was the "hem" which the poor woman touched, supposing there was some peculiar virtue in it. So the people of Gennesaret brought their sick to Christ for a similar purpose. See Mark vi, 56, where the same word in the original, κράσπεδον, is rendered "border." The Pharisees prided themselves greatly on these tassels, considering them as marks of special sanctity in the wearers, and therefore sought to enlarge their size. See Matt. xxiii, 5.

653.—THE PURSE.

X, 9. Provide neither gold, nor silver, nor brass in your purses. See also Mark vi, 8; Luke x, 4.

"In your purses," is literally "in your *girdles*," (ζώνας.) It is quite common to use the folds of the girdle as a pouch, or pocket, for the reception of money. Money is also sometimes carried in a bag, which is put into the girdle. This is referred to in the parallel passage in Luke, where the word rendered "purse" (βαλαντιον) signifies a bag.

654.—SHOES.

X, 10. Neither shoes. See also Luke x, 4.

From the fact that, in the parallel passage in Mark vi, 9, the disciples are commanded to be "shod with sandals," it has been inferred that our Lord designed to mark a distinction between shoes and sandals, though some commentators treat the idea as absurd. It is certain, however, that in our Lord's time there were, besides sandals, other coverings for the feet more nearly approaching our idea of a shoe. Some of these covered the entire foot, while in others the toes were left bare, as represented in the engraving.

187.—ANCIENT SHOES.

The use of shoes may have been forbidden to the disciples because of their luxury, while sandals were allowed as articles of necessity. Thus the statement in Matthew and in Luke, and that in Mark, may be reconciled. The shoe was forbidden, the sandal permitted.

When the prodigal came back to his father's house shoes were put on his feet. Luke xv, 22.

For a description of sandals, see note on Acts xii, 8.

655.—HEATHEN DUST.

X, 14. When ye depart out of that house or city, shake off the dust of your feet. See also Mark vi, 11 ; Luke ix, 5.

The schools of the scribes taught that the dust of heathen lands was defiling. They therefore objected even to bringing plants or herbs from heathen countries, lest some of the dust should come with them. Some of the rabbins permitted this, provided no dust was brought with the plants. They give this gloss to the rule : "They take care lest, together with the herbs, something of the dust of the heathen land be brought, which defiles in the tent, and defiles the purity of the land of Israel." See LIGHTFOOT, *Horæ Hebraicæ*.

The Saviour, doubtless, alluded to this rabbinical rule, and, by using the expression of the text, conveyed the idea to his disciples that every place which should reject them was to be considered heathen, impure, profane.

When Paul and Barnabas were driven from Antioch, in Pisidia, "they shook off the dust of their feet." See Acts xiii, 51.

656.—COUNCILS—DISCIPLINE OF THE SYNAGOGUE.

X, 17. They will deliver you up to the councils, and they will scourge you in their synagogues. See also Mark xiii, 9.

1. In addition to the Great Sanhedrim or Council (for a description of which see note on Matt. xxvi, 59) there were councils of an inferior degree. There is some obscurity in connection with their history and construction. They are supposed to have been originated by Moses. See Deut. xvi, 18. In later times there were two of them in Jerusalem, and one in each town in Palestine. The rabbins say there were twenty-three judges to each of these councils in every place where the population was a hundred and twenty, and three judges where the population was less. Josephus, however, says that there were seven judges to each council, and that each judge had two Levites to assist him.

These councils had power not only to judge civil cases, but also such criminal cases as did not come within the jurisdiction of the Supreme Court, or Sanhedrim. In the provinces they at first met in the market-place, but afterward in a room adjoining the synagogue. Some writers suppose that these local provincial councils are identical with the "elders" and "rulers of the synagogue," so often mentioned in the New Testament. See article "Synagogue," in Kitto's *Cyclopedia*, vol. iii, p. 902 *b*. See, further, note on Acts xiii, 15. The connection in the text between councils and scourging seems to indicate this, unless it can be shown, as some have asserted, that the "rulers of the synagogue" formed a council apart from the smaller Sanhedrim.

2. The discipline of the synagogue was severe. Besides excommunication, (see note on John ix, 22,) scourging was sometimes practiced. The number of the stripes was limited by law to forty. Deut. xxv, 3. To prevent the possibility of excess, by mistake in counting, the legal number was reduced by one. Paul was thus beaten five distinct times. 2 Cor. xi, 24. It is said, however, that in aggravated cases the stripes were laid on with greater severity than usual.

The rabbins reckon a hundred and sixty-eight faults to be punished by scourging; in fact, all punishable faults to which the law has not annexed the penalty of death. "The offender was stripped from his shoulders to his middle, and tied by his arms to a pretty low pillar, that he might lean forward, and the executioner might more easily come at his back. . . . It is said that, after the stripping of the criminal, the executioner mounted upon a stone, to have more power over him, and then scourged him both on the back and breasts with thongs made of an ox's hide, in open court, before the face of the judges."—Burder, *Oriental Customs*, No. 949.

Scourging in the synagogues is also referred to in Matt. xxiii, 34. Paul admits that in his days of wickedness he had in this manner maltreated Christians. Acts xxii, 19.

For an account of Roman scourging, see note on Matt. xxvii, 26. •

657.—PUBLIC PROCLAMATIONS.

X, 27. **What ye hear in the ear, that preach ye upon the house-tops. See also Luke xii, 3.**

Public proclamations are still made from the housetops by the governors of country districts in Palestine. Thomson says: "Their proclamations are generally made in the evening, after the people have returned from their labors in the field. The public crier ascends the highest roof at hand, and lifts up his voice in a long-drawn call upon all faithful subjects to give ear and obey. He then proceeds to announce, in a set form, the will of their master, and demand obedience thereto."—*The Land and the Book*, vol. i, p. 51.

In the contrast expressed between hearing privately and proclaiming publicly, there may also be reference to the mode of instruction in the schools of the rabbis. Lightfoot expresses this opinion, and says: "The doctor whispered, out of the chair, into the ear of the interpreter, and he, with a loud voice, repeated to the whole school that which was spoken in the ear." —*Horæ Hebraicæ.* He also suggests that the reference to the house-tops may be an allusion to the custom of sounding the synagogue trumpet from the roof to usher in the Sabbath. See note on Matt. vi, 2.

658.—THE ASSARIUS.

X, 29. Are not two sparrows sold for a farthing?

'Ασσάριον is one of the two words rendered "farthing" in our version. It was the Roman *as* or *assarius*, a copper coin, equal in value to a tenth of a *denarius*, (see note on Matt. xx, 2,) or three farthings English, or one cent and a half American.

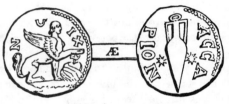

138.—ASSARION.

In Luke xii, 6, two *assaria* are spoken of. It is thought that a single coin is there intended of the value of two *assaria*. The Vulgate has *dipondius*. Madden says: "It is very clear from the fact of the word *dupondius, or dipondius,* which was equal to two *asses,* and was a coin of itself, being substituted for the two *assaria* of the Greek text, that a single coin is intended by this latter expression. This idea is fully borne out by the coins of Chios. The Greek autonomous copper coins of this place have inscribed upon them the words ACCAPION, ACCAPIA ΔΥΩ or ΔΥΟ and ACCAPIA TPIA."—*History of Jewish Coinage,* p. 243.

659.—GAMES OF CHILDREN.

XI, 16, 17. It is like unto children sitting in the markets, and calling unto their fellows, and saying, We have piped unto you, and ye have not danced; we have mourned unto you, and ye have not lamented. See also Luke vii, 31, 32.

There is allusion here to the habits of children, who, in the East as elsewhere, imitate in sport what they see performed in sober earnest by adults. The public processions and rejoicings on Oriental wedding occasions, and the great lamentations at funerals, make such an impression on the young mind that children introduce imitations of them into their plays. Some of them play on imaginary pipes, while others dance, as at weddings. Again, some of them set up an imitation of a mournful wail, to which others respond in doleful lamentations, as at funerals. Then at times there will be found some stubborn little ones, of perverse spirit, who will not consent to take part in any play that may be proposed. They will not dance while others pipe, neither will they lament when others mourn. They are determined not to be pleased in any way; they will play neither wedding nor funeral. Thus it was that the people would receive neither Jesus nor John; but, like perverse children, they refused to be satisfied with any proposition made to them.

Travelers have noticed that children in Palestine, at the present day, keep up this ancient custom of playing weddings and funerals.

660.—FREE CORN FOR THE HUNGRY.

XII, 1. His disciples were an hungered, and began to pluck the ears of corn, and to eat. See also Mark ii, 23; Luke vi, 1.

It was perfectly lawful for persons when hungry to help themselves to as much of their neighbor's growing grain as they wished for food. They were not allowed to cut any, but must simply gather what was needed with the hand. "When thou comest into the standing corn of thy neighbor, then thou mayest pluck the ears with thine hand: but thou shalt not move a sickle unto thy neighbor's standing corn." Deut. xxiii, 25. The Pharisees did not complain that the corn was plucked, but that it was gathered on the Sabbath.

This ancient freedom of a handful of grain for a hungry traveler is still in existence in Palestine.

661.—TESTIMONY GIVEN STANDING.

XII, 41. The men of Nineveh shall rise in judgment with this generation, and shall condemn it. See also Luke xi, 32.

The Saviour may have alluded to a custom among the Jews and Romans, whereby the witnesses rose in their seats when they made accusation or bore testimony. The "Queen of the South" is in like manner represented as rising in judgment. See verse 42, and Luke xi, 31. The dying Stephen saw "the Son of man standing on the right hand of God." Acts vii, 56. May he not have risen to bear testimony against Stephen's persecutors?

The same custom is alluded to in Luke xxiii, 10.

662.—FISHING-BOATS.

XIII, 2. He went into a ship, and sat. See also Mark iv, 1.

We have no special description of the ships which were used on the Sea of Galilee. The most of them were probably small boats used for fishing purposes, and propelled by oars, while some had masts and sails. There were doubtless others which were used for pleasure or for passage; and Josephus tells us of some in his day that were vessels of war. Frequent mention is made by the evangelists of the ships on the Sea of Galilee.

22

663.—GOING FORTH TO SOW.

XIII, 3. Behold, a sower went forth to sow. See also Mark iv, 3;
Luke viii, 5.

According to Dr. Thomson, this statement is more literally true than would
appear to a hasty reader. The farmers in Palestine *go forth* to sow their
seed, the fields being at a considerable distance from their homes, sometimes
six or eight miles. See *The Land and the Book*, vol. i, pp. 115–118.

664.—THE WAY–SIDE.

XIII, 4. When he sowed, some seeds fell by the way-side. See
also Mark iv, 4; Luke viii, 5.

The ordinary roads or paths often lead by the side of uninclosed fields;
hence it must often happen that the seed thrown by the hand of the sower
will be scattered beyond the plowed field, and fall on the beaten path.

665.—WICKEDNESS AT NIGHT.

XIII, 25. But while men slept, his enemy came and sowed
tares among the wheat, and went his way.

Roberts states that the exact counterpart of this nocturnal villainy may
be found in India at the present day. A man wishing to do his enemy an
injury, watches for the time when he shall have finished plowing his field,
and in the night he goes into the field and scatters *pandinellu*, or "pig-
paddy." "This being of rapid growth springs up before the good seed, and
scatters itself before the other can be reaped, so that the poor owner of the
field will be some years before he can rid the soil of the troublesome weed.
But there is another noisome plant which these wretches cast into the
ground of those whom they hate: it is called *perum-pirandi*, and is more
destructive to vegetation than any other plant. Has a man purchased a field
which another intended to buy, the disappointed person declares, 'I will
plant the *perum-pirandi* in his grounds.'"—*Oriental Illustrations*, p. 530.

666.—LEAVEN.

XIII, 33. The kingdom of heaven is like unto leaven. See also
Luke xiii, 21.

The usual leaven among the Jews consisted of dough in a high state of
fermentation, though the lees of wine were sometimes employed.

667.—HIDDEN TREASURE.

XIII, 44. The kingdom of heaven is like unto treasure hid in a
field.

The possession of wealth often becomes, in the East, a source of great
perplexity because of its insecurity. Every man being his own banker,

ingenuity is taxed to devise some plan of concealment, or to find some place where money, jewels, and other valuables may remain free from molestation or suspicion. Sometimes these treasures are hidden in secret closets in the house, or in vaults under the house; sometimes they are buried in the field, in a spot unknown to all save the owner. It not unfrequently happens that the owner goes away and dies before the time of his intended return, his secret dying with him. Times of war and pestilence carry off great numbers, who leave treasures concealed, no one knows where. There are, no doubt, deposits of immense value thus buried in different parts of the East. The people are always ready to notice any indication of subterranean wealth, and to dig for it when they get the opportunity. The archæological explorations of travelers are often seriously retarded by the suspicions aroused that they have some secret means of ascertaining the location of hidden treasures, and that the great object of all their exploring is to get money and jewels.

These facts illustrate the text. A man who discovers the place where treasure is hid keeps the discovery to himself, buys the field, and the treasure is his own. Other references of a similar character are made in different parts of the Bible, showing how ancient and how widespread is the custom of concealing treasures. It was thus that Achan hid the spoils of war in the earth in the midst of his tent. Josh. vii, 21. Job represents men who are weary of life, longing for death with the eagerness of treasure-seekers. They "dig for it more than for hid treasures." They "rejoice exceedingly, and are glad, when they can find the grave." Job iii, 21, 22. Solomon, perhaps, alludes to this custom when he speaks of those who search after wisdom "as for hid treasures," (Prov. ii, 4,) though the reference may be, as some think, to mining operations. He may also refer to it when he says that "the abundance of the rich will not suffer him to sleep." Eccl. v, 12. The more treasure one has the more care he must take to conceal it, and the fear of discovery would naturally create sleeplessness. God's promise to Cyrus is a further illustration: "I will give thee the treasures of darkness, and hidden riches of secret places." Isa. xlv, 3. In the parable of the talents, the servant who had but one talent buried it in the earth. Matt. xxv, 18.

Wheat, oil, and other products of the soil, were also buried. See note on Jer. xli, 8.

668.—FISHING NETS.

XIII, 47. The kingdom of heaven is like unto a net, that was cast into the sea, and gathered of every kind.

The precise form of the fishing nets used by the Hebrews is not known; nor do we know the exact difference between the meanings to be attached to the several words which are translated "net." A kind of net very commonly used resembled the modern seine. It is a net of this sort that is referred to here. Some suppose that in John xxi, 6, there is also an allusion to this kind of net, but others think that a net for deep-sea fishing is there meant; a net so arranged as to inclose the fish in deep water. Such a net seems to be intended in Luke v, 4, where the command is given, "Launch out into the deep, and let down your nets for a draught."

In the Old Testament, fishing nets are referred to in Hab. i, 15, 16.

669.—EXTRAVAGANT PROMISES.

XIV, 7. He promised with an oath to give her whatsoever she would ask. See also Mark vi, 23.

It is common for public dancers at festivals in great houses to ask for rewards from the company. An instance is recorded by Thevenot, in his *Travels in Persia*, which reminds us of this extravagant promise of Herod. Shah Abbas was on one occasion so pleased with the performances of a dancing-woman that he gave her the fairest khan in all Ispahan, one which yielded large revenues to the royal treasury. He was drunk at the time, and, when he became sober, repented of his rash generosity, and compelled the girl to accept, instead, a sum of money very far below the value of the khan.

670.—THANKS AT MEALS.

XIV, 19. He took the five loaves, and the two fishes, and looking up to heaven, he blessed, and brake. See also Mark vi, 41; Luke ix, 16; John vi, 11.

It was customary among the Jews to give thanks to God at the commencement of every meal. The usual form was, "Blessed be thou, O Lord our God. the king of the world, who produced bread out of the earth." They also had a form of blessing for the wine: "Blessed art thou, O Lord, the king of the world, who created the fruit of the vine." These, or similar forms, were used at the celebration of the passover. See note on Matt. xxvi, 20. Paul, in allusion to this custom, calls the wine used in the Lord's supper "the cup of blessing." 1 Cor. x, 16. The expression "bless the sacrifice" in 1 Sam. ix, 13, is also an allusion to the custom of asking a blessing before eating, the reference being to those parts of the peace-offering which were to be eaten by the offerer and his friends. See note on Lev. vii, 11.

In compliance with the ancient Jewish custom, the Saviour, before feeding the five thousand, blessed God for the gift bestowed. At another time, when four thousand were fed, "he took the seven loaves and the fishes, and gave thanks, and brake them." Matt. xv, 36. See also Mark viii, 6, 7.

671.—BASKETS.

XIV, 20. They took up of the fragments that remained twelve baskets full. See also Mark vi, 43; Luke ix, 17; John vi, 13.

The baskets now used in the East resemble very much those which are represented on the monuments of Egypt. They are often like our own in shape, material, and workmanship.

The baskets here referred to (κόφινοι) were probably the ordinary traveling baskets which the Jews took with them when on a journey. They carried their provisions in them, so that they might not be polluted by eating the food of the Gentiles; and it is also said that they sometimes carried hay in them, on which they slept at night. Thus they kept aloof from the Gentiles in food and lodging. This will account for the contemptuous description which Juvenal gives of the Jews, when he represents that their household goods consisted of a basket and hay!

In the corresponding miracle, where four thousand were fed, a different kind of basket was employed. See Matt. xv, 37; Mark viii, 8; and especially Matt. xvi, 9, 10; Mark viii, 19, 20; where, in the original, two different terms are used. It is impossible, however, now to tell the precise difference between the two sorts of baskets mentioned.

672.—TRADITION.

XV, 8. Why do ye also transgress the commandment of God by your tradition? See also Mark vii, 9.

Lightfoot (*Horæ Hebraicæ*, on verse 2) gives a number of curious illustrations from the old Talmudical writers, showing the value which they set on traditions: "The words of the scribes are lovely, above the words of the law; for the words of the law are weighty and light, but the words of the scribes are all weighty." "The words of the elders are weightier than the words of the prophets." "A prophet and an elder, to what are they likened? To a king sending two of his servants into a province. Of one he writes thus: Unless he shows you my seal, believe him not; of the other thus: Although he shows you not my seal, yet believe him. Thus it is written of the prophet. He shall show thee a sign or a miracle; but the elders thus: According to the law which they shall teach thee."

673.—BINDING AND LOOSING.

XVI, 19. Whatsoever thou shalt bind on earth shall be bound in heaven: and whatsoever thou shalt loose on earth shall be loosed in heaven.

Lightfoot gives a large number of citations from rabbinical authorities to show the common usage in the Jewish schools of the words "bind" and

" loose," and also the meaning of these figurative terms. To "bind" is to forbid; to "loose" is to allow. Rosenmüller says: "Binding and loosing—that is, prohibiting and permitting—were, in the Aramaic language, which Jesus used, a customary expression to denote the highest authority. So in the *Syriac Chronicle* of Gregory Bar-Hebræus, or Abul-faraj, it is said (p. 593 :) 'The Jew who yesterday was the highest ruler, could *bind and loose*, and wore royal garments, to-day wore a smock-frock. His hands were no longer blackened with writing, but with painting. He was a beggar, and no more lord.' "—*Morgenland*, vol. v, p. 67.

674.—THE TEMPLE-TAX.

XVII, 24. They that received tribute-money came to Peter, and said, Doth not your Master pay tribute ?

Literally, Doth not your master pay the *didrachm*, or *double drachma?* This was not the tax for the support of the civil government, but the half-shekel tax for the support of the temple-service, which every Jew was expected to pay. It was founded by Moses, in connection with the tabernacle service. See Exod. xxx, 13. It is also referred to in 2 Kings xii, 4; 2 Chron. xxiv, 6, 9. Its value was about thirty cents.

675.—THE STATER.

XVII, 27. When thou hast opened his mouth, thou shalt find a piece of money : that take, and give unto them for me and thee.

This " piece of money " was a *stater*, which term was applied to coins of gold, of silver, and of an alloy of the two precious metals of the color of amber, and therefore called *electrum*. The *stater*, which was miraculously provided for tribute-money, is supposed to have been one of the tetradrachms of the cities of Syria. It was a silver coin, having the same weight as the shekel, and its value was about sixty cents of our money. This one coin was thus of sufficient value to pay the temple-tax of both Jesus and Peter.

676.—MILLSTONE—DROWNING.

XVIII, 6. It were better for him that a millstone were hanged about his neck, and that he were drowned in the depth of the sea. See also Mark ix, 42; Luke xvii, 2.

1. The ordinary upper-stone of the Eastern hand-mill is from eighteen inches to two feet across, and might easily be hung around the neck of a person to be drowned. Some commentators, however, are of the opinion that, by the "ass-millstone," as the original in both Matthew and Mark may be rendered, is meant a stone larger than that used in the ordinary mills—one so large as to require brute-power to turn it. Such a stone would sink a body in the depths of the sea beyond the possibility of recovery.

2. There is no evidence to show that the mode of punishment named in the text was ever practiced by the Jews. It was in use, however, by the ancient Syrians, the Romans, the Macedonians, and the Greeks. It was inflicted on the worst class of criminals, especially on parricides, and on those guilty of sacrilege.

677.—" NINETY AND NINE."

XVIII, 12. If a man have a hundred sheep, and one of them be gone astray, doth he not leave the ninety and nine, and goeth into the mountains, and seeketh that which is gone astray? See also Luke xv, 4, 7.

This mode of expression was very common with the Jews. Lightfoot cites from the Talmud a passage illustrative of it: " When a man is dividing nuts among the poor, though ninety-nine call upon him to divide them, and one call on him to scatter them, to him they must hearken. With grapes and dates it is not so. Though ninety-nine call on him to scatter them, and one to divide them, to him they must hearken."

678.—" TWO OR THREE."

XVIII, 20. Where two or three are gathered together in my name.

This is a common Oriental form of speech to express an indefinite number. There are other instances of it in the Bible. See 1 Kings xvii, 12; Isa. vii, 21; xvii, 6; Jer. iii, 14; Hos. vi, 2. Some commentators, however, suppose the passage in Hosea to refer to the resurrection of Christ; but it is by no means certain.

679.—TORMENTORS.

XVIII, 34. His lord was wroth, and delivered him to the tormentors, till he should pay all that was due unto him.

The "tormentors" are the jailers, who were allowed to scourge and torture the poor debtors in their care in order to get money from them for the grasping creditors, or else to excite the compassion of friends, and obtain the amount of the debt from them. " In early times of Rome there were certain legal tortures, in the shape, at least, of a chain weighing fifteen pounds, and a pittance of food barely sufficient to sustain life, (see ARNOLD'S *History of Rome*, vol. i, p. 136,) which the creditor was allowed to apply to the debtor for the purpose of bringing him to terms; and no doubt they often did not stop here."—TRENCH, *Notes on the Parables*, (Am. ed.,) p. 133.

680.—BENEDICTIONS ON CHILDREN.

XIX, 13. Then were there brought unto him little children, that he should put his hands on them, and pray. See also Mark x, 13; Luke xviii, 15.

It was common among the Jews to bring their children to men noted for piety, to have their blessing and their prayers. On the first anniversary of the birth of a child, it was usual to take it to the synagogue to be blessed by the rabbi.

The laying-on of hands when in prayer was also a customary form when invoking the Divine blessing. Thus Israel, when his eyes were dim with age, laid his hands on the heads of Ephraim and Manasseh, and blessed them and prayed for them, (Gen. xlviii, 14;) and thus Jesus took these children "up in his arms, put his hands upon them, and blessed them." Mark x, 16.

681.—THE "NEEDLE'S EYE."

XIX, 24. **It is easier for a camel to go through the eye of a needle, than for a rich man to enter into the kingdom of God.** See also Mark x, 25; Luke xviii, 25.

There is supposed to be here a reference to a proverbial form of expression common in the Jewish schools, when one desired to express the idea of great difficulty or of impossibility. Lightfoot gives several quotations from the rabbis, where the difficulty is represented by the image of an elephant going through the eye of a needle.

Some writers, however, think that there is allusion in the text, not only to a proverbial form of speech, but also to a fact. They refer to the low, narrow entrances to Oriental houses, and to the difficulty a camel would experience in entering, though even a camel might enter if he would take off his load and kneel down; which may be considered a hint to rich men who would enter the kingdom of heaven.

A recent English writer says: "In Oriental cities there are in the large gates small and very low apertures, called, metaphorically, 'needles'-eyes,' just as we talk of certain windows as 'bulls'-eyes.' These entrances are too narrow for a camel to pass through them in the ordinary manner, or even if loaded. When a laden camel has to pass through one of these entrances it kneels down, its load is removed, and then it shuffles through on its knees. 'Yesterday,' writes Lady Duff Gordon from Cairo, 'I saw a camel go through the eye of a needle, namely, the low-arched door of an inclosure. He must kneel, and bow his head to creep through; and thus the rich man must humble himself.' "—*Bible Animals*, by the Rev. J. G. WOOD, p. 243.

682.—HIRING LABORERS.

XX, 1. **Went out early in the morning to hire laborers into his vineyard.**

Lightfoot (*Horæ Hebraicæ*) gives several citations from Jewish writers to show that the customary time of working was "from sun-rising to the appearing of the stars, and not from break of day." The laborers, however, may have been *hired* before sunrise.

683.—THE DENARIUS.

XX, 2. When he had agreed with the laborers for a penny a day, he sent them into his vineyard.

The *denarius* (penny) was the principal silver coin of the Romans. It was originally ten times the value of the *as*, (see note on Matt. x, 29,) from which

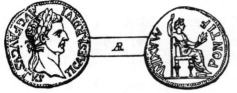

139.—DENARIUS OF TIBERIUS CESAR.

circumstance it derived its name. When, afterward, the weight of the *as* was reduced, the *denarius* was made equal to the weight of sixteen *asses*. The value of the earlier *denarius* was a little over eightpence half-penny, or about seventeen cents; that of the later was sevenpence half-penny, or fifteen cents. This was the ordinary price of a day's labor.

Under the Republic the *denarius* had on one side the head of Hercules, Apollo, Mars, Janus, or Jupiter; but under the Empire it bore the title and effigies of the reigning Cesar. See Matt. xxii, 19-21; Mark xii, 15-17.

The "ten pieces of silver" mentioned in Luke xv, 8, are supposed to have been *denarii;* and so are the "fifty thousand pieces of silver" mentioned in Acts xix, 19, though authorities vary in opinion.

684.—THE MARKET-PLACE.

XX, 3. He went out about the third hour, and saw others standing idle in the market-place.

The place for trading was often at the gates of walled cities. See note on 2 Kings vii, 1. Here, also, laborers went to seek employment, and employers went to seek laborers. Sometimes, in Oriental cities, a large public square is used for similar purposes. Morier says: "The most conspicuous building in Hamadan is the Mesjid Jumah, a large mosque now falling into decay, and before it a *maidan* or square, which serves as a market-place. Here we observed every morning, before the sun rose, that a numerous body of peasants were collected with spades in their hands, waiting, as they informed us, to be hired for the day to work in the surrounding fields."— *Second Journey through Persia,* p. 265.

685.—DAILY PAYMENT OF LABORERS.

XX, 8. So when even was come, the lord of the vineyard saith unto his steward, Call the laborers, and give them their hire.

This was according to the Mosaic law, which sought thus to protect the poor laborer from any employer who might wish to keep back his hire.

"The wages of him that is hired shall not abide with thee all night until the morning." Lev. xix, 13.   "Thou shalt not oppress a hired servant that is poor and needy, whether he be of thy brethren, or of thy strangers that are in thy land within thy gates: at his day thou shalt give him his hire, neither shall the sun go down upon it; for he is poor, and setteth his heart upon it." Deut. xxiv, 14, 15.

686.—POST OF HONOR.

XX, 21. Grant that these my two sons may sit, the one on thy right hand, and the other on the left, in thy kingdom. See also Mark x, 37.

It was evidently the intention of this ambitious mother to have positions of the greatest honor for her two sons.   The right hand is usually considered the post of the highest honor.   See 1 Kings ii, 19; Psa. xlv, 9; lxxx, 17. For this reason Jesus is said to be at the right hand of God.   See Psa. cx, 1; Mark xiv, 62; xvi, 19; Luke xx, 42; xxii, 69; Acts ii, 34; vii, 55, 56; Rom. viii, 34; Eph. i, 20; Col. iii, 1; Heb. i, 3, 13; viii, 1; x, 12; xii, 2; 1 Pet. iii, 22.   As an apparent exception to this usage, Sir John Chardin states that among the Persians the *left* hand of the king is esteemed the most honorable.   See *Coronation of Solyman III.*, p. 42.   In the East generally, although the right hand may be esteemed more honorable than the left, yet a position on either hand near the king is considered a post of great honor. Josephus represents Saul at supper with Jonathan his son on his right hand, and Abner the captain of his host on his left. *Antiquities*, book vi, chap. ii, § 9. The same fact is intimated, though not expressed, in 1 Sam. xx, 25.   In the Sanhedrim the vice-president sat on the right hand of the president, and the referee, who was the officer next in rank, sat on the left.   See note on Matt. xxvi, 59.

687.—GARMENTS AND BRANCHES STREWN.

XXI, 8. A very great multitude spread their garments in the way; others cut down branches from the trees, and strewed them in the way. See also Mark xi, 8; Luke xix, 36; John xii, 13.

1. The "garments" were the large outer mantles.   See note on Deut. xxiv, 12, 13.

2. It was usual to strew flowers and branches, and to spread carpets and garments in the way of conquerors and great princes, and of others to whom it was intended to show particular honor and respect.   In a similar way Jehu was recognized as king: "Then they hasted, and took every man his garment, and put it under him on the top of the stairs, and blew with trumpets, saying, Jehu is king." 2 Kings ix, 13.   When Xerxes crossed the Hellespont his way was strewed with myrtle branches.   When Cato left his army and returned to Rome garments were strewn in his way.

The cus'om is still sometimes seen in the East. Roberts was surprised, shortly after his arrival in India, to find, on paying a visit to a native gentleman, that the path through the garden was covered with white garments on which he was expected to walk. They were spread as a token of respect for him. Dr. Robinson relates that shortly after a rebellion which had taken place among the people of Bethlehem, " when some of the inhabitants were already imprisoned, and all were in deep distress, Mr. Farran, then English consul at Damascus, was on a visit to Jerusalem, and had rode out with Mr. Nicolayson to Solomon's pools. On their return, as they rose the ascent to enter Bethlehem, hundreds of the people, male and female, met them, imploring the consul to interfere in their behalf, and afford them his protection; and all at once, by a sort of simultaneous movement, ' they spread their garments in the way' before the horses."—*Biblical Researches*, vol. i, p. 473.

688.—THE TEMPLE MARKET.

XXI, 12. Jesus went into the temple of God, and cast out all them that sold and bought in the temple, and overthrew the tables of the money-changers, and the seats of them that sold doves. See also Mark xi, 15; Luke xix, 45.

In John ii, 14, is an account of a similar occurrence which took place during the first year of Christ's ministry.

This temple market is supposed to have been established after the captivity, when many came from foreign lands to Jerusalem. Lightfoot says: " There was always a constant market in the temple in that place, which was called ' the shops ; ' where, every day, was sold wine, salt, oil, and other requisites to sacrifices; as also oxen and sheep in the spacious Court of the Gentiles."
—*Horæ Hebraicæ.*

The money-changers made a business of accommodating those who had not the Jewish half-shekel for the annual temple tax. See note on Matt. xvii, 24. Every one, rich and poor, was expected to pay the half-shekel for himself during the month of Adar. It thus became necessary sometimes to change a shekel into two halves, or to exchange foreign money for the Jewish half-shekel. The men who followed this business made their living by charging a percentage for the exchange, and carried on their traffic within the temple area.

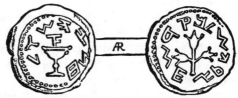

140.—HALF-SHEKEL. ASCRIBED TO SIMON MACCABEUS.

Loftus found a curious resemblance to this practice in the court of the mosque of Meshed Ali at Nedjef: " A constant fair is carried on at stalls, which are supplied with every article likely as offerings to attract the eye of the rich or pious—among these, white *doves* are particularly conspicuous."— *Travels in Chaldea and Susiana*, p. 53.

689.—THE CHILDREN'S SONG.

XXI, 15. The children crying in the temple, and saying, Hosanna to the son of David.

The Jewish children, when very young, were taught to wave the branches of palm and boughs of myrtle and willow bound together, which were used at the Feast of Tabernacles; and also, while shaking them, to join in the chorus of Hosanna. It is a fact worth noticing, we think, that these children shouted Hosanna, not simply in childish imitation of the multitude. (verse 8,) but in recollection of what they had been taught to do; and although this was not the Feast of Tabernacles, yet when they heard the shout of Hosanna they were ready to respond. The point which the text illustrates is, the custom of early training the Jewish children in the worship of God. Lightfoot (*Horæ Hebraicæ*) quotes on this subject from the Gemara: "The rabbis teach that so soon as a little child can be taught to manage a bundle. he is bound to carry one; so soon as he is known how to vail himself, he must put on the borders; as soon as he knows how to keep his father's phylacteries, he must put on his own."

690.—VINEYARDS—FENCES—WINE-PRESSES—TOWERS.

XXI, 35. There was a certain householder, which planted a vineyard, and hedged it round about, and digged a wine-press in it, and built a tower. See also Mark xii, 1; Luke xx, 9.

1. There appear to have been several ways of planting vineyards in Palestine. Sometimes the vines were planted in rows and trained on stakes. Dr. Robinson describes the celebrated vineyards near Hebron as arranged in this manner: The vines "are planted in rows eight or ten feet apart in each direction. The stock is suffered to grow up large to the height of six or eight feet, and is there fastened in a sloping position to a strong stake, and the shoots suffered to grow and extend from one plant to another, forming a line of festoons. Sometimes two rows are made to slant toward each other, and thus form by their shoots a sort of arch. These shoots are pruned away in autumn."—*Biblical Researches*, vol. ii, pp. 80, 81.

The vines are sometimes planted on the side of a terraced hill, the old branches being permitted to trail along the ground, while the fruit-bearing shoots are propped with forked sticks.

An ancient mode of planting vineyards was by training the vines over heaps of stones. Palmer discovered large numbers of these stone-heaps while traveling through the Negeb, or south country of Palestine. Near the ruins of El-'Aujeh he found some. "The black, flint-covered hill-slopes which surrounded the fort are covered with long, regular rows of stones, which have been carefully swept together and piled into numberless little black heaps. These at first considerably puzzled us, as they were evidently artificially made, and intended for some agricultural purpose; but we could not conceive what plants had been grown on such dry and barren ground. Here again Arab tradition came to our aid, and the name *teleilat-el-'anab*, 'grape-mounds, solved the difficulty. These sunny slopes, if well tended, with such supplies of water and agricultural appliances as the inhabitants of El-'Aujeh must have possessed, would have been admirably adapted to the growth of grapes, and the black flinty surface would radiate the solar heat, while these little mounds would allow the vines to trail along them, and would still keep the clusters off the ground."—*Desert of the Exodus*, p. 367. In another place (p. 352) he represents these "grape-mounds" as forming one of the most striking characteristics of the Negeb, the hill-sides and the valleys being covered with them for miles.

2. The vineyards were sometimes fenced with walls of stone, (see Num. xxii, 24; Prov. xxiv, 31,) and sometimes with a hedge of thorny plants, (see Psa. lxxx, 12,) and again with stone-walls and hedge combined. The last method is probably referred to in Isa. v, 5, where hedge and wall are both spoken of. Maundrell mentions another sort of wall which he saw surrounding the gardens near Damascus. "The garden-walls are of a very singular structure. They are built of great pieces of earth made in the fashion of brick, and hardened in the sun. In their dimensions they are two yards long each and somewhat more than one broad, and a yard thick. Two rows of these, placed edgeways, one upon another, make a cheap, expeditious, and, in this dry country, a durable wall."—*Journey from Aleppo to Jerusalem*, under date of April 27.

3. The wine-press consisted of two parts—the receptacle for the grapes, and the vat for the liquor. Either part, by itself, is sometimes called the press. Some very primitive wine-presses are spoken of by travelers, consisting of a single excavation in the rock, lower at one end than at the other, so that the wine when pressed out might find a place to settle. In some instances a trench is dug in the ground in a similar way, and lined with stone or cement. Usually, however, the receptacle for the grapes and the vat for the wine are distinct. The place where the grapes are put may be of stone, or of wood. Near the bottom on one side, or else in the bottom, is a closely-grated hole, through which the wine flows into the vat beneath.

Dr. Robinson found a very ancient wine-press at Nableh, not far from Kefr Sâba, the Antipatris of Paul's time. "Advantage had been taken of a ledge of rock; on the upper side, towards the south, a shallow vat had been dug out, eight feet square and fifteen inches deep, its bottom declining slightly towards the north.   The thickness of rock left on the north was one foot; and two feet lower down on that side another smaller vat was excavated, four feet square by three feet deep.   The grapes were trodden in the shallow upper vat, and the juice drawn off by a hole at the bottom (still remaining) into the lower vat. . . . Such is its state of preservation that, were there still grapes in the vicinity, it might at once be brought into use without repair."—*Biblical Researches*, vol. iii, p. 137.

The grapes were put into the upper part of the wine-press, and trodden by the feet of men.   Reference is made to this in Judges ix, 27; Neh. xiii, 15; Amos ix, 13.   At least two trod together, and often seven or more.

141.—Wine-press.   From an ancient Egyptian painting, Thebes.

To tread "the wine-press alone" was an expression indicative of desolation. Isa. lxiii, 3.   The treaders usually supported themselves by ropes which hung from a cross-beam over their heads.   Some think a reference to this custom is made in Isa. lxiii, 5, where it is said, "my fury, it upheld me;" the idea being that there were no ropes on which this lonely treader could hang, but that he was sustained solely by the strength of his passion.

The pressure of the grapes by the feet naturally spattered the red juice over the upper garments.   Thus we read of Judah in the prophecy of the dying Jacob: "He washed his garments in wine, and his clothes in the blood of grapes." Gen. xlix, 11.   Thus also the question is asked in Isaiah: "Wherefore art thou red in thine apparel, and thy garments like him that treadeth in the winefat?" Isa. lxiii, 2.   The grape-treaders accompanied their labors with songs and shouts.   See note on Isa. xvi, 10.

4. The tower was designed as a place of temporary dwelling for the guard, who watched over the vineyard while the fruit was ripening, to keep off thieves and wild beasts.   It was also sometimes used as a temporary

abode by the owner during the season of vintage. Though many of the towers were frail edifices, scarcely lasting longer than one season, others were more durable, being built of stone. They were either circular or square in shape, and varied in height from fifteen feet to fifty. In a garden near Beirut Maundrell saw an unfinished tower, which had been built to the height of about sixty feet, and was twelve feet thick. These lofty towers could be used not only as guard-houses for the vineyards, but also as watch-towers, to detect the coming of an enemy in the distance. Similar towers were built in the open country for the protection of the shepherds. See note on 2 Chron. xxvi, 10.

The vineyard, the hedge, the wine-press, and the tower, are also referred to in Isa. v, 1, 2.

691.—DOUBLE INVITATIONS.

XXII, 8. Sent forth his servants to call them that were bidden to the wedding.

This double invitation was customary among the wealthy in giving entertainments, and is still observed in some parts of the East. The invitation is given some little time in advance, as with us, and when the feast is ready a servant comes again with the announcement of the fact. Esther invited Ahasuerus and Haman to a feast, and when it was ready the king's chamberlains were sent to notify Haman. Compare Esther v, 8; vi, 14. The custom also finds illustration in the parable of the Great Supper narrated by Luke, which some expositors consider identical with this, though others treat the two accounts as belonging to separate parables. The narrative in Luke says: "A certain man made a great supper, and bade many: and sent his servant at supper-time, to say to them that were bidden, Come, for all things are now ready." Luke xiv, 16, 17. Here the two invitations are distinctly marked. Additional interest is given to this parable by the fact that the second invitation was given only to those who had accepted the first.

692.—HOST AND GUESTS.

XXII, 11. When the king came in to see the guests, he saw there a man which had not on a wedding-garment.

1. It was customary for monarchs and others who gave magnificent banquets to come in to see the guests after they were assembled. Allusion is doubtless made to this custom in the text, and also in Luke xiv, 10: "When he that bade thee cometh." The context plainly intimates that the guests had assembled and occupied their places before the host made his appearance.

2. The surprise manifested by the king at finding one of the guests without a suitable garment, when it could not be expected that people who had thus been suddenly called, and from the poorer classes too, would furnish

themselves with festive apparel, is an indication that the bounty of the king had provided a supply for the guests from his own wardrobe. The beauty of the parable, as well as its deep spiritual significance, is more clearly seen in the fact that beggars are represented as clothed in the garments of royalty! Although there is no direct evidence to show that it was customary thus to furnish wedding-guests with robes, the intimation is clearly made in the parable, and there are, in profane history, accounts of kingly generosity of a character somewhat similar. Extensive wardrobes were a part of Eastern wealth. See note on Job xxvii, 16. Garments were often given as presents; it was a special mark of honor to receive one which had been used by the giver, and kings sometimes showed their munificence by presenting them. See notes on Gen. xlv, 22; 1 Sam. xviii, 4; Esther vi, 8.

693.—THE PHARISEES.

XXII, 15. Then went the Pharisees, and took counsel how they might entangle him in his talk.

The Pharisees were a politico-religious party among the Jews. Their origin is involved in obscurity, but it is commonly supposed that the beginning of the party dates from a time shortly after the Babylonish Captivity. A Pharisee is, literally, one who is separated; and it is thought that the name was given because these people separated themselves from all Levitical impurity. They were doubtless a pure people in the beginning, their design being to preserve the law from violation, and the Jewish people from contamination. As their influence increased, and political power came into their hands, they lost much of their original simplicity. In the time of Christ they were very numerous and influential, and occupied the chief offices among the Jews. They were divided into two schools: the School of Hillel, and the School of Shammai.

The Pharisees were especially distinguished for belief in an Oral Law of Moses, as well as a Written Law. This Oral Law was supposed to be supplementary to the Written Law, and, with various comments added from time to time, had been handed down by tradition. The Pharisees had great veneration for this traditionary code, and for the traditionary interpretations. They placed them in authority on a level with the Written Law, and even above it. See note on Matt. xv, 3. As a body, they were not chargeable with immorality in life; on the contrary, there were many zealous and conscientious men among them, and many things which they taught were worthy of being observed, as Jesus himself admitted. See Matt. xxiii, 3. These teachings were from the law; it was when they attempted to make their traditions valid that Jesus denounced them. The great error of the most of them consisted in substituting human tradition for divine law, and in observing mere external forms, many of them of a most wearisome as well as puerile character, instead of seeking for inward purity of heart, which would have been accompanied by corresponding blamelessness in life.

It was but natural that such teachers should be bitterly opposed to Christ, and that he should vehemently denounce them and warn the people against them. They endeavored in various ways to "entangle him in his talk," (literally, to ensnare or entrap him,) and in every possible manner they exhibited their hatred. His stinging rebukes tingled in their ears and rankled in their hearts, and made them threaten his life.

694.—THE HERODIANS.

XXII, 16. They sent out unto him their disciples, with the Herodians.

These Herodians were rather a political than a religious party. They were Jews who attached themselves to the political fortunes of the Herodian family, hoping thereby to promote the interests of the Jewish people. They were not very strict in observing the requirements of the Jewish ritual; and, although in this respect they were the opposite of the Pharisees, they easily united with that powerful body in efforts to ruin Jesus, as appears from this verse in connection with the fifteenth. See also Mark iii, 6; xii, 13. Some suppose, from comparing Matt. xvi, 6, with Mark viii, 15, hat the Herodians were all Sadducees; that they belonged to what is known ·s the Bœthusian branch of that body.

695.—THE SADDUCEES.

XXII, 23. The same day came to him the Sadducees, which say that there is no resurrection.

The time when the Sadducees appeared as a party among the Jews is unknown. It is generally supposed that they had their origin about the same time as the Pharisees. The derivation of the name is a matter of dispute. Some derive it from the Hebrew *tsedek*, "righteousness," and suppose that the name was given because of their piety. Others say that the Sadducees were organized by Zadoc, a scholar of Antigonus Socho, president of the Sanhedrim, and a disciple of Simon the Just. This Zadoc died B. C. 263, and from him the name Sadducee is thought to be derived. Others seek a derivation from Zadok the priest, who lived in the time of David. See 1 Kings i, 32.

The vital point of difference between the Pharisees and the Sadducees was in their opinion of the Law. The Sadducees rejected the traditionary interpretations of the law, to which the Pharisees attached so much importance. They did not believe in any Oral Law as a supplement to the Written Law, but they took the Hebrew Scriptures, with the authoritative explanations which were developed in the course of time, as the only rule of faith and practice. They accepted those traditional explanations of the law

23

which could be deduced from the Scriptures, but rejected all which the Pharisees, without authority, had added. In some respects they were more rigid interpreters of the law than the Pharisees. A number of illustrations of this are given by Dr. Ginsburg, in his article on "Sadducees," in KITTO's *Cyclopedia.*

The Sadducees denied the doctrine of the resurrection because they considered there was no proof of it in the Hebrew Scriptures. Whether they also denied the soul's immortality, as is commonly represented, is a point on which critics are not agreed. The statement in Acts xxiii, 8, is sometimes adduced as proof of this denial: "For the Sadducees say that there is no resurrection, neither angel, nor spirit: but the Pharisees confess both." It is claimed, however, that this does not show that the Sadducees did not believe in angelic or spiritual existence, but that they did not believe in any manifestation of the angels or spirits to human beings in their own day. Reuss, in HERZOG's *Real-Encyklopädie, s. v. Sadducäer,* suggests that the ninth verse gives a key to the interpretation of the eighth. The Pharisaic scribes there admit the possibility of a spirit or an angel having spoken to Paul. The Sadducees might easily deny the reality of such appearances in their day without denying the actual existence of such beings, or the accounts of their appearances which are given in the Old Testament. This opinion is adopted by Twistleton in SMITH's *Dictionary of the Bible,* and also by Dr. Milligan in FAIRBAIRN's *Imperial Bible Dictionary.*

The Sadducees were not so numerous as the Pharisees, nor were their doctrines so acceptable to the people. They were an ancient priestly aristocracy, having considerable wealth and great political power. From Acts v, 17, compared with iv, 6, it has been inferred that many of the kindred of the high priest at that time, as well as himself, were of the Sadducean party, and that probably the priestly families in general belonged to them. They were too cold and austere in their manners to make many converts, and disappeared from history about the close of the First Century of the Christian era.

696.—SUMMARY OF THE LAW.

XXII, 40. On these two commandments hang all the law and the prophets.

1. It was customary among the Jews to hang a copy of their laws in a public place, and some commentators suppose an allusion to this custom to be made here.

2. Jewish teachers have at various times attempted to make compendiums of the law. Tholuck gives a very interesting account of one of the most remarkable of these made by Rabbi Samlai, and contained in the Gemara. The following is a condensed statement of Samlai's compendium

of the law: Moses gave six hundred and thirteen commandments on Mount Sinai. David reduced these commandments to eleven, which may be found in the fifteenth Psalm, in answer to the question, "Lord, who shall abide in thy tabernacle?" Afterward Isaiah came and reduced the eleven to six, as may be seen in Isa. xxxiii, 15. Then came Micah and reduced the six to three. See Micah vi, 8. Once more Isaiah brought down the three to two. Isa. lvi, 1. Lastly came Habakkuk, and reduced them all to one: "The just shall live by faith." Hab. ii, 4. See THOLUCK'S *Commentary on the Sermon on the Mount,* (Am. Ed.,) p. 139.

697.—PHYLACTERIES.

XXIII, 5. They make broad their phylacteries.

Whether the commands in Exod. xiii, 9, 16; Deut. vi, 8; and xi, 18, concerning the duty of binding the word upon the hand and head, were designed to be interpreted figuratively or literally, is a disputed point among commentators. The Jews have for ages attached to them a literal meaning, though some writers claim that this was not done until after the captivity. Whatever the original design of the injunction may have been, in the time of the Saviour it was supposed by all the Jews (excepting the Karaites, who gave to the passages above cited a figurative meaning) to be a duty to wear upon their persons certain portions of the law.

The passages selected were Exod. xiii, 1–10; Exod. xiii, 11–16; Deut. vi, 4–9; and Deut. xi, 13–21. These four sections were written in Hebrew on strips of parchment with ink prepared especially for the purpose. There were two sorts of phylacteries —one for the arm, and one for the head. That for the arm consisted of one strip of parchment on which the above texts were written. This was inclosed in a small square case of parchment or black calf-skin, and fastened with a long, narrow leather strap

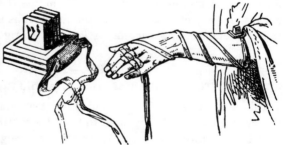

142.—PHYLACTERIES FOR THE HEAD AND ARM.

to the inside of the arm, between the bend of the elbow and the shoulder, that when the arm touched the body the law might be near the heart. The strap was carefully wound around the arm and the fingers until the ends came out by the tip of the middle finger. The Sadducees, however, wore the phylacteries in the palm of the left hand instead of on the arm. The case for the forehead consisted of four cells, and had four strips of parchment on which the before-mentioned texts were written. It was fastened by leather straps on the forehead, between the eyes, and near the roots of the hair; or, as the rabbins say, "where the pulse of an infant's brain is."

The phylacteries were worn by the men only. The common people wore them only during prayers, but the Pharisees wore them continually; and as they sought by inclosing the parchment strips in larger boxes than ordinary to attract the attention of the people, the Saviour denounces them for making "broad their phylacteries." He does not condemn the wearing them, but the ostentation connection with it. They became badges of vanity and hypocrisy; and, not unlikely, were used as amulets, though some writers deny this.

Modern Jews continue the use of the phylacteries, which they call *tephillin;* that is, *prayer-fillets,* because they use them in time of prayer.

698.—PLACES OF HONOR.

XXIII, 6. The chief seats in the synagogue. See also Mark xii, 39; Luke xi, 43; xx, 46.

These "chief seats" were seats of honor which were prepared for the elders of the synagogue and for the doctors of the law; and hence called, in the second verse of this chapter, "Moses' seat." They were placed in front of the ark, which contained the law, in the uppermost part of the synagogue, at the "Jerusalem end." See note on Matt. iv, 23. Luke calls them "uppermost seats." Those who occupied them sat with their faces to the people. These seats were considered positions of great honor, and were eagerly sought by the ambitious scribes and Pharisees. It is probable that James refers to this custom of honor in the Jewish synagogue when he speaks of "a good place," where the rich man is invited to sit in the Christian "assembly," or *synagogue,* as it is in the original. See James ii, 2, 3.

699.—RABBI.

XXIII, 7. To be called of men, Rabbi, Rabbi.

This was a title of distinction given to teachers, and literally means Master, or Teacher. It is supposed to have been introduced during our Lord's ministry. Lightfoot says: "We do not too nicely examine the precise time when this title began; be sure it did not commence before the schism arose between the schools of Shammai and Hillel; and from that schism, perhaps, it had its beginning."—*Horœ Hebraicœ.* Gamaliel I., who was patriarch in Palestine from A. D. 30–50, was the first who was honored with this title. It will thus be seen that Jesus was assailing a new fashion which had come into use in his own time.

There were three forms of the title used: Rab, Rabbi, Rabbon; respectively meaning, Master, My Master, Our Master. The precise difference between these terms, in their practical application, is not, however, very clear Ginsburg, in KITTO's *Cyclopedia, s. v. Rabbi,* quotes from two ancient Babylonian Jews to the effect that the title Rab is Babylonian, and was given to those Babylonian sages who received the laying-on of hands in their colleges ; while Rabbi is the title given to the Palestinian sages, who received it with the laying-on of hands of the Sanhedrim.   They also state that Rab is the lowest title, Rabbi next higher, and Rabbon highest of all, and given only to the presidents.

There is, however, a different explanation of these titles given in the *Aruch,* or Talmudical lexicon.   According to this, a Rabbi is one who has disciples, and whose disciples again have disciples.   When he is so old that his disciples belong to a past generation, and are thus forgotten, he is called Rabbon ; and when the disciples of his disciples are forgotten he is simply called by his own name.

These distinctions probably belong to a later age than Christ's ministry. The terms Rabbi and Rabbon seem to have been used with the same general meaning.   Jesus was called both.   See John i, 38; xx, 16.

Witsius states that the title was generally conferred with a great deal of ceremony.   Besides the imposition of hands by the delegates of the Sanhedrim, the candidate was first placed in a chair a little raised above the company; there were delivered to him a key and a table-book: the key as a symbol of the power and authority conferred upon him to teach others, and the table-book as a symbol of his diligence in his studies.   The key he afterward wore as a badge of honor, and when he died it was buried with him.—BURDER's *Oriental Literature,* No. 1,220.

700.—HYPOCRISY.

XXIII, 14. Woe unto you, scribes and Pharisees, hypocrites! for ye devour widows' houses, and for a pretense make long prayer. See also Mark xii, 40; Luke xx, 47.

1. The scribes and Pharisees had peculiar facilities for obtaining property under false pretenses.   The scribes, on account of their knowledge of law, were often consulted on property questions; and the Pharisees, by reason of their supposed piety, exercised great influence over the people.   Those who were inexperienced in business intrusted their property to these men for safe keeping, and many lost by it.

2. Some of the Pharisees prayed an hour, besides meditating an hour before and an hour after prayer.   This, repeated three times a day, made nine hours spent in pretentious devotion.   One of the rabbis says: "Since, therefore, they spent nine hours every day about their prayers, how did they perform the rest of the law? and how did they take care of their worldly affairs?   Why, herein—in being religious, both the law was performed and

their own business well provided for." And again: "Long prayers make a long life."—LIGHTFOOT, *Horæ Hebraicæ.*

701.—WINE–STRAINING.

XXIII, 24. Ye blind guides, which strain at a gnat, and swallow a camel.

This would be more correctly rendered by "strain *out* a gnat." The *at* is supposed to have been originally a typographical error, which has since been universally copied. Alford, however, doubts this, and supposes that it " was a deliberate alteration, meaning, ' strain [out the wine] at [the occurrence of] a gnat.' " In either case the meaning is the same. The reference here is to an old proverb, which, in turn, refers to an old custom. The Jews, in common with other Oriental people, strained their wine before drinking it, not only to keep the lees from the cup, but also to get rid of the insects, which, in a hot climate, collected around the fluid.

Wincklemann describes an instrument, evidently intended for a wine-strainer, and which was found in the ruins of Herculaneum. It is made of white metal, of elegant workmanship, and consists of two round and deep plates, about four inches in diameter, with flat handles. Plates and handles fit into each other so exactly that when put together they seem to make but one vessel. The upper plate is perforated, and the wine, passing through the holes, fell into the deeper vessel below, whence it was drawn into drinking-cups. The dregs and insects remained on the upper plate.

702.—WHITEWASHED TOMBS.

XXIII, 27. Ye are like unto whited sepulchres, which indeed appear beautiful outward, but are within full of dead men's bones, and of all uncleanness.

The tombs were whitened with lime, so that they could be easily distinguished, and thus prevent the Jews from being ceremonially defiled by approaching them. See Num. xix, 18. This whitewash became soiled and washed off by the rains, and it was therefore necessary to renew it at intervals. This was usually done in the middle of the month Adar, when the streets and sewers were mended.

It is still customary in Palestine to whitewash the tombs. Mohammedans, as well as Jews, are very particular about this. See engraving on the opposite page.

703.—DECORATED TOMBS.

XXIII, 29. Ye build the tombs of the prophets, and garnish the sepulchres of the righteous.

The Jews not only whitewashed the tombs, but, in common with other p ople, they ornamented them in various ways. This is still customary in the East. The graves of the most eminent Mohammedan saints are each covered with a stone or brick edifice called *welee*. It has a dome or cupola

143.—Sheik's Tomb.

over it, varying in height from eight to ten feet. With it lamps are often hung, and the grave proper is covered with carpet and strings of beads. Sometimes more costly ornamentation is used.

704.—HEROD'S TEMPLE

XXIV, 1. **Jesus went out, and departed from the temple: and his disciples came to him for to show him the buildings of the temple.** See also Mark xiii, 1; Luke xxi, 5.

This is what is commonly known as Herod's temple, and was a restoration or reconstruction of the temple of Zerubbabel; that structure being taken down piecemeal, and this gradually substituted for it. It was, however, larger and more splendid than the temple of Zerubbabel; its courts occupied more ground than those which surrounded that old temple, and far exceeded them in magnificence

According to the Talmud the entire temple area was five hundred cubits square Around the edge of this square, and against the massive stone wall which inclosed it, cloisters were built, (1, 2, 3, 4,*) their cedar roofs being supported by rows of Corinthian columns of solid marble. The cloisters on

---

* The figures refer to the corresponding figures on the diagram. See next page.

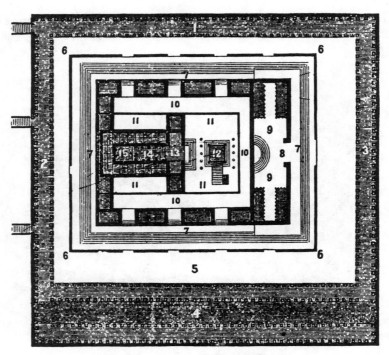

144.—GROUND-PLAN OF HEROD'S TEMPLE.

1. North Cloister.
2. West Cloister.
3. Solomon's Porch.
4. King's Porch.
5. Court of the Gentiles.
6. Wall of Separation.
7. Platform.
8. Beautiful Gate.
9. Court of the Women.
10. Court of the Israelites.
11. Court of the Priests.
12. Great Altar of Burnt-Offering.
13. Porch of the Temple.
14. Holy Place.
15. Most Holy Place.

the north, west, and east sides (1, 2, 3) were alike in height and width, the columns which upheld the roof being twenty-five cubits high, and the halls themselves thirty cubits wide. The colonnade on the east (3) was called Solomon's Porch, and is mentioned in John x, 23; Acts iii, 11; v, 12. The cloisters on the south (4) formed an immense building known as the *Stoa Basilica*, or King's Porch. It was much wider than the cloisters on the other sides, and consisted of a nave and two aisles. This immense building, with its high nave, its broad aisles, and its marble columns, presented a grand appearance. Josephus says: "Its fineness, to such as had not seen it, was incredible; and to such as had seen it was greatly amazing." The south-eastern corner of this building is supposed to have been the "pinnacle of the temple," where the devil took Jesus in the Temptation. See note on Matt. iv, 5. In these cloisters the Levites resided. Here the doctors of the law met to hear and answer questions. See Luke ii, 46. They were favorite places of resort for religionists of different sorts to discuss various points of doctrine. Jesus often spoke here to the people; and after his death his followers met here. See Acts ii, 46.

North of the center of the large area inclosed by these cloisters stood the sacred inclosure of the temple, its boundaries extending nearer to the cloisters on the west than to Solomon's Porch on the east. The space surrounding this inclosure was the Court of the Gentiles (5), and was open to all comers. It was paved with stones of various colors. It was here that the cattle-dealers and money-changers desecrated the house of God. See note on Matt. xxi, 12. This court was also called the Outer Court, the Lower Court, and, by the rabbins usually, the "Mountain of the Lord's house."

The inclosure of the temple proper was on a terrace about six cubits higher than the Court of the Gentiles. It was approached by steps, and was surrounded by a wall three cubits high (6). This wall was designed to shut off the Gentiles, and there were pillars erected in the wall at certain distances with inscriptions in Latin, Greek, and Hebrew, warning all Gentiles to come no further under penalty of death. The Jews, on one occasion, accused Paul of having brought "Greeks" up the steps, and into the sacred inclosure, in violation of the standing order. See Acts xxi, 28. To this wall of separation Paul is thought to refer: "For he is our peace, who hath made both one, and hath broken down the middle wall of partition between us." Eph. ii, 14. At the top of the terrace, and going entirely around it, was a platform (7) ten cubits wide extending to another wall.

In the eastern side of the latter wall was a gate (8) of elegant workmanship, forty cubits wide, and supposed to have been the "Gate Beautiful," mentioned in Acts iii, 2, 10. It was sometimes called the "Gate Susan," because it had a representation of the town of Susa sculptured in relief on it. Though there were gates on the north and south sides, this was the grand entrance to the Court of the Women (9), which was the general place of public worship at the time of the sacrifices. It received its name, not because it was exclusively appropriated to the women, but because the women were not allowed to go beyond it. There were smaller courts in the four corners of this; and on the north, east, and west sides were galleries supported by columns. In front of these columns were distributed the eleven treasure chests of the temple, in addition to the two at the gate Susan, for the half-shekel tax. It was into one of these that the poor widow threw her two mites. Mark xii, 41, 42; Luke xxi, 1, 2. It was near these treasure chests that the incidents recorded in the eighth chapter of John took place. See John viii, 20.

West of the Court of the Women, separated from it by a wall, and on a terrace higher still, was the Court of the Israelites (10). This was a narrow hall completely surrounding the Court of the Priests, and had cloisters on all sides supported by beautiful columns. The rooms of these cloisters were devoted to various purposes connected with the service of the temple. This court was entered from the Court of the Women by a flight of semi-circular steps and through the Gate of Nicanor. The session room of the Sanhedrim was in the south-east corner of the Court of the Israelites.

On a terrace fifteen steps higher still, and separated from the Court of the Israelites by a low stone balustrade, was the Court of the Priests (11). In the eastern part of this was the great altar of burnt-offering (12), directly west of which arose the Great Temple itself. The building was of white marble, and some of the foundation-stones were of immense size. It was divided into two parts, forming the Holy Place (14) and the Most Holy Place (15), the two being separated by a vail. See note on Matt. xxvii, 51. The internal arrangements of these two sacred places were probably like those of the temple of Zerubbabel. See note on Ezra vi, 3, 4. Above these were rooms used for various purposes, and on the sides were three stories of chambers. In the front part of the building was the porch (13), which projected a short distance beyond the building, north and south, giving it this form : ⊣

A striking feature in the general appearance of the temple and its various courts is the series of terraces; the different courts rising one above the other, until the temple itself was reached on a platform highest of all. The structure—the paved courts, the beautiful columns, the white marble cloisters, the gate-ways, which in themselves were high and massive buildings, and, crowning all, the white temple standing high above the rest, its front walls ornamented with thick plates of gold—produced an effect which was magnificent beyond description. See, further, note on Luke xxi, 5.

705.—GETTING DOWN FROM THE HOUSE-TOP.

XXIV, 17. Let him which is on the housetop not come down to take any thing out of his house. See also Mark xiii, 15; Luke xvii, 31.

Some commentators have endeavored to show how those who were on the flat tops of the houses might escape without coming down, by going over the roofs of the other houses until they reached the city wall. But a comparison with the narrative as given by Mark and Luke shows that the direction was intended as a caution against stopping in any of the rooms of the house on their way down in order to collect their valuables. Mark's account says: "Let him that is on the housetop not go down into the house, neither enter therein, to take any thing out of his house." Luke has, "In that day, he which shall be upon the housetop, and his stuff in the house, let him not come down to take it away." They are not told that they are not to come down in order to escape, but they are not to come down for the purpose of entering the house. According to our method of building it would be impossible to come down from the roof without entering the house; but in the Oriental houses there are stairs on the outside of the house landing in the court, from which one could escape into the street through the porch. Occasionally, though not often, we are told of stairs which come directly from the roof on the street side of the house into the street below. Some travelers deny the existence of such external stairs, while others positively affirm it. Anderson, for instance, says: "The house in which I lodged in Jerusalem had an outer as well as an inner stair, by which, without descending into the court, I could at any time go out into the street." —*Bible Light from Bible Lands*, p. 183.

706.—THE MILL.

XXIV, 41. **Two women shall be grinding at the mill.** See also Luke xvii, 35.

The ordinary hand-mill of the East consists of two circular stones from eighteen inches to two feet in diameter and about six inches deep. The

lower, or "nether," is sometimes, though not always, of heavier and harder stone than the upper. See Job xli, 24. The upper, or "rider," is slightly concave, and covers like the lid of a vessel the lower, which is convex. From the center of the lower stone there rises a pivot, on which the upper stone

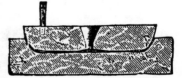

145.—SECTION OF EASTERN HAND-MILL.

revolves. Near the edge of the upper stone is the perpendicular stick or handle by which it is turned, and at the center is a hole for the pivot, and also for the grain to fall through upon the stone below. The lower stone has a projection on a part of the edge two or three inches long, slanting downward, and hollowed so as to carry off the meal.

The work of grinding meal is usually performed by the women, and is very laborious. Sometimes one works alone, but usually two work together, sitting on the ground with the millstones between them, and both taking hold of the handle and moving it entirely around, to and from them. The usual time for grinding is at early dawn, or else at the evening in preparation for the following day. The stones, as they crush the grain, send forth a grating sound, which, though not very musical in itself, is melodious enough to a hungry traveler. Reference is made to this noise in Eccl. xii, 4; Jer. xxv, 10; Rev. xviii, 22. In addition to this, the women often sing while grinding.

The women who ground were, among the families of wealth, either slaves or the lowest servants. Thus, in Exod. xi, 5, we read of "the maid-servant that is behind the mill." In this passage the expression "behind the mill" can be readily understood by what is said above of the position of the servants when grinding. The prophet Isaiah represents the "virgin daughter of

Babylon" as compelled to sit on the ground like a servant to grind meal. See Isa. xlvii, 1, 2. We also have more vividly brought before us the indignity which the Philistines put on Samson when they compelled him to "grind in the prison-house." See note on Judges xvi, 21.

The millstones were considered so important and necessary a part of household furniture that the Mosaic law would not allow them to be pawned. "No man shall take the nether or the upper millstone to pledge: for he taketh a man's life to pledge." Deut. xxiv, 6.

146.—Women Grinding Corn with the Hand-mill of modern Syria.

707.— MARRIAGE PROCESSION.

XXV, 1. Ten virgins, which took their lamps, and went forth to meet the bridegroom.

On the occasion of a marriage the bridegroom, attended by his friends, went to the house of his bride, and brought her with her friends in joyful procession to his own house. The virgins mentioned in the text were probably some of the friends of the bride, who were to meet and join the procession at some convenient place.

708.—TORCHES.

XXV, 3, 4. They that were foolish took their lamps, and took no oil with them; but the wise took oil in their vessels with their lamps.

It is difficult to tell whether lamps proper or torches are here meant. The rabbins speak of a staff used on such occasions, on top of which was a brazen dish containing rags, oil, and pitch. Chardin says that, in many places of the East, instead of torches they carry a pot of oil in one hand and a lamp full of oily rags in the other. The account given by Forbes is similar. He says: "The massaul or torch in India is composed of coarse rags rolled up to the size of an English flambeau, eighteen or twenty inches long, fixed in a brass handle. This is carried in the left hand; in the right the massaulchee (or torch-bearer) holds a brass vessel containing the oil, with which he feeds the flame as occasion requires."—*Oriental Memoirs*, vol. ii, p. 417.

Whether these virgins carried torches, or merely lamps, as some commentators suppose, they needed a supply of oil to replenish their light, and

147.—Marriage Procession.

148.—Torches

hence were obliged to carry "vessels" to contain the supplies of oil.   Great efforts are made to have an abundance of light at Oriental weddings, which always take place at night.   Reference is made to this custom of night-weddings, not only in these two verses, but also in the first verse, and in the fifth and sixth verses.   Lamps, torches, and lanterns are freely used in the marriage procession, and also at the house of the bridegroom, where the ceremony is performed.   Only vegetable oil, chiefly olive, is used for illuminating purposes.

709.—THE CLOSED DOOR.

XXV, 10.   The bridegroom came; and they that were ready went in with him to the marriage : and the door was shut.

At all formal banquets the invited guests presented their tablets or cards to a servant stationed at the entrance-door for the purpose, care being taken to keep out uninvited spectators.   When the company were assembled the "master of the house" shut the door, and after that the servant was not allowed to admit any one, no matter how great the importunity.   This illustrates not only the text, but also Luke xiii, 24, 25.

710.—SHEEP AND GOATS.

XXV, 32.   He shall separate them one from another, as a shepherd divideth his sheep from the goats.

Sheep and goats are allowed to mingle during the day while at pasturage, but at night are separated.   Thus the Saviour seeks to illustrate the truth that though righteous and wicked are now together, there will come a time of separation.

711.—THE ACQUITTED AND THE CONVICTED.

XXV, 33.   He shall set the sheep on his right hand, but the goats on the left.

Some think there is a reference here to a custom in the Sanhedrim of putting the acquitted prisoners on the right of the president, and those who were convicted on his left.   If so, the illustration of the text is derived from two customs; the *separation* of the two classes being taken from the shepherds, and their *position* from the Sanhedrim.

712.—ALABASTRA—OINTMENTS—RECLINING AT MEALS.

XXVI, 7.   There came unto him a woman having an alabaster box of very precious ointment, and poured it on his head as he sat at meat. See also Mark xiv, 8; John xii, 8.

A similar incident, though occurring at another time and place, is recorded in Luke vii, 36–38.

1. In Alabastron, in Egypt, vessels were anciently made of a peculiar stone, a kind of soft, white marble, which was found in that vicinity, and which was supposed to be specially adapted to preserve the odor of perfumed

ointments. The Greeks named the vessels from the town where they were made. The stone afterward was called by the same name, and at length all perfume vessels, of whatever form or substance, were called *alabastra*. They have been found made of gold, glass, ivory, bone, and shells. Specimens of these ancient perfume-boxes, or vases, made of alabaster and of other materials, some of them richly ornamented, are in the British Museum, and also in the Abbott Collection, New York.

The *alabastra* were of various shapes and sizes, though they were commonly long and slender at the top, and round and full at the bottom, like a Florentine oil-flask. According to Epiphanius, the *alabastron* ordinarily used for fragrant ointments contained about half a pint.

149.—ALABASTRA.

2. The Eastern people not only make a free use of simple oil for the purpose of anointing, (see note on Psa. xxiii, 5,) but they prepare fragrant ointments, some of which are very costly. The custom is very old, and prevails among various nations. Even among the rude Parthians the kings had a "royal ointment," which Rawlinson describes as "composed of cinnamon, spikenard, myrrh, cassia, gum styrax, saffron, cardamom, wine, honey, and sixteen other ingredients." He does not, however, give them the credit of inventing this odoriferous compound, but suspects that they adopted it from the more refined Persians, whose "monarch applied to his own person an ointment composed of the fat of lions, palm-wine, saffron, and the herb *helianthus*, which was considered to increase the beauty of the complexion. He carried with him, even when he went to the wars, a case of choice unguents, and such a treasure fell into the hands of Alexander, with the rest of Darius's camp-equipage, at Arbela."—*Five Ancient Monarchies*, vol. iii, p. 212.

The holy ointment of consecration among the Jews, though it was not permitted to be used for ordinary purposes, gives us an idea of the variety of ingredients used in compounding ointments. This "holy anointing oil" was composed of myrrh, sweet cinnamon, sweet calamus, cassia, and olive oil. See Exod. xxx, 23, 24.

In later times greater attention seems to have been paid to the perfume of the ointments which were used for hospitality or for personal purposes. The fragrance of some ointments is said to have remained in the *alabastra* for hundreds of years. The ointment mentioned in the text is called by Mark

150.—RECLINING AT TABLE.

'ointment of spikenard," probably because that costly aromatic plant was one of the principal ingredients.

From Job xli, 31, it appears that the different ingredients of which ointments were anciently compounded were boiled together. The h gh estimamation in which the more costly ointments were held is manifested not only in the expression "very precious" in the text, and in the remarks of the disciples as indicated in the eighth and ninth verses, but in several other passages. See 2 Kings **xx**, 13; Psa. cxxxiii, 2; Eccl. vii, 1. That such ointments were sometimes very expensive is evident from a comparison of John **xii**, 3, 5, where we find that a pound cost three hundred pence. Reckoning the penny at fifteen cents, (see note on Matt. **xx**, 2,) and the pound at twelve ounces avoirdupois, (see note on John xii, 3,) this would make the value three dollars and seventy-five cents an ounce. The fragrant character of ointment is also referred to in Sol. Song i, 3; iv, 10; Isa. lvii, 9; Rev. xviii, 13.

3. The expression "sat" at meat would be more correctly rendered by "reclined," since the guests were lying on a bed, according to the fashion of the times. When or by whom the custom of having dinner-beds was introduced is not known; the Persians usually have the credit of it. The Jews, no doubt, learned it from them, as did also the Greeks. The Romans, who likewise practiced it, are said to have derived it from the Carthagenians. We find reference to the custom in Esther i, 6; vii, 8; and in Ezek. xxiii, 41.

Among the Romans three beds were generally used in the dining-room, and thus combined were called the *triclinium:* they were arranged around the sides of a square in the center of the dining-room, which was itself sometimes called *triclinium.* The tables were in front of them, and within easy reach of the guests, and the left side was open, to allow the servants to pass in and out. The *triclinia* varied in style at different periods. The frames on which the couches were placed were sometimes made of costly wood and highly ornamented. The beds themselves were stuffed with various substances: straw, hay, leaves, woolly plants, sea-weed, wool, and, among the wealthy and luxurious, with feathers and swan's-down. Cushions or pillows were placed on the beds, so that the guests might rest the left arm, on the elbow of which they usually leaned, the right hand being left free to reach the food. See note on John xiii, 23. Some authorities, however, state that when the guests began eating they lay flat upon the breast, and afterward, when hunger was satisfied, they turned upon the left side, leaning on the elbow.

The Romans allowed three guests to each bed, making nine in all. It was the rule of Varro that "the number of guests ought not to be less than that of the Graces, nor to exceed that of the Muses." Sometimes, however, as many as four lay on each couch. The Greeks went beyond this number, and so did the Jews.

The front of the bed was somewhat higher than the table, and as the *triclinium* was on an inclined plane, the feet of the guests lay toward the floor. In the incident recorded by Luke the woman anointed the feet of Jesus. This she could easily do by passing between the rear of the *triclinium* and the wall of the room. In the account given in the text and its parallels, Matthew and Mark speak of the woman's anointing the head of Jesus, while John speaks of anointing his feet. By comparing the two accounts it thus seems that she anointed both head and feet. She probably first entered the passage where the servants waited by the table. Here she could reach the head of the Saviour, and then going behind the *triclinium* she could easily find access to his feet, as did the other woman in the house of the other Simon mentioned by Luke.

Reclining on the dinner-bed is also referred to in Matt. ix, 10; xxvi, 20; Mark xiv, 18; xvi, 14; John xii, 2. In all these passages the expression "sitting at meat" has the meaning above given.

The "tables" mentioned in Mark vii, 4, are dinner-beds.

713.—PIECES OF SILVER.

XXVI, 15. They covenanted with him for thirty pieces of silver.

It is difficult to ascertain what coins are here meant. Mr. Poole, of the British Museum, one of the best authorities on numismatics, suggests (see SMITH'S *Dictionary of the Bible, s. v.* PIECE OF SILVER) that the thirty *arguria*, mentioned here and in Matt. xxvii, 3, 5, 6, 9, were not denarii, as many commentators suppose, but shekels, and that shekels must also be understood in the parallel passage of Zech. xi, 12, 13. Thirty shekels of silver was the price of blood when a slave was accidentally killed. See Exod. xxi, 32. As there were probably no current shekels during our Lord's time, Mr. Poole supposes that the tetradrachms of the Greek cities of Syria were the coins which composed the thirty pieces of silver paid to Judas. These tetradrachms have the same weight as the shekels of Simon Maccabæus; and the *stater* found by Peter in the fish was a specimen of them. See note on Matt. xvii, 27. This would make the sum which Judas received equivalent to about eighteen dollars, United States coin, or a little over three pounds ten shillings, English.

714.—PASSOVER GUESTS.

XXVI, 17. Where wilt thou that we prepare for thee to eat the passover? See also Mark xiv, 12; Luke xxii, 9.

The Israelites who came to Jerusalem to celebrate the Passover were received by the inhabitants as brothers, and apartments were gratuitously furnished them where they might eat the feast. In return, the guests gave their hosts the skins of the paschal lambs and the vessels they had used in the ceremonies. According to this custom the disciples, wishing to make arrangements for the Passover, inquired of the Lord if he had any special house in view where he desired to go.

715.—PREPARING FOR THE PASSOVER.

XXVI, 19. The disciples did as Jesus had appointed them; and they made ready the passover. See also Mark xiv, 16; Luke xxii, 13.

The two disciples, Peter and John, who represented the company who, with Jesus, were to celebrate the Passover together, went, as was customary, to the temple with the paschal lamb. There, taking their turn with others who thronged the temple on the same errand, they killed the lamb, the nearest priest catching the blood in a gold or silver bowl, and passing it to the next in the row of priests until it reached the priest nearest the altar, who instantly sprinkled it toward the altar's base. The lamb was then flayed and the entrails removed, to be burnt with incense on the altar. All this was done in the afternoon. As soon as it was dark the lamb was roasted with great care. Thus the two "made ready the Passover." They likewise provided unleavened bread, wine, bitter herbs, and sauce. See also note on Exod. xxiii, 15.

716.—PASSOVER CEREMONIES IN CHRIST'S TIME.

XXVI, 20. Now when the even was come, he sat down with the twelve. See also Mark xiv, 17; Luke xxii, 14.

The ceremonies of the Passover supper in the time of Christ were as follows:

1. A cup of wine was filled for every one of the company, over which he who presided at the feast pronounced a blessing, after which the wine was drank.

2. The bitter herbs, the unleavened bread, the *charoseth*, and the flesh of the *chagigah*, were then brought in. The *charoseth* was composed of vinegar and water, according to some authorities; others say that it was a mixture of vinegar, figs, almonds, dates, raisins, and spice, beaten to the consistence of mortar or clay, to commemorate the toils of the Israelites when they worked in the brick-yards of Egypt. The *chagigah* was a special voluntary peace-offering which was made at the Passover and other great festivals.

3. When these were all placed upon the table, the president of the feast, who in a family celebration of the Passover was the head of the family, took a portion of the bitter herbs in his hand, dipped it into the *charoseth*, and, after thanking God for the fruits of the earth, (see note on Matt. xiv, 19,) ate a piece the size of an olive, and gave a similar portion to each one, who, according to custom, reclined with him on the dinner-bed. See note on Matt. xxvi, 7. (Some Jewish writers say that they reclined on couches

24

while they ate the Passover in order to show that they were no longer slaves, but free. and at rest.) The unleavened bread was then handed round, and the paschal lamb placed on the table in front of the president.

4. A second cup of wine was poured out and drank, after which an explanation of the feast was given, in accordance with Exod. xii, 26, 27. The first part of the "Hallel," or hymn of praise, was then sung. This consisted of Psalms cxiii and cxiv, and was followed by a blessing.

5. After the singing, unleavened bread and bitter herbs, dipped in the *charoseth*, were eaten. Then the flesh of the *chagigah* was eaten, and next the paschal lamb. A third cup of wine was then poured out and drank, and soon after a fourth. After the fourth cup the rest of the " Hallel" was sung. This consisted of Psalms cxv to cxviii, and is the "hymn" referred to in verse 30 and in Mark xiv, 26.

It was while partaking of this Passover feast that the Lord's Supper was instituted by the Saviour. A number of interesting and important questions, some of them of great difficulty, arise in connection with this subject, but their discussion would be out of place here. The different standard commentaries may be consulted for their solution.

717.—CHIEF PRIESTS—ELDERS.

XXVI, 47. Judas, one of the twelve, came, and with him a great multitude with swords and staves, from the chief priests and elders of the people.

1. David divided the whole staff of the Aaronic priesthood into twenty-four classes, sixteen of which belonged to the house of Eleazer and eight to that of Ithamar. This arrangement was continued by Solomon, and was probably kept up with more or less regularity by his successors. Compare 1 Chron. xxiv, 1–19, with 2 Chron. viii, 14; xxxv, 4. We find allusion to it in the time of Christ, Zacharias, the father of John the Baptist, being a priest of " the course of Abia." Luke i, 5. The heads or presidents of these twenty four classes are the " chief priests," of whom mention is made in the Old Testament as well as in the New. See 1 Chron. xxiv, 3, 4; 2 Chron. xxvi, 20; Ezra x, 5; Neh. xii, 7, etc. They are called " governors of the sanctuary " in 1 Chron. xxiv, 5, and " princes of the sanctuary " in Isa. xliii, 28.

Some authorities affirm that, in the New Testament, the term " chief priests " has a broader meaning than that just given; that it includes not only the heads of the twenty-four classes, but also the high priests and ex-high priests. Others include those priests who were of the immediate kindred of the high priest. See ROBINSON, *New Testament Lexicon*, *s. v.* ἀρχιερεύς, 2. The Rabbins include among the chief priests the twenty-four heads of the " Ephemeries," or courses, the heads of the families in every course, the presidents over the various offices in the temple, and any priests or Levites, although not of these orders, that were chosen into the chief council. See LIGHTFOOT, *Horæ Hebraicæ*, on Matt. ii, 4.

2. The term "elders" was no doubt originally applied to the heads of families, and to the oldest persons in tribes or states. When it became an official title is not known. The elders among the Israelites seem to have been recognized as a distinct body very early. See Exod. iii, 16, 18; iv, 29; xii, 21; Num. xi, 16, 25. They were probably the leading persons in each tribe. Traces of them appear all through the Old Testament history. In the New Testament the elders of the Jewish people are often referred to. Each synagogue had its company of elders, though there seem to have been other officials of the same title not connected with the synagogue. In the Sanhedrim they were the representatives of the people, as the "chief priests" were representatives of the priesthood.

The expression "chief priests and elders," sometimes with the word "scribes" added and sometimes without, is often used to denote the Great Sanhedrim described in the next note. See Matt. xvi, 21; xxi, 23; xxvii, 1, 12, 41; Mark xv, 1, 31; Luke xxii, 66.

718.—THE SANHEDRIM.

XXVI, 59. All the council sought false witness against Jesus, to put him to death.

This was the supreme court of the Jewish nation, which heard appeals from inferior courts, and tried cases of greater gravity than those which came before them. It is commonly known as the Sanhedrim, though the word is sometimes written Sanhedrin, and occasionally Synhedrium, Synedium, Synedrion. It is the Hebraizing of the Greek word συνέδριον, *a sitting together*, or, as in the text and in numerous other places, a *council*.

The number of members in the Sanhedrim is usually considered to have been seventy-one, though on this subject there is a diversity of opinion among authorities, some fixing the number at seventy, and others at seventy-two. Twenty-three members were necessary to make a quorum.

The origin of this council is thought by some writers to be found in the company of seventy elders who were appointed to assist Moses in the government of the Israelites. See Num. xi, 16, 17. Others, however, deny that this could have been the origin of the Sanhedrim, and affirm that the seventy elders were only intended to serve a temporary purpose, since no trace of them is found after the death of Moses. They could hardly have been judges, as the members of the Sanhedrim were, since there were more than sixty thousand judges among the Israelites already. See MICHÆLIS, *Laws of Moses*, vol. i, p. 247. Those who agree with Michælis in his views on this subject suppose that the Sanhedrim was instituted after the captivity. It is quite likely, however, that the council of Moses may have been the germ from whence the idea of the Sanhedrim was developed.

The members of the Sanhedrim were chosen from the chief priests, elders, and scribes. It was necessary to have priests and scribes in the body, and they were usually quite numerous, though the majority of the members are thought to have been laymen. The relative numbers of the three classes are not definitely known. The Pharisees and the Sadducees were both represented, sometimes the one and sometimes the other being in the majority. Most of the scribes probably belonged to the Pharisees.

Great care was taken in the selection of members, who were required to be morally and physically blameless. They were also expected to be learned in law, in sciences, and in languages. It was necessary for them to have been judges in their native towns; to have been transferred from there to the small Sanhedrim, which met at the temple mount; and thence to the second small Sanhedrim, which met at the entrance of the temple hall. They were not eligible unless they were the fathers of families, in order that they might be able to sympathize when cases involving domestic affairs were brought before them. If this rule was in force at the time of Stephen's trial, and if, as many suppose, Saul of Tarsus was a member of the Sanhedrim at that time, then Saul must have been a married man and a father. See CONY BEARE AND HOWSON, *Life and Epistles of St. Paul*, vol. i, p. 71.

The officers of the Sanhedrim were a president, a vice-president, and a sage or referee, all of whom were elected by the members. The president was called *Nasi*, that is, "prince" or "elevated one." He represented the civil and religious interests of the Jewish nation before the Roman government abroad, and before the different Jewish congregations at home. In the Sanhedrim he occupied the highest seat, summed up the votes of the elders, and determined traditions. The high priest was eligible to the office of president of the council, but had no right to preside *ex officio*. He must first be elected to the office. The vice-president was called *Ab-beth-din*, that is, "father of the house of judgment." He led and controlled the discussions on disputed points. The sage or referee was called *Chakam*, that is, "wise one." It was his duty to put into proper shape the subject for discussion and present it to the council. The vice-president sat on the right of the president, and the sage or referee on his left.

The council held daily sessions, lasting from the close of the morning sacrifice to the commencement of the evening sacrifice. On Sabbaths and festival days, however, they held no sessions. The place of their meeting is not precisely known; it seems to have varied at different times. A number of years before the birth of Christ a building was erected within the temple inclosure, and called the "Hall of Squares," or "Hall of Stones," because of the square-hewn stones which made the floor. Talmudical authorities do not agree as to the position of this hall, whether north or south of the temple proper; but all agree that it was situated to the east. In the most carefully arranged plans of the temple it is usually put to the south-east. Here the Sanhedrim met until shortly before the death of Christ, when they removed to a place in the Court of the Gentiles, and were not even confined to that. They met in the high-priest's palace when Jesus was brought before them. They subsequently settled at Tiberias.

When in session the Sanhedrim sat in a semicircle, the officers being in the center. The members sat cross-legged on the low cushions, or on carpets spread on the floor.

The council extended its jurisdiction beyond Palestine to every place where Jews had settlements. See Acts ix, 1, 2; xxii, 5. They could only try cases which involved violations of ecclesiastical law. They condemned to corporeal, and also to capital punishments. The latter were restricted to four modes: stoning, burning, beheading, and strangling. Forty years before the destruction of the temple the power of inflicting capital punishment was limited to those cases where the sentence of the Sanhedrim had been confirmed by the Roman procurator.

The Sanhedrim is often referred to in the New Testament. Besides the frequent mention of it in connection with the history of Christ, we find it engaged as an instrument of persecuting the apostles. Peter and John were brought before it. Acts iv, 1–21. Not long after, all the apostles were arraigned. Acts v, 17–42. In a short time Stephen was brought for trial. Acts vi, 12–15. Paul also, in later years, stood in the presence of this august body. Acts xxii, 30.

In addition to the great Sanhedrim there were smaller councils, for an account of which see note on Matt. x, 17.

719.—SPITTING—BUFFETING.

XXVI, 67. **Then did they spit in his face, and buffeted him; and others smote him with the palms of their hands. See also Mark xiv, 65; John xviii, 22.**

1. Spitting in the face was considered the greatest insult that could be offered to a person. See Deut. xxv, 9; Job xxx, 10. An Oriental, in relating any circumstance of which he desires to express the utmost contempt, will make a motion with his mouth, as if spitting.

2. Graham states that, at the present day in Palestine, when men quarrel and come to blows they strike each other, not with the fists, but with the palms of the hands. The insult offered to Jesus was given in this ordinary form; though, in addition, there were some who buffeted him, or struck him with their fist.

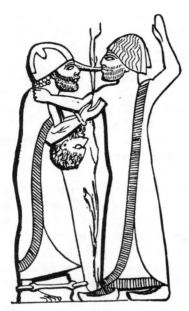

151.—The Accuser Spits upon and Buffets the Accused.

There is a scene represented on the Assyrian marbles which graphically illustrates this text, and at the same time shows the antiquity of the custom referred to. A captive is brought before the king, and in front of him is one who seizes the prisoner with the left hand, while the right hand is extended with open palm as if to smite him. He is also represented as spitting in the captive's face. Around his neck is suspended the head of a slain countryman.

This indignity of spitting and smiting was repeated in the case of Jesus by the Roman soldiers. The first insult of the kind was when he was in the presence of the high priest. Afterward, when Pilate released Barabbas and delivered Jesus up to the brutal soldiery, they again spit upon him and smote him. See Matt. xxvii, 30; Mark xv, 19; John xix, 3.

720.—PETER IN THE PALACE.

XXVI, 69.—Peter sat without in the palace. See also Mark xiv, 66; Luke xxii, 55; John xviii, 16, 18.

The meaning of this is that Peter was in the court of the palace, around which the house itself was built, but yet outside of the rooms. See note on Esther i, 5, and the engraving accompanying it. In this open court a fire was made, and here Peter was warming himself. Mark says that "Peter was *beneath* in the palace." The room in which the trial was held was probably a few steps above the court, opening into it, and separated from it by a railing and pillars. Thus Peter was in the palace, to which John plainly tells us he had been admitted, and yet, at the same time, he was "without" and "beneath."

721.—THE PORCH.

XXVI, 71. When he was gone out into the porch. See also Mark xiv, 68.

The porch is the passage-way from the street to the court. See diagram on page 198. It is sometimes arched, and its floor usually inclines from the direction of the street. A door opens from it into the court; but this door is so arranged that it is not directly opposite to the gate which opens to the street. Thus, though both should be open at the same time, no one, in passing through the street, would be able to look into the court. This was the place to which Peter retreated when he was accused of having been with Jesus. The porch is also mentioned in Judges iii, 23.

722.—POSITION OF THE ACCUSED.

XXVII, 11. Jesus stood before the governor.

It was the custom for the judge to sit while the accused person stood before him. Thus Paul said to Agrippa: "Now I stand and am judged for the hope of the promise made of God unto our fathers." Acts xxvi, 6. Thus Jesus stood before Pilate, as is stated in the text.

The accuser also stood while giving testimony. See note on Matt. xii, 41.

723.—THE PRISONER RELEASED.

XXVII, 15. Now at that feast the governor was wont to release unto the people a prisoner, whom they would. See also Mark xv, 6; Luke xxiii, 17; John xviii, 39.

It is not known whether the custom here mentioned was of Jewish or of Gentile origin. According to Maimonides, the Jews were in the habit of punishing criminals at the three great feasts, because there would then be a greater multitude of people to witness the punishment than at other times. If the custom be of Gentile origin, as many suppose, it is then a question whether it was a Syrian or a Roman custom. Grotius supposed that the Romans introduced it in order to gain the good-will of the Jews. There is, however, no historic mention of the practice aside from what we find in the Gospels.

It is thought that this privilege of demanding the release of a prisoner at the Feast of the Passover was expressly named in the instructions which Pilate had received as *proprætor*, since the governor had not the right of himself to release a prisoner, the right of pardoning a condemned criminal being a prerogative of the emperor alone.

724.—SCOURGING.

XXVII, 26. When he had scourged Jesus, he delivered him to be crucified. See also Mark xv, 15; John xix, 1.

It was customary among the Romans to scourge a condemned criminal before he was put to death. From Luke xxiii, 16, some have doubted whether the scourging of Jesus was a punishment of that character, inasmuch as Pilate there seems desirous to substitute scourging for crucifixion. It is not, however, a question of any practical moment, since the scourging was probably as severe as was usual in the cases of the condemned.

Scourging among the Romans was a more severe punishment than among the Jews. See note on Matt. x, 17. The scourge was made of cords or thongs of leather, and especially of ox-hide. There was one sort with which slaves were beaten, the use of which was particularly dreadful. It was knotted with bones, or heavy, indented circles of bronze. Sometimes the thongs, two or three in number, terminated in hooks. Such an instrument of torture was called a *scorpion*. There was no legal limit to the number of blows, as among the Jews; but the unfortunate culprit, bound to a low pillar, so that his bent back might more readily receive the heavy strokes, was beaten with merciless severity, and death was sometimes the result of this cruel punishment. Paul refers to Roman scourging in 2 Cor. xi, 25.

725.—THE ROMAN COHORT.

XXVII, 27. Then the soldiers of the governor took Jesus into the common hall, and gathered unto him the whole band of soldiers. See also Mark xv, 16.

This " band " (σπεῖρα) was the Roman *cohort*, which was the tenth part of a legion, and consisted of three *maniples*, each having two *centuries*. Ordinarily the *cohort* comprised six hundred men, but the number varied from three hundred to a thousand or more. Cornelius commanded a *century* in the Italian *cohort*. Acts x, 1. The *cohort* is also referred to in Acts xxi, 31; xxvii, 1.

726.—THE ROBE.

XXVII, 28. They stripped him, and put on him a scarlet robe. See also Mark xv, 17; John xix, 2.

The " robe " was probably the Roman *paludamentum*, which closely resembled the Greek *chlamys*. It was an outer garment, which hung loosely over the shoulders, was open in front, reached down to the knees or lower, and was fastened across the chest with a clasp, which, by the motions of the wearer, sometimes shifted to either shoulder. It was commonly either white or purple. Mark and John speak of this one as purple, and Matthew says it was scarlet. The two terms were convertible. The *paludamentum* was a military cloak, and, in mockery of the royalty of Jesus, was put upon him after he had been "stripped" of the outer garment which he usually wore. Compare verse 31, and see note on Deut. xxiv, 12, 13.

727.—EXECUTIONS OUTSIDE THE WALLS.

XXVII, 31. After that they had mocked him, they took the robe off from him, and put his own raiment on him, and led him away to crucify him. See also Mark xv, 20; Luke xxiii, 26; John xix, 16.

Mark says that they led him *out*. So in the Epistle to the Hebrews it is said that Jesus "suffered without the gate." Heb. xiii, 12. Capital punishments among the Jews were executed outside the boundaries of camps or the walls of cities. See Lev. xxiv, 14; Num. xv, 35, 36; 1 Kings xxi, 13; Acts vii, 58. The Romans also observed the same custom, particularly in the crucifixion of malefactors.

728.—PLACE OF CAPITAL PUNISHMENT.

XXVII, 83. **When they were come unto a place called Golgotha, that is to say, a place of a skull.** See also Mark xv, 22; Luke xxiii, 33; John xix, 17.

This is supposed to have been the spot where capital executions for Jerusalem usually took place. It was customary to have certain places set apart for such purposes by the different cities. Rosenmüller (*Morgenland,* vol. v, p. 117) gives several illustrations of this. The Mamertins had such a one on the Pompeian Way, behind their city. The Romans also had a particular place for the crucifixion of slaves. Descriptive names were given to these places. The Romans called their place of execution *Sestertium,* because it was two and a half miles from the city. The Thessalians called theirs *Korax,* the *Raven;* which is similar to the German *Rabenstein,* (ravenstone,) a name given to a place of execution, because the ravens resort there when a criminal is executed and exposed. "To the ravens!" was a very significant ancient curse. The name of the place where Jesus was executed was Golgotha, a corrupt form of the Chaldee name for a skull. This would be a significant title for a place of execution, and many suppose that this is the reason of the name. Others, however, think the name may have been given to the place because of its rounding, skull-like form; and some authorities assert that the Romans had no particular places for crucifixion near Jerusalem, but executed this mode of punishment anywhere outside the walls. Even if this were so, there may have been reasons why one place should be more frequently used than others, and this might properly be known as the "place of a skull."

729.—STUPEFYING POTION.

XXVII, 84. **They gave him vinegar to drink mingled with gall.** See also Mark xv, 23; Luke xxiii, 36.

It was customary among the Romans to give to the person to be crucified a stupefying potion of wine and myrrh. This, according to Mark, is what was offered to Jesus, while Matthew states that they offered vinegar and gall. Some think the wine, being sour, is represented by the word "vinegar," and the myrrh, being bitter, by the word "gall." Lightfoot suggests that Mark gives the ordinary name by which the usual stupefying potion was known, while Matthew tells literally what was offered instead by the soldiers, in mockery, as Luke says. See Luke xxiii, 36. It may be, after all, that two distinct draughts were offered, the one by way of mocking his agony, and the other according to the usual custom.

730.—CRUCIFIXION.

XXVII, 35. **They crucified him, and parted his garments, casting lots.** See also Mark xv, 25; Luke xxiii, 33; John xix, 18.

Crucifixion was not a Jewish punishment, though among the Jews culprits were sometimes tied to a stake by their hands *after* death. See Deut. xxi, 22. It was an ancient mode of capital punishment, and is said to have been devised by Semiramis. It was in use by the Persians, Assyrians, Egyptians, Carthaginians, Scythians, Greeks, Romans, and ancient Germans. It was a most shameful and degrading punishment, and among the Romans was the fate of robbers, assassins, and rebels. It was especially the punishment of criminal slaves.

There were several kinds of crosses used. One consisted of two beams of wood laid across each other in the form of an X. Another had two beams of unequal length, the shorter placed on top of the longer, like the letter T. In a third variety, a small portion of the longer piece appeared above the transverse beam, thus: and on this the inscription was placed. See note on Matt. xxvii, 37. This was doubtless the form of cross on which our Lord was crucified. From the center of the perpendicular beam there projected a wooden plug or horn, on which the body of the condemned rested. The bottom of the cross was sharpened, that it might be more easily driven into the ground. The ordinary representations of the cross in paintings and engravings are incorrect, inasmuch as they make it appear larger and heavier than the reality. It was not generally more than ten feet high, so that when erected, a part of it being in the earth, the feet of the sufferer were not far from the ground.

The condemned man was first stripped of his clothing, which seems to have been the perquisite of the executioners. See John xix, 23, 24. He was then fastened to the cross, which had been previously fixed in the earth—though sometimes he was first fixed to the cross—which was then lifted and thrust into the ground. He sat on the middle bar or horn, already mentioned, and his limbs were stretched out and tied to the bars of the cross. Large iron spikes were then driven through the hands and feet. Sometimes the feet were nailed separately, and at other times they were crossed and a long spike was driven through them both.

In this situation the poor sufferer was left to linger until death slowly came to his relief. This usually required two or three days, though some lingered a longer time before their sufferings ended. The pain was very severe, though not so intense as has sometimes been represented. On this subject Dr Stroud says: "The bodily sufferings attending this punishment were doubtless great; but, either through ignorance or design, have been much exaggerated. The insertion of the cross into its hole or socket, when the criminal was previously attached to it, did not necessarily produce the violent concussion which has been supposed; and, as the body rested on a bar, it did not bear with its whole weight on the perforated extremities. At all events there have been many examples of persons enduring these sufferings with the utmost fortitude, and almost without a complaint, until relieved from them by death. A fact of importance to be known, but which has not been sufficiently regarded, is that crucifixion was a very lingering punishment, and proved fatal, not so much by loss of blood—since the wounds in the hands and feet did not lacerate any large vessel, and were nearly closed by the nails which produced them—as by the slow process of nervous irritation and exhaustion."—*The Physical Cause of the Death of Christ*, p. 55.

After death the body was left to be devoured by beasts and birds of prey. The Romans, however, made an exception in favor of all Jews who were crucified; this was on account of their law, as contained in Deut. xxi, 22, 23. They were permitted to bury the crucified Jews on the day of crucifixion. This usually made it necessary to hasten their death, which was done by kindling a fire under them, or by letting hungry beasts attack them, or by breaking their bones with an iron mallet.

731.—THE GUARD.

XXVII, 36. Sitting down they watched him there.

This refers to the military guard, who were the actual executioners, and whose duty it was to watch the person crucified lest his friends should rescue him. In this instance the guard probably consisted of five men, four of them ordinary soldiers, (a "quaternion;" see note on Acts xii, 4,) and the fifth the centurion in command. Compare Matt. xxvii, 54, with John xix, 23.

732.—THE TABLET ON THE CROSS.

XXVII, 37. Set up over his head his accusation written, THIS IS JESUS THE KING OF THE JEWS. See also Mark xv, 26; Luke xxiii, 38; John xix, 19.

It was a Roman custom in cases of capital execution to put on a tablet the crime for which the condemned suffered, this tablet being placed in full view of all who witnessed the execution. Eusebius states that the martyr Attalus was led around the amphitheater, while before him there was borne a tablet, on which were the words, "This is Attalus the Christian." The tablet was sometimes carried by the condemned man himself, hung around his neck, on the way to execution. In the official language of the Romans it was called *Titulus*. It was a metal plate, having black letters on a white ground. We know not whether Jesus carried this tablet around his neck, or whether it was borne before him; but when the cross was reared it was placed over his head in view of all beholders.

733.—THE VAIL OF THE TEMPLE.

XXVII, 51. Behold, the vail of the temple was rent in twain from the top to the bottom. See also Mark xv, 88; Luke xxiii, 45.

This vail was the curtain which hung between the Holy Place and the Most Holy Place. It was sixty feet in length, and reached from floor to ceiling. The rabbins say that there were two vails in this part of the temple; that while in the first temple there was a wall one cubit thick, in the second temple they placed two vails between the Holy Place and the Most Holy Place, leaving a vacant space of a cubit in width between them. If this were so, they were probably both torn at the time referred to in the text and parallels, since the design of the evangelists evidently is to show that the separation between the two parts of the temple no longer existed.

734.—THE "DOOR" OF THE SEPULCHER.

XXVII, 60. And laid it in his own new tomb, which he had hewn out in the rock: and he rolled a great stone to the door of the sepulcher, and departed. See also Mark xv, 46; Luke xxiii, 53; John xix, 41, 42.

1. For a description of rock-tombs, see note on Isa. xxii, 16.

2. Dr. Barclay, in his account of the "Tombs of the Kings," represents the outer door as consisting of a large stone disc like a millstone, and suggests that this may have been the case with Joseph's tomb, into which the Saviour was put, though he admits that there are other methods by which "a great stone" might be "rolled to the door of the sepulcher." He says: "Immediately in front of the doorway (the top of which is more than a foot below the floor of the porch) is a deep trench, commencing a foot or two west of the door, and extending three or four yards along the wall eastward. The bottom of this trench is a short distance below the sill of the door, and is probably an inclined plane. Along this channel a large thick stone disc traverses, fitting very accurately against its western end, which is made concave, so as to be exactly conformed to the

152.—DOOR OF THE TOMB.

convexity of this large millstone-like disc when rolled to that end—thus closing the door-way most effectually."—*City of the Great King*, p. 192.

Porter has a statement similar to that of Barclay, though he does not give the shape of the slab which is rolled into the groove. See *Giant Cities of Bashan*, etc., p. 139. Of course no one can say that this was the precise arrangement in Joseph's sepulcher, though we see no improbability in it.

The rolling of the stone is also mentioned in Matt. xxviii, 2; Mark xvi, 3, 4; Luke xxiv, 2. The stone at the sepulcher is likewise named in John xi, 38, 39.

735.—SEALING THE SEPULCHER.

XXVII, 66. So they went, and made the sepulcher sure, sealing the stone, and setting a watch.

It is thought by some that this refers to the custom of fastening the stone at the entrance of the tomb with cement, a custom which has been noticed by modern travelers. The context, however, shows that this was an official sealing, which was intended to be so arranged that the seal could not be broken without detection. Thus the lion's den was sealed into which Daniel was put. See Dan. vi, 17. A cord stretched across the stone, with a lump of stamped clay fastening it at each end, would prevent any entrance without detection. Clay was often impressed with the stamp of seals for various purposes. See note on Job xxxviii, 14.

MARK.

736.—THE ROOF BROKEN UP.

II, 4. When they could not come nigh unto him for the press, they uncovered the roof where he was: and when they had broken it up, they let down the bed wherein the sick of the palsy lay. See also Luke v, 19.

From the second verse it appears that the crowd of people was so great as to fill, not only the court, but the porch. (For description of the court, see note on Matt. xxvi, 69; and of the porch, see note on Matt. xxvi, 71.) The precise position of the Saviour is not stated. He may have been in the general reception-room, which opened into the court at the side opposite to the porch, with the people behind him in the room, and before him in the court; or, if the house were two stories high, he may have been on the gallery which surrounded the court, the people thronging the gallery as well as the court below. See note on Esther i, 5. Nor are we told how the four bearers of the sick man contrived to get him to the roof. Some suppose that they carried him up by the stairs which led from the court; but, if the house was so crowded as to leave no room even at the door, it is hard to tell how they could get him through the porch into the court, and thence to the stairs. If the house was joined to others in the same street, they might have taken him through the adjoining building, and lifted him over the parapet which divided the roofs of the two houses, and thus have placed him on the roof of the house where Jesus was teaching; or there may have been a flight of external stairs by which they could ascend from the street to the roof. See note on Matt. xxiv, 17.

Several explanations have been given of the manner in which they found access to Jesus after they reached the roof. Mark says that they "uncovered" the roof, and "broke it up." Luke says, "they let him down through the tiling." Tile-roofs, however, are not common in Syria, though Greek houses are usually covered in this manner. This fact has led to the suggestion that Luke, being probably a native of Greek Antioch, may have used the word "tiling," not in reference to the material of which the roof was made, but because it was to him the most familiar term which signified roofing. See Phillott in SMITH'S *Dictionary of the Bible*, s. v. TILE. Both evangelists undoubtedly mean the covering which was over that part of the house where Jesus was. The following are the principal explanations which have been given of the manner in which the roof was uncovered:

1. That the sick man was let down through the scuttle, or ordinary opening in the roof; this opening being first made large enough for the purpose by breaking the roof around its edge. This is Dr. Lightfoot's explanation. See *Horæ Hebraicæ* on this text.

2. That the court, where Jesus and the people were assembled, was covered by an awning. See note on Esther i, 6. The friends of the sick man, on reaching the roof, loosened this awning, and then let the paralytic down into the court. This is the opinion of Dr. Shaw. See *Travels*, etc., p. 211.

3. That the ordinary roof of the house was actually broken up, the sticks, thorn-bush, mortar, and earth, of which it was composed, being thrown aside, until an aperture was made large enough to let the sick man through. (For structure of roofs, see note on Psa. cxxix, 6.) This view, which is adopted by many commentators, is advocated by Dr. Thomson. He states that the roof could easily be broken in this manner, and easily repaired; that, as a matter of fact, it is often done for the purpose of letting down grain, straw, and other articles. He says: "I have often seen it done, and done it myself to houses in Lebanon, but there is always more dust made than is agreeable." —*The Land and the Book*, vol. ii, p. 7. The doctor, however, supposes that in the case referred to in the text the roof may have been made of materials more easily taken up, such as coarse matting, boards, or coarse slabs.

4. That the Saviour was in the gallery while he addressed the people around him and in the court below, and that it was the roof of this gallery which the friends of the sick man broke up. This is the opinion of Dr. Kitto. He says: "They had only to take up two or three of the loosely-attached boards forming the covering of the gallery, and there was a clear and sufcient opening through which to let their friend down to the feet of our Saviour."—*Daily Bible Illustrations*, vol. vii, p. 260.

This last theory seems to us to present greater probabilities of correctness than any of the others, though every one of them shows how the incident recorded in the text was possible.

737.—BOAT-CUSHION.

IV, 88. He was in the hinder part of the ship, asleep on a pillow.

This "pillow" (προσκεφάλαιον) is supposed by critics to have been different from the soft pillow used for a head-rest in houses. See note on Ezek. xiii, 18. Such an article would hardly be in place in a fisherman's boat. It was rather the cushion or fleece on which the rowers sat when they pulled the oars. "This use of προσκεφάλαιον for 'cushion to *sit* upon,' though rare, is found occasionally in even the purest classical writers."—BLOOMFIELD.

738.—TOMBS FOR DWELLINGS.

V, 2, 3. When he was come out of the ship, immediately there met him out of the tombs a man with an unclean spirit, who had his dwelling among the tombs. See also Luke viii, 27.

Tombs hewn out of the rock were sometimes made hiding-places for criminals, dwellings for poor people, and abodes for the insane. By reading the description of these tombs contained in the note on Isa. xxii, 16, it can be seen that they might readily be converted into places of shelter by persons whose tastes were not fastidious, or whose necessities compelled them to seek a refuge. Isaiah describes the idolatrous Hebrews of his time as a people who "remain among the graves, and lodge among the monuments." Isa. lxv, 4. This is supposed to have been done from the superstitious notion, which they had learned from the heathen, that the dreams which they would have in such desol-te places would be a revelation of future events.

At the present day travelers in Palestine sometimes find a temporary asylum for the night in the old tombs, which are no longer used for burial purposes. Buckingham, who visited a number of tombs in the very region where the incident referred to in the text took place, found a carpenter's shop in an old sepulcher. He went into another which was used as a dwelling. "The tomb was about eight feet in height on the inside, as there was a descent of a steep step from the stone threshold to the floor. Its size was about twelve paces square; but, as no light was received into it except by the door, we could not see whether there was an inner chamber as in some of the others. A perfect sarcophagus still remained within, and this was now used by the family as a chest for corn and other provisions, so that this violated sepulcher of the dead had thus become a secure, a cool, and a convenient retreat to the living of a different race."—*Travels in Palestine*, p. 440.

739.—DILIGENT HAND-WASHING.

VII, 8. For the Pharisees, and all the Jews, except they wash their hands oft, eat not, holding the tradition of the elders.

There is great diversity of opinion among critics as to the proper rendering of πυγμή, "*oft.*" Its primary signification is the *fist*, and hence Robinson renders the text, "*unless they wash their hands* (rubbing them) *with the fist, i. e.,* not merely dipping the fingers or hand in water as a *sign* of ablution, but rubbing the hands together as a ball or fist in the usual Oriental manner when water is poured over them."—*Lexicon of the New Testament.* From this he supposes the word to be taken in the sense of "*sedulously, carefully, diligently.*"

How "diligently" the "traditions of the elders" required the Pharisees to wash is illustrated by Lightfoot in extracts from Rabbinical writers. See *Horæ Hebraicæ* on Matt. xv, 2. He states that they make mention "of the quantity of water sufficient for this washing—of the washing of the hands, and of the plunging of them; of the first and second water; of the manner of washing; of the time; of the order, when the number of those that sat down to meat exceeded five, or did not exceed; and other such like niceties." Not content with the ordinary usage of washing after eating, (see note on 2 Kings iii, 11,) they carefully washed before eating, lest they should be injured by Shibta, "an evil spirit, which sits upon men's hands in the night; and if any touch his food with unwashen hands that spirit sits upon that food, and there is danger from it."

740.—CORBAN.

VII, 11. Ye say, If a man shall say to his father or mother, It is Corban, that is to say, a gift, by whatsoever thou mightest be profited by me; he shall be free. See also Matt. xv, 5.

The *corban* was an offering of any kind consecrated to God. It was right to make such offerings because God had commanded them; but the Saviour charges the Pharisees with placing their traditions above the Divine commands. For instance, God ordained honor and obedience to parents; but the Pharisees, by their traditionary explanation and abuse of the law of *corban*, completely nullified the law of parental honor. Their traditions taught that whatever was *corban*, that is, a gift consecrated to God, could not be alienated for any other purpose; but in the application of this principle, which in itself is correct enough, they manifested a wonderful ingenuity of perversion. If, for instance, parents desired help, and the son should say "My property is *corban*," it released him from all obligation to sustain his parents; nevertheless, strange to say, it did not bind him to consecrate his substance to sacred uses. He could use it for his own purposes, or give it to whom he pleased, except to those to whom he had said, "It is *corban*." No wonder the Saviour charged the Pharisees with "making the word of God of none effect" through their tradition.

741.—STANDING DURING PRAYER.

XI, 25. **When ye stand praying, forgive, if ye have aught against any.**

Standing, as well as kneeling, was, among the Jews, an ancient posture during prayer. There are several other Scripture references to it besides the text. See 1 Sam. i, 26; 1 Kings viii, 22; 2 Chron. vi, 13; Luke xviii, 11, 13. While in this attitude the hands were sometimes stretched out heavenward. See note on 1 Kings viii, 22. The ancient Persians and Egyptians also stood in prayer; the latter sometimes also kneeled. Some of the varied postures of the Mohammedans in prayer are standing.

742.—MITE—FARTHING.

XII, 42. **She threw in two mites, which make a farthing.** See also Luke xxi, 2.

1. The λεπτόν, or "mite," was the smallest Greek copper coin. Its value was the eighth part of an *assarion;* thus making it worth about one fifth of one cent, or three eighths of one farthing. See note on Matt. x, 29. It is also mentioned in Luke xii, 59.

2. The κοδράντης, or "farthing," was the smallest Roman brass coin, and was worth the fourth part of an assarion, and equal to two *lepta*, or mites; that is, about two fifths of one cent, or three fourths of one farthing. It is also mentioned in Matt. v, 26.

743.—NIGHT-WATCHES.

XIII, 35. **Watch ye therefore: for ye know not when the master of the house cometh, at even, or at midnight, or at the cockcrowing, or in the morning.**

The earliest division of the night into watches is noticed in the note on Exod. xiv, 24. After the Jews became subject to the Roman power they adopted the Roman method of dividing the watches. These watches were four: the first being from sunset to three hours later; the second from this time to midnight; the third from midnight to three hours before sunrise; and the fourth from this time to sunrise. These four watches are all alluded to in the text, the first being called "even," the second "midnight," the third "cockcrowing," and the fourth "morning;" the names indicating the time when the watch terminated.

This mode of dividing the night is also referred to in Matt. xiv, 25; xxiv, 43; Mark vi, 48; Luke xii, 38.

744.—AN EXCEPTIONAL CUSTOM—PITCHER.

XIV, 13. There shall meet you a man bearing a pitcher of water. See also Luke xxii, 10.

1. Water is usually carried by women. See note on Gen. xxiv, 15. Therefore the sight of a *man* carrying water would more readily attract attention. Hackett says: "I recollect but two instances in which I saw 'a man bearing a pitcher of water;' and I think that the manner in which the Saviour refers to such a circumstance (he mentions it as a sign) implies that it was not common."—*Illustrations of Scripture*, p. 89.

2. The "pitcher" is supposed to have been an *amphora*. See note on 2 Kings iv, 2.

745.—THE "UPPER ROOM."

XIV, 14, 15. Where is the guest-chamber, where I shall eat the passover with my disciples? And he will show you a large upper room furnished and prepared: there make ready for us. See also Luke xxii, 11, 12.

Some suppose this "guest chamber" and "upper room" to be the *aliyah*, or room above the porch or on the roof. See note on 2 Kings iv, 10. Others, however, think the words refer to a large open room fronting the court, on the side opposite to the entrance from the porch, and elevated above the level of the court. See note on Matt. xxvi, 69. This is a very important apartment in an Eastern house, and is often elegantly fitted up. Here the owner receives his friends, or those who come to him on business. It is the first room that meets the eye of a visitor on entering the court, and frequently presents a splendid appearance. Sometimes a fountain in the court directly in front of this apartment cools the air, while adding beauty to the appearance.

746.—MODE OF EATING.

XIV, 20. One of the twelve, that dippeth with me in the dish. See also Matt. xxvi, 23.

The Orientals at their meals make no use of knives, forks, or spoons. The animal food is so thoroughly cooked as to be easily separated by the fingers, and with the fingers the food of all kinds is mainly taken from the dish. When, however, the food is in a semi-fluid state, or so soft that the fingers cannot conveniently hold it, a piece of bread is dipped into the dish and made the vehicle by which soft food is conveyed to the mouth. This bread formed the "sop" mentioned in John xiii, 26, where see the note.

747.—COUNSELOR.

XV, 43. Joseph of Arimathea, an honorable counselor. See also Luke xxiii, 50.

The expression "counselor" means that Joseph was a member of the Jewish Sanhedrim or Great Council. Luke makes this clear by adding, "The same had not consented to the counsel and deed of them." Luke xxiii, 51. "Them" undoubtedly refers to the Jewish authorities who had condemned Jesus. It is supposed by some that the expression "honorable" was a title of distinction applied to every "counselor" or member of the Sanhedrim. For a description of this Council, see note on Matt. xxvi, 59.

LUKE.

748.—WIVES OF PRIESTS.

I, 5. There was . . . a certain priest named Zacharias, of the course of Abia: and his wife was of the daughters of Aaron.

Great care was taken in the selection of wives for the Jewish priests, so that the line of priests might be kept in every respect unsullied. "It was lawful for a priest to marry a Levitess, or, indeed, a daughter of Israel; but it was most commendable of all to marry one of the priests' line."—LIGHT-FOOT, *Horæ Hebraicæ.* Zacharias was specially honored in having for his wife one of the descendants of Aaron.

749.—NAMING THE CHILD.

I, 59. It came to pass, that on the eighth day they came to circumcise the child; and they called him Zacharias, after the name of his father.

It was customary among the Jews to give names to children at the time of their circumcision. The rabbins say that this was because God changed the names of Abram and Sarai at the same time that he instituted circumcision. It was very rarely that the son received the name of the father; there was, doubtless, some special reason in this case why the friends wished the babe to be called Zacharias. The custom of naming the child at the time of circumcision is also illustrated in the case of Jesus. See Luke ii, 21.

Other nations, as well as the Jews, gave names to their children on special days. Godwyn says: "The Romans gave names to their male children on the ninth day, to the female on the eighth. The Athenians gave names on the tenth. Others on the seventh. These days Tertullian calleth Nominalia. The Grecians, besides the tenth day on which they named the child, observed also the fifth, on which day the midwives took the child, and ran about a fire made for that purpose, using that ceremony as a purification of themselves and the child."—*Moses and Aaron*, book vi, chap. i.

Morier gives an interesting account connected with the naming of children in Persia. He says: "The Persians have no ceremony that corresponds entirely to our christening, because their children become Mohammedans as soon as the Kelemeh Islam has been whispered into their ear; but they have one called the *Sheb be Khair*, or 'Be the night propitious,' which is for the purpose of giving the child a name. If the father of the child be in good circumstances, he collects his friends together and makes a feast. ·He also requires the attendance of several Mollahs; and when the *mejlis* or assembly is complete, sweetmeats are brought in and eaten. The infant is also brought into the *mejlis*, and placed near one of the Mollahs. The father of the child then gives out certain names, five in number, each of which is written separately on separate slips of paper. These slips of paper are placed either within the Koran, or under the edge of the *nummud*, or carpet. The *Fatheh*, which is the first *surai* or chapter of the Koran, is read. One of the slips of paper is then taken out at random by the hand of the father, and the child is called after the name which is there inscribed. A Mollah takes up the babe, pronounces the name in its ear, and places the paper on its swaddling-clothes. The relations of the child then each give it money and other presents, and this custom they call the *Roo-memah*, or *Showing the face*."—*Second Journey*, etc., p. 108.

750.—WRITING–TABLETS.

I, 63. He asked for a writing-table, and wrote, saying, His name is John.

Writing-tablets were in use among various ancient nations. They are referred to in Isa. xxx, 8, and in Hab. ii, 2, and metaphorically in Prov. iii, 3; Jer. xvii, 1, and 2 Cor. iii, 3. They are yet to be seen in modern Greece. Among the Romans they were occasionally made of ivory or of citron-wood, but generally of beach, fir, or some other common wood. They were covered with a thin coating of wax, in which the letters were formed by a *stylus*, an instrument corresponding to the modern pen. It was made of gold, silver, brass, iron, copper, ivory, or bone. One end was pointed for writing, while the other was smooth, flat, and circular, for erasing, and for smoothing the waxed surface so that it might be used again for writing. The outside part of the tablet, which was held in the hand, was not coated with wax, and around the edge of the inside there was a thin, narrow ledge, so that when two tablets came together the waxed surfaces would not touch each other and become marred.

A book was often made of several of these tablets combined, sometimes as many as five or six being fastened together at the backs by means of wires, which also served as hinges. Tablets were used for almost every species of writing, where the document was not of great length. Letters, or even wills, were written upon them. For the purpose of sealing these, and other documents which might require it,

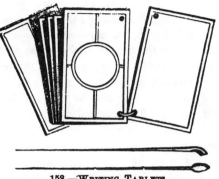

153.—WRITING TABLETS.

holes were made in the outer edge, through which a triple thread was passed and fastened with a seal.

751.—SWADDLING–CLOTHES—MANGER—INN.

II, 7. She brought forth her first-born son, and wrapped him in swaddling-clothes, and laid him in a manger; because there was no room for them in the inn.

1. The "swaddling-clothes" were bandages which were tightly wrapped around a new-born child. The rank of the child was indicated by the splendor and costliness of these bands. A fine white shawl, tied with a golden band, was sometimes used for the purpose; at other times a small purple scarf, fastened with a brooch. The poor used broad fillets of common cloth.

The practice is still followed in the East. Miss Rogers, an English lady, who had opportunities far beyond ordinary travelers for observing the domestic life of the Eastern people, describes the appearance of an infant thus bandaged: "The infant I held in my arms was so bound in swaddling-clothes that it was perfectly firm and solid, and looked like a mummy. It had a band under its chin and across its forehead and a little, quilted silken cap on its head with tiny coins of gold sewed to it. The outer covering of this little figure was of crimson and white striped silk; no sign of arms or legs, hands or feet, could be seen."—*Domestic Life in Palestine*, p. 28. This was in Jaffa. Another infant which she saw in Bethlehem is thus described: "I took the little creature in my arms. His body was stiff and unyielding, so tightly was it swathed with white and purple linen. H s hands and feet were quite confined, and his head was bound with a small, soft red shawl, which passed under his chin and across his forehead in small folds."—P. 62. This custom is referred to in Job xxxviii, 9; Lam. ii, 22; Ezek. xvi, 4; Luke ii, 12.

2. There is a dispute as to the precise meaning of the word φάτνη, here

and in verses 12 and 16 rendered "manger," and in Luke xiii, 15, rendered "stall." Some authorities give it the one meaning, and some the other; while others, as our translators, attach both meanings to the word. It is the Septuagint rendering for the Hebrew *ebus* in Job xxxix, 9, and in Isa. i, 3; a word which, in our version, is translated "crib." The location of the manger or the stall is also a point of discussion; whether it was connected with the stable belonging to the inn, or with some other stable in the neighborhood, as, for instance, in some cave near by. Caves, we know, were used for dwellings, (see note on Gen. xix, 30,) and are so used at this day, and also for stables. The discussion is interesting, but is not pertinent to the object of this book. It is proper, however, to remark, that in many rude houses horses and cattle are stabled in the court, while the family are provided for in apartments raised on a platform of stone some two feet from the level of the court. The food of the animals is placed on this platform, and sometimes there are hollow places in the stone which serve the purpose of mangers. See further in the description of the inn in the next paragraph.

3. The Eastern "inn," or caravanserai, bears no resemblance to the inns with which we are acquainted. There are various kinds of these Oriental inns, some being merely small, rude resting-places, such as are mentioned in the note on Jer. ix, 2, while others are capacious and comparatively comfortable. Such an inn presents, at a distance, the appearance of a fortress, being a quadrangular building about a hundred yards long on each side of the square, having its wall about twenty feet high. An arched gate-way, surmounted by a tower, opens into a large open court, surrounded by a platform, on the level of which are the travelers' rooms. These rooms are not furnished, each traveler being expected to provide for himself every thing but actual shelter. He must carry his own bedding, provisions, and cooking utensils. In case of sickness the porter in attendance may minister to his wants. See Luke x, 34, 35. The horses, camels, and baggage are placed in the extensive court, in the center of which is a fountain. Sometimes, however, there are stables formed of covered avenues, extending between the rear wall of the lodging-rooms and the external wall of the caravanserai, the entrance being at the corners of the quadrangle. These stables are on a level with the court, and thus below the level of the platform on which are the

155.—Diagram of Caravanserai.

travelers' apartments. This platform, however, projects into the stable, thus forming a ledge or bench above the stable floor. On this ledge the cattle can, if they wish, rest the nose-bags of haircloth which contain their food. Dr. Kitto thinks that it was in such a stable as this that our Lord was born. See *Daily Bible Readings*, vol. vii, p. 63.

154.—INTERIOR OF VIZIR KHAN, ALEPPO.

752.—"THE CONSOLATION."

II, 25. The same man was just and devout, waiting for the consolation of Israel.

The *Consolation* was a term used by the Jews of that period, and long after, to designate the Messiah. Lightfoot says that they were accustomed to swear by "the Consolation." When we are told in the text that Simeon was waiting for "the Consolation of Israel," we are to understand that he was waiting for the Messiah.

753.—THE FIRST DAY'S JOURNEY.

II, 44, 45. But they, supposing him to have been in the company, went a day's journey ; and they sought him among their kinsfolk and acquaintance. And when they found him not, they turned back again to Jerusalem, seeking him.

This does not mean that they traveled an entire day before they missed the lad. An ordinary "day's journey" varied from eighteen to thirty miles. See note on 1 Kings xix, 4. But when a party started on a journey the first day's travel was invariably shorter than the usual distance. This is a very ancient custom, and is still practiced. When every thing is ready for the caravan to move they slowly march on, but halt for the first night at a distance of from three to eight miles from the place of starting. The reason assigned for this usage is, that if any thing has been left behind through mistake or forgetfulness, some one may with but little trouble return and get it in time to join the caravan the next day.

In the case before us they made the short journey of the first day, and then halted for the night; so that, instead of traveling all day without missing Jesus, they only traveled a few hours. The first stopping-place of nearly all traveling parties who now leave Jerusalem for the north is el-Bireh, supposed to be the ancient Beer, or Beeroth. It is only eight or ten miles from the city, and is considered a three hours' journey. There is a tradition that this is the very place where the caravan, of which the family of Jesus was a part, made their first halt; and it certainly has greater probability in its favor than many other traditions connected with Palestine. Halting here, or not far from it, when the family gathered together they noticed the absence of Jesus, and immediately went back to the city to find him.

754.—DOCTORS AND DISCIPLES.

II, 46. They found him in the temple, sitting in the midst of the doctors, both hearing them, and asking them questions.

There were several places within the Temple area where doctors of the law met their disciples. One of these places was in the cloisters described in the note on Matt. xxiv, 1. Another was in the synagogue which was in the Temple inclosure. After service the doctors admitted any who wished to converse with them on matters pertaining to the law. There were also other places resorted to for a similar purpose; and Lightfoot declares that it was not impossible for Jesus to have been in the great Sanhedrim itself.

There is no reason to suppose that in the conversation which Jesus held with these learned men there was any thing like controversy. He simply followed the custom of the time, which allowed any one who chose to question the doctors on any points on which they desired information.

755.—PUBLIC SCRIPTURE-READING.

IV, 16. He went into the synagogue on the Sabbath day, and stood up for to read.

When the law and the prophets were read in the synagogue those who read were expected to stand. See note on Acts xiii, 15. Not only priests and Levites but common Israelites were allowed to read the Scriptures publicly. Every Sabbath seven persons read: a priest, a Levite, and five ordinary Israelites.

756.—BOOKS OF PROPHECY.

IV, 17. There was delivered unto him the book of the prophet Esaias. And when he had opened the book, he found the place where it was written, etc.

1. For a description of books, and the mode of opening and closing, (referred to in this verse and in verse twenty,) see notes on Job xix, 23, 24; and on Isa. xxxiv, 4.

2. Each of the prophetical books is supposed to have been in a separate volume, with the exception of the prophecies of the twelve minor prophets, which were perhaps bound together.

757.—THE CHAZAN—POSTURE OF TEACHERS.

IV, 20. He closed the book, and he gave it again to the minister, and sat down.

1. The position of the "minister" in the synagogue bore no resemblance to that of the minister in the Christian Church. He was called *chazan*, and, in the time of Christ and for several centuries afterward, was the lowest servant in the synagogue, his duties resembling those of the sexton in one of our churches. He had charge of the furniture, and kept the building in good order, preparing it for service, and summoning the people at the appointed hour. It was also his duty to call out the names of those whom the ruler of the synagogue selected to read the lesson of the day, and to hand to them the sacred roll, receiving it from them when the reading was

finished. It was the *chazan* who "delivered" Isaiah's prophecy to Jesus, as recorded in verse seventeen, and to him Jesus gave the book when he had done reading, as noted in the twentieth verse.

2. Sitting was the customary posture of a teacher when instructing his disciples. Hence, when Jesus rolled up the manuscript and returned it to the hands of the *chazan*, he sat down on the platform instead of going back to his seat, because he wished to address the people. This custom is also referred to in Matt. v, 1; xxiii, 2; xxvi, 55; John viii, 2. See, further, note on Acts xxii, 3.

758.—NIGHT-FISHING.

V, 5. We have toiled all the night, and have taken nothing.

Night-fishing is very common in the East. Roberts says that in India the fishermen prefer the night to the day. They carry lighted torches to allure the fish. Dr. Thomson gives a lively description of night-fishing in Palestine: "It is a beautiful sight. With blazing torch the boat glides over the flashing sea, and the men stand gazing keenly into it until their prey is sighted, when, quick as lightning, they fling their net or fly their spear; and often you see the tired fishermen come sullenly into harbor in the morning, having toiled all night in vain."—*The Land and the Book*, vol. ii, p. 80.

Night-fishing is also referred to in John xxi, 3..

759.—TAX-GATHERING.

V, 27. He went forth, and saw a publican, named Levi, sitting at the receipt of custom. See also Matt. ix, 9; Mark ii, 14.

1. The publicans were the Roman tax-gatherers, of whom there were several classes. The Roman senate farmed the taxes to rich capitalists, who agreed to pay a certain sum into the public treasury, and reimburse themselves with the taxes they collected. These capitalists were called *publicani*, and often formed themselves into a joint-stock company, appointing one of their number as general manager. He usually resided at Rome, and was called *magister*.

The *publicani* were an influential section of the Roman knights, an ancient order who occupied a kind of middle rank between the senators and the people. These, however, are not mentioned in the New Testament. The "publicans" so frequently referred to there were the *portitores*, or men who were employed by the *publicani* to collect the taxes in the provinces. They were the actual custom-house officers, and were commonly natives of the provinces where they were stationed. They were supervised by the *sub-magistri*, who made the returns to the *magister* at Rome. Zaccheus was a *sub-magister*, or "chief of the publicans." Luke xix, 2. Levi, or Matthew, was one of the *portitores*, or tax-gatherers.

The publicans, of whatever class, were looked upon with disfavor by the masses of the people. The complimentary reference of Cicero to the *publicani*, which has sometimes been cited as an evidence of their high respectability, is thought to have been merely the flattery of an orator who sought to accomplish political purposes thereby. The *portitores*, however, were especially detested. Their duty, if honestly discharged, would have made them unpopular enough; but when, as was often the case, they went beyond their legal rights and levied exorbitant taxes, using all the machinery of the law to help them, their unpopularity greatly increased. Many of them were Jews, and were regarded by their Jewish brethren as no better than the heathen, with whom publicans were often classed. See Matt. xviii, 17. It is said that the Jews would not associate with them, nor allow them in the temple or in the synagogue; nor would they permit them to give testimony in Jewish courts. Even the presents which they brought to the temple are said to have been rejected. They were completely excluded from their fellows.

These statements serve to illustrate the reference made to the publicans in the Gospel narratives. They were classed with sinners. See Matt. ix, 10, 11; xi, 19; Mark ii, 15, 16; Luke vii, 34; xv, 1. They were mentioned with harlots. See Matt. xxi, 31, 32. They were alluded to as occupying the lowest position in morals, the vilest of the vile: "*even* the publicans." Matt. v, 46, 47.

2. *Sitting* at the receipt of custom accurately expresses the posture which is occupied in the East by all who transact business. The merchant sits when he sells, and even carpenters and washerwomen sit at their work No one stands when at work unless it is entirely unavoidable.

3. There were houses or booths built at the foot of bridges, at the gates of cities, at the mouths of rivers, and by the sea-side, where the tax-gatherers transacted their business. Such a place was the τελώνιον, or "receipt of custom."

760.—THE "BOSOM."

VI, 38. **Good measure, pressed down, and shaken together, and running over, shall men give into your bosom.**

The term "bosom" frequently refers, in Oriental usage, to the folds of the garment as they extend beyond and droop over the girdle. This part of the dress is also called the "lap." See 2 Kings iv, 39; and see also note on Neh. v, 13. It is used as a receptacle for various articles, as pockets are used with us; though some things are deposited there which we would not put into our pockets. Fathers sometimes carried their children here. See Num. xi, 12, and note on Isa. xlix, 22. Here also the shepherd carried the lambs. See 2 Sam xii, 3; Isa. xl, 11. To this custom of making a recep-

tacle of the folds of the dress there are frequent allusions. See Job xxxi, 33; Psa. lxxix, 12; lxxxix, 50; cxxix, 7; Prov. vi, 27; xvii, 23; xxi, 14; Isa. lxv, 6.

This is the custom referred to in the text; though we are not authorized to infer, as some have strangely done, that grain and other articles that are measured in the way suggested in the text were literally carried in the bosom. The figure is double, and the design is to express the reflex benefits of good deeds; they will come back in full measure to bless the giver.

761.—FOUNDATIONS.

VI, 48. He is like a man which built a house, and digged deep, and laid the foundation on a rock. See also Matt. vii, 24.

In building the better class of houses it is usual to dig down until the solid rock is reached, in order to have a sure foundation for the edifice. Dr. Robinson says of a new house he visited in Nazareth, by invitation of its owner, "In order to lay the foundations he had dug down to the solid rock, as is usual throughout the country; here to the depth of thirty feet; and then built up arches."—*Biblical Researches*, vol. ii, p. 338. It was of such a house that the Saviour spoke in the text: the builder "digged deep."

762.—SYNAGOGUE BUILDING.

VII, 5. For he loveth our nation, and he hath built us a synagogue.

It was no unusual thing for one man to build a synagogue at his own expense. If, as in this case, a Gentile built the sacred edifice, the Jews had no scruples in receiving the gift, even if he did not become a proselyte, as some suppose this centurion to have been. They held that the holiness of the place consisted, not so much in the building, as in its being set apart and dedicated to holy uses.

763.—CUSTOMS AT FUNERALS.

VII, 12. Now when he came nigh to the gate of the city, behold, there was a dead man carried out, the only son of his mother, and she was a widow: and much people of the city was with her.

1. It was customary, and still is, to bury the dead outside the limits of the city. Heathen nations as well as Jewish observed this usage. Rare exceptions were sometimes made in the case of royal personages. See note on 1 Kings ii, 10. Thus it was that Jesus saw the dead man carried out of the gate.

2. It was usual for all who knew the deceased to accompany the body to

the grave. There were several relays of men to take turns in carrying the bier. This was considered a privilege. Thus we are told that "much people of the city was with" the bereaved mother.

764.—THE BIER.

VII, 14. He came and touched the bier: and they that bare him stood still.

The bier is a wooden frame, partly resembling a coffin and partly a hand-barrow. The deceased is arrayed in grave-clothes, the ankles are bound, the hands are laid on the breast, and a shawl is thrown across the face. Miss Rogers says of a bier she saw: "It was a painted wooden stand, about seven feet by two, raised slightly on four legs, with a low gallery round it, formed of uprights far apart and two cross-bars. Two strong poles projected at each end from the corners. Above it a canopy was raised, made of freshly-gathered elastic palm-branches. They were bent like half-hoops, and then interlaced and secured lengthways with straight fronds."—*Domestic Life in Palestine*, p. 162. The bier was lifted by four men who bore it aloft, the poles resting on their shoulders.

765.—KISSING THE FEET.

VII, 38. Stood at his feet behind him . . . and kissed his feet.

This was no unusual practice among the Jews, and was also customary among the Greeks and Romans. It was a mark of affection and of reverence. It was also the practice of supplicants, and of those who had an important request to present. Kissing the feet of princes was a token of subjection and obedience. See also verse 45.

766.—GUIDING THE PLOW.

IX, 62. No man, having put his hand to the plow, and looking back, is fit for the kingdom of God.

The Eastern plow is of very rude and simple workmanship. See note on 1 Kings xix, 19. It is evident from the text that in our Lord's time the plow usually had but one handle, and many such plows are still seen. One hand guides the plow, while the other holds the long goad (see note on Judges iii, 31) by which the oxen are spurred on to their work. The plow being light, it is necessary for the plowman to lean forward with all his weight on the handle to keep the share in the ground. Many commentators suggest that by looking back the laborer would be unable to make straight furrows. This is true; but it is also true that he could not make any furrow at all, and this fact must not be overlooked in considering the figure used by our Lord in the text.

767.—FORMAL SALUTATIONS.

X, 4. Salute no man by the way.

This was not designed to forbid them from exercising the usual courtesies of life, in giving a mere *salaam* to those they might meet, as is evident from the very next verse, and also from Matt. x, 12, 13. They were, doubtless, allowed to give the usual salutation of "Peace!" See note on John xx, 19. But the text is designed to remind them of the importance of their mission, and of the necessity of diligence in its execution. Hence, they were not to observe the tedious and oft-repeated salutations with which the Orientals love to greet each other. These ceremonies of salutation are numerous and slowly performed. When two friends meet each inquires of the other, again and again, concerning his health and the health of his family; and repeats over and over again the best wishes for his prosperity and peace, thanking God that he is permitted once more to behold his face. These formalities are accompanied by numerous bowings and posturings of the body, and are sometimes repeated as often as ten times, consuming much time and making great delay. Those whom our Lord sent forth were forbidden to do this.

A similar injunction was given by Elisha when he sent his servant Gehazi to the Shunamite's house: "If thou meet any man, salute him not; and if any salute thee, answer him not again." 2 Kings iv, 29.

768.—FORMAL VISITING.

X, 7. In the same house remain. . . . Go not from house to house.

The exhortation to diligence in their work, alluded to in the last note, is repeated in a different form in this text. As salutations are tedious and frequent, so Oriental etiquette requires much visiting from house to house. This consumes time and takes attention from business; hence our Lord commands his disciples not to do it.

769.—NEIGHBORS.

X, 29. He, willing to justify himself, said unto Jesus, And who is my neighbor?

The Jews gave a very narrow definition of the word "neighbor." The rabbins interpreted it to mean only those who were of the Jewish people. The Gentiles were not considered neighbors.

770.—USE OF OIL AND WINE.

X, 84. Went to him, and bound up his wounds, pouring in oil and wine.

This was a favorite application for wounds in ancient surgery. It was considered a sovereign remedy, especially for wounds produced by violence;

wool, lint, or pounded olive being first laid upon the wound. The wine was supposed to cleanse, and the oil to soothe and heal. The two were sometimes made into a compound.

771.—NIGHT-TRAVELING.

XI, 5, 6. Which of you shall have a friend, and shall go unto him at midnight, and say unto him, Friend, lend me three loaves; for a friend of mine in his journey is come to me.

It would, indeed, be a rare circumstance among us to have a friend come at midnight to borrow bread; but in the East, where, on account of the heat, the traveling is often done at night, it might easily occur To an Oriental audience the allusion in the parable would be perfectly natural.

772.—FAMILY BEDROOM.

XI, 7. Trouble me not: the door is now shut, and my children are with me in bed.

It is common for a whole family, parents, children, and servants, to sleep in the same room, different beds being made for them on different parts of the divan. See note on 2 Kings i, 4, and on Matt. ix, 6. "Εἰς τὴν κοίτην [*in bed*] may best be rendered by our *a-bed*, for *at-bed*. Μετ' ἐμοῦ [*with me*] does not necessarily imply in the same *bed*; rather, according to the simplicity of ancient manners, in the same *room*."—BLOOMFIELD.

773.—NEGLECTED TOMBS.

XI, 44. Ye are as graves which appear not, and the men that walk over them are not aware of them.

There is an allusion here to the custom spoken of in the note on Matt. **xxiii**, 27, though the reference in this text is to the neglect of the custom rather than to its observance. When the customary whitewashing of a flat tomb was neglected its presence was easily concealed from view, and the passer-by might walk upon it and thus become ceremonially defiled.

774.—MONEY-BAGS.

XII, 33. Provide yourselves bags which wax not old, a treasure in the heavens that faileth not.

Money was kept in the royal treasuries in bags, the value of the contents being first ascertained and marked upon each bag, which was then sealed. Thenceforth, as long as the seal remained unbroken, the bag was estimated at its marked value, without re-counting. This was customary in ancient Egypt, and is still the usage in Persia and in other parts of the East. It is not confined to royal treasuries; but private bankers pursue a similar plan, so that in some parts of the Levant a "purse" is the word used for a particular sum of money. These bags are made of cotton-cloth, and are of different sizes, as they are used for carrying gold, silver, or copper pieces. A similar custom seems to be referred to in 2 Kings xii, 10.

Money-bags are alluded to in 2 Kings v, 23, and Job xiv, 17. The "bag" which Judas carried (John xii, 6; xiii, 29) was probably a small box or chest. A different word is used in the original, in John, from the one rendered "bag" in the text in Luke. It originally signified a box carried by musicians for the purpose of holding the mouth-pieces of their instruments.

775.—TREES IN VINEYARDS.

XIII, 6. A certain man had a fig-tree planted in his vineyard.

Vineyards were not devoted exclusively to vines. Fruit-trees of various kinds were planted within their limits, so that it is perfectly correct to speak of a fig-tree being planted in a vineyard. The ancient Egyptians planted their vines and fruit-trees in the same inclosure.

776.—SABBATH–FEASTING.

XIV, 1. He went into the house of one of the chief Pharisees to eat bread on the Sabbath day.

The strictness with which the Jewish Sabbath was kept did not prevent the Pharisees, as well as other Jews, from having a better provision of food on that day than on ordinary days. They did this as a religious duty in honor of the day. Lightfoot gives several curious instances of this custom from the rabbins, of which this is one: "'Rabba Bar Rabh Houna went to the house of Rabba Bar Rabh Nachman. He set before him three measures of rich cake; to whom he, How did you know of my coming? The other answered, Is there any thing more valuable to us than the Sabbath?' The Gloss is: 'We do by no means prefer thee before the Sabbath; we got these things ready in honor of the Sabbath, not knowing any thing of thy coming.'"—*Horæ Hebraicæ.*

777.—PLACE OF HONOR AT FEASTS.

XIV, 7. He marked how they chose out the chief rooms.

"Room" is old English for "place," and indeed is still sometimes used in that sense, as when we say, "Make room."

The Orientals have always been punctilious in reference to positions of honor at formal feasts. The chief rooms or places at feasts differed among different nations. Among the Greeks and Romans the middle place in each *clinium* of the *triclinium,* or dinner-bed, was the coveted position of honor. See note on Matt. xxvi, 7. This was the place which the Pharisees eagerly desired: "They chose out the chief rooms." For this they received a merited rebuke from Jesus.

See also Matt. xxiii, 6; Mark xii, 39; Luke xx, 46.

778.—ARRANGEMENT OF GUESTS.

XIV, 9, 10. Give this man place ; . . . Friend, go up higher.

The host did not hesitate to regulate the position of his guests after they had settled it for themselves. He gave the highest in rank the chief place, sending the men up or down as circumstances required. Even in modern times there are instances of this. Schulz was at a wedding-feast at St. Jean d'Acre where two persons who had seated themselves at the top were compelled by the master of ceremonies to go down. Morier was at an entertainment in Persia where the governor of Kashan entered and took the lowest place. The host, on discovering him, pointed with his hand to an upper seat, which the governor took, the other guests making way for him. See BURDER, *Oriental Illustrations*, No. 1304.

779.—DIVISION OF PROPERTY.

XV, 12. The younger of them said to his father, Father, give me the portion of goods that falleth to me. And he divided unto them his living.

Neither Jewish nor Roman law permitted the father to have the arbitrary disposal of all his estate. The property was entailed on the sons at the father's death, the daughters not being allowed to inherit unless there were no sons. See Gen. xxxi, 14; Num. xxvii, 8. The general application to this law is seen in the fact that, when Job gave an inheritance to his daughters as well as to his sons, special mention is made of the act as though it were a remarkable occurrence. See Job xlii, 15. The first-born son received a double share. See Deut. xxi, 17.

Some commentators, in illustrating this text, suppose that the sons had a right to demand a division of the property during the father's life-time, and that the father could not refuse such a demand. The text, however, does not necessarily imply this. For all that here appears, it may have been merely a request urged by the son and granted by the father. There is nothing to show that the father was compelled to comply. He did comply, it is true but whether by compulsion or of his own volition is not stated. Mr. Burder (*Oriental Customs*, 1086) gives an extract from Halhed's *Code of Gentoo Laws*, in which it is stated that under certain circumstances the sons had a right to demand of their father a division of his property during his life-time. There is no evidence, however, that either Jews or Romans had any such law, though they may have been acquainted with it as existing in India.

The verisimilitude of the parable is sufficiently observed, without any reference to a law of compulsion, by supposing it customary sometimes for fathers of their own volition to divide their estate among their sons. This is said to have been sometimes done among the Romans, and that it may have been an occasional custom among the Jews is evident from the example of Abraham, who "gave all that he had" to his son Isaac. See Gen, xxiv, 36; xxv, 5.

780.—FEEDING THE SWINE.

XV, 15. He sent him into his fields to feed swine.

This was considered one of the most degrading employments, not only by the Jews, but by other nations. Among the Egyptians, for example, the swineherd was completely shut off from society. The Saviour makes use of this antipathy to illustrate the depth of misery to which the dissipation of the young prodigal had brought him.

781.—THE STEWARD.

XVI, 1. There was a certain rich man which had a steward.

The steward had general charge of the business of the house, and especial care of the heir. This is referred to in Gal. iv, 2, where the word else-where rendered "stewards" is translated "governors." The office is a very ancient one. Abraham had a steward, Eliezer. See Gen. xv, 2, and note on Gen. xxiv, 2. The steward was generally an old faithful slave, though some-times free men were so employed. The honorable position of the steward is seen in the fact that he was considered to be ruler over the household. See Luke xii, 42. His duties are also referred to in the parable of the la-borers. See Matt. xx, 8.

782.—DISPOSITION OF CRUMBS.

XVI, 21. Desiring to be fed with the crumbs which fell from the rich man's table: moreover the dogs came and licked his sores.

Some suppose that by these "crumbs" are meant the pieces of bread wherewith it was customary at table to wipe the fingers, an act rendered necessary by the practice of conveying the food to the mouth by means of the hand. When the fingers were thus wiped, the fragments of bread which had been used for the purpose were thrown to the ground, where the dogs were allowed to get them. This will help to illustrate the witty turn of the Syrophenician woman, who, when the Saviour said to her, "It is not meet to take the children's bread, and to cast it to dogs," quickly replied, " Truth, Lord: yet the dogs eat of the crumbs which fall from their masters' table." Matt. xv, 26, 27. See also Mark vii, 28.

We also see by this the connection with the closing part of the text: "moreover the dogs came and licked his sores." With the dogs he had his food of the discarded fragments of the table, and the compassionate beasts not only permitted him to partake of their food, but also nursed him in his sickness.

26

783.—SEMI-WEEKLY FASTS.

XVIII, 12. I fast twice in the week.

It is said that these semi-weekly fasts were observed by the Jews because continuous fasting might be injurious. The days selected were the second and fifth. The reason assigned for the selection of these days is because it was supposed to be on the second day of the week that Moses went up into Mount Sinai to receive the two tables of the law, and it was on the fifth day of the week that he came down on account of the idolatry concerning the golden calf. These days were chosen, not only when public fasts were to be observed, but also when individuals fasted privately.

The only fast commanded in the Mosaic law was in connection with the celebration of the Great Day of Atonement. See note on Lev. xvi, 34. Other fasts were observed, however, in later periods of Jewish history until, in our Lord's time, the Pharisees carried the practice to an extreme. They fasted often, (Matt. ix, 14,) and disfigured their faces. Matt. vi, 16. In the text the Pharisee is represented as regarding this frequent fasting as an evidence of his piety.

784.—SMITING THE BREAST.

XVIII, 13. The publican standing afar off, would not lift up so much as his eyes unto heaven, but smote upon his breast.

This is one mode of expressing great grief among the Orientals, especially in mourning for the dead; and its insertion in the parable is very expressive of the deep sorrow of the penitent publican. His grief on account of his sins was like the grief of those who mourned for their dead.

Morier gives an interesting account of the ceremonies observed annually in Persia in commemoration of the death of Hossein, the grandson of Mohammed, who was slain. One part of the ceremonies consists in beating the breast as a token of grief. Morier says: "In front of the palace a circle of the king's own tribe were standing barefooted, and beating their breasts in cadence to the chanting of one who stood in the center, and with whom they now and then joined their voices in chorus. Smiting the breast is a universal act throughout the mourning; and the breast is made bare for that purpose by unbuttoning the top of the shirt."—*Second Journey*, etc., pp. 178, 179.

785.—THE "POUND."

XIX. 13. He called his ten servants, and delivered them ten pounds.

The *mina*, or "pound," was not a coin, but a sum of silver reckoned by weight, and was worth £3 15s. 6d. sterling, or about $19

786.—ORNAMENTS OF THE TEMPLE.

XXI, 5. Some spake of the temple, how it was adorned with goodly stones and gifts.

The temple of Herod was built of stones so exceeding white that Josephus says the building from a distance looked like a mountain of snow. It was also gilded in many places, so that the reflection from the sun's rays was sometimes painful to the eye of the beholder. It was likewise adorned with barbaric spoils taken in war, and with the voluntary offerings of those who desired in this way to express gratitude to God for past favors, or to manifest a hope for future benefits. According to Josephus there were among these costly gifts golden vines from which hung clusters of grapes as tall as a man. See *Wars of the Jews*, book v, chap. v, §§ 4 and 6.

This custom was very common among the heathen. Their idol temples were richly ornamented with valuable articles, such as shields, chaplets, golden chains, and candlesticks, and the spoils of battle. The treasures of many pagan temples to-day are beyond computation.

For a more complete description of Herod's temple, see note on Matt. xxiv, 1.

787.—TEMPLE CAPTAINS.

XXII, 4. He went his way, and communed with the chief priests and captains, how he might betray him unto them.

These "captains" were not Roman military officers, but the Levitical officers who had charge of the temple watch. The "captain of the temple" mentioned in Acts iv, 1; v, 26, was probably the chief officer of the whole guard of the temple.

788.—GAME OF BLINDFOLDING.

XXII, 64. When they had blindfolded him, they struck him on the face, and asked him, saying, Prophesy, who is it that smote thee ? See also Matt. xxvi, 67, 68; Mark xiv, 65.

Reference is thought to be made here to a sport very common in ancient times, resembling what is known among us as "blind-man's-buff." One person was blindfolded and the others struck him in turn, and then asked him to guess the name of the one who smote him. He was not released until he gave the name correctly. In this way the persecutors of Jesus mocked him, challenging him, if he were a prophet, to tell the names of his tormenters.

789.—DIVISION OF JEWISH SCRIPTURES.

XXIV, 44. In the law of Moses, and in the prophets, and in the psalms.

This is the ordinary Jewish division of the Scriptures. The Jews have, *first*, the *Law*, which includes the Pentateuch; *secondly*, the *Prophets*, in which are included Joshua, Judges, the two books of Samuel, the two books of Kings, and all the prophets except Daniel; and *thirdly*, the *Hagiographa*, or Sacred Writings, in which are comprised, in the order here named, Psalms, Proverbs, Job, Solomon's Song, Ruth, Lamentations, Ecclesiastes, Esther, Daniel, Ezra, Nehemiah, and the two books of Chronicles. This third division was called "the Psalms," because that book was the first in the division. In the text it is so called by our Lord.

790.—PRIESTLY BENEDICTION.

XXIV, 50. He led them out as far as to Bethany, and he lifted up his hands, and blessed them.

The priests in blessing the people lifted up their hands. Maimonides states that the ordinary priests raised their hands above their heads; but the high-priest raised his hands to a level with the plate of gold on his forehead, but not above it.

———◆———

JOHN.

791—THE SHOE-LATCHET.

I, 27. Whose shoe's latchet I am not worthy to unloose.

The latchet was a leathern thong by which the sandal was fastened to the shoe. It was the work of a servant to loosen this, and thus John expressed his deep humility and consciousness of insignificance when contrasted with his master. See also Mark i, 7; Luke iii, 16; Acts xiii, 25. The shoe-latchet is likewise referred to in Isa. v, 27.

See also note on Matt. iii, 11.

792.—THE FIRKIN.

II, 6. Six waterpots of stone, . . . containing two or three firkins apiece.

The *metretes*, "firkin," was the principal Greek liquid measure, and contained a little more than eight gallons and seven eighths. It corresponded to the Hebrew *bath*. See note on Ezek. xlv, 10.

793.—THE "GOVERNOR OF THE FEAST."

II, 8. He saith unto them, Draw out now, and bear unto the governor of the feast.

Among the Greeks, at all formal feasts, there was a "symposiarch," who was one of the guests, and was selected to take charge of the feast. It was his duty to preserve order, to maintain liveliness among the guests, to assign each one his proper place, to decide what proportion of water should be mingled with the wine, and how much each of the company was to drink. Among the Romans was a corresponding officer who was called *rex convivii*, or *arbiter bibendi*. It is thought by many that the ἀρχιτρίκλινος, or "governor of the feast" mentioned in the text, was an officer of the same kind. This, however, is denied by other authorities, who assert that the ἀρχιτρίκλινος was not a guest, but a servant hired for the purpose, whose business it was to take charge of the other servants and see that they properly performed their work. He had some duties in common with the symposiarch, among which was that of tasting the wine before it was offered to the guests. Thus when Jesus had miraculously changed the water into wine, he directed the servants to take some of it to "the governor of the feast."

794.—THE "FRIEND OF THE BRIDEGROOM."

III, 29. The friend of the bridegroom, which standeth and heareth him, rejoiceth greatly because of the bridegroom's voice.

"The friend of the bridegroom" was the person selected by the bridegroom to conduct the marriage negotiations on his part. It was he who carried messages between the bridegroom and the bride during the time of the betrothal. See note on Matt. i, 18. When, on the occasion of the marriage, they were brought to see each other in a private room or under a canopy provided for the purpose, the "friend of the bridegroom" stood without, eager to catch the first words of delight which came from the bridegroom's lips, expressive of the satisfaction he experienced on conversing with his betrothed.

This position John the Baptist claims for himself figuratively. He is not the Christ, but bears a relation to him similar to that borne by the *paranymph* to the bridegroom. He makes the arrangements for bringing Christ, the bridegroom, to the Church, his bride. He waits with reverence and respect to hear words of joy coming from the lips of Christ because he has found a waiting and a willing Church. As the services of the *paranymph* only occupied a short time, so the Baptist's mission would soon be over: "He must increase, but I must decrease." Verse 30.

795.—DRAWING WATER.

IV, 11. The woman saith unto him, Sir, Thou hast nothing to draw with, and the well is deep.

The wells in Palestine are usually deep. The depth of Jacob's well has been variously estimated by travelers from sixty-five feet to over a hundred. The best authorities give from seventy-five to eighty feet. To get water from such a depth a rope is fastened to the leathern bucket or earthen jar, which is let down into the well, sometimes by means of a pulley, and sometimes by merely sliding the rope over the stone curb of the well. It is no

156.—WOMEN DRAWING WATER.

uncommon thing to find well-curbs with deep furrows in them, worn by the friction of the ropes which have for many years passed over them.

796.—CONTEMPT FOR WOMEN.

IV, 27. Upon this came his disciples, and marveled that he talked with the woman.

Their astonishment was not only because of the non-intercourse of the Jews and the Samaritans, but also because it was unusual for a Jewish teacher to converse with women in a public place. The rabbins expressed their contempt for women by teaching that they were not to be saluted or spoken to in the street, and they were not to be instructed in the law.

797.—SEALING.

VI, 27. Him hath God the Father sealed.

Burder (*Oriental Customs*, No. 1120) suggests that there may be an allusion here to the sacrificial death of Christ, and cites from Herodotus an account of the ceremonies accompanying the selection of a victim for sacrifice among the ancient Egyptians. If, after careful search, the animal was found without blemish, the priest bound a label to his horns, applied wax to the label, and sealed it with his ring. This set it apart for sacrifice, and no animal could be offered unless thus sealed. We have no knowledge of any such ceremony among the Jews, though they were careful in selecting their victims; but the sacrificial customs of other nations were doubtless known to them. The meaning of the text may, therefore, be, that Jesus had been set apart or "sealed" as a sacrifice in order that he might obtain eternal life for those who believe on him.

On the other hand, Lightfoot interprets the passage to mean that God had confirmed Jesus by his seal to be "the great Ruler both of his kingdom and family;" and he refers for illustration to a rabbinical form of instruction which declares the seal of God to be *Truth*, one of the names which Jesus applies to himself. See John xiv, 6. Compare also John iii, 33.

References to the sealing or setting apart of the people of God are made in 2 Cor. i, 22; Eph. i, 13; iv, 30; Rev. vii, 2. For a description of seals and sealing in a literal sense, see notes on 1 Kings xxi, 8, and Job xxxviii, 14.

798.—CEREMONIES AT THE FEAST OF TABERNACLES.

VII, 37. In the last day, that great day of the feast, Jesus stood and cried, saying, If any man thirst, let him come unto me and drink.

In addition to the ceremonies originally prescribed at the institution of the Feast of Tabernacles, (see note on Exod. xxiii, 16,) were several others of a later date. Among these was the daily drawing of water from the pool of Siloam. Every morning of the seven days of the feast proper, at day-break, a priest went to the pool of Siloam and filled with water a golden pitcher, containing about two pints and a half. He was accompanied by a procession of the people and a band of music. On returning to the temple he was welcomed with three blasts from a trumpet, and going to the west side of the great altar he poured the water from the golden pitcher into a silver basin, which had holes in the bottom through which the water was carried off. This ceremony was accompanied with songs and shouts from the people and with the sound of trumpets. It is supposed to have been designed to represent three distinct things : 1. A memorial of the water provided for their fathers in the desert. 2. A symbol of the forthcoming "latter rain." 3. A representation of the outpouring of the Holy Spirit at the coming of the Messiah. To the last reference is made in verses 38, 39, and to the pouring out of the water Jesus no doubt refers in the text.

Nearly all the authorities agree in saying that on the eighth day this ceremony was dispensed with. There is great diversity of opinion, however, as to the meaning of "the last day, that great day of the feast;" some supposing it to be the seventh, and others the eighth. It is urged that the eighth day was not properly a part of the feast, but a special day of "holy convocation," the peculiar ceremonies of the feast having ceased at the close of the day previous, although the ritual provided special offerings for the eighth day. On the other hand, it is affirmed that the Jews held the eighth day in higher esteem than any of the seven others because they thought the solemnities of the day were designed especially for them, whereas on the other days all the nations of the world were included in the supplications that were offered. It is sufficient for our present purpose to say that, if the seventh day be intended by "the last," the Saviour probably uttered the words of the text at the time when the water was poured out by the officiating priest. If the eighth day be meant, then it is probable, as Alford suggests, that the words were used after the singing of the Hallel, just at the time when, on previous days, the water had been poured out.

It is thought by some that this custom of drawing water from Siloam and pouring it out by the side of the great altar was introduced before the Babylonish captivity, and that Isaiah refers to it when he says, "With joy shall ye draw water out of the wells of salvation." Isa. xii, 3.

799.—FREEDOM BY THE SON.

VIII, 86. If the Son therefore shall make you free, ye shall be free indeed.

It was a custom among some of the Grecian cities to permit the son and heir to adopt brothers, and thereby give them a share in the rights and privileges enjoyed by himself. To this some think reference is made in the text. Others think the reference is to a Roman custom by which the son, after his father's death, might, if he chose, give freedom to the slaves that were born in the house during his father's time.

800.—JEWISH HATRED OF SAMARITANS.

VIII, 48. Say we not well that thou art a Samaritan and hast a devil?

The contempt and hatred which the Jews entertained toward the Samaritans was manifested, not only in their refusal to have any dealings with them beyond what was demanded by necessity, (see chap. iv, 9,) but also in the fact that the Jews made the name of Samaritan a synonym for every thing that was vile and contemptible. As Lightfoot remarks, they could not in this instance have mistaken Jesus for a Samaritan literally, because, according to verse 20, he was in the treasury of the temple, a place where no Samaritan was permitted to come. They used the term figuratively as a reproach. Rosenmüller says: "There was a notorious and deadly hatred between the Jews and Samaritans on account of religion. For this reason the Jews, in the language of common life, applied the epithet 'Samaritan,'

not only to one who belonged to Samaria, but to every one whom they supposed had the mode of thinking and the principles of a Samaritan; and
they, therefore, often designated by this name a sworn enemy of the Jewish people and the Jewish religion, and a morally bad man. So, in our own
language, a man who has a propensity to cruelty and despotism we call a
Turk, and a covetous rich man a Jew."—*Morgenland*, vol. v, p. 241.

801.—PERIOD OF MATURITY.

**VIII, 57. Thou art not yet fifty years old, and hast thou seen
Abraham ?**

The Jews considered fifty years as a period of maturity in human life.
The expression in the text is therefore not to be considered, as some have
strangely done, to imply that Jesus was nearly fifty years old at this time,
but simply that, still being a young man, it was impossible that he could have
seen Abraham.

802.—EXCOMMUNICATION.

**IX, 22. The Jews had agreed already, that if any man did con-
fess that he was Christ, he should be put out of the synagogue.**

According to the Talmud and the rabbins there were two, and perhaps
three, grades of excommunication among the Jews. The first was called
niddin, and those on whom it was pronounced were not permitted for thirty
days to have any communication with any person save at a distance of four
cubits. They were not prohibited from attending public worship, though
they could not during the thirty days enter the temple by the ordinary gate.
They were not allowed during that time to shave, and were required to wear
garments of mourning. The second was called *cherem*, and was pronounced
on those who remained contumacious under the first. It was of greater
severity than the other, and required the presence of at least ten members
of the congregation to make it valid. The offender was formally cursed, was
excluded from all intercourse with other people, and was prohibited from
entering the temple or a synagogue. The third was called *shammatha*, and
was inflicted on those who persisted in their contumacy. By this they were
cut off from all connection with the Jewish people, and were consigned to
utter perdition. It is not clear, however, that there was any real distinction
between the second and third grades here noted.

Lightfoot suggests (in *Horæ Hebraicæ*, on 1 Cor. v, 5) that the penalty of
excommunication was probably inflicted for those faults for which neither
the law nor tradition made any certain provision. The Talmud assigns as
the two general causes of excommunication, *money* and *epicurism*. The first
refers to those who refused to pay the moneys which the court directed them
to pay; and the second refers to those who despised the word of God or
of the scribes. Some rabbinical writers enumerate twenty-four different

offenses for which excommunication was inflicted, some of them being frivolous in the extreme.

Excommunication is alluded to in Matt. xviii, 17; John ix, 34; xii, 42; and xvi, 2. Some think our Lord, in Luke vi, 22, refers to the several grades above noticed: "Blessed are ye, when men shall hate you, and when they shall separate you from their company, and shall reproach you, and cast out your name as evil, for the Son of man's sake."

803.—THE SHEEP-FOLD.

X, 1. He that entereth not by the door into the sheep-fold, but climbeth up some other way, the same is a thief and a robber.

In this beautiful figure reference is made to the place of shelter for the sheep where they might repose at night, and be safe from the attacks of wild

157.—SHEEP-FOLD.

beasts. The modern sheep-folds of Syria, which no doubt resemble those of ancient times, are low, flat buildings opening into a court, which is surrounded by a stone wall, protected on the top by a layer of thorns. A doorway carefully guarded forms the entrance. Sheep-folds are referred to in a number of passages. See Num. xxxii, 16, 24, 36; 1 Sam. xxiv, 3; 2 Chron. xxxii, 28; Psa. lxxviii, 70.

804.—SHEPHERD AND SHEEP.

X, 3–5. He calleth his own sheep by name, and leadeth them out. And when he putteth forth his own sheep, he goeth before them, and the sheep follow him: for they know his voice. And a stranger will they not follow, but will flee from him; for they know not the voice of strangers.

1. The Eastern shepherds give names to their sheep, as we do to dogs and horses. Every sheep recognizes his own name, and comes when called.

2 Travelers have noticed the wonderful readiness with which the sheep of a large flock will recognize the shepherd's voice. Though several flocks are mingled they speedily separate at the command of the shepherd, while the word of a stranger would have no effect on them. Porter thus describes a scene he witnessed among the hills of Bashan: "The shepherds led their flocks forth from the gates of the city. They were in full view, and we watched them and listened to them with no little interest. Thousands of sheep and goats were there, grouped in dense, confused masses. The shepherds stood together until all came out. Then they separated, each shepherd taking a different path, and uttering as he advanced a shrill, peculiar call. The sheep heard them. At first the masses swayed and moved as if shaken by some internal convulsion; then points struck out in the direction taken by the shepherds; these became longer and longer until the confused masses were resolved into long, living streams, flowing after their leaders."—*Giant Cities of Bashan*, p. 45.

805.—THE FEAST OF DEDICATION

X, 22. It was at Jerusalem the feast of the dedication, and it was winter.

This was a feast instituted in honor of the restoration of divine worship in the temple, and its formal rededication to sacred uses after it had been defiled by the heathen under Antiochus Epiphanes. This dedication took place B. C. 164, and an account of it is given in the apocryphal book of 1 Maccabees iv, 52–59. The feast lasted two days, and could be celebrated not only in Jerusalem but elsewhere.

In later times it was known by the name of the "Feast of Lamps," or the "Feast of Lights," because of the custom of illuminating the houses while celebrating it. The rabbins have a tradition that, when the Jews under Judas Maccabeus drove the heathen out of the temple and cleansed it from its pollution, they found a solitary bottle of sacred oil which had escaped the profane search of the heathen. This was all they had for lighting the sacred lamps; but by a miracle this was made to last for eight days, which period was therefore the time for the duration of the feast.

806.—THE HOURS OF THE DAY.

XI, 9. Are there not twelve hours in the day?

The Jewish day was reckoned from evening to evening. See note on 1 Cor. xv, 4. The word "day" was, however, used in another sense also, as with us, to denote that portion of the twenty-four hours during which the sun shone. While the night was divided into watches, (see note on Mark xiii, 35,) the day was divided into hours; each of these hours being one twelfth of the time between sunrise and sunset. Thus the hours varied in length according to the time of year, the summer hours being longer than those of winter. In the latitude of Palestine the longest day has, according to our reckoning, fourteen hours and twelve minutes, and the shortest nine hours and forty-eight minutes. This makes a difference of four hours and twenty-four minutes between the longest day and shortest. If we divide the day into twelve hours, there will be found a difference of twenty-two minutes between the longest hour and the shortest, the length of the hour varying from forty-nine minutes to seventy-one.

The first hour began at sunrise, the sixth ended at noon, and the twelfth ended at sunset. The third hour divided the period between sunrise and noon, and the ninth between noon and sunset. The first at its close corresponded nearly to seven o'clock A. M. of our time, and the twelfth hour to six o'clock P. M.

The "third hour" is mentioned in Matt. xx, 3; Mark xv, 25; Acts ii, 15. It may, be roughly reckoned at nine o'clock A. M. of our time. The "sixth hour" is named in Matt. xx, 5; xxvii, 45; Mark xv, 33; Luke xxiii, 44; John iv, 6; xix, 14; Acts x, 9. It corresponded exactly to twelve o'clock noon of our time. The "seventh hour" is mentioned in John iv, 52. It was about one o'clock P. M. The "ninth hour" is spoken of in Matt. xx, 5; xxvii, 45, 46; Mark xv, 33, 34; Luke xxiii, 44; Acts iii, 1; x, 3. It was about three o'clock P. M. The "tenth hour" is named in John i, 39. It was about four o'clock P. M. Some commentators, however, contend that John, writing this Gospel in the later years of his life, referred to Roman time and not to Jewish, thus making the hour ten o'clock A. M. This could hardly be, unless all his other estimates of time were reckoned in the same way, which, from a consideration of various texts, is highly improbable; besides, as Lücke (cited by Alford) remarks, even among the Romans the division of the day into twelve equal hours was, though not the *civil*, the popular way of computing time. The "eleventh hour" is mentioned in Matt. xx, 6, 9, and corresponds nearly to five o'clock P. M.

There also seems to have been a popular mode of reckoning the hours of the night in a similar way, as well as by watches. "Midnight" is mentioned as a particular "hour." Compare Acts xvi, 25, with xvi, 33. "The third hour of the night" is named in Acts xxiii, 23. This was about nine o'clock P. M.

807.—DOUBLE NAMES.

XI, 16. Thomas, which is called Didymus.

Both these names have the same signification, a twin; Thomas being Aramaic, and Didymus, Greek. It is said to have been customary for the Jews when traveling into foreign countries, or familiarly conversing with the Greeks or Romans, to assume a Greek or Latin name of similar meaning to their own.

808.—RABBINICAL NOTIONS OF SOUL AND BODY..

XI, 17. Then when Jesus came, he found that he had lain in the grave four days already.

The three days after death were called "days of weeping," which were followed by four "days of lamentation," thus making up the seven "days of mourning." See note on Gen. xxvii, 41. According to the rabbinical notion the spirit wanders about the sepulcher for three days seeking an opportunity to return into the body; but when the aspect of the body changes it hovers no more, but leaves the body to itself. The friends of the deceased were in the habit of visiting the sepulcher for three days after death and burial, (see note on Acts v, 6,) probably because they supposed they would thus be nearer to the departed soul. When the fourth day came and decomposition took place, and the soul, as they supposed, went away from the sepulcher, they beat their breast and made loud lamentations. This explains the allusion to the "four days" in this text and in verse 39. To say that one had been in the grave four days was equivalent to saying that bodily corruption had begun.

809.—THE FURLONG.

XI, 18. Bethany was nigh unto Jerusalem about fifteen furlongs off.

The *stadium*, or "furlong," mentioned here and in Luke xxiv, 13; John vi, 19; Rev. xiv, 20; xxi, 16, was not so long as our English furlong, being six hundred and six feet and nine inches in length.

810.—FORMAL CONDOLENCE.

XI, 19. Many of the Jews came to Martha and Mary to comfort them concerning their brother.

The formal visitation of condolence from friends took place immediately after burial, and lasted several days. As soon as they returned from the grave the mourners stood in a row, and their friends passed by, each speaking a word of comfort while passing. There were afterward visits of sympathy at the house, those on the third day being specially marked. It was thus that a large company assembled at the house of the sorrowing sisters.

811.—WEEPING AT THE GRAVE.

XI, 31. She goeth unto the grave to weep there.

It is very common for the friends of deceased persons—especially for the women—to make formal visits to the grave for the purpose of audibly expressing their grief. Prof. Hackett, on visiting a Syrian town, was compelled by the quarantine officers to pitch his tent in a grave-yard, where he observed a great number of women who surrounded the graves of their friends, and shrieked and wept for a long time. See *Illustrations of Scripture*, p. 111. Porter noticed a similar custom in the Druse country, where he found a long procession of women near a clamp of newly-made graves. "As they marched with stately steps around the tombs they sung a wild chant, that now echoed through the whole glen and now sunk into the mournful cadence of a death-wail."—*Giant Cities of Bashan*, etc., p. 39. When the Jews saw Mary hastily arise and leave the house they supposed she was going to the grave according to custom. It was thus the two Marys visited the sepulcher of the Lord. See Matt. xxvii, 61; xxviii, 1.

812.—THE POUND.

XII, 3. **Then Mary took a pound of ointment of spikenard, very costly.**

The λίτρα, "pound," varied in weight in different countries. The Roman *libra*, which is supposed to be the weight mentioned in the text, was equal to nearly twelve ounces avoirdupois.

813.—NEED OF FEET-WASHING.

XIII, 10. **He that is washed needeth not save to wash his feet.**

The meaning of the passage will be more readily perceived if, for *washed*, we read *bathed*, which is the idea conveyed by the original word. Allusion is probably made to the fact that one who has been to the bath need only, on returning to his house, wash the dust of the road from his sandaled feet. Thus he that has bathed need "not save to wash his feet."

814.—POSITION AT TABLE.

XIII, 23. **Now there was leaning on Jesus' bosom one of his disciples, whom Jesus loved.**

Reclining on the *triclinium*, or dinner-bed, the guest lay usually upon his left side, leaving his right hand free to reach the food. See note on Matt. xxvi, 7. His head would thus easily come into contact with the breast of the person on his left. It was in this way that John leaned on the bosom of Jesus while at supper. This is also mentioned in John xiii, 25; xxi, 20. A figurative use of the custom referred to is made in Luke xvi, 22, 23; John i, 18.

815.—THE "SOP."

XIII, 26. **Jesus answered, He it is, to whom I shall give a sop, when I have dipped it. And when he had dipped the sop, he gave it to Judas Iscariot, the son of Simon.**

It was customary for the host to give to such of his guests as he chose a "sop," or thin piece of bread dipped into the food in the dish, and saturated

158.—Women Mourning at the Grave.

with its fluid part. See note on Mark xiv, 20. Jowett, in speaking of an entertainment at which he was a guest, says: "When the master of the house found in the dish any dainty morsel, he took it out with his fingers and applied it to my mouth."—*Researches*, etc, p. 210.

This verse is of interest, since, taken in connection with the twenty-third verse, (see note preceding,) it indicates the position of Judas at the feast. He must have been very near to Jesus since he was within reach of his hand. He was very probably next to him; and since John lay to the right of the Saviour, Judas in all probability was at his left. If so, the Saviour must at times have laid his head on the traitor's breast; and thus the base treachery of Judas is seen in a most revolting aspect. While the Master was pillowing his head upon him he was meditating on the chances of securing the blood-money for which he had contracted to betray his Lord!

816.—PLACE FOR GARDENS.

XVIII, 1. He went forth with his disciples over the brook Cedron, where was a garden.

Gardens were made outside of the cities. The rabbins assign as a reason for this the foul smells which arose from the weeds and from the manure which was necessary for fertilizing. "Upon this account there were no gardens in the city, (some few gardens of roses excepted, which had been so from the days of the prophets,) but all were without the walls, especially at the foot of Olivet."—LIGHTFOOT, *Horæ Hebraicæ*, Matt. xxvii, 60.

817.—LANTERNS.

XVIII, 3. Judas then, having received a band of men and officers from the chief priests and Pharisees, cometh thither with lanterns and torches and weapons.

There are several varieties of lanterns in use in Palestine at the present day. One of these commonly used is made of waxed linen, or even of paper, stretched over rings of wire, and having a top and bottom of tinned copper. When folded the candle projects above the top of the folds, so that the lantern may, in the house, serve the purpose of a candlestick. This style of lantern is of ancient use. Transparent horn lanterns were also used; and bladder was sometimes substituted for horn.

The lanterns used by the officers on the occasion of the arrest of Jesus were doubtless of some strong serviceable material, perhaps of horn. The dark lantern was sometimes used by civil and military officers. It was square, with a

159.—LANTERN.

white skin on one side and black skins on the three other sides. See SMITH'S *Dictionary of Antiquities, s. v.* LATERNA.

818.—FEMALE DOOR-KEEPERS.

XVIII, 17. The damsel that kept the door.

Women were often employed by the ancients as porters. Classical writers make frequent allusion to the custom. It is mentioned also in the account of Peter's deliverance from prison, wherein it is stated that the house of Mary, the mother of John Mark, had a female porter. See Acts xii, 13.

819.—CHARCOAL.

XVIII, 18. Made a fire of coals, for it was cold; and they warmed themselves.

Charcoal is of ancient origin, and is still used for fuel in Palestine, though not so commonly employed for that purpose as sticks and other articles. See notes on 1 Kings xvii, 10; Psa. lviii, 9; and Matt. vi, 30. It was doubtless the material used for the fire spoken of in the text, and was probably burning in a pan or brazier made of metal or earthenware.

Charcoal is also referred to in Prov. xxvi, 21, (where the distinction is finely made between dead and burning coals;) Isa. xliv, 12; liv, 16; and John xxi, 9.

820.—BEARING THE CROSS.

XIX, 17. And he bearing his cross went forth.

A cross sufficiently large and strong to hold the body of a man, and long enough to allow a suitable portion to rest in the ground, would be too heavy for any ordinary man to carry. Some have, therefore, supposed that the cross which the condemned bore, according to the Roman law, was merely a miniature representation of the cross on which he was to suffer death; and that he was compelled to carry it to the place of execution to indicate to the spectators in the streets through which he passed the kind of death he was about to suffer. It would thus be a public badge of his shame. Lipsius, however, says that only a part of the cross was borne by the condemned, and that this part was the horizontal beam, which was the lighter of the two pieces of which the cross was composed. The heavier part, the perpendicular, was either planted in the earth before the arrival of the procession, or was ready to be set up as soon as the condemned man arrived with the transverse beam.

821.—THE TUNIC.

XIX, 23. The coat was without seam, woven from the top throughout.

χιτών was a tunic or inner garment which was worn next to the skin. It usually had sleeves, and generally reached to the knees, though sometimes to the ankles. It is mentioned in Matt. v, 40; Luke vi, 29; Acts ix, 39. Sometimes, for luxury, two tunics were worn at the same time. This our Lord forbade his disciples. See Matt. x, 10; Mark vi, 9; Luke iii, 11; :x, 3. When a person had on no garment but this he was said to be "naked." See note on 1 Sam. xix, 24.

These tunics were sometimes woven in one piece. Braun, a German theologian of the seventeenth century, wrote a quarto volume in Latin descriptive of the dress of the Jewish priests. In this he describes at length the manner in which seamless coats were woven, and gives pictorial illustrations. He had one of them made for himself by a weaver, according to directions which he gave, and on a loom made for the purpose. Seamless coats are still found in India and in other parts of the East.

822.—PREPARATION FOR BURIAL.

XIX, 40. **Then took they the body of Jesus, and wound it in linen clothes with the spices, as the manner of the Jews is to bury.**

This was not embalming, according to the Egyptian method, as described in the note on Gen. l, 2, 3. The Jews simply anointed the body, and wrapped it in fine linen, putting spices and ointments in the folds. In our Saviour's case the operation was not completed, owing to the coming of the Sabbath. As soon as the Sabbath was over the pious women came to complete the work. See Mark xvi, 1. The use of ointment in burial is referred to in Matt. xxvi, 12; Mark xiv, 8; John xii, 7.

John and Luke are the only evangelists who speak of the ointment and spices at the burial of Christ. See text, and Luke xxiii, 56. All four of them, however, mention the linen clothes. See Matt. xxvii, 59; Mark xv, 46; Luke xxiii, 53; text; and John xx, 5–7. These are also named in connection with the burial of Lazarus. See John xi, 44. It is there said that he was "bound hand and foot with grave-clothes," and skeptics have made themselves merry with the absurdity of the story that a man having both feet bound together should be able to "come forth." That the feet were bound *together* is, however, a gratuitous assumption. If each leg and each arm were separately swathed in linen bandages the assertion of the evangelist would still be strictly true, for Lazarus would then have been "bound hand and foot," while at the same time able, at the command of Christ, to move, though not to walk easily.

A "napkin" is also mentioned in connection with the burial of Lazarus. It was bound about his face. See John xi, 44. One was also used at the burial of Jesus. See John xx, 7. This was a handkerchief which was employed to tie up the chin of a corpse.

Reference to the use of linen bandages in burial is also seen in the account of the burial of Ananias, wherein it is said that "they wound him up." See Acts v, 6.

823.—SALUTATION.

XX, 19. Came Jesus and stood in the midst, and saith unto them, Peace be unto you.

This was the most common form of salutation among the Hebrews, and is often referred to in the Scriptures. In the history of Joseph it is said that "when his brethren saw that their father loved him more than all his brethren, they hated him, and could not speak peaceably unto him." Gen. **xxxvii, 4.** That is, they refused to give him the ordinary salutation of the day, "Peace be unto you." See also Judges xix, 20; 1 Sam. xxv, 6; Matt. **x, 12, 13.** These salutations of peace were often merely ceremonial, having in them no real hearty meaning; but Jesus informed his disciples that when he uttered the word "Peace," it was something more than a mere conformity to a worldly custom: "Peace I leave with you, my peace I give unto you: not as the world giveth, give I unto you." John xiv, 27.

THE ACTS OF THE APOSTLES.

824.—A SABBATH DAY'S JOURNEY.

I, 12. Then returned they unto Jerusalem from the mount called Olivet, which is from Jerusalem a Sabbath day's journey.

This was the distance beyond which it was considered unlawful for a Jew to travel on the Sabbath day. Its limitation is supposed to have originated in the rabbinical comment on Exod. xvi, 29, where every man is commanded to abide in his place on the Sabbath. Our Lord is thought to have in mind the customary limit of a Sabbath day's journey when he directs his disciples to pray that their flight be not on the Sabbath day. See Matt. xxiv, 20.

The distance to be understood by this limited Sabbath travel is variously estimated at three quarters of a mile, one mile, one mile and three quarters, and two miles. The best authorities represent it as three quarters of a mile.

825.—TIME FOR EATING.

II, 15. For these are not drunken, as ye suppose, seeing it is but the third hour of the day.

It was not usual to eat or drink on any day before the third hour, at which time the morning sacrifice was performed. Lightfoot, on authority

160.—House-top.

of Baronius, says: "And on these solemn festival-days they used not to eat or drink any thing till high-noon."—*Horœ Hebraicœ.* This custom furnished a ready answer from Peter to the charge of drunkenness.

826.—TIME FOR BURIAL.

V, 6. The young men arose, wound him up, and carried him out, and buried him.

It was usual in Palestine to bury a corpse on the day of death. The heat of the climate, doubtless, had much to do with this custom; besides which, so far as the Jews were concerned, their law made any one unclean for seven days who touched a dead body, or who was even in a house where a dead body lay. See Num. xix, 11, 14. Lazarus was probably buried on the day of his death. See John xi, 17, 39. Sapphira, the wife of Ananias, was, like her husband, buried immediately after death. See Acts v, 10.

827.—READING ALOUD.

VIII, 28. Sitting in his chariot read Esaias the prophet.

From verse thirty it is evident that the eunuch was reading aloud. It is still a common custom of the "Orientals generally to read aloud, even when they do it for their own instruction only, and without any intention of being heard by others. They swing the head, and even the entire upper part of the body, from one side to the other as they perform the act, and utter the words with a tone which comes nearer to singing or cantillation than to our unimpassioned mode of reading."—HACKETT'S *Illustrations of Scripture,* p. 224.

828.—COMPLIMENTARY NAMES.

IX, 36. There was at Joppa a certain disciple named Tabitha, which by interpretation is called Dorcas.

Dorcas means *antelope,* or *gazelle.* This beautiful animal is much admired in the East, and it is a common compliment to tell a woman that she has the eyes of an antelope. It is also no uncommon thing among Eastern nations to name their girls after various animals noted for beauty.

829.—PRAYER ON THE HOUSETOP.

X, 9. Peter went up upon the housetop to pray about the sixth hour.

The housetop was used, not only as a place of idolatrous worship, (see note on Lev. xxvi, 30,) but also for the worship of the true God. To us this would seem to be a singular place for prayer, unless one wished to indulge in Pharisaic ostentation; but the battlement around the flat roof of an Oriental dwelling (see note on Deut. xxii, 8) might readily be used as a screen from public observation. It may be that one reason why the Jews prayed upon the housetop was that they might more readily look in the direction of the temple in Jerusalem. See note on Dan. vi, 10.

830.—THE MILITARY NIGHT-WATCH.

XII, 4. **When he had apprehended him, he put him in prison, and delivered him to four quaternions of soldiers to keep him.**

The usual number of a Roman military night-watch was four, and the watch was changed every three hours. Thus during the twelve hours of night there would be four of these watches or "quaternions." Of these two were in the prison, (see verse 6,) and two were sentinels before the door. See verse 10, and the latter part of verse 6.

831.—PRISONERS CHAINED.

XII, 6. **Peter was sleeping between two soldiers, bound with two chains.**

Among the Romans the prisoner was bound to the soldier who had charge of him by means of a chain, which joined the prisoner's right wrist to the left wrist of the soldier. Sometimes, for greater security, the prisoner was chained to two soldiers, one on each side of him. This was the case with Peter. Paul was at one time bound in a similar way. See Acts xxi, 33. At another time he was fastened to a single soldier. See Acts xxviii, 16, 20.

832.—SANDALS.

XII, 8. **The angel said unto him, Gird thyself, and bind on thy sandals.**

The sandal consists of a wooden or leathern sole, which is fastened to the foot by thongs or latchets. The Bedawín of Mount Sinai wear sandals

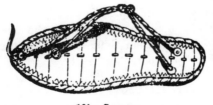

made of "fish-skin," or rather of the hide of a species of Dugong obtained from the Red Sea, near Sherm. See PALMER's *Desert of the Exodus*, p. 81. The leathern thongs which are used to keep the sandals on the feet are referred to in Mark i, 7, and in Luke iii, 16.

161.—SANDAL.

833.—KNOCKER—STREET-DOOR.

XII, 18. **As Peter knocked at the door of the gate, a damsel came to hearken, named Rhoda.**

1. The door of an Eastern house usually has an iron knocker, consisting of a thick ring.

2. "The door of the gate" is the outer or street door; the door of the porch, or entrance way to the house. This outer door or gate sometimes has a smaller door cut into it, which can be more readily opened, and is more frequently used than the large door of which it forms a part. Some writers think that a door of this description is referred to in the text.

834.—THE LAW AND THE PROPHETS—RULERS OF THE SYNAGOGUE.

XIII, 15. After the reading of the law and the prophets, the rulers of the synagogue sent unto them.

1. The custom of reading the law publicly was very ancient. The "prophets" are said to have been added in a singular way. "When Antiochus Epiphanes burnt the book of the law, and forbade the reading of it, the Jews, in the room of it, selected some passages out of the prophets which they thought came nearest in words and sense to the sections of the law, and read them in their stead; but when the law was restored again they still continued the reading of the prophetic sections."—STEHELIN's *Traditions of the Jews*, cited by BURDER, *Oriental Customs*, No. 1160. Hence the expression "the law and the prophets" was used to denote the portion of Scripture that was read in the synagogue, and, by synecdoche, the whole of the Jewish Scriptures. See Matt. v, 17; Luke xvi, 29. As a matter of fact, however, the *Hagiographa*, or "Holy Writings," which composed the third part of the Jewish Scriptures, (see note on Luke xxiv, 44,) was not read in the synagogue.

2. The "ruler of the synagogue" occupied a very important position. In the temple synagogue he was the third officer in rank; the first officer being the high priest, and the second the chief of the priests. In provincial synagogues the "ruler" was supreme. No one was eligible to this office until he had a certificate from the Great Sanhedrim that he possessed the requisite qualifications. His election, however, was by the members of the synagogue. It was his duty to supervise all matters connected with worship.

Sometimes this office is mentioned in the singular number, as if there were but one ruler to the synagogue. See Mark v, 35, 36, 38; Luke viii, 49; xiii, 14. At other times the plural form is used, as in the text. See Mark v, 22. The idea of plurality is also implied in the expression, "a ruler of the synagogue," (Luke viii, 41,) and in the words "chief ruler." Acts xviii, 8, 17. Neander suggests that "we must make the limitation, that in smaller places an individual, as in larger towns a plurality, stood at the head of the synagogue. It is most probable that, although all presbyters were called ἀρχισυνάγωγοι, yet one who acted as president was distinguished by the title of ἀρχισυνάγωγος; as *primus inter pares*."—*Planting and Training*, (Edition, Bohn,) vol. i, p. 36, *note*. Thus the "rulers" would be the same as the "elders" mentioned in Luke vii, 3, and elsewhere. Some suppose them to be identical with the local Sanhedrim. See note on Matt. x, 17.

835.—GODS IN HUMAN FORM.

XIV, 11. The gods are come down to us in the likeness of men.

It was a common opinion among the ancient heathen that the gods were accustomed to visit men in human form. Frequent reference is made to this opinion by classical writers. There was a tradition among this very people that Jupiter and Mercury had once appeared in Phrygia to an aged couple, Philemon and Baucis. In this visit the two gods were entertained by Lycaon, whence the name of the province, Lycaonia.

836.—JUPITER AND MERCURY.

XIV, 12. They called Barnabas, Jupiter; and Paul, Mercurius, because he was the chief speaker.

Jupiter, called Ζεύς by the Greeks, was the supreme head of all the heathen divinities. He had a temple at Lystra. Mercury, called Ἑρμῆς by the Greeks, was a son of Jupiter, and the herald or messenger of all the gods. Hence he was the god of eloquence. These two deities were supposed to travel together. Thus the people, having decided that Paul, by reason of his eloquence, must be Mercury, inferred that his traveling companion was Jupiter. This renders unnecessary the suggestion of Chrysostom, that Barnabas was probably of more majestic mien than Paul, and therefore was thought to be Jupiter.

837.—IDOLATROUS GARLANDS.

XIV, 13. Then the priest of Jupiter, which was before their city, brought oxen and garlands unto the gates, and would have done sacrifice with the people.

It was customary to build temples to the tutelar deities in the suburbs of the cities, and to set up their images before the city at the gates. These images, and the victims which were sacrificed to them, were crowned with garlands of cypress, pine, or other leaves, or of flowers. The garlands were sometimes placed upon the altars, and then again upon the priests.

In India, flowers are used in idolatrous worship on gods, priests, and worshipers, and are presented to friends as a mark of respect. Roberts says: "In the latter part of 1832 I visited the celebrated pagoda of Rami-seram, the temple of Ramar. As soon as I arrived within a short distance of the gates, a number of dancing-girls, priests, and others came to meet us with garlands. They first did me the honor of putting one around my neck, and they presented others for Mrs. Roberts and the children."—*Oriental Illustrations*, p. 567.

838.—PLACES OF PRAYER.

XVI, 13. We went out of the city by a river side, where prayer was wont to be made.

Many writers suppose that there is reference here to the Jewish custom of having *proseuchæ*, or places of prayer, distinct from synagogues, and in locations where there were no synagogues. Though some commentators deny the reference to the custom in this passage, yet the existence of the custom itself is undeniable. The *proseuchæ* were places for prayer outside of those towns where the Jews were too poor to have synagogues, or were not permitted to have them. They were generally located near the water for the convenience of ablution. Sometimes a large building was erected: but frequently the *proseucha* was simply a retired place in the open air or in a grove.

Rivers seem to have been favorite places of resort for God's people. In captivity they assembled "by the rivers of Babylon." Psa. cxxxvii, 1. Ezekiel speaks of being among them "by the river of Chebar." Ezek. i, 1. Daniel was "by the river of Ulai" when he beheld one of his visions, (Dan. viii, 2;) and he saw another when he was "by the side of the great river, which is Hiddekel." Dan. x, 4. Dr. Pusey quotes from a decree of the Halicarnassians, which gave leave " that those of the Jews who willed, men and women, should keep the Sabbaths, and perform their rites according to the Jewish laws, and make oratories by the sea according to their country's wont."—PUSEY *on Daniel*, pp. 110, 111.

839.—STOCKS.

XVI, 24. Who, having received such a charge, thrust them into the inner prison, and made their feet fast in the stocks.

Some would understand by ξύλον, "stocks," simply a bar of wood to which the feet of the prisoner were chained. Others suppose the instru-

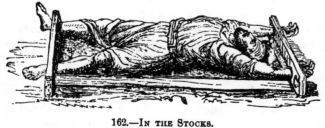

ment to have corresponded to the modern stocks, consisting of a frame of wood in which the two feet, separated far apart, were placed.

162.—IN THE STOCKS.

There were some ancient stocks in which were five holes for fastening feet, hands, and head. In Ceylon, at the present day, an instrument similar to this is used, only the head is allowed to be free.

The use of the stocks is very ancient. See Job xiii, 27.

840.—RESPONSIBILITY OF JAILERS.

XVI, 27. **He drew out his sword, and would have killed himself, supposing that the prisoners had been fled.**

According to the Roman law, if a prisoner escaped, the jailer who had him in charge was compelled to suffer the penalty which was to have been inflicted on the prisoner. This accounts for the despair of the jailer in this case. He preferred death by his own hands to the death by torture, which probably awaited some of the condemned prisoners whom he supposed to have escaped.

841.—ROMAN CITIZENS NOT TO BE BEATEN.

XVI, 37. **They have beaten us openly uncondemned, being Romans, and have cast us into prison.**

The treatment of these prisoners, being Roman citizens, was illegal in three different ways: 1. In binding them in the stocks. 2. In beating them. 3. In failing to give them a trial. The Valerial law forbade the binding of a Roman citizen. The Porcian law forbade his being beaten. Cicero, in his celebrated *Oration against Verres*, asserts that "it is a transgression of the law to bind a Roman citizen; it is wickedness to scourge him. Unheard, no man can be condemned."

This will account for the fear expressed by the magistrates when they heard that the prisoners were Romans. See verse 38. Paul had a similar experience afterward in Jerusalem: "As they bound him with thongs, Paul said unto the centurion that stood by, Is it lawful for you to scourge a man that is a Roman, and uncondemned." Acts xxii, 25.

842.—DEBATES IN THE MARKET PLACE.

XVII, 17. **Therefore disputed he . . . in the market daily with them that met with him.**

The market was not only a place for buying and selling, for hiring and being hired, (see note on Matt. xx, 3,) but it was also a public resort for all who wished to inquire the news or to hold disputations. For this reason the Pharisees loved to go there, because, amid the crowds assembled, they would receive the ceremonious salutations in which they delighted. See Matt. xxiii, 7; Mark xii, 38; Luke xi, 43; xx, 46.

The Athenian market, or *Agora*, must not be imagined to be "like the bare spaces in many modern towns, where little attention has been paid to artistic decoration, but is rather to be compared to the beautiful squares of such Italian cities as Verona and Florence, where historical buildings have closed in the space within narrow limits, and sculpture has peopled it with impressive figures."—CONYBEARE AND HOWSON, *Life of St. Paul*, vol. i, p. 354.

843.—EPICUREANS—STOICS.

XVII, 18. Then certain philosophers of the Epicureans, and of the Stoics, encountered him.

1. Epicurus, the founder of the sect which bore his name, was born at Samos about 340 B. C. He early adopted the atomic theory of Democritus, and taught philosophy in Athens for nearly forty years, his place of instruction being a beautiful garden in the heart of the city. According to the Epicureans the universe consists of matter and space. Matter is uncreated and indestructible. It is composed of minute atoms, infinite in number and imperceptible to the senses. These atoms may change in mutual relation and in combination, but they cannot be annihilated. They are perpetually moving in space, and are constantly undergoing transpositions of form, but are regulated by no law save that of blind chance. Epicurus believed in the existence of the gods, but this belief was practically no better than atheism, since he denied that the gods had any part in the operations of nature. There was in his system no room for conscience, no place for moral obligation. Pleasure was the chief object of life. Though it is claimed that the ideal of Epicurus was not pleasure of a degrading nature, and that he taught a strict morality, yet the system inevitably tended to sensuality, and had natural attractions for those who were fond of debasing pleasures. It made no provision for a future life, for it knew of no other life than this. Its creed may be briefly summed up in this: "Let us eat and drink, for to-morrow we die."

2. The Stoics were founded by Zeno of Citium in the fourth century before Christ. Their place of meeting was in the "Painted Porch," or *Stoa*, of Athens, whence they derived their name. They believed in two fundamental principles, the active and the passive. The passive was matter, the active was God. They were pantheists, denying the independent existence of the soul, and affirming that all souls were emanations of Deity. They also taught that God and man were both alike inexorably subject to Fate. In opposition to the Epicureans they held that men ought to have no regard to pleasure, but to act only for the right. They were not agreed in their views of a future life. Some believed that all souls were absorbed into Deity at death; others that they maintained their separate existence until a general conflagration of the universe took place; others still, that only the good thus maintained a separate existence.

844.—TRADES LEARNED.

XVIII, 3. Because he was of the same craft, he abode with them, and wrought: for by their occupation they were tentmakers.

Among the Jews the boys were all compelled to learn trades. It was considered disreputable not to be acquainted with some branch of handicraft, a practical knowledge of a trade being regarded as a requisite to personal independence. This custom has been found, not only among the Jews, but among some other nations. One of the Sultans of Turkey was taught to make wooden spoons!

845.—EPHESIAN LETTERS.

XIX, 19. Many of them also which used curious arts brought their books together, and burned them before all men.

Ephesus was the great center of magic in the time of Paul. The "books" here mentioned were probably made up of directions for producing magical results, and were reckoned of great value to all who practiced sorcery. One of the "curious arts" consisted in the use of the "Ephesian letters," celebrated in ancient times. These are supposed to have been copies of certain characters which were engraved on the crown, the girdle, and the feet of the statue of the goddess Diana. See note on verse 35. They were written on strips of parchment, and worn as amulets. The "books" may have taught how to use these to the best advantage. Hesychius (cited by BURDER, *Oriental Literature*, No. 1429) says: "The Ephesian letters, or characters, were formerly six, but certain deceivers added others afterward; and their names, according to report, were these: askion, kataskion, lix, tetrax, damnameneus, and aision. It is evident that askion means darkness; kataskion, light; lix, the earth; tetrax, the year; damnameneus, the sun; and aision, truth: these are holy and sacred things."

846.—SHRINES OF DIANA.

XIX, 24. A certain man named Demetrius, a silversmith, which made silver shrines for Diana, brought no small gain unto the craftsmen.

These shrines were miniature representations of the most sacred portion of the heathen temple; that part of it where the statue of the goddess was situated. They were made of wood or precious metal, and were worn as charms. A little door on one side concealed the image of the goddess within. Roberts found a similar practice in India, where shrines of idols are often made in the shape of a temple and suspended from the neck of the wearer.

For a description of the temple represented by the shrines mentioned in the text, see the next note.

847.—THE TEMPLE OF DIANA.

XIX, 27. That the temple of the great goddess Diana should be despised, and her magnificence should be destroyed, whom all Asia and the world worshipeth.

This was the largest of the Greek temples, and the most magnificent of the ancient world. It is said to have been burned and rebuilt no less than seven times, the temple referred to in the text being the eighth of the series. This and the two which immediately preceded it were built on the same foundation, which was laid by Theodorus about B. C. 500. The first temple of the three built on this foundation was burned about B. C. 400. The second was burned on the same night that Alexander the Great was born, B. C. 356. Great efforts and sacrifices were made to replace this by a building which should far excel all the others in magnificence, and it was this splendid edifice on which the eyes of the Apostle Paul gazed. It is said to have been two hundred and twenty years in building, though some writers claim that this period is intended by the ancient historians to include the time from the foundation by Theodorus to the completion of the great temple. It was four hundred and twenty-five feet long, and two hundred and twenty feet wide. In the interior was a chapel containing the image of the goddess. See note on verse 35. The roof of this chapel was of cedar. The rest of the vast building was open to the sky, and consisted of colonnades, the columns of which were sixty feet high and seven feet and a half in diameter. It is commonly said that there were one hundred and twenty-seven of these columns, each the gift of a king, and Pliny is referred to as the authority for this statement. There are late commentators, however, who, by punctuation, give a different translation to the statement of Pliny, making it read: " The columns were one hundred and twenty, seven of them the gifts of kings." Leake suggests the probability of an error in transcribing: " It is very possible that the early copiers of Pliny made the common oversight of omitting an unit, writing cxxvii instead of cxxviii."—*Tour in Asia Minor*, p. 347. Either of these interpretations makes the number of columns even. Thirty-six of the columns were richly carved, and ornamented with precious metals and stones. Some suppose that Paul makes reference to this great temple in 1 Cor. iii, 9–17, and in Eph. ii, 19–22.

818.—THE THEATER AT EPHESUS.

XIX, 29. They rushed with one accord into the theater.

This was an immense semicircular structure, the largest of which any account has come down to us from ancient times. It was open to the sky, with ascending seats, tier above tier, and is said to have been capable of holding thirty thousand persons. Its ruins are yet to be seen. Among the Greeks, (though rarely among the Romans,) theaters were used, not only for spectacular entertainments, but also for assemblages for political or business purposes. Hence it was perfectly natural for the excited multitude to rush into the theater on this occasion.

It was in a theater that Herod Agrippa I. gave audience to the Tyrian deputies, and was smitten with disease and death. See JOSEPHUS, *Antiquities*, book xix, chap. 8, § 2. See also Acts xii, 20–23.

849.—THE ASIARCHÆ.

XIX, 31. Certain of the chief of Asia, which were his friends, sent unto him, desiring him that he would not adventure himself into the theater.

The *Asiarchæ* were officers who were chosen to superintend the public games which were held in honor of the gods and of the Roman emperors. Their duties being semi-religious, they are by some authorities called priests, and their office is called a priesthood. Every year ten of the most prominent citizens of the chief cities of proconsular Asia were chosen to the office of Asiarch for the term of one year, though eligible to reappointment. They were of necessity men of great wealth, since the games at which they officiated were very costly, and the *Asiarchæ* were themselves obliged to meet the entire expense. When officiating they were clad in purple and crowned with garlands. Whether the entire number superintended the games, or only one was selected from the ten to preside while the others assisted, is a point of controversy not yet settled.

850.—TOWN-CLERK—DIANA OF EPHESUS.

XIX, 35. When the town-clerk had appeased the people, he said, Ye men of Ephesus, what man is there that knoweth not how that the city of the Ephesians is a worshiper of the great goddess Diana, and of the image which fell down from Jupiter?

1. The *grammateus*, scribe, or "town-clerk," as the word is here rendered, seems to have been charged with duties of a higher order than those of the ordinary scribes among the Greeks. It is supposed that, under the Roman rule in Asia Minor, the work of the scribes was not limited to recording the laws and reading them in public. They presided over popular assemblies, and sometimes legally assumed the functions of magistrates. The title is preserved on ancient coins and marbles, and the scribes were evidently regarded as governors of cities or districts.

2. While the Diana of the Romans corresponded to the Artemis of the Greeks, this Ephesian Diana or Artemis was a totally distinct divinity of Asiatic origin. Her worship was found by the Greeks in Ionia when they settled there, and to her they gave the name of Artemis. There was in many respects a resemblance between the Ephesian Artemis and the Syrian Astarte. See note on 1 Kings xi, 5. Her worship extended over a vast region, and cities vied with each other for the honor of being called *neokoron*, sweeper, or keeper, of the temple; "worshiper" in the text. The original Ephesian image was said to have fallen from heaven, as was also asserted of images of other deities in other cities. This has given rise to the opinion that this and similar images were ærolites, and were worshiped according to

the ancient superstition which gave sanctity and divinity to certain stones. See note on Isa. lvii, 6. Ancient authorities, however, assert that the Ephesian Artemis was of wood, some say of ebony, others of vine-wood. Whatever the material, the figure was very coarse and rude. The later image of the Ephesian goddess was elaborately made, and was covered with carefully-wrought symbols and mystic figures. See note on verse 19.

The following is the description given of this statue by Mr. Falkener (*Ephesus*, pp. 290, '91): "The circle round her head denotes the nimbus of her glory, the griffins inside of which express its brilliancy. In her breast are the twelve signs of the zodiac, of which those seen in front are the ram, bull, twins, crab, and lion; they are divided by the hours. Her necklace is composed of acorns, the primeval food of man. Lions are on her arms to denote her power, and her hands are stretched out to show that she is ready to receive all who come to her. Her body is covered with various beasts and monsters, as sirens, sphinxes, and griffins, to show she is the source of nature, the mother of all things. Her head, hands, and feet are of bronze, while the rest of the statue is of alabaster, to denote the ever-

163.—Diana of Ephesus, from an Antique Statue in the Naples Museum.

varying light and shade of the moon's figure. . . . Like Rhea, she was crowned with turrets, to denote her dominion over terrestrial objects."—Fairbairn, *Imperial Bible Dictionary*.

851.—VOWS—NAZARITES.

XXI, 23, 24. We have four men which have a vow on them; them take, and purify thyself with them, and be at charges with them, that they may shave their heads.

1. The custom of making vows to God is very ancient. We read of it as far back as the days of Job. Eliphaz refers to it in Job xxii, 27. Jacob practiced it. Gen. xxviii, 20–22; xxxi, 13. We read in later times of the vows of Jephthah, (Judges xi, 30, 31;) Hannah, (1 Sam. i, 11;) and Absalom, (2 Sam. xv, 8, 9;) though the last-mentioned probably pretended to vow for the purpose of furthering his rebellion. Heathens vowed as well as Jews. See Jer. xliv, 25; Jonah i, 16.

Vows usually involved free-will offerings to be given to God as a recognition of his goodness, either subsequent to the reception of blessings desired, or in anticipation of them. There was no law compelling any one to make vows, but, when once made, they came within the limit of the law, and their fulfillment became obligatory. See Num. xxx, 2; Deut. xxiii, 21, 22; Judges xi, 35; Prov. xx, 25; Eccl. v, 4, 5.

The offerings to be devoted to the service of God in the fulfillment of vows were houses or land; animals for sacrifice; or the person of the one making the vow, his child, or his slave. These personal offerings could be redeemed, (see Lev. xxvii, 1–7;) so also could houses and land. Lev. xxvii, 14–25. Animals for sacrifice were not redeemable. Lev. xxvii, 9, 10, 33.

Besides the texts above mentioned, vows are referred to in Psa. xxii, 25, l, 14; lvi, 12; lxvi, 13; cxvi, 14, 18; Isa. xix, 21; Nahum i, 15.

2. The vow specially alluded to in the text is supposed by most commentators to be the vow of the Nazarite. The origin of this peculiar vow is unknown, and even the etymology of the word is disputed, though most authorities derive it from *nazar*, to "consecrate," to "separate." The law regulating it is found in the sixth chapter of the book of Numbers, where the subject is treated, not as a novelty, but as a well-established custom.

The Nazarite vow was a consecration to the Lord. There were a few instances in which this consecration was for life. Persons thus set apart were called "Nazarites of perpetuity." Samson was one of these. See Judges xiii, 4, 5. So was Samuel. See 1 Sam. i, 11. John Baptist is also thought to have been a Nazarite for life. See Luke i, 15.

The Nazarites generally were, however, limited in the duration of the obligation imposed by their vow. These were called "Nazarites of days." The ordinary time was thirty days, but sometimes it extended to sixty, or even to a hundred, days. During the time the obligation lasted the Nazarite was to be separate in three particulars: 1. He was not to partake of wine or strong drink in any form. 2. He was not to allow his hair to be cut. 3. He was not to come in contact with a dead body.

At the close of his term of separation the Nazarite was to perform certain ceremonies, which are detailed in Num. vi, 13–21. Among other things, he was to cut off his hair and put it into the fire of the peace-offering. After the wave-offering was presented he might drink wine. In addition to the usual offerings required by the law, it was customary for those who were able to give something to help the poorer Nazarites procure their regular offerings. Paul is supposed to have complied with this custom, thus "being at charges with them," and enabling them to finish the term of their vows by shaving their heads. This will explain, not only the text, but also verse 26. In this way the apostle was able to show to his sensitive Jewish brethren that he did not mean to "forsake Moses." Paul's vow, which is spoken of in Acts xviii, 18, is also thought by many commentators to have been a Nazarite vow, though some dispute this view.

Various theories have been devised in explanation of this singular custom of the Nazarite. Perhaps none is more satisfactory than that which represents it to be the "typical representation of a holy life." Fairbairn says: "It sets forth in a striking and beautiful manner the leading features of a life devoted to God. It originates in a solemn resolve of the free-will, and is in this respect an interesting emblem of a godly life, which is the spontaneous outgoing of a heart renewed by the Spirit of God."—*Imperial Bible Dictionary, s. v.* NAZARITE. See also FAIRBAIRN'S *Typology,* vol. ii, p. 346.

A resemblance to at least one of the practices of the Nazarites may be found in the customs of other ancient nations besides the Jews. (The authorities are given in WINER, *Biblisches Realwörterbuch, s. v.* NASIRAER.) Among the Egyptians, Syrians, Greeks, Romans, and Arabs, it was customary in times of impending peril to consecrate the hair and beard to the gods. Morier gives a singular illustration of a similar practice among the modern Persians. Speaking of customs concerning young children, he says: "It frequently happens after the birth of a son that if the parent be in distress, or the child be sick, or that there be any other cause of grief, the mother makes a vow that no razor shall come upon the child's head for a certain period of time, and sometimes for all his life. If the child recovers and the cause of grief be removed, and if the vow be but for a time, so that the mother's vow be fulfilled, then she shaves his head at the end of the time prescribed, makes a small entertainment, collects money and other things from her relations and friends, which are sent as *Nezers* (offerings) to the mosque at Kerbelah, and are there consecrated."—*Second Journey,* etc., p. 108.

852.—POSITION OF TEACHER AND SCHOLAR.

XXII, 8. Brought up in this city at the feet of Gamaliel, and taught according to the perfect manner of the law of the fathers.

In Jewish schools the master sat on a high chair, the elder pupils on a lower bench, and the youngest on the ground. The general custom at present in the East is for the teacher and pupils to sit upon the ground, and, according to Maimonides, this was once the ancient practice. The custom probably varied at different periods, but in either case the pupils were literally "at the feet" of their instructor. This is referred to in Luke x, 39, where we are told that Mary "sat at Jesus' feet, and heard his word."

853.—APPEAL—ROMAN COUNCILORS.

XXV, 11, 12. I appeal unto Cesar. Then Festus, when he had conferred with the council, answered, Hast thou appealed unto Cesar? unto Cesar shalt thou go.

1. The Roman governors exercised supreme jurisdiction over the provinces; but all Roman citizens had the inalienable right of appeal. This

right Paul saw fit to use, and thereby took the case out of the hands of Festus and removed it to a higher court.

2. The *assessores*, or councilors, were men learned in the law, whose business it was to sit in judgment with the governor, and advise with him on points of law. Festus turned to them to ascertain whether the appeal of Paul was admissible.

854.—THE HAND STRETCHED FORTH.

XXVI, 1. Then Paul stretched forth the hand, and answered for himself.

This was a customary form of dignified oratory, designed to show the earnestness of the speaker. The orator stretched forth the right hand, having the two lowest fingers shut in on the palm of the hand, while the other fingers were extended. It is said that Demosthenes often used this gesture.

This is not to be confounded with the "beckoning" mentioned in Acts xiii, 16. That was simply a motion of the hand for the purpose of gaining attention. See also Acts xii, 17.

855.—THE SKIFF.

XXVII, 16. We had much work to come by the boat.

The skiff, or small boat, which accompanied the ancient sailing vessel was not taken on board, as with us, but was usually allowed to follow in the wake. In this instance, by reason of the storm, it was thought advisable to take it on board, but the task was one of great difficulty.

856.—" UNDERGIRDING."

XXVII, 17. Which when they had taken up, they used helps, undergirding the ship.

Every ship carried large cables, which were used in case of necessity for passing around the hull, thus "undergirding " it, and saving it from the strain which resulted from the working of the mast in a storm

857.—ANCHORS, HOW USED.

XXVII, 29. They cast four anchors out of the stern.

1. Ancient vessels had not so heavy anchors as ours, and therefore carried more.

2. It was customary to anchor ancient ships by the stern, though they were sometimes anchored at the bow. The anchors were carried in the skiff to a suitable distance from the vessel and there dropped. In modern times ships-of-war in action have sometimes been anchored from the stern. Lord Nelson pursued this plan at the battle of the Nile, and at the battle of Copenhagen. See the account in ALISON, *History of Europe*, (Edition, Harper,) vol. i, p. 513 ; vol. ii, p. 154.

858.—DOUBLE RUDDERS.

XXVII, 40. **They committed themselves unto the sea, and loosed the rudder bands.**

More correctly, the bands of the *rudders;* the word in the original being plural. Each ship had two rudders, or paddles, for steering, one on each quarter. The hinged rudder at the stern is comparatively a modern contrivance.

859.—SHIPS NAMED.

XXVIII, 11. **A ship of Alexandria, which had wintered in the isle, whose sign was Castor and Pollux.**

Ancient ships had the name on each side of the bow, as with us, and represented by a sculptured figure. The vessel in which Paul now sailed was the "Castor and Pollux," named after twin deities who were regarded as the special patrons of sailors.

———◆———

ROMANS.

860.—CAPITAL PUNISHMENT.

VII, 24. **O wretched man that I am! who shall deliver me from the body of this death?**

It is thought by some commentators, though the opinion is controverted by others, that there is an allusion here to a horrible mode of punishment mentioned by ancient writers, by which the criminal condemned to death was fastened by chains to a dead body and left to die by inches in the loathsome companionship of a putrefying corpse.

861.—ADOPTION.

VIII, 15. **Ye have received the Spirit of adoption, whereby we cry, Abba, Father.**

Among the Greeks and Romans, when a man had no son he was permitted to adopt one even though not related. He might, if he chose, adopt one of his slaves as a son. The adopted son took the name of the father, and was in every respect regarded and treated as a son. Among the Romans there were two parts to the act of adoption: one a private arrangement between the parties, and the other a formal public declaration of the fact. It is thought by some that the former is referred to in this verse, and the latter in verse 23, where the apostle speaks of "waiting for the adoption." The

28

servant has been adopted privately, but he is "waiting" for a formal public declaration of the fact.

After adoption, the son, no longer a slave, had the privilege of addressing his form er master by the title of "father." This he had no right to do while a servant. See also Gal. iv, 5, 6.

862.—THE KISS.

XVI, 16. Salute one another with a holy kiss.

The kiss was not only used among men as a token of friendship, (see note on Gen. xxix, 13,) and of homage to a superior, (see note on Psa. ii, 12,) but as one of the ceremonies connected with divine worship, and intended to express mutual love and equality. As such it is supposed to have been used in the synagogues, and thence transmitted to the Christian Church. There is nothing said in the New Testament in reference to the part of the service where the kiss was introduced, but early Christian writers state that in the apostolic age it was given after prayers and before the communion service. The minister first said, "Peace be unto you," and the people responded. Then "a deacon goes on to proclaim solemnly that they should salute one another with a holy kiss; and so the clergy salute the bishop, and laymen their fellow-laymen, and women one another."—BINGHAM, *Antiquities*, book xv, chap. 3, § 3.

See also 1 Cor. xvi, 20; 2 Cor. xiii, 12; 1 Thess. v, 26; 1 Pet. v, 14. In the last passage it is called "a kiss of love."

————•————

I CORINTHIANS.

863.—SET FORTH LAST.

IV, 9. For I think that God hath set forth us the apostles last; as it were appointed to death: for we are made a spectacle unto the world, and to angels, and to men.

The apostle may have had in his mind the public exhibition of the *bestiarii* and gladiators; the former were men who fought with beasts, and the latter men who fought with each other. Some thus fought for pay, while others were criminals who were compelled to contend with beasts or with armed men as an expiation of their crimes, and as a source of amusement to the spectators. In the early part of the day of such an exhibition the prisoners were given arms wherewith to defend themselves, but at the close of the exhibition, at noon, the poor wretches had nothing to protect them, and soon fell easy and certain victims to the destroyer. Thus the apostles were set forth *last*.

864.—TEMPERANCE—CHAPLETS.

IX, 25. **Every man that striveth for the mastery is temperate in all things. Now they do it to obtain a corruptible crown; but we an incorruptible.**

Among the four sacred games of the ancient Greeks the Olympic and the Isthmian were the most celebrated, the former taking the precedence. To these familiar games the apostle makes many allusions in his writings. (See further, note on Heb. xii, 1.) There are two of such in this text.

1. Every competitor in these games was obliged to undergo a severe and protracted training, sometimes lasting nearly a year, during which time he carefully avoided excesses of every kind. A passage from Epictetus so beautifully illustrates this text that it is cited by most commentators: "Would you be a victor in the Olympic games? so in good truth would I, for it is a glorious thing; but pray consider what must go before, and what may follow, and so proceed to the attempt. You must then live by rule, eat what will be disagreeable, refrain from delicacies; you must oblige yourself to constant exercises at the appointed hour, in heat and cold; you must abstain from wine and cold liquors; in a word, you must be as submissive to all the directions of your master as to those of a physician."—*Enchiridion*, chap. xxxv.

Thus Paul says in the text: "Every man that striveth for the mastery is temperate in all things."

2. The victor was rewarded with a crown or chaplet of leaves. The Olympic crown was made of the leaves of the wild olive, the Isthmian was made of pine or ivy. From the earliest periods of history chaplets of leaves were bestowed upon heroes who had conquered on the field of battle. Thus the Psalmist says of the triumphant Messiah: "Upon himself shall his crown flourish." Psa. cxxxii, 18. The idea of a crown *flourishing* is very expressive when spoken of a leafy chaplet; though some commentators render the word *shine*. This is the sort of crown to which Paul refers in the text as "corruptible." The crown of thorns which was placed on the Saviour's head was a mockery of these wreaths of triumph, as well as of the golden crowns of kings. See Matt. xxvii, 29; Mark xv, 17; John xix, 2, 5.

The leafy crown given to the victor in these ancient games doubtless furnishes the metaphor which is used in 2 Tim. ii, 5; iv, 8; James i, 12; 1 Pet. v, 4; Rev. ii, 10; iii, 11.

865.—BOXING.

IX, 26. **So fight I, not as one that beateth the air.**

The allusion here is to boxing. It was customary for the boxers while training to strike out at an imaginary adversary merely for exercise. This was "beating the air." The text may refer to this, or to the efforts which, when the real contest took place, each made to avoid the blows of his adversary, so that these blows should fall upon the air. The apostle struck real blows at a real adversary.

The "beating" was done by means of leather bands which were fastened around the arms and wrists, and were sometimes studded with nails and loaded with lead or iron. This made the blow heavy, and frequently dangerous. Fighting in this way was "resisting unto blood;" this is the ground of the image in Heb. xii, 4.

866.—THE HERALD.

IX, 27. **Lest that by any means, when I have preached to others, I myself should be a castaway.**

In the word "preached" we have reference to the office of a herald. Such an office was employed, not only by kings to announce their decrees, (see Dan. iii, 4.) and to proclaim their coming. (see Mal. iii, 1, and note on Isa. xl, 3,) but also by those who had charge of the ancient games, to which reference has been made in the preceding verses. The herald proclaimed at the opening of the games the name and country of each candidate, and the rules of the contest. Most commentators suppose the apostle here to represent himself as such a herald. He has announced the opening of the contest, and the laws which regulate it; he is now to be careful lest after all he himself should not succeed. for, unlike the herald in the games, he is also a competitor. Bloomfield, however, thinks that there is here, at best, only an "under-allusion" to the office of herald. See his note *in loco.*

867.—GLASS.

XIII, 12. **For now we see through a glass, darkly; but then face to face.**

Critics differ as to the meaning of the word rendered "glass" in this verse. Many suppose it means a metallic mirror, as it evidently does in James i, 23. (For an account of ancient mirrors, see note on Exod. xxxviii, 8.) Such a mirror, covered with a thin vail, as was often done to protect from dust and dampness, would present a dim, shadowy reflection, causing the beholder to see "darkly," or more literally, *enigmatically.* Others think that the "glass" in this text was the *lapis specularis,* a kind of talc of which the ancients sometimes made their windows. Through this the indistinct outlines of an object could be seen, but the beholder was left to guess what the object might be. He was looking at an *enigma;* he saw "darkly."

We have thus a beautiful illustration of the difference in clearness of vision between the present life and the future. The vail will be taken from the mirror, so that the reflection will be clear; or, the semi-transparent window will be removed, so that nothing shall obstruct the sight.

868.—MODE OF RECKONING TIME.

XV, 4. That he was buried, and that he rose again the third day according to the Scriptures.

Among the Jews the day was reckoned from evening to evening, (see Lev. xxiii, 32,) though this reckoning was sometimes varied. In popular language a part of a day was reckoned for the whole. The Saviour was buried at the close of the day, just before the Sabbath began. He remained in the tomb during the whole of the Sabbath, which ended the following evening. Another day then began, and when the night of this day passed and its morning came he rose from the dead. Though but a short time of the first day was spent in the grave, it is still reckoned according to Jewish usage as the first day of his burial, the Sabbath being the second, and the next day the third.

See also Matt. xvi, 21; xvii, 23; xx, 19; Mark ix, 31; x, 34; Luke ix, 22; xiii, 32; xviii, 33; xxiv, 7, 21, 46.

869.—ENEMIES UNDER THE FEET.

XV, 25. For he must reign, till he hath put all enemies under his feet.

There is a similar passage in Joshua x, 24, on which see the note. The monuments of ancient Egypt, Assyria, and Persia give numerous illustrations of the custom of conquerors trampling on the vanquished. In the cave at Beit el Walley in Nubia is a hieroglyphic description of Rameses II. trampling on his enemies. It reads: "Kol, the strange land, is beneath thy sandals." At the foot of a wooden mummy case in the British Museum are painted the soles of two shoes, and on each is the figure of a man with his arms and hands tied behind him, and his feet tied at the ankles. In this helpless state he is supposed to be trampled on by the wearer of the shoes. It was a very expressive illustration of mingled triumph and contempt.

These customs strikingly illustrate

164.—ENEMIES TRAMPLED ON.

the text, and numerous parallel passages.   See Psa. viii, 6; cx, 1; cxix, 118; Isa. xiv, 19; xxv, 10; xxviii, 3, 18; lxiii, 6; Lam. i, 15; iii, 34; Dan. viii, 13; Micah vii, 10; Mal. iv, 3; Luke xxi, 24; Rom. xvi, 20; Heb. x, 29.

II CORINTHIANS.

870.—ROMAN MILITARY TRIUMPHS.

II, 14. Now thanks be unto God, which always causeth us to triumph in Christ, and maketh manifest the savor of his knowledge by us in every place.

A Roman military triumphal procession was one of the grandest spectacles of ancient times.   It was granted to a conqueror only when certain conditions had been fully complied with.   Among these it was required that the victory be complete and decisive; that it should be over a foreign foe; that at least five thousand of the enemy should be slain in a single battle; that the conquest should extend the territory of the state, and put an end to the war.   When the senate decided that all the required conditions had been met a day was appointed, and every necessary arrangement was made for a splendid pageant.   When the day arrived the people crowded the streets, and filled every place from which a good view of the procession could be obtained.   The temples were all open and decorated with flowers, while incense smoked from every altar.   Fragrant odors from burning spices were profusely scattered through the temples and along the streets, loading the air with their perfume.   In the procession were the senate and chief citizens of the state, who thus by their presence honored the conqueror.   The richest spoils of war, such as gold, silver, weapons of every description, standards, rare and costly works of art, and every thing that was deemed most valuable by either conqueror or vanquished, were carried in open view of the crowded city.   The prisoners of war were also compelled to march in the procession.   The general, in whose honor the triumph was decreed, rode in a chariot which was of peculiar form and drawn by four horses.   His robe was embroidered with gold, and his tunic with flowers.   In his right hand was a laurel bough, and in his left a scepter; while on his brow there was a wreath of Delphic laurel.   Amid the shouts of the soldiers and the applause of the populace the conqueror was carried through the streets to the temple of Jupiter, where sacrifices were offered, after which there was a public feast in the temple.   (For a more detailed account, see SMITH's *Dictionary of Antiquities, s. v.* TRIUMPHUS.)

To the splendors of such a scene the apostle doubtless alludes in this text, and also in Col. ii, 15: " And having spoiled principalities and powers, he made a show of them openly, triumphing over them in it." Here Christ is referred to as the Great Conqueror, making public exhibition of the spoils of war. In the text at the head of this note it is also Christ who is the conqueror, Paul being merely an instrument used by him for the accomplishment of his work. Thus, wherever he preached Christ triumphed; and as in the Roman triumphs odors were profusely scattered around, so the knowledge of Christ was every-where proclaimed by the apostles: "Maketh manifest the savor of his knowledge by us in every place." In the Roman triumph the fragrance which filled the air was inhaled alike by the captives of war doomed to death, and by the people who by means of the victory were saved from a similar fate. Thus the Gospel is preached to all, but with different results: to the believer, salvation; to him who rejects, eternal death. So Paul says in the fifteenth and sixteenth verses: "For we are unto God a sweet savor of Christ, in them that are saved, and in them that perish: To the one we are the savor of death unto death; and to the other the savor of life unto life."

871.—WALL—WINDOW—BASKET.

XI, 33. Through a window in a basket was I let down by the wall. See also Acts ix, 25.

1. The wall of a house is sometimes also a portion of the city wall, and thus windows may be placed in the wall through which access may be had to the region outside of the city. The floor of an upper story sometimes extends beyond the wall, giving an opportunity for a bay window projecting outside the wall. Either of these methods would afford a chance to escape from the city without passing through the gates. Thus the spies escaped from Jericho. See Josh. ii, 15. David seems to have escaped in a similar manner by the help of Michal. See 1 Sam. xix, 12.

2. The basket by which Paul was let down probably resembled the large round shallow baskets which are still used in Damascus and in other parts of the East for various purposes. When Prof. Hackett was in Damascus he saw a couple of men come to the top of the wall with a basket full of rubbish, which they emptied over the wall. A friend said to him: "Such a basket the people use here for almost every sort of thing. If they are digging a well and wish to send a man down into it, they put him into such a basket; and that those who aided Paul's escape should have used a basket for the purpose was entirely natural, according to the present customs of the country. Judging from what is done now, it is the only sort of vehicle of which men would be apt to think under such circumstances."—*Illustrations of Scripture*, p. 69.

GALATIANS.

872.—THE PEDAGOGUE.

III, 24. The law was our schoolmaster to bring us unto Christ.

The παιδαγωγός, "schoolmaster," was not an instructor, but a trustworthy slave, to whom was committed the care of his master's sons from the time they were six or seven years of age until puberty. "His duty was rather to guard them from evil, both physical and moral, than to communicate instruction, to cultivate their minds, or to impart accomplishments. He went with them to and from the school or the gymnasium; he accompanied them out of doors on all occasions; he was responsible for their personal safety, and for their avoidance of bad company."—SMITH'S *Dictionary of Antiquities*, *s. v.* PÆDAGOGUS.

873.—THE MARK.

VI, 17. I bear in my body the marks of the Lord Jesus.

Slaves were branded with a peculiar mark to designate their masters. So Paul had in his body marks, received in persecution for Christ's sake, which showed to whom he belonged. Some think there is an allusion here to his "thorn in the flesh," which was a perpetual mark put upon him by his lord and master.

See also notes on Lev. xix, 28; Isa. xlix, 16; Ezek. ix, 4.

EPHESIANS.

874.—MILITARY SANDALS.

VI, 15. Your feet shod with the preparation of the gospel of peace.

The military sandals of the Roman private soldiers and centurions were made of very strong leather, and the soles were thickly studded with hobnails in order to give a sure footing. Thus the Christian soldier, having the Gospel as a sure footing, can stand firmly against the attacks of his spiritual foes.

875.—FIERY DARTS.

VI, 16. The shield of faith, wherewith ye shall be able to quench all the fiery darts of the wicked.

Some have thought that the allusion here is to poisoned arrows. See note on Job vi, 4. There were darts, however, sometimes used in ancient warfare that were literally "fiery." They were hollow reeds filled with naphtha or some other combustible material, and, being set on fire, were shot from slack bows. Whatever the arrows struck, the flames consumed. Water served to increase their violence; they could only be extinguished by being covered with earth. Large shields were used by the soldiers against whom these "fiery darts" were thrown, and thus their persons were protected

---

PHILIPPIANS.

876.—REGISTER OF CITIZENS' NAMES.

IV, 3. With other my fellow-laborers, whose names are in the book of life.

It was customary to have registers of citizenship, in which were entered the names of citizens, both natural and adopted. Heaven is represented as a city, and its inhabitants are registered. Some, who have not yet reached the heavenly city, are regarded as citizens on their way home. Their names are registered with the others. Such were the "fellow-laborers" to whom Paul refers in the text. See also Isa. iv, 3; Dan. xii, 1; Luke x, 20; Rev. xiii, 8; xvii, 8; xx, 15; xxi, 27. When one was deprived of citizenship his name was erased from the roll of citizens. Reference may be found to this in Exod. xxxii, 32; Psa. lxix, 28; and Rev. iii, 5.

II TIMOTHY.

877.—ROMAN MILITARY DISCIPLINE.

II, 3. Thou therefore endure hardness, as a good soldier of Jesus Christ.

The discipline of the Roman army was very severe. Every soldier was compelled to "endure hardness." The weapons were heavy, and in addition to them the ordinary foot soldier was compelled to carry a saw, a basket, a pick-ax, an ax, a thong of leather, and a hook, together with three days' rations. He was treated more like a beast of burden than a man. See JOSEPHUS, *Wars of the Jews*, book iii, chap. v.

878.—SINGLENESS OF AIM.

II, 4. No man that warreth entangleth himself with the affairs of this life; that he may please him who hath chosen him to be a soldier.

The Roman soldier was expected to keep one thing in view, and only one: the service of his commander. He was not allowed to marry, nor could he engage in agriculture, trade, or manufactures.   He was a *soldier*, and could not be any thing else.

The figure is very suggestive of the singleness of aim which characterizes the true minister of Jesus Christ.   He is not allowed to engage in any employment which will, by its entanglements, interfere with his usefulness. This is what Paul, in the text, designs to intimate to Timothy.

879.—OBLIGATIONS OF LAW.

II, 5. And if a man also strive for masteries, yet is he not crowned, except he strive lawfully.

No man could hope to obtain the reward in the ancient games of running, leaping, boxing, or wrestling, unless he complied with the regulations which were prescribed; first, in the necessary previous training, (see note on 1 Cor. ix, 25,) and then in the conduct of the games.   He must "strive lawfully."   Thus the apostle says in 1 Cor. ix, 24: " *So* run, that ye may obtain."   That is, keep all the rules if you wish to succeed.   It is thought by some that Paul also refers to these rules of the games when he says, in 1 Cor. ix, 26: "I therefore so run, not as uncertainly."   That is, I have a knowledge of all the rules which regulate the race, and I know what I am engaged in.

880.—MURAL INSCRIPTIONS.

II, 19. Nevertheless the foundation of God standeth sure, having this seal, The Lord knoweth them that are his. And, Let every one that nameth the name of Christ depart from iniquity.

The word "seal" is here used in the sense of *inscription*.   Ancient seals frequently had inscriptions on them; though the allusion here is to inscriptions that were placed on buildings.   Besides writing on doors, (see note on Deut. vi, 9,) it was customary to inscribe on some of the foundation-stones of large buildings words indicating the purpose for which the building was erected, or containing some striking apothegm.   Allusion to this custom is also made in Rev. xxi, 14: "The wall of the city had twelve foundations, and in them the names of the twelve apostles of the Lamb."

881.—THE CLOAK.

IV, 18. The cloak that I left at Troas with Carpus, when thou comest, bring with thee.

The φελόνης was a thick upper garment corresponding to the Roman *panula*, and was used in traveling instead of the toga as a protection against the weather.   It was sometimes worn by the women as well as by the men.   It was usually made of wool, though occasionally of leather, and was a long sleeveless garment, made like a sack, with an opening for the head.

HEBREWS.

882.—THE GOLDEN CENSER.

IX, 8, 4. After the second vail, the tabernacle which is called the holiest of all; which had the golden censer.

Commentators are perplexed as to the meaning of θυμιατήριον, rendered "censer" in this text. Some suppose the golden altar of incense is meant; but it is difficult to reconcile this opinion with the fact that this altar was not in the Most Holy Place. Others refer it to the censer which the high-priest used on the Great Day of Atonement. This utensil, however, is not said to have been made of gold. On the contrary, Exod. xxvii, 3, 19, indicate that it was made of brass. Reference seems to be made to a special vessel of gold which remained perpetually in the Most Holy Place of the Mosaic Tabernacle. It is not alluded to in any other part of the Bible.

Meyer, in his *Bibeldeutungen*, has an essay discussing this subject, in which he advances the opinion that there were two kinds of incense used in the Tabernacle; the first described in Exod. xxx, 7, 8, and the second in Exod. xxx, 34–36. "The first or holy incense was used daily for burning on the coals; but the other, or most holy incense, that which was hallowed, was used cold, like our smelling-salts, and was set in the Most Holy Place before the Ark of the Covenant, diffusing a perpetual fragrance. In order that the mixture might accomplish the end designed it was pulverized, **and** possibly some other chemical process was added, (verse 35.) That it might remain before the Testimony, the place where it was positively ordered to be, it was proper that there should be a vessel, a *thumiaterion,* an open perfume dish or cup; this vessel was undoubtedly of gold, as were the other vessels of the Most Holy Place."—*Bibeldeutungen*, pp. 7, 8.

Meyer thinks he has thus discovered the meaning of the word "censer" in the text. His explanation is certainly plausible, and not liable to the difficulties which beset the others.

883.—SAWING ASUNDER.

XI, 37.—They were sawn asunder.

This terrible mode of punishment is said to have originated either with the Persians or the Chaldeans, and was occasionally practiced by other ancient nations. It is supposed by some to be mentioned in 2 Sam. xii, 31, and 1 Chron. xx, 3, though commentators are by no means agreed on this point. There is a very old tradition that Isaiah suffered death by this means. The Saviour is thought to refer to it in Matt. xxiv, 51, and Luke xii, 46. Dr. Shaw says that the Western Moors practiced this barbarous punishment during his travels among them. "They prepare two boards of a proper length and breadth, and having tied the criminal betwixt them, they proceed to the execution by beginning at the head."—*Travels*, p. 254.

884.—THE RACE.

XII, 1. Wherefore, seeing we also are compassed about with so great a cloud of witnesses, let us lay aside every weight, and the sin which doth so easily beset us, and let us run with patience the race that is set before us.

Running was one of the most popular of the Olympic games. The place prepared for the race was called the *stadium* because of its length, which was a *stadium*, or six hundred Greek feet. This was equal to six hundred and twenty-five Roman feet, or six hundred and six and three quarters feet English. See note on John xi, 18. The word appears in the original of 1 Cor. ix, 24, where it is translated "race" in our version. The *stadium* was an oblong area, with a straight wall across one end, where were the entrances, the other end being rounded and entirely closed. Tiers of seats were on either side for the spectators or "witnesses." The starting-place was at the entrance end, and was marked by a square pillar. At the opposite end was the goal, where sat the judge holding in his hand the prize. The eyes of the competitors were fixed on him: "Looking unto Jesus." Heb. xii, 2. The goal, as well as the starting-place, was marked by a square pillar, and a third was placed midway between the two. The goal is the

165.—Ancient Foot-race.

"mark" referred to in Phil. iii, 14. The competitors, through severe training, had no superfluous flesh, and all unnecessary clothing was put off. Flesh and clothing alike were laid aside as a "weight" which might hinder in the race. The distances run were various. The most common was the space between the starting-point and the goal. Sometimes this was doubled, the race terminating where it began. Sometimes the terms of the race required a still longer distance to be run. Seven, twelve, twenty, and even twenty-four times the length of the stadium were occasionally run. This required severe effort, and was a great tax on the strength. The runners might well be exhorted to "run with patience."

There are other passages where allusions are made to the game of running. In 1 Tim. vi, 12, Paul says, as rendered in our version, "Fight the good fight of faith;" and in 2 Tim. iv, 7, "I have fought a good fight." Some commentators understand that, in both these passages, *running* rather than *fighting* is designed by the original terms. The idea is one of contest for superiority. The kind of contest seems to be indicated in 2 Tim. iv, 7, where Paul says, "I have finished my course;" that is, "My race is run." The "course" is also mentioned in Acts xx, 24, and 2 Thess. iii, 1. Phil. iii, 13, 14, also refers to the race: "Brethren, I count not myself to have apprehended: but this one thing I do, forgetting those things which are behind, and reaching forth unto those things which are before, I press toward the mark for the prize of the high calling of God in Christ Jesus." Here the course is not yet finished; he has not yet "apprehended" or seized the prize. Not looking behind, he reaches forth, just as the runners inclined their bodies forward the better to get over the ground. He presses toward the mark or goal, just as they eagerly put forth their utmost endeavor to get the prize. He is in earnest, and determined to succeed.

JAMES.

§85.—TRAVELING MERCHANTS.

IV, 18. Go to now, ye that say, To-day or to-morrow we will go into such a city, and continue there a year, and buy and sell, and get gain.

It is not usual among us for merchants to get rich by going from one city to another. A steady pursuit of trade in one place is deemed essential to success. In the East, however, it is different. There the merchants are itinerant. Professor Hackett says: "Many of those who display their goods in the Eastern bazars are traveling merchants. They come from other cities, and after having disposed of their stock in trade, either for money or other commodities, proceed to another city, where they set up in business again. They supply themselves in every instance with the merchandise best suited to a particular market, and thus, after repeated peregrinations, if successful in their adventures, they acquire a competence and return home to enjoy the fruits of it. The process, therefore, agrees precisely with the apostle's representation. The way to become rich was to go into this or that city and sojourn for awhile and trade, and then depart to another city."— *Illustrations of Scripture*, p. 63.

The men to whom the brethren of Joseph sold him were traders of this sort. See note on Gen. xxxvii, 25.

I PETER.

886.—ADORNMENTS OF THE HEAD.

III, 8. Whose adorning, let it not be that outward adorning of plaiting the hair, and of wearing of gold, or of putting on of apparel.

1. The Oriental ladies are exceedingly fond of golden ornaments and of costly array. See notes on Gen. xxiv, 22, 53; and also on Isa. iii, 16, 18, 20, 22, 23, 24, where a variety of these adornments are described.

2. Especial attention is paid to the hair. Long hair is greatly prized. See 1 Cor. xi, 15. Great care is taken in dressing the hair. Costly ointments are used. See note on Matt. xxvi, 7. The tresses are carefully braided. Lady Montague counted a hundred and ten of these tresses on the head of a Turkish lady, and all of natural hair. The custom of plaiting the hair is very ancient. The Egyptians practiced it, and some specimens of old plaited hair are yet to be seen in museums on the heads of mummies. The women of other nations were not behind them. "In the daily use of cosmetics they bestowed the most astonishing pains in arranging their long hair; sometimes twisting it round on the crown of the head, where, and at the temples, by the aid of gum, which they knew as well as the modern belles, they wrought it into a variety of elegant and fanciful devices—figures of coronets, harps. wreaths, diadems, emblems of public temples and conquered cities. being formed by the mimic skill of the ancient friseur; or else, plaiting it into an incredible number of tresses, which hung down the back, and which, when necessary, were lengthened by ribbons so as to reach to the ground, and were kept at full stretch by the weight of various wreaths of pearls and gold fastened at intervals down to the extremity. From some Syrian coins in his possession, Hartmann (*Die Hebräerin am Putztishe*) has given this description of the style of the Hebrew coiffure; and many ancient busts and portraits which have been discovered exhibit so close a resemblance to those of Eastern ladies in the present day, as to show that the same elaborate and gorgeous disposition of their hair has been the pride of Oriental females in every age."—KITTO'S *Cyclopedia*, *s. v.* HAIR.

Among the interesting specimens of antique pottery discovered by Mr. Barker in Cilicia in 1845 are two terra cotta heads of women with the hair plaited and dressed as shown in these engravings. See BARKER's *Lares and Penates*, pp. 158, 168. In the valuable antiquities from the island of Cyprus in the Cesnola collection (Metropolitan Museum of Art, New York) there is a stone head which bears a close resemblance to one of these terra cotta heads from Cilicia. See engraving No. 167. The Apostle Paul also makes reference to braiding the hair in 1 Tim. ii, 9.

167.—PLAITED HAIR OF ROMAN LADIES.

166.—HEAD DRESS OF ROMAN EMPRESS.

887.—THE CHIEF SHEPHERD.

V, 4. When the chief Shepherd shall appear, ye shall receive a crown of glory that fadeth not away.

In Heb. xiii, 20, Jesus is called "that great Shepherd of the sheep." This corresponds to the "chief Shepherd" in the text. Where the flocks were numerous and a large number of shepherds were necessary, one was placed in charge of all the others. This was true of the herdmen also. Pharaoh told Joseph to take the most active of his kinsmen and make them "rulers" over his cattle. Gen. xlvii, 6. Doeg was the "chiefest of the herdmen" of Saul. 1 Sam. xxi, 7.

Burder gives an interesting quotation from the *Gentlemen's Magazine* for May, 1764, wherein there is a description of the sheep-walks of Spain: "Ten thousand compose a flock, which is divided into ten tribes. One man has the conduct of all. He must be the owner of four or five hundred sheep, strong, active, vigilant, intelligent in pasture, in the weather, and in the diseases of sheep. He has absolute dominion over fifty shepherds and fifty dogs, five of each to a tribe. He chooses them, chastises them or discharges them at will. He is the *præpositus*, or the *chief shepherd*, of the whole flock."—*Oriental Customs*, No. 1310.

Thus we have an illustration of the text. Christian ministers are pastors or shepherds; but there is one over them all. Jesus is the "chief Shepherd." He superintends them, cares for them, assigns them their several positions, and rewards or punishes them.

III JOHN.

888.—INK—PENS.

13. I had many things to write, but I will not with ink and pen write unto thee.

1. For a description of the ink used in the East, see note on Jer. xxxvi, 18.

2. There were two sorts of pens. One was of iron, for use on metallic or waxed plates. See Jer. xvii, 1, and notes on Job xix, 23, 24, and on Luke i, 63. The other was a reed pointed in the same manner as the quill pens of modern times, though not usually slit. This was used with the ink for writing on parchment, or on papyrus.

JUDE.

889.—LOVE-FEASTS.

12. These are spots in your feasts of charity, when they feast with you, feeding themselves without fear.

The *agapæ* or love-feasts, here called "feasts of charity," were feasts which were celebrated in connection with the sacrament of the Lord's Supper; whether before or after is a disputed question. Possibly the precedence varied at different periods of Church history. Bingham gives this account of it from Chrysostom: "The first Christians had all things in common, as we read in the Acts of the Apostles; and when that ceased, as it did in the apostles' time, this came in its room, as an efflux or imitation of it. For though the rich did not make all their substance common, yet, upon certain days appointed, they made a common table; and when their service was ended, and they had all communicated in the holy mysteries, they all met at a common feast: the rich bringing provisions, and the poor and those who had nothing being invited, they all feasted in common together."

The same authority also quotes from Tertullian, who represents the order of service of the *agapæ.* "Our supper, which you accuse of luxury, shows its reason in its very name—for it is called ἀγάπη, which signifies *love* among the Greeks. Whatever charge we are at, it is gain to be at expense upon the account of piety. For we therewith relieve and refresh the poor. There is nothing vile or immodest committed in it. For we do not sit down before we have first offered up prayer to God; we eat only to satisfy hunger, and drink only so much as becomes modest persons. We fill ourselves in such manner as that we remember still that we are to worship

God by night. We discourse as in the presence of God, knowing that he hears us. Then, after water to wash our hands, and lights brought in, every one is moved to sing some hymn to God, either out of Scripture, or, as he is able, of his own composing; and by this we judge whether he has observed the rules of temperance in drinking. Prayer again concludes our feast; and thence we depart, not to fight and quarrel, not to run about and abuse all we meet, not to give ourselves up to lascivious pastime; but to pursue the same care of modesty and chastity, as men that have fed at a supper of philosophy and discipline, rather than a corporeal feast." See BINGHAM'S *Antiquities of the Christian Church*, book xv, chap. 7, §§ 6–9.

Most commentators suppose an allusion in 1 Cor. xi, 21, to the feasts of love, which were used in connection with the eucharist. Dr. Lightfoot, however, while conceding that there were such feasts, denies that they are the *agapæ* mentioned by Paul and by Jude. He supposes that both Paul and Jude refer to entertainments which were provided for traveling brethren at the cost of the Church, in imitation of the custom of the Jews in their synagogues. His entire comment is curious and interesting. See his *Works*, (Edition, Pitman,) vol. xii, p. 522.

REVELATION.

890.—THE CHŒNIX.

VI, 6. A measure of wheat for a penny, and three measures of barley for a penny.

The *chœnix*, "measure," was an Attic dry measure, and was nearly equivalent to one quart English. Its measurement was the usual daily allowance for a soldier or a slave.

891.—PALM-BRANCHES.

VII, 9. Clothed with white robes, and palms in their hands.

Palm-branches were used on occasions of festivity. See Lev. xxiii, 40; Neh. viii, 15. They were regarded as tokens of joy and of triumph. Kings and conquerors were welcomed by having palm-branches strewn before them, and waved in the air, with shouts and acclamations of joy. Thus they were waved before the Messiah on the occasion of his entry into Jerusalem. See John xii, 13. Conquerors in the Grecian games returned to their homes triumphantly waving palm-branches in their hands. Thus in the New Jerusalem John sees the triumphant followers of the Messiah with 'palms in their hands."

29

892.—TEMPLE-WATCHMEN.

XVI, 15. Behold, I come as a thief. Blessed is he that watcheth, and keepeth his garments, lest he walk naked, and they see his shame.

Lightfoot supposes that there is a reference here to the duties of a certain officer of the temple, called "The Ruler of the Mountain of the House." He went about the temple at every watch with lighted torches, to see whether or not the guards were at their posts. If he found one of them sleeping "he struck him with a stick; and it was warrantable for him to burn the garments of such an one. And when it was said by others, What is that noise in the court? the answer was made, It is the noise of a Levite under correction, and whose garments are burning, for that he slept upon the watch. R. Eliezer Ben Jacob said, They once found my mother's son asleep, and they burnt his clothes."—*Hebrew and Talmudical Exercitations* on Luke xxii, 4.

893.—MANY CROWNS.

XIX, 12. His eyes were as a flame of fire, and on his head were many crowns.

Monarchs who claimed authority over more than one country wore more than one crown. The kings of Egypt were crowned with the *pshent*, or united crowns of Upper and Lower Egypt. When Ptolemy Philometer entered Antioch as a conqueror he wore a triple crown, two for Egypt, and the third for Asia.

John saw him who was "King of kings and Lord of lords," and "on his head were *many* crowns." Thus, in a beautiful figure, the universal dominion of our blessed Lord is set forth.

INDEXES.

[The figures on the right hand refer to the numbers of the NOTES.]

I. ANALYTICAL INDEX.

I. RELIGIOUS CUSTOMS.

1. SACRED PLACES.

1. Jewish tabernacle, 141.
   Altar of burnt-offering, 145.
   Altar of incense, 144.
   Ark of covenant, 142.
   Brazen laver, 146.
   Golden candlestick, 143.
   Golden censer, 882.
   Table of show-bread, 143.
2. Temples :—
   First temple—Solomon's, 295.
   Second temple — Zerubbabel's, 375.
   Third temple—Herod's, 704.
      Doves sold in it, 688.
      Gifts to it, 786.
      Pinnacle, 635.
      Solomon's porch, 721.
      Vail, 733.
3. The synagogue, 636, 762.

2. SACRED PERSONS.

1. Chief priests, 717.
2. Dress of priests, 148.
3. Levites, 178.
4. Levitical captains, 787
5. Minister of the synagogue, 757.
6. Priestly investiture, 182.
7. Prophet's mantle, 182.
8. Ruler of the synagogue, 834.
9. The "Consolation," 752.
10. Wives of priests, 748.

3. SACRED OFFERINGS.

1. Burnt-offering, 151.
2. Drink-offering, 169.
3. Hands laid on victim, 160.
4. Meat-offering, 152.
5. Peace-offering, 156.
6. Sacrifice of the red heifer, 181.
7. Sin-offering, 153.
8. Time of evening sacrifice, 311.
9. Trespass-offering, 154.
10. Use of hyssop, 437.
11. Use of salt, 150.
12. Wood-offering, 385.

4. SACRED SEASONS.

1. Agapæ, 889.
2. Feast of dedication, 805.
3. Feast of harvest or pentecost, 131.
4. Feast of tabernacles, 131, 798.
5. Feast of trumpets, 170.
6. Great day of atonement, 161.
7. New moon and sabbath, 335.
8. Passover, 130, 714, 715, 716.
9. Preparation for the festivals, 129.
10. Sabbatical year, 171.
11. Visitors during festivals, 132.
12. Year of jubilee, 172.

5. VARIOUS CEREMONIES CONNECTED WITH WORSHIP.

1. Clothes washed before worship, 126.

Magicians, 76.
Necromancer, 195.
Observer of times, 195.
Wizards and witches, 195.
2. Various kinds of divination:—
By arrows, 578.
By divining cups, 90.
By the liver, 578.
By rods, 597.
By teraphim, 60, 578.
3. Books of magic, 845.

8. ECCLESIASTICAL COURTS.

1. Discipline of the synagogue, 656, 802.

2. The great sanhedrim, 718, 747.
3. The lesser sanhedrim, 656.

9. MISCELLANEOUS.

1. Corban, 740.
2. Cursing, 115, 262.
3. Dancing, 123.
4. Fasting, 783.
5. Lots, 463.
6. Pharisees, 672, 693, 700, 739.
7. Sacred numbers, 468.
8. Sadducees, 695.
9. Swearing by the uplifted hand, 5.
10. The burning lamp, 6.
11. Vows, 851.
12. Washing the hands, 431.

II. CIVIL AND POLITICAL CUSTOMS.

1. OFFICIAL.

1. Kings and queens:—
Coronation, 346.
Crowns, 893.
King's pillar, 347.
King, how approached, 395.
Persian queen, 394.
Pharaoh, the name, 3.
Roads made ready for monarchs, 513.
Scepters, 576.
Silence in presence of royalty, 619.
Solomon's throne, 303.
2. Other officers :—
Asiarchæ, 849.
Captain of the guard, 71.
Chamberlains, 391.
Cup-bearer, 378.
Herald, 513.
Tirshatha, 383.
Town clerk, 850.

2. LEGISLATIVE.

1. Concerning persons:—
Personal liberty :—
Adoption, 861.
Compulsory help, 642.
Freedom by a javelin, 260.
Freedom given by the son, 799.
Opening a servant's ears, 434.
Rights of a Roman citizen, 841.
Responsibility of jailers, 840.

2. Concerning property :—
Ass fallen under burden, 128.
Goel, 245.
Landmarks, 197, 550.
Law of inheritance, 779.
Patrimony not to be sold, 322.
Payment of tribute, 674.
Tax-gathering, 759.
Transfer of property, 27.
3. Unalterable laws, 596.

3. JUDICIAL.

1. Courts.—
Accused standing before the judge, 722.
Agreeing with adversary, 640.
Appeal to Cesar, 853.
Condemnation to death, 398.
Debtor arrested by creditor, 640.
Roman council, 853.
Testimony given standing, 661.
2. Punishments :—
Capital punishments:—
Burning alive, 591.
Chaining to a corpse, 860.
Crucifixion, 727, 729, 730, 820.
Cutting in pieces, 589.
Drowning, 676.
Face of the condemned covered, 399.
Guard at executions, 731.
Hands bound, 270.

III. MILITARY CUSTOMS.

IV. SOCIAL AND DOMESTIC CUSTOMS.

8. Servants :—
  Carrying sandals, 633.
  Doorkeepers, 818.
  Pedagogue, 872.
  Promoted, 78.
  Stewards, 29, 781.
  Watchful, 451.
9. Sickness:—
  Egyptian physicians, 98.
  External applications, 457.
  Oil and wine, 770.
  Ointments, 712.
  Treatment of wounds, 480.
  Use of hyssop, 437.

2. HABITATIONS.

1. Cities and villages :—
  Camping-grounds, 186.
  Cities of the giants, 187.
  City gates:—
    Between the two, 282.
    In the midst of, 268.
    Places of assembly, 15.
    Places of justice, 199.
    Shut at sundown, 531.
  Market-places, 339, 684, 842.
  Quarters of the city, 16.
  Watchmen, 283, 479.
2. Dwellings :—
  Booths, 319.
  Caves, 18.
  Houses :—
    Court:—
      Bath, 275.
      Cisterns, 536.
      Hangings, 388.
      Pillars, 238, 454.
    Dedication of a new house, 198.
    Entrance :—
      Gate, 462, 833.
        Hinges, 467.
        Inscriptions, 190.
        Keys, 224, 502.
        Locks, 224.
      Low gateways, 462.
      Porch, 721.
      Porter, 283.
    Interior :—
      Chamber on the wall, 333.
      Chamber over the gate, 284.
      Chimney, 600.

Decorations, 548, 604.
Guest-chamber, 745.
Hearth, 553.
"House of the women," 392.
Pegs, 503.
Storage-room, 345.
Winter and summer houses, 604.
Roof:—
  Battlements, 201.
  "Broken up," 736.
  Dwelling on, 464.
  Place of assembling, 499.
  Place of drying, 215.
  Place of prayer, 829.
  Place of promenade, 275.
  Proclamations from, 657.
  Stairs from, 705.
  Grass growing on, 452.
  Leaky, 469.
  Mode of construction, 452.
Walls :—
  Built of clay, 411, 415.
  Deep foundation, 761.
  Inscriptions on foundation, 880.
  Wood sometimes used, 618.
Windows :—
  Glass, 867.
  In the wall, 871.
  Latticed, 228.
Tents :—
  "Door" of, 8, 14.
  Materials and mode of pitching, 474.
  Wife's tent, 40.
Tombs used for dwellings, 738.
3. Furniture and utensils:—
  Alabastra, 712.
  Amphoræ, 332.
  Barrel, 308.
  Baskets, 671, 871.
  Beds, 325, 388, 606, 649.
  Bedsteads, 188.
  Bottles, 218, 450, 545, 546, 651.
  Box of oil, 341.
  Cruse, 266, 327.
  Drinking-cups, 89.
  Divan, 325.
  Flesh-pots, 124.
  Frying-pan, 155.

II. TEXTUAL INDEX.

Where a text and number are printed in **full face,** it indicates that the text has an article especially devoted to it.

II KINGS.

Ch. Ver.	No.
13. 15	348
13. 17	228, 349
13. 21	350
15. 29	352
16. 3	163
17. 10	222
17. 16	189, 222
17. 17	163
17. 30, 31	351
18. 11	352
18. 13	352
18. 31	536
18. 32	353
18. 34	354
18. 37	70
19. 1	70
19. 15	295
19. 24	191
19. 26	452
19. 28	512
19. 29	172
19. 32	565
19. 37	355
20. 11	356
20. 13	357, 712
20. 17, 18	391
21. 3	189, 222
21. 6	163
21. 7	222
21. 13	327
21. 18	292
21. 26	292
23. 3	347
23. 5	189, 621
23. 6	222
23. 7	222
23. 10	163
23. 11	358, 391
23. 12	333
23. 13	304
23. 17	359
23. 24	60
23. 34	371
24. 14	352
24. 17	371
25. 1	565
25. 4	366
25. 7	360
25. 8	71
25. 11	352
25. 19	391

I CHRONICLES.

Ch. Ver.	No.
2. 34, 35	361
6. 54–60	178
9. 26	587
10. 9	362
12. 2	363
12. 8	555
13. 8	432
15. 16	432, 456
15. 28	447
16. 3	477
16. 5	432
16. 36	364
20. 3	883
21. 23–25	27
21. 23	508
21. 25	26
23. 5	283
23. 24–27	178
24. 1–19	717
24. 3, 4	717
24. 5	717
25. 1	432
25. 5	365
25. 6	456
26. 13	283, 463
27. 25	554
27. 28	554
28. 1	391
28. 2, 3	295
28. 11–19	295
29. 24	560

II CHRONICLES.

Ch. Ver.	No.
2. 16	294
3. 1	295
3. 3	134
3. 4	295
3. 5	295
3. 7	295
3. 10–13	142, 295
3. 14	295
4. 1–6	295
4. 7, 8	295
4. 9	295
5. 13	456
6. 12	300
6. 13	347, 741
6. 34	595
8. 5	366
8. 14	283, 717

II CHRON.

Ch. Ver.	No.
9. 4	378
9. 15	301
9. 16	302
9. 17	303
9. 24	64, 93
11. 5–10	366
11. 15	162
12. 3	122
13. 5	150
13. 11	295
15. 14	447
15. 16	306
15. 24	447
16. 14	367
18. 33	251
21. 19	367
22. 11	345
23. 9	302
23. 11	346
23. 13	347
24. 6	674
24. 7	222
24. 9	674
24. 18	222
25. 12	368
26. 10	369
26. 14	251
26. 15	366, 370
26. 20	717
27. 4	369
28. 3	163
28. 27	292
29. 18	295
29. 34	151
30. 6	407
30. 8	560
31. 11	587
32. 5	366
32. 27	357
32. 28	803
32. 33	292
33. 3	222
33. 19	222
34. 4	174
34. 31	347
35. 4	717
35. 13	327
35. 24	80
35. 25	541
36. 4	371
36. 20	372

Ch. Ver.	Job.	No.	Ch. Ver.	Psalms.	No.	Ch. Ver.	Psalms.	No.
30. 10		719	18. 40		96	74. 5		556
30. 23		265	21. 9		591	75. 3		387
30. 31		455	22. 25		851	75. 4, 5		249
31. 7		212	23. 4		256	75. 8		460
31. 17		**419**	**23. 5**		**429**	76. 11		64
31. 21		199	**24. 7**		**430**	78. 70		803
31. 26-28		189	**26. 6**		**431**	**79. 2**		**443**
31. 27		427	28. 1		444	79. 12		760
31. 32		9	28. 2	300,	595	80. 1		295
31. 33		760	30. *Title.*		198	80. 12		690
32. 19		195	30. 3		444	80. 17		686
33. 24		444	31. 4		598	81. 6		544
37. 18		139	**33. 2**		**432**	**88. 4**		**444**
38. 9		751	35. 7		575	88. 9		300
38. 14		**420**	**35. 13**	161,	**433**	89. 6		650
38. 25		426	38. 2		348	89. 17		249
38. 30		50	**40. 6**		**434**	89. 24		249
39. 9		751	40. 7		511	89. 50		760
39. 23		252	**41. 9**		**435**	**91. 3**		**445**
39. 25		447	44. 20		300	92. 3		432
40. 7		314	45. 3		318	**92. 10**	249, 429,	**446**
41. 1		497	45. 7		429	92. 12, 13		387
41. 2		**421**	**45. 8**	**436,**	604	93. 1		314
41. 7		**422**	45. 9	36,	686	94. 13		575
41. 24		706	45. 13, 14	36,	229	**98. 6**		**447**
41. 29		252	47. 1		346	99. 1		295
41. 31		712	50. 14		851	104. 2		388
41. 34		650	**51. 7**		**437**	104. 3		333
42. 10		**423**	51. 19		151	104. 13		333
42. 11	65,	**424**	52. 8		387	104. 15		429
42. 12		402	55. 17		595	**106. 19, 20**		**448**
42. 14	342,	**425**	56. 6		428	**106. 28**		**449**
42. 15		779	**56. 8**		**438**	106. 37, 38		163
			56. 12		851	110. 1	686,	869
Psalms.			57. 6		598	112. 9		249
1. 3		**426**	**58. 4, 5**		**439**	113-118		716
1. 4		634	**58. 6**		**440**	116. 3		289
2. 2		346	**58. 9**	307,	**441**	116. 14		851
2. 12		**427**	60. 8		247	116. 18		851
3. 7		440	61. 3		369	118. 12		441
5. 7		595	62. 3		415	**119. 83**		**450**
5. 12		253	63. 1		21	119. 118		869
7. 15		575	63. 6		121	119. 148		121
8. 6		869	65. 6		314	**123. 2**		**451**
9. 15	575,	598	66. 13		851	124. 7		445
10. 8	186,	**428**	68. 31		300	127. 1		479
15. 1-5		696	69. 12		15	127. 5	15,	199
16. 4		192	**69. 22**		**442**	**129. 6**		**452**
18. 5		289	69. 28		876	129. 6-8		240
18. 28		412	72. 10		64	129. 7		760
18. 34	348,	594	73. 13		431	132. 3		325

496 BIBLE MANNERS AND CUSTOMS.

Ch. Ver. EZEKIEL.	No.	Ch. Ver. EZEKIEL.	No.	HOSEA.	
17. 18	461	41. 8	134	Ch. Ver.	No
17. 20	598	44. 31	168	2. 7	222
19. 4	**575**	**45. 10**	**584**	2. 8	184
19. 8	598	**45. 12**	**585**	2. 13	66
19. 11	**576**	**45. 14**	**586**	3. 1	477
20. 6–8	138	46. 21	295	3. 4	60
20. 28	194			**4. 12**	**597**
20. 31	163	DANIEL.		4. 13	194
20. 37	176			5. 8	447
21. 12	549	**1. 2**	**587**	5. 10	197
21. 14	**577**	**1. 5**	**588**	6. 2	678
21. 21	**578**	1. 6, 7	371	**7. 12**	**598**
21. 22	565	1. 20	76	9. 4	210
21. 27	534	2. 2 76, 520, 630		9. 8	445
22. 13	577	**2. 5**	**589**	10. 5	621
22. 28	572	2. 14 71, 287		10. 11	207
23. 12	**579**	2. 27	630	**11. 4**	**599**
23. 14	**580**	2. 35	634	13. 2	427
23. 24	251	2. 48	630	**13. 3** **600**, 634	
23. 25	**581**	3. 4	866	14. 6	436
23. 40	342	**3. 5** 365, **590**			
23. 41	712	**3. 6**	**591**	JOEL.	
23. 42	35	3. 7 365, 590		2. 1	447
24. 17 208, 210, 486, 612		3. 10 365, 590		3. 10	482
24. 22	612	3. 15 365, 590			
24. 23	486	**3. 20**	**592**	AMOS.	
25. 6	577	**3. 21**	**593**	1. 3	508
26. 8	565	3. 29 71, 589		2. 2	447
26. 9	565	4. 9	630	**2. 6**	**601**
26. 20	444	4. 29	275	**2. 8**	**602**
27. 10	251	5. 2	390	2. 16	261
27. 20	579	**5. 4**	**594**	3. 5	445
27. 30	279	5. 7	476	**3. 12**	**603**
28. 8	444	5. 11	630	**3. 15**	**604**
29. 4	512	5. 16	476	5. 12	199
31. 3, 4	426	5. 29 93, 476		5. 16	541
31. 14	444	6. 8	596	5. 23	432
32. 3	598	**6. 10** 228, 333, **595**		**5. 26** 163, **605**	
32. 14	418	6. 12	596	**6. 4**	**606**
32. 18	444	**6. 15**	**596**	6. 5	432
32. 27	**582**	6. 17	735	6. 10	367
33. 2	283	7. 9	472	**6. 12**	**607**
33. 6	283	8. 2	838	**7. 14** 326, **608**	
33. 7	283	8. 13	869	8. 5	335
37. 20	**583**	9. 21	595	8. 6	601
38. 4	512	10. 3	429	**9. 9**	**609**
38. 5	251	10. 4	838	9. 11	319
39. 15	359	12. 1	876	9. 13	690
40	295	12. 4	381		
40. 5	134	12. 7	5	OBADIAH.	
41. 7	295	12. 9	381	7	435

31

III. TOPICAL INDEX.

Sacrifices, of the dead, 449.
Saddles, 21.
Sadducees, 695.
Saharonim, 231.
Salt applied to infants, 574.
 in sacrifices, 150.
 Savorless, 637.
Salutation—"Peace!" 823.
 "Well!" 336.
Salutations, 84, 240, 767.
Samaritans, Jewish hatred of, 800.
Samson and the pillars, 238.
 making sport, 237.
Sandals, 832.
 Military, 874.
 representative of worthlessness, 601.
Sanhedrim, The Great, 718.
 The Lesser, 656.
Sawing asunder, 883.
Saws, 298.
Scepters, 576.
"Schoolmaster," 872.
Schools of the prophets, 326.
Scourging, Jewish, 656.
 Roman, 724.
Scribes, 648.
Scrip, 256.
Scriptures, Jewish, how divided, 789.
Sculpture, Colored, 580.
Sealing of Christ, 797.
Seals, 323, 420.
Seats, Chief, 698.
 without backs, 248.
Sebat, The month, 622.
Seeds, Mixed, forbidden, 202.
Seirim, 162.
Sepulcher, Stone door of, 734.
Sepulchers, garnished, 703.
 Rock, 501.
 sealed, 735.
 Whited, 702.
Serpent-charming, 439.
Servant, "Eldest," 29.
Servants, watching eyes of master, 451.
Seven, The number, 468.
Shadow desired, 406.
Shaving, Egyptian custom of, 77.
Sheepfold, 803.
Sheets, 488.
Shekel, 26.
 Half, 674.

Shekel, of the sanctuary, 175.
Shepherd and sheep, 804.
 Chief, 887.
Shepherds, abomination to Egyptians, 95.
 Wandering, 106.
Shield, (*kidon*,) 252.
 (*magen*,) 302.
 (*tsinnah*,) 253.
 "uncovered," 500.
Shields, anointed, 498.
 reddened, 615.
Ship, 662.
Shoe, a symbol of ownership, 247.
 loosed, 208.
Shoes, 654.
 carried by servants, 633.
 when removed, 107.
Shoulder, Burden on, 20.
Shrines of Diana, 846.
"Sign" on ships, 859.
Silence, in presence of royalty, 619.
Singing at work, 495.
Sin-offering, 153.
Sistrum, 272.
Sitting, at work, 759.
 posture of teacher, 757.
Sivan, The month, 400.
Skin for skin, 403.
Skirt, Spreading the, 245.
Slaughter of animals for food, 83.
Slaves elevated to power, 78.
Sling, 256.
Smiting the breast, 784.
Snares of fowler, 445.
 of hunter, 289.
Snow, Use of, in summer, 466.
Snow-water, Supposed virtues of, 408.
Soap, 626.
Soldier, Roman, Discipline of, 877.
 Roman, to have no other occupation, 878.
Son, Use of the word, 650.
Songs of Victory, 258.
 Responsive, 259.
"Sop," 746.
 given to another, 815.
Sower, "going forth," 663.
Sowing beside all waters, 510.
Span, 136.
Spear, (*chanith*,) 253.
 (*kidon*,) 252.

THE END.